## Selina Hastings

Selina Hastings is a writer and literary journalist. For fourteen years she worked for the *Daily Telegraph* book page and subsequently became literary editor of *Harpers & Queen*. She has published biographies of Nancy Mitford, Evelyn Waugh and Rosamond Lehmann. Her biography of Waugh won the Marsh Biography Prize.

## Praise for *The Secret Lives of Somerset Maugham*

'One of the fascinating pleasures of this superb biography [is] to see the veils being stripped away and the messy truth about Maugham's life and relationships exposed . . . Selina Hastings's great merit as a biographer is that not only does one sense that the scholarly groundwork has been thoroughly achieved but also that the places and people she describes are portrayed with such graphic clarity and assurance . . . [She] recounts the mass of detail and the massive literary output with great sagacity and the sharpest of eyes. I read this biography with total fascination'   William Boyd, *Observer*

'[Selina Hastings] provides a searing emotional history . . . her closing chapter . . . is so powerfully written, in places so shocking, as to give a series of physical jolts to the reader. Hastings's book cannot be bettered'
Richard Davenport-Hines, *Sunday Telegraph*

'Hastings is the cream of biographers'   David Hare, *Guardian*

'[Selina Hastings] provides an acute, penetrating, yet wonderfully sympathetic portrait of that hypersensitive and sometimes spiteful man. Literary biography could hardly be better done'   Philip Ziegler, *Spectator*

'[Selina Hastings is] a biographer who is second to none . . . [the story] is told with a clear eye and the benefit of an incisive mind. But be warned: once picked up, this . . . biography is impossible to put down'
Thomas Boyle, *Herald*

# The Secret Lives of
# Somerset Maugham

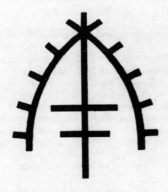

SELINA HASTINGS

JOHN MURRAY

First published in Great Britain in 2009 by John Murray (Publishers)
An Hachette UK Company

First published in paperback in 2010

1

© Selina Hastings 2009

The right of Selina Hastings to be identified as the Author of the Work
has been asserted by her in accordance with the
Copyright, Designs and Patents Act 1988.

A CIP catalogue record for this title is
available from the British Library

ISBN 978-0-7195-6555-7

Typeset in Monotype Bembo by Ellipsis Books Limited, Glasgow

Printed and bound by Clays Ltd, St Ives plc

John Murray policy is to use papers that are natural, renewable and
recyclable products and made from wood grown in sustainable forests.
The logging and manufacturing processes are expected to conform to the
environmental regulations of the country of origin.

John Murray (Publishers)
338 Euston Road
London NW1 3BH

www.johnmurray.co.uk

To Neil and Reiden Jenman
with gratitude and affection

# Contents

# I

# A Blackstable Boyhood

In 1955 Somerset Maugham at the age of eighty-one was asked in a
newspaper interview if he liked the idea of having his biography written.
No, he did not. It would be a pointless exercise, in his view. 'The lives
of modern writers are not interesting in themselves,' he said dismissively.
'A life of myself is bound to be dull . . . [and] I don't want to be associated with dullness.' In truth there was little danger of that. Disingenuous,
as in this statement, maybe; dull, never. For much of his long life – he
lived to be over ninety – Somerset Maugham was the most famous writer
in the world, acclaimed everywhere for his superb short stories and for
his novels, the best known, *Of Human Bondage*, becoming one of the most
widely read works of fiction of the twentieth century. His books were
translated into almost every known tongue, sold in their millions and
brought him celebrity and enormous wealth. For nearly forty years
Maugham in his luxurious villa in the south of France was filmed and
photographed and written about, until it seemed there was little the
public were not at liberty to know about this legendary figure. And yet
since his early youth there had always been other, secret facets to Maugham,
important aspects of himself, of his career, that he had no intention of
revealing. In a very true sense he lived much of his life under cover: he
was a homosexual when homosexual practice was against the law; in both
world wars he worked for British intelligence, sometimes at considerable
risk to his personal safety; and as a writer of fiction he spent much of
his day in a private world of the imagination, peopled by characters often
more real to him than men and women in the world outside. He was
further distanced by developing in childhood a stammer that made him
agonisingly self-conscious; it inhibited him, and as an adult he formed
the habit of having by his side an interpreter, a sociable, outgoing chap,
usually also his lover, who would act as intermediary, make the initial
contact and enable Maugham himself to keep more or less in the background. Yet with all his elaborate defences Maugham remained intensely
vulnerable; he was a passionate, difficult man, capable of cruelty as well

as of great kindness and charm, and despite all his worldly success he never found what he wanted. A wretchedly unhappy marriage wrecked years of his existence and the great love of his life remained unrequited.

For many of his readers Somerset Maugham is identified with the British Empire and the Far East, with Maugham himself a symbol of the English gentleman, the pukka sahib, with generations of old-established county family behind him. Yet in fact Maugham's parents were recent arrivals among the professional middle classes, and they lived not in England but in France: it was on French soil that Maugham's life both began and ended. Maugham's father, Robert Ormond Maugham (1823–84), was a solicitor, the third generation to practise law in a family who were descended from farmers and small tradesmen in Westmorland. It was Robert Maugham's grandfather who had first come to London, where he had risen no higher than a lawyer's clerk, although his son had gone on to achieve distinction not only in his legal practice but as one of the founders of the Law Society. Robert himself had done so well in the family business that in the 1840s he had moved to Paris to open a branch there, his partner, William Dixon, remaining behind to run the London office. The premises of Maugham et Dixon, *juriconsultes anglais*, were at 54 rue du Faubourg Saint-Honoré, situated immediately opposite the magnificent Hôtel de Charost, home of the British Embassy, and here Maugham et Dixon prospered, especially after the firm's semi-official appointment as legal adviser to the Embassy itself.

By his mid-thirties Robert Maugham was making a good living, doing well from the boom years of Louis Napoleon and the Second Empire, when in Paris everyone seemed to be making money – 'Enrichissez-vous!' was the cry. New shops and businesses were opening almost daily, and in the centre of the city Haussmann's grandiose constructions were rising rapidly from the rubble of demolition. The population of the capital was enormously expanding, and so was the English community upon which much of the business of Maugham et Dixon naturally depended. Eventually Robert Maugham felt sufficiently well off to take a wife, and on 1 October 1863 at the age of thirty-nine he married Edith Mary Snell, a ravishing young woman sixteen years his junior. The wedding, conducted by Robert's brother, the Rev. Henry Maugham, took place in the British Embassy, after which the Maughams settled into an apartment at 25 Avenue d'Antin (now Avenue Franklin D. Roosevelt), a broad street lined with chestnut trees just below the *rond-point* of the Champs-Elysées and a convenient five-minute walk from the office. The apartment, on the third floor of one of the new purpose-built buildings, was light-filled and spacious. In the large drawing-room the walls were hung with Doré engravings, and also displayed were the Tanagra statuettes, Rhodes ware and ornate Turkish daggers which Robert Maugham as a young man had brought back from his travels. In the billiard-room were two dark-walnut bookcases filled with sets of Scott, Dickens, Charles Kingsley and Captain Marryat as well the Tauchnitz novels which Edith Maugham loved.

Young Mrs Maugham was the product of a rather more exotic background than her husband's. Although she had lived in France most of her life, Edith had been born in India. Her father, Charles Snell, a captain in the Madras Native Infantry, had died at the age of fifty, barely a month after her first birthday. Within a couple of years her mother, Anne Alicia, left India and returned to England, bringing with her an ayah to look after Edith and a posthumous younger sister, Rose. Soon afterwards the widow and her two small daughters moved to France where they remained, the girls attending a convent school while Mrs Snell supplemented her meagre pension by writing novels and children's stories in French and by composing music for drawing-room ballads. Clearly a woman of culture, character and resource, Anne Alicia was not only much younger than her husband but socially his superior. While Charles Snell was the son of a Falmouth sailmaker, Anne Alicia, née Todd, was the daughter of a well-to-do Yorkshire squire who had lost most of his money after moving to Cornwall and investing in a tin mine which failed. Her mother was a Brereton, a landed Cheshire family tracing its descent back to the twelfth century, and it was one of Anne Alicia's Brereton uncles who was christened Somerset in honour of a distinguished godfather, General Sir Henry Somerset. It was Henry Somerset Brereton's middle name which was to be passed on to his famous great-nephew, who never cared for it. After Edith married and settled in Paris, Anne Alicia moved with Rose to Saint-Malo, where six years later Rose, aged twenty-seven, died of tuberculosis. Throughout the nineteenth century tuberculosis was the leading cause of death in France; it killed Rose and later her sister Edith, and was very nearly to kill her nephew William Somerset. Anne Alicia Snell lived for another thirty-five years, dying in 1904 at the age of eighty-nine in Le Mans.

For nearly seven years the Maughams enjoyed an agreeable existence in the French capital. Robert, 'lively and gregarious', worked hard at his business, while Edith ran the household and supervised the upbringing of the three boys who arrived in quick succession. Her two closest women friends were Mary ('Minnie') Wodehouse, a vivacious American, and the English Isabella Williams-Freeman, both married to second secretaries at the Embassy. It was often in their company that she shopped at the great new department stores, drove out for carriage exercise in the Bois de Boulogne, and paid calls on her acquaintance – English afternoon tea, *le five-o'clock*, had newly become fashionable among the French. At this period Robert was making a considerable amount of money and was happy for his wife to spend as she pleased. The two of them enjoyed a lavish style of living, keeping a carriage, frequently attending the theatre and operá, and entertaining generously; Edith was stylishly dressed, the apartment was always filled with flowers, and the finest hot-house fruit, grapes and peaches out of season, appeared on the table. Much of the Maughams' social life inevitably revolved around the Embassy, but Edith also numbered among her friends writers and painters, among them Prosper Mérimée and Gustave Doré. Regarded as the reigning beauty of the English community, Mme Maugham was much admired for her qualities of empathy and charm. She was one of the few foreigners whose name was listed in the annual directory, *La Société et le High Life*, and after her death she was described as an habituée of the most elegant salons, 'une femme charmante, qui ne comptait que des amis dans la haute société parisienne, où elle occupait une des premières places'.* Such a eulogy almost certainly owes more to flattery than fact – however cultured and charming, it is unlikely that an English solicitor's wife would be received by the Duchesse de Guermantes – but it is nonetheless clear that Edith Maugham was a woman of exceptional allure.

Both Maughams were small in stature, but while Robert's appearance verged on the brutish – he was plump, with a large sallow face, yellow whites to his eyes and a bulbous chin framed by moustache and bushy side-whiskers – Edith was doll-like and beautiful. Her hair was a rich auburn, her pale complexion flawless, and her dark-brown eyes large and set wide apart. Edith's diminutive figure looked exquisite in the tight-waisted, bell-skirted crinolines still fashionable for most of the 1860s – there was a sumptuous black ball-dress covered in lace in which she appeared to stunning effect – and if the great couturier Worth, patronised by the Empress and most of the French court, was beyond her means, she nonetheless showed considerable flair, dressing with an elegance and chic that owed more to her long residence in France than to her English blood. When the Maughams were seen together the contrast was almost risible, and they became affectionately known

---

* 'a charming woman, with countless friends in Parisian high society, in which she occupied one of the highest positions'.

as 'Beauty and the Beast'. Minnie Wodehouse once asked Edith how she could love such an ugly little man. 'Because he never hurts my feelings,' Edith replied.

In October 1865 the couple's first child was born, a boy, Charles Ormond, followed a year later by Frederic Herbert, and in June 1868 by Henry Neville. The youngest had barely reached his second birthday when the Franco-Prussian War broke out, shortly followed by Napoleon III's humiliating surrender in September 1870 at Sedan. With the Prussian army advancing on Paris, the Maughams, like many others in the English community, departed for England, leaving behind them at the Avenue d'Antin a couple of servants to look after the apartment and a Union Jack fastened to the balcony. The little boys were deposited with their Maugham grandmother at her house in London while their parents went to Italy. This was a holiday much needed by them both, Robert exhausted by the pressure of work in his office, Edith by bearing a trio of children in less than three years. The terrible siege of Paris was by now under way, with the starving populace reduced to eating rats and animals from the Zoo. As nothing could penetrate the German blockade, messages arrived from the Avenue d'Antin by carrier pigeon, one of them requesting to know whether Madame desired the summer covers to be put on the furniture in the drawing-room. The five-month siege was succeeded by the bloody civil war known as the Commune, during which great swathes of the city were destroyed and more than 20,000 people killed. But by the end of May 1871 government forces had regained control, and in August the Maughams returned to Paris, met at the Gare du Nord by their loyal manservant François, who was able to tell them that the apartment had been left untouched by the Germans largely thanks to their prominently displayed Union Jack.

The apartment may have remained intact but most of the centre of the city presented a scene of desolation, the Tuileries a blackened ruin, the Hôtel de Ville a heap of rubble, the Colonne Vendôme toppled to the ground. Although rebuilding began at once and progressed with speed, it was some time before the business life of the city fully recovered and, with so many English having gone for good, Robert Maugham found himself perilously out of pocket, obliged to start almost from scratch in rebuilding his practice.

Edith meanwhile resumed her domestic round, a loving and much loved mother to her three boisterous boys, and in 1873 she again found herself pregnant. At that time the government, understandably anxious to strengthen its military might, was threatening the introduction of legislation imposing French nationality on all boys born in France to foreign parents, a measure which would automatically make them eligible for conscription. To circumvent this, the British Ambassador, Lord Lyons, had authorised the rigging up of a maternity ward on the second floor of the Embassy, so that the wives of those immediately connected to the Chancery could safely give birth on British soil. And here on 25 January 1874 Edith's fourth child was born, another boy, to be christened William Somerset.

The years of Somerset Maugham's early childhood were almost certainly the happiest of his life. By the time he was old enough to take notice, his three brothers, Charlie, Freddie and Harry, had gone, sent off to school in England and coming home only for the holidays. The result was that little William led the life of a much indulged only child, and with his father away at his office all day, returning only after the boy had been put to bed, he was in the happy position of having his adored mother entirely to himself. After the departure of his wet-nurse, Willie was looked after by a French nursemaid, his 'nounou', with whom he shared a bedroom, and it was she who would take him in to see his mother in the morning while she was resting after her bath, a private interlude of perfect intimacy and love, the memory of which stayed with him always, to be poignantly recalled nearly forty years later.

> [The servant] opened the door of a room on the floor below and took the child over to a bed in which a woman was lying. It was his mother. She stretched out her arms, and the child nestled by her side . . . The woman kissed his eyes, and with thin, small hands felt the warm body through his white flannel nightgown . . .
> 'Are you sleepy, darling?' she said.
> . . . The child did not answer, but smiled comfortably. He was very happy in the large, warm bed, with those soft arms about him. He tried to make himself smaller still as he cuddled up against his mother, and he kissed her sleepily. In a moment he closed his eyes and was fast asleep . . . the woman kissed him again; and she passed her hand down his body till she came to his feet; she held the right foot in her hand and felt the five small toes; and then slowly passed her hand over the left one.

After visiting his mother, Willie was taken out, usually to play in the Champs-Elysées, a broad avenue in those days lined with private houses and luxurious apartment buildings. He and his nurse would make their way through the horse-drawn traffic and fashionably dressed pedestrians to the gardens at the end nearest the Place de la Concorde. Here were roundabouts, a Punch-and-Judy, little booths selling gingerbread and barley sugar, and near the *rond-point* a stirringly realistic panorama of the siege of Paris, with guns, and 'dead bodies' in real French uniforms. There were always other children in the gardens, and as he grew older Willie was allowed to play with them, dashing in and out of the shrubbery in vigorous games of 'La tour prend garde' or 'Balle à l'ennemi'. With his pale skin, fair curls and large brown eyes, Willie in his black-belted suit was indistinguishable from the little French boys in their short trousers and lace-up boots who were his playmates; indeed he spoke French far more fluently than English, sometimes mixing the two. Edith was amused when one day her small son, catching sight of a horse from the window of a railway carriage, cried out, 'Regardez, Maman, voilà un 'orse.' His first extant letter, written at the age of six and addressed to his parents, is in French: 'cher papa, chere maman, votre petit willie est heureux au jour de noel de vous exprimer ses meilleurs souhaits, et sa reconaissante affection. croyez-moi, cher papa, chere maman, votre fils respectueux, willie maugham.'* In the afternoons, either his mother had nursery tea with him, or Willie went to the drawing-room to be shown off to her guests, once memorably to Georges Clemenceau, the future Prime Minister. Occasionally he was asked to recite a fable of La Fontaine after which, if he were lucky, some kind gentleman might tip him. On his seventh birthday one of his mother's friends gave him a twenty-franc piece which he chose to spend on his first visit to the theatre; accompanied by his eldest brother Charlie he saw Sarah Bernhardt in an 'atrocious' melodrama by Sardou, which thrilled him to the core. On Sundays Willie accompanied his mother to the English church in the rue d'Aguésseau opposite the Embassy, where she always took him out before the sermon.

For Willie his mother was the centre of his entire existence. He loved her unreservedly and felt completely secure in her love for him. While his father remained a shadowy presence and barely impinged upon his consciousness, his mother's attention, he knew, was always his; nothing mattered to him much that did not concern the sweet intimacy that existed between himself and her.

Willie's education was begun at a little French day school, unlike his brothers who had had their first lessons with English governesses at home. The older boys' arrival in Paris for the holidays brought with it an exciting disruption of routine. Edith was a talented amateur actress and she regularly staged shows for an invited adult audience which the children were

---

* 'dear papa, dear mama, your little willie is happy on christmas day to give you his best wishes and grateful affection. Believe me to be, dear papa, dear mama, your respectful son, willie maugham.'

allowed to attend, productions which were 'well above the ordinary amateur standard', according to one diplomatic spectator. Her friends the Williams-Freemans were also keen on amateur dramatics, and Willie frequently accompanied his mother on the calls she paid at their apartment in the Avenue de l'Alma (now George V) on Sunday afternoons, when Isabella Williams-Freeman was 'at home'. His exact contemporary among the family was Violet, who had also been born in the Embassy, and Violet, her sister and brother, impressed by this cheerful, confident, imaginative and rather daring little boy, willingly appointed him their *chef du bande*. He held them spellbound with his stories and was ingenious at thinking up games. Once Willie's eldest brother Charlie took them all to the circus, and often the children played together in the Champs-Elysées, where they ate sugared *gaufrettes* while watching the Guignol, and Willie, with an air of great innocence, delighted his companions by passing off fake sous at the kiosk selling balloons.

Violet was sometimes taken to tea on her own at the Avenue d'Antin, as Edith was her godmother. The little girl worshipped her godmother and hated to see how frail and often how ill she looked; her beautiful brown eyes were sad, and there seemed to be an aura of melancholy surrounding her, of the origins of which Violet had no idea, later speculating that perhaps there had been an unhappy love affair before Edith married. In fact illness could well have accounted for her depression, for, like her sister Rose, Edith was consumptive, and depression is a familiar concomitant of tuberculosis.

By now a semi-invalid, Edith was advised to avoid extremes of temperature, and as summers in Paris could grow uncomfortably hot and the stifling air was considered unhealthy, she used to take the children in July to a rented house at the seaside for three months. Parisians of rank and fashion favoured Trouville, but the Maughams chose to go a few miles along the Normandy coast to less expensive Deauville, then still as much a fishing village as a resort, with a busy harbour as well as a small casino, racecourse and *plage de famille*. Willie was looked after by his nurse while his brothers raced about on the wide sands and paddled at the water's edge, their mother sitting on a camp stool working on her embroidery and chatting to the other *estivants*. On Saturdays Robert Maugham took the train down from Paris to join them for a couple of days, once turning up in a 'bone-shaker' car with iron tyres in which he took the boys for juddering rides along the front.

When Willie was five, Edith again became pregnant. In those days it was believed that childbirth fortified women who had consumption, a theory which may have had something to do with Willie's birth in 1874, five and a half years after the arrival of Harry, the youngest of his three brothers. This time, the baby, another boy, was still-born, and in order to recuperate Edith, accompanied by Willie, travelled south to winter in Pau, a town at the foot of the Pyrenees popular with the English for the curative powers of its mild climate and pure mountain air. But whatever the benefits, they were short lived, and not long after Edith had returned home her condition worsened. As his mother grew weaker, Willie's time with her was curtailed, partly no doubt in an attempt to shield him from the more harrowing symptoms of the disease, the racking cough bringing up phlegm and blood, the agonising chest pain, the fevers and drenching sweats. Typically, periods of paralysing lassitude alternated with hectic bursts of energy and optimism, when for a brief period a semblance of normality could be resumed. But increasingly daily life at the Avenue d'Antin came to revolve around the visits of frock-coated doctors with their sinister black bags bearing the cumbersome treatments then in vogue. Bleeding had largely been abandoned, replaced by cupping, which was thought to draw the infection out; drinking milk was also believed to be important, cow's milk, goat's milk, but best of all ass's milk, and every morning a little string of donkeys stopped at the door to provide Edith with her tonic.

In the spring of 1881, not long after the return from Pau, Edith found she was once more expecting a child, but by this time she was too ill for there to be much hope that such a remedy could save her. Towards the end of that year she realised she was dying and that her boys would shortly be left motherless. Although eight months pregnant and desperately ill, she summoned the last of her strength and somehow managed to dress herself, putting on the bodice of a favourite white damask evening gown over a black skirt. Quietly letting herself out of the apartment she went to have herself photographed so that her sons would always remember how their mother looked. On 24 January 1882 Edith gave birth to a son, who was quickly baptised Edward Alan before dying the following afternoon. Less than a week later, at the age of forty-one, Edith herself died, on the 31st of the month, six days after Willie's eighth birthday.

With his mother's death the world in which Willie had been so safe and happy ended abruptly and for ever. His brothers, who had been summoned to the death-bed, shortly afterwards returned to England, and Willie was left to cope with his profound and terrible grief as best he could. The child's love for his mother was passionate and unreasoning, and having lost her when he did he was never able to come to terms with her loss. He kept the last photograph of her beside his bed throughout his life, together with a long tress of her hair, his two most treasured possessions, and even in great old age he would admit that he had never got over his mother's death. Over thirty years later, in his autobiographical novel *Of Human Bondage*, he recalled the immediate aftermath, when the boy enters his dead mother's room:

> [He] opened a large cupboard filled with dresses and, stepping in, took as many of them as he could in his arms and buried his face in them. They smelled of the scent his mother used. Then he pulled open the drawers, filled with his mother's things, and looked at them: there were lavender bags among the linen, and their scent was fresh and pleasant. The strangeness of the room left it, and it seemed to him that his mother had just gone out for a walk. She would be in presently and would come upstairs to have nursery tea with him.

His father, himself utterly crushed by the loss of his wife, did what he could to console him, but he had seen little of his youngest son and the two were comparative strangers. As before Robert Maugham spent six days a week at his office, while Willie was looked after by his mother's much loved French maid, who now took over the role of nurse. Willie was taken away from his little school, going for his lessons instead to the English clergyman of the church attached to the Embassy. This gentleman, realising that his pupil's English was far from adequate, made the boy read aloud from police reports in the newspaper, details of some of the grislier cases haunting the child for years afterwards. 'I can still remember the horror of reading the ghastly details of a murder in the train between Paris and Calais,' Maugham wrote later.

Only on Sundays did the boy spend any time with his father. Robert Maugham's one indulgence was the building of a summer house at Suresnes, a few miles west of the centre of Paris, close to the Seine and the Bois de Boulogne. On Sundays father and son, companions in grief, would take the *bâteau-mouche* downriver to inspect progress on the house, built in an eccentric style, part Japanese, part Swiss chalet, painted white with red shutters, and overlooking a splendid panorama of the Seine, of the racecourse at Longchamps and beyond them of the whole of Paris. Robert Maugham, described by his youngest son as having a 'romantic mind', had never forgotten the travels he had made in his youth, to Morocco, Greece and Asia Minor, and in his imagination his little house near the Seine in suburban Suresnes was a villa on the Bosphorus. To emphasise the exotic effect he had the Moorish sign against the Evil Eye engraved on the windows, a sign which was famously adopted by the writer Maugham as his personal insignia. 'My father was a stranger to me when he was alive,' Maugham was later to say. 'Yet somehow that sign against the Evil Eye seems to have bound us together.'

Before long the building was complete, the garden laid out and furniture delivered, but Robert Maugham had no time to enjoy it. Since his wife's death he himself had grown progressively weaker, his complexion more sallow, dogged by nausea, exhaustion and pain, symptoms of the stomach cancer that was shortly to kill him. As he could no longer cope with the load of work at his practice, he asked Albert Dixon, brother of his original partner, to find him a French-speaking solicitor, and John Sewell, the young man who arrived from London to take on the job, was soon judged sufficiently competent to be made a partner.

On 24 June 1884, two and a half years after losing his wife, Robert Maugham himself died. He was sixty years old, and despite his long, hard-working career he left behind him less than £5,000 to be shared between his four sons. 'It was the end of a home,' Freddie Maugham sadly recalled. 'My brothers and I were soon separated by the force of events, and therefore we did not see much of each other.' Appointed the boys' guardians were the good-natured old lawyer from the London office, Albert Dixon, and Robert Maugham's only brother and Willie's godfather, Henry Macdonald Maugham, Vicar of Whitstable in Kent. These two men came briefly over to Paris to cope with the crisis. A three-day auction was held to dispose of the contents of the apartment, personal possessions were packed and labelled, servants paid off, and all necessary arrangements made to transfer the brothers' domicile from France to England. For the three older boys, accustomed to life on the other side of the Channel, the change was not so great, Charlie returning to Cambridge, Freddie and Harry as before to school. But for ten-year-old Willie it was all strange and unfamiliar, impossible to imagine what he would encounter in the unknown country where he was to live from now on with his uncle and aunt.

Willie made the nine-hour journey accompanied by his faithful nurse, excited, as any young boy would be, but also deeply apprehensive at the prospect of what lay ahead. After the Channel steamer docked at Dover, in the midst of all the bustle of disembarkation – Willie from force of habit calling out, 'Porteur! Cabriolet!' – they saw waiting for them on the quayside the sombre figure of the Rev. Henry Maugham, black-coated, bewhiskered and severe. As they covered the twenty-odd miles to Whitstable Willie kept close to the kindly Frenchwoman, the 'one link with all the happiness and affection I'd known in the Avenue d'Antin . . . my last link with my mother and all that she had meant to me'. By the time they arrived at the vicarage, it was late and the travellers were exhausted. Before Willie went up to bed, however, his uncle had something to say: he informed him that there was no question of being able to afford a nurse and that she was to be sent back to France as soon as possible. And next day she was gone.

For the rest of his life Maugham looked back on his childhood in England as a period of utter desolation. 'I shall never forget the misery of those next few years,' he used to say, and even in old age the memory was so painful that it gave him the 'cold shudders'. Indeed, given the circumstances it is hardly surprising the boy was wretched: an orphan at ten years old, still suffering agonies of grief for his mother, and placed in the care of strangers in what was in effect a foreign country. Instead of cosseting and indulgence, of the warmth, gaiety and lavishness of his parents' life, of their comfortable apartment and sophisticated society, he found himself in a bleak and alien environment, unloved and of importance to no one. In a revealingly autobiographical novel written in his early twenties and never published, Maugham gives a portrait of himself as a young man, one who had experienced so little happiness in life that he did not know how to cope when people were kind to him; and forty years later there appears a telling entry in his notebook: 'He had had so little love when he was small that later it embarrassed him to be loved . . . He did not know what to say when someone paid him a compliment, and a manifestation of affection made him feel a fool.'

Neither his uncle nor his aunt was deliberately unkind, but they were a dull, unimaginative pair, childless themselves and with no experience of dealing with children; perhaps understandably, they were nervous of having their well-regulated existence disrupted by the presence of a small boy who might well turn out to be noisy, cheeky and rough. Willie's uncle in particular was selfish and set in his ways. As his nephew Freddie later said of him, 'he was very narrow-minded and a far from intelligent cleric, and I cannot truthfully praise him as a guardian of boys'. Like his brother Robert, Henry Macdonald Maugham was small in stature but, although inclined to corpulence, much better looking. Then in his late fifties he had been Vicar of Whitstable for the previous thirteen years, a living that he found suited him well. A lazy man, he was fortunate in having a curate, Mr Ellman, who took much of the work of the parish off his hands. He was fortunate, too, in that his wife Sophie was submissive by nature and accepted without question that the comfort and convenience of her husband should be considered paramount. Sophie, born Barbara Sophia von Scheidlin, was German, the daughter of a Nuremberg merchant, though for reasons no longer known she was living in Staffordshire at the time of her marriage in 1858 when she was thirty, her husband a year younger. Plump and almost pretty, her blonde hair coiled in thick plaits on the crown of her head, Sophie was a quiet, modest woman, straitlaced and conventional, but while prim in manner and embarrassed by any display of emotion, she had a kind heart and desired to do her best by her nephew, as long as he in no way impinged on the wellbeing of her husband or the smooth running of the household.

The vicarage, two miles outside Whitstable on the Canterbury Road, was a gloomy place, built only a few years previously of yellow brick in a bastardised Gothic style. Maugham memorably described the interior of the house with its self-consciously ecclesiastical atmosphere: 'the hall was paved with red and yellow tiles, on which alternately were a Greek Cross and the Lamb of God. An imposing staircase led out of the hall . . . The balusters were decorated with emblems of the Four Evangelists.' Downstairs were the dining-room, in which much of the family's daily life was led, the drawing-room, kept pristine for receiving company, and the study in which the Vicar wrote his weekly sermon. Upstairs Willie had a tiny bedroom at the front overlooking the drive. The house, not yet converted to gas, was lit by oil-lamps, with candles for the bedrooms. Outside was a large garden, and at the back of the house a semicircular lawn gave on to fields in which sheep grazed; a mile away the square stone tower of the medieval parish church, All Saints', could just be glimpsed through the trees.

The memory of the deep unhappiness suffered by Willie during those first days and weeks at the vicarage weighed on him for many years, and provided the inspiration for his most famous work of fiction. '*Of Human Bondage*', Maugham wrote, 'is not an autobiography, but an autobiographical novel . . . the emotions are my own . . . [but] fact and fiction are inextricably mingled.' He was in his late thirties when it was published in 1915, after which at last, 'I found myself free from the pains and unhappy recollections that had tormented me.' Particularly in the section dealing with the childhood of the hero, Philip Carey, there is plenty of evidence, from Maugham's own testimony as well as elsewhere, to support the assumption that the narrative is closely based on fact. Certainly the figures of the Vicar and his wife are recognisably portrayed, and much of the blame for the wretchedness of the motherless boy must be laid at their door. The Rev. Henry Maugham was not popular in the parish; snobbish, blinkered and magnificently self-centred, he was a man who inspired neither affection nor esteem; and his wife was timid and unquestioningly accepted her husband at his own inflated valuation. And yet they were not bad people; the Vicar was no Mr Murdstone; it would never have occurred to him for a moment that he was not satisfactorily fulfilling his obligations towards his brother's boy. But Maugham's feelings about him and about that period of his life were entangled with grief over his mother's death, with his rage at having been abandoned. Nobody could have replaced Edith Maugham, certainly not such a stiff and starchy couple as the Rev. Henry and his wife.

However, within his own narrow limits, it is clear the Vicar made an effort to be kind. In *Of Human Bondage* the episode of Philip's arrival at the vicarage demonstrates his uncle's parsimony but it also shows a genuine attempt to make contact with the boy.

> The vicar, having said grace, cut the top off his egg.
> 'There,' he said, handing it to Philip, 'you can eat my top if you like.'
> Philip would have liked an egg to himself, but he was not offered one, so took what he could . . .
> 'How did you like that top, Philip?' asked his uncle.
> 'Very much, thank you.'
> 'You shall have another one on Sunday afternoon.'
> Mr Carey always had a boiled egg at tea on Sunday so that he might be fortified for the evening service.

And he is making an effort, too, when he explains to Philip, as the sort of modest joke a child might enjoy, about the two pokers set beside the dining-room fireplace: '[Mr Carey] pointed out to his nephew that there were two pokers. One was large and bright and polished and unused, and was called the Vicar, and the other, which was much smaller and had evidently passed through many fires, was called the Curate.'

As one of his neighbours said, the trouble with Henry Maugham was that 'he was fond of children but unable to understand them'. He certainly never understood his nephew, and it was only in later life that Maugham realised that his uncle was not quite the stern and solemn figure he had taken him to be. For instance, the Vicar's proverbs – 'A parson is paid to preach, not to practise' and '"Do unto others as you would they should do unto you." An excellent maxim – for others' – were taken with absolute seriousness by Willie at the time, and only with hindsight did it occur to him that they were intended to amuse.

Nevertheless, if there was no deliberate cruelty, Henry Maugham was capable of an obtuseness that came very near it. In Maugham's short memoir, 'Looking Back', he describes his first Sunday at the vicarage. After church in the morning the boy is sat at the dining-room table and told by his uncle to learn the collect of the day.

'I'll hear you say it at tea time,' he said, 'and if you say it properly you shall have a piece of cake.' Then he went into his study to rest after the morning's exertions and my aunt went to lie down in the drawing-room. I was left alone. An hour or so later she went into the garden to have a stroll and as she passed the dining-room windows peeped in to see how I was getting on. My face was buried in my hands and I was crying, crying bitterly. She hurried into the dining-room and asked me what was the matter. Crying all the more, I sobbed, 'I can't understand it. All those words, I don't know what they mean.' 'Oh, Willie,' she said, 'your uncle wouldn't want you to cry. It was for your own good that he wanted you to learn the collect. Don't cry.' She took the prayer book away from me and I was left alone once more to sob my heart out. When the table was set for tea my uncle did not speak to me. I could see that he was cross. I think my aunt must have persuaded him that I was too young to learn a collect by heart; anyhow I was never asked to do so again.

Sophie plainly was touched by the boy's unhappiness and did what she could to make the situation better, but nevertheless she and Willie remained shy and awkward with each other. And he himself was not altogether easy: in Paris he had been spoilt by his adoring female coterie, and when crossed had quite a temper. Rather than spend time with his aunt, he much preferred to take his toys and play in the kitchen, an arrangement that suited everybody. 'His aunt was not sorry. She did not like disorder, and though she recognized that boys must be expected to be untidy she preferred that he should make a mess in the kitchen. If he fidgeted his uncle was apt to grow restless and say it was high time he went to school.'

The Whitstable living, worth £300 a year, included with the vicarage twenty acres of glebe land. This was not wealth but it enabled the Vicar and his wife to live respectably and in modest comfort. Henry Maugham was frugal by nature: for the sake of economy he even shared his daily copy of *The Times* with two neighbours; but one indulgence he did allow himself was the occasional trip to the Continent for the sake of his health, when he would stay at some German spa to take the waters and rest from the exigencies of his parochial duties. Sophie was rarely invited to accompany him, remaining at home to oversee the running of the household, which comprised a gardener, who fed the hens and looked after the stoves, two maids, a cook-general and a housemaid. In the cosy back offices it was the maids who provided Willie with a version of the warm feminine company with which he had been so happily surrounded in the Avenue d'Antin. Interestingly, in the two novels drawing most nearly on Maugham's own experience, *Of Human Bondage* and *Cakes and Ale*, the kind-hearted maternal figure in both instances is the cook-general, Mary-Ann, in real life Mary-Anne Tilley, who was in her late twenties when Willie arrived in England. In the novels it is Mary-Ann who looks after the boy and whom he comes to love; she, not his aunt, who nurses him through his childhood illnesses, gives him his bath, tucks him up in bed, and tells him stories. The story-telling was important, for while he listened Willie would become wholly absorbed, forgetting his misery and his longing for his mother. As he later wrote of himself at this period, it was when he was unhappy that he wanted stories most, a form of addiction that was to stay with him for life. Mary-Ann, in her mid-thirties, fresh-faced and snub-nosed, was a Whitstable girl ('Blackstable' in the novels). 'She was never ill. She never had a holiday. She was paid twelve pounds a year. One evening a week she went down the town to see her mother, who did the vicarage washing; and on Sunday evenings she went to church. But Mary-Ann knew everything that went on in Blackstable.'

As the days passed the sense of strangeness began to wear off, and by the end of the autumn of 1884 Maugham had largely grown accustomed to his new life. It was a lonely life because his uncle considered himself a cut above most of Whitstable society, shamelessly toadying to the local squire, Sydney Greystone of Tankerton Castle, while refusing to have anything to do with the tradesmen, or with the fishermen and their families; nor, as a pillar of the Church of England, would he speak to chapel folk, crossing the road rather than pass on the same side as the Baptist minister, Mr Laurence, or the Wesleyan, Mr Walter. The congregation at All Saints' was never large. Whitstable was made up of two ecclesiastical parishes, Anglican and Nonconformist, with the majority of townspeople belonging to the latter. Henry Maugham was a high-church Anglican with a pronounced sympathy for Rome – 'in his secret soul he yearned for processions and lighted candles' – a tendency which won him little respect among the chapel-goers. During the General Election of 1880 some irreverent character had written in large letters on the vicarage fence, 'Change here for Rome', a facetious graffito which had annoyed him exceedingly. Unsurprisingly, 'Old Maugham', as he was referred to behind his back, was 'a cracking snob', and considered few children suitable as playmates for his nephew. A Whitstable contemporary, one of the Board School boys, recalled how isolated the child appeared. 'His guardians would rigidly take care that he should be kept apart from common people,' he said. 'He was too remote from our way of living to encourage familiarity.' This remoteness is reflected in a scene in *Of Human Bondage*, in which a well-to-do banker takes a neighbouring house for the summer.

> The banker had a little boy of my own age . . . I still remember the discussion that ensued when I asked if I might bring him to the vicarage; permission was reluctantly given me, but I was not allowed to go in return to his house. My aunt said I'd be wanting to go to the coal merchants next, and my uncle said: 'Evil communications corrupt good manners.'

As a consequence of his enforced isolation, and of the lack of love, Maugham changed from a child naturally sociable and outgoing to one guarded and withdrawn. Sometimes he was overwhelmed by sadness and a longing for his mother, but he soon learned to hide his emotions, particularly when hurt or unhappy, and could never bear to be seen crying. He spent hours playing on his own in the garden, fishing for roach in the pond or aimlessly swinging on the big five-barred gate at the end of the drive. Charlotte Etheridge, the doctor's daughter, remembered being struck by the aura of loneliness that surrounded the little boy, by glimpsing his forlorn figure, unsuitably clad in a Frenchified velvet suit with a white lace collar, standing alone and aimless outside the house.

And there was another reason for Maugham's apartness. He had developed a bad stammer which made him painfully self-conscious. In France there had been no sign of such an impediment. Yet since Maugham's arrival in England the stammer had become marked, and it caused him, and for much of his life continued to cause him, anguish and humiliation. Shy and unsure of himself, he now also had to cope with this added horror, only too well aware that it made him conspicuous and caused other children to laugh at him. For a child feeling his way in a foreign environment, it was particularly terrifying to be at the mercy of such a cruel encumbrance, never knowing when his speech, his chief medium of communication, might not be hideously distorted and he himself made to look slow-witted and ridiculous. Inevitably, a sense of anger and frustration was compounded by a deep, if irrational, feeling of self-disgust, a feeling unknown in his previous unclouded existence but which from now on was to remain with Maugham always. A harrowing occasion for Maugham, never to be forgotten, was when his uncle took him on the train up to London for the day, sending him back on his own.

> There was a long queue outside the third-class ticket office, so I took my place in the queue. But when it came to my turn to ask for my ticket to Whitstable I couldn't get the word out. I just stood there stammering. People behind me were getting impatient, but I still couldn't say 'Whitstable'. Suddenly two men stepped out of the queue and pushed me aside. 'We can't wait all night for you,' they said. 'Stop wasting our time.' So I had to go to the back of the queue and start all over again. I'll never forget the humiliation of that moment – with everyone staring at me.

One of the strangest aspects of Maugham's life in Kent is the absence of any sign of communication between himself and his brothers. In Paris, it is true, he had led the existence of an only child and there had been no strong bond formed between himself and the three older boys. They had been sent to the newly founded Dover College, chosen mainly for its ease of access from France. From Dover College the eldest, Charlie, who used to take his small brother to the circus and theatre during the holidays, had gone up to Cambridge to read law, while Freddie and Harry were still at school. Although Dover is only just over twenty miles from Whitstable, there seems to have been little contact with the vicarage. According to Maugham's nephew, Robin, 'The three older brothers were absorbed in their own careers and could spare no time for the sorrows of their very much younger brother.' It is possible that the Vicar discouraged visits, and entirely probable that Willie never thought to complain. Freddie also was living with a clergyman relation, the Rector of Paston, near Peterborough, married to one of Robert Maugham's sisters, but this aunt and uncle were cheerful and affectionate and he was happy there, and it may have been only later that he discovered how miserable his brother's situation had been.

Daily life at the vicarage was strictly regulated and monotonous, its timetable rigidly designed around the Vicar's unchanging habits. Money was spent carefully and in private some rigorous economies were practised: family meals were extremely plain, no carriage was kept, a fly being hired from the Bear and Key when required. Willie's annuity of £150 was just sufficient to pay for his keep and education. The day revolved around four meals, breakfast, followed by prayers, then dinner at one o'clock, tea at five, and a cold supper (bread and butter and a little stewed fruit) at eight, followed by more prayers. Afterwards on winter evenings there was sometimes a game of whist, in which the boy was allowed to take part.

'My uncle always took dummy, and though of course we played for love, when my aunt and I lost I used to retire under the dining-room table and cry.' This was the routine for six days of the week leading up to Sunday. Sunday was the high point, the great day when the Vicar delivered his sermon, an effort for which he required substantial bolstering up in advance, a reverential hush during composition in his study, an egg beaten up in a glass of sherry at breakfast, and another egg for tea to support him through Evensong. Willie, who was not allowed to play on Sundays or make any noise, rode with his uncle and aunt to church in the hired fly, which smelt strongly of stale straw. His aunt was invariably dressed in a black silk cloak and feathered bonnet, his uncle imposing in his cassock, a gold cross hanging over his stomach from the gold chain round his neck. In the evening the boy again accompanied his uncle to church, this time on foot. 'The walk through the darkness along the country road strangely impressed him . . . At first he was shy with his uncle, but little by little grew used to him, and he would slip his hand in his uncle's and walk more easily for the feeling of protection.'

Apart from attending church, Maugham left the house only to escort his aunt on her occasional trips into town. There was little for him to do on these expeditions except trail after her while she did her shopping, or wait fidgeting while she conducted her business at the bank, but there was often something interesting to look at. In the 1880s Whitstable, on the windswept north coast of Kent looking out over the North Sea, was a town of just under 5,000 souls and still primarily a fishing community famous for its oyster beds. The harbour was always full of activity, with the coming and going of fishing boats and oyster dredgers, of shabby little colliers bringing coal from Newcastle, and luggers carrying cargoes of hay and wheat up the Thames to Tower Bridge. On the beach there was usually a gathering of oyster porters and their carts, of grimy colliers unloading coal, and of blue-jerseyed fishermen with ruddy faces and gold rings in their ears. Leading up from the harbour was a web of narrow streets of wooden fishermen's houses, outside which on fine days the men sat smoking and mending their nets. Sometimes Maugham was allowed inside one of these low-roofed dwellings, tangled with sails and fishing tackle, and invited to admire some treasure brought back from the other side of the world, a lacquer box from Japan, a decorated dagger from the bazaars of Istanbul, whose owner would readily tell him the story of the distant voyages of his youth. The lengthy high street was lined with shops displaying the centuries-old Kentish names, Gann, Kemp, Cobb, Driffield; there was also a bank, two or three small yellow-brick houses belonging to the coal-ship owners, a tiny museum and a circulating library, and three taverns, the Bear and Key, the Duke of Cumberland and the Railway Arms. Apart from the rank of horse-drawn cabs drawn up outside the station there was little wheeled traffic, and if Aunt Sophie stopped in the street to gossip with an acquaintance she rarely had to step aside for anything other than the doctor's dogcart or the baker's trap. In winter, Whitstable could be bitterly cold and the icy east wind drove people indoors. But in summer when the weather was fine the little town took on a holiday aspect, with visitors from London strolling down to the beach where they could hire a bathing machine, take a turn on the swing-boats and buy a shrimp tea for sixpence.

Gradually as Willie grew accustomed to his new surroundings he came to love the green and gentle Kentish countryside. The shore between Whitstable and the mouth of the Thames was wild and the marshes when overcast appeared grey and desolate, but only half a mile inland the landscape changed. Here was rich farming country, with lush pastures full of sheep, with hawthorn hedges and clumps of ancient elms, with shady lanes and wooded hills. At intervals set back from the road were the farmhouses, with their spacious barns and oast-houses overlooking the hop fields, and in clusters between them the farm-workers' cottages, their tiny gardens ablaze with wallflowers, hollyhocks and tiger lilies, with near by the little whitewashed inns, the Jolly Sailor, the Merry Ploughman, the Crown and Anchor, their squat doorways draped in honeysuckle. In winter the wind came straight off the North Sea and sometimes it rained for days on end, but even then Maugham found something that moved him in the harshness of that barren coastline. 'In winter it was as if a spirit of loneliness, like a mystic shroud, had descended on the shore . . . when the sea-mist and the mist of heaven are one, when the sea is silent and heavy, and the solitary gull flies screeching over the grey waters.' The boy gazing out over the cold waters of the North Sea could imagine what might lie in the grey distance, even if for the present he was firmly anchored to England, with no possibility of venturing beyond.

During his first year in Whitstable it was arranged for Maugham to do his lessons at Ivy House, home of Dr Charles Etheridge, a neigh-bour of the Maughams and one of the town's two physicians. As the boy's education to date had been mainly in French, it was important that as well as learning his three Rs he should concentrate on perfecting his English, a task that was not made any easier by his newly devel-oped stammer. In fact, however, he made greatest progress on his own, unconsciously familiarising himself with the language during the hours he passed reading in his uncle's library, one of the few of his chosen methods of recreation which was popular with the grown-ups as it kept him quiet and out of the way. Spending so much time in his own company, insensibly he formed 'the most delightful habit in the world, the habit of reading . . . Haphazard among the sermons and homilies, travels, the lives of the Saints, the Fathers, the histories of the church, were old-fashioned novels; and these . . . [he] at last discovered. He chose them by their titles, and the first he read was *The Lancashire Witches*, and then he read *The Admirable Crichton*, and then many more. Whenever he started a book with two solitary travellers riding along the brink of a desperate ravine he knew he was safe.' And thus, making his way on his own through the books in his uncle's library, devouring everything from travel literature to the perfumed exoticism of *The Arabian Nights*, Maugham discovered one of the great passions of his life, a passion that would provide both pleasure and inspiration, that would encourage and clarify his own formidable skills as a story-teller, but which would also increase his isolation: in later life he found it difficult to be in anyone's company for more than a few hours before the longing came over him to be alone with a book. Books were to be his great comfort and resource, his most reliable retreat. At this early stage in his development, however, Maugham was aware of none of this. 'He did not know that thus he was providing himself with a refuge from all the distress of life; he did not know either that he was creating for himself an unreal world which would make the real world of every day a source of bitter disappointment'.

The vicarage library provided a welcome haven, but if Maugham believed his way of life was now settled he was mistaken. In May 1885, less than nine months after his arrival in England, his world was again turned upside down when he was sent away to school.

The King's School in Canterbury, situated in the precincts of the great cathedral, was one of the oldest schools in the country, founded by Henry VIII in 1541 on the basis of a much older abbey school established by St Augustine in the sixth century. By the mid-nineteenth century, Canterbury had become something of a provincial backwater, and with the coming of the railways the more prosperous Kentish families sent their sons to Eton, Harrow and Westminster, leaving the King's School to cater mainly for sons of local clergy, of the officers at the cavalry depot and of the better-off tradesmen and manufacturers. Yet, if it could not be ranked among the leading public schools, it was highly regarded within the county and boasted among its old boys several famous names, among them Christopher Marlowe and Walter Pater; Dickens paid it the compliment of sending David Copperfield to school there. Its character was emphatically Anglican, with all its teaching staff in holy orders, and the education it provided was solid and traditional, with a heavy bias towards Classics.

Accompanied by his uncle, Maugham made the short journey from Whitstable to Canterbury by train. Apart from his kindergarten in Paris, Maugham at eleven years old had had no experience of school, knew no other boys and, his head filled with alarming scenes from *Tom Brown's Schooldays*, he felt sick with apprehension. Most of all he dreaded being mocked for his stammer. Driving in a cab past the medieval walls and gateway and along the narrow streets, they came to a door in a high wall behind which stood the red-brick Georgian house which was the preparatory school for the junior boys. They were shown into the parlour, and while waiting for the headmaster to arrive Maugham in panic blurted out, 'Tell him I stammer, Uncle.'

The head of the Junior School was R. G. Hodgson, a giant of a man over six foot tall, with a bushy red beard and jovial manner. He gave the newcomers a hearty greeting, after which the Vicar immediately took his leave, abandoning his nephew to his fate. Maugham's trunk and play-box were carried upstairs and he was shown where he was to sleep, in a dormitory of narrow, green-curtained cubicles each furnished with bed, wash-stand and chair. In the morning the boys were woken by a bell and descended to the form-room, a long, bare room with two tables at which were benches, or forms, on either side, and here prayers were said before a breakfast of tea and bread-and-butter. By now the day boys were assembling, and Maugham felt overwhelmed by the boisterous crowd surging into the house, all known to each other, pushing and shouting, excitedly bragging about their holidays and taking little notice of the new boy in their midst. But by the end of the first morning's school Maugham, as he had feared he would be, had become a target of derision. His stammer, immediately apparent and intensified by anxiety, was regarded as a huge joke, and when the class was released into the large, walled playground boys fell over themselves imitating his stuttering speech, choking with laughter as in their own eyes their attempts became ever more outrageously comical. Maugham desperately struggled not to give way to tears. 'His heart beat so that he could hardly breathe, and he was more frightened than he had ever been in his life.'

Even without his stammer Maugham was singularly ill-equipped for school life. Small for his age and far from robust, he suffered from a weak chest and was often unwell, indeed missed much of his first term through illness. Longing to blend in, he was fatally different from the other boys: he had no parents, no friends, knew nothing of current schoolboy customs or slang, had never played cricket or football, and was still not entirely at ease with the English language. 'I have never forgotten the roar of laughter that abashed me', he wrote, 'when in my preparatory school I read out the phrase "unstable as water" as though unstable rhymed with Dunstable.' In this last area, his brothers' experience had been similar: they, too, were mocked for their French accents, referred to as 'froggies' by their schoolfellows. Yet for them the situation was easier: not only did they have each other for company but they were far sturdier than their little brother and excelled at sport. At Dover College both Charlie and in his turn Freddie had been made head prefect, while Charlie was Victor Ludorum, Freddie won his caps for rugger and cricket, and Harry was in the school rugger fifteen. Maugham in contrast was not much good at games, the *sine qua non* at any boys' public school, and at first was considered a dunce because his stammer made him appear inarticulate and stupid. In his memoir, 'Looking Back', Maugham describes one of many such humiliating incidents.

> The Master was a Scot called Gordon.* I was placed at the bottom of the form and on the first day of the term he told me to construe a passage. The Latin was simple and I knew very well how to put it in English, but I was shy and nervous. I began to stammer. One of the boys started to giggle, then another, then a third, and in a minute or two the whole class was shouting, screaming, yelling with laughter. I pretended not to notice, but went on stammering my head off. At last the master thumped the table at which he sat with his clenched fist and, shouting to be heard in the uproar, yelled, 'Sit down, you fool. I don't know why they put you in this form.'

By the time he arrived in Canterbury, Maugham had already grown accustomed to solitude. Wholly unprepared for communal life, he hated the lack of privacy and was awkward with the ragging, the easy banter and backchat of the other fellows. The torment and ridicule he suffered over his stammer caused him to shrink into himself, and although he longed to be popular he lacked the ability to make himself liked, lacked 'that engaging come-hitherness that makes people take to one another on first acquaintance'. Despite these obstacles, however, Maugham did

---

* In fact the Rev. E. J. Campbell: Gordon was the name Maugham gave to the character based on Campbell in *Of Human Bondage*.

well at his work, and at the end of his three years at Hodgson's was awarded a scholarship and the privilege of wearing a short black gown.

In the senior school Maugham found the quality of life considerably improved. The school itself was an eccentric jumble of houses of various styles and periods, from medieval to modern, grouped round a quadrangle beyond which was a wide lawn bordered with fine old trees, the whole dominated by the great grey Gothic cathedral, soaring upwards with its arches and buttresses and its massive central Bell Harry Tower, which 'rose like the praise of men to their God'. By now Maugham was on comradely terms with a good many of the boys, to whom his disability had become of little interest, and although he made no close friend he was tacitly accepted as one of the herd. It was generally recognised that Maugham was no longer an easy target. He was exceptionally observant and had a sharp wit, much appreciated by those at whom it was not directed, and this was coupled with a fiendish instinct for homing in on others' weakness. Time and again he would come out with some clever criticism to raise a laugh, not understanding that its very accuracy would cause it to rankle long after. He fell into the habit of saying these things 'because they amused him, hardly realising how much they hurt, and was much offended when he found that his victims regarded him with active dislike'. Longing to be popular while knowing he was not, Maugham developed a singular habit, one which, although he had no inkling of it then, would stand him in good stead as a novelist. He would take as a model a boy he particularly admired, and would imagine he was that boy, would talk with his voice, laugh with his laugh, imitate his gestures and mannerisms. The impersonation became so vivid in his own mind 'that he seemed for a moment really to be no longer himself. In this way he enjoyed many intervals of fantastic happiness.'

In schoolboy terms Maugham was clever – he had an excellent memory and won prizes in Music, Divinity, History and French – so that on the whole he had little to fear from the teaching staff, with the exception of the bad-tempered Mr Campbell, nicknamed 'Scraggs' for his habit of 'scragging', or violently shaking boys by the neck. Campbell was a bully, both physical and mental, one of his favourite techniques being to seize a victim and force him to rub out his mistake on the blackboard with his nose. Campbell's previous post had been in Devon, at Westward Ho!, where he had taught the young Rudyard Kipling, who in *Stalky & Co.* portrays him as the hated and irascible Mr King. Maugham's portrait is even more savage, and Campbell seen through the eyes of Philip Carey is a terrifying figure.

He was impatient and choleric. With no one to call him to account, with only small boys to face him, he had long lost all power of self-control. He began his work in a rage and ended it in a passion . . . His large face, with indistinct features and small blue eyes, was naturally red, but during his frequent attacks of anger it grew dark and purple.

The other masters, long set in their ways, Maugham regarded with a mixture of tolerance and contempt. He found much of the teaching uninspired, the curriculum having remained unchanged for generations, with heavy emphasis on the teaching of Latin and Greek, and modern languages regarded as unimportant. As might be expected, Maugham was particularly scornful of the lessons in French, taught by masters who although they had a good grasp of grammar made no attempt to reproduce what they considered an entirely unnecessary foreign accent. None of them, in Maugham's disdainful view, could have 'got a cup of coffee in the restaurant at Boulogne'.

Fortunately, not only for Maugham but for the entire school, in 1886 a new headmaster was appointed. The Rev. Thomas Field, son of a Canterbury linen-draper, had distinguished himself brilliantly at Oxford, and having made a success teaching at Harrow arrived at the King's School, aged only thirty-two, full of energy and fresh ideas. Tall and lean, with a black beard and thick black hair falling untidily over his forehead, Field had an immediately galvanising effect on both masters and boys. He was friendly and approachable, and his conversation was wide-ranging and full of topical reference. He was a mesmerising teacher, and would arrive in a form-room unannounced to take a class, surprising his audience by talking not of Horace or Homer but of French novels and German philosophy, drawing comparisons between Disraeli and Alcibiades, and enthusiastically discussing the pros and cons of the current Prime Minister, Gladstone, and Home Rule. As one of the high achievers, Maugham early came to the notice of Mr Field, who was kind to him, talked to him as an adult and encouraged him in his interests. Starved of approval and attention, Maugham responded eagerly, bestowing on Field a fervent hero-worship. 'I adored him,' he was later to say. Field became easily the most important figure in the boy's life, and for a time his disaffection for the school diminished and he felt there was little he would not do to please such a sympathetic and imaginative headmaster.

Maugham had a highly developed visual sense, all his life was passionately interested in painting and to a lesser extent architecture, and it was while at Canterbury that he became aware of the first stirrings of an aesthetic perception. As his mood lightened and he no longer needed to dread every aspect of his day, he began consciously to respond to the beauty of his surroundings. 'There was a wonderfully cobwebbed feeling about their dizzy and intoxicating antiquity . . . The whole atmosphere was strangely light and airy, full of the sound of bells and the cries of jackdaws floating around the great Bell Harry Tower . . .' He loved the wide lawns and wisteria-clad walls of the school, the melancholy cry of the rooks in the elm trees, above all the sight of the famous cathedral grandly rooted in all its medieval magnificence. Maugham describes Philip Carey buying a photograph of the cathedral to pin up in his study, surprised by the emotion its beauty awakens in him, aware as he looks at it of 'an odd feeling in his heart, and he did not know if it was pain or pleasure'. In adult life, when in distant parts of the globe, Maugham was sometimes overcome by nostalgia when reminded of Canterbury Cathedral, when the sight of some great edifice in Russia, China or Malaya would suddenly evoke emotional memories of his boyhood.

As conditions improved at school, so did they at home. All holidays were spent at the vicarage, but Maugham was older now and disinclined to submit so completely to his uncle's diktats. He was not in the least afraid of him, knew himself to be a great deal more intelligent, and was fairly confident of getting his own way when it mattered. Of Aunt Sophie he had grown genuinely fond; she was affectionate and kind, and Maugham had no trouble in twisting her round his little finger, particularly when his uncle was not present to witness the process. For long periods now Henry Maugham was away from home, an increasingly fragile state of health obliging him to go off to the Continent for lengthy periods of recuperation, sometimes taking his wife with him, as she too was growing frail. With the Vicar's self-serving presence removed from the house, the atmosphere was noticeably relaxed and Maugham had considerable licence to enjoy his independence. During the 1880s a craze for bicycling had gripped the youth of the nation, and Maugham, having persuaded his uncle to buy him one of the new safety bicycles, took a keen pleasure in riding about the countryside, exploring the network of little lanes and on warm days pedalling down to the beach with towel and bathing-drawers for a swim.* By the age of fifteen Maugham, although not tall, had grown into an attractive boy, with thick dark hair, brown eyes and pale complexion. He had become quite a dandy, taking trouble with his clothes and priding himself on his elegant turn-out in white flannels,

---

* His youthful bicycling was to be vividly recalled nearly fifty years later in a crucial scene in the novel *Cakes and Ale*.

blue blazer and a black-and-white straw boater. Anxious to be considered grown up, he smeared his top lip with Vaseline in the hope of encouraging a moustache, and resented being addressed still as 'Master Willie'. 'In fact, I did not like either of my names, and spent much time inventing others that would have suited me better. The ones I preferred were Roderic Ravensworth and I covered sheets of paper with this signature in a suitably dashing hand. I did not mind Ludovic Montgomery either.' Following the lead of his uncle and aunt, he 'accepted the conventions of my class as if they were the laws of Nature'. Regarding himself as a superior youth, he took on their snobbish attitudes, adopting an air of lordly patronage with the tradespeople and complaining fastidiously of the holidaymakers from London who invaded Whitstable in the summer. 'We thought London people vulgar. We said it was horrid to have all that rag-tag and bob tail down from town every year.'

Both at the vicarage and at school there was a heavy emphasis on religion, and Maugham could not help but be influenced by it. His uncle's speech was garnished with biblical reference, all the masters at school were ordained, and attendance at church both in Whitstable and Canterbury was frequent and compulsory. Imbibing the pious atmosphere surrounding him, Maugham like many children went through an intensely religious phase, serious and devout, reading and re-reading the Old and New Testaments, and taking a great deal of time and trouble over his prayers. According to the version related in *Of Human Bondage*, almost certainly derived from the actual event, Philip prays to God to cure his hated affliction, his club-foot. Having been taught to believe that true faith can move mountains, it never occurs to the boy that God will not grant his petition. 'He prayed with all the power of his soul. No doubts assailed him. He was confident in the word of God.' In a state of rapturous excitement at the miracle about to be performed, Philip's disappointment when it fails to take place is painful and profound; bitterly disillusioned he feels betrayed, both by his uncle and by his uncle's God. This incident marks the first step in Maugham's loss of faith; and yet he retained throughout his long life a strong interest in religion, in all religions, his emotional attraction towards religious belief always at war with his intellectual rejection of it, subliminally searching for a spiritual resolution that he was never able to achieve. When soon after leaving school he finally abandoned the strong and innocent faith of his boyhood he felt it as a liberation, but also as a loss. At the time hardest to accept was the knowledge that with no expectation of an afterlife he would never see his mother again.

The King's School may have prided itself on its close affiliations with the Anglican Church but its student body was no more high-minded than any other group of boys shut up for weeks at a time with scarcely a glimpse of the opposite sex. Among the two hundred boarders it is inconceivable that there did not exist the usual sexual experiment between boys, the lustful, purely physical encounters, as well as more emotionally charged affairs. It is unlikely that Maugham would have remained aloof from this. (In later life while dining with a companion at the Garrick Club he pointed out an elderly gentleman respectably eating his dinner as 'someone I went to bed with at King's'.) His was a passionate nature: in Whitstable he had conceived an emotional attachment to one of the boys in the town, who was, according to his brother Harry, 'since our mother died . . . the only person you've ever been able to love'; but of greater significance is the indication of a serious attachment to a fellow pupil. In both versions of Maugham's autobiographical novel, in *Of Human Bondage* as well as in the earlier, unpublished draft, 'The Artistic Temperament of Stephen Carey', there is a section dealing with the hero's intense infatuation with a classmate. In the earlier novel, the reader is left in no doubt about the physical aspect of the crush, although in the later version Philip's sexual feelings are more obliquely conveyed, and in both instances it is his desperate need for affection that is paramount. In *Of Human Bondage* the object of his passion is the handsome Rose,★ good-natured, easy-going and popular, the antithesis of the solitary Philip, and when Rose carelessly befriends him, Philip is both amazed and grateful, his gratitude transmuting into a jealous love, to which Rose, inevitably, is completely indifferent. It is possible that Rose's original was a boy called Leonard Ashenden, a classmate of Willie Maugham's. Ashenden is the name Maugham gives his narrator in *Cakes and Ale*, a novel which draws heavily on his own experience, and Ashenden is the name, too, of the protagonist in his collection of First World War spy stories, again auto-biographical. In all probability Leonard Ashenden would have been known to his schoolfellows as 'Ash' (a single syllable, like 'Rose'), and in a letter written in 1954 in answer to a query from the real Ashenden's widow, Maugham tells her, 'I chose the name Ashenden because like Gann, and Driffield, it is a common surname in the neighbourhood of Canterbury . . . [and] the first syllable had to me a peculiar connotation which I found suggestive.'

During the Michaelmas term of 1888, when Maugham was fourteen, he suffered a bad attack of pleurisy and had to be dispatched home for

★ The name Rose clearly had significance, as Maugham also gave it to the object of Stephen Carey's passion and to the irresistible heroine of *Cakes and Ale*.

the rest of term. By Christmas he was better, but given his clinical history it was considered imprudent for him to return to school until the weather grew warmer, and so he was sent to Hyères, near Toulon in the south of France. Here he stayed with an Englishman who had settled in the town and made his living tutoring convalescent boys. It was a strange experience for Maugham to be back in France, the country he had left four years before, whose language he had barely heard spoken intelligibly since. Like Pau, where he had been taken by his mother, Hyères was much frequented by the English, prized for the health-giving properties of its mild climate. The soft pine-scented air, the colours in the market-place, the beaches and palm trees, the strong, earthy flavour of Provençal cooking, presented a striking contrast to Whitstable and Canterbury and stirred poignant memories of the past.

When Maugham returned to school after Easter the following year, 1889, he found himself out of step. A few months is a long time in the life of a school, his old friends had made new friends, he had been moved up to a different form where the work was unfamiliar, and the bullying of the hot-tempered Campbell seemed intensified. Maugham's hatred of the man possessed him. 'I made up my mind, then and there, that I would never spend another term with that beast of a master.' The plan had been for Maugham to go to Cambridge, like his brothers, and in this he was warmly encouraged by Mr Field, who had no doubt of the boy's ability to win the necessary scholarship if only he would apply himself. But now his ambitions in that direction were diminished by his loathing for the school. His overwhelming desire was to leave as quickly as possible, and if that meant sacrificing his Cambridge career then sacrifice it he would. 'I knew exactly what to do. I was small for my age and frail, but cunning. I had no difficulty in persuading my uncle that with my delicate health it would be safer for me to spend the following winter again with the tutor at Hyères rather than take the risk of another winter in the cold and damp of Canterbury, with the happy result that at the end of that mortifying term I left the King's School for good.'

Maugham had got his way, but the indications are that his relief at effecting his escape did not bring him the happiness he had anticipated. Philip Carey, desperate to leave school, also gives up his chance of the famous university. Expecting to feel nothing but excitement on his final day he is instead tormented by regret.

In a flash there appeared before him the life which he had heard described from boys who came back to play in the OKS match or in letters from the University read out in one of the studies . . . His school-days were over, and he was free; but the wild exultation to which he had looked forward at that moment was not there. He walked round the precincts slowly, and a profound depression seized him . . . He wondered whether he had done right. He was dissatisfied with himself and with all his circumstances.

# 2

# At St Thomas's Hospital

After his second winter at Hyères Maugham returned home to the vicarage very much at a loose end. At sixteen he had no idea what he wanted to do with his life, except leave Whitstable again as quickly as possible. It was Aunt Sophie, sympathetic to his situation, who suggested he go to Germany to learn the language, and she wrote to relations of hers asking them to recommend a family with whom her young nephew could stay. The Vicar approved of the scheme, no doubt relieved to have the boy once more off his hands. 'He did not much like me,' Maugham wrote, 'for which I cannot blame him, since I do not think I was a likeable boy, and as it was my own money that was being spent on my education, he was willing enough to let me do as I chose.' Thus it was arranged that Maugham should travel to Heidelberg, where he would lodge with a professor and his wife who ran a pension for foreign students.

Arriving in Heidelberg on a sunny May morning in 1890, Maugham was enchanted by what he saw of the city as he walked up from the station, following the porter with his luggage-laden barrow up through the narrow medieval streets and along a shady avenue to the large white house that was to be his home for the next year. The Herr Professor, a tall man in middle age with greying fair hair, was courteous and correct, addressing Maugham in a formal, slightly archaic English, while his wife by contrast was a stout, red-faced little woman, bright-eyed and bustling, who chattered away in a mixture of German and broken English. At dinner the first evening Maugham came face to face with his fellow guests: a couple of American theology students; a Frenchman and a Chinese, both studying at the university; and a lanky New Englander, James Newton, who taught Greek at Harvard and had come to Germany to broaden his horizons. Maugham's priority was to learn the language, and in this he was given daily tuition by the Professor, who turned out to be an excellent teacher, hitting on the clever device of setting his pupil to translate into German one of the Shakespeare plays he had studied at school. With his retentive memory and good ear Maugham learned quickly, and as soon as he was reasonably proficient embarked on a study of Goethe, for whose work his teacher had a fervent enthusiasm. Maugham also enrolled in courses at the university, where he heard the distinguished philosopher Kuno Fischer electrify his audiences with his discourses on Schopenhauer, whose pessimistic theories, that the reason for human existence is unknown, free will an illusion and the afterlife does not exist, came to Maugham as a revelation.

Maugham was a keen student and spent many hours reading and writing in his little turret room overlooking the treetops. He read not only the German authors to whom he was now introduced but French writers, unknown in Whitstable but whose works had filled the bookshelves at the Avenue d'Antin: La Rochefoucauld, Racine, Stendhal, Balzac, Flaubert, Maupassant and Anatole France. He began writing himself, ambitiously embarking on a centenary life of the composer Meyerbeer, but destroyed the manuscript after it was rejected by the first publisher to whom it was sent. Maugham was very happy. After the tedium and restrictions of school and the vicarage, he revelled in his freedom and responded eagerly to the stimulus of his new environment. The other young men at the pension were by several years his senior, and Maugham was impressed by what seemed to him their exceptional intelligence and sophistication. They were friendly towards him and included him in their vigorous discussions on art, literature and theology that often continued late into the night. Religious faith was a subject hotly debated and one which particularly fascinated Maugham, who at first was shocked and excited by the radicalism of some of the views expressed, until one day he realised he himself no longer believed. The relief was enormous. He felt as though a huge burden had been removed: a weight of prejudice and retribution, of the suffocating dullness of church services and learning the collect by heart, of living daily in fear of eternal punishment. 'The whole horrible structure, based not on the love of God but on the fear of Hell, tumbled down like a house of cards,' he wrote, exhilarated by his newly won sense of freedom. 'He was responsible only to himself for the things he did . . . He was his own master at last.'

The American, James Newton, paid Maugham particular attention, kindly offering to show him the best walks within easy reach of the city. Almost daily they set off together to explore the famous ruined castle or tramp up the Königstuhl to admire the view of the Neckar valley, of the tall roofs and spires of Heidelberg, and further off the misty outlines of Mannheim and Worms and in the distance the glinting waters of the Rhine. Sometimes they took tea in a leafy beer-garden and in the evenings strolled round the Stadtgarten listening to the band. When Newton planned a fortnight's holiday in Switzerland, Maugham, having obtained his uncle's permission, accepted the older man's invitation to go with him, all expenses paid. It seemed an idyllic friendship; and Maugham later claimed it was only with hindsight he realised that his mentor's interest in him had been primarily sexual, that Newton's attentions were inspired less by generosity than by physical attraction.

Soon after their return to Heidelberg, Newton left for Berlin, his place at the pension taken by an Englishman, John Ellingham Brooks. Brooks was recently down from Cambridge, and having wasted a year failing to study law in London had come to Germany in search of culture. Handsome, with blue eyes, a wide sensual mouth and wavy fair hair, Brooks was charming, kind-hearted, sentimental and vain. Passionate about literature he talked with hypnotic intensity about his favourite authors, all new to Maugham, about Meredith, Swinburne, Walter Pater and Omar Khayyám, and with only the slightest encouragement would recite reams from 'Dolores' or the *Rubáiyát*. He also wrote poetry himself, mostly of a pessimistic nature, and recited that too, tossing back his blond locks and gazing into the middle distance with a vatic blue-eyed stare. He frequently declared his intention to devote his life to literature and enumerated the books he had in mind to produce. Maugham was entranced. He sat spellbound as Brooks held forth on the glories of Italy and Greece, on Shelley and Plato and Oscar Wilde, on Cardinal Newman and Matthew Arnold. Avidly he read what Brooks told him to read, swallowed whole his unremarkable opinions, and was flattered when this charismatic character began to single him out, defending him when the others ridiculed his arguments, as they not infrequently did.

Before long Brooks, like his predecessor, was inviting Maugham to accompany him on walks, during which he would boast of his aesthetic sensibility, his indifference to worldly success, and his disdain for the pitifully humdrum lives he saw his contemporaries leading. Brooks had big plans for himself, and it was only lack of time that so far had prevented his writing the important work that would ensure his place in the pantheon. Such talk was heady stuff for a lonely and intelligent boy, and when it became clear that Brooks required more of him than to be simply an admiring acolyte, Maugham was happy to oblige. Years afterwards Maugham confided to a friend that he had lost his virginity to Brooks, but it seems not to have meant very much, only taking one step further the kind of activity that had been common practice at school. Indeed for Maugham at sixteen, an impressionable and highly sexed adolescent, it was intensely exciting to be the lover of such an apparently brilliant and original young man. In time he came to see through Brooks, dismissed him as a wastrel and poseur, and his embarrassment at having been taken in led him to treat Brooks harshly both in life and in print. The character based on Brooks in *Of Human Bondage* is summarised as a man who 'honestly mistook his sensuality for romantic emotion, his vacillation for the artistic temperament, and his idleness for philosophic calm. His mind, vulgar in its effort at refinement, saw everything . . . in a golden mist of senti-mentality. He lied and never knew that he lied, and when it was pointed out to him said that lies were beautiful.' But during those early days in Heidelberg Maugham's relationship with Brooks was inspiring and added greatly to his sense of liberation, to his conviction that at last he was on the threshold of the real world.

One of Brooks's enthusiasms was for the theatre, and when the winter repertory season began he and Maugham went two or three times a week to the little Stadttheater, animatedly discussing the production in the tavern afterwards. They saw *Die Ehre* by Hermann Sudermann, then a young playwright in the vanguard of the realist movement, and also several plays by Ibsen, a writer admired by the intelligentsia but regarded by most decent folk as outrageous and obscene: in Heidelberg his works were greeted fairly evenly by both boos and cheers. To Maugham Ibsen's plays were a revelation. During his time in Germany he went several times to Munich, where it is possible in January 1891 that he was present for the first-ever production of *Hedda Gabler*, and perhaps, too, in June for the revival of *The Vikings at Helgeland*, which Ibsen himself attended. It was in Munich that he caught his one and only sight of the great Norwegian, peacefully reading his paper over a glass of beer at the Maximilianerhof. Except at the age of seven when he had seen Bernhardt in Paris, Maugham before he arrived in Germany had never been to a play – the modest touring productions occasionally given at the Assembly Rooms in Whitstable had been considered unsuitable entertainment by the Vicar – and he was now seized by a passion for the stage. The moment he entered the theatre he felt excited and engaged, and the more drama he saw the more he became fascinated by the technique of play-writing, eagerly sketching out plots and writing down snatches of dialogue. Heavily under Ibsen's influence, he studied the dramatist's technique by translating into English German versions of Ibsen's plays, and he began experiment-ing with one-acters, characterised by an unflinching realism and much concerned with shameful secrets and venereal disease.

Shortly before Christmas Brooks left Germany for Florence, where he intended to immerse himself in Dante and Boccaccio, and Maugham was able to resume his studies uninterrupted. But the influence of Brooks had unsettled him, and 'the delights of those easy, monotonous and exciting days in Heidelberg' began to pall. Now he was impatient to go home, assert his independence and begin earning his living.

In July 1891 Maugham returned to Whitstable after his year's absence to find his aunt and uncle visibly diminished: both had aged, his uncle stouter and balder, Aunt Sophie wizened and obviously unwell. With no idea what to do with himself – writing as a profession was considered out of the question – Maugham asked his uncle for advice. The Vicar naturally favoured the Church, but even he accepted that his nephew's stammer made this an unlikely proposition. Maugham's brothers had followed their father into the law, Charlie, assisted by Harry, now working for the family firm in Paris, while Freddie had recently been called to the Bar by Lincoln's Inn; but the law, too, demanded a high level of fluency. An old friend of Henry Maugham's was consulted about openings in the Civil Service, but he was dissuasive, explaining that since the introduction of a competitive examination it was in his view no longer quite the place for a gentleman to make his career. Eventually Maugham went up to London to see his father's old partner, Albert Dixon, who arranged for him to try out for a few weeks in an accountant's office in Chancery Lane; but the work was unbearably boring and Maugham was soon back in Whitstable. Finally it was Dr Etheridge, the family doctor, who came to the rescue by suggesting that young Maugham might do worse than train as a physician at his own alma mater, St Thomas's Hospital. By this time Maugham was prepared to consider almost anything that would effect his escape, and so after a few weeks at a crammer's preparing for the necessary examination, on 3 October 1892 at the age of eighteen he entered St Thomas's Hospital Medical School as a student.

It had long been Maugham's ambition to live in London. Since returning from Heidelberg he had chafed more than ever at the dull domesticity of Whitstable, and recently the gloomy atmosphere at the vicarage had turned even gloomier following the death of Aunt Sophie at the end of August 1892. In poor health for some time Sophie had gone to Bad Ems in Germany in the hope that the waters would restore her, and there she had died. Maugham had grown fond of his aunt, but he had been too much away from home to feel her loss more than slightly. A house of mourning was not the ideal place, nor a moping widower the ideal companion, for an eighteen-year-old boy, who moreover had no wish to be reminded of the harrowing bereavements of his early childhood, and

Maugham had been desperate to get away. Since his schooldays he had been aware of the lure of London, in his imagination a city of infinite promise. A couple of boys at school had been Londoners and Maugham had been intrigued by their boasted familiarity with the seamier sides of the capital. 'There emerged the vague rumour of the London streets by night . . . the surging throng round the pit-door of theatres, and the glitter of cheap restaurants, bars where men, half drunk, sat on high stools talking with barmaids; and under the street lamps the mysterious passing of dark crowds bent upon pleasure.'

Such sinister glamour was little in evidence at 11 Vincent Square, Maugham's home for the next five years. A large, slightly shabby Georgian square to one side of the busy thoroughfare of Vauxhall Bridge Road, with its pawn shops and rattling trams, Vincent Square is close by the Thames Embankment in Westminster, only a short distance from the Houses of Parliament. For £1 a week Maugham had two rooms on the ground floor of number 11, a bedroom at the back, furnished with a narrow iron bed, wash-stand and chest-of-drawers, and a sitting-room with a bay-window in the front overlooking a row of enormous plane trees and the wide green expanse of Westminster School playing-fields which the square enclosed. Here he was looked after by his landlady, Eliza Foreman, assisted by Mrs Foreman's husband, who cleaned the boots and helped with the washing-up, and by Florrie Johnston, a little maid-of-all-work. Mrs Foreman was a friendly soul, cheerful and energetic, with a sallow face and large black eyes; she was an excellent cook who took pride in looking after her gentlemen, for whom she provided two meals a day, a substantial cooked breakfast and a rather more frugal dinner. Maugham took trouble to make his little parlour comfortable, draping the chimneypiece with a Moorish rug, putting up some thick green curtains, and hanging on the wall a print of a soulful peasant girl holding a mandolin which he had found as a special offer in a Christmas edition of the *Illustrated London News*. Later, as his taste grew more sophisticated, he replaced this luscious piece of kitsch with mezzotints of paintings by Perugino, Hobbema and Van Dyck bought for a few shillings apiece from a shop in Soho Square.

Classes at the hospital began at 9.00, and every morning Maugham woke to the sound of his landlady lighting the fire in his sitting-room – 'If you don't get up at once you won't 'ave time to 'ave breakfast, an' I've got a lovely 'addick for you,' she would call through the door. Bathing hurriedly in the tin bath kept under his bed, he ate his breakfast and then walked briskly down to the Embankment, with its noisy bustle of horse-drawn traffic, threading his way through the rush-hour crowds surging over Lambeth Bridge, then left along Lambeth Palace Road to St Thomas's. On his way home to Vincent Square he bought an evening paper, and this he read until his dinner was served at 6.30. At the same table off which he had eaten he studied his textbooks, worked at his own writing, then sat in his armchair reading until it was time for bed. From Monday to Friday he was fully occupied, but during the first few week-ends the time hung heavy and Maugham was lonely. He wandered through the National Gallery, strolled round the West End, ate his modest meals in an ABC,* and most Saturday evenings he went to the theatre. Sometimes in the queue for the gallery the man next to him would try to start a conversation; but according to Maugham's published version of these early encounters he refused to be drawn, answering 'in such a way as to prevent any further acquaintance'. It was a relief when Monday morning dawned and he could return to regimented timetables and hospital routine.

St Thomas's, one of the great London teaching hospitals, was founded as a charitable institution in the twelfth century for the purpose of treating the diseased poor, which 700 years later still remained its primary purpose. A development of eight vast blocks of solid Gothic architecture, the size of a small town, St Thomas's had been forced by the expansion of the railways to move from its original location in Southwark to the south bank of the Thames at Lambeth, and here the magnificent new build-ings had been opened by Queen Victoria in 1871. A notable distinction was conferred on the hospital when Florence Nightingale established her School of Nursing there, and Miss Nightingale's dominating influence not only over her School but over the running of the entire complex ensured that high standards were rigorously maintained. At the Medical School most students took the Conjoint Board of the College of Surgeons and the College of Physicians, a course costing a little over £300 per annum and stretching over five years, the winter term lasting from October to March, the summer session from May to the end of July.

The subjects of study during the first months were Anatomy, Biology, Physics and Chemistry, and most of this Maugham found ineffably tedious. Dutifully he attended the lectures, learned hundreds of requisite facts by heart, and having equipped himself with a microscope, a mahogany instru-ment case and a copy of *Heath's Dissector* carried out his practical work in the Dissecting Room, which was painted an ominous red and reeked

* A popular chain of tea shops run by the Aerated Bread Company.

of disinfectant. This part of the course first-year students often found difficult to stomach, although Maugham never suffered from squeamishness and proved dextrous with the scalpel. The hospital provided the corpses, purchased at £5 each from the local workhouse and preserved with a mixture of vermilion and arsenic (the former to highlight the arteries, the latter to prevent putrefaction), and the students worked in pairs, clubbing together to buy their body parts, arms and legs 12s 6d, abdomen 7s 6d, head and neck 15s. As a guard against nausea, the lighting of cigarettes and pipes was encouraged, a privilege that naturally fostered a sociable atmosphere, and as a result 'a good deal of gossip went on over the dissection of a "part"'. Indeed at the end of the morning, when the Demonstrator had left and the mangled parts been returned to the students' lockers, the Dissecting Room took on quite a cosy atmosphere, a home from home where shirt-sleeved young men with a few minutes to spare could drop in for a quick smoke and a gossip.

At the end of the morning's work, Maugham lunched off cocoa and a buttered scone for 4d in the basement canteen and then leafed through the daily papers in the students' common-room; in fine weather, it was pleasant to sit outside on the terrace with a textbook, occasionally looking up to gaze across the river at the Houses of Parliament. As at school Maugham craved popularity and acceptance, but he was still shy, still inhibited by his stammer, and although he was well disposed towards his contemporaries there was little common ground. Those who had been to university were inclined to be stand-offish, or so Maugham felt, still touchy at having missed the opportunity of a place at Cambridge; he had no interest in the seemingly universal enthusiasm for cricket and football; neither did he wish to take part in the prodigious after-hours drinking bouts, having learned from unpleasant experience that more than a small quantity of alcohol made him sick. There were one or two handsome fellows with whom he became silently infatuated, envying their charm and high spirits, but by now he was better at hiding his feelings, skilful at adopting protective colouring. His guarded manner made any real intimacy impossible and by his classmates he was regarded as an aloof, almost forbidding individual.

The students at St Thomas's, like young men everywhere, talked exhaustively about sex and constantly bragged about their sexual exploits, a subject that interested Maugham a good deal. Until now his physical relations had been only with men and he felt ashamed of his lack of experience with women. One Saturday evening he walked up to the Strand to pick up a prostitute, who for £1 agreed to spend the night with him. Reassured by

her youthful, almost countrified appearance, he accompanied her to a small
hotel off Shaftesbury Avenue where he was led into a bare little room
smelling of stale tobacco, with greasy stains on the wallpaper and furnished
only with a chair, a wash-stand and a big wooden bed with dirty sheets.
The result of the encounter, unsurprisingly, was a dose of the clap, necessitating a discreet visit to one of the house physicians for treatment. But,
far from embarrassment, Maugham felt pleased with himself, proud to be
able to join in boasting with the other chaps, and perhaps privately relieved
to discover he was able to function 'normally'.

Throughout his life an appearance of conventionality was of profound
importance to Maugham. The fact of his bisexuality had to be kept secret
from most sections of the society in which he moved, and this need for
secrecy was something which subliminally he recognised early on. His
French upbringing and his stammer had set him apart from the boys at
school, and now to be categorised as an invert, as the term then was, and
thus a member of yet another unpopular minority, would have been
painfully difficult to accept. He was struck by an incident which took
place while he was going over his dissected part with the Demonstrator;
he failed to find the specified nerve and, when it was pointed out to
him, protested that it was in the wrong place. 'I complained of the
abnormality, and he [the Demonstrator], smiling, said that in anatomy it
was the normal that was uncommon . . . The remark sank into my mind,'
wrote Maugham afterwards, 'and since then it has been forced upon me
that it is true of man as well as of anatomy.'

Learning in childhood how to live under cover, Maugham rarely revealed
himself except to his closest intimates. At twenty he was well aware of
his sexual orientation, of his feelings for men, although for years he tried
to convince himself that such feelings were no more than a minor
aberration. 'I tried to persuade myself', he said in later life, 'that I was
three-quarters normal and that only a quarter of me was queer – whereas
really it was the other way round.' In the notebook he kept at this period
and published many years later he describes the purely physical attraction he sometimes felt for his own sex, although typically he was careful,
for public consumption, to deny the existence of any explicitly sexual
ingredient. 'The friendship of animal attraction . . . [is] unreasoning and
unreasonable; and by the irony of things it is probable that you will have
this feeling for someone quite unworthy of it. This kind of friendship,
though sex has no active part in it, is really akin to love: it arises in the
same way, and it is not improbable that it declines in the same way.'
Looking back he comments, 'I do not remember who the persons were

who occasioned these confused reflections, but . . . I surmise that I had found my feeling for someone to whom I was drawn unreciprocated.'

'I entered little into the life of the hospital and made few friends there,' he recalled, 'for I was occupied with other things.' Certainly medicine was of small interest: he knew he needed to qualify, as that would provide him with a career on which to fall back if all else failed; but he was determined to make his living by his pen, and single-minded in this pursuit he allowed nothing and nobody to get in its way. A passionate autodidact and exceptionally disciplined and industrious, Maugham read prodigiously, not only in English literature – novels, plays, poetry – but also in French, German, Russian and Italian. In the course of two months he read three plays by Shakespeare, two volumes of Mommsen's *History of Rome*, much of Lanson's *Littérature française*, several novels in English and French, two scientific works and an Ibsen play. He copied out passages from Swift, from Dryden, from Jeremy Taylor, committing parts of them to memory. His head was filled with ideas and he covered page after page in his notebooks with outlines for stories and dramatic plots, with scraps of dialogue and with observations and reflections. 'I was writing', he said, 'because I could not help it.' His immediate ambition was to write a play, and he continued to go regularly to the theatre, often in the company of a good-looking young man whom he had first met in Heidelberg, Walter Adney Payne.

Payne's father, George Payne, was a leading figure in the London music-hall and, as manager of the Tivóli in the Strand, the New Oxford in Oxford Street and the London Pavilion in Piccadilly, enjoyed a virtual monopoly over the West End. As Maugham the medical student and Payne, studying to be a chartered accountant, were both chronically short of funds, Payne senior was a valuable source of free tickets, enabling them to go nearly every Saturday afternoon to the halls to see Marie Lloyd, Dan Leno, Vesta Tilley and Albert Chevalier. In the evening they went to the theatre, where from their cheap seats in the pit they saw such memorable productions as Wilde's *A Woman of No Importance*, *The Second Mrs Tanqueray* with Mrs Patrick Campbell and George Alexander's staging of *The Importance of Being Earnest*. On 5 January 1895 they were among the fashionable audience at the St James's Theatre for the disastrous first night of Henry James's play *Guy Domville*, when the distinguished author while taking his bow was humiliatingly booed. It was a distressing scene which Maugham never forgot. '[James] was greeted with such an outburst of boos and catcalls as only then have I heard in the theatre,' he wrote many years later.

'He confronted the hostile audience, his jaw fallen so that his mouth was slightly open and on his countenance a look of complete bewilderment. He was paralysed. I don't know why the curtain wasn't immediately brought down.'

Pictures were another passion of Maugham's, and here he had a mentor in the eccentric form of one Wentworth Huyshe. A generation older than Maugham, Huyshe, a small, slender man with an Elizabethan beard and pale-blue eyes, had been a distinguished war correspondent for both the *New York Herald* and the London *Times*. He had lived and worked in London, Paris and New York, and had married twice, first to an American, secondly to the daughter of an uneducated farm labourer. With his second wife, by whom he eventually had nine children, Huyshe settled in the country near Harlow in Essex, where he led a bohemian existence in pursuit of his many and varied interests. These included heraldry and armour, historical costume (on the subject of which he had corresponded with Oscar Wilde), literature, music and painting. A friend first of Harry Maugham, one of whose poems he had set to music, Huyshe, by then nearing fifty, saw considerable promise in Maugham; he encouraged him with his writing and took him to concerts, galleries and museums, teaching him how to look at pictures and introducing him to new names in various branches of the arts. Maugham stayed with the Huyshes at Besom Cottage, where in the mornings, oblivious of the racket made by the junior members of the household, he sat and wrote at Huyshe's desk, showing his work to his host when he had done. 'Why, this is fine! This is wonderful!' Huyshe would exclaim. When Maugham's first novel was published a few years later he inscribed a copy to Wentworth Huyshe and sent it to him with a grateful letter. 'I can never forget how kind you were to me when I was a stupid boy, & you took me about & showed me things, & inspired me with all sorts of new ideas. I can honestly say that I owe a very great deal to you, and now it is a great pleasure to me to be able to send you my first-born.'

Meanwhile at the hospital Maugham had moved on to study Practical Pharmacy and Materia Medica, subjects which he found marginally less tedious than Anatomy, quite enjoying the business of rolling pills, mixing ointments and grinding up powders. But it was not until he took his turn as a clerk in the Out-Patients' Department that suddenly his attention was fully engaged. Here for the first time he found his work of consuming interest, fascinated not by the range of ailments but by the men and women themselves, who day after day came to the hospital for help.

Lambeth in the 1890s was one of the poorest and most overcrowded areas of London. Families tended to be large, and although infant mortality was high (deaths of the under-fives accounted for nearly 50 per cent of the total mortality rate) many couples had ten, eleven or even twelve children, with whom they lived in dark, cramped houses backing on to filthy courts with open drains, or in overcrowded tenements where conditions were squalid in the extreme. Many of those fortunate enough to be employed worked in sweatshops, where sometimes seventeen or eighteen men and women were crammed into a tiny top-floor room, inadequately lit and heated, with water closets without water and the only ventilation coming from broken windows nailed shut, the empty panes filled up with canvas. Disease ran rife, and drink, easily available and comparatively cheap, was the most popular panacea, with the result that high levels of domestic violence were commonplace. Death from starvation was not infrequently the end for the elderly and the unemployed. Such was the population which depended on St Thomas's for its free medical care, and with which Maugham was now in daily contact.

From early afternoon the waiting-room was thronged with men, women and children, some decently dressed, others ragged and dirty; and despite the strong odour of disinfectant the stench of unwashed bodies grew sickeningly pungent as the day wore on. The men were seen first, most suffering from chronic bronchitis, or 'a nasty 'acking cough', as it was usually described, as well as venereal disease and every possible variety of drink-related disorder. With the women, aged prematurely by frequent confinements, the main problems stemmed from malnutrition and from the split lips, black eyes and broken ribs regularly dealt them by their drunken husbands. Maugham assisted the house physician, who allotted him the more straightforward cases to deal with on his own, and it was now that he heard the stories of these frequently harrowing lives. For the patients it was unusual to find among the hard-pressed medical staff someone who took such an interest in their personal problems, and they responded gratefully to this sympathetic young doctor with his gentle manner and expressive dark eyes. Unlike many of his colleagues, Maugham never patronised his patients: it was understanding they wanted, not pity, and through his genuine interest he came to learn more about their lives and of their teeming, claustrophobic world than did many of the highly qualified doctors who saw their patients only as medical specimens. Like his alter ego in *Of Human Bondage*, Philip Carey, Maugham came to realise that the poor:

did not want large airy rooms; they suffered from cold, for their food was not nourishing and their circulation bad; space gave them a feeling of chilliness, and they wanted to burn as little coal as need be; there was no hardship for several to sleep in one room, they preferred it; they were never alone for a moment, from the time they were born to the time they died, and loneliness oppressed them; they enjoyed the promiscuity in which they dwelt, and the constant noise of their surroundings pressed upon their ears unnoticed. They did not feel the need of taking a bath constantly, and Philip often heard them speak with indignation of the necessity to do so with which they were faced on entering the hospital . . .

Never before had Maugham been confronted by such a variety of character and human type, and he was enthralled by the narratives that day after day were spun out before him, excited by their indefinable potential. So absorbed did he become in these glimpses of life in the raw, of human nature at its most unguarded, that when he himself fell ill – with septic tonsilitis contracted after performing a post-mortem on a badly decomposed corpse – in spite of being nursed in the private wing and 'treated like a crowned head', he could hardly wait to resume his duties.

Busy although he was at the hospital, and in his spare time immersed in his own reading and writing, Maugham nonetheless maintained his links with family and friends. One of the latter was John Ellingham Brooks, last seen in Heidelberg, who now came wafting in from the Continent, where he had been travelling extensively and writing flowery letters about love and art and the glories of Italy, particularly as seen through the eyes of Ruskin and Pater. As before in Germany, Maugham found Brooks's company inspirational, and falling again under his influence he took the opportunity of his first Easter vacation, six weeks in the spring of 1894, to visit Italy. Already the previous year at Brooks's instigation he had begun to study Italian, and now with £20 in his pocket he set off, spending a few days in Paris on the way in order to see his brothers Charles and Harry and to visit the Louvre. Fired by Pater's essay on the *Mona Lisa*, he made excitedly for Leonardo's famous portrait, but 'I was bitterly disappointed. Was this the picture Pater had written about with such eloquence and in prose so ornate?' He continued on to Genoa and Pisa, and then to Florence, where he stayed for over a fortnight, lodging in a house overlooking the Duomo with a kindly widow whose spinster daughter gave him lessons in Italian. Eager to learn, Maugham made good use of his time. 'I lived laborious days,' he recalled, beginning each morning with a couple of hours studying Dante before setting off to see the sights, Ruskin in hand. 'I admired everything Ruskin told me to admire,' he wrote,'and turned away in disgust from what he condemned. Never can he have had a more ardent disciple.' Only in the evening did he allow himself a little recreation, wandering out after dinner in search of adventure but, according to the account written years later, 'such was my innocence, or at least my shyness, I always came home as virtuous as I had gone out'.

Back in London Maugham was introduced to Brooks's friends, a group of aesthetically inclined young men who dazzled him by their zest and creativity. They seemed to fizz with imagination and original ideas while he in juxtaposition appeared dull and ordinary. 'They could write and draw and compose with a facility that aroused my envy,' Maugham wrote, '[and] they had an appreciation of art and a critical instinct that I despaired of attaining.' It was presumably one of these budding geniuses who told him airily that there was only one picture in the Louvre worth looking at and that was by Chardin. 'That was strong meat to set before a youth just turned twenty. I was too shy to tell the young man that I thought Titian's *Man with the Glove* a beautiful portrait and that Titian's *Entombment* had deeply moved me.' It was only later that Maugham came to recognise that the group's effusions owed more to youthful high spirits than to genuine talent, and that their mentor, Brooks, was temperamentally flawed and would never fulfil the much trumpeted promise of his early years.

Shortly after returning from Italy, Maugham had two family weddings to attend. The first, and much the more unexpected, was that of the Rev. Henry Maugham, who, a widower for not quite two years, had proposed marriage to Ellen Matthews, the fifty-year-old spinster daughter of a General Henry Matthews of Bath. The wedding took place on 6 June 1894, after which the new Mrs Maugham was brought to Whitstable, where she was soon discovered to be a merry creature, in every way a lively contrast to her predecessor. During Aunt Ellen's occupation the vicarage became a much more cheerful house to visit, and it was clear that she made the Vicar very happy.

Two weeks later, on 21 June, Charlie, eldest of the four Maugham brothers, was married in London to Mabel Hardy, daughter of the animal-painter Heywood Hardy. For the previous five years Charlie had been working in Paris, a junior partner in the family law firm, now Sewell et Maugham, and it was here that he had met his future wife who was studying at the Conservatoire. They returned to Paris after the wedding, where they embarked on the kind of prosperous, sociable way of life that the Maugham parents had enjoyed a generation earlier. Like his father,

Charlie was good-natured and clever, while Mabel, or Beldy as she was known, a talented amateur artist, was vivacious and fun, both popular members of Parisian expatriate society. For a time Charlie's younger brother Harry worked with him at Sewell et Maugham, but the arrangement had not been a success. Harry was an unconventional character who had little interest in the law; his real ambition, like Maugham's, was to be a writer. Gentle, kind-hearted, but also thin-skinned and neurotic, Harry spent most of his spare time composing lengthy verse dramas and sitting in cafés in company with like-minded young men, artists and poets; soon he gave up any pretence at pursuing a legal career, left Paris and after a spell in London moved to Italy. He and Maugham had much in common, aesthetically and intellectually; they were both outsiders, shy and insecure; they were both sexually nonconformist; they both wanted to write; and yet they never became close, separated geographically, but also by a lack of that fraternal bond that never had the chance properly to form between Maugham and his brothers.

With Charlie and Harry living on the Continent, Maugham saw most of Freddie, the second eldest, who had remained in London and joined chambers in Lincoln's Inn. Ironically it was their relationship that came to be most strained, the ultra-conventional Freddie coming to regard his younger brother with a censoriousness deeply resented by Maugham, who with part of himself would have liked to have attained the iron-clad respectability of his sibling. As young men, however, this mutual hostility was mild and intermittent, and they had enough of a shared past and interests in common – the theatre, golf, looking at pictures – for them to enjoy each other's company, at least in small doses. Freddie, in adulthood always addressed as F.H., was a handsome, athletic man of dour demeanour, his icy reserve effectively concealing a sensitiveness and vulnerability that was rarely revealed, even within the family. In December 1896, F.H. had married Helen ('Nellie') Romer, daughter of a High Court judge, Robert Romer, soon to become a lord justice of appeal. While F.H. appeared joyless and austere, Nellie was affectionate, gregarious and high-spirited, possessed of enormous charm and a rumbustious sense of humour, with a love of slapstick and silly jokes. If her boisterous jollity sometimes grated, F.H. nevertheless depended on his wife for the sympathy and warmth he craved but could not show. She and Maugham took to each other at once and quickly became close friends, Nellie inviting her brother-in-law to family occasions, including him in amateur theatricals, and often asking him to tea on her own, when the two of them would gossip amicably, before her husband with his blighting presence returned to the house in the evening. At this period F.H. was making painfully slow progress in his career, with few briefs coming in; he was tormented by financial worries and frustrated ambition, and the strain of this made him more than usually distant and cold. 'The waiting for work is a terrible drawback to a young barrister,' he wrote fifty years later, 'and tends to sour his whole existence. I shall never forget those unhappy days.'

When Maugham resumed his studies at the hospital after the summer of 1894, he moved from Out-Patients to working on the wards, accompanying the house physician on his rounds, carrying out tests and writing up case-notes. The wards at St Thomas's were pleasant places, long, light rooms with a row of spotless white beds down each side, the clinical atmosphere softened by generous arrangements of flowers and potted plants. As before, Maugham enjoyed contact with the patients, and yet the wards lacked the drama and excitement of his previous post, and he welcomed the transition to surgical clerk, assisting at operations, standing beside the surgeon ready to hand him his instruments. If the operation were an unusual one, the theatre galleries would fill up with observers, but on most days there was not more than a handful of students watching, which gave the proceedings a cosiness that Maugham relished.

Occasionally his sang-froid deserted him, as he recounts in a description of watching an operation that painfully brought back memories of his mother's death. 'The other day I went into the theatre to see a Caesarian,' he records in his notebook for 1897.

> Before starting Dr C. made a short discourse . . . He told us that the patient couldn't have a child naturally and had had to be twice aborted; but she'd set her heart on having one now that she was pregnant again and though he'd explained the danger to her and said that it was only an even chance that she'd come through, she'd told him that she was prepared to risk it . . . The operation appeared to go very well and Dr C's face beamed when he extracted the baby. This morning I was in the ward and asked one of the nurses how she was getting on. She told me she'd died in the night. I don't know why, it gave me a shock and I had to frown because I was afraid I was going to cry. It was silly, I didn't know her, I'd only seen her on the operating table. I suppose what affected me was the passion of that woman, just an ordinary hospital patient, to have a baby, a passion so intense that she was willing to incur the frightful risk; it seemed hard, dreadfully hard, that she had to die.

In both the Easter and summer vacations of 1895 Maugham went again to Italy, this time to Capri in the company of Ellingham Brooks. Describing the island as 'the most enchanting spot I had ever seen',

Maugham was bewitched by the romantic beauty of the place, revelling in the warmth, in the scented air and in the atmosphere of dreamy tranquillity that Capri possessed in those days when it was still a rural community with a small foreign population and was visited by only a few tourists who tended to avoid the summer months. Arriving on the little steamer from Naples, the two men were rowed ashore, their luggage carried up the steep road from the harbour by a couple of burly female porters who left them with their belongings in the main square. On this first visit Maugham and Brooks lodged in a modest *pensione* where four shillings a day bought board, lodging and a view of Vesuvius from the bedroom window. The two men went for long walks up the steep hillsides covered in sweet-smelling shrubs, past vineyards and lemon orchards and little white-washed houses draped in roses, jasmine and bougainvillaea. Reaching the summit they could turn to look down at the sea far below, at the Faraglioni, two great grey rocks rising like a cathedral out of the clear green water. Mornings were dedicated to study, after which at midday they swam off the rocks at the Bagnio Timberino and basked in the sun before lazily wending their way uphill for lunch under a vine-covered pergola. Every evening after dinner they joined the throng at Morgano's, the wine shop beside the Piazza Grande. Here, the expatriate community gathered to exchange news and gossip, Maugham listening intently as Brooks and his new acquaintance, writers, painters, sculptors, held forth on art, philosophy and literature. Lacking their learning and fluency Maugham felt himself at a disadvantage; he sat smoking and saying little, never mentioning his own attempts at composition.

> I thought it all grand. Art, art for art's sake, was the only thing that mattered in the world . . . They were all agreed about this, that they burned with a hard, gem-like flame. I was too shy to tell them that I had written a novel and was half-way through another and it was a great mortification to me, burning as I was too with a hard, gem-like flame, to be treated as a philistine who cared for nothing but dissecting dead bodies and would seize an unguarded moment to give his best friend an enema.

Inhibited in conversation he may have been, yet the tongue-in-cheek reference to giving his best friend an enema indicates confidence in other areas. Maugham at twenty-one took care with his appearance and had begun to dress, insofar as his modest income allowed, with a certain elegance; with his slim build and expressive features he was an engaging young man, sexually magnetic and well aware of the glances he attracted.

The powerful creative impulse, which inspired so many ideas and drove him to write for hours every night, materialised also in a sexual energy which, even while he was sitting mainly motionless and silent as during the evening sessions at Morgano's, was potent. The fact that he and Brooks were lovers would have caused little comment on Capri, where irregular relationships were accepted almost as the norm. The island had long enjoyed a reputation for tolerance towards its foreign community, many of whom were drawn there as much by the good-looking Capresi youth as by the beauty of the setting. As a later inhabitant, Compton Mackenzie, wrote of Capri, 'Its reputation as a decomposer of character was classic.' A blind eye was turned to the conduct of most of these exotic imports, for instance, the notorious Count Fersen, paedophile and opium-addict; or the ex-Vicar of Sandringham, who had arrived suddenly after trouble with choirboys at home; or Lord Alfred Douglas, trailing clouds of infamy and seen openly misbehaving with a pretty cabin-boy on his yacht. Only occasionally did one of them go too far, like the arms magnate Friedrich Krupp, reports of whose behaviour with under-age boys were beginning to cause alarm, eventually resulting in his having to leave the island. Nonetheless the moral climate was unusually relaxed and, to those who found the laws and attitudes of northern Europe a serious hindrance to their preferred way of life, Capri was a welcome haven. Such a one was John Ellingham Brooks, who within a couple of weeks felt so entirely at ease that he decided not to return to England but to remain on Capri for good.

Brooks's decision was timely. In the same month that he and Maugham first visited Capri, April 1895, the trial was taking place in London of Oscar Wilde. Wilde's was not the only nor indeed the first such trial to be exhaustively reported since the passing ten years earlier of the Criminal Law Amendment Act,★ but it made a greater impact and reached a far wider audience on account of the fame of the accused, the social status of the accuser, the Marquess of Queensberry, and the headline-grabbing wit, flamboyance and panache with which Wilde, fatally, conducted himself in court. Here a world was revealed of rent-boys and male brothels and perverse sexual practices hitherto undreamt of by the majority of the nation's newspaper-reading population. Wilde's subsequent sentencing to two years' hard labour struck terror into the hearts of many men who had imagined that a modicum of discretion was all that was necessary to keep them out of trouble. A significant number decided there and then

★ The Criminal Law Amendment Act of 1885 proscribed all homosexual acts between males.

to leave for the Continent, and it was said that on the night after Wilde's arrest, instead of the usual sixty or so crossing from England to France, six hundred gentlemen took passage on the Channel steamers. The trial of Oscar Wilde was to cast a long shadow, and for seventy years Maugham's generation had to live with the very real fear of blackmail, exposure, public scandal and arrest. It is unlikely that Maugham at only twenty-one fully understood the relevance of these events to his own life, but the Wilde case could not fail to increase his determination to keep areas of his private life under cover, to encourage the habit of concealment.

In London on the occasions when he was seen by one of his fellow students outside the hospital it was noted that he was always with the same young man, almost certainly his theatre-going friend Walter Adney Payne. Payne, 'dear companion of my lonely youth', as Maugham described him, was the first in a series of close male associates on whom throughout his life he depended heavily. There is a visible pattern that runs through these relationships, beginning with a sexual affair which then evolves into an intimate friendship, with the one-time lover becoming part secretary, part companion and facilitator. Although nothing remains of any personal correspondence (on Payne's death all letters between them were on Maugham's instructions destroyed), the two men were close for over twenty years, with Payne the first to take on the role of secretary–companion that in later years was most notably filled by Gerald Haxton and then Alan Searle. The probability is that, like Haxton's and Searle's, Payne's early friendship with Maugham contained, if only briefly, some sexual element, before developing into a more stable and long-lasting commitment. And like his successors Payne from the beginning was able to provide one essential service: he enabled Maugham to make contact with strangers. Because of his stammer Maugham found it next to impossible to initiate the kind of exchange so easily struck up with others in public places. His stammer was a torment to him and at times made him excruciatingly inhibited and self-conscious, as he himself painfully described.

> Few realised the exhaustion it caused him to speak. What to most men is as easy as breathing was to him a constant strain. It tore his nerves to pieces. Few knew the humiliations it exposed him to, the ridicule it excited in many, the impatience it aroused, the awkwardness of feeling that it made people find him tiresome, the minor exasperation of thinking of a good, amusing or apt remark and not venturing to say it in case the stammer ruined it. Few knew the distressing sense it gave rise to of a bar to complete contact with other men.

Thus, knowing that he could not speak without the risk of making a fool of himself, Maugham liked to rely on someone else to start the conversation, and in this respect Payne with his good looks and pleasant manner was the ideal companion.

On their regular outings to the play and music-hall the opportunities for casual encounters were numerous. Along the Strand, in Piccadilly, around the newly built theatres in Shaftesbury Avenue were dozens of shops, cafés and public houses that stayed open till the early hours attracting crowds of men and women, not all of them engaged in respectable pursuits. At night the streets were crowded, alive with opportunity, as Maugham was fondly to recall. 'There was a part [of the West End] . . . they called the Front, the street on the north side that led from Shaftesbury Avenue to the Charing Cross Road, where from eleven to twelve people walked up and down in a serried throng . . . There was a sense of adventure in the air. Eyes met and then . . .' Indoors, the Criterion Bar and the promenade at the Pavilion were two popular locations for casual pick-ups, and at the Tivoli in the Strand and at the Empire and Alhambra in Leicester Square the staff had long learned to turn a blind eye to the all-male activity that went on in the dark upper tiers of the auditorium. Out-of-doors two popular homosexual cruising areas were the Embankment Gardens by the river and the statue of Achilles in Hyde Park★ ('Really, the things that go on in front of that work of art are quite appalling. The police should interfere,' says Mabel Chiltern in Wilde's *An Ideal Husband*).

Maugham was irresistibly drawn to the sexual underworld. He soon learned that a man about town never went to the music-hall before nine, as that was the hour when prostitutes of both sexes arrived to ply their trade, strolling enticingly up and down among the gentlemen smoking and drinking in the Promenade bar. Maugham's early attempt at picking up a tart, an alarmingly self-possessed young woman, ended in humiliation when she simply turned her back and walked contemptuously away from his stammered offer to buy her a drink. Outside in the Strand trade was relatively cheap, the pricier rent-boys and 'daughters of joy' concentrating on prosperous Piccadilly. A slender figure in his hat and dark overcoat, Maugham, fascinated, would watch them as they sauntered along looking for custom, invisible to the ordinary couples and family parties making for omnibus and Underground after an evening's blameless entertainment. In his notebook for 1896 Maugham records a fragment

---

★ Nearly forty years later in the short story 'The Creative Impulse', Maugham as a private joke gave the title *The Achilles Statue* to a thriller written by a respectable lady novelist.

of dialogue that is undeniably flirtatious in tone, as it might have taken place between himself and an older man.

'Oh, I should hate to be old [says the younger]. All one's pleasures go.'
'But others come.'
'What?'
'Well, for instance, the contemplation of youth. If I were your age I think it not improbable that I should think you a rather conceited and bumptious man: as it is I consider you a charming and amusing boy.'

Preparing it for publication half a century later, Maugham teasingly adds that he could no longer 'remember who said this . . .'

In October 1896 Maugham arrived at the final stage of his training at St Thomas's, the study of Obstetrics and Gynaecology. The first morning's lecture was memorable. 'Gentlemen,' the instructor began, 'woman is an animal that micturates once a day, defecates once a week, menstruates once a month, parturates once a year and copulates whenever she has the opportunity.' Recently a new requirement had been introduced, a course in practical midwifery, for which students were expected to be on call for a period of three weeks, and within a mile's radius of the hospital to attend a minimum of twenty confinements. During his tour of duty Maugham was called out on sixty-three occasions. Temporarily lodged in a room opposite the main gates where he could be quickly summoned by the porter, he was rarely able to snatch more than a couple of hours' sleep, and yet he was almost unaware of his exhaustion so absorbed was he in what he witnessed of his patients' lives. It was the first time he had worked outside the hospital precincts, and it was only now that he saw for himself the frightening reality of the poverty in which large numbers struggled to exist, experienced at close quarters the noise, the stench, the overcrowding, the filthy, verminous conditions from which for many there was no chance of escape. If the head of the family were in work, then life was tolerable; if not, then the situation was desperate, and in such cases the arrival of another baby was regarded with despair. 'Accidents' were not infrequent: mothers rolled on their babies while they slept, and errors of diet were not always the result of carelessness.

In a passage written fifty years later Maugham recalls his induction into the slums of Lambeth. It was usually the husband or a small child of the expectant mother who led him through the dark and silent streets,

up stinking alleys and into sinister courts where the police hesitated to penetrate, but where your black bag protected you from harm. You were taken to grim houses, on each floor of which a couple of families lived and down into a stuffy room, ill-lit with a paraffin lamp, in which two or three women, the midwife, the mother, the 'lady as lives on the floor below' were standing round the bed on which the patient lay. Sometimes you waited in that room for two or three hours, drinking a friendly cup of tea with the midwife and going down in the street below now and then to get a breath of air. The husband was sitting on the step and you sat down beside him and chatted.

In cases of emergency Maugham could summon help from the Senior Obstetric Clerk, but by the time the SOC arrived it was often too late: the baby had failed to breathe or the mother had bled to death and there was nothing to be done. After nights like these it was a relief to come out at dawn into the fresh air and walk beside the Thames, watch the sky turn pink and the early-morning mist dissolve over the water.

It was during Maugham's training in midwifery that the idea came to him for a novel. Over the past few years he had experimented with a number of projects, his chief ambition being to write for the theatre. The plays he had submitted, however, had been rejected, and so he planned instead to complete two or three novels in the hope that if these were published managers would look more favourably on his dramatic work.

This was an exciting time in publishing. During the 1890s a number of lively new publishing houses had been founded – Heinemann, Hutchinson, Methuen, the Bodley Head; and as the sway of the three-decker novel and the circulating library had recently collapsed, the way had been left clear for young writers to experiment with different and shorter forms. While browsing in the bookshops Maugham had been attracted by the Pseudonym Library, a popular series of cheap paper-bound books published by the enterprising Thomas Fisher Unwin. Unwin, a tall, handsome man, blue-eyed and black-bearded, known almost as well for his flamboyant ties as for his irascible personality, had set up his own business in the 1870s and was notorious both for taking risks and for driving a hard bargain. Supported by, in the words of Ford Madox Ford, a 'heaven-sent' team of readers which included the influential Edward Garnett and, briefly, G. K. Chesterton, Unwin had made some notable discoveries, numbering among his authors Yeats, Galsworthy, H. G. Wells, George Moore and Joseph Conrad. Maugham sent in a couple of short stories, one of which, 'A Bad Example', about a good man whose good-ness leads his selfish family to regard him as mentally unbalanced,\* was passed to Garnett, who advised against publication. 'There is some ability in this, but not very much. Mr Maugham has imagination and he can

---

\* A theme Maugham was to return to nearly forty years later in his final play, *Sheppey*.

write prettily, but his satire against society is not deep enough or humorous enough to command attention. He should be advised to try the humbler magazines for a time, and if he tries anything more important to send it to us.' As a result of this report Unwin rejected both stories, on the excuse that they were too short to stand on their own; he added, however, that if in the future Mr Maugham chose to submit a full-length novel he would be pleased to read it. Intensely excited by this morsel of encouragement, Maugham immediately set to work

*Liza of Lambeth*, or *A Lambeth Idyll*, as it was originally entitled, is set in the slums with which Maugham's medical training had lately made him so familiar. Eighteen-year-old Liza Kemp is a factory girl living in a small single room with her alcoholic mother. Pretty and spirited, Liza is fond of a good time and popular in her neighbourhood. She has a faithful follower, Tom, who hopes to marry her, but she is not yet ready to settle down to a life of domestic drudgery and years of child-bearing – she herself is one of thirteen, which is nothing out of the ordinary in Vere Street. Full of ill-defined longings for love and something greater than her narrow world can offer, she is more than ready to respond when she meets Jim Blakeston, an older man who has recently moved into the street with his wife and five children. Jim seduces her, and the two of them embark on a passionate affair, conducted in secret wherever they can be together away from prying eyes, in Battersea Park, on the Embankment, sheltering from the rain in Waterloo Station. But inevitably they are discovered, and Liza, now pregnant and therefore disgraced, is exposed to jeering and contempt; she is physically attacked by Jim's wife, who in turn is half killed by her husband in a beer-sodden rage. Liza, battered and distraught, goes into labour while helplessly drunk, dying as she miscarries, with her tipsy mother watching over her, assisted by a garrulous midwife who has witnessed such a scene many times before.

As Maugham's literary taste over the past few years had been strongly influenced by John Ellingham Brooks, he might well have chosen to model his style on Brooks's beloved Pater, or on one of the fin-de-siècle Decadents, such as Huysmans or Wilde; but in the event it was the French realists whom he chose to follow, Zola and Maupassant, the latter in particular, whose vernacular style of narrative exactly suited the unromantic nature of his subject. In an introduction to a later edition of *Liza*, Maugham wrote, 'I had at that time a great admiration for Guy de Maupassant . . . who had so great a gift for telling a story clearly, straightforwardly and effectively,' three adverbs which may justly be applied to *Liza*, by any standards an accomplished work of fiction and impressive indeed for a first novel. In writing *Liza*, Maugham explained, 'I described without addition or exaggeration the people I had met in the Out-Patients' Department at the Hospital and in the District during my service as an Obstetric Clerk . . . My lack of imagination . . . obliged me to set down quite straightforwardly what I had seen with my own eyes and heard with my own ears.' He was later to claim that *Liza* was 'the first of the realistic descriptions of the London slums that the English public had had a chance of reading', although in fact it was only one of a number published in that period giving an authentic depiction of the lives of the urban poor, coming after such works of fiction as George Gissing's *The Nether World* (1889), Kipling's terrifying story 'The Record of Badalia Herodsfoot' (1890) and the harrowing *Esther Waters* (1894) by George Moore.

As might be expected, the Lambeth scenes are vividly drawn, their shabbiness and squalor a sombre contrast to the cheeriness of the factory girls with their huge feathered hats and frizzed-up fringes, backchatting saucily with each other and with their young men. The dialogue, at which Maugham had had plenty of practice in his numerous failed attempts at play-writing, is effective and naturalistic; as he rightly said, 'I caught the colloquial note by instinct.' There are some enjoyably comic passages, one scene especially, describing an outing to the theatre to see a third-rate melodrama, although another, centred on a Bank Holiday picnic, is less successful, mainly because of the adoption of an ill-judged mock-pastoral style. Yet in the main the novel keeps a firm grip on reality, and the portrayal of this threadbare society is wholly without sentimentality: the author regards his characters with sympathy but also with an almost clinical detachment, passing no moral judgment on their behaviour: he understands very well that the young women must enjoy themselves where they can, for their futures hold little but hard labour, with drunkenness and domestic violence accepted as the norm. Liza's best friend Sally, for instance, so excited at the prospect of her wedding, soon learns to accept that regular beatings are an unavoidable part of married life. '"It wasn't 'is fault," put in Sally, amidst her sobs, "it's only because 'e's 'ad a little drop too much. 'E's arright when 'e's sober."' Maugham shows a mature awareness of the brutalising nature of poverty as well as of the invincible, if short-lived, optimism of youth. Significantly he also shows a profound understanding of the human craving for love and of the overwhelming power of sexual attraction. The reader is left in no doubt of the nature of Liza's passion for Jim Blakeston:

They sat there for a long while in silence; the beer had got to Liza's head, and the warm night air filled her with a double intoxication. She felt the arm round her waist, and the big, heavy form pressing against her side; she experienced again the curious sensation as if her heart were about to burst, and it choked her – a feeling so oppressive and painful that it almost made her feel sick. Her hands began to tremble, and her breathing grew rapid, as though she were suffocating. Almost fainting, she swayed over towards the man, and a cold shiver ran through her from top to toe. Jim bent over her, and, taking her in both arms, he pressed his lips to hers in a long, passionate kiss. At last, panting for breath, she turned her head away and groaned.

*Liza of Lambeth*, written in three French school-exercise books, was completed in six months, and on 14 January 1897 the manuscript dispatched to Unwin, with a descriptive note, typically pessimistic, attached. 'This is the story of a nine days wonder in a Lambeth slum . . . [which] shows that in this world nothing very much matters, and that in Vere Street, Lambeth, nothing matters at all.' Of the three readers who were shown the text, one, Vaughan Nash, disliked it – vulgar, revoltingly frank and lacking in romance – but the other two, of whom one was Edward Garnett, declared enthusiastically in its favour. 'A very clever realistic study of factory girls and coster life,' wrote Garnett. 'If Fisher Unwin does not publish *A Lambeth Idyll* somebody else certainly will . . . Mr Maugham has insight & humour, & will probably be heard of again . . . N.B. The conversation is remarkably well done.' On the strength of these recommendations and after only one requested alteration – the changing of the word 'belly' to 'stomach' – a contract was signed in April between T. Fisher Unwin and William Somerset Maugham of St Thomas's Hospital. *Liza of Lambeth* was to be published not, as originally intended, in the Pseudonym Library but under Maugham's own name, selling at 3s 6d in a first edition of 2,000, with no royalty on the first 750 copies, and only a small one of 10 per cent on the following 1,250. These terms could hardly be described as generous, but neither were they unusual: Unwin was taking a risk with an unknown author at a period when it was customary for advances to be small and royalties frequently deferred until production costs had been recovered, a process which would have been accelerated had Unwin succeeded in selling the book to the United States, which he failed to do. The American publisher, Charles Scribner, reporting back to his firm in New York, wrote, 'Unwin is indeed a most troublesome person and I am glad I escaped him in London until the last day. Of the projects submitted to us by him, I myself declined the slum story . . .'

*Liza* was published in September 1897, the year of Queen Victoria's Diamond Jubilee. Among other new novels were *Captains Courageous* by Rudyard Kipling, Bram Stoker's *Dracula*, *The Invisible Man* by H. G. Wells and *What Maisie Knew* by Henry James, yet despite such formidable competition the unknown W. Somerset Maugham attracted considerable attention, critics on the whole applauding the author's talent while regretting his shocking subject-matter. 'The whole book reeks of the pot-house and is uncompromisingly depressing,' wrote the reviewer in the *Daily Mail*, 'but it is powerfully and even cleverly written and must be recognized as a true and vivid picture of the life which it depicts.' A similar opinion was expressed in the *Athenaeum*: 'Readers who prefer not to be brought into contact with some of the ugliest words and phrases in the language should be warned that Mr Maugham's book is not for them. On the other hand, those who wish to read of life as it is, without exaggeration and without modification, will have little difficulty in recognizing the merits of the volume.' An enthusiastic entry appeared in the *St Thomas's Hospital Gazette*, which made a point of noticing books written by members of staff. After a review of Dr Anderson's *Deformities of Fingers and Toes*, William Somerset Maugham was congratulated on a 'great and well-deserved success . . . [with *Liza of Lambeth* whose] uncompromising vigour of both plot and style will appeal strongly to all lovers of realism'.

Unwin, a sharp operator who thoroughly understood the value of publicity, sent the book to a number of high-profile personalities who he hoped might bring it to a wider notice, among them Basil Wilberforce, future Archdeacon of Westminster, who obligingly made it the subject of his sermon one Sunday at the Abbey. Another recipient was Joseph Conrad, whose *The Nigger of the 'Narcissus'* was also published by Unwin that year. 'I've just finished reading Liza of Lambeth,' Conrad wrote to Unwin. 'There is *any amount* of good things in the story and no distinction of any kind. It will be fairly successful I believe, for it is a "genre" picture without any atmosphere . . . He just looks on – and that is just what the general reader prefers. The book reminds me of du Maurier's drawings – same kind of art exactly, only in another sphere.' Maugham was delighted with the attention his book was receiving, and even more delighted when only a couple of weeks after publication he called at Paternoster Square and was told that the first edition was sold out and a second already printing.

It was at this point that *Liza* came under attack. An unsigned article appeared in a literary journal, the *Academy*, accusing Maugham of plagiarism, pointing out similarities between *Liza* and another 'slum' novel published at the end of the previous year, *A Child of the Jago* by Arthur Morrison. 'Mr Arthur Morrison may afford to smile at the sincere flatteries of *Liza of Lambeth*. The mimicry, indeed, is deliberate and unashamed . . . Unfortunately the qualities which touch Mr Morrison's work with something akin to genius are precisely the qualities which are here omitted.' Quick to defend himself Maugham wrote to the *Academy*, 'I have not yet had an opportunity of reading Mr Arthur Morrison's books, so I cannot tell what similarity there may be between them and my own . . . It is perhaps a little annoying to be charged with plagiarism, when my book was finished three months before the *Child of the Jago* appeared.' Maugham was always notoriously vague about dates and his statement is not strictly accurate: *A Child of the Jago* was published at the end of 1896, when Maugham had not quite completed *Liza*; yet it is unlikely he would have read Morrison's novel before finishing his own, and moreover, although *A Child of the Jago*, like *Liza*, is set in the London slums, there are few true parallels to be drawn, since Morrison's work, with its pathetic child hero, portrays a desperation, a hopelessness and a violence far more savage than anything depicted by Maugham. There is, however, a strong possibility that Maugham was influenced by an earlier work of Morrison's, *Tales of Mean Streets*, a collection of short stories published in 1894, in the first of which, 'Lizerunt', there are clear similarities to the later *Liza*, although as before Morrison's perspective is much bleaker: where Maugham allows his Liza to escape her wretchedness in death, Morrison's Liza, worn out with beatings and childbearing, is forced into prostitution by her drunken husband in a final attempt to fend off starvation.*

The author's six complimentary copies were sent to family and friends, first among them Walter Adney Payne, inscribed to 'Adney, with the author's love'. Another went to Maugham's mentor, Wentworth Huyshe, and one to each of the Maugham brothers, none of whom expressed much pleasure in the present, Harry disparaging his brother's literary talent, while Charlie expressed himself disgusted by the novel's content, an opinion shared by Freddie's wife Nellie, who noted in her diary that *Liza of Lambeth* was 'a most unpleasant book'. A copy was also dispatched to the vicarage inscribed, 'To the Vicar and Aunt Ellen, with the author's

---

* Within the genre Maugham was not the only one to attract charges of plagiarism: shortly after *A Child of the Jago* was published, Morrison himself was accused of copying from *Life in Darkest London* by Arthur Jay, who in turn had been accused by George Gissing of lifting sections of one of his novels, *The Nether World*.

love'. But the Rev. Henry had no time to read it for he died a few days later, aged sixty-nine, having been in poor health for some time. Maugham and Harry went down to Whitstable for the funeral on 21 September, an event that was well attended by the little town, whose respect, if not affection, the Vicar had won over the years. For his part, Maugham felt neither respect nor affection. Like Philip Carey, 'He had no feeling for the old man, he had never liked him; he had been selfish all his life, selfish to the wife who adored him, indifferent to the boy who had been put in his charge; he was not a cruel man, but a stupid, hard man, eaten up with a small sensuality.'

In October 1897, Maugham received his diploma from St Thomas's qualifying him to practise as MRCS (Member of the Royal College of Surgeons) and LRCP (Licentiate of the Royal College of Physicians). Somewhat to his surprise the Senior Obstetric Physician offered him an appointment, but with his ambition set on a career as a writer he turned it down. He had proved himself competent in medicine and in later life he would always acknowledge the debt he owed to his training. 'I think', he wrote in old age, 'I learned pretty well everything I know about human nature in the 5 years I spent at St Thomas's Hospital.' Had *Liza* failed, his plan had been to take a job as a ship's doctor, which would at least have provided him with the chance to travel; as it was, the success of his novel gave him the assurance to leave medicine altogether, a decision which with hindsight he came to regret. 'I am sorry I abandoned medicine so soon,' he said. 'It was idiotic. Absolutely idiotic. I could just as well have written at night and avoided the desperate financial struggle I had.'

Maugham went to see Fisher Unwin, who asked him what his plans were.

> I told him that I was throwing up medicine . . . and meant to earn my living as a writer. He put his arm round my shoulder.
> 'It's very hard to earn a living by writing,' he said. 'Writing is a very good staff, but a very bad crutch.'
> I shrugged my shoulders with scorn. My first book was a success. I was full of confidence.

Unwin was at his most genial, pressing Maugham to start work on another, much longer novel about life in the slums, which now his name was known would have an even greater success than *Liza*. Maugham was unenthusiastic. 'I was no longer interested in the slums once I had written a book about them,' he dismissively remarked. Instead he surprised his publisher by telling him he had already completed his next work, *The*

*Making of a Saint*, a historical novel written during the previous summer on Capri.

Leaving the manuscript with Unwin, Maugham shortly afterwards departed for Spain, where he was to stay for nearly a year. He hoped that when he returned, by which time, if all went well, there would be a second novel in print, his reputation as a professional man of letters would be established. In this expectation he was to be disappointed.

# 3

# A Writer by Instinct

As a boy reading in his uncle's library, Maugham had found his imagination profoundly stirred by stories and travellers' tales about foreign lands. Enthralled by *The Arabian Nights* and by several accounts of journeys through the Levant (the Vicar liked to collect such works for their illustrations), he had longed to explore the exotic and unknown, a desire that remained unfulfilled while in Whitstable where all he could do was gaze out over the cold North Sea and dream of escape. But now he was entirely independent, with nothing and nobody to constrain him or require his presence. 'Life was before him and time of no account. He could wander, for years if he chose, in unfrequented places, among strange peoples . . . He did not know what he sought or what his journeys would bring him; but he had a feeling he would learn something new about life and gain some clue to the mystery.' Intoxicated by this unfamiliar sense of emancipation, Maugham at first planned to take off for a couple of years, beginning with twelve months in Spain, then going on to Italy and Greece, and finally Egypt where he intended to become proficient in Arabic. Seductive though these ideas were, he was level-headed enough to realise that for a professional writer London was the market-place, and to London he must return before too long an absence caused his name to be forgotten. Thus he decided to confine himself to the first part of his plan, an eight-month sojourn in Seville.

During his time as a medical student Maugham had read widely in Spanish literature and had fallen in love with the idea of Spain, the country which to him more than any other represented romance. And for once reality exceeded expectation, the light and warmth of southern Spain producing in Maugham an intense feeling of happiness. Equipped with a small collection of books – Stanley Lane-Poole's *The Moors in Spain*, George Borrow's *The Bible in Spain*, *Voyages en Espagne* by Théophile Gautier and Richard Ford's *Handbook for Travellers in Spain* – he arrived in Seville on 7 December 1897 and immediately fell in love with the city, with the people and with the Spanish *dulcera de vivir*, revelling in a sense of liberation which up to now he had never known. 'I came to it after weary years in London, heartsick with much hoping, my mind dull with drudgery; and it seemed a land of freedom,' he wrote. 'There I became at last conscious of my youth.'

Maugham's lodgings were at 2 Calle Guzman el Bueno in the fashionable quarter of Santa Cruz, at the house of the British Vice-Consul, Edward Johnston, probably arranged through diplomatic contacts of his brother Charles at the law firm in Paris. Here the narrow streets were lined with large white-washed houses, discreetly hidden behind wrought-iron gates through which could be seen patios dense with foliage. In the heat of summer canvas awnings shaded the street, stretching from house to house until they were taken down in the evening to let in the cooler air. Maugham was glad of the quiet in which to write, for it was a peaceful district and during the day there were few sounds except for the trickle of a fountain, the occasional cry of a beggar or the delicate tap-tap of a donkey's hooves on the cobbled paving. After he had finished his morning's work Maugham explored the city; he liked to walk through the gardens and orange groves of the magnificent Alcázar, past the old men scanning the bullfight news under the palm trees in the Plaza Nueva, and into the great Gothic cathedral where he stood transfixed before the paintings of Murillo and Zurbarán; sometimes his route took him by the government-owned cigarette factory, famous as the location of *Carmen*, just as the raucous groups of gypsy girls, the *cigarreras*, came streaming out. In the evening at the hour of the *paseo* Maugham joined the crowds strolling through the Delicias, the gardens by the Guadalquivir, or along the main thoroughfare, the Calle de las Sierpes, looking at the fashionable ladies driving by in their landaus and at the well-stocked shops, many open to the street as in an oriental bazaar.

As his Spanish improved Maugham entered more into the life of the city. He grew a moustache, smoked Filipino cigars, learned the guitar and bought a broad-brimmed hat with a flat crown; he hankered after a cape lined with green and red velvet, but decided it was too expensive and bought a poncho instead; he went to the theatre and to bull-fights, and drank sherry in dark taverns hung with strings of sausages and hams. He was invited to private houses for dinner, where he listened to heated debates over the conduct of the Spanish–American War being fought over distant Cuba, and he took part in country picnics, where he delighted in watching the girls and young men dance the flamenco. He even managed to arrange a visit to the prison, conducted there one day by the prison doctor when doing his rounds. Maugham was lent a horse, Aguador, on which he rode out into the surrounding country, over the broad Guadalquivir river and through the flat cornfields surrounding the city walls. With the arrival of spring he went further afield, to Ronda, Écija, Granada, a revolver in his belt, a couple of saddlebags carrying his shaving kit and a change of clothing. When riding through the harsh open country he often spent the night in a farmhouse or shepherd's hut, whose owners were not always welcoming, their reserved manner very different from the spontaneity and gregariousness of the Sevillanos. Yet even the easy charm of the city was not quite what it seemed. The people of Andalusia, Maugham concluded, 'have no openness as have the French and the Italians . . . but on the contrary an Eastern reserve which continually baffles me . . . I feel always below the grace of their behaviour the instinctive, primeval hatred of the stranger.'

His bafflement notwithstanding, Maugham was captivated by the Spanish and by Spain. His perspective was highly coloured and romantic, and during his months in Seville he responded eagerly to the erotic atmosphere, the easy availability, in certain quarters, of sexual encounter. In Spain, as in France and Italy, anticlerical feeling had swept away the authority of the Catholic Church and the Church's ancient laws against sodomy, making possible a freedom unknown in the Protestant north; and nowhere more so than in Andalusia, where the legacy of 800 years of Moorish occupation was evident not only in the architecture but in the relaxed Arab attitude towards homosexuality. Beneath a surface formality, courtship rituals between men and women were also conducted with unusual licence. Strolling the quiet streets at night Maugham looked enviously at the cloaked young men clinging to the barred windows while they whispered passionate enticements to their girlfriends within, often with disastrous consequences.

> In Spain the blood of youth is very hot . . . The Spaniard, who will seduce any girl he can, is pitiless . . . so there is much weeping, the girl is turned out of doors and falls readily into the hands of the procuress. In the brothels of Seville or of Madrid she finds at least a roof and bread to eat; and the fickle swain goes his way rejoicing.

Maugham describes a visit to one such brothel, where when his pale-faced girl undressed he was appalled to see the thin body of a child.

> 'How old are you?'
> 'Thirteen.'

'What made you come here?'
'Hambre,' she answered. 'Hunger.'

In *The Land of the Blessed Virgin*, an account of his experience of
Andalusia, Maugham states that, while he never fell in love, he nonetheless was infatuated by a certain Rosarito, about whom he writes in a
ponderously highfalutin manner: 'But when I write of Spanish women
I think of you, Rosarito . . . it is your dark eyes that were lustrous, soft
as velvet, caressing sometimes, and sometimes sparkling with fiery glances.
(Alas! That I can find but hackneyed phrases to describe those heart-
disturbers.)' Rosarito may well have been a Rosario, or indeed never
existed at all except as a literary conceit; in a later account Maugham
refers much more convincingly to conducting numerous light-hearted
affairs, and also to a passion for 'a young thing with green eyes and a gay
smile', gender carefully unspecified, whose charms were sufficiently
magnetic to draw him back to Seville the following year.

When describing this period, Maugham wrote that in Seville 'life was
too pleasant to allow me to give an undivided attention to literature';
nonetheless he was resolute in maintaining his usual habit of industri-
ousness, in eight months completing a travel book, four short stories and
a full-length novel. It was with these in his luggage that he arrived back
in London in the autumn of 1898.

The young man of twenty-four who returned to resume his life in
England was very different from the callow graduate who had left for
Spain the previous year. Maugham had grown considerably in confidence:
he had enjoyed himself immensely in Seville: he was personable, attractive to both men and women, and he was possessed of an enormous
creative energy and appetite for hard work. Now he was intent on taking
his career forward, determined to make of his writing a paying business.
'Your successful man of letters is your skilful tradesman,' says a character
in Gissing's *New Grub Street*. 'He thinks first and foremost of the markets.'
Maugham was to become adept at judging his market. In the 1890s the
literary market was rapidly expanding, focused on a large educated middle
class, with dozens of new magazines and periodicals launched every year
and more than 400 publishing houses in London alone. However, his start
was discouraging: expecting to find waiting for him a substantial sum in
royalties earned from *Liza of Lambeth*, Maugham was taken aback to
discover that the total came to no more than £20. The fact that Fisher
Unwin was unlikely to have made more than that himself weighed not
at all with his author, who remained convinced that the publisher had

pulled a fast one. As he crossly remarked, with *Liza* '[Unwin] did me thoroughly in the eye.' Fortunately he would be unlikely to have the chance to do so again as Maugham before going abroad had appointed a literary agent, W. M. Colles, to act for him: it was Colles who would from now on negotiate with Unwin, and indeed Colles who had succeeded in obtaining an advance of £50 for *The Making of a Saint*, the novel written on Capri the previous summer.

Maurice Colles, a big, burly, Falstaffian figure, was one of a new breed, the role of literary agent having only recently come into existence. Predictably it was looked on with disfavour by publishers ('parasite' was the word used by William Heinemann in describing the species), who were accustomed to dealing directly with their authors, many of whom had a conveniently limited understanding of financial matters. One of the first literary agents was A. P. Watt, who dominated the profession for many years, but at the turn of the century Colles was almost as well known, with a number of distinguished writers on his books, Hardy, Meredith and Arnold Bennett among them. Having trained as a lawyer, Colles in 1890 had taken over the Authors' Syndicate, a literary and dramatic advisory service started by that tireless campaigner for writers' rights Walter Besant, and he acted also as legal counsel to the Society of Authors, with his office in the same building as theirs in Portugal Street, near the Aldwych. Colles was a decent, likeable man, good-humoured and easy to talk to, and for most of his clients, Maugham included, it was some time before they realised the extent of his incompetence.

*The Making of a Saint* had made its appearance in Maugham's absence during the summer of 1898, published in June by Fisher Unwin, a month earlier by L. C. Page in the United States. Maugham had been inspired to attempt a historical novel after reading an article by the prolific man of letters Andrew Lang, who posited that the form was ideal for the young writer as story and characters were ready-made and no experi-ence of real life was necessary. 'Seduced by this bad advice', as Maugham put it, he set to work, basing his plot on an episode in Machiavelli's *History of Florence*, which he had come across while browsing in the British Museum Reading Room during his spare time from St Thomas's. Revolving round Caterina Sforza's bold defiance of her captors at the siege of Forlì, *The Making of a Saint* follows the fortunes of Filippo Brandolini, a young mercenary who is caught up in the revolt of the townspeople against the grasping lord of Forlì. It is a fast-moving tale, with plenty of dangerous conspiracy, fighting, violent stabbings, swordplay and bloodthirsty execu-tions, as well as a hot-blooded love affair between Brandolini and a beautiful but promiscuous Donna Giulia. Towards the end of the novel Giulia finally agrees to marry Brandolini, who is ecstatically happy until, inevitably, he catches his faithless wife in the arms of a lover. Enraged, he kills them both, and then is overcome with remorse, penitently taking holy orders before entering a monastery.

In later years Maugham expressed unalloyed contempt for *The Making of a Saint*; he left it out of the collected edition of his work, went to considerable lengths to have it suppressed, and in the copy he gave his nephew Robin wrote, 'A very poor novel by W. Somerset Maugham'. And yet the book has many good qualities if judged fairly for what it is, a fast-paced and well-plotted adventure of the kind that Maugham as a schoolboy eagerly devoured, a worthy successor to Henty and Harrison Ainsworth, with the addition of a sexy love-story woven in. According to its author's gloomy recollection, the critics received *The Making of a Saint* with coolness and the public with indifference, although in truth the novel's reception was far from unfavourable. Unwin's reader Edward Garnett had reported with enthusiasm that 'So far as we can see Mr Maugham is going *strong* . . . the novel [is] a strong unusual piece of work, full of vigour . . .', and critics drew attention to its pace and readability, to its 'marvellous intensity and force'. As with *Liza of Lambeth*, a couple of reviewers professed themselves affronted by the explicit nature of the love scenes, but in the main it was judged a highly creditable effort. '[Mr Maugham] has written a good novel,' said the *Spectator*, 'and he ought some day to write much better ones.'

Having given up his Vincent Square lodgings when he left for Seville, Maugham now moved into a small flat which he shared with his old friend Walter Payne, in Albany Chambers, Westminster, near St James's Park. Shortly afterwards they moved to another in Carlisle Mansions, an apartment block behind Victoria Station, the two men employing a maid of all work to cook for them and do the housework. In the play Maugham was working on at the time, *The Man of Honour*, he describes typical bachelor quarters, as it might be his and Walter's.

> A writing-desk littered with papers and books . . . a fire-place with arm-chairs on either side; on the chimney-piece various smoking utensils . . . numerous bookshelves filled with books; while on the walls are one or two Delft plates, etchings after Rossetti, autotypes of paintings by Fra Angelico and Botticelli. The furniture is simple and inexpensive . . . the dwelling-place of a person who reads a great deal and takes pleasure in beautiful things.

Like the play's hero, Basil Kent, Maugham 'loved the smell of smoke, the untidy litter of books, the lack of responsibility', and indeed it was an ideal arrangement in more ways than one. Maugham was devoted to and trusted Payne, who was amiable and level-headed, providing a reassuring counter-balance to his friend's more volatile temperament; they both had a passion for the theatre and continued to go regularly to plays together; and Payne, a qualified chartered accountant with a good business sense, now agreed to take on the handling of Maugham's financial affairs, as well as dealing with all the correspondence with publishers, agents and magazine editors which lay outside Maurice Colles's remit. And there were other advantages to living with Payne: as he was out all day – he had recently given up accountancy to read for the Bar – Maugham had the place to himself in which to write; and when Payne returned in the evening he often brought attractive company with him. As Maugham put it, looking back on this period with the cold and cynical eye of his extreme old age,

> He [Payne] was very good-looking, and had no difficulty in getting girls to go to bed with him . . . small-part actresses, shop-girls or clerks in an office. About one evening a week Walter would arrange to go out and the girl I was then friends with came and dined with me, after which we indulged in sexual congress. Later in the evening we dressed and went downstairs, I put her in a cab, paid the fare and made an appointment with her for the following week. There was no romance in it, no love, only appetite: on looking back, these experiences of mine seem dreadfully sordid, but after all, I was in my early twenties and my sexual proclivities demanded expression.

Determined to make his mark as quickly as possible, Maugham ener-getically set to work, fortunately unaware that it would be nine long years before he was to achieve any substantial success. In those days, 'I had a natural lucidity and a knack for writing easy dialogue . . . to write was an instinct that seemed as natural to me as to breathe, and I did not stop to consider if I wrote well or badly.' His immediate priority was to sell the works he had written in Spain, the first of which to appear was a short story, 'The Punctiliousness of Don Sebastian', published in October 1898 in *Cosmopolis*, a journal printed in three languages, a third of it in English, a third French and a third German. Unsurprisingly it failed to prosper and folded a month after Maugham's story appeared, without paying its contributor. 'Of course I was disappointed at getting no money from *Cosmopolis*,' Maugham wrote robustly to Colles, 'but I was scarcely surprised since I knew from the Paris solicitor who has charge of the editor's affairs & who is also my brother that Oltman was the very shadiest of characters.' Bound by the terms of his contract, Maugham had no choice but to submit his work to Fisher Unwin as the firm had first refusal of his next two books. Unwin expressed not the least interest in the sketches of Andalusia, *The Land of the Blessed Virgin*, and declined to pay the £100 Maugham was asking for his novel, 'The Artistic Temperament of Stephen Carey'; he was, however, prepared to issue the short stories as a collection, a decision which pleased Maugham who was anxious that these should appear before the novel. 'It is true that "Stephen Carey" is finished,' he wrote to Colles, 'but as it is a little strong I particularly wish to publish something milder first, so that I may not be known as a writer of the George Moore type.'*

Of the six stories that make up *Orientations*, four were written in Spain, while two, 'A Bad Example' and 'Daisy', were thoroughly reworked versions of stories which Maugham had composed earlier. Edward Garnett had read the original 'A Bad Example' and had not cared for it, and nor, with one exception, did he much care for what was put before him now. The stories, he reported, 'are all a little flat, a little heavy . . . [and] we feel that Mr Maugham's reputation will suffer if he publishes the present collection'. The exception was 'Daisy', to which Garnett responded with enthusiasm, describing it as 'excellent . . . *modern*, done with insight & done with spirit'. If only Maugham could produce five more of this quality, 'well, *that* will be a very different thing'.

'Daisy' is set in Blackstable, Maugham's fictional rendering of Whitstable, its heroine a carpenter's daughter, a warm-hearted and lovely young woman who is rejected by her uncharitable family when she has an affair with a married man. Abandoned and near to starvation, Daisy begs them to forgive her and take her back, but they turn her away. Time passes, and Daisy makes her name on the stage, eventually resurfacing, to her family's horror, as a star in pantomime, appearing in the nearby town of Tercanbury (Canterbury).

> Daisy as Dick Whittington, bounded on the stage – in flesh-coloured tights, with particularly scanty trunks, and her bodice – rather low. The vicar's nephew sniggered . . .
>   Daisy began to sing, –
>
>> 'I'm a jolly sort of boy, tol, lol,
>> And I don't give a damn who knows it . . .'
>
> . . . The piece went on to the bitter end, and Dick Whittington appeared in many different costumes and sang many songs, and kicked many kicks,

* Moore was known for novels of disturbing social realism.

till he was finally made Lord Mayor – in tights. Ah, it was an evening of bitter humiliation . . .

Soon afterwards Daisy marries a rich young baronet with whom she returns to live near Blackstable. By this time her parents have fallen on hard times, and her snobbish and avaricious mother, desperate to be well in with her titled daughter, schemes to persuade her to come to the rescue. Clear-sighted about their motives, Daisy is also generous and forgiving, and agrees to settle an income on her parents, bearing no rancour.

Significantly, the final version of 'Daisy' was written shortly after the death of the Rev. Henry Maugham, when Maugham's memories of his boyhood had been vividly refreshed by attending his uncle's funeral. His portrait of Whitstable is vengeful, showing its people as mean-spirited and hypocritical; and yet there is an underlying sadness for something loved that was now lost. After leaving her parents' house, Daisy walks alone through the town to the sea, overcome with nostalgia for what she is yet relieved to be leaving behind her.

> Daisy walked down the High Street slowly, looking at the houses she remembered, and her lips quivered a little . . . At last she came to the beach, and in the darkening November day she looked at the booths she knew so well, the boats drawn up for the winter, whose names she knew, whose owners she had known from her childhood . . . And she looked at the grey sea; a sob burst from her; but she was very strong, and at once she recovered herself. She turned back and slowly walked up the High Street again to the station . . . her heart full of infinite sadness – the terrible sadness of the past.

*Orientations* was published in June 1899, dedicated to Mrs Edward Johnston, wife of the Vice-Consul with whom Maugham had stayed in Seville. The title of the collection was dreamt up by the author, who wanted to find something suitably sententious: the word 'orientations', as he rightly observed, 'at the time was not very familiar to the general public'. After leafing through various French moralists and failing to find a suitably relevant quotation, he decided to invent one: 'C'est surtout, par des nouvelles d'un jeune écrivain qu'on peut se rendre compte du tour de son esprit. Il y cherche la voie qui lui est propre dans une série d'essais de genre et de style différents, qui sont comme des orientations, pour trouver son moi littéraire.'*

* 'Above all it is through the new work of a young writer that one is made aware of the range of his abilities. It is here he tries out the genres and the different styles that best suit him, which act as directions guiding him towards his true literary self.'

Despite an unenthusiastic notice in the *London Bookman*, describing it as 'an average book, fairly readable, but with no serious interest or promise about it', *Orientations* was generally praised by the critics: 'The best writing we have yet seen from Mr W. S. Maugham,' according to the *Athenaeum*, while even the previously hostile *Academy*, which had savaged *Liza* and been no more than lukewarm about *The Making of a Saint*, admitted itself impressed. 'Mr Maugham begins to be interesting. This book is much better than either the shrill and hysterical *Liza of Lambeth* or the rather mediocre *Making of a Saint* . . . [*Orientations* is] trenchant, sincere, candid, humorous, witty, and flippant . . . Mr Maugham . . . has an abundance of vitality, which is perhaps the scarcest thing in modern literature.'

It was this abundance of vitality that was such a distinctive ingredient of Maugham's magnetism as a young man. Although he was not tall, he was strikingly attractive, with his dark hair and moustache and his pale skin; to one acquaintance, the writer Louis Marlow,* Maugham's face had an almost oriental beauty, 'the dark brown eyes, congruous with his lustrous dark hair . . . [suggesting] the eyes of some painted portrait. They gave that same effect of rich pigmentation in sudden contrast with skin pallor.' As his earnings increased, Maugham was able to spend more on clothes, and soon developed an elegant sartorial flair. In retrospect he liked to represent himself as shy and socially awkward at this stage of his life, and it is true he was always self-conscious about his lack of height. 'The world is an entirely different place to the man of five foot seven from what it is to the man of six foot two,' he wrote in his notebook. Yet by the time he returned from Spain he was well able, despite his stammer, to hold his own in most company, and certainly had few inhibitions in pursuing his amorous adventures. 'I saw no reason to subordinate the claims of sense to the tempting lure of spirit,' he wrote, 'and I was determined to get whatever fulfilment I could out of social intercourse and human relations, out of food, drink and fornication.' Possessed of an urgent sexual energy, Maugham was always on the look-out for opportunity, and yet at the same time he was emotionally vulnerable, with a hunger for love and affection, 'almost continuously in love', as he described himself, 'from the time I was fifteen to the time I was fifty'. He may have liked to see himself when young as tough and heartless, but the reality was different: in love affairs with both men and women he was almost too susceptible, and often suffered great anguish as a result. One woman with whom in his twenties he had a brief affair said of him, 'He is a fearfully emotional man, sexually.'

---

* Pen-name of Louis Wilkinson.

Although no overt evidence survives, there are clear indications that when Maugham was in his late teens and early twenties he experienced some powerful sexual and emotional upheavals. In the early novels, *Liza of Lambeth*, *The Making of a Saint*, *The Hero*, *Mrs Craddock* and *The Merry-Go-Round*, sexual passion is the dominant theme; and there is one work from this period that is particularly revealing, 'The Artistic Temperament of Stephen Carey'. 'Stephen Carey' was never published, and when late in Maugham's life he presented it to the Library of Congress in Washington it was on the strict understanding that it could be neither quoted from nor copied. And indeed the novel is a raw and revealing work, in which a number of important autobiographical motifs first appear which later are given far greater weight and polish in *Of Human Bondage*. Written in Spain in 1898, the year after Maugham left St Thomas's, 'Stephen Carey' was, Maugham had warned his agent, 'a little strong' as regards subject-matter; and so indeed it proved, considered 'too indecent for publication', even after considerable toning down. After revising his original version, Maugham told Colles that 'finally I have erased all that might bring a blush to the cheek of the most modest journalist.' Even this was not enough to satisfy the Mrs Grundys of the publishing world, however, although in the event Maugham came to feel profoundly grateful that the novel never appeared as it would have made impossible the writing of the infinitely superior *Of Human Bondage*. 'I should have lost a subject which I was then too young to make proper use of,' he explained with hindsight. 'I was not far enough away from the events I described to see them reasonably and I had not had a number of experiences that later went to enrich the book I finally wrote.'

In later years Maugham dismissed his third novel 'as merely an insignificant curiosity', an unduly harsh judgment of an immature but intriguing work which shows strong promise of a notable talent. 'Stephen Carey' relates the story of the early years and young manhood of the eponymous hero, which closely, but not completely, follows the author's own experience. An orphan, Stephen is unhappy at school and in young manhood is bored by his job in a lawyer's office in London. It is during his indenture that he meets and falls passionately in love with a waitress, Rose, a thin, plain young woman, good-natured and cheerfully promiscuous. Consumed by lust for Rose, Stephen is led into appalling levels of degradation, from which he eventually emerges to find salvation of a kind in marriage to an innocent and pretty cousin. 'Stephen Carey' is a closely autobiographical and extraordinarily interesting document, pedestrian in

the early sections, compelling once Rose enters the story, and the big
central theme, Stephen's obsession with Rose, must correspond to an experience undergone by Maugham while he was studying at the hospital.
Here, Rose is presented as shallow and unrefined, and yet there is something engaging about her: she is placid and prepared to be pleased – a
very different type from the malevolent Mildred, her reincarnation in *Of
Human Bondage*. In the later novel Maugham is dealing with a scarring
sado-masochistic affair, and it is no wonder that in the earlier version,
written when he was only twenty-four, he was not yet prepared to reveal
it; he softened the story, blurred the edges, and inevitably turned it into
something else.

Despite his failure to win the critical attention he needed to advance
his career, the name Somerset Maugham was beginning to be known,
and Maugham soon found himself moving in wider social circles than
before. After the publication of *Liza of Lambeth*, he had been asked to a
couple of bookish salons, mainly centred in Notting Hill and Kensington,
and he had come to the attention of that literary panjandrum Edmund
Gosse, who invited him to his famous Sundays at his house near Regent's
Park. Gosse, distinguished as both critic and author, wielded powerful
influence; with many celebrated writers as friends, he also liked to make
the acquaintance of promising newcomers, and an invitation from Gosse
served as a ticket of entry to the inner circle of letters. As one admirer
described the process, 'Young writers were not introduced to him, they
were brought up to be *presented*, and beforehand they would feel nervous
– if they did not, he could be trusted to see that they felt nervous afterwards.' Gosse was a vain man, touchy too, but he had a keen sense of
humour and a nice line in malice. His personal acquaintance with some
eminent Victorians – Tennyson, Browning, Swinburne and Gissing –
provided a fascinating link to a past age; he was formidably well read,
and Maugham judged him 'the most interesting and consistently amusing
talker I ever knew'. At Gosse's parties you might meet Henry James or
Thomas Hardy, although often the room was uncomfortably overcrowded,
which made it difficult to drink tea and eat cucumber sandwiches while
listening intelligently to the conversation of the literati as they discussed
publishers and agents and shredded the reputations of their absent colleagues.
At such literary parties Maugham was particularly intrigued by the
women, some flamboyantly dressed in loud patterns and big beads, others
mousy little spinsters who hardly spoke above a whisper. 'I never ceased
to be fascinated by their persistence in eating buttered toast with their
gloves on, and I observed with admiration the unconcern with which

they wiped their fingers on their chair when they thought no one was looking.'

Outside these predominantly literary circles, one of the most influential of Maugham's new acquaintance was that eccentric figure, Augustus Hare. Impressed by *Liza of Lambeth*, Hare had asked a clerical friend of his who knew Maugham to invite the young man to dinner. The evening had been a success, and shortly afterwards an invitation was issued for a weekend in Sussex at Holmhurst, Hare's house near St Leonard's-on-Sea.

Augustus Hare, part scholar, part snob, part fussy old maid, had enjoyed his greatest success during the 1870s and 1880s, when his idiosyncratic guidebooks, in particular to Italy, France and Spain (*Walks in Rome*, *Days near Paris*, *Wanderings in Spain*), had been widely read and admired. Holmhurst was crammed with little treasures picked up on his travels – stuffed birds, photographs, ornamental pots and plaster busts – each with its history or sentimental memory, each dear to its owner. Formidably knowledgeable in his chosen subjects, Augustus nursed a lifelong passion for the aristocracy, and in England there was hardly a country house of importance at which he was not an appreciative guest, his hosts flattered by the enthusiastic interest he took in their noble mansions and their contents. He had enjoyed considerable acclaim in these exalted spheres with two of his biographical works, *The Life and Letters of Frances, Baroness Bunsen* and *The Story of Two Noble Lives*, about Countess Canning and Louisa, Marchioness of Waterford. Now in his sixties but looking much older with his white hair and walrus moustache, Augustus divided his time between London, where he dined out grandly every night, and the country, where he led 'a curious little home life very much centred on the befriending of boys'. As Maugham remarked of his new friend, 'He was not what people call a man's man,' and when entertaining was much more at ease in the company of middle-aged ladies, preferably titled. 'I do not think he was of a passionate nature,' Maugham continued.

> He told me once that he had never had sexual intercourse till he was thirty-five. He marked the occasions on which this happened, about once every three months, with a black cross in his Journal. But this is a matter on which most men are apt to boast, and I dare say that to impress me he exaggerated the frequency of his incontinence.

Maugham grew fond of Augustus, whom he saw as 'innately and intensely frivolous . . . [but also] kind, hospitable and generous'. The two men had a bond in that they were both survivors of wretchedly unhappy childhoods – Augustus's appallingly so – and Maugham, touched by the older man's kindness in taking him under his wing, genuinely enjoyed his weekends in Sussex. Holmhurst was far from being one of the great houses, but it was a gentleman's residence, a substantial if unbeautiful early-nineteenth-century house, greystone and vaguely gothicised, surrounded by a lovingly landscaped garden, with a terrace, wide lawns and a view across woods and fields to the sea. Augustus was proud of his property and liked to invite friends to stay, usually a couple of well-born ladies and two or three cultured old gentlemen happy to enjoy a quiet Friday to Monday in the country. The house was well run by an entirely female staff and the standard of comfort was high. After a bath in front of the bedroom fire, guests descended to a plentiful cooked breakfast served downstairs at nine, before which Augustus liked to read two or three prayers from a leather-bound Bible; here and there passages had been heavily scored out, because, Hare explained, 'God is a gentleman, and being a gentleman he would have thought the fulsome praise of Him in very bad taste.' During the rest of the day there would be three more substantial meals, little guided tours of the garden, perhaps some sketching, and in the evening music, conversation and 'an intolerably tedious' game of Halma. The proceedings were often rounded off with a dramatic recitation by Hare of one of his famous ghost-stories, ensuring that his guests collected their candles for bed in a state of nervous apprehension.

As someone who preferred to listen rather than talk, Maugham fitted in well with this somewhat staid company. The house was grander than anything he had known before and he was quick to learn everything his host set out to teach him. In Augustus's view Maugham lacked polish: it was not enough, he told him, just to sit and listen: he must make conversational contributions of his own and sharpen up his small talk. There were, too, some vulgar phrases of which Maugham must break the habit. Augustus was displeased to hear his young friend talk of going somewhere by bus: 'I prefer to call the conveyance to which you refer an omnibus,' he reproved him; he winced at another ill-bred nuance: 'Yesterday when we came in from our walk you said you were thirsty and asked for a *drink* . . . A gentleman does *not* ask for a *drink*, he asks for *something to drink*.' Hare had admired *Liza of Lambeth* but he was anxious that Maugham should now leave the subject of the lower orders and acquire a knowledge of the manners and customs of the nobility and gentry. To this end he started taking his protégé with him when he called on his well-born acquaintance, encouraging them to invite his promising young friend to their parties.

Among the hostesses who at Hare's suggestion took Maugham up was

Blanche Crackanthorpe, wife of a distinguished barrister and mother of the writer Hubert Crackanthorpe. At her salon in Rutland Gate, Mrs Crackanthorpe specialised in entertaining literary celebrities, bringing together promising beginners such as Maugham with well-known figures like Hardy, Galsworthy and Henry James. Somewhat higher up the social scale was the tuft-hunting Lady St Helier, who at her house in Portland Place liked to mix aristocratic society with professional people, lawyers and doctors, as well as with artists and writers. During the last years of Queen Victoria's reign, as Lady St Helier described them in her memoirs, 'the conventional rules were swept away . . . [and] I found the most unlikely people generally appreciated and enjoyed meeting such well-known representatives of literature, art, and politics as Sir John Millais, Sir Frederick Leighton . . . Mr Thomas Hardy, Lord and Lady Iddesleigh, Sir William and Lady Harcourt, Miss Braddon, and others'. A promising young writer such as William Somerset Maugham was an asset in such company, and Maugham for his part relished the opportunity to observe the upper classes in their natural habitat. It was at the end of a dazzling dinner at Portland Place that Maugham found himself sitting next to the elderly Duke of Abercorn. 'Do you like cigars?' the Duke asked him, taking out of his pocket a large cigar-case. 'Very much,' said Maugham, who could rarely afford them. 'So do I,' continued the Duke, selecting one and inspecting it carefully. 'And when I come to dinner,' he continued lighting up, 'I always bring my own.' He snapped the case shut and returned it to his pocket. 'I advise you to do the same.'

Another patron of Maugham's was the wife of Basil Wilberforce, the Archdeacon of Westminster who had preached a sermon on *Liza of Lambeth*. Since then Mrs Wilberforce had taken a kindly interest in Maugham, including him in her lively parties at the house in Dean's Yard and introducing him to several fashionable hostesses, who were delighted to ask the clever, attractive and unattached young man to their luncheons, dinners and dances. Maugham took pleasure in his grand new social life, even if it came at a cost: the people who entertained him were extremely well off, which he was not, obliged to economise where he could. Dining out meant dressing in white tie and tails, with kid gloves and silk top hat; as cabs were beyond his means, Maugham came and went by omnibus, with its upper deck open to the weather. When invited to the country for a Friday to Monday, greater expenditure was unavoidable, with half-sovereigns to be dispensed to the butler, to the footman who brought the morning tea, and often to a second footman who unpacked his bag and acted as valet. At a large house-party young bachelors were sometimes obliged to share a bed, which not infrequently led to sex. 'Often it turned out to be very pleasant,' Maugham recalled.

Years later, pondering on what it was that these rich and worldly people saw in him, he put the question to one of the hostesses of his youth. 'You were different from other young men,' she said. 'Though quiet . . . you had a sort of restless vitality that was intriguing.'

A success in society, Maugham found that success in his professional life continued to elude him. Discouraged by having had two books turned down and reluctant to spend the winter in England, at the end of 1898 he again went abroad, first to Rome, then back to Seville, where the young creature 'with green eyes and a gay smile' was still much on his mind. Leaving Andalusia after a couple of months he continued on to Morocco – a natural step after immersion in the Moorish culture of southern Spain – before returning to London in April 1899. After the sensual seductiveness of the Mediterranean, London appeared particularly drab: the soot and fog, the muddy streets reeking of manure, the crowds, the clatter and jangle of trams. Even more lowering to the spirit was the fact that Colles had failed to place elsewhere either of the works rejected by Unwin, 'Stephen Carey' and *The Land of the Blessed Virgin*; and, on top of this, a one-act play Maugham had written while in Rome, 'Son & Heir' (never produced or published and now lost), was also languishing from lack of interest, a particular disappointment as he was still determined on a career as a dramatist. Indeed apart from a couple of short stories published in *Punch*, for more than two years little was heard from Somerset Maugham until the appearance of a third novel in July 1901.

*The Hero* was suggested by the Boer War, 'the first rent', as Maugham later saw it, 'in that great fabric, the British Empire'. The war had broken out in 1899, and in 1900 with the sieges of Mafeking and Ladysmith was currently much in the news. The story tells of James Parsons, a gallant young soldier just home from the Cape. James has been recommended for the Victoria Cross for his brave attempt under fire to save the life of a brother officer, yet his attitude towards the war is far from the black-and-white view unquestioningly held in Little Primpton. The main theme of the novel is not war but a tormenting question of personal honour: five years earlier, before leaving for abroad, James had proposed marriage to Mary Clibborn, the girl next door; he was never in love, but she was a decent sort, his parents were all for it, and it seemed a good idea at the time. During his absence, however, he had become obsessed with the wife of a regimental colleague, and he now feels that he would rather die than marry plain, priggish Mary when his thoughts are all of the wickedly seductive Mrs Pritchard-Wallace. In the course of struggling both with his conscience and with the suffocating conventions of village society, he hears that Mrs Wallace, now a widow, has arrived in London. He goes to see her and finds her spell as potent as ever; while in her intoxicating presence, 'the recollection of Mary came back to him, in the straw hat and the soiled serge dress . . . Mrs Wallace was lying in a long chair, coiled up in a serpentine, characteristic attitude; every movement wafted to him the oppressive perfume she wore; the smile on her lips, the caress of her eyes, were maddening.' Although he knows Mrs Wallace is out of his league, he also knows he cannot return to Mary. 'To James . . . that physical repulsion which at first had terrified him now was grown into an ungovernable hate . . . "Oh, no," he said to himself, "I would rather shoot myself than marry you!"' And this is exactly what he does, James's shocking suicide bringing the book to an abrupt end, apart from a brief epilogue describing Mary's eventual and entirely suitable union with the local curate.

Here again the subject of physical desire was plainly much on the author's mind. Bossy, frumpish Mary Clibborn, with her good works and sensible shoes, provides the perfect foil to the unscrupulous Mrs Wallace, whose appeal to James, it is made very clear, is based entirely on sex. 'The touch of her fingers sent the blood rushing through his veins insanely; and understanding his condition, she took pleasure in touching him, to watch the little shiver of desire that convulsed his frame . . .' In James's view, marriage without passion 'is ugly and beastly', a trap to be avoided at all costs, a belief he certainly shared with his creator.

With hindsight, Maugham judged *The Hero* 'an honest piece of work', if more appropriate as a short story, an opinion with which it is easy to agree. Much of the social comedy is enjoyable, especially as played out between James's parents and their neighbours, with their love of backgammon, blancmange and the novels of Marie Corelli; but there are too many meandering conversations and characters in need of further development for the reader not to wish for the celerity and concision of the shorter form. Maugham continues his retrospective analysis by regretting that under the influence of Walter Pater he had been led into attempting an embarrassingly euphuistic style – 'an oak tree, just bursting into leaf, clothed with its new-born verdure, like the bride of the young god, Spring'. This is typical of the kind of exercise at which he was trying his hand, some extravagant examples of which – 'The western clouds of the sunset were like the vast wing of an archangel, flying through the void on an errand of vengeance' – appear in his notebooks. The interesting fact about these, however, is not the occasional exaggerated efflorescence, as in the instance quoted above, but how remarkably accomplished many of the notebook experiments in dialogue and description are and how diligently worked at.

The novel, received by the critics with temperate approval, was published by Hutchinson, the three-book contract with Unwin, to Maugham's relief, having finally expired. *The Hero*, for which an advance of £75 was paid, was the first of Maugham's works to bear on its cover the Moorish sign against the Evil Eye, adopted by his father Robert Maugham after his travels in the Near East, and which was famously to become Somerset Maugham's insignia – in this case unfortunately printed upside-down.

Before writing *The Hero*, Maugham had finished another novel, one for which yet again he had experienced considerable difficulty in finding a publisher. The problem was as before, that Maugham's work was earning a reputation for impropriety, his content considered too sexually explicit, with the consequence that publishers were beginning to regard him as a risky proposition. With the new work, *Mrs Craddock*, he was again sailing very close to the wind: not only was the subject, of female sexual desire, considered shocking but the language, too, was found offensively frank. Publisher after publisher turned it down, including the prestigious William Heinemann; fortunately, however, the renowned critic Robertson Nicoll, a partner at Hodder & Stoughton, recognised the book's quality, and while acknowledging its unsuitability for his own imprint persuaded the more adventurous Heinemann to reconsider. This time it was read by the head of the firm himself, who agreed to take it on condition that some particularly inflammatory passages were excised.*

*Mrs Craddock* is a fascinating novel, the most mature and sophisticated of Maugham's work to date. When the story opens, Bertha Ley, a beautiful young orphan of eighteen, cultured and well read, has recently returned to her family seat in Kent after three years' travelling on the Continent. Out walking one day Bertha's eye falls on one of her tenant farmers, Edward Craddock, a sturdy and handsome young man, for whom she instantly conceives an overwhelming passion. Sweeping aside the snobbish objections of the county families, Bertha weds her honest yeoman, and at first is blissfully happy, charmed by her

---

* That the new novel was considered dangerously risqué had little effect in bridling Maugham. More than a quarter of a century later the French critic Paul Dottin wrote, 'Maugham will doubtless be recognised in time as one of the novelists who have contributed most to removing from the English literary vocabulary the word "improper".'

husband's simplicity and good nature, and intoxicated by his rough masculinity. Gradually, however, she begins to perceive that the man she has married, although virtuous and dependable, is stupid, complacent and cold, his infrequent embraces causing Bertha, an intensely passionate woman, much misery by their mechanical nature. For a while she pins her hopes on having a child, but when her baby is still-born she sinks into despair, her devouring love for Edward eventually turning to revulsion and contempt.

Bertha takes to leaving home for months at a time, and while staying with an aunt in London she meets a young cousin, nineteen-year-old Gerald Vaudrey, charming, dissolute and divinely good-looking. Despite the difference in age (Bertha is now thirty), the two of them work themselves up into a lustful frenzy. In a few weeks Gerald is due to sail for America and Bertha, convinced she is in love, decides to defy caution and run away with him to Florida. But when she arrives at the station there is something in Gerald's manner, previously so ardent, that gives her pause.

> Bertha looked at him. She wanted to say that she adored him and would accompany him to the world's end, but the words stuck in her mouth. An inspector came along to look at the tickets.
> 'Is the lady going?' he asked.
> 'No,' said Gerald.

Heartbroken, Bertha returns home, where Edward is touchingly pleased to see her. His feelings, however, are now a matter of indifference to his wife, as is his death, which occurs shortly afterwards as the result of a hunting accident. The novel ends with Bertha finally grieving, not for the loss of her husband, but for the loss of the love she had for him; and with this understanding comes a sense of freedom. In the last scene Bertha settles down quietly by the fire to read her book, in tranquil preparation for whatever the next stage of her life may bring.

In his remarkable portrait of Bertha, Maugham created a vital, complex, captivating and fully rounded woman, exigent and spoilt but also sympathetic and endearing. He knows her through and through, catches every nuance of her self-deception, of her skewed falling in love, sees through her wiles, gently mocks her affectations, yet at the same time identifies whole-heartedly with every surge and current of her passionate nature, almost as though he were her alter ego, his own divided sexuality giving him a kind of double vision, a deeper insight into the feminine psyche. The influence of Flaubert is evident, with Bertha Craddock in character a close cousin of Emma Bovary. Like her French counterpart Bertha is sensual, wilful and highly strung, and like Emma suffers agonies of boredom in her husband's company. Bertha, though, is well placed in the world and her yearnings are not for social advancement but for romance. At the beginning she sees in Edward Craddock a romantic hero, and running parallel to her feelings of sheer carnality is her mistaken perception that the stolid farmer is a kind of noble savage whose innate sensitivity needs only to be released by the power of her love. Sadly, this is not the case. Edward, self-satisfied and unnoticing, ignores his wife's demands for attention, treating her outbursts of furious frustration with irritating good-humour. 'Women are like chickens,' he is fond of repeating. 'When they cluck and cackle sit tight and take no notice.'

Bertha is drawn with the unerring psychological accuracy for which Maugham would become known, particularly in his treatment of women; yet so, too, is Edward: if deserving of far less sympathy, he is nonetheless entirely credible, and the reader is shown fairly how the situation appears from his point of view. Edward is a clod and a bore, but he is not a bad man; he is a dull, decent, ordinary chap, stubbornly convinced of the rightness of his banal opinions. He will never understand his wife – during their courtship, 'It puzzled him sometimes to catch her smile of intense happiness when he was discussing the bush-drainage of a field' – but within his narrow limits he loves her and means to treat her well. The man who supplants him in Bertha's affections, Gerald Vaudrey, is also a three-dimensional figure, and of a type, sexy, rakish and amusing, that was attractive not only to Bertha but to her author. (In an interview given twenty years later Maugham admitted that of all his fictional characters, 'My recollection lingers with most pleasure on a youth called Gerald Vaudrey in *Mrs Craddock*.') '[Gerald] was certainly not at all shy, although he looked even younger than nineteen. He was quite a boy, very slight . . . with a small girlish face . . . His hair was dark and curly; he wore it long, evidently aware that it was very nice; and his handsome eyes had a charming expression. His sensual mouth was always smiling.' Maugham knows, if Bertha does not, how dangerous such young men can be; and it is perhaps not wholly irrelevant that the novel was written very shortly after Maugham returned from his second visit to Seville, where he had gone, he said, to continue his affair with his green-eyed paramour.

Written in 1900 in the last year of Queen Victoria's reign, *Mrs Craddock* was published in Britain at the beginning of the Edwardian age, in November 1902, not appearing in the United States till 1920. The novel was widely noticed and generally acclaimed, although several critics felt it their duty to warn readers of the daring nature of the content. '[If] you are afraid to look life in the face,' said St John Adcock in the *Bookman*, 'you had better leave Mr Maugham alone.' Indeed the cuts insisted on by Heinemann had done little to blur the candid fact of Bertha's passion, and it is surprising, given the prudishness of the period, that so little was taken out. Yet, even by Maugham's pessimistic standards, his fourth novel was 'a substantial success', if for its author there remained a sense of frustration: his ambition was to write for the theatre, and he still regarded his novels mainly as a means of making his name well enough known so that managers would look with favour on his drama, none of which had yet been accepted. Now with *Mrs Craddock* in the public eye he was about to put this theory to the test with his first full-length play, for which he had the highest hopes.

# 4

## Le Chat Blanc

In his autobiographical work *The Summing Up*, Maugham, in typically self-deprecating mode, states that he began to write plays simply because 'it seemed less difficult to set down on paper the things people said than to construct a narrative'. There was, of course, more to it than that, but with his finely attuned ear he was quick at picking up the rhythms of colloquial speech, and in his preferred role of listener was as intrigued by the manner in which people expressed themselves as by the content. From the age of sixteen Maugham had been passionately interested in the theatre, had read widely not only the English dramatists, but French, Spanish, German and others in translation, and he went as often as he could to the play. It had not escaped his attention either that a success in the theatre brought more substantial and immediate financial rewards than were ever likely with a novel. Maugham was to become phenomenally popular as a dramatist, his play-writing extending over three decades, bringing him fame and glamour and making him an immensely rich man; he wrote thirty full-length plays, and his work, staged all over the world, has been filmed, constantly revived and widely translated. Yet such an outcome would have been hard to predict from the extremely modest beginnings of Maugham's theatrical career: none of his early attempts at play-writing found favour with the managers to whom they were sent, and it was only a steely determination that prevented him from giving up during ten years of rejection and discouragement. The first dramatic work by Maugham actually to be produced was *Marriages Are Made in Heaven*, a one-act play originally written in 1898, with the popular theme of the society woman with a guilty past. Having failed to place it in London, Maugham translated the piece into German, and as *Schiffbrüchig* (*Shipwreck*) it was taken up by Max Reinhardt's company in January 1902 for the tiny Schall-und-Rauch cabaret theatre in Berlin, where it ran for a mere eight performances.

The same year, 1898, Maugham had also completed his first full-length work, *A Man of Honour*, strongly influenced by Ibsen, in his eyes the greatest of all modern dramatists. On his first visit to Italy Maugham had taken with him a German version of *Ghosts*, familiarising himself with the play by rendering it into English. The plot of *A Man of Honour* is recognisably Ibsenite in approach, dealing with the pressures of society, the struggle for personal integrity and the disastrous consequences of ignoring instinct in a blind adherence to convention. But the West End was no more receptive to Maugham than it had been to Ibsen himself, and the play was turned down, first by the distinguished Johnston Forbes-Robertson and then by the American impresario Charles Frohman, who had recently taken over the Duke of York's Theatre in St Martin's Lane. After this second rejection, Maugham made some extensive revisions before trying a completely different tack and submitting the play to the Stage Society, which to his delight accepted it for two performances in February 1903.

The Stage Society had been founded in 1899, the successor to the short-lived Independent Theatre Club set up by the pioneering J. T. Grein. Playwright, critic and manager, Grein saw it as his mission to produce plays of artistic merit which were unlikely to prove popular in the mainstream. West End audiences in the 1890s had been fed an almost exclusive fare of society drama, plays about the upper and well-to-do middle classes, preferably with a plot involving a parvenu and a shameful secret, usually that of a woman with a past. Typical titles of the period were *Lady Huntsworth's Experiment*, *Lady Gorringe's Necklace*, *Lady Epping's Lawsuit* and *Lord & Lady Algy*, with the plays of Oscar Wilde offering the supreme example, from *Lady Windermere's Fan* to the guying of the genre in *The Importance of Being Earnest*. Along with Wilde, whose career in the theatre had been so abruptly curtailed, the most popular playwrights of the period were R. C. Carton, Haddon Chambers, Henry Arthur Jones and Arthur Wing Pinero, author of the immensely successful *The Second Mrs Tanqueray*. Jack Grein was interested in a different genre. It was Grein who in 1892 had put on *Widowers' Houses*, the first ever performance of a play by George Bernard Shaw, and Grein the previous year who had staged a single performance of Ibsen's *Ghosts*, an occasion greeted with howls of outrage. In the words of its translator, William Archer, 'The shriek of execration with which this performance was received by the newspapers of the day has scarcely its counterpart in the history of criticism.'

With Grein's acceptance of *A Man of Honour*, Maugham felt that at last he was within reach of the career for which he had been unsuccessfully aiming for nearly a decade. The Stage Society was a private members' club and audiences were small, but it was the only organisation presenting experimental theatre and consequently its productions attracted a good deal of attention. Maugham was further encouraged by the fact that a member of the committee, the eminent scholar and journalist W. L. Courtney, had offered to publish the script in the March 1903 issue of the prestigious *Fortnightly Review*, of which he was editor. This was a notable accolade: Courtney was widely respected for his flair in spotting new talent and under his editorship the *Review* was considered the leading literary journal of the day, counting among its contributors Meredith, Kipling, H. G. Wells, George Moore and Henry James.

Described by its author as a tragedy, the play deals with the wretched consequences for an honourable young man of insisting on his moral duty by marrying beneath him. Basil Kent, a hero of the Boer War, proposes marriage to Jenny Bush, barmaid at the Golden Crown in Fleet Street, because she is expecting his child. Despite his friend John Halliwell attempting to argue him out of it, Basil insists on sticking to his disastrous commitment, although he and Jenny have nothing in common and he is in love with a young widow, Hilda Murray, Halliwell's sister-in-law. The marriage is miserably unhappy: the baby dies at birth; Basil is both bored and irritated by his good-natured but ill-educated wife, and bitterly resents having to support her grasping family. By the last act, Basil has finally decided to leave Jenny and marry Hilda when the news is brought that his wife has drowned herself in the river. At first overcome by remorse, Basil begins to realise that he is at last free to live life as he pleases, his horror at what he has escaped expressed with a striking depth of feeling. 'You don't know what it is when your prison door is opened,' Basil exclaims ecstatically to Halliwell.

Maugham attended rehearsals, delighted to see his work come to life in the hands of an accomplished cast led by Harley Granville Barker. Granville Barker, handsome, serious and immensely talented, was one of the initiators of the modern movement, shortly to become known, both as actor and director, for his association with Shaw. The actor's portrayal of Basil Kent was everything the author could have wished, even if backstage the young man was found to be rather less rewarding, arrogant and 'brimming over with other people's ideas', in Maugham's view. '[Granville Barker] is a difficult person to deal with,' he complained to his agent, 'very vain & full of self-conceit.'

The first night, on 22 February 1903, at the Imperial Theatre, Tothill Street, was well attended by friends and family and generally judged a success, although Maugham was in an agony of nerves throughout. His sister-in-law Nellie wrote in her diary, 'Went to the first night of Willie's play . . . Very enthusiastic audience, and it was quite well acted. Willie was pale with terror!' Afterwards there was a party at the nearby Westminster Hotel at which Harry Maugham arrived late, attracting attention by his dishevelled appearance, wearing not evening dress like everyone else but a rumpled blue suit, and visibly the worse for wear. 'I'm glad my little brother has had some success at last,' he declared in an embarrassingly loud voice. The production attracted a gratifying amount of attention, even if the notices were mixed: most of the establishment critics found the subject-matter depressing (the *Athenaeum* likened it to 'a long Scandinavian night') although on the whole the playwright was thought to show promise. J. T. Grein himself, writing in the *Sunday Times*, was by far the most enthusiastic, favourably comparing Maugham to Pinero and expressing admiration for the author's linguistic style. 'Not for a long time had I heard such fine and nervous English,' he stated. 'Simplicity is throughout the keynote of Mr Maugham's dramatic vein . . . His drama is true.' Balanced between these two positions was Max Beerbohm, who had succeeded Shaw as theatre critic for the *Saturday Review*. In an article headed 'A Chaotic Play' Beerbohm wrote that the second act 'is admirably conceived and written; and the third act is a fine piece of emotional drama. The rest of the play falls to pieces. Mr Maugham becomes too bitter . . .'

Maugham had learned some valuable lessons in stagecraft while watching rehearsals, how to shape dialogue, the importance of changing speed, how to get laughs in the right places and position the pauses; he was pleased with the level of response from the audience; and yet he was left with a feeling of frustration after the two performances were over. The experience seemed to have advanced his career very little. The Stage Society was admirable in its way, but Maugham's ambitions were focused on a much wider horizon: the commercial theatre of the West End. 'I was not satisfied with the appreciation of a small band of intellectuals,' he wrote. 'I wanted no such audience as this, but the great public.'

As a first step in this direction Maugham sent the play to Muriel Wylford, manager of the Avenue Theatre (now the Playhouse Theatre) at Charing Cross. Miss Wylford agreed to put it on, with herself in the part of Jenny Bush, for a four-week run in February 1904, together with a one-act farce Maugham had completed earlier, *Mademoiselle Zampa*,* as

---

* Never published and no known manuscript exists.

a curtain-raiser. This was a flop and had to be withdrawn, but *A Man of Honour* proved moderately popular. 'Now that the author has softened down its cynical ending,' said the *Illustrated London News*, '[the play] ranks as the most interesting and observant work our stage has known for many a day.' Max Beerbohm, who also attended this second production, wrote about it at length, considering that, although it had its flaws and was notably inferior to the author's novels, the play was genuinely poignant and full of insight. 'There is no reason to suppose', he concluded, 'that anon Mr Maugham as playwright will not be the equal of Mr Maugham as novelist.' On the first performance the final curtain was followed by a storm of enthusiastic clapping and calls for the author. One of the actors standing by the pass door watched as Maugham took in what was happening, hardly able to believe his ears. 'I can see now the shy young author, quite shaken by the cheers and prolonged applause, coming through to the stage but unwilling to take a call.'

Of the three brothers, it was Harry who showed the most interest in Maugham's writing for the theatre, as he, too, had ambitions as a playwright and had published a collection of plays in verse. Unfortunately this was an unfashionable genre, and the collection had met with little more success than the rest of Harry's writings, his poetry, an anthology of travel writing about Italy and a short-lived series of articles in *Black and White* magazine under the by-line 'The Amiable Egoist'. In 1902 he and Maugham had collaborated on a play, *The Fortune Hunters*, but Maurice Colles failed to place it and it was never produced. Serious and intellectual, Harry was worried by what he saw as his brother's superficiality, warning him that his ambitious social life would have a deleterious effect on his work. 'Harry told me that my plays . . . were well constructed and neatly contrived but they were also trivial and shallow because the life I was leading was trivial and shallow.' Plump, handsome and permanently dishevelled, Harry had never felt at home in the world; he was sensitive and shy and had become increasingly reclusive, drinking too much, struggling with depression and finding it difficult to make friends. He was a bit of a bore, according to Maugham. 'He needed a lot of understanding,' said Charlie's wife Beldy, 'and very few people could understand him.' In 1899 Harry had left Italy where he had been living since leaving the family law firm in Paris, and returned to England, taking rooms in Cadogan Street, Chelsea, where he led a largely solitary existence. 'Very much homosexual', according to a contemporary, Harry was nervous of women and much preferred the company of men; his few friends were drawn from the

bohemian circle of writers and painters of which Maugham's old mentor
Wentworth Huyshe was the centre. Years later Harry's niece Honor
spoke of a well-known writer, unnamed, who told her he had been a
lover of Harry's.

Harry was too sweet-natured to begrudge his younger brother his
success yet it undoubtedly added to his own feelings of inferiority.
Whether it was fear of failure, unhappiness over a love affair, the threat
of scandal or simply the engulfing nature of his chronic depression, in
July 1904 Harry killed himself. Freddie Maugham – F.H. – briefly
noted in his appointment diary the course of events, that on 20 July
he was summoned by wire to Cadogan Street to find Harry blue in
the face and in agony, having swallowed nitric acid three days earlier.
He took him to St Thomas's Hospital, where for nearly a week Harry
lingered, dying at 7.45 on the evening of the 27th, three-quarters of
an hour after the arrival of Charlie and Beldy from Paris. The inquest,
at which it was recorded that Harry had ended his life 'while of
unsound mind', took place two days later, followed immediately by
the funeral at Lambeth Cemetery. At no stage in F.H.'s account is there
any mention of Maugham being present, and yet in Maugham's own
version, recounted some years later, he states that it was he who was
summoned, he who found Harry, he who took him to hospital. The
probability is that both brothers were involved, that George Barlow,
the friend who was the first on the scene, sent a wire to the two of
them; attempting suicide was a criminal offence, and as it would therefore have been risky to call a doctor, Maugham's medical expertise was
vital; so, too, his familiarity with St Thomas's, where he could use his
influence to persuade the authorities to keep the matter quiet. The
week after the funeral Maugham went to stay with Charles and Beldy
at Meudon, near Versailles, where they had taken a house for the summer,
and the brothers talked endlessly about Harry, speculating about the
reasons that drove him to death. 'I'm sure it wasn't only failure that
made him kill himself,' Maugham significantly concluded. 'It was the
life he led.'

Harry's suicide was shocking and horrific, even if, true to form, it
was rarely referred to within the family. All four of Robert Maugham's
sons suffered from depression: Charles was portrayed by his family as
'pale and grave . . . melancholy . . . a rather sad man', while F.H. in his
appointment diaries regularly defines his own state of mind as 'depressed'
and 'very sad'; Maugham was an unhappy child who evolved into a
deeply melancholic man, 'violently pessimistic', as he characterised himself,

and both he and F.H. in later life suffered frequently from nightmares. One of Maugham's nieces had a theory that the Maugham boys as small children 'must at some time have been ill-treated, perhaps by some French nurse'; while her younger sister wrote of her father and her uncle Willie that 'both wept easily at plays and over novels . . . yet remain[ed] dry eyed throughout any of life's tragic events. Perhaps they had insulated themselves as best they could from unbearable sorrows, which resulted at times in an icy coldness which could chill and sometimes destroy human relationships.' Maugham at least was fortunate in that his abundant vitality, his ambition and his insatiable curiosity made his life for most of the time seem worth living. But for Harry it was not, and although he could rarely bring himself to speak of it, his brother's pathetic self-destruction was to haunt Maugham for many years.

Having turned his back on the Stage Society, Maugham believed he now understood what commercial managements were looking for, and already during the previous twelve months he had completed three plays which in his view were ideal for the West End: *The Explorer*, *Loaves and Fishes* and, with Harry, *The Fortune Hunters*. And yet not one of them had been accepted. There was, too, a farce, *The Middle of Next Week*, written for the actor–manager Charles Hawtrey, but Hawtrey demanded so many changes that Maugham in a fury tore up the script. All this was a grave disappointment not only in terms of establishing a reputation but also financially, because at this period his only income, apart from his tiny patrimony, was generated by the occasional short story sold to magazines. Sharing a flat with Walter Payne, Maugham was able to live modestly, but in both his professional and social life appearances were important. He was making new friends, was admired as a promising young writer and was beginning to be much sought after in the more intellectual social circles. He liked to dress well, to give dinners on occasion, and recently he had joined a gentlemen's club, the Bath Club in Dover Street, which offered its members a swimming-pool, squash-courts, a Turkish bath and a card-room well known to serious bridge-players. None of this was cheap, and Maugham grew increasingly frustrated by his financial insecurity. 'Times are very hard & publishers very moneyless at present,' Maugham wrote to Wentworth Huyshe. 'I cannot tell when the clouds will roll by!'

The easy-going Colles was continually being nagged by his client to try to interest managers in his plays, solicit commissions from journals, reissue old work, explore new sources, press for payment from dilatory editors, anything, in fact, that would bring in some money. 'If you hear of anyone wanting a play translated from French, German, Italian or Spanish, or adapted, I should be glad to do it,' ran a typical plea. 'I was anxious to see you about a sixpenny edition of *Liza*,' ran another. 'Also I wondered if you could get me an *Arrowsmith Annual* to do. I have sketched out a rather sensational murder story (quite proper!) somewhat in the manner of Edgar Allan Poe . . .' 'Behold three short stories,' begins a businesslike communication written in July 1904. '"The Criminal", 2300 words, somewhat better than the others, would do for *Lloyds*. "Flirtation", 300 words, might suit the *D. Mail*. "A Rehearsal", 3000 words, is bad enough to suit anything.'

His financial situation may have been precarious but Maugham nonetheless was regarded with respect as a promising young member of the literary intelligentsia, 'an honourable condition', he remarked, 'which, some years later, when I became a popular writer of light comedies, I lost.' To his already heavy workload he was now invited to add the co-editorship of what was intended to be a prestigious annual anthology, a successor to *The Yellow Book*, a project on which he collaborated with the writer and illustrator Laurence Housman, a younger brother of the poet A. E. Housman. *The Venture*, subtitled *An Annual of Art and Literature*, was a luxurious production, in hard covers, copiously illustrated and printed on thick, cream-coloured paper with an elegant black typeface. On a distinguished list of contributors were John Masefield, G. K. Chesterton, James Joyce, Havelock Ellis, Thomas Hardy and E. F. Benson, with illustrators Gordon Craig, T. Sturge Moore and Charles Ricketts; in the first number Maugham included a piece of his own, *Marriages Are Made in Heaven*, the original English version of the curtain-raiser that had been staged the previous year in Berlin. It was agreed that all participants should be paid a share of the profits in place of a fee, but no profits were ever forthcoming. The first issue appeared, a little late, in the autumn of 1903, followed by a second in 1905, after which no more was heard or seen of *The Venture*. 'The whole thing was, of course, too highbrow to be popular,' Laurence Housman loftily concluded. 'Perhaps had it been published at a guinea instead of at five shillings, it would have done better.'

Among the few women writers appearing in *The Venture* was the novelist Violet Hunt, whom Maugham had first met in 1902. A woman who inspired extremes of liking and loathing, Violet, now in her forties and notorious for her turbulent love-life, was tall and thin with a mass of dark hair, large eyes, a beaky nose and pointed chin. Born in 1862 she had been brought up among artists and poets, her father, Alfred Hunt, a landscape painter, friend of Ruskin, Burne-Jones, Millais and Robert Browning; Violet had modelled for Burne-Jones and Sickert, and from childhood had been encouraged to regard herself as a Pre-Raphaelite beauty. At eighteen she had been admired by the young Oscar Wilde, who called her 'the sweetest Violet in England', and in her twenties she had had a number of affairs with older men, including the diplomat and publisher Oswald Crawfurd, from whom she contracted syphilis; later she became one of the many mistresses of H. G. Wells and conducted a tormenting ten-year relationship with Ford Madox Ford, eleven years her junior. A novelist of the 'new woman' genre, Violet was a frequent contributor to magazines and very much in the swim in bookish circles; she was well known as a literary hostess, with her bi-monthly luncheons at the Writers' Club in Norfolk Street and her garden parties at South Lodge, her house on Campden Hill near Holland Park. Among the distinguished habitués were Henry James, Ezra Pound, Joseph Conrad, Wyndham Lewis, Wells, Arnold Bennett and D. H. Lawrence, who strolled about the lawn sipping iced coffee and encouraging their hostess in her scandalous conversation. 'I rather like her,' Lawrence remarked. 'She's such a real assassin.' The novelist Hugh Walpole remembered seeing Maugham at one of Violet's summer parties, wandering among the trees, elegant in a grey top hat. Indeed it was Violet's keen appetite for gossip that primarily appealed to Maugham, who was amused by her high spirits and malicious tongue; she, sexually voracious, was strongly attracted and lost little time in luring him into bed. It was Violet who remarked of Maugham, 'He is a fearfully emotional man, sexually.'

The physical side of the friendship was unsatisfactory and mercifully brief, Violet still suffering the after-effects of her affair with Crawfurd, but the two remained fond of each other, Maugham writing Violet long flirtatious letters and even confiding in her, up to a point, about his love-life. 'My "affair" is over THANK GOD,' he had written in a postscript at about this time, possibly a reference to an entanglement with one of the attractive prospects brought to the flat by Walter Payne.

Much of the correspondence with Violet Hunt is devoted to a discussion of their literary enterprises, Maugham expanding on his own projects and offering a considered judgment of hers. 'I am wishing I need never write another novel all my life,' he admitted after coming to the end of *Mrs Craddock*. 'But I suppose I shall – I have got a sort of sneaking desire to do a minor *Comédie Humaine* for England.' And when in 1904 Violet published a fictionalised account of her ill-fated affair with Crawfurd,

Maugham told her, 'I think you have done it with very great skill. I confess I should have liked a little more "obscenity", because Appleton's charm is obviously sexual, but I recognize that this was impossible.' In 1908 Violet dedicated to him her novel *White Rose of Weary Leaf*, in graceful recognition of his dedication to her of his sketches of Andalusia, which was eventually published in 1905; unfortunately, he had neglected to ask her permission first and she had taken offence, 'chiefly, I think, because it was called *The Land of the Blessed Virgin* & she could not imagine what the hell would be her business in such a country', Maugham jokingly remarked. Violet soon recovered her good humour, however, and the friendship endured, she ebullient and demonstrative, he amiable and reserved. Nearly twenty years later Maugham was to draw her portrait in *The Moon and Sixpence* as Rose Waterford, who was torn 'between the aestheticism of her early youth, when she used to go to parties in sage green, holding a daffodil, and the flippancy of her maturer years, which tended to high heels and Paris frocks . . . No one was kinder to me', he wrote, 'than Rose Waterford. She combined a masculine intelligence with a feminine perversity . . . No one could say such bitter things; on the other hand, no one could do more charming ones.' As she grew older, Violet grew increasingly touchy and tiresome, but Maugham always treated her with gentleness, and unlike many of her acquaintance refused to cold-shoulder her for her frequently outrageous behaviour.

It was a sign of his confidence in Violet's critical judgment that Maugham asked her to read his new novel, *The Merry-Go-Round*, before he submitted it for publication, at her suggestion cutting out several whole chapters as well as undertaking some minor pruning. *The Merry-Go-Round*, somewhat reluctantly accepted by Heinemann for a royalty of £60 and as part of a package with *The Land of the Blessed Virgin*, presents a reworking of *A Man of Honour*, a fleshing out of the story of Basil Kent and his miserable marriage to the barmaid Jenny, with the addition of two subsidiary plot-lines. The first of these tells the story of Bella, a clergyman's homely daughter, who, having devoted her life to her selfish and irascible father, in middle age falls in love with the gentle Herbert, a poetic young man not only years her junior but considerably below her in social class; despite her father's fury, the two marry and are blissfully happy until Herbert contracts tuberculosis and dies. The second and much the more interesting theme describes the helpless passion of a well-to-do married woman for a venal, caddish young man, several years her junior and very much on the make.

This story is narrated with a far more lively style and spirit than the other two. Reggie Barlow-Bassett, like Gerald Vaudrey in *Mrs Craddock*, has a sensual beauty that enslaves Grace Castillyon. From their first encounter Grace is smitten; sitting next to her at dinner, '[Reggie] told her little scabrous stories in a low, suave voice, staring meanwhile into her eyes with the shameless audacity of a man conscious of his power.' Soon the besotted woman is lavishing money and every luxury on her worthless lover, risking her marriage and her standing in society, desperate to please him even though she knows he cares nothing for her and is only after what he can get. Like Mrs Craddock's love for her husband and Jenny's love for Basil Kent, Mrs Castillyon's love for Reggie is a humiliating bondage: Grace Castillyon is in a state of 'utter abasement', her desperate passion for Reggie making her 'careless into what abyss of shame and misery it led'. Eventually she is saved from ruin and persuaded to return to her husband by the stern intervention of Miss Ley, an outspoken spinster first encountered in *Mrs Craddock* as standing *in loco parentis* to Bertha before her marriage.

*The Merry-Go-Round* has definite merits, if it cannot be said to display Maugham at his best. The unhappy-marriage plot, transplanted from *A Man of Honour*, despite minor changes and additions shows signs of authorial weariness at trudging round the track a second time; while the happy-marriage plot, the union of Bella and Herbert, is spoiled by too sentimental a treatment, liberally sprinkled with examples of those Pateresque sentences practised so assiduously in the notebooks and later vehemently despised. As Maugham himself put it, the book suffered from 'the pernicious influence' of the aesthetes: 'I wrote with affectation . . . I was afraid to let myself go.' Where, with advantage, he did let himself go is in the story of Mrs Castillyon and the appalling Reggie, and here the language is free of artificiality, indeed strikingly modern ('I was simply dying for a fag,' says one female character to another). The problem is that in terms of the book as a whole the account of this consuming obsession is so vivid that it damagingly overshadows the rest.

There are two characters in the novel who stand apart, their role mainly that of observers, useful links between the three discrete story-lines, the spinster Miss Ley and her much younger friend and confidant, the doctor Frank Hurrell. Miss Ley, the author tells us, cultivated 'a certain primness of manner which made very effective the audacious criticism of life wherewith she was used to entertain her friends'. Her original was an interesting woman, Mrs George Steevens, widow of a *Daily Mail* correspondent who died while covering the Boer War. Plain of feature but stylish – she dressed always in severe black and white – she was elderly when Maugham met her, a bright-eyed old lady full of charm and vitality, as well as outspoken and capable of stunning rudeness to those she disliked. There was an air of notoriety surrounding Christina Steevens: during her first marriage, as Mrs Rogerson, she had been barred from polite society after her scandalous involvement in the divorce case which ruined the career of the Liberal MP Sir Charles Dilke. She once startled Henry James by confiding that she had poisoned her first husband. 'If she had been beautiful and sane,' James concluded, 'she would have been one of the world's great wicked women.' Mrs Steevens lived at Merton Place in Surrey, on the site of the house that had once belonged to Admiral Nelson, where her precarious finances never prevented her from offering her wide circle of friends an abundant hospitality. Merton, near Wimbledon, was within easy reach of London, and a stream of visitors would drive out by hansom on Sundays for lunch or tea, in fine weather wandering through the garden and along the banks of the river; among them were actors, writers, painters and their hangers-on, 'a queer lot', as Maugham said of a group which included Violet Hunt as well as others who were to become important to him, Max Beerbohm, Oscar Wilde's disciple Reggie Turner and the popular playwright Henry Arthur Jones.

It was Jones who told Maugham that when he read *Liza of Lambeth* he had immediately recognised Maugham's potential as a dramatist, a flattering statement in direct contradiction of the opinion proffered by another of Mrs Steevens's guests. While strolling one afternoon on the lawn at Merton Maugham had had a long talk with the gentle and charming Max Beerbohm. In those days Max had not yet perfected his supremely elegant sartorial style: in Maugham's view the dandyism 'didn't quite come off. His very narrow shirt cuffs, protruding a good two inches out of the sleeves of his tail coat, were generally a trifle grubby, the coat needed a brushing & the trousers pressing . . . You had the impression of a small part actor in a provincial company dressed as a swell.' Although himself a dramatic critic and half-brother of Herbert Beerbohm Tree, one of London's foremost actor–managers, Max's youthful love for the theatre had largely evaporated, and sometimes when sitting on duty through some dire production he would try to keep his spirits up by reminding himself, '[at least] I am not a porter on the Underground Railway'. Now he earnestly entreated Maugham to give up writing for the stage: in Max's opinion Maugham's talents were primarily as a novelist, and that for one capable of such subtlety of characterisation the drama was too crude a medium. Of course, Max continued, there was a great deal of money to be made out of the theatre by some people, but 'you, my boy, are not one of those people'. Maugham nodded politely and Max, 'sorry for him, yet conscious of having done a good afternoon's work, briskly changed the subject'. But if Max believed he had influenced his companion, he was wrong. 'He little knew,' said Maugham. 'I was young, poor and determined.'

Despite such dispiriting advice, Maugham's friendship with the witty and fastidious Max, begun at Merton, lasted a lifetime. Indeed Maugham had much to be grateful for in Mrs Steevens's hospitality, and he responded warmly to the old lady's liveliness and generosity, admiring her impatience with humbug and her frankness in speaking her mind, both qualities which he bestowed upon her fictional counterpart, Miss Ley. In *The Merry-Go-Round* he drew on his own relationship with Mrs Steevens in portraying that between Miss Ley and Frank Hurrell, the doctor, who in both appearance and character bears a striking resemblance to his author. Frank, we are told, was:

> a strong man, of no very easy temper, who held himself in admirable control. Silent with strangers, he disconcerted them by an unwilling frigidity of manner . . . an extremely reserved man, few knew that Frank Hurrell's deliberate placidity of expression masked a very emotional temperament. In this he recognized a weakness and had schooled his face carefully to betray no feeling; but the feeling all the same was there, turbulent and overwhelming . . . He kept over himself unceasing watch, as though a dangerous prisoner were in his heart ever on the alert to break his chains.

If *The Merry-Go-Round* is not among the most distinguished of Maugham's novels, in autobiographical terms it is undoubtedly important. Not only is there a substantial element of self-portrayal in the drawing of Frank Hurrell but, more crucially, there is a revealing picture of Maugham's emotional state. In describing Grace Castillyon's passion for Reggie Barlow-Bassett, Maugham gives powerful expression to an obsession of his own, also for a much younger man. Shortly after he had completed the novel Maugham wrote to Violet Hunt, 'Most of what one writes is to a greater or lesser degree autobiographical, not the actual incidents always, but always the emotions . . . When one has to suffer so much it is only fair that one should have the consolation of writing books about it.' And years later he said of this period of his life that he urgently wanted to write a novel that would make money, 'because I was at the

time much taken with a young person of extravagant tastes . . . I determined to write a book that would enable me to earn three or four
hundred pounds with which I could hold my own with my rivals. For
the young person was attractive.'

Maugham was always careful to cover his tracks, and the young
person in question is left unidentified, although evidence points firmly
in the direction of a handsome youth called Harry Philips. Studying
at Oxford when Maugham first met him, Henry (Harry) Vaughan Philips
was the son of the Rev. Edward Philips, Rector of Hollington, near
Stoke-on-Trent in Staffordshire. One of five boys, he was intended for
an ecclesiastical career, and the first step in this direction was three years
at Keble, a relatively new college founded primarily to perpetuate the
aims of the Oxford Movement and to provide a breeding-ground for
Anglican curates. Keble was not the right place for Harry. Described
by a fellow undergraduate as 'quite the most dazzling figure for charm,
good looks, and brilliant wit that I had ever encountered', he was
proving a grave disappointment to his father, having no interest in the
Church and regarding his time at Oxford as an opportunity to enjoy
himself to the full and whenever possible to shock his pious college
contemporaries by outré behaviour. Having failed the set papers at the
end of his first year, playboy Harry had left Keble – 'a nice fellow',
his tutor had reported, '[but] a little too aesthetic & sentimental for his
intellect, which is not strong' – and enrolled instead in Marcon's, one
of the more respectable of the gentlemen's halls attached to the university, where he could be crammed for his degree, a qualification which
in the end was never conferred. 'I was constantly failing in my exam-
inations,' as he cheerfully admitted.

Like Oscar Wilde who ten years earlier had haunted Oxford in
pursuit of Lord Alfred Douglas at Magdalen, so Maugham became a
familiar figure, strolling down the High with Harry or encountered
sitting smoking in his rooms. 'We took a great liking to each other,'
said Harry, '& I invited him to stay with my parents in Staffordshire.
My Father thought him clever but did not like his views on religion.'
This was hardly surprising given Maugham's agnosticism and his support
of Harry's determination not to enter the Church. 'I cannot help
thinking it a very cruel thing to force anyone into a distasteful profession,' said Maugham, no doubt remembering the similar pressure exerted
on him by the Vicar at Whitstable, '& doubly so, into one that needs
faith & self-sacrifice, & a "call", when the wretched man cannot bring
himself to believe any of the dogmas which his people find self-evident.'

Despite this lack of agreement, however, no parental objection was made to the friendship and the two men continued to see each other constantly.

In *The Merry-Go-Round* Grace Castillyon, helplessly infatuated, is forever having to bribe Reggie to be nice to her. 'She had a certain hold over him in his immense love of pleasure. She could always avoid his peevishness by taking him to the theatre; he was anxious to move in polite circles, and an invitation to some great house made him affectionate for a week.' As with Reggie, so with Harry; but providing the young man with entertainment did not come cheap, and Maugham had to work at full pressure, desperate to earn money. 'Money was like a sixth sense,' he wrote, 'without which you could not make the most of the other five.' Every penny counted, and in perusing the statements sent in by Colles he allowed no detail to escape his attention. 'I see that you have charged me some 15/- for postage; this you have never done before, & I don't see why you should suddenly begin,' he complained in August 1904. He was relying on the new novel to rescue his finances and he stressed to Colles the importance of having the book properly publicised and promoted. 'I hope', he wrote, 'you will impress upon Heinemann the necessity of advertising *The Merry-Go-Round* well.' In the event its appearance on 19 September 1904 was a flop, and in spite of a few good reviews sales were poor, an outcome for which Maugham blamed both publisher and agent. 'I should like you to observe', he suggested sarcastically to Colles three months after publication, 'with what energy Heinemann is making the public see what an excellent book *The Merry-Go-Round* is.' The firm did no better at the beginning of the following year with *The Land of the Blessed Virgin*, which had finally made its appearance in January 1905; this, too, failed to sell many copies in spite of a couple of appreciative notices, including one, unsigned, in the *Times Literary Supplement* by the young Virginia Stephen. '[Mr Maugham] has his pen well under control,' she wrote, 'and he has a sincere desire to find the right word for the beauty which he genuinely loves.'

As Maugham continued his ardent pursuit of the tantalising Harry, the need for cash grew ever more pressing, and he continued to drive himself hard. 'I wrote', as he put it, 'with jealousy gnawing at my heart-strings.' Dazzlingly attractive, Harry was much sought after, and it was mortifying to have to sit by while richer men treated him to suppers at the Savoy and lunches by the river at Maidenhead. Harry's 'frivolous soul' delighted in such spoiling; he saw no reason to deny himself, and his lover's anguish was treated with an indifference that drove Maugham nearly to distraction. When in the summer of 1904 Harry came down from Oxford without a degree, vaguely intending to pursue some kind of career as an artist, Maugham saw his chance and encouraged him to think seriously of training in Paris; he himself would leave London and take an apartment on the Left Bank which he and Harry could share. From the innocence of his country parish, Philips senior saw nothing wrong in the proposal: Maugham seemed a sensible chap, a hard-working writer with an established reputation who might well prove a good influence on his feckless son. Immediately Maugham put his plan into action, invigorated not only by the prospect of having his beloved boy to himself but also by the chance of breaking new ground. For over six years he had struggled for success in London, and it suddenly began to look pointless and as though nothing would ever change. 'It was all very nice, but I couldn't see that it was leading me anywhere,' he noted. 'I was thirty . . . I was in a rut and I felt that I must get out of it. I talked the matter over with Walter Payne with the result that we got rid of the flat we had shared, sold for a song the little furniture we had and I, thrilled, went to Paris.'

Throughout his twenties Maugham had visited Paris at intervals, sometimes staying with his eldest brother Charlie and his young family, sometimes in a hotel, neither entirely satisfactory, as he explained to Violet Hunt. 'When I am with my brother I am somewhat overwhelmed by domesticity & when I stay at a hotel I am ruined.' Now in looking for somewhere to live Maugham enlisted the help of a new friend, Gerald Kelly, a young painter currently living in France whom he had met one Sunday in 1903 while staying with Charles and Beldy at the house they rented for the summer in Meudon.

Five years younger than Maugham, Gerald Kelly (of the family that published *Kelly's Directories*) was the son of a well-to-do clergyman, the Vicar of St Giles in Camberwell. Possessed of abundant nervous energy and an irascible Irish charm, Gerald was short and stocky, with finely drawn features, eyes alert behind big round spectacles and a head of thick, untidy black hair. Spoilt and sickly as a child, he had been educated at Eton and Cambridge, although the formative experience of his early years were his visits to Dulwich Picture Gallery which first inspired his love of painting. Without any formal training in art, he had moved to Paris in 1901, where he bought a large studio in the rue Campagne-Première in Montparnasse, and helped by the dealer Paul Durand-Ruel began assiduously visiting the studios of Monet, Degas and Cézanne, even succeeding in persuading the sculptor Rodin to take him on as an assistant. Concentrating on portraiture, with landscapes as a sideline, Kelly was beginning to become known. One of his paintings had been bought by the French government in 1903, and the following year, still only twenty-five, he was made a member of the Salon d'Automne.

At Meudon Maugham and Kelly had taken to each other at once, Maugham captivated by the younger man's exuberant volubility, his passion for art and ideas, while Kelly was impressed by Maugham's intelligence, his dry sense of humour and his wide-ranging curiosity. He was also fascinated by Maugham's appearance which he longed to paint: 'his whole face was just one colour – very pale . . . [and] his eyes were like little pieces of brown velvet – like a monkey's eyes'. The two men were very different in manner. 'While I have leaned on his patience and on his wisdom, he has often been exasperated by my verbosity,' Kelly wrote. Nonetheless they had a number of attributes in common: they were both tolerant and unshockable, both had a quick wit and a hot temper, although Maugham was better at controlling his; they both had a passion for travel; and they took pride in their intellectual integrity. 'Both of us obstinately refused to pretend to admire what really we did not admire – even when we had been told we should admire it,' said Kelly. 'Willie dared to find Meredith and Pater overrated; I was bold enough to love Ingres and Manet – unfashionable judgments at the beginning of this century.'

It was during this time, while he was living in Paris with Harry, that Maugham's education in the visual arts was seriously begun, and Kelly had much to do with this. It was Kelly who lent him books, taught him how to look at paintings, and explored with him the works of the Old Masters as well as introducing him to the new. Kelly inspired his friend with his own passion for Velázquez, Maugham responding with fervour to the Spanish master's vision of Spain as well as to his uncompromising realism and profound humanity; and it was Kelly who first showed Maugham work by the Impressionists, by Monet, Renoir, Manet and Cézanne, taking him to see the collection at the Luxembourg. But despite Kelly's energetic enthusiasm Maugham at this stage remained unimpressed by the latter: 'to my shame,' he wrote later, 'I could not make head or tail of them'. When apart, the two men wrote at length to each other about art, and after Maugham became famous, Kelly was his principal portraitist, painting him a total of eighteen times. Despite Kelly's superior knowledge, Maugham never hesitated to instruct his friend, candidly criticising his work, pointing out where he was going wrong, and taking advantage of his five years' seniority to adopt the tone of an affectionate but bossy elder brother. 'My dear Gerald,' he wrote in July 1905,

I am very sorry, though by no means surprised, that you have fallen ill again. It is obvious to the meanest intelligence that if you lead such a life as you led in Paris you are quite sure to be ill . . . I cannot write to you with any patience. By the stupidest carelessness (and I daresay at the bottom of your heart the feeling that it's very romantic & picturesque to cultivate a fine frenzy which ignores the matter of fact) you are throwing away all your chances of becoming a better painter than Tom, Dick, or Harry. For the work you do when you're not well is rotten . . .

With Kelly Maugham enjoyed the kind of fraternal relationship he had never formed within his own family, and although there were areas of his life that remained off-limits, his miserable childhood, for instance, and his brother's suicide, he confided in Kelly freely about almost everything else. And Kelly did the same with Maugham, on several occasions turning to him for advice when his tempestuous affairs with women went wrong. Their friendship was close and it lasted a lifetime. After Maugham's death Gerald Kelly's words were reported in *The Times*: 'Willie was a duck,' he said, 'an absolute duck.'

At Maugham's request Kelly found him a small apartment near his own in Montparnasse, on the fifth floor of 3 rue Victor Considérant, with a view over the cemetery where Maupassant is buried, and near the great bronze Lion de Belfort. Consisting of two rooms and a kitchen, the rent was 700 francs a year, the equivalent of £28; some second-hand furniture and basic utensils were purchased and a *bonne-à-toute-faire* engaged to come in the mornings to make breakfast and do the housework and laundry. Kelly's help had also been enlisted in recommending drawing classes for Harry Philips, 'who has the ingenious idea of cultivating the smaller arts – costume, posters, illustration, & so forth', Maugham had written from London, adding that 'He is a very charming person . . . [and] I think you cannot fail to like him.' The version for general consumption was that the young man was accompanying Maugham as his secretary, but as Harry frankly admitted, 'I cannot say that I was his secretary, although we used that *nom de plume*. I was his companion & wrote a few notes, social & otherwise for him.'

Harry's allowance was only £120 a year and, as Maugham's annual earnings amounted to barely as much, the two men were obliged to lead a frugal existence, economising where they could and feeding themselves as cheaply as possible at the local restaurants and cafés. Despite his poverty, Maugham wished to indulge his young companion, desperately anxious to keep him happy. 'He was exceedingly kind in every way,' said Harry, remembering the many evenings at the theatre, the excursions to Versailles, the afternoons in the Louvre and the Luxembourg. '[Willie's] interest in paintings was immense . . . His favourite artist at that time was Velasquez. He did not care then for the modern painters whose pictures he bought at a later date.' Although not much of a reader himself, Harry was impressed by Maugham's knowledge of literature and even more by his gifts as a linguist, not only in French but in German, Spanish and Italian. Harry had the sense, or perhaps the insensitivity, to respect Maugham's reticence: vaguely aware that his early life had been unhappy, that there was a profound sadness over the death of his brother, he never probed, preferring instead to encourage the light-hearted side of his nature. 'Maugham adored a laugh,' Harry recalled, '& had a generous sense of humour.'

Paris in the early 1900s was still the Paris of the Belle Epoque. There was an elegance and spaciousness about the city particularly pleasing to Maugham after the narrow streets and dinginess of London. Changes had taken place since he had lived there with his parents twenty years before: then there had been no Métro, no motor vehicles among the horse-drawn omnibuses and yellow fiacres, no Eiffel Tower soaring above the skyline; nor had there existed such an efflorescence in the arts: now there were over forty theatres, with Sarah Bernhardt the reigning queen; and in the new *salles d'expositions* there was much excited talk about the Impressionists. Montparnasse had long been popular with artists, although the new wave of painters and sculptors was tending to settle in Montmartre, which was cheaper and still retained something of a village atmosphere. Montparnasse at the turn of the century had the peaceful air of a provincial town, with its own Métro station, its neighbourhood theatres, its dance-halls and *cafés-chantants*, as well as bars and restaurants where a decent two-course meal with half a carafe of wine could be had for less than a couple of francs. In the evening the possibilities were lively and various, dancing at the cheap and cheerful Bal Bullier, watching Houdini at the Alhambra or La Goulue at the Bal Tabarin, or for a mere seventy-five centimes suffering the hard seats and crush of people to listen to classical music at the Concerts Rouges in the rue Taitbout.

Paris may have been cheaper than London but amusements still had to be paid for, and Maugham was inflexible in keeping to a strict working routine, writing all morning till 12.30, when he and 'the Gilded Youth', as he somewhat drily referred to Harry, would go out for a modest lunch, on Sundays treating themselves to an aperitif first at the Café de la Paix. In the afternoons they usually visited the Louvre, or some other gallery or museum, while at night Harry liked to explore a wide variety of entertainment. 'I began this letter three days ago,' Maugham wrote to Gerald Kelly after a brief visit to England, 'but various debauches into which the G[ilded] Y[outh] has led me have prevented me from finishing it. I have been to a Bal Tabarin and various other haunts of vice & am astounded that in the short time I spent in London & he was safe from my watchful eye, he should have learned ten times more about Paris than you or I know.'

Most evenings the two men dined at Le Chat Blanc, a little restaurant in the rue d'Odessa recommended by Gerald Kelly. Here they became part of a group of painters, writers and sculptors, a few French but mostly English and American, who nightly dined together at a communal table upstairs, where over an inexpensive couple of courses and plenty of wine the rival merits of the leading artists of the day were noisily debated. These gatherings were the nearest that Maugham, in later life always careful to conform to the outward appearance of respectability, came to the bohemian way of life. Conversation often grew hotly argumentative, carried on in a fug of cigar smoke in a mixture of English and French; when the volume grew too loud and the atmosphere too boisterous Maugham, who never enjoyed rowdy behaviour, would often slip out to walk the dark streets on his own. Among the regulars were Gerald Kelly, who would sometimes bring in his patron Rodin, bearded and pungent; Clive Bell, a young English art student; Ivor Back, a trainee surgeon and friend of Kelly's; Penrhyn Stanlaws, the American 'pretty women' painter; the Canadian Impressionist James Wilson Morrice, regarded with awe for his acquaintance with Bonnard, Matisse, Vuillard and Lautrec; and the formidable Irish painter Roderic O'Conor, tall, swarthy, misanthropic. 'I suspect he was a tragic figure,' wrote Clive Bell, one of the few who succeeded in befriending the surly Irishman, 'though he kept his tragedy to himself.'

It was O'Conor who interested Maugham the most, mainly because of his friendship with Gauguin. In 1903 Maugham had been taken by Kelly to the famous Gauguin exhibition at the Galérie Vollard and had become fascinated with both the man and his work. Learning that O'Conor had spent some months with Gauguin in Brittany, Maugham was eager to ask him about it, 'but unfortunately he took an immediate dislike to me which he did not hesitate to show. My very presence at the dinner table irritated him and I only had to make a remark for him to attack it.' One evening the two men had a furious row about the merits of the poet Hérédia, during which the Irishman remained 'coldly and bitingly virulent'. Refusing to be cowed, however, and genuinely admiring the man's work, Maugham a few days later called on O'Conor in his studio and asked to buy a couple of small still-lifes. O'Conor was taken aback. 'After a moment's hesitation, with a sullen look on his face, he mentioned a price, a very modest one, and I took the money out of my pocket and went away with the pictures in my hands.' This gesture did little to improve relations, however, and O'Conor was overheard comparing Maugham to 'a bed bug, on which a sensitive man refuses to stamp because of the smell and the squashiness'.

This disobliging remark was relayed by another member of the group, a big, bull-like man with a savage, sensual face, flamboyantly dressed in a bejewelled red waistcoat and large silk cravat with an enormous ring on one pudgy white hand. Aleister Crowley had been at Cambridge with Kelly, and in 1903 had married Kelly's sister Rose – who coincidentally counted as her best friend Charles Maugham's wife Beldy. Claiming to be a master of the occult and recently created 'Khan of the East', Crowley was a compulsive show-off, declaiming dramatically and making fantastic boasts of his mental and physical prowess, and most sensationally of his supernatural powers: he himself, it appeared, had led many past lives, and was presently reincarnated as none other than the Great Beast of the Apocalypse; he liked to be known as Brother Perdurabo, under which guise he dabbled in Satanism and had been much involved in the occult goings-on of the Hermetic Order of the Golden Dawn. He had experimented copiously with drugs and was indefatigable in exploring his complex sexuality, avidly pursuing every kind of debauch with both men and women, preferably of a sadistic and sanguinary nature. As might be expected, this preposterous person fascinated Maugham. 'I took an immediate dislike to him,' he wrote, 'but he interested and amused me.' Certainly Maugham had no wish to befriend Brother Perdurabo, but the mesmerising performance and undeniably sinister aura caught at his imagination, shortly to emerge re-formed in the character of the infamous Oliver Haddo in *The Magician*.

One of the few who saw good qualities in Crowley was an occasional diner in the rue d'Odessa, ex-editor of the magazine *Woman* and known to the journal's readers under the by-lines 'Barbara' and 'Cécile'. Having had a modest success with a first novel, Enoch Arnold Bennett had resigned from the magazine, had published two more novels, *The Grand Babylon Hotel* and *Anna of the Five Towns*, and in 1902 had moved to Paris, where he lived with his fox terrier Fly in a modest apartment in Montmartre. Like Maugham, Bennett had been introduced by Gerald Kelly to Le Chat Blanc, and had formed the habit of dining there once a week. Both Maugham and Gerald Kelly tended to patronise Bennett, or 'Enoch Arnold', as they referred to him between themselves. With his receding chin, snub nose, bristly moustache and rabbity teeth, they thought he looked vulgar, 'like a managing clerk in a city office', in Maugham's snobbish phrase; behind his back they mocked his clothes and Midlands accent, found his manners uncouth and dismissed the successful *Grand Babylon Hotel* as populist tosh. Bennett's French was clumsy, whereas Maugham spoke like a native, but at their very first meeting it was Bennett who, unforgivably, put Maugham in the wrong. As Kelly related it, at the end of dinner,

> Willie – with his impeccable French accent – said to the waitress: 'Vous me donnerez un anneau,' meaning that he wanted a napkin ring . . . 'You know, Maugham,' observed Bennett heavily, 'the French don't call it an "anno", they call it a "rong".' (He meant a 'rond'.) Willie became quite grey with rage; to have made this absurd mistake and thus laid himself open to correction by a quite unspeakable individual whose knowledge of French was rudimentary!

A further cause for division was the embarrassing fact that Bennett, like Maugham, suffered from a bad stammer, and Maugham was well aware that the two of them at the same table struggling to get the words out ran a high risk of looking grotesque. As he admitted, 'I am dreadfully afraid of being ridiculous.'

Fortunately the amiable Bennett either failed to notice or refused to be offended by Maugham's *de haut en bas* manner, enjoying his company and taking pleasure in the younger man's style. Describing an afternoon visit of Maugham's to his flat in the rue de Calais, Bennett wrote in his journal,

> [Maugham] has a very calm almost lethargic demeanour. He took two cups of tea with pleasure and absolutely refused a third; one knew instantly from his tone that nothing would induce him to take a third. He ate biscuits and gaufrettes very quickly, almost greedily, one after the other without a pause, and then suddenly stopped. He smoked two cigarettes furiously, in less time than I smoked one . . . . I liked him.

Maugham by contrast wrote of Bennett, 'I didn't very much like him . . . He was cocksure and bumptious . . . [although] I always enjoyed spending an evening with him.' Sometimes after dinner Maugham and Kelly would accompany Bennett home, where he would play Beethoven to them on an upright piano. On one of these occasions Bennett startled Maugham by making him an unexpected proposal: would Maugham like to share in his mistress? She spent two nights a week with him, two nights with another gentleman, liked to take Sundays off, but was on the look-out for someone who would take the two nights she still had available. 'I've told her about you,' said Bennett. 'She likes writers [and] I'd like to see her nicely fixed up.' The offer was declined.

Despite the unpromising start to the friendship, Maugham eventually became genuinely fond of Bennett, 'a very lovable man', as he called him, and he greatly admired Bennett's later masterpiece, *The Old Wives' Tale*, which he thought in its author's lifetime never received the critical accolade it deserved. Violet Hunt, also in Paris at that time, was one of Maugham's circle whom he introduced to Enoch Arnold, and when Maugham was otherwise engaged she promoted Bennett to position of favourite escort. As before in London, Violet and Maugham met regularly, spending much of their time in sharp-tongued gossip about fellow members of the British colony. As well as Gerald Kelly's circle of artists this included a little contingent of women writers, with whom Maugham became a great favourite – women of earnest intention if modest talent, such as Netta Syrett, author of *Nobody's Fault* and *Roseanne*, and Ella d'Arcy, whose short stories had appeared in *The Yellow Book*. They entertained Maugham to tea, were delighted when he escorted them to the theatre and were grateful when on one of his absences from Paris he lent them his apartment.

It was only to Violet, however, that he let down his guard and talked about his private life and emotions. At this period he was suffering a good deal of wretchedness over Harry Philips, and Violet, whose own love affairs were invariably passionate and unhappy, provided a sympathetic ear. 'I never saw Maugham moved except one . . . time in Paris,' she noted in her diary, almost certainly a reference to Maugham's unburdening himself about Harry's behaviour. Something had happened between the two men, most probably an infidelity on Harry's part, which had upset Maugham a good deal and which he was later to use in *Of Human Bondage*. Looking back Harry regretted his behaviour. 'I was somewhat ashamed,' he said, 'as I realized that I had hurt his feelings more than I thought.' In May 1905 Harry decided to return to England for a while, leaving his lover despondent. In a letter to Kelly, temporarily absent from Paris, Maugham complained of his low spirits. 'I miss you sadly,' he told Gerald, '[and] I know not how I shall do when the Gilded Youth has abandoned me . . . I am sick to death of my work & seized by panic that all my imagination has left me: sometimes I fear that I shall never be able to do any good again. I feel like a well run dry.'

The work with which he was having such difficulty was a novel, *The Bishop's Apron*, a reworking of *Loaves and Fishes*, one of the three plays, as yet unproduced, written after *A Man of Honour*. The *Bishop's Apron* is a much improved version, more complex and substantial, of what in dramatic form is a rather formulaic comedy about a snobbish clergyman with some very worldly ambitions. Theodore Spratte, Vicar of St Gregory's in South Kensington, is handsome, pompous and vain (Maugham rarely has a good word to say for the Anglican clergy). A widower, he lives with his sister and two grown-up children, devoting his considerable energies to bettering the standing of himself and his family: he is immensely proud that his elder brother is Lord Spratte, their father, although of humble origins, having been ennobled as lord chancellor. If all goes as planned, his son and daughter will marry rank and money, and he himself be offered the see of Barchester, thus the reference to the episcopal vestment of the title. At first it looks as if none of his ambitions will be realised: his daughter, Winnie, falls in love with a lower-class young man; his timid son fails to propose to his rich girlfriend; and the bishopric is offered elsewhere. With typical contrariness, however, Maugham reverses expectation, and by the last chapter the Rev. Theodore Spratte has everything he wanted and more: a bigger and better bishopric than Barchester, Winnie wed to a wealthy peer and he himself betrothed to the well-endowed beauty his son feebly failed to claim for himself. 'You are a downy old bird, Theodore,' his brother tells him, laughing.

If *The Bishop's Apron* reads a little like a novel-by-numbers, it is nonetheless an extremely efficient piece of work. The world of the Rev. Theodore Spratte is a milieu Maugham knew well from mixing with fashionable clergy, such as the Wilberforces, in London society. There are neat twists in the plot, some highly comic passages of dialogue, particularly those between the Vicar angling for his see and the canny old Prime Minister, Lord Stonehenge, determined not to give it; and the characters are very much more than the sum of their parts. Theodore, for instance, although ridiculously conceited, undeniably has charm: his high spirits and enjoyment of life are very winning, as are his moments of deflating self-knowledge, most enjoyably exposed during a scene (taken almost verbatim from an early short story, 'Cupid and the Vicar of Swale') in which he proposes to a well-to-do widow, who knows exactly what he is up to and is determined not to let him get away with it.

With both the novel and the play Maugham was consciously aiming to appeal to the upper bourgeoisie. The pretentiousness of Theodore Spratte, so thrilled by his family's recent ascent to the peerage, raises a comfortable laugh; and so, at the time, would the scene of Winnie's common young man bringing his family to tea at the vicarage. This has been arranged by Theodore with the sole purpose of curing his daughter of any desire to marry into the lower orders, a scheme that is wholly successful: Winnie is appalled by the Railings from Peckham, by their dropped aitches, by their lack of education and by garrulous Mrs Railing's fondness for gin, and afterwards has little compunction in breaking off her engagement to Bernard. (In the play Winnie's epiphany comes when she discovers that Bernard wears detachable shirt-cuffs.) As with Basil Kent's miserable marriage to his barmaid in *A Man of Honour*, much emphasis is placed on the potential for unhappiness in a relationship in which class and education are unequal.

With the novel completed, Maugham was anxious to have it published as soon as possible, but not by Heinemann, condemned as culpably negligent in having failed to promote *The Merry-Go-Round*. A large share of the blame was laid also at the door of Maurice Colles, whose genial indolence had come to irritate Maugham intensely. Determined to put his affairs in the hands of someone more focused and businesslike, he talked the matter over with Arnold Bennett, another disaffected Colles client, who was now with J. B. Pinker, with whom he was much pleased. Urging Maugham to follow his example, Bennett offered to effect the introduction. 'I think I have got you a new client in the person of W. Somerset Maugham,' he wrote to Pinker. 'He seems to me a man who will make his way.'

James Brand Pinker, because of his cockney accent known affectionately as 'Jy Bee', had set up his agency in 1896, having worked for a number of years on newspapers and magazines, an experience that had gained him useful contacts and an intimate knowledge of the British literary world. From his office in Arundel Street off the Strand, Pinker, clean-shaven and rosy-cheeked, dealt with the rights and contracts of a growing number of distinguished writers, including Wells, Galsworthy, Conrad, Gissing, Joyce, Jack London and Ford Madox Ford. With A. P. Watt and Curtis Brown he was regarded as one of the leading players in the field, respected by authors and publishers alike for his considerable business acumen. Even William Heinemann, who had been such a vigorous opponent of the literary agent, enjoyed cordial relations with him, and indeed it was at Heinemann's suggestion that Henry James was added to Pinker's list. He had his detractors, among them D. H. Lawrence and Oscar Wilde, for whom he had failed to find an American publisher for *The Ballad of Reading Gaol*, but most of his clients were devoted to him.

Maugham's association with Pinker was to make an important difference to his professional career, and he quickly came to appreciate his new agent's dedication and expertise. Immediately, however, he was faced with the task of disengaging himself from his old agent, Maurice Colles, who was shocked and hurt by Maugham's proposed defection and by his accusations over the handling of *The Merry-Go-Round*. But Maugham was adamant. 'I think we must agree to differ,' he told Colles firmly. 'I do not wish to enter into recriminations; but I cannot help thinking that what is obvious to me now your experience might have suggested to you then, namely, that when a publisher does not like a book & has made up his mind that it will not sell, one might just as well throw it in the Thames as let him publish it.' With the old connection severed, Maugham then wrote to his new agent: knowing exactly what he wanted, he took trouble to set out his expectations, making clear that he intended to consign all his writing to Pinker with the exception of the plays, which would be handled by the theatrical agent Reginald Golding Bright. As to *The Bishop's Apron*, he suggested it should be offered to Chapman & Hall, 'because they have no one of any particular importance & it would be worth while for them to boom me. I am sick of playing third fiddle to Hall Caine.'* Moreover, Chapman & Hall had already expressed an interest in publishing Maugham, '& I imagine they will give an advance of £150 & a good royalty'. But here Maugham's imagination had run away with him: Arthur Waugh, the firm's director, told Pinker that there was no question of increasing his offer of exactly half that sum, £75, and with that Maugham was obliged to be content. Dedicated to Harry Philips, *The Bishop's Apron: A Study in the Origins of a Great Family* was published in a small edition in February 1906, without Maugham's Evil Eye insignia and with little advertisement, its critical reception, good-humoured if somewhat sparse, along much the same lines as that accorded to *The Merry-Go-Round*.

Much of the correspondence with Colles and Pinker had been written by Maugham from Capri, where, having patched up his relationship with Harry, he had gone with him in July 1905 for an extended holiday. The two men had taken a little house, the Villa Valentino, and Maugham was revelling in the Mediterranean warmth and indolence and in the return

---

* Hall Caine (1853–1931) was a popular romantic novelist.

of Harry's companionship. 'We have been here nearly a week,' Maugham wrote contentedly to Gerald Kelly in early July,

> [with] nothing whatever to do from morning till night . . . The Gilded Youth, somewhat overcome by the heat at present, cannot make it out: he murmurs plaintively that it is such a rush to do nothing . . . We have both suffered agonies by lying out, naked, in the sun too long on our first day & our backs & legs were so scorched that we could hardly bear ourselves. G. Y.'s snowy skin suffered terribly . . . The bathing is of course delightful; the water so warm that one can play about in it the whole morning.

Under these idyllic conditions, Maugham found it difficult to get down to work. 'I have not an idea in my head,' he told Kelly,

> & except that I'm rather afraid I shall never have any more in my life, I'm much pleased with myself. Only, being of a damned dissatisfied temper, it is only with difficulty that I prevent myself from making plans for the future. I find it one of the hardest things in the world to enjoy the present moment: my impulse is always to neglect it for the consideration of the wonderful things I shall do & see & feel three months hence.

One whom Maugham had looked forward to seeing again was his old friend from Heidelberg, John Ellingham Brooks, but he was disappointed to find Brooks no longer the stimulating companion he once had been. The handsome, vibrant character, so full of ideas and enthusiasm, had developed into something of a bore, his innovative theories now seeming stale and old-fashioned; his hair was thinning, he had put on weight and his blue eyes had a slightly watery look. Having squandered his small fortune, Brooks had been rescued from penury by a wealthy American painter, Romaine Goddard, who, herself homosexual, had taken pity on him and agreed to a marriage of convenience, imagining that Brooks might provide her with pleasant companionship when she was on the island, while leaving her free to follow her own distinctively bohemian life in London and elsewhere. The marriage proved a disaster, however, with Brooks shocking his wife by his grasping attitude towards money, his dreadful manners and his insistence on a *ménage à trois* with a sulky peasant boyfriend forever in the background. Having married in June 1903, they formally separated a year later, Romaine buying her husband off with an income of £300 a year, a sum which was more than adequate to provide Brooks with a comfortable life lotus-eating on Capri. As his friend E. F. Benson phrased it, 'In the process of making a complete failure of his life as far as achievement of any sort went, he made himself for many years very happy.'

While Maugham was writing of his summer to Gerald Kelly in Paris, Kelly was describing a passionate love affair he had embarked upon with a young dancer; he was proposing to move her in with him but wanted to know what Maugham thought of the scheme. Not much, was the answer; his reasons are given in a letter that clearly refers to a harrowing experience of Maugham's own, and goes some considerable way to explaining his horror of the kind of relationship he depicts in both *The Man of Honour* and *The Bishop's Apron*, a relationship between two people disastrously unequal in intellect and social station. 'I'm sure a lot of people will think you a devilish lucky fellow,' Maugham wrote to Kelly,

> [but] you must not mind if I congratulate myself rather than you . . . I cannot help rubbing my hands & gloating because I do not stand in your shoes . . . I remember all I've suffered from the frightful exacting-ness of women & I am willing to offer whole stacks of candles to the saints so that they may leave me my freedom. You wait, my boy, till you are asked when you'll be back each time you go out, & where you've been the moment you come in, till you have to put up with sulks if you don't agree to the most unreasonable things, & quarrels for the absur-dest trifles . . . Ouf! I sweat when I think of it. Women can never leave a man his freedom, they use every imaginable device to load him with chains, & they don't rest till they've bound him hand & foot so that he can't stir . . . Before you set up housekeeping with your dancer arrange in your own mind quite clearly how you're going to separate. For it's a devil of a job & if you've got any decency in you, you'll be made to feel an absolutely heartless, mean beast . . . You'll find every penny is important. Taking a woman about with one is not cheap, because one has to go in cabs instead of buses, & they have all sorts of little whims which have to be satisfied. And you'll want more money, because you'll go a great deal more to theatres & out in the evenings. You'll find that when one lives with a person of no particular education . . . time hangs rather heavily on one's hands; one racks one's brains for conversation & at last is driven to going somewhere. So whatever you do, don't hamper yourself by being short of money . . . Having said all this I give you my blessing & wish you well . . . For myself I only hope that I shall never again be imprisoned by any passion.

The idyll on Capri failed to last the summer. At the beginning of August Harry decided he had had enough and left to return to his family in Staffordshire. 'It was there I decided I was really getting nowhere &

should he tire of me I would be pretty useless,' Harry recalled. 'His cynicism distressed me & . . . I found it difficult to live with someone who believed that no one did anything without a motive.' To gregarious Harry, intent on having fun, Maugham's periods of moodiness and introversion were incomprehensible, their growing lack of communication something of which Maugham himself was miserably aware; as he wrote in his notebook,

> one places all one's love, all one's faculty of expansion on one person, making, as it were, a final effort to join one's soul to his . . . But little by little one finds that it is all impossible, and however ardently one loves him, however intimately one is connected with him, he is always a stranger . . . Then one retires into oneself and in one's silence builds a world of one's own which one keeps from the eyes of every living soul, even from the person one loves best, knowing he would not understand it.

The two men parted on good terms, however. Harry shortly afterwards joined the army for a spell, before marrying a rich woman whose substantial fortune enabled him to live in idleness for the rest of his days.

With Harry gone, Maugham expected to be heartbroken; but in fact he soon recovered. Having received the first payment from Chapman & Hall for his novel it was gratifying to realise that the sum was all his with which to do as he pleased. 'By the time I received the money the passion that I had thought would last for ever was extinct and I had no longer the slightest wish to spend it in the way I had intended.' Instead he spent it on travel, first to Tuscany with his dependable old friend Walter Payne, then skiing in Switzerland, and in January the following year to Egypt for a couple of months. Passing through Paris only to tidy up his affairs, Maugham returned to London in the spring of 1906, extremely hard up but more determined than ever to make the breakthrough into fame and prosperity. While abroad he had written some travel articles as well as a couple of short stories, and Pinker, like Colles before him, was being urged to chase payments. 'Has the *Lady's Realm* or whatever it was stumped up?' Maugham was anxiously enquiring in July. 'This is the season when my tailor & hatter send in bills.' Fortunately Maugham's living expenses were minimal. Payne, who continued to handle his friend's financial affairs, had taken rooms in Pall Mall, at number 56, and as before Maugham was able to make use of these, needing to rent only a bedroom next door. Here he set himself to work on a new novel, inspired by the grotesque figure of Aleister

Crowley. *The Magician* was finished by the end of the year, but the horrific nature of its content shocked the publishers to whom it was shown and Pinker had failed to sell it.

Beginning to grow slightly desperate, Maugham now resorted to the quick fix of recycling old material. He had already excavated his rejected play *The Explorer*, digging out one of its subplots for use as the short story 'Flirtation', and now, like a thrifty housewife determined not to let anything go to waste, he sat down to rewrite the entire play as a novel. It was a tedious exercise, and Maugham was ashamed of the finished product, which 'irked my conscience like the recollection of a discreditable action'. Suggested by the adventures of the great African explorer H. M. Stanley, the man who 'found' Livingstone, the plot revolves round Alec Mackenzie, one of the strong, silent men who built the Empire, and Mackenzie's noble refusal to clear his own reputation by breaking his word to a scoundrel. In love with a pure young woman, Lucy Allerton, Mackenzie promises to take with him on a dangerous expedition to East Africa her worthless brother George, in the hope of reforming his character. George behaves despicably, but Alec offers him the chance of salvation through leading a dangerous attack against a gang of dastardly slave-raiders. George is killed, and Alec returning to England is faced with a growing rumour that he sent George to his death to save his own skin, a rumour he cannot refute as he promised George never to reveal the truth about his shameful behaviour. By the final chapter Lucy's love and her belief in Alec triumphs, and although the story ends with Alec again departing for the white man's grave the implication is that he will return. '"Have no fear; I will come back. My journey was only dangerous because I wanted to die. I want to live now, and I shall live." "Oh, Alec, Alec, I'm so glad you love me."'

*The Explorer*, dedicated 'To My dear Mrs W. G. Steevens', reads like the mechanical exercise which indeed Maugham had found it to be. 'I *do not like* it,' he told Violet Hunt. 'The characters are all too virtuous for me & the nobility of their sentiments bores me to extinction'; while to Gerald Kelly, in whose copy were inscribed the words, 'Gerald Kelly from W. S. Maugham, his worst book', he wrote, 'The people were too heroic for me to live with . . . I vomited daily at the exalted sentiments that issued from their lips, & my hair stood up on end at the delicacy of their sense of honour.'

By the end of the summer of 1907 Maugham was exhausted and had seen little reward for his unrelenting industry. *The Explorer* had been accepted by Heinemann but would not appear till the following year; *The Magician* had still not found a publisher; and none of the plays which had been circulating round the London managements had found any takers, despite the tenacity of Maugham's play agent, Golding Bright. But there was one glimmer of light. While in Paris Maugham had written a comedy, *Lady Frederick*, which he had designed specifically to provide a succulent part for a leading actress. At first the play met with no greater enthusiasm than its predecessors, but then suddenly Maugham's luck seemed to change: George Tyler, an American producer in Paris on the look-out for material, read it, liked it and offered to buy an option on it for $1,000. Tyler invited Maugham to his hotel to discuss the proposition, telling him that the piece packed a hell of a punch, though it needed gingering up with a few more epigrams (within a couple of hours Maugham added twenty-four). He gave his visitor a couple of cocktails, the first of his life, '[and] Maugham told me afterwards', said Tyler, 'that, when he left me that afternoon with his check for a thousand in his pocket, he was stepping on his left ear with his right hind foot . . . He struck me as a nice young fellow with a possible future.' Convinced he had a hot property, Tyler returned with the script to London, only to find that no actress, in the words of one to whom he showed it, would touch the part with a ten-foot pole. The problem was that the eponymous heroine, Lady Frederick, a fascinating adventuress not quite in her first youth, is required in the pivotal scene to appear literally and shockingly bare-faced: brightly lit, wearing no make-up and without the false hair which most fashionable women then used in considerable quantities. Under these conditions none of the big stars who might otherwise have leaped at the role would look at it: Ellis Jeffreys, elegant and sophisticated comedienne, was appalled by the very idea; Mrs Pat Campbell declared she had never been so insulted in her life; the American star Violet Allen said she wouldn't consider it for a moment. Charles Frohman was approached but saw little merit in the play, and so reluctantly Tyler was forced to abandon the project, 'feeling pretty melancholy on Maugham's account and pretty sore on my own'.

Dejected but resolute, Maugham immediately started on a new work, *Mrs Dot*, also with a strong female lead, yet carefully designed to cause offence to nobody; this, however, was turned down on the grounds that it was too bland. 'I began to think that I should never be able to write a piece that a leading lady liked,' Maugham wrote despairingly, 'and so tried my hand at a man's play . . . *Jack Straw*.' When this, too, failed to find favour Maugham came near to giving up: there seemed to be nothing for it but to return to his abandoned medical career, go back to St Thomas's for a year's revision and then try to find a post as a ship's surgeon, which would at least give him the opportunity to travel.

It was at this point that interest was suddenly revived in *Lady Frederick*. Otho Stuart, manager of the Royal Court Theatre in Sloane Square, had had a play fail unexpectedly and was now faced with an empty six weeks before his next presentation. Maugham's comedy was not at all his kind of thing but no doubt it would adequately fill the short time available. Maugham was on his travels when he heard the news. From Sicily he wrote excitedly to Golding Bright, 'Your letter filled me with exultation, & now the likelihood of an early production makes me realise that the world is not hollow & foolish.' A courageous actress had been found, Ethel Irving, to play the lead, and rehearsals, which Maugham was desperate to attend, were due to start within a few days.

It was a Sunday when Bright's letter reached Maugham in Girgenti and he learned of the sudden change in his fortunes. Now he urgently needed to be in London the following Thursday. Almost penniless, he found he had enough money only for the train to Palermo and the evening packet to Naples. At Naples he disembarked on Monday morning.

I went to Cook's and found that a boat was going to Marseilles that afternoon and took a ticket, but when I offered a cheque in payment the agent firmly refused to accept anything but cash . . . I expostulated, I raged, I stormed; and at last (I am not a dramatist for nothing) flung out of the office . . . I went to the office of the steamship company and asked for a first class ticket to Marseilles . . . and without a word wrote a cheque for the amount due. The clerk, young and timid, looked a trifle doubtful, but my assurance was such that I think he had not the nerve to refuse; in a minute I was out of the office with my ticket to Marseilles in my pocket. But I had to get to London . . . The shipping agents were also bankers, the banking part of the establishment being in another part of the building; I went in and walked boldly up to the desk. I took out my cheque book and the ticket I had just received.

'I'm going to Marseilles on one of your boats this afternoon. You might cash me a cheque for a fiver, will you?' I smiled ingratiatingly . . .

I did not linger in the bank long after I had the five sovereigns in my pocket . . . I was in great spirits, for now I had enough money to take me to Paris, and I felt confident that I could get on from there without delay . . . The sea was calm and the sky blue. I sat on deck reading . . .

When I got to London I still had a shilling for my cab. On Thursday morning at eleven o'clock I strolled into the Court Theatre. I felt like

Phileas Fogg after his journey round the world in eighty days entering the Reform Club as the clock struck eight.

*Lady Frederick*, rejected by seventeen managements, was for Maugham the first step on the path to enormous celebrity and wealth. The play, written on the back of a discarded typescript because, said the author, '[I was] very short of money . . . [and] could not afford to waste pages of good clean paper,' opened on 26 October 1907. So great was its success that Maugham became famous almost literally overnight, 'England's Dramatist', as he was dubbed by the press. *Lady Frederick* ran for more than a year, and by the following year four of Maugham's plays were running concurrently in the West End, a record which for a living playwright was to remain unbroken for a generation.

# 5

## England's Dramatist

'The years between the beginning of the century and the beginning of the [1914] war', wrote the distinguished theatre critic James Agate, 'mark a period of the greatest dramatic energy in this country since the Elizabethans.' It was in 1907, exactly in the middle of this productive period, that with *Lady Frederick* Maugham enjoyed his first great triumph and laid the foundations of his reputation as one of the most sought-after playwrights of the age. In an era dominated by Shaw, with Galsworthy and Granville Barker among the best known of the serious dramatists, it was Somerset Maugham and James Barrie who for a number of years and in terms of fashionable reputation were pre-eminent in the world of West End comedy, although Barrie, despite the annual revivals of *Peter Pan*, never quite approached Maugham's popularity or earning power. This period saw the final phase of the type of society drama, witty and urbane, at which Maugham excelled: his acute intelligence enabled him to gauge what his audiences wanted; his expert craftsmanship delivered it. The staging of *Lady Frederick* at the Royal Court Theatre owed a great deal to luck, but its subsequent success was largely due to the care with which its author had weighed and measured his ingredients. Before beginning on *Lady Frederick*, Maugham explained, 'I reflected upon the qualities which the managers demanded in a play: evidently a comedy, for the public wished to laugh; with as much drama as it would carry, for the public liked a thrill; with a little sentiment, for the public liked to feel good; and a happy ending.' Equally important, what kind of part would be most tempting to a leading lady? A beautiful adventuress with a title and a heart of gold was the obvious answer. 'Having made up my mind upon this the rest was easy.'

A deft if ephemeral society comedy, *Lady Frederick* is light, sophisticated and absolutely true to its well-established genre. Set in 1890, the action takes place in the Hôtel de Paris in Monte Carlo, where we find Lady Frederick Berolles, a charming and attractive widow in her late thirties, teetering on the verge of bankruptcy. Pleasure-loving and extravagant, she is also, despite appearances and some scandalous rumours to the contrary, a woman with a strong sense of honour. The play opens with the entrance of Lady Mereston, distraught because her son is passionately in love with Lady Frederick and determined to marry her, despite the fact that she is almost old enough to be his mother. Marriage to Charlie Mereston, a marquess with £50,000 a year, would solve all Lady Frederick's problems and the young man is very pressing; but desperate though her situation is Lady Frederick will not stoop to such a venal solution, bravely resolving to quench her youthful suitor's passion by appearing to him in her natural state. Act Three, the scene that had frightened off so many actresses, opens in Lady Frederick's dressing-room, the blinds pulled up to let in strong sunlight; the stage instructions read, '[Lady Frederick] wears a kimono, her hair is all dishevelled, hanging about her head in a tangled mop. She is not made up and looks haggard and yellow and lined. When Mereston sees her he gives a slight start of surprise.' In full view of the audience the transformation is then unflinchingly effected, the false hair, the grease paint, rouge, pencil and powder, each step in the process mercilessly explained to an appalled Charlie Mereston. 'Now for the delicate soft bloom of youth,' says Lady Frederick gaily, picking up her pot of rouge. 'The great difficulty, you know, is to make both your cheeks the same colour.'

The ruse is successful: Mereston is persuaded to give up his pursuit and all ends happily, with the heroine agreeing to marry Paradine Fouldes, a wealthy old admirer, who as he takes her in his arms says sentimentally, 'D'you suppose I don't know that behind that very artificial complexion there's a dear little woman called Betsy who's genuine to the bottom of her soul?'

Always fascinated by the feminine, Maugham was clearly intrigued by the subject of women and cosmetics, and by the moral implications involved: in the Edwardian era no respectable young lady would dream of using make-up and even in the most sophisticated circles there was still an aura of questionable respectability about older women who were known to paint. The theme had first been given an outing by Maugham in 'Lady Habart', a short story published in *Punch* in 1900. Where Lady Frederick is at heart virtuous and unselfish, Lady Habart, equally seductive, is conniving and corrupt, reaching for her powder-puff whenever she has to bring off some particularly devious piece of plotting. The subject is given even greater emphasis in *The Merry-Go-Round*, in which Mrs Castillyon during her adulterous affair with Reggie always appears heavily made up, anxiously increasing the amounts of powder and rouge as the relationship deteriorates, a fact remarked upon by her straitlaced friend Miss Ley.

> 'I surmised you were in some trouble,' murmured Miss Ley, 'for I think you've rather overdone the – slap. Isn't that the technical expression?'
> Mrs Castillyon put both hands to her cheeks . . . Instinctively she took a puff from her pocket, and quickly powdered her face; then she turned to Miss Ley.
> 'Did you never make up?' she asked.
> 'Never. I was always afraid of making myself absurd.'

With *Lady Frederick* Maugham had carefully calculated the impact the final act would make, and when the audience watched the leading lady, Ethel Irving, artificially construct her character's girlish complexion they were as shocked and thrilled as audiences sixty years later when first confronted with full-frontal nudity on the stage in *Hair*.

The elation and enthusiasm shown by the audience on the first night were echoed in most of the reviews. 'Exhilarating entertainment,' said *The Times*, while Reginald Turner in the *Academy* extolled 'a delicious evening, full of delight from start to finish . . . [the author] was completely, splendidly successful'. Such a reception naturally came as an immense relief to Maugham: when he had arrived at the theatre that evening he had not known, he said, whether he should leave it 'as an accomplished dramatist or an embryo bank clerk'. During the performance he sat in white tie and tails pale and silent at the back of a box, as always excruciatingly self-conscious at hearing his lines spoken in public; as he explained to Gerald Kelly, 'it is not a moment at which I commonly feel myself fit for company'. By the end of the first act, however, it was clear that he had a hit on his hands, and at the supper-party he gave at the Bath Club afterwards he was seen to be in high spirits, warmly thanking the actors, especially Ethel Irving, unanimously praised by the critics, and also Charles Lowne, who played Paradine Fouldes. 'You succeeded in making Paradine very fresh & natural,' Maugham told him. '[And] a great deal of the success of the play was due to you.' Throughout his life Maugham was to remember the first night of *Lady Frederick* as the most exciting moment of his theatrical career.

*Lady Frederick* quickly became the talk of the town, transferring from the Royal Court to the Garrick Theatre, then to the Criterion, the New and finally the Haymarket, where it completed an impressive run of 422 performances. The American impresario Charles Frohman, who had originally turned the play down, now 'ate crow', and bought the US rights for twice what he would originally have had to pay, putting it on in New York to great acclaim the following year with Ethel Barrymore in the lead.

Suddenly Maugham as a dramatist was much in demand, and his play agent Golding Bright was inundated with requests from eager managers for scripts which previously they had had no hesitation in declining. Fortunately Bright was well placed to make the most of the situation: member of a theatrical family, brother of the well-known agent Addison Bright, he was married to the playwright George Egerton (real name Mary Chavelita Dunne), and from an early age had been steeped in the business. After his brother's death in 1906, Golding Bright had taken over a number of his clients, including Barrie and for a time Shaw. Over the last couple of years this keen, hard-working young man had proved himself indefatigable in promoting Maugham's work, refusing to be discouraged by the many rejections, and now was delighted that his faith in his client was being rewarded. In quick succession he sold three plays that had been written earlier and turned down, *Mrs Dot*, *The Explorer* and *Jack Straw*, and was kept busy fielding requests for Maugham to undertake commissions. Exhilarated by this sudden turn in his fortunes, Maugham believed that finally he had arrived exactly where he wished to be, a playwright, not a novelist. This moment of epiphany came to him one evening while walking past the Comedy Theatre in Panton Street:

> I happened to look up and saw the clouds lit by the setting sun. I paused to look at the lovely sight and I thought to myself: Thank God, I can look at a sunset now without having to think how to describe it. I meant then never to write another book, but to devote myself for the rest of my life to the drama.

To this end he wrote to his literary agent J. B. Pinker to sever the association between them, explaining that he now had so many requests for plays he would no longer have time to write stories, a letter which Pinker sensibly chose to ignore.

Willing to try his hand at almost anything that would pay, Maugham accepted an offer from the musical-comedy king George Edwardes. Edwardes, owner of Daly's Theatre and the Gaiety, founder of the famous Gaiety Girls, had had a huge hit the previous year with Lehar's operetta *The Merry Widow*, a success he understandably wished to repeat, having his eye on a frivolous piece of frou-frou, *Ein Walzertraum*, by Lehar's chief rival, Oscar Straus. In January 1908 Maugham duly went over to Vienna to take a look, reporting to Gerald Kelly that although the music was pretty the book was 'inconceivably silly': no doubt he would be able to make something of it, however, if allowed a free hand. But Edwardes knew precisely what he wanted and Maugham's version came nowhere near. '*The Waltz Dream* & my dealings with Edwardes are done with,' Kelly was told a few weeks later. 'He did not like what I did, complaining that I had left out what he wanted put in, & so forth; & I did not at all want my name to be attached to the stuff he proposed, so I have got him to give me a round sum down, take my name off, & do what he damned well likes with my book.'

By the time Edwardes's *Waltz Dream* began its run ('not much of a success . . . I am delighted to see') Maugham's next play, *Jack Straw*, was already in rehearsal, opening at the Vaudeville in the Strand on 26 March; this was quickly followed by *Mrs Dot* at the Comedy on 27 April; and lastly, on 13 June, *The Explorer* at the Lyric. Maugham was now in the astonishing position of having four plays in the West End, with only *The Explorer* failing to make a respectable run, with a mere forty-eight performances against *Lady Frederick*'s 422, *Jack Straw*'s 321 and 272 for *Mrs Dot*. 'My success was spectacular and unexpected,' Maugham recalled with satisfaction. His name and the titles of his plays, 'the Maugham quartet', were everywhere: Walter Payne leafing through the sporting pages even came across two racehorses called Lady Frederick and Mrs Dot. 'I was much photographed and much interviewed. Distinguished people sought my acquaintance' and 'I thoroughly enjoyed myself.'

Predictably Maugham, as the celebrity of the moment, was much pursued by fashionable hostesses. Among these was Julia Frankau, who wrote novels under the name Frank Danby. Mrs Frankau, a lively widow of charm and intelligence, was a serious play-goer and had served on the committee of J. T. Grein's Independent Theatre. Befriending Maugham, she included him in the glamorous first-night parties she gave at her house in Mayfair, and encouraged him to attend her weekly salon of well-known actors and writers: Sir Henry Irving had been a regular, and so now were George Moore, Max Beerbohm and Arnold Bennett. In return he accompanied her to the theatre, sometimes taking her on after-wards to dine and dance at the Supper Club in the Grafton Galleries.

Another avid hostess was Lady St Helier, who had originally taken Maugham up in the 1890s at the request of Augustus Hare, and who now began to pursue him with vigour. 'Great ladies', Maugham cynically observed, 'cultivate those occupied with the arts as in former times they kept buffoons.' It was at Lady St Helier's house in Portland Place that he had his sole encounter with two great literary figures, Edith Wharton and Thomas Hardy. Invited to a luncheon given in the American novelist's honour, he was led up to talk to her. Beautifully dressed and magnificently condescending, Mrs Wharton lectured him for twenty minutes with exquisite refinement on a range of well-chosen cultural topics, until Maugham, feeling suffocated by her intellectual patronage, blurted out a question about the thriller-writer Edgar Wallace. Mrs Wharton looked at him with distaste.

> 'Who is Edgar Wallace?' she replied.
> 'Do you never read thrillers?'
> 'No.'
> Never has a monosyllable contained more frigid displeasure . . . her eyes wandered away and a little forced smile slightly curled her lips.
> 'I'm afraid it's getting very late,' said Mrs Wharton.

Thomas Hardy was far more congenial. The occasion was a large, formal dinner-party of eminent figures in politics and the arts.

> When the ladies retired to the drawing-room I found myself sitting next to Thomas Hardy. I remember a little man with an earthy face. In his evening clothes, with his boiled shirt and high collar, he had still a strange look of the soil. He was amiable and mild. It struck me at the time that there was in him a curious mixture of shyness and self-assurance. I do not remember what we talked about, but I know that we talked for three-quarters of an hour. At the end of it he paid me a great compliment: he asked me (not having heard my name) what was my profession.

Mrs Wharton living in Paris may have been unaware of Maugham's celebrity, but in London his name could hardly be avoided. J. T. Grein in the *Sunday Times* wrote, 'One has to go back to the early days of Sardou★ to find a popularity similar and so sudden'; *Punch* ran a cartoon by Bernard Partridge showing the ghost of William Shakespeare scowling enviously at the sight of a wall covered in posters for Maugham's four plays; and Max Beerbohm in the *Saturday Review* hailed Somerset Maugham as 'the hero of the year . . . [whose] name is a household word even in households where the theatre is held unclean.' With four plays running, why not five? Max speculated. 'Five plays running simultaneously! Stupendous! . . . Yet, after all, what are five theatres among so many? Why shouldn't *all* the theatres in London be Maughamised?'

It was Grein, an energetic supporter of Maugham's since he had first produced *A Man of Honour* at the Stage Society, who wrote one of the

★ Victorien Sardou (1831–1908), popular French playwright.

most enthusiastic reviews of the next play, *Jack Straw*, which he described as 'light as a feather and as saucy as a sparrow'. An exuberant, intricately plotted piece, *Jack Straw* had been dashed off in a couple of weeks during Maugham's sojourn in Paris in 1905. The plot was suggested by a story told him by Harry Philips about some people he knew back home in Staffordshire. Thomas Twyford, a manufacturer of sanitaryware, had moved into a handsome manor house only a few miles from Harry's people, the Philipses, in Hollington. The newcomers were cold-shouldered by the gentry who snobbishly refused to call, until Twyford, a keen huntsman and philanthropist, was taken up by his neighbour, the Grand Duke Michael of Russia, who was leasing a house near by. After this, according to Harry, the Twyfords 'suddenly became much sought after'. In the play the parvenus are the (recently hyphenated) Parker-Jenningses from Brixton, now living not in Staffordshire but in the neighbouring county, Cheshire, where, like the Twyfords, they are despised for their origins in trade. While Thomas Twyford first encountered his duke in Hamburg, the Parker-Jenningses befriend theirs, the Archduke Sebastian of Pomerania, in the Grand Babylon Hotel, 'the best hotel in Europe'; and it is when the Archduke comes to stay with them in Cheshire that his hosts instantly become socially acceptable. The parallels were not difficult to draw, and after the play opened Harry found himself in hot water, banned from a number of houses in the locality. This experience was an early instance of what was to evolve into a familiar pattern: a story relayed to Maugham by a third party, then redesigned by him in fictional form but with so little attempt at disguise that the work's appearance frequently resulted in shocked recognition and hurt feelings. Harry Philips may have been the first but he was certainly not the last of these purveyors of tales to suffer from the furious fall-out consequent upon publication, a fall-out which generally left Maugham himself singularly undisturbed.

The twist in the plot which gives *Jack Straw* its irresistible dramatic tension is the triple identity of the hero: an archduke posing as a waiter posing as an archduke. Jack Straw first appears waiting on tables at the Grand Babylon Hotel (the hotel's name a tipping of the hat to Arnold Bennett whose novel of that title had been published in 1902). Among the guests are the nouveaux-riches Parker-Jenningses with their son and daughter; Count de Bremer, the Pomeranian Ambassador; Ambrose Holland, a gentleman in his middle thirties; and Lady Wanley, one of those fascinating widows of indeterminate age who manipulate their way through Maugham's early work. Holland and Lady Wanley, offended by the Parker-Jenningses' rudeness and vulgarity, decide to play a trick on them by passing off the waiter as a Pomeranian archduke. Jack Straw agrees, having fallen for their daughter Ethel, who, unlike her parents, is modest, pretty and refined. The Parker-Jenningses eagerly swallow the story and invite their new acquaintance to stay, ambitious to show him off to the county and secure him as a son-in-law. Back home in Cheshire, as the grandees arrive to meet the Parker-Jenningses' guest, Jack's apparently humble station is revealed and his hosts furiously order him from the house – at which precise point the Pomeranian Ambassador, who, with the audience, has known all along that Jack Straw really is the Archduke, makes a timely appearance waving a telegram from the Emperor consenting to his son's marriage to Ethel.

*Jack Straw*, with its split-second timing, epigrammatic wit and tightly linked subplots, shows great confidence on the part of the author in handling this kind of sophisticated semi-farce. The genre was previously practised with great expertise in England by Pinero, whose plays of the 1880s such as *The Magistrate* and *Dandy Dick* delighted audiences for years, and in France by the incomparable Georges Feydeau, whose immensely popular *Une puce à l'oreille* (*A Flea in Her Ear*) had opened in Paris the previous year and had almost certainly been seen by Maugham. In *Jack Straw* the leading roles were played by two expert practitioners, Lottie Venne as Mrs Parker-Jennings and as Jack Straw the great Charles Hawtrey, 'the most finished comedian of his generation'. Hawtrey, who also directed, scored a great personal success in the play, which might well have enjoyed as long a run as *Lady Frederick* if he himself had not had to pull out with ill health in December, thus bringing the show to an end.

At this stage in his career, Maugham as the author had little say in the matter of casting, and indeed had failed in the one attempt he made to secure a role for a friend. In *Jack Straw*, 'I tried to get a small part for Sue, but could not manage it,' he had written to Kelly in February 1908.

Ethelwyn Sylvia Jones, known as Sue, was a young actress, daughter of the playwright Henry Arthur Jones, who, like Maugham, had become one of Mrs Steevens's regular visitors at Merton Place. Jones, an amusing, energetic man in his late fifties, was a farmer's son who by sheer determination had established himself in the theatre; he had enjoyed considerable success during the 1890s, although his career was now on the wane. As Jones had much admired *Liza of Lambeth*, he and Maugham quickly established a rapport, with Jones voluble on the subject of the drama, talking energetically of his vision of the founding of a national theatre and eager to involve the younger man in his campaign to abolish the Lord Chamberlain's punitive system of censorship.

It was one afternoon in 1906 that Jones had arrived at Merton Place accompanied by Sue, then a ravishing young woman of twenty-three with pale-gold skin, fair hair piled high on her head, blue eyes and a voluptuous figure. She had first walked on in one of her father's plays at only fourteen, after which she had served her apprenticeship in the provinces without making much of a mark. Unhappily married, she was living apart from her husband, Montague Leveaux, manager for Arthur Bourchier's company at the Garrick, and trying to find work in the West End. Maugham was immediately captivated by Sue's luscious beauty: 'she had the most beautiful smile I have ever seen on a human being', he wrote; he was charmed, too, by her sense of humour and direct way of talking; she was generous and tender-hearted and had a delicious gurgling laugh which was irresistibly sexy. The two of them flirted and talked, and Sue agreed to dine with him; the occasion was a success, and after a further couple of evenings in inexpensive restaurants Maugham took her back to his single room in Pall Mall and made love to her. While he escorted her home in a hansom afterwards, she asked him how long he thought the affair would last. 'Six weeks,' he teasingly replied. In fact Maugham was to fall seriously in love with Sue and their affair continued for nearly eight years.

When he met Sue Jones that afternoon at Merton, Maugham had only recently come to the end of his relationship with Harry Philips. Reserved in manner and apparently detached, Maugham took pains to conceal the fact that he was a man of powerful, often turbulent feeling: a largely love-less childhood had made him adept at disguise.

> He had acquired calmness of demeanour and under most circumstances an unruffled exterior . . . People told him he was unemotional; but he knew that he was at the mercy of his emotions: an accidental kindness touched him so much that sometimes he did not venture to speak in order not to betray the unsteadiness of his voice.

Sexually passionate, Maugham also desperately craved love, and until well into middle age was given to a series of intense infatuations. His misfortune lay in an inability ever to find affection equally returned: magnetically attractive to both sexes as a young man, he was much pursued – 'I have often acted a passion that I did not feel,' he admitted – and frequently in the position of having to extract himself from unwanted entanglements, 'with gentleness when possible, and if not, with irritation'. The irony was that he himself never experienced what he described as 'the bliss of requited love'. Expert at covering his tracks, Maugham left little documentary evidence of specific attachments; nevertheless there are numerous signs – references casually made in letters, fictional versions lightly disguised – of his love affairs and of emotional neediness only partly hidden behind the reserve. When looking back in old age, Maugham declared that he had never completely let down his guard, never surrendered wholly to anyone; and yet there are indications that this was not entirely true, and that for a time with Sue Jones his carefully erected defences were thoroughly undermined.

Apart from her sex appeal, Sue had a number of qualities which to a man as highly strung and vulnerable as Maugham were infinitely seductive. Wholly at ease with herself, she was totally accepting, possessed of a benign tranquillity, an unruffled calm that was wonderfully soothing to his spirits. She was good-humoured, too, with an endearingly childlike sense of mischief; she loved to laugh, yet at other times was happy to sit in silence, not needing to be talked to or entertained. Despite her failed marriage and undistinguished career, Sue had a tremendous zest for life, her optimism and vitality a welcome counterbalance to those moods of depression and uncertainty to which her lover was prone. Most importantly, she possessed in abundance a maternal warmth, which for obvious reasons was irresistible to Maugham.

Unfortunately no correspondence between the two has ever come to light, but an indelible impression has been left of Sue as the lovely, warm-hearted Rosie in his novel *Cakes and Ale*, the most adorable of all Maugham's heroines. Over the years Maugham made a number of references to Rosie as the portrait of 'a woman of whom I had been extremely fond for years', plainly pointing to Sue, and Gerald Kelly, in whom full details of the affair were confided, confirmed the identification. Sue, he said, 'came of common family – her mother was particularly so – and had married at the age of 19 . . . She led a miserable life . . . & then met Willie, the only man she ever really loved.' It was his impression, Kelly added, that Willie and Sue 'had a very happy love affair together . . . She was one of the most delightful women I have ever known, I thought her wonderfully beautiful.' To Maugham himself he wrote that Sue was 'a dear' and as Rosie she was 'the most perfectly realized woman you ever got into a book'.

In *Cakes and Ale* Maugham's love affair with Sue is naturally transposed, and yet its essence is unmistakable. Here is the passage describing the first night the lovers spend together, during which the nameless narrator, a very young man at this point, takes Rosie back to his lodgings in Victoria.

I opened the door and lit the candle. Rosie followed me in and I held it up so that she should be able to see herself. I looked at her in the glass as she arranged her hair. She took two or three pins out, which she put in her mouth, and taking one of my brushes, brushed her hair up from the nape of her neck. She twisted it, patted it, and put back the pins, and as she was intent on this her eyes caught mine in the glass and she smiled at me. When she had replaced the last pin she turned and faced me; she did not say anything; she looked at me tranquilly, still that little friendly smile in her blue eyes. I put down the candle. The room was very small and the dressing-table was by the bed. She raised her hand and softly stroked my cheek . . .

. . . A sob broke from my tight throat. I do not know whether it was because I was shy and lonely . . . or because my desire was so great, but I began to cry. I felt terribly ashamed of myself; I tried to control myself, I couldn't; the tears welled up in my eyes and poured down my cheeks. Rosie saw them and gave a little gasp.

'Oh, honey, what is it? What's the matter? Don't. Don't!'

She put her arms round my neck and began to cry too, and she kissed my lips and my eyes and my wet cheeks. She undid her bodice and lowered my head till it rested on her bosom. She stroked my smooth face. She rocked me back and forth as though I were a child in her arms. I kissed her breasts and I kissed the white column of her neck; and she slipped out of her bodice and out of her skirt and her petticoats and I held her for a moment by her corseted waist; then she undid it, holding her breath for an instant to enable her to do so; and stood before me in her shift. When I put my hands on her sides I could feel the ribbing of the skin from the pressure of the corsets.

'Blow out the candle,' she whispered.

It was she who awoke me when the dawn peering through the curtains revealed the shape of the bed and of the wardrobe against the darkness of the lingering night. She woke me by kissing me on the mouth and her hair falling over my face tickled me.

'I must get up,' she said. 'I don't want your landlady to see me.' . . .

Her breasts when she leaned over me were heavy on my chest. In a little while she got out of bed . . . It was a body made for the act of love. In the light of the candle, struggling now with the increasing day, it was all silvery gold: and the only colour was the rosy pink of the hard nipples.

We dressed in silence. She did not put on her corsets again, but rolled them up and I wrapped them in a piece of newspaper. We tiptoed along the passage and when I opened the door and we stepped out into the street the dawn ran to meet us . . .

I kissed her and I watched her walk away.

Intoxicated by his new love affair, Maugham went over to Paris to see Gerald Kelly; he told him he was 'desperately in love' and that he wanted to commission Kelly to paint Sue's portrait. The result is the beautiful *Mrs Leveaux in White*, painted in 1907, in which Sue is shown standing full length, voluptuous in a low-cut evening dress, her mouth half open, her eyes gazing languidly into the middle distance. Equally striking is a second Kelly portrait, even more candidly erotic, of Sue sitting on a sofa, again in décolleté evening dress, looking straight ahead with an expression of heavily sensual promise on her lovely face. 'She posed beautifully for the picture, so patiently,' said Kelly later, 'and both of us did our best, and I think Willie loved the portrait.'

*Jack Straw* had been running for barely a month when *Mrs Dot* opened at the Comedy. The play was produced by the American Charles Frohman, whose theatrical empire in London was fast expanding, his biggest success to date the original 1904 production of *Peter Pan*, which, annually revived, made Barrie a millionaire. Frohman was one of the seventeen managers who had rejected *Lady Frederick*, and not wishing to make the same mistake twice was quick to make an offer for *Mrs Dot*, securing Marie Tempest for the title role and the well-known producer Dion Boucicault to direct. Maugham could hardly believe his luck that two such stars should have been engaged. 'When I went to the first rehearsal . . . it was with trepidation,' he recalled. Marie Tempest 'was the greatest comedienne on the English stage. I expected her to be wilful, exacting, petulant & tiresome . . . To my surprise [she] never showed a trace of impatience . . . She listened to what Boucicault told her with attention & did it without question . . . It warmed the author's heart to see what she made of his lines . . .'

The play was based on a version Maugham had worked on with his brother Harry in 1903, under the title *The Fortune Hunters*, the plot revolving round the machinations of Mrs Dot Worthley, a wealthy young widow, to disentangle the man she loves, Gerald Halstane, from an unhappy engagement so that she may marry him herself. After an ingenious series of complications and reverses, it all ends as it should, with Gerald and Mrs Dot in each other's arms and the discarded fiancée happily engaged to Mrs Dot's nephew, Freddie. As with *Jack Straw*, the technique owes much to the influence of the French farceurs, but also something to an influence nearer home. In Act Three there is this short scene between Mrs Dot and Freddie, who, acting as her secretary, has the job of replying to the many begging letters received by the philanthropic widow.

> [MRS DOT reading a letter drafted by Freddie]: 'To lose one leg in a railway accident is a misfortune, but to lose a second in a colliery explosion points to carelessness.' That's not original, Freddie.
> FREDDIE: I'm so hard up I can only afford to make other people's jokes.'*

Witty and stylish, the play opened on 27 April 1908 to a favourable reception from the critics, nearly all of whom singled out Marie Tempest for particular praise.

No one interested in the theatre could now be unaware of Maugham's prominence, a prominence which inevitably attracted a certain amount of envy. Arnold Bennett, who had had a play produced for the Stage Society earlier in the year, wrote in his journal for 29 April, 'Noticed in myself: A distinct feeling of jealousy on reading yesterday and to-day accounts of another very successful production of a play by Somerset Maugham – the third now running.' And one evening when dining alone in his club Maugham overheard two men at the next table discussing him. 'D'you know him at all?' said one. 'I suppose he's about as swollen-headed as he can be.' 'Oh, yes,' said the other. 'He can't get a hat big enough to fit him.' In fact Maugham was remarkably unchanged by his success, although inevitably his level-headed manner struck some observers as a form of vanity. He was pleased by the acclaim, of course, but he had worked hard through ten long years to achieve it and he saw very clearly the nature of that achievement: he had discovered a knack, a facility for writing light comedy that audiences found amusing; it was not an ability he rated very highly, nor did he see himself continuing with it for very long, but while there was a demand and he enjoyed the exercise he planned to make the most of it: after all, the effort involved could hardly be described as arduous when a play could be turned out in less than a month. 'I regularly wrote one act in five days,' he recalled, 'took the week-end off, and wrote the second and third acts in the same time. Then I gave five days of the fourth week to revising what I had written.'

For Maugham the most significant change brought about by success was financial: for the first time in his life he was free of money worries, and the relief was enormous. His plays had not yet made him rich, as

---

* 'To lose one parent, Mr Worthing, may be regarded as a misfortune; to lose both looks like carelessness.' Lady Bracknell in Wilde's *The Importance of Being Earnest*, Act I.

they were soon to do, but the popularity of *Lady Frederick* marked the point at which he left poverty behind him. 'I hated poverty,' he wrote in his notebook for 1908. 'I hated having to scrape and save so as to make both ends meet.' Fond of his creature comforts, he had never been attracted by the colourful squalor of bohemian life, and being in debt had always troubled him. On a number of levels money meant a great deal to Maugham, and few people in his opinion fully understood 'the great, the insinuating . . . the overwhelming significance of money in the affairs of life'. Money ensured his artistic independence, insulated him from unwelcome intrusion, enabled him to travel where and when he pleased, and provided him with the considerable level of luxury in which he chose to live; more than that, for a man who from childhood had been wholly lacking in emotional security, financial security became a vitally important substitute. That it was a subject which interested him profoundly is shown by the many references to money in Maugham's work, in his correspondence and also in his conversation. 'Sometimes after an evening with Willie,' said the writer Beverley Nichols, 'one felt that one had been dining with a stockbroker.' In 1908, the immediate result of his newly affluent status was that he could afford to leave his single room in Pall Mall and with the faithful Walter Payne move into a smart little flat in Mayfair, at 23 Mount Street, off Park Lane.

Aware that he must quickly capitalise on his current popularity, Maugham immediately set to work making the final alterations to the scripts he still had in hand, and on 13 June 1908 the curtain went up on a fourth play by Somerset Maugham, *The Explorer*. Shortly also to be published as a novel, *The Explorer* after numerous rejections in the past had eventually been accepted by Lewis Waller, one of the most successful actor–managers of his day, adored for his matinee-idol good looks by a large and mainly female following, his more devoted fans wearing badges reading 'K.O.W.', for 'Keen on Waller'. In the eponymous role of the high-minded Alec Mackenzie, Waller was able to give full rein to his flamboyant technique, Max Beerbohm, tongue delicately in cheek, describing him as almost godlike in the part: 'See him standing in the centre of the drawing-room, his heels joined, his shoulders squared, his fists clenched, his lips compressed as by a vice of steel . . . If he is like this in a London drawing-room, what, we rapturously wonder, must he be like in the heart of Central Africa?'

Maugham had long been angling to get a work taken by Waller. The previous year Violet Hunt in her journal had somewhat sourly noted, 'Somerset M., a dramatic genius, making les yeux doux at Beatrice Lewis, whom I know as a vulgar South Kensington art student, because she happens to be the sister of Lewis Waller.' Persuading Waller of *The Explorer's* potential had not been easy, and the play had been submitted and substantially rewritten four times before it was eventually accepted. It was Maurice Colles who had dealt with the earliest version back in 1903, failing to sell it, and when Maugham severed his connection with the agency he naturally assumed that Colles's part in the business was over. But now here was Colles claiming commission, a claim which his ex-client felt was wholly unjustified. 'Practically nothing remains of the play which you tried to place,' Maugham told him. 'If you who are concerned with the Authors Society in protecting authors from dubious claims, consider you have one in this case, I shall lose my faith in responsible agencies.' But Colles did consider he had a claim and was not prepared to be put off, successfully suing for the money in court, the case of *Colles* v. *Maugham* heard in the High Court of Justice, King's Bench Division, with the plaintiff awarded a payment of £21 10s.

The trouble Maugham had with *The Explorer* closely followed on trouble he encountered with the publication of his new novel, although in this instance the affair was settled without legal intervention. *The Magician*, inspired by the grotesque figure of Aleister Crowley, had been written in 1906 and accepted by Methuen, with Maugham signing an agreement for three novels for each of which he would be paid an advance of £75. It was not until *The Magician* was actually set up in print that the head of the firm read it and was so profoundly shocked that publication was cancelled forthwith and the work returned. 'I have always thought that publishers should never learn to read,' Maugham crossly remarked. However, he was sufficiently shaken by the reaction to remove the name of the book's dedicatee, Gerald Kelly, from the manuscript in order to protect his friend from association with an obscene work. The book was then sold to William Heinemann – which in the event proved to be a move of considerable consequence: Heinemann remained Maugham's publisher for the rest of his life. At the time the Heinemann deal was struck Maugham's name was on hoardings all over London and it occurred to Methuen's director that it might be timely to remind their author that he still owed them three novels. Maugham was outraged. 'I, as you know, make a point of cultivating the *beau geste*,' he told Gerald Kelly, '& in a few moving words told him that he could go to hell.'

Methuen's rejection of *The Magician* cannot have come as a complete surprise as Maugham had been uneasy for some time about the story's reception. As early as October 1906 he had written to Pinker, 'I wanted to consult you about taking out the chapter in the lunatic asylum. I do not want to horrify people more than need be.' *The Magician* is in the fullest sense a horror story, and there is little sign that Maugham reined himself in, on the contrary relishing going to the limits in terms of terror and taste. In Paris at the turn of the century there was a considerable vogue for the occult, a vogue greatly encouraged by the novels of the Decadent writer Huysmans, in particular by his 1891 novel *Là-Bas*, which according to Maugham 'had a palpitating horror that many found strangely fascinating . . . [*The Magician*] would never have been written except for the regard I had for Joris-Karl Huysmans.' Strong echoes can be found, too, of other practitioners of the genre such as Mary Shelley and Edgar Allan Poe, and, more recently, of H. G. Wells's savage and sadistic story *The Island of Doctor Moreau*.

The dominating figure in the novel, the Magician himself, is Oliver Haddo, closely based on Aleister Crowley, with all Crowley's vanity and bombast. The story begins in Paris with Arthur Burdon, an English doctor, come to visit his fiancée Margaret, who is staying with her friend Susie prior to her forthcoming marriage. The two women, together with a French savant, Dr Porhoët, take Arthur to dine at their local restaurant. Here the lively company of writers and artists is suddenly silenced by the arrival of Haddo. Haddo immediately draws the attention of everyone in the room with his dramatic stance and flamboyant delivery, although he fails to impress Arthur with his ludicrous claims to be a master of the magic arts. When Haddo informs the company that he is known as the Brother of the Shadow, Arthur, looking at the man's immense girth, makes a facetious rejoinder.

This turns out to be a fatal mistake. Haddo, enraged by the ridicule, decides on a terrible revenge, casting a spell over Margaret so that she becomes obsessed by him, gripped by an overwhelming sexual passion. 'Margaret . . . horribly repelled yet horribly fascinated . . . had an immense desire that he should take her again in his arms and press her lips with that red voluptuous mouth . . . She trembled with the intensity of her desire.' Helpless, Margaret leaves the heartbroken Arthur and marries Haddo. From time to time there are sightings of the couple staying at expensive hotels on the Continent; then one night in London Susie and Arthur find themselves at a dinner-party where it is clear that Margaret is in desperate need of rescue. Eventually with the help of Dr Porhoët, Susie and Arthur track her down to Skene, Haddo's estate in Staffordshire. True to tradition, the place is bleak and remote, with terrible rumours circulating about what is going on inside the house. In the end the forces of evil are defeated, although Margaret dies in the process, and Skene with its wicked Magician and the loathsome horrors it contains is destroyed by fire.

To those in the know it was obvious whence Maugham had drawn much of his inspiration, his portrait of the regulars at Le Chat Blanc (Le Chien Noir in the novel) depicted with little attempt at camouflage. 'I hear that Maugham has crucified us of the White Cat in a new satirical novel,' the painter Roderic O'Conor, who appears as O'Brien, wrote gloomily to Clive Bell. But as might be expected the most extravagant reaction came from the Magician himself, Aleister Crowley, who was infuriated (or pretended to be), and at the same time perversely flattered, by Maugham's wicked caricature, describing the novel as 'an appreciation of my genius such as I had never dreamed of inspiring'. He had come across the book by chance, he said. 'The title attracted me strongly, *The Magician*. The author, bless my soul! No other than my old and valued friend, William Somerset Maugham, my nice young doctor whom I remembered so well from the dear old days of the Chat Blanc. So he had really written a book – who would have believed it!' In a review for *Vanity Fair* signed 'Oliver Haddo', and later in his memoirs, Crowley attacked Maugham, accusing him of plagiarism, not only of plundering his life but of transposing without acknowledgment long passages from books on the occult which Maugham had found in the studio of Crowley's brother-in-law Gerald Kelly. 'Maugham had taken some of the most private and personal incidents of my life, my marriage . . . my magical opinions, ambitions and exploits and so on. He had added a number of the many absurd legends of which I was the central figure. He had patched all these together by innumerable strips of paper clipped from the books which I had told Gerald to buy. I had never supposed that plagiarism could have been so varied, extensive and shameless.'

Crowley had a point. The portrait of Haddo is undeniably drawn from life, and yet, repulsive though he is, it is Haddo who provides the novel's powerful nexus. As to the rest, the adventure story works well enough, and as might be expected the theme of sexual degradation is treated with enthralling veracity; but in artistic terms what sinks the story is exactly what Crowley objected to, Maugham's incorporating hefty chunks from works on the Kabbalah, the Seven Genii, the Keys of Solomon and 'the many things in the East which are inexplicable by science'. None of this really interested him – he thought it all 'moonshine' – and it shows, his lazy extracts making those parts of the book cumbrous and dull. When Maugham showed the script to Violet Hunt she put her finger on just this fault, and in acknowledging her reservation he wrote, 'I daresay you are quite right in saying that the trail of the lamp is over it all, but it was deliberately that I gave so many dates & authorities . . . I wanted to impress upon the reader the fact that all those things had been seriously believed in their time, & I was very anxious to prevent the book from being a mere shocker.' Crowley's detailed cataloguing of *The Magician*'s plagiarised passages did little to endear him to its author: after Gerald Kelly had painted Crowley's portrait, Maugham suggested he submit it to the Royal Academy, 'with the title SON OF A BITCH (arrangement in black & green)'.

*The Magician* was published in November 1908 to mixed reviews, some castigating the author for obscenity, others congratulating him for providing such 'a real thrill of horror'. By this time Maugham's reputation was standing high, very different from the position he had occupied only twelve months before. With Barrie, Pinero, Alfred Sutro and other notable playwrights he was one of the founders of the Dramatists' Club; he was made a member of the Garrick, the old-established gentlemen's club in Covent Garden for actors and men of letters; and he was among seventy notable signatories, including Shaw, Barrie, Galsworthy, Pinero, Yeats and H. G. Wells, of a letter to *The Times* protesting about theatre censorship. On 1 December that year Maugham was one of 180 guests at a dinner held at the Ritz, the purpose to honour Robbie Ross, the loyal friend and executor of Oscar Wilde – and also, indirectly, to rehabilitate eight years after his demise the reputation of Wilde himself. H. G. Wells in an embarrassingly emotional speech proposed Ross's health, and Maugham, sitting next to Wilde's son, Vyvyan Holland, was heard to mutter, 'First and last things that one would rather have left unsaid.'

Maugham's presence that December evening at the Ritz is significant, a gesture of homage to a figure whose impact on his life and writing, although largely unexpressed, was considerable. Maugham never wrote about Wilde – too dangerous a subject – and yet Wilde's influence was formative: as a medical student at St Thomas's Maugham had read *Salome* and *The Picture of Dorian Gray* and seen *The Importance of Being Earnest*; echoes of Wilde appear unmistakably in much of his early dramatic work; and in *The Magician*, a novel with an indisputably Wildean flavour, there is a substantial, if unattributed, quotation, Salome's 'I am amorous of thy body, Iokanaan!' Wilde's declared belief that 'It is not for anyone to censure what anyone else does, and everyone should go his own way, to whatever place he chooses, in exactly the way that he chooses' was one with which Maugham passionately identified and constantly returned to in his work, even if he could not bring himself fully to follow it in life. The exposure of Wilde's homosexuality and its terrible consequences, the loss of family, of home, of reputation, had made a deep impression on Maugham, who could hardly avoid seeing a number of potential parallels in his own situation. Haunted by the tragedy and fascinated by the man, he was strongly attracted by Wilde's social and literary circles, many members of which were present that night at the Ritz, several of whom were to become important as friends of his own.

Key among them were the guest of honour himself, Robbie Ross, and his old friend, Reginald Turner, who together had accompanied Wilde to France after his release from prison. Ross was a small, neat man with a tidy moustache, discreetly homosexual – he had been Wilde's first male lover – with a roguish sense of humour and infectious laugh. As art critic of the *Morning Post* and director of a small gallery, the genial Ross was knowledgeable about paintings, in particular the French Impressionists, a subject guaranteed to interest Maugham who found this recent acquaintance most engaging. 'You are a perfect dear,' he wrote to Ross the day after the dinner, 'and I'm so glad to have known you.' Reggie Turner had become a friend after Maugham had written to thank him for an appreciative review of *Lady Frederick*. Teasingly referred to by Wilde as 'the boy-snatcher of Clement's Inn', Reggie was spinsterish by temperament and unfailingly decorous in mixed company, if capable of delirious promiscuity in all-male gatherings. Unprepossessing in appearance, with thick lips, a snout-like nose and perpetually blinking eyes, he was generous, charming and a brilliant conversationalist, 'the most amusing man I have known', according to Maugham. Max Beerbohm in describing Reggie's wit remarked that he was not very responsive to other people's humour, a comment which worried Reggie, who asked Maugham if he thought it were true. 'I didn't want to hurt his feelings, so I said, "Well, Reggie, you never laugh at any of my jokes." He blinked . . . & puckered up his ugly little face, & with a grin replied, "But I don't [think] they're funny."' Possessed of an adequate private income, Reggie persisted in pursuing a career as a writer, turning out a series of dismally amateurish novels none of which sold more than poorly. Once when Maugham was boasting of the rarity value of his first editions, Reggie declared, 'Ah, it's my second editions which are almost impossible to procure.' It was Reggie who had encouraged Beerbohm to join the Wilde circle, but while Max immensely admired Wilde he never quite became an intimate: unlike Reggie Turner and Ross he was not homosexual and had no wish to follow in that direction, although happy to join in the general talk of straight men as 'mulierasts' and of man's love for man as 'the love that dares not speak its name'. At an early point in their friendship Max had hoped, vainly, that he might save Reggie from this particular primrose path. 'I really think Reg is at rather a crucial point of his career,' he had written to Robbie Ross, 'and [I] should hate to see him fall an entire victim to the love that dares not tell its name.'

Max and Reggie Turner had been inseparable since they were under-graduates at Oxford, and it was a compliment to Maugham that he was now invited to join their clique. Reggie had an apartment on the edge of Berkeley Square, only a couple of minutes' walk from Maugham in Mount Street and from Upper Berkeley Street, where Max lived with his mother and sisters. It was at Upper Berkeley Street that on one mem-orably awkward occasion Maugham was invited to tea.

> I remember that the room was in semidarkness, Mrs Beerbohm, in black, seemed rather shy, the two young women, also in black, conversed with the few guests in undertones. One had the uneasy feeling that in the next room a corpse might be lying in an open coffin. I was evidently not a success at the party for I was never invited again.

A far more informal atmosphere was to be found at Reggie's flat, where Maugham often dropped in on his way to or from Mount Street. It was here one afternoon that he first met H. G. Wells, who had been lunching with Reggie and had returned to the flat to continue their conversation. Wells, regarded as one of the country's leading intellectuals, was then at the height of his fame, and Maugham, uncomfortably aware of the trivial nature of his own celebrity, felt wrong-footed and subtly patronised. 'I received the impression that he looked upon me with a sort of off-hand amusement as he might have looked upon [the music-hall comedians] Arthur Roberts or Dan Leno.' Some of the jolliest evenings spent by the friends were with the eccentric Mrs Steevens. All three young men had been regular visitors to Merton Place which Mrs Steevens had recently left, moving to Kensington where her generous if somewhat chaotic hospitality continued undiminished. 'I'm sure there are various old women as delightful as Mrs Steevens was,' Max wrote after her death to Maugham. 'But I rather doubt whether in these democratic days there are many old women who are so *odd* – so outlandish and unabashed and sure of them-selves and of their own ways of doing and saying things.' Maugham remembered her Tuesday evenings as particularly lively, with:

> Max, Reggie Turner, George Street [the writer G. S. Street], a certain Hipperley, who was an authority on Roman roads, & I. They were very

gay parties, chiefly because Reggie kept us all laughing our heads off. Max did not say much, but when he did, you remembered it. It was pretty sure to be witty or caustic. When the evening came to an end we drove on the top of a bus to go to our respective homes.

An important friendship Maugham made among the 'Oscarians' was with Ada Leverson, who had also been present at Ross's dinner. A faithful friend to Wilde, who called her his 'Sphinx', she had stood by him when the scandal broke and was one of the few to greet him early in the morning on his release from gaol. A finely featured, soft-spoken woman in her forties, slender, with a cloud of dyed-blonde hair, a pale little face and pointed chin, Ada, separated from her husband, was regarded as the Egeria of a mainly homosexual coterie that included Robbie Ross, Reggie Turner, Max Beerbohm and Lord Alfred Douglas. Attracted by and attractive to effeminate young men – she had once tried, unsuccessfully, to seduce Aubrey Beardsley – she was much loved as a discreet and unshockable confidante, treasured as a gifted if somewhat eccentric hostess. 'Her conversation was artificial, in several senses elusive, chaotic and often captivatingly absurd,' according to one of her devotees. At her little house in Radnor Place near Hyde Park, the Sphinx, though far from well off, held delightful soirées, where she always appeared exquisitely dressed, wearing little jewellery and favouring muted colours, beautifully cut and in fine materials. Obliged to supplement her income, Ada had written a couple of novels and she contributed articles to *Black and White* and *Punch*. One of her circle, Robert Hichens, author of *The Garden of Allah*, encouraged her to try her hand at writing plays. '*Write a light comedy at once,*' he wrote to her in 1908. 'I wish it, I command it. Cut out Somerset Maugham.'

There was little chance of that, but the friendship between Ada Leverson and Maugham soon became warm. As in the case of Violet Hunt, a strong emotional attachment developed on the side of the Sphinx, who found this handsome, clever young man disturbingly attractive: she wrote to him constantly, filled his room with flowers when he was ill, and gave him a lucky charm to keep about his person. 'My dear Sphynx,' he wrote to her, using his own idiosyncratic spelling of the word, 'It is too kind of you to send me that lovely horse-shoe. I will wear it on my watch-chain, watch-chain; & the flowers in my hair, my hair. You see your kindness throws me into a lyric rapture . . .' She invited him to dinner and the opera, attended all his plays and relied on him to criticise her work. In 1908 she dedicated to him her novel *Love's Shadow*, 'a great honour', as he recognised. '[Maugham's] visits were looked forward to eagerly,' her daughter recalled, 'and a large photograph of him became part of her personal surroundings.' For his part Maugham was fond of the Sphinx, knew of her feelings and played the relationship skilfully, indulging in a delicate flirtatiousness that scrupulously stopped just short of anything more serious. He allowed her to call him 'Billie', a name used only by his closest intimates. The two of them had a number of interests in common: the writing business – the Sphinx, too, was a client of J. B. Pinker – and also the theatre – among Ada's friends were George Alexander, Charles Hawtrey and Beerbohm Tree, and she had been closely involved with Jack Grein and the Independent Theatre Club. Her association with Wilde was of consuming interest to Maugham, who was touched when she gave him her own precious first edition of Wilde's poem *The Sphinx*, in which, inscribing it for Maugham, she had written lines beginning, 'Oh dark tormenting face of beauty, loved . . .' Maugham was curious about Lord Alfred Douglas, unforgettably encountered thirteen years before during his first visit to Capri, to whom he hoped Ada would introduce him. 'I wish you would ask me to meet Bosie one day,' he wrote to her in December 1908, a request with which Ada was more than willing to comply.

Shortly after this, in January 1909, Maugham's next play opened, and the Sphinx, anxious to promote her friend's career, wrote to Lord Alfred, who was then editor of the *Academy*, asking if she might review it for his journal. He agreed, on condition that there was to be no 'log-rolling', no writing '"something nice" . . . because the author happened to be a friend'. Unfortunately this is exactly what the piece turned out to be, and Douglas returned it with a sharp rebuke. 'My dear Sphinx, I am very sorry, but this article won't do at all,' he began.

> It is a much too obvious 'puff' of a personal friend of yours . . . Maugham's play may be quite amusing and worth seeing and all that, but your criticism would have applied to a really great comedy like one of Oscar's, the sort of thing that only appears once in 20 years . . . When you asked me to dinner to meet him I began to be rather suspicious. I have been living in London on and off for the last 10 years, and if Maugham, whom I remember meeting years ago at Capri, was so anxious to meet me it is a pity he did not do so before I became Editor of a paper which is capable of being very useful to him.

The play in question was *Penelope*, which opened at the Comedy on 9 January 1909, with Marie Tempest again in the title role. Witty and urbane, the plot deals with the worldly wiles employed by Penelope, the devoted wife of a successful London doctor, to win back her husband from his tiresome and tenacious mistress. The theme was not original: Barrie had used something like it the year before in *What Every Woman Knows*, as had Sardou in his popular 1883 farce *Divorçons!*, and it was one to which Maugham himself was to return nearly twenty years later in *The Constant Wife*. But according to Maugham *Penelope* was chiefly inspired 'by the young woman . . . with whom I was having an affair', a statement which opens up the intriguing possibility that Sue Jones dealt with her lover's extramural liaisons in a similar manner. Whatever the actuality, it provided an excellent scenario, and with its topical relevance presented audiences with a work that was thoroughly up to date. In *Penelope*, and in his next play, *Smith*, Maugham for the first time dealt with the modern woman in the modern age, exchanging the grandeur, opulence and Victorian values of *Lady Frederick* and *Jack Straw* for bridge parties, telephones, mansion flats and light, bright sitting-rooms furnished in floral chintz.

*Penelope*, which was to prove yet another popular success, had been commissioned by Charles Frohman, who was now to figure significantly in the promotion of Maugham's reputation as a dramatist. Tubby and bald, Frohman had for some years been the biggest producer in New York as well as establishing himself as a leading impresario in London. Modest in manner, of quick intelligence and a dry wit, he was possessed of a dynamic energy that, said Barrie, 'was like a force of nature . . . They could have lit a city with it.' For Frohman the theatre was his life, and within the profession he was both liked and respected, regarded as a fair man whose word was his bond. It was largely as a result of his efforts that a system of exchange for successful plays was set up between London, Paris and New York, with the emphasis on London as the source of all that was best in contemporary drama: a much repeated saying of Frohman's was that he would rather earn £15 in London than $15,000 in New York. But in fact personal gain meant little; as Bernard Shaw wrote of him, '[Charles Frohman] is the most wildly romantic and adventurous person of my acquaintance. As Charles XII became an excellent soldier because of his passion for putting himself in the way of being killed, so Charles Frohman became a famous manager through his passion for putting himself in the way of being ruined.' Having taken a long lease on the Duke of York's, Frohman had made it his business to establish good working relations with a number of prominent managers, in his record year, 1901, mounting productions in a total of five London theatres; he put under contract one of the best directors in the West End, Dion Boucicault; and, like Grein before him, set up a venue for experimental plays. Frohman kept a permanent suite at the Savoy, from which he would trot along the Strand in a large fur coat and a cloud of cigar smoke on his way to oversee rehearsals. Once in the theatre he stationed himself in the orchestra pit where he discreetly conducted operations, talking in quiet asides to the director, or nodding to an actor to whom he wished to give notes afterwards. He had a childishly sweet tooth, never without a sticky little cache of cakes and sweets, and when he emerged from the theatre his favourite recreation was visiting the Regent's Park Zoo.

By the early 1900s Frohman held a virtual monopoly on importing British drama to the United States, responsible for bringing to America works by Barrie, Pinero and Oscar Wilde. Thus his enthusiasm for the plays of Somerset Maugham was crucial to Maugham's establishing himself across the Atlantic. The collaboration between the two had begun well, with Frohman producing *Lady Frederick* in New York and *Mrs Dot* in London, followed by his commissioning of *Penelope*. 'I want to tell you how glad I am that *Penelope* is a success,' Maugham wrote to him three weeks into the run. 'It is always rather nervous work to accept a commission.'

As with his novels and short stories, Maugham was extremely businesslike when dealing with the marketing of his plays, and a beady eye was kept on Golding Bright, who received a steady stream of instructions and suggestions. 'I should much like to know a variety of things,' begins one letter written in September 1908:

> Have you been able to do anything with *The Explorer* in America, & do you know if there is any chance of a provincial tour for it?
>
> Mrs Wooldridge kindly sent me the takings of the provincial tours of *Lady Frederick* & *Mrs Dot*; but since I know nothing of provincial takings, I do not know if they are doing ill or well. Which? . . .
>
> Has it been possible to make any arrangement for translating *Jack Straw* into French, & if not, would it not be better to accept one of the numerous suggestions that reach us? . . .

A few weeks later he was telling Bright that he was:

> relieved and pleased to hear that Frohman likes the new play [*Penelope*] . . . I think we must ask for good terms, or he will not have the respect for me he should . . .
>
> . . . I should like to hear that you have arranged for the translation and immediate production of all my plays in Paris . . .

At this period of his life Maugham, while never stage-struck, found he enjoyed his involvement in the process of putting on a play. He liked attending rehearsals, where he appeared always immaculately dressed, and he was one of the few authors whose presence was welcomed as he was prepared to settle quietly in the stalls without interfering, always willing to pencil in any changes that might be required. He worked well with the director, Dion ('Dot') Boucicault, though Boucicault's wife, the actress Irene Vanbrugh, said of him that 'It astonished me a little that he and Dot worked so completely in harmony. I am sure they had a sincere admiration for each other's achievements, but I wonder if they really understood or liked each other very much, apart from the common interest they shared in a production.' Maugham loved the pared-down working atmosphere, with the auditorium in darkness and the stage bare; and he relished the easy camaraderie, the gossip and banter in stuffy gas-lit dressing-rooms, 'the hurried lunch at a restaurant round the corner with a member of the cast, and the cup of strong bitter tea, with thick bread and butter, brought in by the charwoman at four o'clock'. The only moment to be dreaded was the first night, when Maugham always suffered agonies from nerves. 'I tried to go to my own first nights as though they were somebody else's,' he wrote, 'but even at that I found it a disagreeable experience . . . Indeed I should never have gone to see my plays at all, on the first night or any other, if I had not thought it necessary to see the effect they had on the audience in order to learn how to write them.' The opening night of *Penelope* was the last time he took a bow in response to cries of 'Author!', as he had recently been stung by a newspaper article complaining that he was promoting himself too energetically. 'I read that I had neither decorum nor decency . . . [and] I determined not again to appear before the curtain on first nights.'

Maugham counted among his friends a number of playwrights, including Henry Arthur Jones, St John Ervine, Alfred Sutro and, after a less than promising start, Harley Granville Barker; he enjoyed talking shop with colleagues and discussing the techniques of the trade. He and Sutro, for instance, regularly read each other's plays and proffered advice, Sutro proving particularly helpful over the writing of *Smith*, while Maugham gave good advice on Sutro's comedy, *The Perplexed Husband*. 'I venture to suggest', he wrote after seeing the play, 'that you will find it useful generally in a comedy to work up to a powerful situation at the end of your penultimate act; I mean of course powerfully comic. And it does not matter there if you are next door to farce. My feeling is that it is enough to tickle the audience all through, but just there it is wise to make them hold their sides.' In actors, on the other hand, Maugham was never much interested outside the confines of the theatre. Indeed even in the informal atmosphere backstage his manner could come over as somewhat aloof. 'I was always nervous with Maugham,' said Irene Vanbrugh, 'and pleasantly surprised by an unexpected word of appreciation.' And it was true that, although he admired the acting profession's talent and courage and was frequently amused by a gift for mimicry or anecdote, in private life he rarely found actors rewarding company.

The one exception of course was the beautiful Sue Jones, to whom he remained passionately attached. Sue was as delightful and alluring as ever, and yet there was something elusive about her, and Maugham found it frustrating that he seemed to be making little progress – that, sweet and generous as Sue was to him, she appeared to be equally sweet and generous to everyone else. He appealed to Gerald Kelly for help. 'The brave has not yet won the fair, indeed the brave has only succeeded in boring the fair to extinction; & now my only hope is in you,' he told him, begging Kelly to come over from Paris to give him support. Meanwhile Maugham did what he could to keep Sue happy: having failed to land a role for her in *Jack Straw*, he now used his influence to secure the part of the maid, Peyton, in *Penelope*. Maugham had no illusions about Sue's capabilities: 'she was not a particularly good actress', he said, 'but good enough for me to be able to get her understudies or small parts'; and as Peyton she looked adorable in her maid's uniform, even winning a pat on the back from the *Sunday Times*, which referred to 'the stoic and impeccable maid of Miss Ethelwyn Arthur Jones'. Her lover had done her a better turn than he realised: this modest success resulted in Sue being asked to join Beerbohm Tree's Shakespeare season at His Majesty's. Here she soon caught the roving eye of Tree himself, who in an attempt to undercut his rival told Sue over supper at the Savoy one evening that she was wasting her time with Maugham as 'he's a queer', information which left Sue remarkably unfazed.

Gerald Kelly acted a crucial part in Maugham's affair with Sue, fond as he was of Sue and closer than anyone else to Maugham. Yet Maugham, while dependent on his friend's much greater experience in dealing with women, in other areas still treated Kelly like a cherished but exasperating younger brother, lecturing him on his career and ticking him off for failing to make the most of his opportunities. He encouraged him to travel. 'I think it wants a good long stay in Italy or Spain or both to get rid of the influence of l'oncle Whistler,' he wrote to him in March 1908.

'I am hoping that now you have got over these amorous entanglements you will really spend some time in parts of the world where the brilliancy of light can have its influence upon you.' Kelly took this advice to heart, and after he had decided that the brilliancy of light was best in Burma, Maugham lent him the money to go there. With Kelly hoping to make a career as a portrait-painter, Maugham also made a point of introducing him to prominent people, and he impressed upon him the importance of providing what his public wanted, a subject which in his own area of expertise he was in a position to understand very well. 'I implore you to take advantage of your forthcoming visit to England to paint a pretty woman. You cannot expect anyone to give you a commission when all that can be shown as an example of your work is a series of masterly presentments of a slut.' Above all, Kelly must get it into his head that he could not afford to slack off. 'I look upon Orpen & Nicholson as your most serious rivals at the moment, & while both of them have recently advanced in public estimation you have stood still . . . I am extremely disappointed that you will have nothing for the summer exhibitions. Do not be angry with me for thrusting all this good advice upon you: it is caused by a real affection & a great admiration.'

Maugham's real affection was undented even after he discovered that Kelly had slept with Sue, his friend's 'odious treachery' referred to by letter in a self-consciously jocular tone. Increasingly it was being borne in on Maugham that Sue was by nature promiscuous, and that she regularly slept not only with him but with a dismayingly large number of his acquaintance, including not only Kelly but also Walter Payne and Ivor Back, Kelly's chum from the Chat Blanc. 'All my friends had been to bed with her,' Maugham wrote, with understandable exaggeration. 'That sounds as though she was something of a wanton. She wasn't. There was no vice in her . . . It wasn't lasciviousness. It was her nature.' Quite simply, Sue enjoyed sex, had no moral inhibitions about it and took it for granted when a man took her out to dinner that she would go to bed with him afterwards. As Kelly put it, Willie was 'the only man she ever really loved . . . [but] this did not keep her from continuing her promiscuous ways'. But now Maugham, who, as he justly admitted, was fairly promiscuous himself, began to believe that he might want to marry her. For a while he had been passionately in love and he still adored her: did it matter that she was not exclusively his? Now that the physical side of the affair was less urgent, was sexual jealousy really an issue? 'There was no one I liked better,' he reasoned, '[and] why should I bother . . . that she had been to bed with so many of my friends?. . . notwithstanding her moral looseness, she was a very good and a very sweet woman.' He was now in his mid-thirties and if he were going to settle down he should do it before long; Sue had recently obtained a divorce from her husband, and without exactly putting it into words gave the impression that she would not be averse to marrying again; so the time seemed to be right.

It was a courageous decision to take, but, like most men of his class and generation whose sexual tastes were unorthodox, Maugham set enormous store by an appearance of conventionality. While by no means wishing to suppress his homosexual tendencies, he was encouraged by the fact that he could also find women attractive, and this misled him into believing that he was, as he put it, three-quarters 'normal' and only a quarter 'queer'. Marriage might swing the balance further in the desired direction, and would at least allow him to pass as straight in polite society. As John Halliwell expresses it in *A Man of Honour*, 'One has to be very strong and very sure of oneself to go against the ordinary view of things. And if one isn't, perhaps it's better not to run any risks, but just to walk along the same secure old road as the common herd. It's not exhilarating, it's not brave, and it's rather dull. But it's eminently safe.' Sue's accepting nature was an important part of her appeal, and so was the fact that she was from a theatrical milieu, with the theatre's traditional tolerance of the irregular and nonconformist, a tolerance Maugham knew very well he was unlikely to find among his own kin. Both his surviving brothers, Charles and F.H., were solidly established husbands and fathers, both hardworking lawyers, both pillars of bourgeois respectability. After Harry's shocking suicide all evidence of undesirable friendships in that quarter had been successfully hushed up, and clearly it was unthinkable that anything of the kind could be allowed to surface again within the family. Maugham, ever the outsider, had little wish to lead the life his brothers led, six days a week in the office and a bucket-and-spade holiday once a year; and yet there was a part of him that felt a strong urge to conform, to play the role of English gentleman, with a wife to run his home, entertain his friends and provide him with children.

And marriage need not necessarily mean a complete change in direction, as long as the proprieties were observed. In the capital, with its vast homosexual population, a thriving subculture existed, a discreet network of contacts, with every variety of male prostitution, from expert professionals in Mayfair brothels to rent-boys in Piccadilly, from the off-duty Guardsman hanging round the music-halls, manly in his scarlet uniform, to the part-time amateurs, the waiters, shop-boys and domestic servants who cruised the parks and loitered on street corners on their evenings off in the hope of picking up a 'tante', as the slang expression had it, and adding a few shillings to their weekly wage. Famous throughout Europe were the Turkish Baths in Jermyn Street, where not only the clients but the entire staff from management to masseurs and chiropodists were homosexual. The running of the Baths was conducted so decorously that the police turned a blind eye to what they knew perfectly well was going on inside, an arrangement much appreciated particularly by the more socially prominent of the Baths' patrons. For a man like Maugham, highly sexed but extremely guarded, and terrified of exposure, consorting with rent-boys was too risky (Wilde told Reggie Turner that his doom was sealed when he saw the rent-boys outside Swan & Edgar's, the Piccadilly department store, while shopping with his wife); the Jermyn Street Baths were more secure, but for his fastidious nature there was something distasteful about such a blatantly open market-place. Preferable by far were the 'safe houses' provided by sympathetic hostesses, among whom Ada Leverson was queen, where like-minded gentlemen, married and single, could meet and make their arrangements without any fear of scandal ensuing.

In conventional society Maugham's ambidexterity was unsuspected, and his good looks, growing fame and an attractive diffidence in manner charmed many. Both men and women found his appearance intriguing. 'What has stayed clear in my memory', wrote the novelist Louis Marlow, 'is the look of that unbelieving and guarded face that seemed so beau-tifully and smoothly, so strongly worked, as in rare ivory: that look of an ancient civilization, Orientally luxurious and wise.' Women were particularly fascinated by him, by his way of seeming to give them his undivided attention, apparently absorbed in their every word; and there was, too, a slight air of mystery about him, about his personality and his emotional focus that unquestionably added to his glamour. Ada Leverson in one of her novels drew a portrait of him at this period, remarkable for the acuteness of its observation. In *The Limit*, the character closely based on Maugham is Gilbert Hereford Vaughan, known to his friends as Gillie. Vaughan, a 'pale, dark, and rather handsome young man' of thirty-four, is an immensely popular playwright, much sought after as a guest at fashionable parties.

> He behaved like anybody else, except that perhaps his manner was a little quieter than the average. Unless one was very observant . . . he did not at first appear too alarmingly clever. He had one or two characteristics which must have at times led to misunderstandings. One was that whatever or

whoever he looked at, his dark opaque eyes were so full of vivid expression that women often mistook for admiration what was often merely observation.

The Sphinx caught exactly Maugham's technique of dealing with reactions to his success, his way of deflecting jealousy and accusations of vanity.

> Knowing that Miss Luscombe, hoping for a part, would be painfully 'nice' to Vaughan, Harry had good-naturedly placed them as far apart as possible. Nevertheless she leaned across the table and said –
>
> 'How *do* you think of all these clever things, Mr Vaughan? I can't think how you do it!'
>
> 'Yes, indeed, we'd all like to know that,' said Captain Foster . . .
>
> 'It's perfectly easy, really,' said Vaughan, 'it's just a knack.'
>
> 'Is it though?'
>
> 'That's all.'
>
> 'How do you get the things taken?'
>
> 'Oh, that's a mere fluke – a bit of luck,' said Vaughan . . .
>
> Vaughan always used this exaggerated modesty as an armour against envy . . . he remained quiet, reserved, and as apparently modest as ever.

Discreet reference is made to a secret private life, the nature of which is of great interest to many an unattached young lady hoping to ensnare him, and the Sphinx deals cleverly with the subject by inventing an entanglement with an innkeeper's daughter, which has to be kept from the public gaze. The appearance in the story of Gladys, 'who is coarse and common', may well indicate something of Ada's feelings about Sue, who was likely to have been resented as the young and beautiful object of Maugham's affections.

As with *Penelope*, the theme of Maugham's next play, *Smith*, has echoes of a work by Barrie, of his 1902 play, *The Admirable Crichton*, in which the servant turns out to be an infinitely superior being to his masters. In *Smith* it is a pretty young parlourmaid, a farmer's daughter, whose integrity is in such striking contrast to the venality and selfishness of her employers that she wins the heart of the hero, the young man of the family. *Smith*, produced by Frohman at the Comedy Theatre, had its first night on 30 September 1909, the third Maugham play to be staged that year: *Penelope* had opened in January, and in March *The Noble Spaniard*, an adaptation by Maugham of a French farce, *Les Gaietés de veuvage*, by Ernest Grenet-Dancourt. In the role of Smith was the ravishingly pretty nineteen-year-old Marie Löhr, for whom the part had been written. Although so young,

Marie Löhr was already making her mark, having enjoyed a notable success the previous year in Shaw's *Getting Married*, and it was hardly surprising if rumours began circulating about her relationship to one of London's most celebrated playwrights. Nellie Maugham, F.H.'s wife, and an inveterate matchmaker, had been energetic in her attempts to introduce her brother-in-law to eligible girls, and Marie Löhr had been one, invited to dinner at Kensington Park Gardens to meet him. A slender ash-blonde, she had arrived looking wonderfully romantic in pink tulle with a rose in her hair. Maugham took her to a dance, she went down to join him for a few days in the country where he was staying to put the finishing touches to *Smith*, and Gerald Kelly was soon being urged to paint her portrait, although, unlike the portraits of Sue, there was no suggestion that Maugham would pay for it. However, if Nellie hoped that anything further would develop she was to be disappointed: it remained nothing more than a friendship. 'I was very fond of him,' said Miss Löhr, 'and we used to have great fun.'

With so many demands on his time, Maugham found it increasingly necessary to leave London in order to write. Sometimes he would run down to Brighton for a few days and put up at the Metropole, and there was an inn at Taplow in Buckinghamshire which he liked as it was near a golf-course, and golf had become something of a passion. With writing such a sedentary occupation, Maugham was aware that exercise was important: he was vain about his figure, but more importantly he needed to keep fit in order to bolster the fragile health that had been his since childhood, which left him vulnerable particularly to respiratory and lung infections. To this end he rode, he walked, he played squash at the Bath Club once a week, but there were few pastimes he enjoyed more than a game of golf. When working on *Penelope* in 1908 he had found a hotel in an idyllic location, Varenna, on the shores of Lake Como, and he returned there the following year to convalesce after a bout of what was probably pleurisy, and to write *Smith*. Varenna was beautiful, the mountain air was exactly what he needed after several weeks in a nursing-home, and there was an excellent golf-course. When his play was nearing completion he invited Kelly and several other friends to join him, Walter Payne, Mrs Steevens, Netta Syrett, who had remained a friend since their time together in Paris, and his brother F.H., also a keen golfer. 'Lovely day. Golf afternoon . . . After d[inner] won 12f at bridge,' F.H. noted contentedly in his diary.

Leaving England in search of seclusion in order to write had little to do with Maugham's wanderlust, which was to be one of the great driving forces of his life – 'that aching to be off & abroad which I know so well', as he described it to Kelly. 'I am neither so happy, nor so amused, nor so comfortable on my travels as I am in London, & yet I cannot get over the restlessness which drives me forth.' Right into extreme old age, it was this restlessness which compelled him to be frequently on the move, and whenever he could spare time from his professional commitments he would take off. As well as to Varenna, he went in 1908 to Madrid, Constantinople, Bursa, Capri and Corfu; in 1909 to Paris, Antwerp and Brussels and for a walking holiday in the Peloponnese; in 1910, the year of his first visit to the United States, he was also in the south of France, Milan, Athens and Venice. 'Really it is with the greatest difficulty that I can keep that purple patch out of my letter,' he wrote to Kelly from Greece. 'Birds are singing all round me. There is a wood just below, olive-trees & cypresses, poplars breaking into leaf, & fig-trees; & then rolling hills, ramp upon ramp, snow-capped in the distance & all rosy in the setting sun . . . it is all beautiful.'

Sometimes Walter Payne went with him, more often he was on his own. In cities he liked to go the theatre and spend hours in picture galleries, the contents of which would be discussed at length in letters to Kelly. Other matters were touched on, too. In their different ways both men fully appreciated the freedom of being out of reach of the pressures of English society. Kelly in Paris revelled in the intoxicating sense of liberty brought about by escape from what he called 'the fantastic conventions and prejudices that surrounded people's sex-experiences in London'. For obvious reasons this applied in even greater measure to Maugham. Brought up in France, he was frequently reduced to a state of exasperation by English prudishness. 'To me England has been a country where I had obligations that I did not want to fulfil and responsibilities that irked me,' he observed. 'I have never felt entirely myself till I had put at least the Channel between my native country* and me.' Whenever the chance offered he took it. 'An amiable person has offered to take me on a motor tour through France,' he wrote cheerily to Kelly in 1907, confident his friend would pick up the implication. At sea en route to Naples in 1907 he reported, 'I met an Egyptian pasha who fell a victim to my charms & made me proposals of a nature which could not be mistaken . . . [though] I declined with a haughty gesture, I could not remain insensible to the compliment.' In 1909 he went with Reggie Turner to Florence,

---

* Although born in the British Embassy and thus technically on British soil, in literal terms France was Maugham's native country, but he always regarded himself as English to the core.

like Capri home to a sizeable community of homosexual expatriates; they stayed in an apartment on the Lung'Arno, where they were joined by Louis Marlow and a young friend of his, and Reggie held centre-stage with his stories about the late, great Oscar. Reggie, 'a living link with Oscar and all those ancient buggeries', in Marlow's words, liked and admired Maugham. 'Ah, yes, yes, I know. He's very good, I know. And good to be with. But not as good as Oscar. Not like Oscar. Oh, no, he'd never be like Oscar!'

It was in Varenna in October 1909 that Maugham wrote most of his next play, *The Tenth Man*, which was something of a departure from form. With the exception of *A Man of Honour* and *The Explorer*, all Maugham's dramatic work so far had been light-hearted social comedy. Only one play, 'Mrs Beamish',* had failed to find a producer; the others, from *Lady Frederick* to *Smith*, had been popular with audiences and highly rewarding in financial terms for their author. Maugham had been candid, perhaps too candid, about his facility in turning out this kind of material, not troubling to conceal how effortlessly ideas came to him, how easily and quickly the plays were written. 'I think the difficulty of play-writing has been much exaggerated,' he wrote airily. 'I had always half a dozen plays in my head, and when a theme presented itself to me it did so divided into scenes and acts, with each "curtain" staring me in the face, so that I should have had no difficulty in beginning a new play the day after I had finished one.'

Rather rashly he had given a newspaper interview in which he expressed his impatience with tragedy and with the weighty play of ideas, light-heartedly arguing that it was most unwise for playwrights to take themselves seriously as the first, perhaps the only, aim of the playwright was to entertain. Such self-deprecating mockery was misplaced, and widely misunderstood by the critics. Max Beerbohm was one of several who went on the attack. 'If light comedy is the only form that he cares to practise now, let him devote himself to that, by all means. But it is hardly gracious in him to gibe at other men who, conscientiously, but unre-muneratively, are treading the path to which his own first ambitions led him.' William Archer, who had criticised *Penelope* for slovenly work-manship, accused Maugham of failing to make allowance 'for the wide divergency of tastes, and for the fact that many people . . . are at least as

---

* 'Mrs Beamish', about a respectable middle-aged couple forced into revealing the shocking fact that they are not married and that their priggish son is therefore illegit-imate, was never produced nor published and exists only in manuscript, deposited in the Library of Congress in Washington.

willing to be entertained by plays with "a great central idea" as by empty trivialities'. The dramatist St John Hankin, a ruthless realist whose plays were said to make even Ibsen look cheerful, came in at slightly different angle. In an article headed 'The Tragedy of Mr Maugham's Dramatic Success', he argued that it was bitterly ironic that when Maugham was writing plays of substance and quality they were consistently rejected, but now that he was producing mere lightweight confections, theatrical London was at his feet.

But Maugham knew what he was doing: he understood his audiences and knew how to provide them with what they wanted. As the critic Desmond MacCarthy wrote of Maugham's plays, 'They were just cynical enough to make the sentimental-worldly think themselves tough-minded while they were enjoying them, and just brilliant enough to satisfy a London audience's far from exacting standard of wit.' Popular success, however, did not mean he was unaffected by adverse criticism, and over the years he repeatedly returned to a defence of his stance. 'The critics accused me of writing down to the public,' he wrote in his autobiographical work *The Summing Up*. 'I did not exactly do that . . . [but I] wrote my comedies with those sides of myself only that were useful to my purpose. They were designed to please and they achieved their aim.' It was from this point, when he first achieved fame as a dramatist, that he believed his rejection by the intelligentsia began, a rejection that continued to rankle, despite frequent denials, for the rest of his life. 'The intelligentsia, of which I had been a modest, but respected member, not only turned a cold shoulder on me . . . but flung me, like Lucifer, headlong into the bottomless pit. I was taken aback and a trifle mortified.' In an attempt to redress the balance, with his next two plays, *The Tenth Man* and *Grace*, he deliberately set out to change tack and return to more serious treatment and themes. Unfortunately, neither was successful and it was more than two years before Maugham felt able to return to playwriting. 'I am tired & bored,' he wrote to Golding Bright at the end of 1909. 'After this I am going to give play-writing a rest for some time. Four plays in the last two years & eight productions! I really think I have the right to slack off for a few months.'

*The Tenth Man*, produced by Frohman and Arthur Bourchier, deals with greed, corruption and a wretchedly unhappy marriage, with divorce denied the miserable wife as it would ruin the careers in Parliament both of her husband, whom she hates, and of the man she loves. The shocking denouement is brought about by a shrewd North Country politician. 'You've got through the world by knowing that nine men out of ten are rascals,' he tells the unscrupulous husband. 'You've forgotten that the tenth man must cross your path at last.' The play opened at the Globe on 24 February 1910, was described as 'dull' and 'stale' by the press, and ran for a mere six weeks. 'It went very flat on the first night,' Maugham reported to Ada Leverson, '& the critics are unduly severe. Mais je m'en fouts, j'm'en refouts, et j'm'en triple fouts . . .'

*Grace*, later retitled *Landed Gentry*, is based on a theme from *The Merry-Go-Round*, that of Grace Castillyon (Insoley in the play) and her caddish lover, Reggie. In this later version the Reggie character is a much nicer young man than his original, and the plot treats not of his affair with Grace, which is more or less over before the action begins, but of Grace's crisis of conscience: she is forced to compare her own moral status with that of a gamekeeper's daughter who commits suicide after bearing an illegitimate child. Presented by Frohman at the Duke of York's on 15 October 1910, *Grace* ran for only slightly longer than *The Tenth Man*, despite enthusiastic reviews for the star, Irene Vanbrugh, in the title role and for Lady Tree, wife of Sir Herbert Beerbohm Tree, in the part of Grace's horrible old mother-in-law. Among a number of carping notices, particularly damning was the critic in the *Saturday Review* (not Max Beerbohm, who had recently resigned), who concluded that Maugham has 'worked his puppets too long . . . [and] lost the trick of handling flesh and blood'. The author himself accepted his two failures philosophically enough, recognising that the plays 'were neither frankly realistic nor frankly theatrical'.

Certainly he was not cast down by two such minor setbacks. At thirty-six Maugham was riding high and enjoying his life immensely. 'I was happy, I was prosperous, I was busy,' as he remarked; he was also famous, and everyone wanted to know him. Under a sedate exterior the fashionable playwright was energetic and high-spirited, capable of a flippant gaiety that was as unsuspected as it was engaging. Described as 'one of London's wittiest bachelors and most indefatigable dancers', he was deluged with invitations and was seen everywhere: in white tie and tails at dances and first nights; two-stepping in Spanish fancy-dress at the Chelsea Arts Ball; joining a vigorous barn-dance at a charity evening at Covent Garden. He attended luncheons and dinners in Mayfair and Kensington, the next afternoon, immaculate in frock coat, top hat and spats, calling, as etiquette demanded, on his hostess of the night before.

> If she was not at home, which you fervently prayed she would not be, you left two cards . . . but if she was . . . [you] were shown upstairs to the drawing-room. You made such conversation as you could for ten minutes,

and then, picking up your hat, which you had laid on the floor beside you, took your leave. When the front door was closed behind you, you heaved a great sense of relief.

Gerald Kelly brilliantly captured Maugham at this period in his portrait *The Jester*. Recently returned to London, Kelly had taken a studio in Knightsbridge, and here Maugham had called on him one day wearing morning dress and a grey topper. '[He] had started to dress himself in a very dapper way,' Kelly recalled, 'and came in delightedly to show me his grey hat.' On a chair in front of an ornate Coromandel screen, the play-wright is seen sitting bright-eyed and alert, one leg casually crossed over the other, hat slightly tilted, shoes shining, gloves immaculate, one hand resting on a slender gold-tipped cane, the perfect picture of the Edwardian dandy, the debonair man-about-town.

With a substantial income at his disposal, Maugham had bought for £8,000 an 800-year lease of an elegant, five-storey Georgian house, 6 Chesterfield Street, right in the heart of Mayfair, jokingly referred to as 'the house that Frohman built'. Here he planned to move with Walter Payne, but first there was a great deal of work to be done on it and furniture to buy: 'your house is being entirely redecorated', he told Frohman. 'You will not know 6 Chesterfield Street when you come.' Maugham's greatest pleasure was in buying pictures for the house, including an Orpen, a couple of landscapes by Wilson Steer, whom he knew slightly, and on the advice of Sir Hugh Lane, founder of the Municipal Gallery of Modern Art in Dublin, a Samuel de Wilde of two actors in a scene from *Sylvester Daggerwood*; this was followed by the purchase of a Zoffany, for £22, of David Garrick and Mrs Cibber in *Venice Preserv'd*, and a small version of Reynolds's *Garrick between Comedy and Tragedy*, both paintings once owned by Sir Henry Irving. These two pictures were the first in what was to grow into a notable collection of over forty theatrical paint-ings, some picked up in junk shops for only a few pounds, eventually bequeathed to the National Theatre.

Between periods of intensely concentrated work, Maugham continued his busy and glamorous social life, as always fascinated to observe the morals and mores of the sophisticated circles which he was invited to join, all stored away as useful material for his fiction. As the critic Desmond MacCarthy wrote of him, Maugham moved through London society 'with the reserve and detachment of a professional man of letters'. Maugham was intrigued to learn, for instance, that the upper classes 'still talked as though to run the British Empire were their private business. It gave me a peculiar sensation to hear it discussed, when a general election was in the air, whether Tom should have the Home Office and whether Dick would be satisfied with Ireland.' Among his recent acquaintance was an ambitious political hostess, daughter of Lady St Helier and wife to a wealthy member of Parliament. With Dorothy Allhusen, Maugham conducted the same kind of affectionate, flirtatious friendship that he maintained with other older women friends, such as Ada Leverson and Violet Hunt. ('My dear Mrs Allhusen, You are a faithless woman. You promise me with all the earnestness in the world that you will write to me, though you have left me without so much as a picture postcard . . . I miss you very much.') The Allhusens had a large country house at Stoke Poges in Buckinghamshire, and here Maugham became a frequent guest at weekend house-parties, where there was always an interesting mix of politicians, writers and eminent members of the armed forces. 'Thank you so much for my jolly week-end,' he wrote to his hostess after one such occasion. 'It is just the sort of rest I like, getting so tired that you go to bed for the remainder of the week.'

It was at Stoke Court that Maugham first met Winston Churchill, then a Cabinet minister in Asquith's government and recently married to Dorothy Allhusen's cousin Clementine Hozier. There was a golf-course near by and the two men often played together in the afternoon, returning to the house for a substantial tea followed by a glittering and formal dinner. It was late one night when the ladies had retired to bed and the men, changed into smoking jackets, were talking over their brandy and cigars that Churchill was startled by an intervention of Maugham's: a young man, very full of himself, had been holding forth at length, in the writer's view talking complete nonsense, when suddenly Maugham broke in and with one sentence, witty but devastating, silenced him. Everyone burst out laughing, but the next morning Churchill came up to Maugham as he was peacefully reading the Sunday papers. 'I want to make a compact with you,' he said. 'If you will promise never to be funny at my expense, I will promise never to be funny at yours.'

Gratified although he was to be in such demand, and much as he relished seeing this side of life, Maugham was by no means at everyone's beck and call. In February 1910 he felt obliged to rebuke Ada Leverson, who had made the mistake of presuming too much on her intimacy by allowing a friend of hers whom Maugham did not know to approach him. 'My dear Sphynx, Pray thank your friend for her kind invitation,' he began. 'I will not accept it. It is a very impertinent thing to invite a total stranger to dine with you. There are certain recognized methods of making the acquaintance of anyone one wants to know & I do not see why they should be neglected because I happen to be a writer . . '

The London season of 1910 had barely begun when on 6 May the death was announced of Edward VII, thus technically bringing to an end the Edwardian era, although it was to continue in all but name until 1914. Maugham was in Italy most of that month, writing to Violet Hunt that he was glad to be out of England 'during the dreary time of public mourning', when theatres were doing little business and society was in the doldrums. It was fortuitous that it was at this time that he was preparing to make his first journey across the Atlantic. For some while Frohman had been urging him to come. *Mrs Dot*, *Smith* and *Penelope* had opened in New York, and *Lady Frederick*, as Maugham proudly told Pinker, 'is one of the greatest successes they have had lately in America'. Originally having planned to go to the States the previous year, he had been forced by illness to postpone the trip. Now, however, he was ready. 'I am sailing by the *Caronia* on the 22nd of October,' he wrote to Frohman, full of high spirits, picturing himself setting out to sea, he told Bright, 'like Christopher Columbus in conquest of America'.

# 6

## Syrie

On 22 October 1910 Maugham sailed from Liverpool on the SS *Caronia*, one of the largest and most elegant vessels in the Cunard fleet. The days of travelling on the cheap were over: from now, wherever possible during the next half-century, Maugham was to journey *en prince*, enjoying a standard of comfort which nowhere was to be more sumptuously provided than by the European liners on the North Atlantic route. On this, the first of numerous crossings over many years, Maugham found the first-class accommodation discreetly luxurious, if not quite comparable to the operatic levels of opulence soon to be displayed in ships such as the *Aquitania*, the *Mauretania* and the ill-fated *Titanic*. On the *Caronia*, for instance, private bathrooms were almost non-existent, even top-echelon passengers mostly making do with baths down the corridor and a commode beside the bed. The crossing took six days, and on arrival in New York Maugham went straight from the noise and bustle of the pier to his hotel, the de-luxe St Regis, a seventeen-storey Beaux Arts bastion on Fifth Avenue in the heart of midtown Manhattan. Built in 1903, the St Regis was the first of the high-rise hotels, regarded as the last word in grandeur and modernity, with electric elevators, bedside telephones and even a primitive form of air-conditioning. Near by on Fifth Avenue the old order was imposingly represented by the monolithic mansions of the Astors and Vanderbilts, while all around was evidence of the new, with fast-rising skyscrapers, neon signs, honking motor traffic, the subway, electric trams and elevated railway.

On Broadway Maugham's name was already familiar: there had been an acclaimed production of *Lady Frederick* with Ethel Barrymore, followed by *Mrs Dot* with Billie Burke, by Marie Tempest in *Penelope*, and *Smith* which had opened at the Empire in September and was doing excellent business with Mary Boland in the title role. Thanks to Charles Frohman's enthusiastic welcome and a number of prominent introductions, Maugham found himself much in demand, lavishly entertained at the most expensive restaurants. 'I am booked up for luncheon & dinner every day for the next week . . . [and] enjoying myself like anything,' he reported soon after his arrival. He quickly became quite a celebrity, with his courteous manners, 'English' reserve and exquisitely tailored clothes. The *New York Times*, taking note of the 'host of social entertainments [given] in his honor', observed that 'Mr Maugham [is] the most socially popular English playwright that has visited America in years.'

One New Yorker on whom he made an unforgettable impression was his 'Mrs Dot': Billie Burke. A vivacious redhead, whose father had toured Europe and America as a clown in P.T. Barnum's circus, Billie Burke had begun her career singing in music-hall in England at the age of fourteen, and was now a popular comedienne working to establish herself as a straight actress, an ambition considerably furthered by her success in Maugham's play. To her, Maugham's elegance was more Parisian than Bond Street, 'with his swallowtails and striped trousers, piping on his coat, smart gloves, a stick, beautifully made shoes, a grey top hat with a black band, and his briskly clipped moustache'. Maugham, who liked the company of pretty women, was entertained by the actress's high spirits and flattered by her obvious admiration. After the show the two went dancing together and to theatrical parties, often in the company of the beautiful star, Maxine Elliott, and, also over from England, Johnston Forbes-Robertson, whose actress wife was Maxine Elliott's sister. One night after a party it was decided they should all go on to a nightclub at the Astor. 'We were not members and it was late, about 2 A.M.,' Billie Burke remembered, '[but] over we went to the party . . . [and down] the red-carpeted grand staircase of the Hotel Astor ballroom . . . I can permit myself to say "made an entrance", for no actress in her right mind would attempt less in descending a great staircase on the arm of Somerset Maugham.' In her memoirs she recalled 'his great smouldering brown eyes', adding wistfully, 'Ah yes, Mr Maugham, so you had, and I was a little in love with you, sir.'

Miss Burke was not the only one to be smitten, and it was inevitable that a number of women came to consider Maugham as ideal husband-material. After all, here was a man, handsome, famous and rich, whose subject was marriage, and yet he was not married. His continuing relationship with Sue Jones was known only to a few, and his penchant for members of his own sex was kept even more of a secret. He was frequently teased by matchmaking ladies anxious to be the one to find the playwright a wife. Replying to one of these, Maria Fleming, an American divorcée living in England, Maugham wrote jokingly, 'I note that you have found me a wife & I shall be interested to see her . . .

[I expect] she is thin & peaky with a narrow sunken chest & bent shoulders.'

A friendship Maugham was particularly anxious to renew while in New York was with a fellow playwright, the twenty-four-year-old Edward (Ned) Sheldon, known as the Boy Wonder of Broadway. Sheldon, son of a wealthy Chicago real-estate dealer, had made a sensation by writing two immensely successful plays, one while he was still at Harvard. Obsessed by the theatre from an early age, Sheldon, tall and dark, was clever, sensitive, charming and urbane; he was also rich and very handsome: there had been an intense infatuation with the actress Doris Keane, although it had come to nothing. Sheldon, like Maugham, was somewhat ambivalent in his sexuality. In 1909 he had visited Europe, which was probably when he and Maugham first met, returning in the summer of 1910, when he saw Maugham in London. Maugham found him intensely attractive and hoped for a more physical relationship, but Sheldon was evasive and quick to shy away, with the result that 'there was never the least frankness between them upon the subject of sex'. Nonetheless the two men had a great deal in common and they became devoted friends, with Maugham when in New York often staying at Sheldon's exotically furnished apartment on Gramercy Park – French furniture, Venetian glass, gunmetal mirrors, thick black carpets and live macaws on perches.

From New York Maugham went for a few days to Boston, where he dined with Henry James, who was then staying with his recently widowed sister-in-law in Cambridge. Maugham's attitude to James's work over the years was to grow increasingly equivocal, a mixture of impatience and admiration, impatience with what he saw as a lack of that empathy essential to a novelist and admiration for a superb technique. 'The great novelists, even in seclusion, have lived life passionately,' Maugham wrote. 'Henry James was content to observe it from a window . . . He had humour, insight, subtlety, a sense of drama; but a triviality of soul that made the elemental emotions of mankind . . . incomprehensible to him.' Maugham had met James on a couple of occasions in London and had been intrigued by him, if slightly irritated by the atmosphere of *cher maître*, the great man's expectation of reverence and homage. Nonetheless he found him good company, witty when in the mood, and he was pleased to see him again, enjoying the intimate evening *à trois*, although it was obvious that James on this occasion was in a nervous and unhappy frame of mind: grieving over the death of his brother William, he was also pining to return to England, restless and ill at ease in the land of his birth. As Maugham prepared to leave, James insisted on accompanying him to the corner where he would catch the street-car back to Boston.

> I protested that I was perfectly capable of getting there by myself, but he would not hear of it, not only on account of the kindness and the great courtesy which were natural to him, but also because America seemed to him a strange and terrifying labyrinth in which without his guidance I was bound to get hopelessly lost . . . The street-car hove in sight and Henry James was seized with agitation. He began waving frantically when it was still a quarter of a mile away. He was afraid it wouldn't stop, and he besought me to jump on with the greatest agility of which I was capable . . . I was so infected by his anxiety that when the car pulled up and I leapt on, I had almost the sensation that I had had a miraculous escape from certain death. I saw him standing on his short legs in the middle of the road, looking after the car, and I felt that he was trembling still at my narrow shave.

Before returning to New York Maugham spent four days in Washington. It was here that he received a letter from a Joseph Beaumont Maugham, a member of the American branch of the Maughams, inviting him down to Tenafly, New Jersey to meet the head of the family, Ralph S. Maugham, a schoolteacher and local dignitary. Joseph Beaumont, known as Monty, turned out to be a sensitive-looking young man of eighteen, with dark hair and eyes. Maugham was taken aback by the similarities. 'There was a striking family likeness,' he recalled. 'But the oddest thing of all was that the young man spoke with a pronounced stammer.' Following instructions, Maugham went by trolley-car to Tenafly, a village a few miles up the Hudson, where he had a long talk with his kinsman: Ralph Maugham's father, it transpired, had emigrated from London to Connecticut in the 1850s; although no definite connection was established between his branch of the family and that of Robert Ormond Maugham, Willie Maugham's father, it appeared that they, too, were of humble stock and came from the same area of the north of England.

Upon his arrival back in England in December 1910, Maugham was immediately faced with two conflicting demands, his work and the decoration and furnishing of Chesterfield Street. The first and most urgent requirement was to put the finishing touches to *Loaves and Fishes*, the comedy about the irrepressible Canon Spratte, which was due to go into rehearsal after Christmas. Written as long ago as 1903, *Loaves and Fishes* had failed to arouse any interest at the time, and having subsequently been reshaped as a novel, *The Bishop's Apron*, was now returned to the form for which it had originally been intended. It opened at the Duke of York's on 24 February, yet despite a polished Frohman–Boucicault production and an enthusiastic first night it ran for only a few weeks. Maugham had been much congratulated by his colleagues: 'Barrie thinks it far & away the best thing I have ever done, Sutro is enthusiastic, & others – Knoblock*, for instance – have written to me long & excited letters'. He himself had been well pleased with it, and consequently he was bemused by the audience's reaction: 'The public goes & laughs, but on the way out expresses its dislike – it is the parson that does it.' As he explained, 'People are shocked to see a clergyman made fun of on the stage & they won't come.' Continuing to ponder, he reached a further conclusion, one that was characteristically clear-sighted in the assessment of his professional standing. 'I think it possible that the public is just tired of me,' he told Gerald Kelly.

> That is an eventuality to which I have always looked forward, & it leaves me calm. I can give them a rest for a year or two, & then they will have forgotten, & come back to my work with avidity. I have put into three years & a half what most dramatists would have given ten years to, & it would not be surprising if my characteristics have become tedious.

Fortunately Maugham could easily afford to step back and consider his position. For the past fifteen years, since the writing of *Liza of Lambeth*, he had worked unceasingly, producing an astonishing quantity of material; now, thanks to the large sums coming in every week from both sides of the Atlantic and to Walter Payne's prudent investments, he could allow himself some leisure. For such a prolific and successful writer, the failure of one production, regrettable, of course, was no serious matter. Frohman was unconcerned, indeed was offering the enormous sum of £10,000 for a new play as a vehicle for Billie Burke, but Maugham was uninterested in the proposal and turned it down. Billie Burke after her triumph in New York was going to California in *Mrs Dot*, 'which will bring me in anything from two to three thousand pounds', as Maugham told Kelly, '& John Drew† goes on with *Smith* till June so I shall still be able to pay for the house without touching my capital.'

The workmen were finally on the point of leaving, and Maugham was anxious to give the house his full attention. He and Walter Payne were to continue their amicable arrangement of cohabiting, Payne having left the

---

* Edward Knoblock (1874–1945), American playwright who spent most of his professional life in England.

† John Drew (1853–1927), American actor, popular in light comedy; his sister Georgiana was the mother of the three famous Barrymores, Ethel, Lionel and John.

Bar in order to take over his late father's music-hall and theatrical business. The two men, with the assistance of a decorator friend, a Mr Howard, now threw themselves into the creation of an elegant townhouse, choosing furniture, buying carpets and giving careful thought to the hanging of pictures. 'Howard has been very kind to us,' Maugham reported to Kelly. 'His advice has been extremely useful, & his taste seems excellent . . . [although] I do not share his admiration for the massive & gilded: the only thing I am quite sure I like gilded is sin.' Kelly, who on his friend's recommendation was spending some months in Spain, was in receipt of a stream of letters asking him to find various ornaments – pottery, glass, pictures, fabric. In pride of place opposite the fireplace in the drawing-room was Kelly's *Jester*, 'one of the best things you have done', as Maugham told him. 'You cannot think how fine my portrait looks in its new frame, so distinguished, & it is real decoration,' he wrote, adding proudly, 'Everyone who comes expresses admiration of the house . . . [and] my own room, the long one upstairs, is a great success.' This was Maugham's writing-room, and in contrast to the lower floors was sparsely equipped, a wide, bare room with two narrow sash windows facing the street and in the centre a rough deal table serving as a desk. The final task before moving in was the hiring of staff – cook, housemaid and a butler, Croft, who doubled as valet, accompanying his employer when he went away for the weekend. The finished results were entirely satisfactory. 'I have never been so comfortable in my life,' Maugham declared. One of the early visitors to Chesterfield Street, the novelist Hugh Walpole, described number 6 as 'a gay discreet bandbox of a house in Mayfair that became for many of us one of the happiest, most hospitable, most amusing houses in London'. Walpole never forgot being shown round by his host. 'I was, I remember, from the very first struck by the strange contrast of the lower social part of the house and the room on the top floor where he did his work. That top floor remains, after all these years, as the most ideal spot for a writing man that I have ever seen.'

With the house more or less completed, Maugham was aware of the familiar restlessness taking hold. At Easter he stayed in Paris for a few days. 'This morning I walked down the boulevard,' he wrote to Kelly, '& I felt once more that wonderful elation of one's first day in Paris. My mind was so active, I seemed to walk on air: I caught on the wing (& pinned down for inspection) that rarest of all prizes, a moment of pure, complete happiness.'

In June, a month of stiflingly hot weather, he went with Payne to Le Touquet to avoid the festivities surrounding the coronation of George V, and then also with Payne for a golfing holiday in Ireland, followed by a short trip to the Balearics before returning to London to prepare for another visit to New York in the autumn. But now he was longing to go further, his mind filled with visions of the Far East, 'with pictures of Bangkok and Shanghai, and the ports of Japan . . . [with] palm-trees and skies blue and hot, dark-skinned people, pagodas; the scents of the Orient'. One mooted project involved Kelly, who was planning a lengthy sojourn in Burma. 'I have half a mind to join you in Burmah for a little,' Maugham told him, '& shall try & persuade you to come on to China with me.' But escape was not to prove as easy as in his imaginings it seemed.

For the previous five years Maugham had been wholly engaged with the theatre, but now his interest had waned. True, there were still minor commissions to be fulfilled: a preface for an edition of his plays to be published by Heinemann in September; two adaptations from the French: *A Trip to Brighton*, from a sketch by Abel Tarride, and a version of *Le Bourgeois Gentilhomme* for Sir Beerbohm Tree. Yet more and more he felt himself drawn towards the writing of a novel. 'After submitting myself for some years to the exigencies of the drama I hankered after the wide liberty of the novel,' he wrote. 'I knew the book I had in mind would be a long one and I wanted to be undisturbed, so I refused the contracts that managers were eagerly offering me and temporarily retired from the stage. I was then thirty-seven.' His theme was predominantly autobio-graphical, much the same as that attempted at the age of twenty-four in 'The Artistic Temperament of Stephen Carey': the story of his childhood and young manhood and of a degrading sexual obsession. This time, however, with greatly increased maturity and confidence, it would be approached without flinching and with an uncompromising adherence to psychological truth. The subject began increasingly to absorb him, the compulsion he felt to write different from anything he had previously known; his memories were literally forcing themselves upon him: 'I had all that stuff choking me, occupying my thoughts by day & my dreams by night, and I wanted to be free of it.'

In order to begin on the work undisturbed he went to stay at the Sunningdale Golf Club in Berkshire, from where he reported that he was making good progress.

> Now that I am well on with it I am very happy. It is a great satisfaction to sit down to it every morning & peg away, without having to bother about whether it is long or dull, or whether this will get across the foot-lights or whether an actress will ever be able to say the other. I am afraid it will be much longer than I could wish, but there is no help for it: I have so much to say . . .

In August he was in Ireland, motoring and again playing golf. 'I brought my book away with me,' he told Dorothy Allhusen,

> but I have done nothing; & yet it is in my thoughts night & day . . . I am so hoping it will be good. So many novels are written in these days that there seems no reason to write one unless it is out of the common, except the pleasure it gives the writer; & that, thank heaven, is something that is independent of the result.

From then on over the next two-and-a-half years came regular reports that the novel was almost finished – and yet somehow the end continued to lie just out of reach, an unfamiliar experience for Maugham, accustomed to completing a work in a matter of weeks. Begun in the autumn of 1911, for an unprecedented advance of £500, the novel was apparently nearing its end the following spring, Maugham writing to Kelly that after a period of intense concentration he had gone over to Paris for a few days 'to clear my brain & rest. I found myself with a month's more work on my novel, but so tired that I feared if I went on I should hurry the end or grow mechanical; & since all I had to write was so clear before me I thought there could be no harm in putting it aside.' But in mid-July William Heinemann received a letter explaining that 'The book is not ready & will not be in time for the autumn season.' The next reference appears in a letter to Kelly dated May 1914: 'I am working hard at the novel & shall have a great deal for you to read when you come back'; yet it is not until autumn of that year that it is clear the book was at last in Heinemann's hands and being prepared for publication for the following August.

Such an unusually long period of gestation was due not only to the size of the project but also to Maugham's reluctance to stay sequestered for more than a few days at a time: there were simply too many distractions. The winter season of 1911, the first after the coronation, was particularly brilliant: the Russian ballet, with Pavlova and Nijinsky, was in London and there were new plays by Sutro, Shaw and Arnold Bennett, all attended by Maugham. Bennett's play, *The Honeymoon*, was 'a disastrous failure . . . monstrously verbose', as Maugham reported to Kelly with a certain relish. 'I met him [Bennett] afterwards at supper chez Marie Tempest,' he continued, lapsing into the kind of mocking commentary he and Kelly used to amuse themselves with on the subject of Enoch Arnold when in Paris.

> He plays the celebrity very well . . . He asked after you, & bade me pass on to you a few kind words of encouragement. His wife has aged in the

last two or three years, & is now thin, lined, & unattractive . . . quite commonplace & provincial . . . She gives an impression of self-effacement. Can it be that Arnold Bennett rules her with the iron rod of the Five Towns?

Another diversion at this time was a brief love affair with a Russian woman, Princess Alexandra Kropotkin, the daughter of Prince Peter Kropotkin, the anarchist–intellectual then living in exile in London. 'Sasha' Kropotkin was a big, voluptuous woman, handsome, with high cheekbones, a wide mouth and slightly protuberant dark eyes. Clever and intense, a friend of socialists such as William Morris and Bernard Shaw, Sasha moved in a circle of Russian artists and revolutionaries, and in this period of European fascination with all things Russian Maugham found it exciting at her parties to make such close contact with Russian history and literature, to meet Diaghilev and Pavlova, to drink vodka and discuss Tolstoy and Dostoevsky with passionate intensity. The two of them went over to Paris for a few days where they stayed at a little hotel on the Left Bank; they visited the Louvre and the Comédie Française, went dancing in a Russian nightclub, and Sasha ate her way through a number of enormous meals with an appetite that slightly appalled her lover.[*] Maugham introduced her to his brother Charles, who was visibly impressed that Willie should be on such intimate terms with a real princess. 'He simply couldn't believe I was fucking anyone so grand,' as Maugham somewhat indelicately phrased it. The affair provided a pleasant interlude, ending after a few weeks 'without acrimony on either side', leaving Maugham free to travel, a lure which he was never able to resist for long. In March 1912 he went to Spain for six weeks, and in August, accompanied by Walter Payne and his brother and sister-in-law, F.H. and Nellie, he undertook a tour to Paris, Prague, Marienbad and Munich; in September while the others returned home he went on by himself to Rome. He was back in London in November, but left again the following month for New York, in order to undertake an unusual piece of research, nothing at all to do with his novel, but for a new play. Entitled *The Land of Promise*, this was first staged in the United States in November 1913, opening in London the following February, where a successful run at the Duke of York's was brought to an abrupt end by the outbreak of war. It was only then that Maugham put the finishing touches to his novel.

---

[*] Maugham drew on this episode for his short story 'Love and Russian Literature' in the *Ashenden* collection.

*Of Human Bondage* is a flawed and magnificent work, showing all the strengths as well as the weaknesses of Maugham as novelist. At 300,000 words and filling sixteen medium-sized notebooks it is the longest and also the most intensely personal of all Maugham's novels, written with an astonishing vitality and drive. 'The teeming memories' which had been so insistently pushing at his consciousness were of his own boyhood and youth, the story of which provides the novel's main plot, a linear narrative told in a style deliberately spare and unadorned: there is none of the softening and prettification that found their way into 'Stephen Carey'. The dominant theme is of the hero's journey towards self-discovery, mainly through the terrifying experience of a masochistic sexual obsession; he believes his search to be for the meaning of life, for the figure in the carpet, which turns out to be as elusive as in Henry James's famous story; although here the revelation that there is no meaning comes as an immense liberation. 'His insignificance was turned to power . . . for, if life was meaningless, the world was robbed of its cruelty.'

The hero, Philip Carey, is a small boy and already fatherless when the story begins with the harrowing death of his mother in childbirth. The boy is put in the charge of his uncle, the Vicar of Blackstable in Kent, a selfish, unloving man, and of his German wife Louisa. As soon as he is old enough Philip is sent to board at the King's School, Tercanbury, where he is wretchedly unhappy: hampered by a club-foot, about which he is painfully self-conscious, he is mercilessly teased, driven into a surly state of friendlessness eventually alleviated by an intense infatuation for another boy, Rose. At sixteen Philip goes for a year to Heidelberg, falling under the influence of an intellectual dilettante similar in every respect to John Ellingham Brooks. Returning to England Philip is taken on as a clerk in a chartered accountant's office in London, but finding the work intolerable gives it up in order to study art in Paris.

It is at this point that the novel first diverges from the precise path of Maugham's life, while still keeping close to the context of his own Parisian experience: the little apartment in Montparnasse, the friendship with Gerald Kelly (Lawson in the novel), the expatriate artists' community, the argumentative dinners at the Chat Blanc (here renamed Gravier's). As Maugham made clear, 'not all the incidents are related as they happened, and some of them are transferred to my hero not from my own life but from that of persons with whom I was intimate'. One such incident involves a fellow student of Philip's, a plain and talentless young woman who develops a hopeless infatuation for him and eventually ends up killing herself, an event which shakes Philip badly. It is soon after this, realising he will never be first rate as a painter, that he returns to London to train as a doctor at St Luke's Hospital.

Philip and one of his fellow students form the habit of dropping in at a nearby tea-shop, and it is here that Philip first sets eyes on his nemesis. Mildred, one of the waitresses, is a pretty but pasty-faced young woman with an offensively offhand manner. 'She was tall and thin, with narrow hips and the chest of a boy . . . the faint green of her delicate skin gave an impression of unhealthiness.' At first annoyed by her snubbing indifference, Philip gradually finds himself perversely attracted, excited by her obvious contempt: 'it was absurd to care what an anaemic little waitress said to him; but he was strangely humiliated'. And so his destructive obsession takes hold. He courts Mildred slavishly, begs for her attention, lavishes whatever presents and treats he can afford on her, and the more scornfully she treats him the more abjectly he crawls back for more. The few times she carelessly allows him to make love to her, his desire, instead of being slaked, burns stronger than ever. He clearly sees that Mildred is stupid, vulgar, humourless and avaricious; he despises himself for his passion but is helpless in its grip. Mildred taunts him, bores him, enrages him; they quarrel violently; sometimes he wants to kill her; but away from her he can think only of seeing her again, of begging her forgiveness, of meekly accepting the humiliations she heaps upon him.

Twice she leaves him for other men, the first time coming back penniless and pregnant, asking Philip to take her in, which he gratefully does. When she leaves him a second time, with Griffiths, a colleague from the hospital, Philip abases himself still further, providing money for the two to go away together, appalled to find that even his feelings of jealousy excite him. '[Philip] was sick with anguish, and yet the torture of it gave him a strange, subtle sensation . . . he was seized with a desire to do horrible, sordid things . . . his whole being yearned for beastliness.' After this Philip loses touch with Mildred, until one day he catches sight of her in Shaftesbury Avenue obviously touting for trade. Horrified, he agrees once more to take her in, but this time realises to his relief that his passion is spent. Mildred is nonplussed, unable to understand that she no longer has any hold over him, and she sulks when he refuses to sleep with her. Typically contrary, she finds his indifference arouses her. 'He never even kissed her now, and she wanted him to . . . She often looked at his mouth.' Eventually there is a hideous scene during which Mildred tries to seduce Philip and fails; his obvious revulsion enrages her, and when he comes home from the hospital the following evening he finds her gone, his two little rented rooms wrecked, his clothes and few possessions in tatters.

It is now that Philip reaches the nadir of his existence. Through an unwise investment of his tiny patrimony, he loses all his money and is left penniless. Not only can he not afford to continue his training, he cannot pay his rent, nor, after the few shillings in his pocket are spent, can he afford to buy food. 'Though he had always been poor, the possibility of not having enough to eat had never occurred to him; it was not the sort of thing that happened to the people among whom he lived . . .' Unable to find work and desperate with hunger, he starts sleeping rough, fortunately rescued at this point by a kindly if eccentric character, Thorpe Athelney, whom Philip had befriended when Athelney was a patient at the hospital. An ebullient, Micawberish figure, father of nine, Athelney takes Philip temporarily into his threadbare but jolly household and procures him a job in a large linen draper's in Oxford Street, a strange world to Philip, required to stand all day at the top of the stairs directing customers, at night sleeping in a squalid dormitory with the other male assistants. After a few months in this ill-paid employment, Philip hears once again from Mildred, asking for his help. Reluctantly he calls at her lodgings, where he finds her ill with venereal disease. He prescribes medicine for her, making her promise to find honest work; the baby is dead, she has only herself to support. Then one evening a few weeks later he catches sight of her in Tottenham Court Road, painted, befeathered and riddled with infection, obviously, despite all her pledges to reform, back on the game. 'He turned away and walked slowly down Oxford Street. "I can't do anything more," he said to himself. That was the end. He did not see her again.'

Soon after this, Philip's fortunes improve. His uncle dies, leaving his nephew just enough money to complete his training, which will eventually enable him to secure a post as ship's surgeon and so travel the world, an ambition he has held since childhood. During the summer Thorpe Athelney invites him to join his family hop-picking in Kent, and it is here surrounded by the soft green countryside of his boyhood that Philip finds himself attracted by the eldest Athelney daughter, the sweet and modest Sally. 'He lost his head. His senses overwhelmed him . . . He drew her into the darker shadow of the hedge.' When a few weeks later Sally tells him she is pregnant he gloomily accepts, although not in love, that he must marry her, thus giving up all hope of freedom and adventure. Shortly after this, the story ends unexpectedly: Sally discovers she was mistaken and frees Philip from his obligation; he, however, is struck with the sudden realisation that he had deceived himself: 'it was no self-sacrifice that had driven him to think of marrying, but the desire for a wife and a home and love . . . What did he care for . . . the pagodas of Burma and the lagoons of South Sea Islands?'

This abrupt finale is the only unconvincing part of an otherwise extraordinarily compelling novel. Maugham's explanation for choosing this particular resolution is that he himself was much preoccupied at the time with a wish to marry. 'I sought freedom and thought I could find it in marriage,' he wrote. 'I conceived these notions when I was still at work on *Of Human Bondage*, and turning my wishes into fiction, as writers will, towards the end of it I drew a picture of the marriage I should have liked to make.' Up to these last few pages, however, the work is enormously impressive, much of it standing comparison with some of the best of Maugham's contemporaries, with the novels of Bennett, Gissing and George Moore, as well as with an important earlier influence, Samuel Butler's *The Way of All Flesh*, a novel much admired by Maugham. Butler's influence is clearly detectable, especially in the matchless early sections covering Philip's boyhood at the vicarage and his schooldays – poignant, funny and minutely observed.

Throughout it is evident that Maugham draws widely from his own experience: even apart from the boyhood sections and the dominant central theme of the affair with Mildred, there are numerous places, situations and subsidiary characters recognisable from life. Gerald Kelly, for instance, contributes both to Lawson, the art student in Paris, and to Griffiths, the treacherous friend who runs off with Mildred; Sally Athelney is endowed with Sue Jones's beauty as well as with her sexual magnetism and maternal tenderness; and Sally's father, Thorpe Athelney, is a lively portrait of Maugham's old mentor, Wentworth Huyshe, with his working-class wife and nine children, with whom Maugham used to stay at Besom Cottage in Essex. Interestingly, there is one sequence, vividly described, which was created entirely from a second-hand account, in the chapters dealing with Philip's job in a shop. With no experience of such work himself, Maugham commissioned an account from Gilbert Clark, a young actor who between jobs had been employed at the Piccadilly department store, Swan & Edgar's. At Maugham's request Clark wrote a 6,000-word description of his experience, for which he was paid 30 guineas. 'I can't tell you how pleased I am with what you have given me,' Maugham told him, the truth of this declaration borne out by Clark, who stated that 'Willie used my stuff practically word for word.'

There was no need for outside assistance, however, in treating the theme at the heart of the novel, that of Philip's bondage, his masochistic obsession with the frightful Mildred. The identity of the original of this curiously androgynous character is a mystery: a Lambeth prostitute, according to one theorist, a tea-shop waitress, in the view of another, while Maugham's one-time lover Harry Philips, who might be expected to know, definitely asserted that 'she' was a boy. What is certain is that he or she, or an amalgam of both, existed and that Maugham must have met her when he was very young: her prototype was Rose in 'Stephen Carey', which was written as early as 1898. The likelihood is that in the later novel Maugham added to the portrait various attributes and incidents culled from subsequent experience. Harry Philips when he read the novel recognised one such incident, 'undoubtedly an episode in our friendship not very creditable to me which he attributed to her [Mildred]'. The fictional Mildred must owe something, too, to the young woman about whom Maugham had expressed himself so vehemently to Gerald Kelly in 1905:

> You wait, my boy, till you are asked when you'll be back each time you go out, & where you've been the moment you come in, till you have to put up with sulks if you don't agree to the most unreasonable things, & quarrels for the absurdest trifles, till you have to endure your own jealousy & the other's . . . You'll find that when one lives with a person of no particular education . . . time hangs rather heavily on one's hands; one racks one's brains for conversation & at last is driven to going somewhere.

Every detail of Philip's enslavement rings true. His degradation is relentlessly mapped out, his lust, his abject devotion, his tormented self-loathing. Mildred is diabolical, yet at the same time Maugham allows us to see that she is to be pitied. One of Maugham's greatest strengths as a novelist is his ability to create three-dimensional characters, women as well as men, interacting with each other. Mildred, so cold and callous with Philip, is pathetic when she falls in love with Griffiths and suffers agony when he casually abandons her. Equally, Philip himself is depicted with ruthless honesty, not only eager, vulnerable, tender-hearted, but also priggish, self-pitying and capable of a subtle sadism; when wishing to hurt Mildred, 'he exercised peculiar skill in saying little things which he knew would wound her; but which were so indefinite, so delicately cruel, that she could not take exception to them.'

Despite its flaws *Of Human Bondage* is a major achievement. Maugham, who usually cultivated a fastidious detachment, shows in this work a personal commitment that was unusual, sweeping the reader up in his own passionate intensity. That the novel fails quite to reach the first rank is due partly to its somewhat limited vision; partly to a prose style that at times verges on the pedestrian; and partly to its author's reluctance to jettison extraneous material, Maugham in this instance inclining more towards the encyclopaedic didacticism of an H. G. Wells – improving lectures thrown in on religion, philosophy and art – rather than the disciplined selectivity of a Henry James.

Always an astute judge of his own work, Maugham knew that *Of Human Bondage* was of a different calibre from anything he had previously produced; he also knew that his standing was such that he was now free wholly to please himself. As he explained to Heinemann,

> I am aware that in the past I have compromised too much with what others have thought the public taste . . . Many writers are forced by poverty to consider whether this or that will hurt the sale of their books . . . but I think it would be disgraceful if I allowed any such thoughts to influence me. There are very few of us who can afford to break the bonds which the circulating libraries have placed on the contemporary English novel (bonds which have made it an object of contempt on the continent) and it behoves such as can to do so.

The choice of a title proved difficult, and a list of several was compiled – 'The Road Uphill', 'Experience', 'The Broad Road', 'A Winter's Day', 'The Day's March' – none of which seemed exactly right. Heinemann was in favour of 'Life's Thoroughfare', which Maugham thought commonplace. 'I am sorry to have been so fussy,' he wrote, 'but the book is my ewe-lamb, and I want to get away from the obvious.' Eventually Maugham fixed on 'Beauty from Ashes', a misquotation from Isaiah 61 ('to give unto them beauty for ashes'), but finding this had recently been used decided instead to take the title of one of the books in Spinoza's *Ethics*. *Of Human Bondage* was published by Doran in the United States on 12 August 1915, a day later by Heinemann in England. George Doran, celebrating his firm's recent association both with Maugham and with Heinemann, expressed his unqualified admiration for the work, recording in his memoirs that 'Were I given freedom of choice as to that book which I would first choose to have written had I the genius and wit, it would be *Of Human Bondage*.'

In the press the critical reception was at first rather more muted. With Europe embroiled in war, readers were hardly in the mood for long, serious novels, and on both sides of the Atlantic reviews were respectful rather than excited. By some Maugham was regarded as a follower of the modern realists, of secondary importance to such as Arnold Bennett and Compton Mackenzie; others declared themselves impressed if somewhat bemused, describing the book as puzzlingly difficult to categorise. 'It is on the grand scale, and in some ways beautiful,' wrote Gerald Gould in the *New Statesman*, '[but] the whole is exceedingly strange.' Then at the very end of the year a notice appeared in the *New Republic* by the distinguished novelist Theodore Dreiser placing the work in a different bracket altogether. 'Here is a novel . . . of the utmost importance,' Dreiser wrote, 'unmoral, as a novel of this kind must necessarily be . . . a gorgeous weave, as interesting and valuable at the beginning as at the end.' Somerset Maugham, he concluded, was indeed 'a great artist'. From this point *Of Human Bondage* climbed steadily in terms of critical evaluation, although it was not until the 1920s, when it was rediscovered following the enormous success of Maugham's novel *The Moon and Sixpence*, that it attained canonical status; in 1934 it was made into a film with Leslie Howard and Bette Davis, and for nearly half a century was widely regarded as a classic.

But this was all in the future. When Maugham began writing *Of Human Bondage* in 1911 his novels were considered a minor part of the oeuvre, his reputation based on his remarkable success as a playwright. His publishers, Heinemann and Doran, nevertheless regarded him with respect, his name a prestigious addition to their lists. George Doran, who came over once a year to buy books in London, was Irish-Canadian, a tall, imposing man with a courtly manner, who numbered both Hugh Walpole and Arnold Bennett among his authors, famously selling 100,000 copies in the States of *The Old Wives' Tale*; his association with Maugham and Heinemann he regarded as 'two of the most notable, satisfying contacts of my publishing life'. Maugham's dealings with Doran were solely about business, but with William Heinemann he was on more intimate terms, the two men having much in common. Like Maugham, Heinemann was small, with a slight stutter, was a gifted linguist, well read in French, German and Italian; a man of great charm and vitality, he had a passion for music and painting, and for the theatre (both Ibsen and Pinero appeared under his imprint). It was often said that his genius for friendship was equalled only by his genius for publishing, a judgment supported by a list of authors that included Conrad, Kipling, Robert Louis Stevenson, Galsworthy, Beerbohm, Henry James and H. G. Wells.

The fact that Somerset Maugham would outsell them all could hardly have been predicted in 1915, although in the theatre, in the West End and on Broadway he was undoubtedly regarded as a very valuable property indeed; his intention to abandon writing drama had not unnaturally been received with gloom by Charles Frohman. In reply to a courteous enquiry from Maugham about his health, Frohman had replied that he was unwell, 'partly on account of the weather, but more especially because you are not doing any work'. Finally Frohman had decided to confront the issue. 'I want a new play from you,' he announced. 'All right,' said Maugham. 'Why not rewrite *The Taming of the Shrew* with a new background?' 'All right,' said Maugham. The more he thought about it the more the idea appealed, and as he turned it over in his mind a memory came back to him of an aunt, with whom he used to stay in Tunbridge Wells: Aunt Julia had had a paid companion who eventually left her to go and live with a brother who was farming in Canada. 'I well remembered the shock it caused my elderly relative when her former companion ("very well connected, my dear") wrote and told her that she had married one of the hired men.' It was this recollection that provided the starting-point, the idea explored further by Maugham going out to see for himself what that way of life was like. Perhaps it was Aunt Julia's companion who furnished the introduction, or even herself acted as his hostess on her bleak prairie farm, where at the end of 1912 Maugham arrived from Toronto via New York to spend a month in the bitter winter cold of the Canadian mid-west.

After the comfort and modernity of Manhattan the primitive conditions encountered in Manitoba provided a harsh contrast, and yet Maugham could not help but be intrigued by his rough surroundings, reporting that despite 'a good deal of discomfort and tedium' he found 'that curious and intense life . . . most interesting'. Back in New York at the end of December, he described his experience in a letter to the actress Mabel Beardsley, sister of Aubrey.

> My God, what a life they lead . . . surrounded by the snowy prairie, cut off from their neighbours & absorbed with the struggle of getting three meals a day. Husbands & wives get to such a pitch of irritability that they will pass weeks without speaking to one another. In one house in which I stayed the wife had killed herself, in another there hung a strange gloom of impending madness. I was glad to get away. But it was an interesting experience, & the prairie, even under the snow, had a curious fascination which lingers in my memory.

The play was peculiarly topical, its title, *The Land of Promise*, a deliberate evocation of the phrase familiar from advertisements aimed at attracting British settlers to Canada. Norah, the 'Shrew', a young woman of twenty-eight, passionate and quick-tempered beneath a decorous exterior, has for the past ten years led a wretched existence as the paid companion of a disagreeable old lady in Tunbridge Wells. When the play opens her employer has just died, and Norah, completely penniless, decides to join her brother on his farm in Canada. Here the refined Norah is so miserable that in despair she offers herself as wife to one of the hired men. Frank, the Petruchio figure, strong and manly, with an enjoyably sardonic sense of humour, agrees to take her on but only on certain conditions. 'I give her board and lodging and the charm of my society,' he says. 'And in return she's got to cook and bake and wash and keep the shack clean and tidy.' Predictably, the first night of their married life is tempestuous, with Norah haughtily refusing to obey her husband's orders and Frank determined to subdue her. 'You're nothing but an ignorant woman and I'm your master. I'm going to do what I like with you, and if you don't submit willingly, by God I'll take you as the trappers in the old days used to take the squaws.' Eventually he opens the door to the bedroom and Norah, recognising defeat, slowly walks towards it. (When the film version of *The Land of Promise* was made in 1917 this scene was censored, with Frank spending his wedding night sleeping on the floor.) In the last act six months have passed and we see the shack transformed, muslin curtains at the windows, flowers on the table, and Norah and Frank obviously on amicable terms. Norah's brother arrives with a letter offering her a place as companion to another old lady in England. 'For God's sake take it,' he urges her. But Norah has changed: here in this harsh land of promise there is struggle and hardship but also the hope of a worthwhile future; more importantly, she realises she has fallen in love with her husband.

*The Land of Promise* is a strong piece of drama, courageous in its treatment of sexual dominance and submission, particularly at a time when female suffrage and emancipation were much in the news. As Maugham realised, conveying the play's message enormously depended on how the two main characters were interpreted. In Norah, as well as courage and passion there is a deep hidden sadness rooted in an unexpressed terror of facing a future as a penurious spinster; while it is important that Frank, although unmannered, is basically decent and kind. We know, from the scene played out between them when they first meet, that there is a strong mutual attraction, and it is this, and Frank's good-heartedness despite his tough talk, that prevents the third act from appearing brutal and unpleasant. In the scene leading up to what virtually amounts to marital rape, the subtext must reveal that Norah's fury with Frank, a man she apparently despises, comes as much from fury with herself for physically desiring him. If this is not made evident then the play fails.

*The Land of Promise* opened in Washington in November 1913, before transferring to New Haven, Connecticut, finally coming into New York on 25 December. Billie Burke as Norah was a guaranteed draw. As Maugham told Gerald Kelly, 'the audience of course knew nothing of the play, they just came to see the star'. Unfortunately, Miss Burke, blind to the troubling complexities of Norah's character, saw the piece as a straightforward romantic comedy and Norah as a feisty little firebrand who by perkiness and pouting finally gets her man. Needless to say, this made nonsense of the role: 'the leading part loses by being played as a romantic ingénue', Maugham complained, cross that his play was being so 'rottenly acted . . . by that little slut'. The situation was made worse by the star resenting the fact that the actor playing Frank was receiving all the accolades.

> In scene after scene my poor leading lady was just acted off the stage. There were consequently scenes, quarrels, & recriminations, & at one moment I seriously feared that Billie Burke would not continue to play, but first by flattery & then by cutting out the laughs that the man got (!) we have reconciled her to the part.

That Billie Burke herself was unhappy is made clear in her memoirs. '*The Land of Promise*', she recalls,

> was a beautifully written but dreary kind of play for me. My costumes were not fetching – one black dress and another of a particularly ugly blue – and the problems of Canadian farmers did not interest New York audiences. It was full of integrity and all that . . . but the change of character was perhaps too sudden for me . . . Some other established dramatic actress could have carried this play, but I could not.

In the States the notices were generally good, although there was a certain amount of umbrage taken north of the border. The play 'gives an altogether incorrect conception of the conditions in Western Canada', complained the *Edmonton Journal*, while the *Daily Bulletin* protested that 'No Canadian man would dream of ordering his wife about . . . if there is one thing Canadian men do well, it is the way they treat their wives.' By March the following year indignation had reached such a pitch that the planned tour of Canada had to be cancelled.

When *The Land of Promise* was produced in England in February 1914 a performer of a very different calibre took the lead – Irene Vanbrugh, a subtle and intelligent actress who had no trouble in bringing out the dark shadows and anxieties in Norah's character. The *English Review*, which particularly praised her performance, compared the play favourably to Shaw's *Pygmalion*, which had opened a few weeks afterwards.

The Pygmalion of Mr Maugham is muscular . . . a little brutal, sexual, catastrophic, that of Mr Shaw epicene, bloodless, intellectual, and neuter . . .

Comparing the two plays technically, it is significant to observe how boldly Mr Maugham has freed himself from the entertainment label, what a fresh and strong note he rings, as with what conservative insistency Mr Shaw sticks to the old formula of artificial type designed primarily for the laugh. Though Mr Maugham's situation is theatrical, and it is difficult to believe in the enormity of his lady-help's prudery, the theme makes a good play, and he must be congratulated on having recaptured his true art and made the public swallow it.

In order to oversee the American production of *The Land of Promise*, Maugham had arrived in New York on 15 November 1913, returning home at the beginning of January 1914, a couple of weeks before his fortieth birthday. But on this, his third visit to the United States, he had had an additional purpose in mind. Sue Jones was also due to arrive in America, having landed a small part, obtained for her by Maugham, in Ned Sheldon's play *Romance*, which had had a successful run on Broadway and was now playing at the Princess Theatre in Chicago. Maugham had missed saying goodbye to Sue before he left England and was determined not to miss her again, for he had finally made up his mind to ask her to be his wife. In a telling passage in *The Summing Up* he describes his attitude towards marriage at this stage in his life.

If I meant to marry and have children it was high time I did so . . . It seemed a necessary motif in the pattern of life that I had designed, and to my ingenuous fancy (for though no longer young and thinking myself so worldly wise, I was still in many ways incredibly naïve) it offered peace; peace from the disturbance of love affairs . . . bringing in their train such troublesome complications . . . peace that would enable me to write all I wanted to write without the loss of precious time or disturbance of mind; peace and a settled and dignified way of life.

In terms of society, Maugham could have married well above his station: such an attractive and successful man was considered a good catch, and by no means only in theatrical circles. But Sue was the woman he wanted: he loved her, and he knew despite her promiscuity that she loved him; as he put it to his friend Alfred Sutro, 'Do you really think that A loves B less because B has been to bed with somebody else? And vice versa. I don't.' When not on tour, Sue spent much of her time discreetly lodging at Chesterfield Street, and Maugham had grown used to the safe haven of her warm and welcoming presence. She understood him, accepted him for what he was, and with her easy-going nature never intruded where she was not wanted or presented him with demands that were difficult or tire-some to fulfil. Secure in herself, she gave confidence to Maugham, who for all his sophistication was often anxious and unsure. In short he trusted her, wanted her, and believed the two of them could make a life together.

Before leaving England Maugham prepared with care. He bought an expensive engagement ring, two large pearls encircled by diamonds, and planned his schedule so that after fulfilling his commitments in New York he could stay in Chicago with Sue during the obligatory fortnight she would need to work out her notice with the company. After this there would be a quiet registry-office wedding, and then the two of them would leave at once for a long honeymoon voyage to Tahiti and the South Seas. On the day that Sue's ship was due to arrive in New York Maugham went down to the pier to meet it. Amid the noise and bustle of disembarkation he caught sight of her almost at once, talking to a tall, handsome young man who quickly disappeared. Sue was delighted to see him and kissed him warmly, but was unable to linger as the train for Chicago was leaving within the hour. For the next couple of weeks Maugham was kept busy with his play, but at the beginning of December he went up to Chicago, taking a room at the same hotel in which Sue was staying. He telephoned to arrange a time to meet, and she sounded delighted to hear him but asked him not to come to the theatre as his presence in the audience would make her nervous. She agreed, however, to have supper with him after the performance. At about half-past ten Sue rang to say she was ready, and Maugham went to her small suite. Looking wonderfully beautiful, she gave him her usual loving embrace and started to tell him about the play, but something was wrong: she seemed restless, uneasy, at moments almost on the edge of hysteria. She hardly touched the supper that had been ordered, and soon Maugham rang for the waiter to take it away. Deciding this was the moment he said quietly, 'I've come to ask you to marry me.'

> [Sue] paused for what seemed to me quite a long time. Then, 'I don't want to marry you,' she said. I was taken aback . . . 'D'you mean it?' I asked. 'Yes.' 'Why not?' I asked. 'I just don't want to.' . . . I took out of my pocket the engagement ring I had bought and handed it to her. 'I got this for you.' She looked at it. 'It's very pretty,' she said . . . She handed it back to me . . . 'If you want to go to bed with me you can,' she said, 'but I won't marry you.' I shook my head: 'No, I won't do that.' We sat in silence for a while. I broke it by saying, 'Well, there's nothing more to be said, is there?' 'No,' she answered. I could see that she wanted me to go. I put the ring back in my pocket, got up, kissed her and bade her goodnight.

Although the above account was written nearly fifty years later, fifty years during which the memory had remained ineradicably etched in Maugham's mind, it tallies closely with the letter he sent to Gerald Kelly from New York immediately after his return there from Chicago.

> My schemes for going round the world have come to nothing. I went up to Chicago to see Susan & found her in a very hysterical condition, & I can do nothing with her, I will tell you more in detail when we meet; poor thing, her nerves, her digestion, everything has gone wrong; it is an effect America often has on people, & the only thing for her is a rest cure, but I cannot induce her to be sensible & get back to England & have me.

In his memoir 'Looking Back', Maugham depicts himself walking down Piccadilly soon after his return to London and catching sight of an *Evening Standard* placard on which in large capitals were the words 'ACTRESS MARRIES EARL'S SON'. 'I guessed at once who the actress was and bought a paper. I was right.' In fact Sue had married in Chicago on 13 December, while Maugham was still in New York and less than a fortnight after rejecting his proposal; her husband was Angus McDonnell, a younger son of the Earl of Antrim. Maugham guessed that McDonnell had been the good-looking fellow passenger to whom he had seen her talking when disembarking from the ship; he also guessed, rightly, that McDonnell had made her pregnant ('I knew how careless she was in these matters') which would explain Sue's nervousness and the so-called digestive disorders which he had attributed to stress.

Apart from Kelly, Maugham told almost no one what had happened. Adept at concealment, he gave little sign of his disappointment, although in fact the loss of Sue Jones was a blow from which he took a long time to recover and never ceased regretting: even after many years the mention of her name never failed to stir deep emotion. He had loved her truly, believing that he and she could have made a happy, if not wholly conventional, life together. Of course he would have strayed, and perhaps so would she, but still they might have made it work. Fortunately he could not foresee that with the loss of Sue Jones all hope of such contentment was gone for good.

Maugham never blamed Sue for her decision, expressing the conviction that Angus McDonnell would make her 'a much better husband than I should have done', a generous concession in the circumstances, if not, unfortunately, borne out by events. McDonnell, a handsome adventurer of great energy and charm, took his wife back to England where they settled near Tunbridge Wells. The pregnancy which had panicked

Sue into marriage turned out to be ectopic, and Sue was never to bear children. The marriage was not happy as she and her husband had little in common. By middle age Sue had grown red-faced and fat, her acting career virtually forgotten; she took to drink and Angus to other women, her chief interest in life the breeding of Dandie Dinmont terriers. She died in 1948, and is buried at Glenarm, her husband's ancestral home in Ireland. An obscure figure who made little impact on her profession, Sue would have been long forgotten had it not been for her glorious reincarnation in 1930 as Rosie, the heroine of one of Maugham's finest novels, *Cakes and Ale*.

Heavy-hearted, Maugham returned to London in January 1914 and immediately set about driving himself harder than ever. *The Land of Promise* was doing excellent business, and Frohman was urging him to deliver four more plays for the following season, including one for Marie Tempest, another for Gerald du Maurier. His life was not all work, however, for it was now that he encountered again a woman he had met shortly before leaving for America. He had found her amusing and attractive, but thought little more about her until chance again brought her into view. A brief light-hearted affair with no ties attached seemed the ideal prescription to alleviate his sadness over Sue. Little did he know that he was about to enter the longest, most miserable and most bitterly destructive relationship of his life.

It began harmlessly enough one evening in the autumn of the previous year, 1913, shortly before Maugham sailed for New York. He had been sitting reading in his top-floor study in Chesterfield Street when the telephone rang. A neighbour, Mrs Carstairs, wanted to ask him a favour: she and her husband had invited a couple of friends to dine and go to the theatre, and at the last minute one had dropped out: would Maugham take his place? 'It happened that I had nothing to do and hadn't seen the play,' Maugham recalled, 'so I said I would be glad to come.' Having changed into evening clothes he walked down the street to the Carstairs' house and was shown into the drawing-room where he was introduced to his fellow guest. Mrs Wellcome, in her mid-thirties, was striking rather than conventionally pretty, with a wide mouth, slightly prominent nose, creamy complexion and big brown eyes; she was fashionably dressed and on her fingers wore large cabochon emeralds. It was obvious she found him attractive, and consequently during dinner he was at his wittiest and most entertaining. As they prepared to leave for the theatre, Mrs Wellcome whispered flatteringly, 'I wish we didn't have to go to this play. I'd like to listen to you talking all night.' The next afternoon, during the obligatory call on his hostess, Maugham mentioned that he had found her friend very charming. Syrie Wellcome was the wife of the enormously wealthy Henry Wellcome, the American pharmaceutical manufacturer, Mrs Carstairs told him; the marriage had not been happy and the couple were now living apart.

A few days later Maugham at the opera caught sight of Syrie Wellcome sitting in the stalls and went to speak to her. She was obviously pleased to see him, explaining that she was sorry she was unable to invite him to visit her as she was temporarily living in an 'odious' flat near Marble Arch while her new house in Regent's Park was being decorated. 'She hoped I would come to the house-warming party she intended to give as soon as she moved in.' It was shortly after this that Maugham left for America to oversee rehearsals of *The Land of Promise* and to ask Sue Jones to marry him.

The London production of *The Land of Promise* opened at the Duke of York's Theatre on 26 February 1914, by coincidence the same night that Syrie had chosen for her house-warming. Maugham sent her two tickets for the front row of the stalls, intending to go to her reception as soon as he could get away from the theatre. Tense and nervous as always on a first night, Maugham was irritated to see Syrie slide into her seat late, several minutes after the curtain had gone up, and he almost decided to cut her party, but having refused other invitations in order to accept this he had nothing else to do, and so made his way up to 4 York Terrace in Regent's Park. It was a good party, with an orchestra and a crowd of lively, fashionably dressed people, many of whom congratulated him on the play. Maugham, high on his success, thoroughly enjoyed himself, dancing several times with his hostess, returning home late in the small hours. 'After that', he said, 'I saw Syrie almost every day.'

Syrie Wellcome was not quite the conventional society woman that she appeared. Born in 1879, five years younger than Maugham, Syrie was a daughter of the great reformer Thomas Barnardo, founder of the Dr Barnardo's Homes for destitute children. The eldest girl in a family of six (a seventh, a boy, had died as a baby), Gwendoline Maud, in adult life always known as Syrie, had had an unusual upbringing. Both Barnardo and his wife, who was also called Syrie, although within the family referred to as the Begum, were members of an American religious sect, the Open Plymouth Brethren. Devoutly evangelical, an ardent member of the temperance movement, Dr Barnardo laid heavy emphasis, in the comfortable family house in Hackney, on daily Bible readings and prayers, on strict punctuality and obedience, and on the spurning of worldly pleasures: drinking, smoking and visits to the theatre were all forbidden. A flamboyant personality, aggressive, obstinate, arrogant and overbearing, Barnardo was also capable of considerable charm and personal kindness: he was treated warily by his children, but he was also loved, particularly by his elder daughter, who inherited a number of her father's traits, notably a hot temper, a steely determination to have her own way (as a girl this earned her the nickname Queenie) and a talent for commerce. Barnardo, probably of distantly Jewish origin, was the son of a Prussian furrier who had settled in Dublin; he was a brilliant businessman and made a great deal of money, but spent it faster than it accrued, mainly on his various charities, and was frequently in financial difficulties, his resources strained to satisfy his wife's demands for an ever higher standard of living.

When Syrie was seventeen the Barnardos moved from Hackney to St Leonard's Lodge, Surbiton, a substantial Victorian house standing in its own grounds. It was here that the Begum, a tough, determined woman, in many ways more practical than her husband, started giving occasional parties so that her elder daughter might have the chance to meet some suitable young men. This was a fortunate development for Syrie, who loved social life and longed for the great world, of which she had been given a first taste when her father had taken her with him to Canada for the opening of one of his children's homes. He intended that Syrie should train to be a missionary and go to China, a choice of career that could not have been further from her own ambitions. She longed to leave home, where the atmosphere was gloomy and repressive, with two of her brothers dying from diphtheria and her sister permanently disabled. She loathed the emphasis on religion, and had not the faintest interest in her father's good works, disliking the orphans and the Barnardo Homes and resenting being made to play the piano during the communal hymn-singing. After a brief flirtation with a local youth, Syrie, encouraged by her mother, focused her attention on bigger game, a middle-aged American and friend of Dr Barnardo's, who was temporarily staying at St Leonard's before moving into a house he had rented near by on the banks of the Thames.

Henry ('Hal') Wellcome, a handsome, well-built man of forty-six with blue eyes and a bushy ginger moustache, was immensely rich. Like Thomas Barnardo, whom he much admired, he had been brought up in a religious, temperance environment, and although he had largely sloughed off the influences of his Minnesota childhood, he retained a strong instinct towards altruism and bettering the lot of his fellow man, the great goal of his life the eradication of disease in impoverished parts of the world. He had long been settled in England, and his pharmaceutical company, Burroughs Wellcome, established in London, had become hugely successful, the first manufacturers of the compressed pill or 'Tabloid' which was to revolutionise Western medicine. Wellcome enjoyed female company, although he had never had the time, nor particular inclination, to think of marriage. Syrie, however, attractive and vivacious, definitely caught his fancy, and she on her side found him good fun: he kept a canoe on the river and was always ready for a party, and she was excited by the marked attentions he paid her. Most importantly she saw in Wellcome an escape route from the suffocating atmosphere of home as well as an entrée into the world of the sophisticated and well-to-do of which she longed to be part.

But at the end of the summer Wellcome left for abroad without anything having been said, and it looked as if the big fish had escaped the net. Swift action was necessary, and the wily Begum, knowing that Wellcome was bound for a research trip to the Sudan, dispatched her daughter in pursuit. No one could have been more surprised than Hal Wellcome in Khartoum, immersed in studying the effects of disease on the native peoples, to see the delightful Miss Barnardo disembark one day from a Nile steamer with a befrilled and parasoled party of sightseeing English ladies. The ruse was successful, and Syrie returned to England engaged, becoming Mrs Henry Wellcome at a quiet ceremony in St Mark's Church, Surbiton on 2 June 1901.

The marriage was a disaster almost from the start. Wellcome was a man of the highest principle, intelligent, energetic and sociable, if happier when dealing with large groups than with individuals. He was also set in his ways, wholly dedicated to his work, and as a powerful player in his field who was frequently consulted by governments and heads of state, he was accustomed to deference and inclined to be dictatorial. In marrying the daughter of his public-spirited old friend he believed he had found the ideal wife, high-minded, biddable and self-denying, eager to devote herself to pleasing him and to promoting his numerous charitable interests. This was a serious miscalculation. Syrie, frivolous and self-indulgent, envisaged a high-spending married life in which she would preside over some of the capital's most elegant soirées, with regular vacations at fashionable continental resorts. Her fantasy soon faded. The Wellcomes' first married home was a rented house in Kent, where Syrie found herself acting as hostess not to *gens du monde* but to grey-haired professors and their dowdy wives, who sat in the garden drinking tea and discussing the challenging possibilities of developing a vaccine against diphtheria. When the Wellcomes went out it was invariably to attend crowded functions in hot hotel banqueting rooms, where young Mrs Wellcome was required to sit on a platform stupefied with boredom while distinguished scientists made lengthy speeches prior to an endless series of presentations of cups, medals and diplomas. Worse were the trips abroad. Instead of Le Touquet or Biarritz, Wellcome, who was completely indifferent to physical comfort, took his wife rattling round little-known parts of Europe on an obsessive search for objects for his collection of medical instruments and artefacts, which was eventually to number over one million items. For months at a time they drove over terrible roads in a car that was frequently breaking down, at night putting up in primitive inns, by day trailing round dusty shops and museums or crowded, noisy bazaars. Wellcome considered these expeditions a tremendous adventure; his wife detested every minute.

There were other areas of incompatibility, but of these nothing was said, Syrie only later confiding to one or two intimates her distaste for her husband's sexual demands. With his ginger hair now turning grey, his walrus moustache, his red face, his paunch, and the heavy smell of cigars lingering on his breath, Wellcome at nearly fifty was unlikely to appear an attractive prospect to a young woman of twenty-one. It was more than that, however: there were hints of beatings and brutality, of sadistic tendencies, of pain inflicted in the bedroom which privately appalled her. Fortunately for her peace of mind she is unlikely to have heard the rumours which later emerged involving the savage flogging of native bearers and, swiftly hushed up, of a child strung up by its feet and whipped until it died.

In June 1903, shortly after returning from a long tour of Canada and the United States, Syrie gave birth to a son, Mounteney. Both husband and wife doted on the boy, although his arrival, instead of bringing his parents together, acted instead to drive them further apart. Syrie, with a small baby to care for, objected to being made to continue with her husband's demanding programme, nor was she slow in making her objections clear. She sulked, he was irritable, and there were some ferocious rows, with Wellcome by no means always coming off best. He was proud of his chic young wife, but he expected total obedience and grew increasingly resentful of what he regarded as a culpable failure in her duty towards him; he was not pleased, either, that increasingly she seemed to prefer the company of other, younger men, to whom she was obviously most appealing.

In 1909 the Wellcomes were again in America, by this time on notice-ably bad terms. After visiting New York, Washington and California, they travelled to Ecuador where they stayed at the American Legation in Quito: Wellcome at the request of the United States government was to inspect the sanitary conditions of the disease-infested Panama Canal zone, a project enormously appealing to him, less so to his wife. Also staying at the Legation was an American financier, Archer Harman, and it was with Harman that Henry Wellcome suddenly and furiously accused his wife of adultery. Syrie vehemently denied it, but her husband refused to listen, and the scenes between them grew so violent that Syrie, frightened, left for New York. The pair neither saw nor spoke to each other again. A legal separation was brokered, with a generous personal settlement for Syrie of £2,400 a year, and custody of Mounteney until the age of eleven, during which time all his expenses would be met by his father. Whatever happened or did not happen between Syrie and Harman, Wellcome was convinced of his wife's guilt and considered her a deeply immoral woman; he never forgave her, and remained morbidly miserable for the rest of his life. He forbade her name or the subject of his nine-year marriage to be mentioned in his presence, and passed straight to his lawyers Syrie's emotional letters, most of them filled with plaintive requests for more money and anxiety about Mounteney's health.

After the shock of the break-up subsided, Syrie revelled in her freedom, dividing her time between London and Paris. For the first time in her life she was her own mistress, well provided for and able to indulge her taste for luxury and an artistic bent revealed in her stylish clothes and furnishings and in an almost theatrical flair for entertaining. Her drawing-room at York Terrace provided a striking backdrop for her parties, and Maugham used it later as the setting for one of his most successful comedies, *Caroline*. The heroine's drawing-room in Regent's Park, spacious and airy,

> is furnished in a pleasantly fantastic manner by a woman who desires to be in the latest mode, but who tempers it with her own good taste. The influence of futurism is apparent in the carpet, the cushions, the coverings of sofas and chairs; but there is nothing so outrageous as to make the room merely a curiosity. Here and there large jars of flowers contrast the sobriety of nature with the extravagance of human imagination.

Her father having died in 1905, Syrie moved the Begum in to live with her, glad of the veneer of respectability which the maternal presence would provide. For there was no doubt about it: Mrs Wellcome was not quite respectable. Although she had escaped the stigma of divorce, she was nonetheless looked at slightly askance by the more fastidious sections of society: not only was she guilty of desertion but there was subsequent evidence of flighty behaviour – a passionate affair, for instance, with a glamorous young Hussar, Lieutenant-Colonel Desmond FitzGerald, of whom Syrie had had high hopes, dashed when FitzGerald went off with the Duchess of Sutherland. Other wealthy admirers were the Duc de Gramont and one of the Bourbon princes, as well as the American department-store tycoon Gordon Selfridge, who was reported to pay the rent for the house in York Terrace (for which, it was also reported, Syrie had had a doormat made reading 'WELLCOME'). It was Selfridge, too, it was said, who helped subsidise Syrie's expensive wardrobe, her lavish entertaining and the wages of a sizeable domestic staff, a butler and personal maid, cook, kitchen-maid, car and chauffeur, which could scarcely have been afforded on the £200 a month allowed her by Wellcome.

At the time she began the affair with Maugham Syrie was growing anxious. Selfridge was losing interest; she was in her mid-thirties, 'a courtesan just past her prime', as one commentator put it; and although she enjoyed her life, she was beginning to crave security. Wellcome might divorce her at any time, none of her rich lovers had offered to marry her, and with middle age approaching she felt the need of respectable status and a large disposable income. Syrie also desperately wanted another child. Her devotion to Mounteney was visceral and deep; she had looked after him, worried over his delicate health and backwardness at school, taken him with her whenever she could on her excursions abroad. But Wellcome had grown increasingly obdurate about his son, and when in 1912 Mounteney was sent to boarding school, his father began severely to limit Syrie's access, causing acute anguish not only to her but to the boy, who had always been very close to his mother.

Thus in 1913 when Willie Maugham came into her life, he appeared to be everything Syrie wanted, 'the most charming man in London', rich, fashionable and unattached. It was not long before Syrie determined to have him, and if that meant she had to make all the running, then that is what she would do.

Three or four weeks after the house-warming in 1914, during which time she and Maugham had seen each other daily, Syrie announced she was going to Paris, where she had the use of an apartment on the Quai d'Orsay, and suggested Maugham should come, too. They travelled separately, and on arrival he telephoned from his hotel to arrange to take her to dinner, afterwards going back to her apartment where for the first time they made love. The next morning Maugham returned to London, and when Syrie followed a few days later they fell into an agreeable routine of dining almost every evening at York Terrace, after which they would go to bed. 'It was all very delightful,' said Maugham. 'In the circles in which we moved it was an understood thing that I was Syrie's lover . . . I was proud of her and pleased with myself.' Her compliments were expert, she was sexy, and he delighted in her gaiety and vitality, appreciating the fact that she was always beautifully dressed and groomed, her instinctive chic an aspect he took particular pleasure in showing off. (After taking Syrie to call on his sister-in-law Nellie Maugham, one of his little nieces recorded in her diary, 'Uncle Willie brought Mrs Welcome [sic] to tea in a very funny hat.') Maugham sometimes accompanied Syrie on shopping expeditions in Bond Street, and enjoyed watching her slender figure parade in silk negligées and diaphanous tea gowns – although, still unworldly in some respects, it never occurred to him that in his role as lover he might be expected to settle the bill. Syrie entertained frequently and with panache, with Maugham now a permanent fixture on her guest list. At one of her parties he and the entertainer Elsa Maxwell 'locked horns in an endurance contest', as Miss Maxwell put it. 'I pounded the piano and Willie danced, for three hours, without a break. What an evening!'

All this was good fun. Maugham knew that Syrie was impressed by him, and that his connection with the stage gave her a cachet with her friends; but he regarded their relationship as no more than a light-hearted affair between two sophisticated adults, neither of whom wanted any serious entanglement. So completely was he off his guard that he laughed when Syrie told him she was 'madly in love'; he was touched, and his vanity flattered, but not for a moment did he take the declaration literally.

Then something happened which might have warned Maugham that the situation was far more serious than he had believed. He and Syrie were walking in Richmond Park when to his astonishment Syrie announced she wanted to have his child. Maugham was appalled: he had a weakness for babies, hoped one day to have children of his own, but not by this woman whom he did not love and with whom he had no intention of settling down. In the plainest possible terms he set out the immense difficulties, legal and social, of bringing into the world an illegitimate child, but Syrie brushed them aside, explaining that one of her brothers, married but childless, would be delighted to bring the baby up; then after three or four years she could adopt it and no one would be any the wiser. The plan was deceptively simple; so simple that for a moment Maugham was tempted. But then reason prevailed. He told Syrie that it was out of the question, he would have nothing to do with it, and she must not think of it again.

The following month, April 1914, Syrie invited Maugham to join her and a couple of friends in Biarritz. When after a few days the friends left, Syrie suggested that she and Maugham should drive over the border into Spain, a country he loved and about which he had told her so much. Maugham was instantly wary: it was one thing to conduct an affair with a married woman behind closed doors, but flagrantly to travel alone with her, without a third party as chaperon, was asking for trouble: he had no wish to compromise Syrie's reputation, nor did he wish to become involved in any punitive action that Wellcome might choose to bring against his wife. But Syrie reassured him: she and her husband had agreed an amicable arrangement, she explained, whereby each was free to enter into other relationships. And so they set off, stopping the first night at León before going on to Santiago de Compostela, where they stayed in a suite at the beautiful Reyes Católicos. The weather was warm, they were both relaxed, and for the first time Maugham made love to Syrie without protection, carelessly leaving the precautions to her. After nearly a week in Compostela they drove to Paris and caught the Golden Arrow to London.

It was not long after his return home that Maugham received a shock. Syrie telephoned one morning and said she must see him urgently. When he arrived at her house he found her in bed, looking pale and tearful. She began to cry and told him she had had a miscarriage. 'I didn't want to tell you till I was certain,' she wept. Maugham was stunned, as he had understood her to have given up all idea of having a baby, but he said nothing of his disquiet; he sat down by her bed, held her hand and did his best to comfort her, drying her tears with his handkerchief. 'Would you like to bring the affair to an end?' she whispered. 'Do you want to finish it?' She was ill and unhappy; he knew of the painful situation over Mounteney, and he felt desperately sorry for her. 'Of course not,' he said. 'Why should I?' Within a short time Syrie had completely recovered, and over the next few weeks the couple resumed their familiar routine as though nothing had happened, dining and dancing, going to parties together and lunching at the Ritz. Of Maugham's friends, only Gerald Kelly was let into the secret. 'I have got a great deal to tell you,' Maugham wrote. 'But I dare not write it. I shall tell you of a very curious development, but in the most dreadful confidence.'

Robert Maugham, hard-working legal adviser to the Paris Embassy

The charming and beautiful Edith Maugham

The Rev. Henry Maugham, 'a far from intelligent cleric'

Kind-hearted Aunt Sophie

Willie and his uncle outside the vicarage

A lonely child, guarded and withdrawn

Maugham as a pupil at the King's School, Canterbury

'Life was before him . . .'

The acerbic F. H. Maugham in middle age

Willie, Charlie and Harry Maugham at St Moritz

Kelly's portrait of the irresistible Sue Jones. *Inset:* The painter Gerald Kelly, a lifelong friend

Ethel Irving
shocking audiences
in *Lady Frederick*

Gladys Cooper, Maugham's
favourite actress, in
*The Sacred Flame*

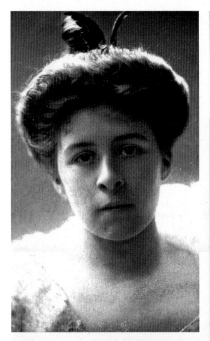

*Above left:* Syrie Wellcome, lively, stylish and unstoppably ambitious

*Above right:* The very fashionable Mr and Mrs Somerset Maugham

*Left:* The Maughams with Liza at Le Touquet

*Right:* Maugham
leaving New York
aboard RMS *Aquitania*

*Below:* Eddie Knoblock,
Maugham, Hugh
Walpole and Gerald
Haxton with Douglas
Fairbanks in Hollywood

A. S. Frere in his office at Heinemann

Eddie Marsh, ruthless 'diabolizer'

Ellen and Nelson Doubleday with Maugham
at Bonny Hall

Maugham believed that he had had a lucky escape; he was perfectly happy to continue seeing Syrie in the short term, especially while she was still emotionally fragile, but the incident had shaken him, and it made him realise that as far as he was concerned the affair had no real future. Fond though he was, he was beginning to feel a little bored by Syrie's company, uneasy at her dependence on him and fretting to be free. It irritated him, for instance, that after each time he took her out her immediate question was, 'When am I going to see you again?' Although Wellcome appeared to show no inclination to divorce his wife, the possibility that he might made Maugham distinctly nervous. Syrie was 'still madly devoted', he reported to a woman friend; 'her husband has gone to Bermuda and there is no talk of getting rid of him; so I breathe again.' However, for safety's sake he decided the best plan was to disappear for a while, and so he left London to spend the month of July with Gerald Kelly on Capri.

It was a short but idyllic period of respite. The two men stayed at the Villa Cercola, a little white-walled house above the town which was shared by the novelist E. F. ('Dodo') Benson and Maugham's old friend from Heidelberg, John Ellingham Brooks. Benson, whose discreetly homo-erotic novel *Colin* vividly evokes this period on Capri, came over from England as often as he could, while Brooks was a permanent resident, the arrangement convenient not because Brooks and Benson were friends but, as one of their neighbours delicately phrased it, because 'they had tastes in common besides literature, which made Capri a desirable retreat for them both'. The villa, facing south and luxuriantly draped in passion-flower and plumbago, had a terrace running along its front and a big studio out at the back; lizards basked on the walls, the orange trees were in flower, and leisurely meals, cooked by the amiable Seraphina, were eaten under the shade of a vine-covered pergola in the garden. Mornings were devoted to study, Maugham working on the first draft of a new play, after which the four men walked down to the Bagno Timberino, where they swam in the translucent water, sunbathed, and eyed the local Capresi youth, as beautiful and as obliging as ever. Following a siesta in the shuttered cool of the house, Maugham had a lesson in Russian, given him by an eccentric émigré from Odessa who came to the villa every afternoon, after which there was usually a game of tennis or a stroll up the slopes of Monte Solaro; and after dinner a short walk to Morgano's in the piazza to drink and play cards with the regulars, among them a newly arrived couple, the novelist Compton Mackenzie and his wife.

The Mackenzies had taken the Villa Rosaio on Anacapri, and there was a considerable amount of toing and froing between the two house-holds, the main focus for Maugham the English newspapers which were regularly delivered there. 'The bundle of papers that arrived by every post from England attracted him, and he did not pretend otherwise,' Faith Mackenzie recalled. 'I did a drawing of him, showing nothing but a chair, an open newspaper and a pair of crossed legs, and called it "Somerset Maugham dines with friends".' Compton Mackenzie, who had recently become something of a celebrity with the publication of his novel *Sinister Street*, relished the company of his fellow writers, even if he was some-times made uncomfortable by the malicious teasing of Brooks by Benson and Maugham, who in his opinion 'treated poor Brooks very badly'. It was easy to see why Brooks got on their nerves: fatter and balder than before, his weak, handsome face burned a rich terracotta, Brooks was otherwise unchanged; lazy, amiable and self-centred, he bored the others by insisting on reading aloud from his translation of Hérédia, endlessly fiddled at but never finished, and tormented them by banging away badly at Beethoven on his upright piano. 'He had fine perceptions,' wrote Benson, '[and] somewhere beneath the ash of his laziness there burned the authentic fire . . . [but] he was inexcusably indolent.'*

The peaceful bachelor routine of the Villa Cercola was suddenly shat-tered at the beginning of August, first by the outbreak of war on the 4th, and secondly by a telegram from Syrie in Rome announcing her immi-nent arrival on the island. Maugham was appalled, his obvious panic infecting the other members of the household. Brooks rushed off 'in a great flutter' to report the news to the Mackenzies, telling them that Maugham had got himself involved with a woman and was terrified he was going to have to marry her. 'I don't know what I shall do if Maugham brings a wife to the Cercola,' Brooks wailed. 'I don't think Benson will like it at all either.' Mackenzie, too, was shocked, and implored Maugham to stand firm. With this support behind him, Maugham immediately wired back begging Syrie not to come as he and Kelly were on the point of leaving for England. Syrie ignored the cable and arrived off the boat in Capri (much as she had arrived off the boat in pursuit of Wellcome fifteen years earlier in Khartoum), only to find Maugham, just as he had said, on the point of departure. Her brief stay can hardly have been passed in a

---

* After Brooks's death on the island in 1929 Maugham wrote a story, 'The Lotos Eater', which was largely based on Brooks and his life on Capri. 'He was of no use to anybody,' he writes of the Brooks character, 'but on the other hand he did nobody any harm. His only object was his own happiness, and it looked as though he had attained it' (*Collected Short Stories* vol. IV (Vintage 2000) p. 221).

happy atmosphere: none of them wanted her there, least of all Maugham.

London was a city in a state of chaotic preparation for war, the excitement and euphoria of the first few days having been quickly subsumed in the confusion of mobilisation. At the age of forty Maugham was too old to enlist (conscription, for unmarried men between eighteen and forty-one, was not introduced until January 1916), but he was passionately patriotic. 'To me the very shape of England on the map is significant,' he wrote, trying to analyse his own particular brand of patriotism. 'It is an emotion compact of pride and longing and love . . . an emotion which makes sacrifice easy.' He was determined to take an active part in the conflict before it ended, as surely it would, before the year was out. Many of his literary colleagues, H. G. Wells and Arnold Bennett among others, regarded their contribution as a literary one, writing about the war, either, like Wells, from home, or, like Bennett, going out to northern France to describe for his readers conditions on the front. But for once Maugham had not the least desire to write: it was action he wanted. Assuming his fluent French was his greatest asset, he contacted his old golfing partner, Winston Churchill, then First Lord of the Admiralty, to offer his services, and was disappointed when Churchill's reply enclosed a letter to be presented to a department head in Whitehall. With no intention of spending the war behind a desk, Maugham ignored this and applied instead to the Red Cross, which was on the point of sending a detachment of ambulances to the front and was in need of interpreters. The maverick Sir Frederick Treves, surgeon-extraordinary to Queen Victoria and a distinguished veteran of the Boer War, had been appointed head of Red Cross personnel at the War Office, and under his galvanising influence a steady stream of doctors, nurses, orderlies, drivers and stretcher-bearers was daily crossing the Channel to France. Their contribution was vital, but it was the flexible, almost amateurish nature of the Red Cross, dependent on assorted, sometimes eccentric groups of volunteers at every level of ability, that appealed to the nonconformist streak in Maugham's nature as well as to his spirit of adventure.

By the third week in October, his application accepted, Maugham was in uniform and ready to leave. Before he could do so, however, there had been a wretchedly unhappy interview with Syrie, during which she told him that she was again pregnant. Maugham was horrified. He felt that this time there was no question but that he had been deliberately trapped; he was angry and dismayed, too upset to be able to disguise his feelings. Syrie, expecting sympathy, was badly shaken by his stony-faced reaction. She burst into tears, sobbing that it was only because she loved him that she wanted to have his child. 'She made me feel a brute,' Maugham recalled. Despite his sense of outrage, he wanted to behave honourably; although he had tired of the affair, he still retained an affection for Syrie, and there was something in the plight of a pregnant woman that never failed to touch him. Nonetheless he was adamant that he would not be panicked into promising any kind of permanent alliance. They talked, and gradually a relative calm was restored, and Maugham was able to set out exactly what he was prepared to do. 'At last I promised that when she could no longer conceal her condition, I would fetch her and take her to some place where she could be confined.' And with that Syrie was obliged to be content.

Maugham landed in Boulogne on 19 October, reporting with other uniformed volunteers to the Hôtel de Paris where the Red Cross had set up headquarters. Rows of canvas-covered ambulances were parked along the quays, and the whole town was seething with khaki; everywhere groups of men in peaked caps and puttees stood about smoking and chatting or roamed the streets in an aimless attempt to pass the time before orders were received. Fierce fighting was taking place only a few miles away at Ypres on the Belgian border, and the sound of gunfire rumbled and thundered intermittently day and night. With the British Expeditionary Force engaged in a desperate struggle to hold back the German advance, the casualty rate was appalling, the numbers of dead and wounded quickly reaching the tens of thousands. Maugham's unit was moved out of Boulogne almost at once to join up with an American Red Cross group in the French zone, its job to transport wounded from the field to the casualty clearing-stations just behind the line; from there they were taken to the base hospitals in towns a few miles further away, to Doullens, Amiens, Montdidier. The weather was cold, the rain relentless. 'There are no candles & nothing but tallow dips,' Maugham reported to Gerald Kelly, 'the roads are horrible, *pavé* with three feet of mud on either side so that if a convoy forces you down nothing but a team of horses will drag you up again.' The makeshift clearing-stations, set up in churches and barns on the edge of the battlefield, were overcrowded and chaotic, but the conditions in the hospitals were little better, all of them overwhelmed by the sheer numbers of wounded, staffed by exhausted medics, with inadequate supplies, and with a basic lack of hygiene that made them breeding grounds for infection.

For Red Cross volunteers like Maugham, frequently required to go on to the field of battle, sometimes under fire, the work was demanding and dangerous. Often the call came at night, when in the freezing cold a convoy of ambulances would have to make its way, without headlights in the pitch dark, along muddy, cratered roads lit only by the flare of gunfire, to pick up their casualties, six stretchers stacked in the back of each vehicle, to be unloaded as gently as possible on arrival at their destination. Maugham's duties were various, as stretcher-bearer, driver and interpreter, his knowledge of both French and German proving invaluable in communications between the English medical staff and their patients. On one such occasion he found himself in a hospital housing two or three hundred wounded, its overcrowded wards airless and stinking of blood and excrement.

> There seemed not to be more than two doctors in charge, and they were assisted by a couple of dressers and a number of women from the town who had no knowledge of nursing. There was one German prisoner with whom I talked a little. He had had his leg cut off and was under the impression that it would not have been amputated if he had been French. The dresser asked me to explain to him that it was necessary to save his life, and with graphic detail explained to me in what a state the leg was.

On another night, after a period of intense fighting near Montdidier, orders came to bring the ambulances to the village church. As the darkened vehicles drew up one after the other and the stretchers were unloaded, the already dead were thrown on a heap outside the door, while the living were laid in rows on the straw-covered floor. The only light came from candles placed on the altar.

> Conversation mingled with groans of pain and the cries of the dying. One young boy, horribly wounded and desperately afraid, kept screaming '*Je ne veux pas mourir*,' while three soldiers standing by him tried to comfort him: one whose hand he held caressingly passed his other hand over the boy's face . . . '*Mais non, mon vieux, tu guériras*' . . . But he went on screaming '*Je ne veux pas mourir*' till he died.★

Some of the volunteers were severely shaken by the constant shelling and traumatised by the sights they were forced to witness, the horrific wounds sustained by many of the casualties, torn apart by the murderous weaponry employed by both sides. But Maugham, brave and unsqueamish, was often exhilarated by enemy action. 'I saw a battle between aeroplanes the other day which was the most horribly thrilling thing I have ever seen,' he told Alfred Sutro, while to William Heinemann he wrote from Dunkirk, 'I was lucky enough the other day to witness the shelling

★ 'I don't want to die' . . . 'No, old chap, you'll get better.'

by the Germans of some French batteries . . . It was splendid to see the bursting shells & the great eruption of earth as the Jack Johnson★ buried itself in the ground . . . On the way home they were shelling the Ypres road which I had to drive down, but missing it with admirable regularity. I went & looked at one of the holes. It was positively enormous.' The carnage was frightful, one engagement alone leaving 300 dead and 1,600 wounded; but with his medical training Maugham never flinched, his practical attitude combined with a notable gentleness and compassion resulting in his soon being asked to apply his long-forgotten skills, cleaning wounds, painting on iodine and tying bandages. 'I had done no work of this kind for many years,' he recorded in his notebook,

> and at first felt embarrassed and awkward, but soon I found I could do the little that it was possible to do . . . I have never seen such wounds. There are great wounds of the shoulder, the bone all shattered, running with pus, stinking; there are gaping wounds in the back; there are the wounds where a bullet has passed through the lungs; there are shattered feet so that you wonder if the limb can possibly be saved.

In the same unit with Maugham was the critic Desmond MacCarthy, a charming, indolent, erudite companion, only three years younger, with whom Maugham was to form a valued friendship. Elected an Apostle at Cambridge, MacCarthy knew such influential figures as Bertrand Russell and E. M. Forster, and through his friendship with Lytton Strachey, Leonard Woolf and Clive Bell had early become involved with the Bloomsbury group. His theatre reviews, particularly his writings on Shaw, were widely admired, as was his introduction for Roger Fry's famous Post-Impressionist exhibition of 1910. With so much common ground between them the two men had a great deal to talk about, and Maugham was one of many who found in MacCarthy an inspired conversationalist, so much so that he was led into being rather more forthcoming than at the time he realised, and was taken aback some years after the war to find his views on his own work retailed in an article as MacCarthy's own. 'I was a trifle vexed,' wrote Maugham tetchily, 'for it is a very different thing to tell the truth about yourself and to have somebody else tell it, and I should have liked the critic to do me the compliment of saying that he had heard it all from my own lips.' Desmond MacCarthy was indeed a shrewd critic of Maugham's fiction, which he admired, the only one of the Bloomsbury intellectuals to pay him any serious attention. Writing on Maugham in the 1930s, he perceptively noted that 'The war had a most important

★ A German artillery shell named after the American heavyweight boxing champion.

influence on the development of his talent . . . He learnt then how good it was for his talent to travel and to be alone.'

Maugham and MacCarthy had crossed over from England together, and on arrival in Boulogne had been warned, as writers, against sending back reports to the press, although neither had the least intention of doing anything of the sort. Eager for action, they found that between periods of intense activity were long periods of idleness, and both were grateful to find in the other a kindred spirit. 'We are either rushed off our legs or bored & idle,' as Maugham explained, and it was a great resource to have MacCarthy for company. When they could get away the two men dined together, sometimes at the Hôtel Meurice in Boulogne, where MacCarthy, safely out of sight of his wife, occasionally managed a date with a girlfriend; on other occasions they lingered over their wine and cigars in country inns, or pottered about sightseeing in the various towns and villages in which they were billeted. Maugham had a lucky escape one day in the Grande Place in Ypres: he had just moved to look more closely at the ruins of the medieval Cloth Hall when the wall against which he had been leaning was blown up by a German shell. 'It makes sightseeing a matter of some delicacy,' as he remarked in a letter to Gerald Kelly. Their unit was constantly on the move. Near Ypres the men stayed in a convent, fifteen to twenty in a room sleeping on straw palliasses on the floor; at Doullens Maugham was more comfortably installed in the house of a retired shopkeeper and his wife, who fussed over him and gave him hot milk before bed; at Steenvoorde near the Belgian border the accommodation was a grim little hotel with disgusting food and no bath, yet Maugham found he was nonetheless enjoying himself.

> The work was hard and tedious. But what a delight it was to have no responsibility! I had no decisions to make. I did what I was told, and having done it my time was my own. I could waste it with a clear conscience. Till then I had always thought it so precious that I could not afford uselessly to waste a minute . . . I was never without a sense of responsibility. To what? Well, I suppose to myself and to such gifts as I had, desiring to make the most both of them and of myself. And now I was free. I enjoyed my liberty. There was a sensual, almost voluptuous, quality in the pleasure of it.

He was not, however, entirely cut off from his professional duties. While they were stationed at Malo near Dunkirk, MacCarthy walked into Maugham's tiny bedroom and found him marking the proofs of his novel by the light of a single candle. MacCarthy, himself congenitally disorganised, was struck by the neatness of the scene, the long strips of paper tidily arranged on the narrow bed, the very few corrections that had been made. 'When I remarked on it, he replied that he always went over his work carefully [in manuscript] before he sent it to the printer.'

By the end of November it was clear that the war was not going to be over soon, and Maugham wrote to Syrie urging her to think again about continuing her pregnancy, now into its third month, as this was no time to have a baby. 'She took no notice of my letter,' he recorded grimly. 'She was determined to have the child.' Reluctantly Maugham decided he must return to England, heavy hearted because he had no wish to involve himself further with Syrie and her situation – but even more because he had recently met the man who for the next thirty years was to be the centre of his life.

# 7

# Code Name 'Somerville'

Shortly after arriving in Boulogne in October 1914 Maugham's unit had joined with a group of American Red Cross volunteers, among whom was a young man of twenty-two. Gerald Haxton, of middle height, with grey-blue eyes, sleek light-brown hair and a neatly trimmed moustache, was a slender, handsome youth. Speaking flawless French and with no trace of an American accent, Haxton was a charming, gregarious fellow, out to enjoy himself. In common with many of his transatlantic contemporaries, he had volunteered for the ambulance service because, unlike the military, it offered excitement and risk without the necessity of a long, dull period of training first, its members classed as officers but without the responsibility of command. By chance he and Maugham were both working in the same makeshift hospital in one of the local châteaux, and Gerald recognised the well-known playwright whose picture he had seen in the paper. Maugham was trying to soothe a badly wounded British soldier who was crying out for water, which the doctors had forbidden him to have. 'I'm sorry, but is there anything else I can do to help? Can I write a letter home for you?' 'Raite a lettah?' the soldier sneered in a ghastly imitation of Maugham's accent. 'Not on your life!' It was at this point that Gerald intervened, walking over to give the man a cigarette and tell him a few dirty stories to distract him from his pain. That night he and Maugham found themselves standing on a balcony overlooking the garden, talking of what they would do when the war was over. Maugham said he wanted to write and to travel: what did Gerald want? 'From you or from life?' the young man asked provocatively. 'Perhaps both,' Maugham replied. 'They might turn out to be the same thing.' Haxton unhesitatingly made clear that what he was interested in was 'fun and games . . . someone to look after me and give me clothes and parties.' The two of them then went up to Gerald's room where he had a bottle of gin, 'and that's how it all began'.

Although the time they spent together was brief both knew their meeting had been significant. Maugham was immediately smitten by this attractive young man, who in both looks and personality was precisely the type he found most irresistible, a bit of a chancer, raffish, self-indulgent and good-natured. Like Reggie Barlow-Bassett in *The Merry-Go-Round* and Gerald Vaudrey in *Mrs Craddock*, Haxton was a sexual opportunist, brimming with vitality – he had 'a habit of walking across a room on his toes, as if he were warming up for a race' – and he was well aware of the potency of his own animal magnetism. In an atmosphere charged with danger, emotions ran high, with the ethos of close male camaraderie fostering intense friendships, friendships that in the trenches, as with boys at school, not infrequently led to something more.★ It was in such an electric atmosphere that Maugham's long love affair with Gerald Haxton started.

Frustratingly, there are few records relating to Gerald's life and circumstances before 1914, and Maugham was careful to conceal or destroy as much as he could that referred to their subsequent relationship. What is certain, however, is that that relationship was the most important of his life, although among Maugham's friends and family opinion was sharply divided as to the character and influence of Gerald himself. Even in appearance there was something paradoxical, his face tantalisingly hard to read, with one eye cheerfully mischievous, the other full of threat. Some saw him as a benevolent charmer whose good humour did much to counter the older man's irritability and bouts of depression: he 'charmed the birds from the trees . . . [and] Willie was always enraptured by him', said the writer Arthur Marshall, an opinion seconded by Hugh Walpole, who wrote in his diary that Haxton was 'charming, full of kindness and shrewdness mixed'. This was a view shared by the critic Raymond Mortimer, who found Gerald 'jolly and delightful, always the life and soul of the party', while the aesthete Harold Acton, with a tinge of envy, wrote that Haxton was 'perennially young . . . as gay and irresponsible a companion as a careworn man could wish for'. There were others, however, who regarded Gerald Haxton almost as the devil incarnate. 'Shifty', 'disreputable', 'a cad', 'just this side of being a crook' are the words and phrases that repeatedly occur; the writer Peter Quennell, who memorably described Haxton as being 'very masculine . . . with a hard tarty face',

---

★ After the Battle of Vimy Ridge, for instance, this limerick went the rounds:

> In his bath mused the Marquess of Byng,
> Ah, Vimy Ridge such memories bring!
> That lovely young trooper –
> I mean, Gladys Cooper –
> My goodness, that *was* a near thing!

was one of many who judged his influence to have been wholly deleterious, holding him responsible for introducing the previously fastidious Maugham to some of the most sordid areas of the homosexual underworld. But perhaps most revealing is the portrait Maugham himself drew of Gerald as Rowley Flint in the 1941 novella *Up at the Villa*. 'He had an air of dissipation and people who didn't like him said he looked shifty . . . [but] what Rowley Flint had which explained everything was sex appeal . . . there was something that swept you off your feet, a sort of gentleness behind the roughness of his manner, a thrilling warmth behind his mockery . . . and the sensuality of his mouth and the caress in his grey eyes.'

Born on 6 October 1892, in the same month that Maugham started his studies at St Thomas's Hospital, Gerald Frederick Haxton was the son of a leading writer and editor on the *San Francisco Examiner*, the flagship in the newspaper empire of William Randolph Hearst. Henry Raymond Haxton, an émigré Englishman, was a tough, ambitious, hard-drinking rogue, a tall, flamboyant figure, bearded and flashily dressed. He married first a little-known actress, Agnes Thomas, whom he soon afterwards left for the beautiful Sara Thibault, member of a socially prominent family which had played an important part in the early history of California. The second Mrs Haxton was cultured and refined: she played the piano almost to professional standard and numbered among her acquaintance the celebrated novelist Gertrude Atherton, protégé of the writer and journalist Ambrose Bierce. In San Francisco the Haxtons appear to have had an interesting circle, as Bierce was a friend also of Harry Haxton's, as was Lloyd Osbourne, stepson of Robert Louis Stevenson. Haxton had travelled widely in Europe, and soon after their marriage the couple left America to settle in Paris, where Gerald was born, an only child adored by his mother, who described him dotingly to a woman friend as 'a rosy roly-poly, fat as butter'. When Gerald was still very young his parents separated and his father is next heard of in New York; Sara meanwhile moved to London, where she and Gerald led an impoverished existence in lodgings at 5 Queen's Road, St John's Wood.

It is probable that Gerald never saw his father again. In 1892 Henry Haxton came over to England to take part in the promotion of the *Encyclopaedia Britannica*, and over a number of years he spent much of his time in London, occupying a suite at the Savoy Hotel and masterminding a series of aggressive advertising campaigns, most famously in *The Times*. In 1904, as a result of the mutually beneficial association of the *Encyclopaedia* with *The Times*, Haxton was moved over to the newspaper, where he remained as advertising manager until ill-health obliged him to retire in 1911.

Strangely, although based in London, Haxton appears to have had no contact with either his wife or his son. In a few surviving letters written by Sara Haxton to Louise Sharon, a friend from California, there is no mention of any communication with her husband. Sara was evidently very hard up and worried constantly about money, more than once reduced to borrowing from the Sharons; she also complains that she has no one to advise her over Gerald's education, which plainly indicates the absence of a father-figure in the boy's life, a deprivation from which he must have suffered, especially as his mother was in poor health and rarely had the energy or resources to go out or entertain. 'I am leading the dullest and most monotonous of lives,' Sara complained to Mrs Sharon. 'But I dare say it's good for me. Only I don't quite see how – there's no doubt a narrow existence contracts all one's thoughts and feelings in the long run.' Sara did her best for her son, taking trouble to find the right school, buying him a dog and taking him for walks in the country on Sundays. But she was right: it was a dull existence, and no doubt by adolescence Gerald was fretting to escape, oppressed by his mother's anxiety and fragility, her constant complaints of colds and neuralgia, and by her suffocating dependence.

Apart from these few details, no other traces have emerged of Gerald Haxton's early years. The next sighting is in 1915 when, a year after meeting Maugham, Gerald got into trouble. On 13 November, while Maugham was abroad, Gerald, aged twenty-three, was arrested with another man in a Covent Garden hotel and charged with six counts of gross indecency (the legal term covering all homosexual acts with the exception of sodomy). Arraigned at the Old Bailey on 7 December both men pleaded not guilty, and with the help of two eminent attorneys, probably paid for by Maugham, they were acquitted on all counts. The judge, however, was convinced that Gerald was a bad lot, and taking advantage of his American nationality, afterwards had him registered as an undesirable alien, forced to leave the country and banned from ever setting foot in Britain again.

But for now this was all in the future. At the beginning of January 1915, Maugham, summoned by Syrie, left his unit and returned to England. The two of them met in Dover, and from there went by train to neutral Italy, to Rome, where Maugham had decided Syrie could be delivered 'without anyone knowing anything about it'. An apartment had been found near the Pincio, and here they settled to await the birth of their child. It was not a happy time for either. Maugham, painfully missing Gerald and worried about his exposure to danger at the front, felt not particularly inclined to respond sympathetically to Syrie's complaints and constant demands for attention. He at least had his writing – he was at work on a play – and there was golf when the weather permitted, whereas Syrie, shut up in the apartment all day, was wholly dependent on his company: she spoke no Italian, showed no interest in reading, sewing or sightseeing, and apart from Maugham saw no one except for the English doctor. To both the days seemed interminable. 'It is bitterly cold here, raining & miserable, & I regret the pleasant hardships of Flanders,' Maugham wrote gloomily to Heinemann; while to Gerald Kelly he expressed more specific anxieties. 'If only I am able to write here & under these conditions. Oh, what a perfect fool I am! But the only thing is to set my teeth & go through with it,' adding fatalistically, 'After all the future must look after itself & when anything may happen why should one bother.'

Certainly as regards the war everyone's future was precarious, and the stated intention of Italy to join the Allied cause seemed to promise very little. In a letter to Heinemann written in March 1915, Maugham expressed his disgust at what he saw as the supine attitude of most Italians.

> Did I tell you that my banker here said to me: What we want is a decisive victory of the allies; then you'll see what we Italians will do! It is the prevailing attitude, & they are none of them conscious of the poor figure they cut. I have read in the English papers of the demonstrations in Rome in favour of intervention, but I have seen two or three, and they were nothing but mild promenades of two or three hundred peaceable citizens. Their motto is: we don't want to fight, but by Jingo if we do, you've got the men, you've got the ships, you've got the money too.

As the time for Syrie's confinement drew near Maugham wrote to her mother, asking her to come out to Rome. He had yet to meet Mrs Barnardo, and was apprehensive about her reaction to his living in sin with her daughter, but there was no need for disquiet: during her years in the East End the Begum had seen it all, and later while staying in York Terrace she had grown accustomed to turning a blind eye to certain aspects of Syrie's behaviour. 'She took it as the most natural thing in the world,' Maugham reported with relief. During the evening of 4 May Syrie went into labour: it was soon clear that all was not well and at midnight the doctor was so worried he called an ambulance to take her to hospital in the Via Lancisi. Here on 6 May, under the name 'Mrs Wells', she was delivered of a daughter by caesarian section, Elizabeth Mary, always known as Liza after *Liza of Lambeth*, her father's first novel. A few days later the doctor told Syrie that she would never be able to conceive again, news which reduced her to despair: despite her age, nearly thirty-six, and her uncertain situation she longed for more children, a longing intensified by the painful separations from her son Mounteney. 'She cried bitterly,' said Maugham. 'I did my best to console her. That was all I could do.' Three weeks later Syrie had recovered sufficiently to travel, and on 9 June the four of them arrived back in London, Maugham returning to Chesterfield Street, Syrie, the Begum and baby Liza to a nearby hotel because the house in York Terrace had been let.

In Maugham's luggage was his new play, *Our Betters*, which he had all but completed, knowing how anxious Frohman was to see it. But suddenly Frohman was no longer there. On 1 May he had sailed from New York on the Cunarder, *Lusitania*, but seven days later just off the Irish coast the ship had been torpedoed with a loss of nearly 2,000 lives, Charles Frohman's among them. From the accounts of survivors it appears that the impresario had behaved with singular sang-froid, handing his lifejacket to another passenger and remaining coolly on deck to finish his cigar. With a flourish that may owe more to journalistic flair than to fact, his last words were reported to have been a quotation from *Peter Pan*, 'To die would be an awfully big adventure.' The news of Frohman's death was a shock to Maugham, who had come to like and trust this dedicated man of the theatre; there was, however, no time to lose in putting into action plans for the play's production. 'I am very glad to know that everything is to be continued just as though poor C.F. were still alive,' Maugham wrote to Al Hayman, Frohman's business partner. 'As I expect you know the idea was to open the Duke of York's Theatre with it in the autumn.'

In the tradition of Restoration comedy, *Our Betters* follows the path set by Goldsmith and Sheridan, but with a reach considerably extended, the twin pivots of the action not London and the country, but England and the United States. Although the treatment is very different, broader and more light-hearted, the plot bears some striking similarities to a short story of Henry James's, 'A London Life'. As in James's story its world is that of the dollar princesses who migrated from America to marry into the more impoverished sections of the British upper class. Leader of this flamboyant flock is the fascinating Lady Grayston who, bored by her dull baronet husband, consoles herself with a series of lovers, the current incumbent, the millionaire Arthur Fenwick, owner of a chain of department stores. Pearl Grayston's little sister, Bessie, has recently arrived in

England, and Pearl plans to marry her off to young Lord Bleane. Bessie, however, has a mind of her own, and although initially dazzled by the splendour of her surroundings, is soon repelled by the cynicism, greed and flagrant immorality of her wealthy compatriots, and returns with relief to America.

*Our Betters*, 'a dazzling icy glitter', as one critic wrote, is a highly polished, highly expert comedy of manners, chic, sophisticated and extremely amusing – just the play, in fact, to appeal to a war-weary London public. Unfortunately that public was to be denied it. First, the Lord Chamberlain's office refused to pass the play unless a change were made to a scene in which Bessie is tricked into discovering Lady Grayston *in flagrante* with a gigolo; this Maugham got round by having a young man, rather than an innocent girl, come upon the shocking sight. But then a more serious obstacle arose: the Foreign Office, nervous about upsetting the sensibilities of its most powerful potential ally, suddenly decided that the play was anti-American and banned it. Instead of being premiered in London *Our Betters* opened in March 1917 in New York, where, ironically, it was a resounding success. Despite a few expressions of outrage at the immorality of the theme – 'morally sordid' and 'offensive' according to the *New York Dramatic Mirror* – critics loved it and audiences came flocking. 'An excoriating . . . and exceedingly interesting comedy', said the *New York Times*, while the scholarly Louis Kronenberger, later drama critic for *Time* magazine, gave it as his opinion that 'no playwright since Vanbrugh . . . had drawn so harsh and unredeemed a picture of London society as Maugham did in *Our Betters* . . . one of the best testimonials to American push ever written.' When in 1923 the play eventually arrived in London, produced at the Globe with Margaret Bannerman and Constance Collier, it was rated just as highly. Desmond MacCarthy praised it in the *New Statesman*, describing it as 'remarkable . . . [and] mercilessly amusing', while the influential James Agate acclaimed it 'one of the most brilliant plays which has ever fallen from the pen of an English dramatist . . . a magnificent piece of satire, and the work of a master of the theatre.'

In the programme for the London production of *Our Betters* there was printed a curious little note from the playwright. 'Owing to various rumours which were circulated when the play was produced in America, the author wishes to state that the characters in it are entirely imaginary,' a statement owing more to a fear of libel than a respect for the truth. The 'various rumours' which six years earlier had raced round New York referred to the close similarity between the character of Lady Grayston's lover, Arthur Fenwick, and Syrie's lover Gordon Selfridge, the department-store tycoon. By his own later account Maugham had based the one on the other, without troubling himself very much about differentiating between the two, even underlining the parallel by giving the fictional version the name of another big London store, Fenwick, and endowing him with all Selfridge's well-known vulgarity, bombast and sentimentality. Of these Maugham had learned during the long weeks when he and Syrie were in Rome awaiting the birth of Liza, and Syrie had told him stories about her former admirers, chief among whom was Selfridge. 'She was very amusing about him,' it transpired. According to Syrie, Selfridge 'had fallen madly in love with her and had offered to settle five thousand a year on her. She refused,' Maugham recorded, adding drily, 'I did not know what to believe and what, with the hope of impressing me, she invented.' In the play the besotted old man lavishes presents and money on Lady Grayston, for which she has an insatiable appetite, but makes her wince by insisting on addressing her as 'girlie'.

> PEARL: I wish you wouldn't call me girlie, Arthur, I do hate it.
> FENWICK: That's how I think of you . . . I just say to myself, She's my girlie, and I feel warm all over . . .

It did not pass unnoticed that Gordon Selfridge, a famous first-nighter, gave the first night of *Our Betters* a miss.

There were other, very private personal references sewn into the text. The character of the gigolo, for instance, a spoilt, sexy young man, unashamedly out for what he can get, is named Tony Paxton, 'a hand-some youth of twenty-five, in beautiful clothes, with engaging manners and a charming smile', a portrait particularly designed to be appreciated by Gerald Haxton. And in Tony Paxton's scenes with his patron, the portly Duchesse de Surennes (née Minnie Hodgson from Chicago), there are echoes of painful scenes between Syrie and Maugham. Like Mrs Castillyon with Reggie Barlow-Bassett, Minnie is infatuated with Paxton, prepared to give him anything he wants in order to please him, repeatedly begging for assurance that he loves her. 'I wish you wouldn't constantly ask me if I love you. It is maddening,' says Tony irritably.

> D'you think it's jolly for me to feel that your eyes are glued on me what-ever I'm doing? I can never put my hand out without finding yours there ready to press it.
> DUCHESSE: I can't help it if I love you.
> TONY: Yes, but you needn't show it so much. Why don't you leave me to do the love-making?

If Maugham had believed that by taking Syrie abroad their relationship could remain undercover he was soon to be disabused. After the acrimonious separation from his wife Henry Wellcome had appeared to show little interest in her activities, indifferent to whom she saw or what she did as long as she behaved herself during those times when she had care of Mounteney. But in fact Wellcome was not indifferent, and his bitterness over Syrie's departure had calcified over the years into a determination to divorce her as soon as the ideal opportunity arose. When Wellcome learned of Syrie's affair with the celebrated playwright he knew he had got her just where he wanted: Maugham was rich, he was unmarried,* and the scandal of being judged the guilty party in such a high-profile divorce should ensure the ruin of Syrie's reputation for ever. As early as January 1912 Wellcome's lawyers had started gathering evidence, hiring private investigators to track the couple's movements, for instance, at the Imperial Hotel, Hythe, where the two of them were observed spending the night, '[Mr Maugham] and Mrs Wellcome occupying adjoining bedrooms'. By the time Maugham and Syrie returned to London after the birth of Liza, Wellcome's legal team was already in Rome collecting information and, with the help of the British Consul, interviewing witnesses, including the nurses at the hospital and the English doctor who had attended 'Mrs Wells' during her confinement.

Maugham, meanwhile, knew nothing of this, his mind set on returning to some kind of war work. 'I was at a loose end,' he complained, 'and nobody seemed to want me.' It was Syrie who came to the rescue: one of her girlfriends was the mistress of a Major (later Captain) John Wallinger, an officer in the foreign section of the Secret Service Bureau (later SIS, the Secret Intelligence Service), and it was arranged that the four of them should dine together one evening. Wallinger, who supervised a network of British agents in Germany and Switzerland, was impressed by Maugham and offered him a job in Geneva. It was arranged that he would go out there at the end of the year.

By this time matters were coming to a head at home, for it was now that Syrie received a letter from Wellcome's solicitors stating her husband's intention to divorce her and to cite Maugham as co-respondent. For Syrie this was an entirely desirable development: she longed to be rid of Wellcome, and she was far too tough a character to care very much about damage to her reputation as a consequence of divorce as long as she could be assured of remarriage at the end of it. For Maugham, however,

* Wellcome might have chosen to cite Gordon Selfridge, but Selfridge was married with four children, and, crucially, was a member of the same Freemasons' lodge as Wellcome.

who had always believed Syrie's assertion that Wellcome had no wish to change the status quo, the news was devastating. The case, unquestionably, was indefensible: he was to be publicly identified as co-respondent and he knew very well it would be considered disgraceful if he refused to wed Syrie after it. He felt trapped, deceived and very angry. Syrie, who had persisted in ignoring the fact that Maugham had never shown any wish to marry her, now felt frightened by his reaction, terrified that he might somehow renege on what she saw as his irrefutable obligation towards her. Desperately she sought a way to win his sympathy.

One evening Maugham was dining quietly with a doctor friend in Chesterfield Street when Syrie telephoned; she told him she had taken an overdose of sleeping pills and that he must come at once. The two men immediately went round to her hotel, where the doctor, as Maugham put it, 'got busy', while he telephoned the Begum, asking her to come and look after her daughter for a couple of days until she was fully recovered.

Frustrating Syrie's hopes, Maugham remained unmoved by her staged attempt at suicide, still reluctant to make the final commitment. In order to prepare himself for the forthcoming case he consulted a leading divorce lawyer, Sir George Lewis, who told him candidly that his situation was bleak: the evidence against him was incontrovertible and Wellcome was preparing to make the most of it, his one concession, agreed at Maugham's particular request, that there should be no mention of the child, Liza, in court. Lewis strongly advised Maugham to buy Syrie off: he had formed a poor opinion of her, seeing her simply as a gold-digger, an ageing adventuress in search of a large income. 'You'd be a fool to marry her,' he told his client, suggesting that instead he offer to give £20,000 or £30,000, which with the £1,000 a year Wellcome had promised if she did not remarry would keep her in comfort for the rest of her life. Maugham was powerfully tempted, and yet his sense of honour was strong; he could not quite bring himself to abandon Syrie, for whom he still had a residual fondness and who was after all the mother of his child. There was another consideration, too, one which he may not have chosen to discuss with Lewis. Syrie was aware of his homosexuality and even had the names of some of the men he had slept with: ruthless as he knew her to be, it was not impossible that she might use this information to blackmail him. 'D'you *want* to marry her?' Lewis asked irritably. 'No,' Maugham replied, 'but if I don't I shall regret it all my life.' Lewis shrugged his shoulders. 'Then there's nothing more to be said.'

It was after this final interview with Lewis that in November 1915 Maugham left for Switzerland, and here shortly before the case was due to be heard that Syrie joined him, hoping to avoid the publicity that the divorce would inevitably attract. It was a miserable period for both: Maugham was obliged to be constantly on the move, leaving Syrie by herself for days at a time; when he returned she was either irritable and resentful, or, in the face of his frigid politeness, tearful and clinging, constantly declaiming her love, imploring him to tell her what she was doing wrong and whether he still had any feeling for her. They bickered endlessly. 'If we were married it would all be different,' Syrie told him. 'B-b-but it might be worse,' Maugham grimly replied. One evening he went to the theatre, and was wryly amused to see enacted on stage an almost exact replica of his own predicament. *Amoureuse* by Georges Porto-Riche is a mordant little piece concerning a married couple, the husband driven frantic by his wife's cloying devotion, her egotism, her over-sensitivity to his moods, the way she will never let him read or work in peace. He explodes in an outburst of bitter complaint to a bachelor friend.

> Tu n'as pas encore perdu le droit d'être seul! ... [Ta maîtresse] n'est pas jalouse, obsédante et questionneuse ... Elle ne se penche pas sur ton épaule, quand tu écris une lettre ... elle n'opère point par de petites phrases vagues, insinuantes, qui n'ont l'air de rien, mais qui se glissent dans l'esprit et entament le courage ... Et si, par hazard, tu dines dehors sans elle, tu ne la retrouves pas à minuit, éveillée dans son lit, le visage immobile, mais la voix altérée et l'oeil plein de jalousie ... je tiens l'existence de cette femme dans mes mains! Je lui suis nécessaire comme l'air, comme la lumière ... Ma présence est non seulement indispensable à son bonheur, mais encore à sa vie. Je l'abandonnerais que je serais un miserable.*

'It positively made my blood run cold as I sat & watched,' Maugham confided to Kelly.

The case finally came to court in February 1916, by which time both respondent and co-respondent were back in London, Maugham having arrived from Geneva as he was obliged to be on hand for the final rehearsals of a new play. With regard to avoiding publicity the timing could hardly have been worse: the case was heard on 14 February, less

---

* 'You haven't lost the right to be alone! ... [Your mistress] isn't jealous, obsessively curious ... She doesn't lean over your shoulder when you're writing a letter ... she doesn't insinuate with those vague little phrases which seem to mean nothing but which lower the spirits and undermine one's courage ... And if by chance you go out to dinner without her, you don't come back at midnight to find her awake in bed, her face expressionless but with a broken voice and an eye full of jealousy ... That woman is entirely dependent on me! I'm as necessary to her as light and air ... My presence is indispensable not only to her happiness but to her life. I'd be an utter wretch to leave her.'

than a week after the opening night of *Caroline* on the 8th, a glamorous occasion, widely reported, ensuring that the playwright's name was already prominently in the public eye. As the case was undefended, neither he nor Syrie was in court to hear the allegations of their adultery and the granting to Wellcome of a decree nisi and custody of Mounteney. In the circumstances the press were remarkably restrained, on the whole confining themselves to briefly summarising the evidence and reporting the judgment. 'I am thankful it is over,' Maugham told Kelly a few days later. 'The case as you saw was published, but the details seem to me of the most harmless character & only the notoriety of the parties can have given any interest to it.' He himself returned almost at once to Geneva, while Syrie retired to a clinic to rest for a few days before going to Paris, which she planned to make her headquarters for the following twelve months. 'You will be doubtless seeing her in a few weeks,' Maugham wrote to Kelly, '& she will tell you the very sensible plan which we have elaborated. I think you will agree on its wisdom.' The details of this 'very sensible plan' remain obscure; what is clear, however, is that Maugham's frame of mind was rather less tranquil than indicated in his letter to Kelly. To his brother F.H. he was more open about the stressful nature of the recent ordeal.

> The whole matter has been a great distress & worry to me, but I try to console myself by thinking it is only through undergoing all varieties of human experience, however distressing some of them may be, that a writer can hope in the end perhaps to produce work of permanent value. I fancy the worst of my troubles are over, but what the final result of the misadventure will be only time can show, and in any case the future can not possibly have in store any worse harassment than I have undergone during the last eight months.

It was perhaps fortunate that Maugham could not foresee the long misery of his future with Syrie, and at least for the moment he was able to put most of his anxiety behind him and take pleasure in the dazzling success of his latest theatrical venture.

Produced by Dion Boucicault at the New Theatre, *Caroline* was an instant hit, a dextrous and supremely efficient piece of the kind Maugham could now write with one hand tied behind his back, 'high comedy at its very best', in the opinion of its star, Irene Vanbrugh. Originally entitled *The Unattainable*, the play's eponymous heroine is a grass widow whose husband, stationed abroad for the past ten years, suddenly dies, leaving her free to marry Robert, a delightful KC with whom she has long conducted an enjoyable and entirely blameless *amitié amoureuse*. Nothing, it seems, could be more suitable, but Robert and Caroline find to their dismay that neither regards the prospect with pleasure, and gradually they arrive at the realisation that their great attraction for each other lay in Caroline's unattainability. Despite the efforts of their friends to see them made man and wife, Caroline eventually contrives to return to the *status quo ante* by 'discovering' that the announcement of her husband's death was a mistake and therefore she and Robert can happily return to their old relationship.

*Caroline* is 'light as a feather', said the *Sunday Times*, 'the quintessence of natural gaiety', according to the *Daily Mail*, and yet the piece derives in part from some painful areas of experience, and the shadow of Syrie is darkly apparent, with the fast-approaching threat of marriage, so deftly avoided in the play, providing a sombre resonance. The subject is first aired in an exchange between Caroline and her maid, Cooper.

> COOPER: Well, ma'am, my belief is that men don't want to marry. It's not in their nature. You 'ave to give them a little push or you'll never bring them to it.
>
> CAROLINE: And supposing they regret it afterwards, Cooper?
>
> COOPER: Oh, well, ma'am, it's too late then.

And in the next act the speech in which Caroline explains to Robert her reluctance to marry could almost have been spoken by Maugham himself:

> Don't you know how you feel when you've been [on] a long journey, and your train steams in at night to some strange city that you've never been in before. All the lights are twinkling. And a wonderful excitement seizes you, and you think any adventure may happen to you . . . Oh, Robert, if you were sitting on the seat opposite me I'd know it never could.

In the playwright's opinion Irene Vanbrugh as Caroline gave 'one of the best performances of her distinguished career', an opinion endorsed by the critics. 'I have never had such an enormous success as *Caroline*,' Maugham boasted to his brother. 'We play to over £2000 a week, which Dion Boucicault tells me is the largest sum he has known a comedy to earn in his whole experience of the theatre. The papers have hailed it with unanimous praise . . . Barring Zeppelins or other such like catastrophes I think we are safe till the end of the summer & perhaps till Christmas.'

By the time this letter was written Maugham had returned to Switzerland, as he had been allowed only a few days' leave from his duties in Geneva. His job there, working for British military intelligence, had materialised after his introduction to Major Wallinger over dinner the previous summer. Having sounded Maugham out and been assured of his willingness to participate, Wallinger had suggested a further meeting at his office in Basil Street. The interview had gone well. Wallinger felt respect for Maugham, and Maugham for Wallinger, who struck him as both unscrupulous and astute, both essential qualities in a spy-master. Nearing fifty, a lean figure with a lined face, thin grey hair and a tooth-brush moustache, Wallinger had been a superintendent in the Indian police, brought to London in 1910 to monitor the subversive activities of Indian nationalists in Britain. In 1915 he had started working in the Secret Service Bureau. So far his operation had met with little success: a keen reader of spy-stories, Wallinger had adopted a number of familiar ruses, including disguising his agents as waiters, but this was quickly rumbled by the Swiss authorities who, fiercely protective of their precious neutrality, were quick to arrest and expel any foreign nationals whose conduct threatened to undermine it. Recently Wallinger had suffered further losses, with one agent denouncing another to the police, who then betrayed two more in his turn; a fifth man had had to be with-drawn after suffering a nervous breakdown, and it was this man whom Maugham was taken on to replace.

To Wallinger Maugham appeared to have not only excellent creden-tials but the ideal cover, that of a writer retiring to the peace and quiet of a neutral country in order to write. His main function, Wallinger explained, would be to act as facilitator rather than as a producer of secret intelligence, relaying messages to and from a network of agents who were working within Germany, in Frankfurt, Koblenz, Trier and Mainz. 'If you do well you'll get no thanks,' Wallinger warned him, 'and if you get into trouble you'll get no help,' conditions which Maugham accepted unques-tioningly. The whole idea of becoming a spy appealed to him enormously. Long a master of disguise, happiest when he could remain under cover, Maugham had no difficulty with the prospect of playing a part; a diffident man, he always preferred listening to talking, and his fascination with other people's lives had developed in him an unusual level of perception. His natural affinity for intelligence work was revealed to a wider public when after the war he wrote a series of stories about his espionage activities, known as the *Ashenden* stories after the name he gave his protag-onist, closely modelled on himself.

In the late autumn of 1915 Maugham, code name 'Somerville', arrived in Geneva, his base the imposing Grand Hôtel d'Angleterre on the banks of the lake. It was immediately obvious that the placid Swiss city had been turned by the war into a hotbed of international intrigue, packed with a moving population of spies and revolutionaries from the various warring nations taking advantage of the safety of the neutral country in their midst. The big hotels were doing a brisk trade catering to an unusually varied clientele. The lobby of the Angleterre became at certain times of day a Babel of European tongues, with a smattering of Russian, Turkish and Arabic besides; and when Maugham dined alone in the evenings he enjoyed identifying other guests who like himself were not quite what they seemed: a Bulgarian working for British intelligence, a prostitute who reported back to Berlin, an Egyptian known to be engaged in anti-British activities, and a German count, Karl Gustav Vollmoeller,★ whom Maugham had known as a playwright in London before the war. 'He had charming manners and was much interested in the Fine Arts. But now Ashenden and he pretended they had never seen one another before. Each of course knew on what work the other was engaged and Ashenden had had a mind to chaff him about it . . . but refrained in case the German looked upon his behaviour as further proof of the British frivolity in face of war.'

Despite the somewhat feverish atmosphere Maugham found that his own duties were on the whole fairly safe and routine, although he usually carried a small revolver in his pocket as a precaution. A large part of his job involved debriefing his agents on their return from sorties into Germany, issuing instructions, and paying their wages. Having made careful note of what he was told and adding his own observations he would then write a detailed report which he transmitted in code. This was a cumbersome business. 'I know nothing so tedious as coding and decoding,' says Maugham as Ashenden.

> [The code] was in two parts, one contained in a slim book and the other, given him on a sheet of paper and destroyed by him before he left allied territory, committed to memory . . . Ashenden deciphered the groups of numbers one by one and as he got it out jotted down each word on a piece of paper. His method was to abstract his mind from the sense till he had finished, since he had discovered that if you took notice of the words as they came along you often jumped to a conclusion and sometimes were led into error. So he translated quite mechanically, without paying attention to the words as he wrote them one after the other.

★ Vollmoeller became best known after the war for his screenplay for the Marlene Dietrich film *Der Blaue Engel* (*The Blue Angel*) and for his collaboration with Max Reinhardt on the play *Der Mirakel* (*The Miracle*).

In addition, on two mornings a week Maugham walked over to the market in the Place du Bourg-de-Four and bought half a pound of butter from an old peasant woman. As she gave him his change she slipped a piece of paper into his hand, the contents of which if discovered would have landed both of them in the dock; it was discreetly done, however, and for Maugham the only real moment of risk was the walk back to his hotel with the paper in his pocket, a distance he tried to cover as quickly as possible.

More hazardous was the weekly journey he made on the little steamer across Lake Geneva to Thonon on the French side, where he met and conferred with a colleague and received orders from London. As this was a round trip beginning and ending in Switzerland, it was conveniently not marked in his passport, but nonetheless Maugham could never be sure he was not being followed, either by an enemy agent or by the secret police, who would not hesitate to arrest and run out of the country any foreigner found to be engaged in espionage. To avoid attracting attention on these crossings Maugham resisted going below to the warmth of the saloon, preferring to remain on deck where he would be less noticeable. But even wrapped in a fur-lined overcoat and muffler, with his hat pulled well down over his ears, the bitter cold chilled him to the bone. In winter the lake was often stormy, and the gusts of sleet blowing down from the mountains cut right through him, and he would think longingly of the warmth of his hotel room, of a hot bath and dinner in front of the fire with his book and his pipe.

The regularity of his timetable led to a certain tedium in an existence which Maugham described as being in many respects 'as orderly and monotonous as a city clerk's'. This was not without advantage, however, as it left him plenty of time for his own work: his greatest anxiety while he was writing *Caroline* had been that he should be discovered and arrested before he had time to finish it. 'Geneva, the centre of all rumours,' as he described it to Kelly a few weeks after his arrival, 'is very quiet & peaceful, & there is nothing in the world to do. I manage to have a pleasant, though a dull, time. I write every morning & am getting along very satisfactorily with my play; I walk about or ride gently in the afternoons; & in the evening go to the play or make a fourth at bridge.' It was, as he admitted, a satisfactory way of life in many ways, sufficiently filled, sufficiently varied, with plenty of time to write and read; 'it was absurd to think that under these circumstances he could possibly be bored and yet, like a little lonely cloud in the sky, he did see in the offing the possibility of boredom'.

There were occasions, however, when boredom was dispelled, and 'Somerville' found himself required to play a more active role. His first mission, undertaken immediately on arrival in Switzerland, was investigating an Englishman, married to a German woman and living in Lucerne, who was suspected of being in the pay of the enemy. Under the pretext of taking German lessons from the man's wife Maugham observed him carefully for a couple of weeks before concluding that he was almost certainly a traitor. A trap was set: Maugham, following instructions, 'indiscreetly' let slip to his new acquaintance that he had connections in the Censorship Department in London. As intended, this information was duly relayed back to German intelligence by the Englishman who, pretending that he wanted to go back home to look for war work, asked Maugham to furnish him with an introduction to his friends in the Department. Shortly afterwards the unsuspecting prey was arrested, and dispatched to England for interrogation.

At another time Maugham was sent by Wallinger to Basle to check on an agent of whom there were suspicions of a different kind. 'Gustav', a Swiss businessman, was supposed to be making regular sorties into Germany under cover of his legitimate business, and on his return sending reports via Geneva to British intelligence. Again Wallinger's suspicions were proved correct, as Maugham mainly by clever questioning managed to discover that in fact 'Gustav' had never left the security of Basle, ingeniously concocting his reports from German newspapers and the gossip he picked up in restaurants and beer-cellars. In February 1916 another job came through, this time on the instructions of none other than Captain Sir Mansfield Cumming, head of the foreign section of the Secret Service Bureau. Cumming passed on his suspicions to Major Walter Kirke, chief of covert operations, that 'Bernard', one of Maugham's agents, 'had been doing us down' by taking large sums of money without sending in a single genuine report. Again Maugham was dispatched to find out what was going on, a scene he later described in *Ashenden*. The two men meet as usual in a café:

[Ashenden] gave him his orders and was prepared to finish the interview.

'Very good,' said Bernard. "But before I go back to Germany I want two thousand francs.'

'Do you?'

'Yes, and I want them now, before you leave this café . . .'

'I'm afraid I can't give it to you.' . . .

The spy leaned forward and, not raising his voice, but speaking so that only Ashenden could hear, burst out angrily:

'Do you think I'm going on risking my life for that beggarly sum you give me? Not ten days ago a man was caught at Mainz and shot. Was that one of your men?'

'We haven't got anyone at Mainz,' said Ashenden, carelessly, and for all he knew it was true. He had been puzzled not to receive his usual communications from that place and Bernard's information might afford the explanation. 'You knew exactly what you were to get when you took on the job, and if you weren't satisfied you needn't have taken it. I have no authority to give you a penny more.'

'Do you see what I've got here?' said Bernard.

He took a small revolver out of his pocket and fingered it significantly.

'What are you going to do with it? Pawn it?'

With an angry shrug of the shoulders he put it back in his pocket . . .

What happened to these men, to the 'Bernards' and 'Gustavs', once their deceptions were found out Maugham rarely had the opportunity to discover; he was, as he put it, 'no more than a tiny rivet in a vast and complicated machine'.

Maugham remained in Switzerland for a period of nearly eight months, from October 1915 to May 1916, broken only by the few days when he returned to London for the first night of *Caroline*. Writers were valued by the intelligence services for their reporting skills and powers of observation, and after Maugham left Geneva he was replaced by his friend and fellow playwright Eddie Knoblock, whose experience of the job was very similar, 'hours of infinite drudgery', as he termed it, 'in which only very rarely there occur moments approaching the dramatic'. Knoblock spent four months in Switzerland before joining Compton Mackenzie, another writer–spy, on a mission in Greece, by which time Wallinger's operation had collapsed in disarray. '[Wallinger's] Swiss show so far as we are concerned is a waste of money,' wrote Major Kirke in July 1916. 'His organization is useless, and has as a matter of fact not produced one report of any real value. He has not the knowledge, nor time to make a success of military secret service work.' On 28 July he recorded in his diary 'the parting of the ways' with Captain Wallinger. Yet unsatisfactory though he was judged to be by SIS, Wallinger was regarded by Maugham with a certain respect, and in the *Ashenden* stories, where Wallinger appears as Colonel R., he is portrayed as very much in control, hard-working, courageous and shrewd.

When Maugham arrived back in England he was in poor health; vulnerable to chest infections he had suffered from exposure during his weekly crossings of Lake Geneva throughout the winter. He was also anxious and depressed. Wellcome was granted a decree absolute on 30 August and there was now no legal barrier to Maugham's marrying Syrie: ultimately, as he very well knew, escape was impossible, but at least he could postpone the inevitable for a little while longer. 'I wanted to recover my peace of mind shattered through my own foolishness and vanity,' he wrote. 'I was willing to marry Syrie, but, the circumstances being as they were, I was not prepared to be rushed into it.' Two plays of his, *Caroline* and *Our Betters*, were to be produced in the States, and so in October 1916 Maugham sailed to New York, intending to oversee rehearsals and also cope with the business of transferring his plays from Frohman's firm, which had proved ineffective since the death of its founder, to John Rumsey, an associate of Maugham's British play agent Golding Bright.

New York six months before America's entry into the war seemed curiously alien, the streets brightly lit, shops full of luxury goods, and theatres and restaurants doing brisk business. The war seemed distant, with most of the newspapers giving greater prominence to reports of the defeat of the Boston Red Sox in the World Series than to those about the terrible slaughter of the Battle of the Somme. Maugham was taken aback by the prevalence of pro-German feeling, with many agreeing with President Wilson's conviction that Britain's ambitions were as objectionable as Germany's. 'There is a great deal of sympathy with Germans,' he told Kelly, '[especially] among the more intelligent part of the population, the professors, literary men, & such like. For the rest there is great admiration of the French, but none of the English . . . I think if the Germans were fighting alone against the English sympathy would be for the most part on the side of Germany.' Maugham had wanted to find more war work, hoping to be sent to Russia, but by now his state of health was too precarious, what he called his 'recurrent lung ailment' making it essential that he take some time, preferably in a warm climate, to convalesce. For many years he had wished to visit the South Seas, having long had an idea in his mind for a novel about Gauguin, and here at last was the opportunity.

Despite their lengthy separation, Maugham had stayed in touch with that dangerously attractive young man Gerald Haxton, currently at a loose end in Chicago, and he lost no time in suggesting that Gerald should accompany him to Polynesia in the nominal role of secretary, like Harry Philips before him, an offer that was enthusiastically accepted. Shortly before they were due to depart Gerald came down to Manhattan, and it was at this point, amid all the cheerful bustle of preparation, that suddenly a telegram arrived from Syrie announcing her imminent arrival, accompanied by child and nursemaid. Since his return from Geneva Maugham for Syrie had been conspicuous mainly by his absence, disappearing first to Paris, then to New York. Unsurprisingly, Syrie was beginning to panic: the decree absolute having been granted, there was no reason why they should not be married immediately,★ and if Maugham intended to evade his responsibilities in that direction then she had no choice but to confront him and insist that he keep his word. In a cold fury Maugham went down to the dock to meet her. They were both tense, Maugham because Syrie was the last person on earth he wanted to see, she terrified that he was somehow going to give her the slip. Having escorted her back to her hotel he told her at once that he was on the point of leaving, that he would be away for several months, and that he had no intention whatever of changing his plans. At this Syrie became hysterical and made a violent scene, which further repelled Maugham. When she eventually calmed down he assured her that he would not renege and that they would be married as soon as he returned. And with that Syrie was forced to be satisfied.

It was with an enormous sense of liberation that Maugham accompanied by Gerald boarded the train to San Francisco, where they were to embark on the first leg of their long sea voyage, the first of many to be undertaken together over the next quarter-century. Maugham was in high spirits, setting off to look 'for beauty and romance', and, he added feelingly, 'glad to put a great ocean between me and the trouble that harassed me'. Since boyhood when he had read Melville and Pierre Loti and the Polynesian novels of Robert Louis Stevenson, his imagination had been fired by dreams of the South Seas; later as a young man in Paris he had been mesmerised by Gauguin, by the pictures of Gauguin's Tahitian period, and while listening to Roderic O'Conor talking about Gauguin during those evenings in Le Chat Blanc he had become fascinated by the man as well as his work, for the past several years mulling over an idea for a novel, eventually to be published as *The Moon and Sixpence*, based on the painter's life. 'I was convinced', Maugham wrote, 'that by going to Tahiti I could get just the material I wanted to enable me to set to work.' He had tried to go as early as 1913, when he had hoped to take Sue Jones with him as his wife; but those plans had come to nothing. Now he was setting off, and with a companion, Gerald Haxton, who was already the focus of his emotional life.

★ In 'Looking Back' Maugham writes of this period, 'The divorce had not been made absolute, and I could not have married Syrie just then even had I wanted to.' But in fact it had and he could.

The distance to be covered was immense, the first section completed on board the SS *Great Northern*, an American liner that regularly plied the Pacific. It was at sea that it first became clear what an important asset Gerald Haxton was to be: gregarious by nature, Gerald effortlessly made friends with his fellow passengers, with whom he was more than happy to pass hours drinking, talking and playing poker, afterwards reporting back to Maugham the stories they had to tell. Maugham himself, intensely curious and ever on the look-out for good material, was nonetheless chary of intimacy, by nature extremely reserved. 'On a journey by sea, however long,' he wrote, 'I would never have spoken to anyone unless someone had first spoken to me.' But with Gerald so 'ebulliently, irrepressibly friendly', Maugham felt released from the strain of social obligation, able to enjoy listening and watching, although he was always affable, always ready to stand his round and take a hand at cards. For Maugham at this stage a game of cards was an absorbing pastime, but for Gerald it was almost a way of life: a reckless, high-risk gambler, he played brilliantly, capable of intense concentration and complex strategy, frequently winning substantial sums at the card-table. On board Gerald was happy to spend most of the day in a fug of cigarette smoke gambling in the saloon, while Maugham joined the others only at meals and in the evening, spending much of his time on deck writing in his notebook and reading. The vast blue emptiness of the Pacific Ocean affected him profoundly, as mile after mile went by without sight of another living soul: 'not a tramp, not a sailing vessel, not a fishing-boat'; 'it is an empty desert; and presently the emptiness fills you with a vague foreboding'.

Among the 400 passengers there was one who made himself particularly agreeable, indeed who was to become a friend for life. Bertram Alanson, three years younger than Maugham, was from a wealthy German-Jewish family, originally called Abrahamson, that owned coffee plantations in Guatemala, where Bert Alanson had grown up and attended university. A gifted financier, Alanson in San Francisco had been the youngest man on the stock-exchange floor, and now a senior partner in the family firm of investment brokers he lived in considerable style in a house over-looking the bay. He was tall and distinguished in appearance, with a passion for golf and Italian opera, as well as for Spanish history and literature, all interests guaranteed to recommend him to Maugham. Although stiff and shy in society, he was intensely snobbish, an energetic social-climber anxious to conceal his Jewish roots. He married rather late in life and always remained closely attached to his mother; within the family he was known to be homosexual. Alanson was by nature a hero-worshipper, and within days he became infatuated with Maugham, excited by his celebrity and impressed by the older man's charm and sophistication. The two of them talked for hours, Alanson fascinated by the breadth of Maugham's knowledge and experience, Maugham delighted to find someone whose financial expertise he could endlessly draw on. He was soon to assign to Alanson total control over his investments, a gesture of confidence which was to have enormous rewards. Their friendship began and remained entirely cloudless, and looking back on it many years later Maugham wrote that no one could have had 'a more devoted, generous, considerate friend than dear Bert'.

The long sea voyage was to take in Hawaii and Samoa, then veer south to Fiji, Tonga and New Zealand, before heading north to Tahiti on the return leg to California. Their first port of call was Honolulu, where they arrived on 14 November 1916 and stayed for three weeks, awaiting the arrival of the *Sonoma*, a small steamship bound for Australia on which they had booked onward passage. Haxton and Maugham, with Alanson for a while in tow, took the opportunity thoroughly to explore the island. A favourite spot was the verandah of a beachside hotel, where well supplied with drinks and cigarettes they could watch the magnificent bronzed bodies of the handsome Hawaiian boys ('sea-gods', Maugham called them) as they surfed the sunlit waves. The two men were fascinated by the contrast between downtown Honolulu, a modern American city with banks, smart shops and pavements lined with Buicks and Fords, and the rough red-light district of Iwilei, openly catering for every variety of sexual taste. On their last night there was a police raid in Iwilei, and the following day, a few minutes before the ship was due to sail, a young woman came hurrying up the gang-plank, clearly in a state of panic. She was a Miss Sadie Thompson, it turned out, an Iwilei prostitute in flight from the law. Once at sea she quickly regained her equanimity, antagonising her fellow passengers, among them a doctor and his wife and an American missionary couple, by playing loud ragtime on her gramophone and drunkenly keeping open house in her cabin for the ship's crew. 'She had a cabin two removed from mine, and she kept that damnable gramophone going night and day,' Maugham recalled. From Honolulu the *Sonoma* sailed to Pago-Pago in Western Samoa, and here the new arrivals were obliged to remain for some days as there was an epidemic of measles in the town. Holed up together in the same squalid boarding-house, confined indoors by the drenching monsoon rain, Maugham and his fellow travellers continued to suffer from the brazen behaviour of Miss Thompson, the 'hot lallapalooza from Honolulu', as one of her boyfriends called her. The missionary was particularly enraged by her, by the ragtime, the drinking, the noise of the rusty bedsprings as she entertained her numerous Samoan clientele, and eventually went to the governor to complain, thus providing Maugham with a crucial episode in what was to become his most famous short story, 'Rain'.

Maugham's first experience of the tropics took powerful hold of his imagination. In Pago-Pago, Apia, Papeete, Suva, Savaii, wherever he went he was entranced by the exotic beauty of his surroundings while at the same time remaining intensely alert to the sometimes tragic, often mundane, unexpectedly suburban life of the colonial community. Pago-Pago in Western Samoa, then under American jurisdiction, displayed exactly this juxtaposition. Once inside the barrier reef the ship entered a large and beautiful lagoon surrounded on three sides by a dramatic backdrop of towering volcanic escarpment covered in lush green vegetation. Along the shoreline were white sand beaches and slender coconut palms, beyond them groves of mango and avocado, interspersed with brilliant bursts of hibiscus, oleander and white tiare. Here and there stood little groups of native huts, with their high thatched roofs like bee-hives; the Samoans themselves were tall and graceful, the men bare-chested, dressed in brightly coloured pareos, while the young women wore their long black hair loose, often crowned with a wreath of heavily scented tiare. But also to be seen from the harbour were two or three trim little bungalows, a Protestant church, the local club, tennis-courts and a modest Government House standing in a neatly kept garden, the Stars and Stripes flapping languidly from a flagstaff.

Maugham's exploration of Samoa and beyond coincided with the rainy season. During their first few days in Pago neither he nor Gerald was prepared for the shock of a tropical climate, the stiflingly high temperatures and the hours a day of deluging rain. With the rain came a breathless heat, sultry and suffocating. The two men dressed in the thinnest of thin shirts and suits of light linen duck, in the evening adopting the local habit of wearing only shirt and pareo. At night they slept naked under mosquito nets, though the nets were often full of holes which the insects diabolically penetrated. During the day, in between downpours, they swam in the freshwater pools, drove in a pony and trap along the wide grassy roads that cut through the plantations, and went to pay homage at Vailima, where Robert Louis Stevenson spent his last years. Stevenson's tomb was up a steep ascent, and the two men, pouring with sweat, had to be physically pushed up the hillside by a couple of giggling Samoan girls, stopping at intervals while Maugham was overtaken by fits of violent coughing. Maugham responded immediately to the languorous, numinous eroticism he had first seen in the paintings of Gauguin. Sex was everywhere: young couples made love in full view and without embarrassment, and at bedtime he often found a dark-eyed *vahine* lying naked and willing under his mosquito net – to be given a handful of coins and briskly shooed away. Everything was open and on offer, and after dark Gerald especially liked to prowl off in search of the all-night saturnalias regularly to be found taking place by the sea-shore.

While spellbound by the prelapsarian beauty of the islands, by the deep blue of the lagoon, the brilliant colours of the vegetation, the immensity of the southern sky at night, Maugham was at the same time intensely interested in the more domestic aspects of life in the tropics, his most valuable material coming from the traders, half-castes, planters, doctors and missionaries with whom he fell into conversation. The dapper, dark-haired Englishman and his 'rather handsome travelling companion' soon became familiar to the regulars who drank at the English Club or on the verandah of the ramshackle Central Hotel. As on board ship, here too it was Gerald who struck up the acquaintance, and Gerald, hanging out in the billiard-room or bar, who first got to know these often eccentric characters, with their strange, sometimes terrible histories. Maugham was enthralled. As he expressed it in his memoir, *The Summing Up*,

> I entered a new world, and all the instinct in me of a novelist went out with exhilaration to absorb the novelty. It was not only the beauty of the islands that took me . . . what excited me was to meet one person after another who was new to me. I was like a naturalist who comes into a country where the fauna are of an unimaginable variety . . . Few of them had culture. They had learnt life in a different school from mine and had come to different conclusions . . . They had their own narrownesses. They had their prejudices. They were often dull and stupid. I did not care. They were different . . . They seemed to me nearer to the elementals of human nature than any of the people I had been living with for so long, and my heart leapt towards them as it had done years before to the people who filed into the out-patients' room at St Thomas's.

Although he stayed in each place for only a matter of weeks, Maugham was quick to absorb the social and cultural nuances, the rivalries, the snobbishness, the delicate balance in relations between native and European, between native and half-caste. Everywhere he went he made detailed notes of the people he met: 'I rarely went to my ship's cabin or lagoon-side hotel room without writing down a description of a special scene . . . or of some conversation with a special character that I might be able to use in a future story'; and gradually, 'from a hint or an incident or a happy invention, stories began to form themselves round certain of the most vivid of them'. Indeed it was now that his interest in writing short stories was strongly revived, and his collection of tales of the South Seas, *The Trembling of a Leaf*,★ marked a triumphant return to the genre of which he was to become a master.

Maugham found inspiration at almost every turn, and as his detailed note-taking makes clear it was this search for inspiration that lay behind his lifelong passion for travel: his restlessness, his wanderlust, was largely driven by an insatiable need to feed the voracious demands of his imagination. As he was to write years later to a young disciple, 'the writer cannot afford to wait for experience to come to him; he must go out in search of it'. Again and again the first tracings of a story can be detected in the jottings in the notebooks. Soon after arriving in Samoa, for instance, he comes across a character called Red, a sullen young man, 'dressed in a sleeveless singlet and a pair of dirty drill trousers', who runs a squalid eating house on the outskirts of Pago. The story that bears his name, constructed from a number of strands to be found in the notebook's pages, is narrated by Neilson, a gloomy Swede living in an isolated bungalow near the beach, who is unexpectedly called on by a fat old skipper come ashore for the night. The sailor is a repulsive specimen: 'His face was red and blotchy, with a network of little purple veins on the cheeks, and his features were sunk into its fatness. His eyes were bloodshot . . . But for a fringe of long curly hair, nearly white, at the back of his head, he was quite bald.' As the two men sit over their whisky Neilson relates to his visitor the romantic story of Red, a young man of outstanding beauty (described by Maugham in one of the very few homoerotic passages in the whole of his fiction).

> The first time you saw him his beauty just took your breath away. They called him Red on account of his flaming hair. It had a natural wave and he wore it long . . . He was tall, six feet and an inch or two . . . and he was made like a Greek god, broad in the shoulders and thin in the flanks . . . [with] that suave, feminine grace which has in it something troubling and mysterious. His skin was dazzling white, milky, like satin; his skin was like a woman's . . . his face was just as beautiful as his body. He had large blue eyes . . . and unlike most red-haired people he had dark eyebrows and long dark lashes. His features were perfectly regular and his mouth was like a scarlet wound. He was twenty.

★ The title comes from a quotation from Sainte-Beuve: 'L'extrême félicité à peine séparée par une feuille tremblante de l'extrême désespoir, n'est-ce pas la vie?' ('In life only a trembling leaf separates great happiness from extreme despair.')

Red falls in love with a native girl with whom he lives in perfect happiness, until one day he is kidnapped by the crew of a whaler and never seen in the islands again. The old sailor shows little curiosity in this affecting tale, far more interested in his whisky and cigar, although he listens amiably enough. It is, therefore, a shock when Neilson suddenly realises the identity of the obese figure slumped in the chair opposite.

> 'What is your name?' he asked abruptly.
> The skipper's face puckered and he gave a cunning chuckle . . .
> 'It's such a damned long time since I heard it that I almost forget it myself. But for thirty years now in the islands they've always called me Red.'
> His huge form shook as he gave a low, almost silent laugh.

Immediately before the account of Red in the notebook are four short paragraphs in which Maugham describes the American missionary couple, a Mr and Mrs Woodrow, whom he encountered on the ship from Honolulu, and also Miss Thompson, the girl who had been run out of the red-light district of Iwilei. The missionaries were on their way back to the Gilbert and Ellice Islands, and Maugham had been struck by the dour and cadaverous appearance of Mr Woodrow, and by the vindictive intolerance of his wife.

> [Mrs Woodrow] spoke of the depravity of the natives in a voice nothing could hush, but with a vehement, unctuous horror; she described their marriage customs as obscene beyond description. She said that when first they went to the Gilberts it was impossible to find a single 'good' girl in any of the villages. She was very bitter about the dancing.

In buoyant contrast to this proselytising pair is Miss Thompson, 'pretty in a coarse fashion . . . she wore a white dress and large white hat, and long white boots from which her calves, in white cotton stockings, bulged'. From these brief jottings Maugham constructed 'Miss Thompson',* the brilliant and terrifying story which was shortly to be retitled and known to the world as 'Rain'. In Maugham's own words, he wanted 'to have Sadie [Thompson] and the missionary experience an emotional collision that would be as shocking in print as censorship at the time would permit'. Written with impressive restraint, the story is set within the claustrophobic confines of a shabby little guest-house in Pago. The plot follows the grimly self-righteous missionary, Mr Davidson, as with sadistic zeal he pursues the prostitute, his declared intention to save her immortal soul. Against a

---

* With his usual indifference to such matters, Maugham did not trouble to give the fictional version of Miss Thompson a different name.

background of an unceasing tropical deluge the drama is played out, with the man of God bullying and hectoring his victim by day, and at night praying with an almost onanistic fervour for her reform. ' "I want her to accept the punishment of man as a sacrifice to God" . . . Davidson's voice trembled with excitement. He could hardly articulate the words that tumbled passionately from his lips.' Under pressure of his relentless persecution the cheerfully immoral Sadie is finally ground down; she becomes miserably convinced of her sinfulness and begs Davidson to bring her to the arms of Jesus. It is during his final interview with Sadie that the missionary, consumed by lust, succumbs, thus destroying himself and for Sadie all belief in the goodness of both God and man.

> [Sadie] gathered herself together. No one could describe the scorn of her expression or the contemptuous hatred she put into her answer.
> 'You men! You filthy, dirty pigs! You're all the same, all of you. Pigs!'

After leaving the missionaries and Miss Thompson in Samoa, the two men continued their voyage south, to Fiji, Tonga and as far as New Zealand. By the time they turned north towards Tahiti they had sailed in many different kinds of vessel, from American steamship to open cutter, to the rusty little traders laden with bananas and copra that regularly plied between the islands; once they spent seven days in an open rowing boat. Most memorable was the passage between Pago and Apia aboard a shabby schooner reeking of paraffin; in a dimly lit cabin the Chinese cook served a supper of meatballs and tinned apricots, followed by tea with condensed milk. 'After supper we went on deck,' Maugham recorded.

> After a while three or four members of the crew came up and sat down smoking. One had a banjo, another a ukulele and a concertina. They began to play and sing, and as they sang they clapped their hands in time. A couple of them stood up and danced. It was a strange, barbaric dance . . . sensual, sexual even . . . At last they grew tired and stretched themselves out on the deck and slept, and all was silence.

On 11 February 1917 they finally reached Tahiti in French Polynesia. This was the island which it had long been Maugham's ambition to visit, impatient to see for himself the place where only fifteen years earlier the great Paul Gauguin had come to paint. In Papeete, the capital, they stayed at the Tiare Hotel, a somewhat eccentric establishment run by Louvaina Chapman, an immensely fat part-Tahitian woman, known throughout the South Seas and beyond for her character and charm. The hotel was only five minutes' walk from the waterfront, which pleased Gerald, who liked to hang about there eyeing the brown-skinned sailors in their scarlet loincloths while Maugham pursued his researches. At first it was difficult to find anyone who had much to say about Gauguin, though Maugham was able to talk to Emile Lévy, a pearl merchant who had known the painter, and also Captain 'Winny' Brander, who had discovered Gauguin's body shortly after his death in 1903. But in fact the best source turned out to be Louvaina Chapman herself, who had befriended Gauguin and was able to provide Maugham with several interesting details as well as a crucial introduction. This was to a female chieftain at Mataiea, about thirty-five miles outside Papeete, who proffered the astonishing infor-mation that there were paintings by Gauguin in a house not far away. The owner of what turned out to be a shabby two-room bungalow was 'a flat-nosed, smiling dark native', who was delighted to invite his visit-ors in. Maugham immediately recognised the artist's work. It transpired that in 1892 Gauguin, ill with the syphilis that was eventually to kill him, had been taken in and cared for by a local farmer, and in gratitude had painted pictures on the glass panels of three interior doors. Two of the panels had been badly damaged, scratched and picked at by children, but the third, representing a sensual Tahitian Eve, dark haired and half naked, a heavy green breadfruit in her hand, was still in a reasonable state of preservation, and it was this panel Maugham immediately offered to buy. His host, uninterested in the painting, was willing to sell, but only at a price that would cover replacing the door.

> 'How much will it cost?' I asked.
> 'A hundred francs.'
> 'All right,' I said, 'I'll give you two hundred.'
> I thought I had better take the picture before he changed his mind, so
> we got the tools from the car . . . unscrewed the hinges and carried the
> door away.

Once back in Papeete the door was carefully packed ready to be shipped via New York to London, eventually to be installed in Maugham's writing-room in the Villa Mauresque, where it remained, one of his most treasured possessions, until shortly before his death.

Maugham and Gerald left Tahiti on 8 April 1917, two days after the United States entered the war. Waiting for Gerald in San Francisco was a telegram from his mother urging him to enlist. He and Maugham took leave of each other, Gerald departing to join the United States army, Maugham to be reunited with Syrie in New York.

Throughout his long liaison with Gerald Haxton, Maugham was to run the gamut of emotion – passion, love, tenderness, fury, frustration, boredom, misery, despair – but at this stage, after their sojourn in the South Seas, Maugham was wholly in love, at the start of what one of his close friends described as 'the first completely beautiful, completely appropriate love affair he had ever had'. According to another, 'Maugham adored Haxton, the one love in his life. Haxton was a cad, but young, attractive, athletic, masculine, and it must have been rapturous for Maugham for a while.' Early on in their relationship Maugham transcribed for Gerald some lines of a poem by Yeats, 'The Lady's First Song', which he felt summed up his feelings: 'I am in love / And that is my shame. / What hurts the soul / My soul adores, / No better than a beast / Upon all fours.' Maugham had surrendered to this young man, who on almost every level had proved to be an ideal companion, handsome, cheerful, sociable, adventurous; he was easy-going, with a good sense of humour and, like Maugham, a vigorous sexual appetite. It was only with Haxton that Maugham could talk through the stories he was evolving in his mind. True, Gerald was inclined to drink too much, and when in his cups his temper could turn nasty, revealing a seam of anger that sober he kept buried. While in the Pacific there had been a couple of violent punch-ups, one in Apia which started when the barman at the Central Hotel had taunted Gerald with dodging the war and evading his patriotic duty. Like his fictional alter ego, Rowley Flint in *Up at the Villa*, when Gerald was drunk 'he was noisy and boastful and vulgar and quarrelsome . . . after two or three drinks there was no holding him . . . Sometimes I couldn't help flying into a passion with him and then we'd have an awful row.' But most of the time he was 'kind and gentle and sweet', and for both sides the relationship was rewarding. For his part Gerald looked up to Maugham, partly as a father-figure, something crucially missing while he was growing up, and also as someone who was more experienced, more sophisticated, and who would introduce him to the kind of life for which he had longed, a life as far removed as possible from the tedium and genteel poverty of St John's Wood. Under Maugham's protection he was indulged and doted on; he was financially secure; and also, by means of his natural sociability, his love of talk, he had found a purpose, a crucial role to play.

In his memoir 'Looking Back', Maugham acknowledged the importance of Gerald's contribution. 'But for him,' he wrote, 'I should never have got the material on our journey to the South Seas that . . . enabled me to write the short stories which later I published in a volume called *The Trembling of a Leaf*.' All six tales appeared first in magazines before they were collected in book form in 1921, dedicated not to Gerald but to Bert Alanson, '[in] trifling acknowledgement of the great kindness you have always shown me.' Ironically, 'Rain', the story that had by far the greatest success, was repeatedly rejected until finally taken by H. L. Mencken's magazine the *Smart Set* only a few months before *The Trembling of a Leaf* appeared. All the stories, fluent, colourful and dramatically succinct, proved popular, but 'Rain' was to cause a sensation: 'a sheer masterpiece of sardonic horror, beyond criticism' ran a typical notice. A showcase both for the author's loathing of intolerant religiosity and for his unillusioned view of the weakness of human nature, 'Rain' has been reprinted again and again, earning its author more than $1 million in royalties. It has been rewritten as a play, turned into a musical, nearly made into a ballet by Roland Petit for the Paris Opéra, and filmed no fewer than three times, with Gloria Swanson (1928), Joan Crawford (1932) and Rita Hayworth (1953) in the part of Sadie Thompson; in 1946 there was an all-black film version entitled *Dirty Gertie from Harlem*; and shortly before her death Marilyn Monroe was signed to play Sadie in an adaptation for television. Among its many admirers was James Michener, author of the Pulitzer Prize-winning *Tales of the South Pacific*.\* 'One of the evil limitations put upon anyone who wants to write about the South Pacific is that he must stop reading Maugham,' Michener wrote.

> [But] I must admit that before I start to do any writing about this vast area I usually take down RAIN and reread those first three paragraphs to remind myself of how completely one can set a physical stage in a few absolutely correct observations. I hold those passages to be about the best beginning of a mood story extant.

But in 1917 this was yet to come. When Maugham parted from Gerald after their six months together he was faced with returning to New York and to Syrie. He had promised he would marry her, and now he had come to fulfil that promise. Had he said nothing else on the subject, Maugham's personal distaste for the concept of the married state could have been deduced from his work. The plot of his play *Caroline*, for instance, is posited on the assumption that love flourishes best outside wedlock and that the institution of marriage is a killjoy and a trap. In 'The Fall of Edward Barnard',† one of the short stories

---

\* It was on Michener's *Tales of the South Pacific* that Rodgers and Hammerstein based their phenomenally successful musical *South Pacific*.

† The plot of 'The Fall of Edward Barnard' was later expanded and reworked in *The Razor's Edge*.

in *The Trembling of a Leaf*, we are asked to applaud the hero's escape from marriage in Chicago to a blissful single life in the South Seas. And in *The Moon and Sixpence,* a novel shot through with anger and written only a year after Maugham's return from Polynesia, he tells the story of the ruthless rejection of marriage and family by the artist, whose creativity up till then has been smothered by domesticity. 'There is no object more deserving of pity', the narrator feelingly remarks, 'than the married bachelor.' But in fact there is no need to search for clues, as Maugham had little hesitation in making his feelings plain. In a letter written only three years into the marriage, he explained to Syrie his view of the situation at the time of their wedding with a candour bordering on the brutal.

> I felt that I had been put in a position which I did not for a moment anticipate was a possibility. I knew that I had made a perfect fool of myself, but I thought I had also been made a perfect fool of . . . I married you because I was prepared to pay for my folly and selfishness, and I married you because I thought it the best thing for your happiness and for Elizabeth's welfare, but I did not marry you because I loved you, and you were only too well aware of that.

In such circumstances it is hardly surprising that the wedding itself was an unjoyous occasion. The formalities took place before a judge in New Jersey at three o'clock in the afternoon of 26 May 1917, all arrangements having been made by Maugham's friend and fellow playwright Ned Sheldon. Sheldon was one of the witnesses, the other, Alexandra Colebrooke, wife of a backwoods British peer, and a friend of Syrie's. The bride gave her age as thirty-two, instead of thirty-seven, but all the groom later recalled of the ceremony was of standing before the judge, 'who first sentenced the drunk in front of us, then married us, then sentenced the drunk behind us'. During the brief exchange of vows Maugham felt so overcome with loathing for his bride that he could hardly bring himself to look at her. Afterwards there was a small reception at the Brevoort Hotel near Gramercy Park, attended by a handful of Maugham's theatrical acquaintance gathered to celebrate the 'doomed entanglement', as one of them termed it, after which the newly married pair retired to a suite at the Devon in midtown Manhattan. As the door closed behind them, Maugham might well have recalled lines from a favourite novel, Samuel Butler's *The Way of All Flesh*: 'There is no time at which what the Italians call *la figlia della Morte* lays her cold hand upon a man more awfully than during the first half hour that he is alone with a woman whom he has married but never genuinely loved.'

Most of June was spent in New York, with Maugham much involved with theatrical business, after which husband and wife left for a seaside holiday in East Hampton, accompanied by two-year-old Liza and a nanny. It was here on Long Island at the beginning of July that Maugham received an unexpected telephone call from a family friend, William Wiseman, asking if he were interested in discussing some possible war work.

Captain Sir William Wiseman, an English baronet still in his early thirties, had been recruited by Mansfield Cumming to work for the American branch of the Secret Intelligence Service. With the myriad animosities between the two countries, the position was a delicate one, but Wiseman, a charming and subtle diplomatist, was making a success of it. By the time the United States entered the war, on 6 April 1917, he had already built up a formidable network of contacts, establishing close links with his American opposite numbers in intelligence as well as between the British Foreign Office and the Department of State in Washington. For both governments it was now an urgent priority to keep Russia in the war. Of the two revolutionary parties, it was the more moderate Mensheviks who were committed to continuing the fight, while the Bolsheviks under Lenin were agitating for peace at any price. The Bolsheviks having recently been ousted, it was the Mensheviks, under the leadership of Alexander Kerensky, who held the majority, and it was thus Kerensky and his coalition Provisional Government that the Allies were anxious to back. To this end Wiseman was mounting a secret operation designed to offer support to Kerensky, whose position, under attack by an increasingly vociferous Bolshevik minority, was beginning to look worryingly insecure. With his project approved on both sides of the Atlantic, Wiseman had recently received generous financial backing, $75,000 deposited to his credit at J. P. Morgan & Co. by the British and a similar sum by the Americans. Now he needed to appoint an emissary who would go to Petrograd, hold talks with the Prime Minister and his colleagues, discreetly disseminate propaganda and regularly report back on the volatile political situation. Somerset Maugham, with his experience in espionage, seemed the ideal choice.

Maugham was astonished by Wiseman's suggestion, flattered and immediately intrigued. The prospect of seeing for himself the country of Tolstoy, Chekhov and Dostoevsky was powerfully appealing; so, too, was the opportunity of involving himself once again in the war; and not entirely to be discounted was the additional satisfaction that such a mission would remove him at least for a time from his marital responsibilities. Against this was the fact that Maugham was far from well. Although his health had temporarily improved during the months in the tropics, it had deteriorated since his return, and now he was always tired, slept badly, was feverish and frequently coughed up blood; recently an X-ray had confirmed what he already suspected, that he was in the early stages of tuberculosis. Maugham was also worried about Gerald, from whom he had heard nothing since the young man had left the States to undergo military training in South Africa; the likelihood of any future communication from Haxton reaching him in Russia was extremely small. The opportunity now offered, however, was too good to miss, and after forty-eight hours' reflection Maugham accepted Wiseman's proposal.

The next few weeks were busy, Maugham travelling by train from Long Island to New York to confer with Wiseman, book his passage, obtain visas and make all other necessary arrangements for travel. He was briefed on the current situation by, among others, Rabbi Stephen Wise, an influential Reform rabbi closely in touch with Jewish communities in Petrograd; by the Polish nationalist Jan Horodyski, who gave him letters of introduction; and by Emanuel Voska, a Bohemian-American secret agent, who as head of the Intelligence Department of the Czechoslovak National Council worked in close alliance with Professor Tomáš Masaryk, the founder and future President of Czechoslovakia, who was currently in Russia helping organise Slav resistance to the Central Powers. As before, Maugham was given the code name 'Somerville', his official identity again that of a writer at work, this time a journalist reporting for the British press. Before leaving, there was one final detail which needed clarification. 'I do not know whether it is intended that I should have any salary for the work I am undertaking,' Maugham wrote to Wiseman.

> I will not pretend that I actually need one, but in Switzerland I refused to accept anything and found afterwards that I was the only man working in the organization for nothing and that I was regarded not as patriotic or generous but merely as damned foolish. If the job carries a salary I think it would be more satisfactory to have it; but if not I am not unwilling to go without. I leave the matter in your hands.

Wiseman took the point, and agreed to provide both salary and expenses.

Having said goodbye to Syrie, who apparently took his going 'without a murmur', Maugham left for San Francisco where on 28 July he was due to embark. Concealed in a belt under his shirt he carried bills of exchange for the enormous sum of $21,000, to be disbursed as he saw fit in the furtherance of Allied interests. His travelling companions were three friendly Americans, en route to Petrograd to join the staff of the United States Embassy there, as well as Voska and a trio of Czech associates, who would act as liaison between Maugham and Masaryk. During the journey it was understood that Maugham would pretend to regard the Czechs as complete strangers. It was also understood that 'Somerville' was acting as a private agent who could, and undoubtedly would, be disavowed by his employers at the first sign of trouble. From California the ship sailed to Yokohama in Japan, giving Maugham his first sight of the Far East, a part of the world which in later years never failed to fascinate. 'It was tantalizing', he told Gerald Kelly, 'to get no more than a brief glimpse of it.' At Yokohama he transferred to a Russian ship as far as Vladivostok, where he boarded a crowded trans-Siberian train for the eleven-day journey to Petrograd. On arrival in the capital he went with Voska straight to his hotel, the Europa on Nevsky Prospekt, in order to rest – he had been feverish and unwell on the train – and prepare for a meeting with the British Ambassador on the following day.

When Maugham arrived in Petrograd at the end of August 1917 he found the city in a state of turmoil. Six months previously the February Revolution had forced the abdication of the Tsar, since when there had been an anarchic period of riot and confusion. Along the broad streets tanks and armoured cars had become a familiar sight, and there was often the sound of gunfire. With the relentless German advance against an army perilously short of arms and apparel, Russian soldiers were deserting in droves, many to be seen roaming the streets, desperate and dangerous. Fighting frequently broke out between the Cossacks, loyal to the Provisional Government, and the Bolsheviks, demanding that the Government should go. Crime was rife, restless crowds surged day and night along the city streets, and there was an acute shortage of all basic supplies; every morning from before dawn long queues of women wrapped in shawls and headscarves waited patiently for deliveries of bread, milk, sugar and tobacco. The great imperial capital, with its magnificent mansions, its canals and bridges, gilded domes and spires, was already beginning to look dingy and dilapidated. Yet despite the crisis there was a level of normality: trams were running, and carriages and motor-cars still plied up and down fashionable Nevsky Prospekt and Morskaia Street, with their shops and restaurants and grand hotels; theatres and concert-halls were open for business as usual, and the cinematographs displayed huge posters of Charlie Chaplin, Douglas Fairbanks and Mary Pickford; cafés were jammed with customers, even if there was little on offer except a sandwich and a glass of tea.

Near the Hermitage on Palace Embankment, opposite the Peter and Paul Fortress, stood the British Embassy, a magnificent eighteenth-century edifice, originally known as the Saltykov House, built by Catherine the Great. It was here that Maugham duly presented himself on the day after his arrival. At Wiseman's request only the vaguest explanation had been provided by London for Maugham's presence in Petrograd: according to the Foreign Office cable, 'Mr Somerset Maugham is in Russia on a confidential mission with a view to putting certain phases of the Russian situation before the public in the United States.' Despite this uninformative statement it was naturally expected that the Embassy should offer him any assistance he required, specifically in the transmission of reports, to be sent in code to the British Consul in New York. Shown into a sumptuously upholstered anteroom hung with massive portraits of Queen Victoria, Edward VII, George V and Queen Mary, Maugham was left to himself for a considerable period before the Ambassador chose to make his entrance; by this time he had worked himself into a nervous state, his stammer intensified by the frigid courtesy with which he was received. Sir George Buchanan was a formidable presence. Tall and lean, with silver-grey hair, a monocle and moustache, Sir George in his black tailcoat and grey trousers looked the perfect cardboard cut-out of an ambassador. 'In his cold and uninteresting way he was really a very handsome fellow,' Maugham grudgingly noted, smarting from the chilliness of his reception. For it was acidulously made clear that the well-known writer was a far from welcome visitor. Sir George, a skilful and distinguished diplomat, was under enormous pressure trying to keep a balance between the various warring factions as well as working to persuade a wavering Kerensky to stay in the war. Now here was this inexperienced amateur arriving on the scene, who not only was to be allowed direct access to Kerensky himself, but whose encrypted cables were to be sent on by the Embassy in a code it could not read and without the Ambassador being made privy to their content. It was this last in particular that Sir George regarded as a grave affront. 'I realized', wrote Maugham after the interview was over, 'that I could not count on much help in that quarter.'

For Maugham the most pressing undertaking was to obtain entrée to the Prime Minister, and with this in mind he made contact with his old flame, Alexandra ('Sasha') Kropotkin. Madame Lebedev, as she now was, had left England to return to Russia in order actively to involve herself in the revolution, already a familiar sight in Menshevik circles with her statuesque figure, lorgnette and well-tailored English clothes. An enthusiastic supporter of the Provisional Government, she knew Kerensky well and was more than willing to provide an introduction. The reality proved disappointing. Once a dynamic and effective leader, Kerensky, still only thirty-six, was a sick man; ensconced in his office in the Winter Palace he had lost the vision and decisiveness that once were his, allowing himself to be easily influenced and constantly changing his mind. He knew he was losing his grip and was terrified by the prospect, which now seemed imminent, of defeat. Kerensky 'looked very unhealthy', Maugham recorded.

> He seemed fearfully on edge. Sitting down and talking incessantly, he took hold of a cigarette-box and played with it restlessly, locking and unlocking it . . . His speech was rapid and emphatic; and his nervousness made me nervous too . . . As the conversation proceeded . . . something pathetic seemed to arise . . . The final impression I had was of a man exhausted . . . He was more afraid of doing the wrong thing than anxious to do the right one.

Maugham's impression on this first meeting, that the Menshevik leader was unworthy of Allied support, was fortified by an incident he witnessed shortly afterwards. Maugham and Sasha Lebedev were in the audience at a vast conference held one wet September evening in the Alexandrovsky Theatre. The theatre was brightly lit and the boxes filled with foreign diplomats, while at long tables on stage sat members of the praesidium. Towards the start of proceedings Kerensky, in a plain brown uniform, clean-shaven, his hair *en brosse*, strode out from the wings and began to address the audience; then suddenly he stopped as if struck as a voice in the audience started to heckle. According to one observer, 'in the middle of his speech . . . [he] rushed from the platform and burst into tears . . . It seemed incredible that this man was holding the reins of great seething Russia.' The British journalist Arthur Ransome was another who recorded the Russian leader's failure of nerve, describing the sweat breaking out on his forehead 'as he faced now one, now another group of his opponents'. Maugham was equally unimpressed. 'I've never seen a man on a public platform whose face actually looked green,' he recalled. 'If I'd been sitting closer I could have smelt the fear.'

This humiliating performance notwithstanding, Maugham continued to confer with Kerensky, their meetings taking place once a week at the Mjedved, the finest restaurant in the city. 'With Sasha acting as hostess and interpreter,' he recalled, 'I provided my guests with quantities of caviare at the expense of the two governments who had sent me to Petrograd, and they devoured it with relish.' Afterwards the conversation would continue in Sasha's apartment, with Kerensky pacing the room and haranguing Maugham as though he were a public meeting. The situation facing the Provisional Government was growing increasingly desperate: abroad the Allies were pressuring Kerensky to continue with the war, while within the country the masses, facing famine and the approach of winter, were demanding peace. For Kerensky the Englishman was becoming an increasingly crucial contact in his dealings with the Allied powers. The American Ambassador, a former grain merchant from St Louis, rarely put his head above the parapet, while His Britannic Majesty's representative was proving impossibly obdurate: at a recent meeting Sir George Buchanan had made it plain that no further help could be expected from his government until the disorganisation in the army, and indeed in the country at large, was substantially resolved. Furious and frustrated, Kerensky had turned his back on the Ambassador and stalked out of the room, a Napoleonic touch, as Buchanan drily described it, but one which if theatrical in effect was awkward in result, leaving the Russian leader with no direct line to Downing Street other than that provided *sub rosa* by Somerset Maugham.

Maugham meanwhile was diligently filing his reports, spending long evenings in his hotel encrypting information, an unwieldy process which it was impossible to hurry. According to the elaborate code with which he had been equipped, Kerensky was to be identified as 'Lane', Lenin as 'Davis', Trotsky as 'Cole', Sir George Buchanan as 'Dewar', while the British government appeared under the guise of 'Eyre & Co.'; if a password were asked for it was 'Friend of Mr King in New York'. His briefings were highly rated by Wiseman, who knew he could rely on Maugham, now the chief British agent in the field, to send back assessments that were both accurate and politically astute. On 24 September Wiseman cabled in cipher to Sir Eric Drummond at the Foreign Office in London, 'I am receiving interesting cables from Maugham . . . [He] asks if he can work with British intelligence officer at Petrograd, thereby benefiting both and avoiding confusion. I see no objection . . . He is very discreet . . .'

As before in Switzerland, Maugham had a team of agents under his control, to be employed as he thought fit. He dispatched a couple of his men to Sweden and Finland to investigate rumours of an alliance between those countries and the Central Powers; and he made strenuous, if ultimately unsuccessful efforts to infiltrate one of his agents into Bolshevik secret meetings, an aim eventually achieved by the Americans. He himself kept closely in touch with a wide range of contacts in Petrograd. There was Voska, of course, and the remarkable Tomáš Masaryk, 'gently spoken, absent-minded and undramatic', whose Czech organisation was run with impressive efficiency; Maugham recommended substantial financial support for Masaryk's Slav Press Bureau, recognising its importance as a front for anti-German propaganda as well as for more covert operations. Maugham also conferred at length with Boris Savinkov, Kerensky's War Minister. Described by Maugham as the most extraordinary man he had ever met, Savinkov had been responsible for some spectacular assassinations of imperial officials, and was crucial to the Allies as a firm believer in the reorganisation of the army and continuation of the war.[*]

At first Maugham was optimistic, believing in the resolve of those at the top and impressed by the general good humour of the crowds in the street, but it was not long before disillusion set in. By the end of September he was already convinced that the cause was hopeless: Kerensky was weak, Lenin and the Bolsheviks were rapidly gaining ground, and there was a general mood of defeatism within the Provisional Government that it was impossible to counter. Looking back Maugham wrote, 'The endless talk when action was needed, the vacillations, the apathy when apathy could only result in destruction, the high-flown protestations, the insincerity and half-heartedness that I found everywhere sickened me with Russia and the Russians.'

And yet, the political situation apart, there was a great deal to be learned and enjoyed, and Maugham was determined to make the most of his time, exploring the city and immersing himself in the language and literature of the country. Every morning he had a lesson in Russian, and he read avidly, the great novelists of the past as well as contemporary authors such as Kuprin, Korolenko, Sologub and Mihail Artzybashev. He went to the ballet, to concerts and to the theatre. (Among the plays on offer was an unknown Russian comedy, which Maugham attended out of curiosity: as the plot unfolded it began to seem increasingly familiar, and glancing at his programme he saw the author's name listed as 'Mum', the title of the play *Jack Straw*.) In fine weather he took long walks, along the great length of Nevsky Prospekt, down the Arcade with its theatres, through the bazaar at the corner of Sadovia Street, across St Isaac's Square, past Pushkin's house by the Fontanka Canal, past mansions and offices, down narrow cobbled streets with decayed wooden tenements. One day strolling round the precincts of the ancient Lavra

---

[*] Savinkov makes an anonymous appearance in Maugham's 1944 novel *The Razor's Edge*, in which the narrator describes himself drinking 'a glass of Russian tea in a prim parlour in Petrograd while a soft-spoken little man in a black coat and striped trousers told me how he had assassinated a grand duke'.

monastery at the end of Nevsky Prospekt he was overwhelmed by a powerful feeling of nostalgia.

> In the birch trees rooks were cawing, and my recollection was carried back to the precincts of Canterbury . . . the same grey clouds hung overhead. I felt homesick. I stood on the steps of the great church, looking at the long line of the monastery buildings . . . but I saw the long nave of Canterbury cathedral with its flying buttresses and the central tower more imposing and lovely to my moved eyes than any tower in Europe.

The homesickness was made worse by the fact that letters were sparse, arriving at irregular intervals in the diplomatic bag. To Eddie Knoblock Maugham wrote, 'I am longing for news of England & have very little; so pray give me half an hour of your time & send me all the current gossip. It seems incredible that one of these days we shall all settle down again to normal existence & read the fat, peaceful *Times* every morning, & eat porridge for breakfast & marmalade.' But the one friend of whom Maugham yearned to have news was Gerald Haxton, from whom he had heard nothing since leaving for Russia. All he knew was that Gerald had sailed for South Africa, but as the weeks passed without any word he began to fear the worst, that his ship had been sunk and that Gerald was dead. In fact Gerald was still at sea: on 26 October 1917 his ship, the Japanese *Hitachi Maru*, had been captured near the Maldives in the Indian Ocean by the notorious German raider *Wolf*. All the passengers and most of the crew were taken off, the Japanese ship being eventually scuttled and sent to the bottom. For the next five months *Wolf* with her cargo of 200 prisoners sailed on a circuitous route north, round the Cape of Good Hope and across the South Atlantic, attacking four more ships on the way, finally reaching her home port of Kiel in the last week of February 1918. From here Gerald was transported to the prison camp at Güstrow in northern Germany, where he remained until the cessation of hostilities the following November.

Meanwhile in Petrograd Maugham took pains to find agreeable society for his spare time. The Europa was filled with Allied agents and there was a good deal of cheerful congress between them, especially after the arrival of the English suffragette Emmeline Pankhurst, who every afternoon kept open house, making tea on a Primus stove in her room for anyone who cared to drop in. With basic supplies growing increasingly scarce – an apple now cost $2.50 and bread was made mainly from acorns and straw – everyone was hungry and talked obsessively about food, about roast beef and roast lamb and real coffee with sugar and cream. Nonetheless, as Voska put it, 'we in the Hotel Europa . . . managed at times to enjoy ourselves and forget the revolution . . . [We] caught the Russian mood – "*Nitchevo!*" ["It doesn't matter!"] – and went about our business as calmly as the natives.'

Hoping to expand his circle Maugham wrote to Knoblock, 'I know that you have friends all over the world, and if you chance to have some here I wish you would let me have a note to them.' The city was full of foreign visitors, diplomats, observers, journalists, businessmen, including a large number of Americans. One of these was an American banker, in Russia to arrange a loan to the Kerensky government; garrulous, self-satisfied and naive, the man was also curiously endearing, and Maugham came to enjoy his company, and was consequently distressed when the banker was killed in a street shooting, an incident recalled in the *Ashenden* story 'Mr Harrington's Washing'. Also among those come to witness the revolution was a glamorous young American couple recently married, John Reed and Louise Bryant, both writers, both convinced Marxists.* Reed, who was to write a classic account of the October revolution, *Ten Days that Shook the World*, had spent time in Mexico with the rebel leader Pancho Villa, and his articles on the subject had caught Maugham's attention. Interested to learn more, he invited the pair to lunch and questioned Reed not only about Mexico but about his prosperous middle-class background and conversion to radicalism. Maugham was in jocular mood and glancing about with an air of mystery whispered to Louise, 'You won't reveal you had lunch with a British secret agent, will you?', a suggestion that struck her as so preposterous she burst out laughing. 'It couldn't have been funnier if he'd said he was an ambassador of the Pope,' she afterwards remarked.

An acquaintance closer to home was the novelist Hugh Walpole. Classified unfit for military service, Walpole had first come to Russia to work for the Red Cross, and was now heading a small intelligence-gathering service, grandly entitled the Anglo-Russian Propaganda Bureau, of no great utility or efficiency although much relied on by the British Embassy; according to Arthur Ransome, 'It organised a certain amount of hospitality and in the end became a joke.' Maugham and Walpole had first met in London in 1911, and both were now pleased to pursue the friendship. Walpole, possessed of the fatal facility of the second rate, was astonishingly prolific; he was also insatiably ambitious, desperate to be accepted by the great and the good, and determined to make his mark as a distinguished man of letters. Shameless at self-promotion, he flattered famous writers by sending gushing fan letters, always including a request

* The 1981 film *Reds*, starring Diane Keaton and Warren Beatty, was based on Reed's life with Bryant.

for a meeting so that he could continue the blandishment in person; and when in receipt of a bad review he never failed effusively to thank the critic concerned for his helpful comments. Bumptious and vain he certainly was, also thin-skinned and embarrassingly sentimental, and many found his craving to be loved irritating; and yet Walpole was not a bad sort: he was friendly and enthusiastic, and except concerning the productions of his own pen was a perceptive critic. Naturally he was thrilled to have come across such a well-known figure as Somerset Maugham, and he gleefully recorded their meetings in his diary. 'Delightful lunch with Willie Maugham. He most amusing,' was the entry for 27 October, and after a concert a few days later, 'Evening with Willie Maugham who was his old delightful self – amusing, clever and extraordinarily kind.'

Maugham also enjoyed these encounters. It was good to talk to someone who was so well read, who moved in much the same world, and with whom he had a number of friends in common. There was the added recommendation of Walpole's rampant homosexuality: Hugh, pink-cheeked and bespectacled, pursued a vigorous sex life. 'I am very sensual but pious and pure if that sensuality is gratified,' he observed of himself contentedly. He was always falling in love, and was famous in queer circles as the only man ever to have got Henry James into bed ('No, it's impossible, it's impossible,' the great man reportedly cried, springing out again in his nightshirt), a story relished and frequently dined out on by Maugham. Indeed Maugham relished Hugh's whole performance, if not quite in the way Walpole imagined. Flattered by his companion's concentrated attention as he happily chattered away, boasting of his successes and confiding the highs and lows of his busy emotional history, Hugh, his pink face aglow, failed to realise how closely he was being observed. Aware he was making an impression, it never crossed his mind that that impression might be ridiculous, and that with his plump face, bulging eyes and little mouth snuffling with excitement he reminded his companion irresistibly of a guinea-pig. Later Maugham was to make devastating use of Walpole in his fiction, but for the time being all was harmonious between them, and Hugh blissfully happy with his kind new friend.

Walpole was intrigued by Maugham's observations on the rapidly changing political scene. 'He watched Russia as we would watch a play, finding the theme, and then intent on observing how the master artist would develop it,' he wrote. But now the play was drawing to a close. By mid-October it was obvious to all that the Bolsheviks would soon be in power, and Wiseman, realising that Maugham as 'the secret agent of reactionary imperialism' was a marked man, decided to have him recalled. When Kerensky learned of Maugham's imminent departure, he summoned him to the Winter Palace and charged him with delivering a message to the Prime Minister, Lloyd George. The crux of the message, which was to be memorised, not written down, was a plea that Britain should offer peace to Germany, but a peace without annexations or compensation, in other words on terms which would make it impossible for the Germans to accept. In such a situation, Kerensky believed, he would have some chance of keeping his mutinous army in the field. 'I must make the Russian soldiers understand what they are fighting for,' he said. 'We haven't got boots or warm clothes or food ... I don't see how we can go on. Of course, I don't say that to the people. I always say that we shall continue whatever happens, but unless I have something to tell my army it's impossible.' A couple of other clauses were added, including the usual request for more guns and ammunition, as well as a demand that Sir George Buchanan be replaced, as 'the Ambassador does not seem able to get into sympathetic relations with the new conditions'.* As soon as the meeting ended Maugham sent a coded communication to London, and shortly afterwards received the reply that to ensure total secrecy a destroyer would be sent to Christiania (now Oslo) in Norway to bring him home.

That same evening, 22 October 1917, Maugham left Petrograd by train from the Finland Station on the first stage of his journey. By this time he was more than ready to go. Not only was there little prospect of achieving anything with Kerensky – two days after his departure saw the outbreak of Lenin's Bolshevik Revolution, 'the ten days that shook the world', during which Kerensky was overthrown – but he himself was seriously unwell. With his lungs badly infected, he was feverish and exhausted, and with the food shortages grown daily more acute he was also malnourished: arriving in Christiania with a day to wait he bought a pound of chocolates which he ate there and then in the street. After a rough crossing to the north of Scotland, he reached London on 17 November, and immediately telephoned Downing Street to make an appointment for the following day. Lloyd George was extremely cordial, expressing his pleasure at meeting the distinguished writer whose plays

* When interviewed in 1962 at the age of eighty-one, Kerensky, then living in New York, had no memory of negotiating with Maugham, recalling that he met him only once at a brief official reception. His failure to remember is perhaps unsurprising given his age, the stresses and myriad claims on his attention in 1917, and the humiliating circumstances of his defeat. However, the Wiseman papers, now in Yale University Library, bear out Maugham's account.

he so much enjoyed. He talked about these a little, then moved on to expound on the war and the current situation, and Maugham began to form the impression that the Prime Minister had a shrewd idea of what he had to say and was determined not to let him say it. Finally, in desperation, Maugham took a paper out of his pocket on which, contrary to instruction, he had written down Kerensky's message, and thrust it at Lloyd George, who scanned it hastily. 'I can't do that,' he said, handing it back. 'What shall I tell Kerensky?' Maugham asked. 'Just that I can't do it,' he repeated, then rising to his feet explained that he had a Cabinet meeting to attend and left the room.

Back in his hotel room Maugham pondered what he should do next. His immediate concern was the state of his health, and from St Thomas's he obtained the name of an eminent lung specialist, who confirmed the diagnosis of tuberculosis and told him he must go immediately to a sanatorium. Scarcely had he had time to take in this information than on 20 November he was called to a debriefing, held in the office of the editor of *The Times* and chaired by the Lord Chief Justice, Rufus Isaacs; among others present were General Sir George McDonough, director of British military intelligence, Gordon Auchincloss, secretary to President Wilson's power-broker, Colonel E. M. House, and, to Maugham's surprise, William Wiseman, recently returned from America. Frightened that his stammer would get the better of him, Maugham handed his report to Wiseman to read aloud. It received little comment, for, as the Foreign Office representative, Sir Eric Drummond, noted on his copy, 'I fear this [is] of only historical interest now.' Depressed by the fact that all his efforts had been in vain, Maugham wrote of his Russian mission, 'I failed lamentably,' although in retrospect, he added, 'it seems to me at least possible that if I had been sent six months before I might quite well have succeeded'. His superiors, however, were impressed by his performance and more than ready to give him further employment. Wiseman suggested he might act as liaison with Polish groups in London and Paris; but more immediately there was a job for him in Bucharest, where he would be required to undertake the same kind of work as before, lending support not to the Mensheviks but to the Cossacks, and encouraging Romania to continue the fight.

And, as before, Maugham was flattered to be asked and, excited by the opportunity, tempted to accept. At the same time he knew he was in no condition to travel.

[I thought] that it was only sensible, since I might crack up, to say that I was suffering from tuberculosis and the doctors advised me to go to a sanatorium, but if they could find no one more trustworthy to do the job, I was perfectly willing to take it on. Rufus Isaacs looked at me. He smiled. 'In that case I don't think we ought to ask you to go,' he said. 'Go to your sanatorium and I hope you'll get well very soon.'

Maugham followed his specialist's advice, repairing to a sanatorium in the north of Scotland. It was to be nearly two years before his recovery was complete, and there was no question but that he had begun treatment only just in time. Nevertheless, part of him regretted his decision to turn the Romanian offer down: 'I knew . . . that I had made a bad mistake. I should have risked the danger and even though I hadn't been of much use the adventure would have been interesting.'

# 8

## Behind the Painted Veil

By the time Maugham left London for Scotland at the end of November 1917 he was a very sick man. Nordrach-on-Dee, just outside Banchory in Aberdeenshire, was a huge private sanatorium dedicated to the treatment of pulmonary tuberculosis. Opened in 1900 and timber-built in the Bavarian style, it was based on the German model, established at Nordrach in the Black Forest, which had pioneered the open-air treatment of TB. Although so far north, the winter climate on Deeside was relatively mild, and patients were exposed to the bracing Scottish air twenty-four hours a day, windows, overlooking smooth green lawns and a thick canopy of conifers, remaining wide open at all times. Besides fresh air, the basic tenets of the cure were bed-rest, gentle graduated exercise, large amounts of nourishing food, particularly fresh meat and vegetables and quantities of milk, and a complete absence of stress. Dr David Lawson, the founder of Nordrach-on-Dee, was insistent that the sanatorium should be a haven of tranquillity, with compulsory naps after meals, a nurse to each patient, and no unnecessary movement allowed: in severe cases even putting the arms behind the head was forbidden for fear of stretching the lungs. Visitors, anyway in the early weeks of a patient's stay, were discouraged. Such ministrations were not cheap – around £3,000 a year; nor was the success rate impressive – many patients died, others remained at Nordrach for years without visible improvement; but until the discovery of antibiotics in the 1940s it was the best treatment available, and at the least it helped stop the spread of infection by isolating sufferers from the world outside.

Maugham was to remain based at Banchory for over a year, and for the first few weeks he barely moved from his bed, exhausted by the symptoms of the disease which had killed his mother and which now had him in its grip. Gradually, however, his condition improved, and before long he was able to take pleasure in his peaceful invalid life, loving the hours spent lying in bed, devoid of all pressure and responsibility. 'I delighted in the privacy of my room with the immense window wide open to the starry winter night,' he wrote. 'It gave me a delicious sense of security, aloofness and freedom . . . The monotonous day, whose only excitement was the books I read and my reflections, passed with inconceivable rapidity.' By degrees as his strength returned he began to enter more actively into the routine of the sanatorium. Between rising at 11.00 and retiring to bed at 4.00, he mingled with the other patients, took some of his meals with them, played cards, and even, on fine days, sat outside wrapped in rugs on the verandah. Little did these men and women know of what consuming interest they were to the writer in their midst. To Eddie Knoblock, Maugham wrote cheerfully,

> There is something that would appeal to your passion for the macabre in the way the tuberculous fall in love with one another, have scenes, scandals, & all the paraphanalia [sic] of the drama; & you cannot imagine the effectiveness of threatening your beloved that you will have a hemorrhage (I never could spell the damned word) if she does not turn a consenting ear to your entreaties . . . One man came here & died four days later. I had quite a success with the remark that it seemed hardly worth while to come to Scotland for so short a time.

During the first few months, Maugham found it impossible to work, but he was avid for news from London, impatient to know what was going on, in the war, in the theatre, among his colleagues and friends. 'The post is always the great thrill of the day,' as he told Alfred Sutro, '& the recipients of letters are the envy of all around.' One interesting event was the opening of a new play of his on 26 January 1918 at the Globe. Written during the previous year, *Love in a Cottage* is an inconsequential little piece which treats with a familiar theme,* that of the rich widow who teases her mercenary suitors by allowing them to propose before revealing that if she remarries she loses her fortune. 'Meant to be nothing but pure entertainment', as the author admitted, the piece had been commissioned by Marie Löhr, who had started in management and was for the first time both producer and star. Described by Desmond MacCarthy in the *New Statesman* only a few years later as 'a play so negligible that I am no longer sure of its name', it was largely thanks to Miss Löhr's sparkling rendition that *Love in a Cottage* racked up a respectable run of 127 performances.

Lacking strength for the physical effort of writing, Maugham was ceaselessly active in his imagination, thinking over his adventures of the past couple of years and planning new work. Closest to hand was the

---

* Previously explored both in 'Cupid and the Vicar of Swale' and in *The Bishop's Apron*.

material gleaned from his fellow patients, a number of whose private dramas were eventually retailed in the short story 'Sanatorium'. Yet richer by far were his own recent adventures, the people and situations he had come across, both mundane and extraordinary, during his work for the intelligence services in Switzerland and Russia. With the nature of that work so secret, and with the war still in progress, there was no question of publishing anything for some time to come. The matter nonetheless was much on his mind, and it was now that he began to compose that seminal series of spy stories, personal, factual and realistic, based on the exploits of his fictional alter ego, Ashenden. The *Ashenden* collection, 'a very truthful account of my experiences during the war when I was in the Secret Service', was not to appear for another ten years, held up by '[Willie's] mysterious bosses in the Foreign Office', as his publisher explained it. According to report there were originally thirty-one stories, but when Maugham showed them to Winston Churchill in draft, Churchill insisted on fourteen being destroyed as he considered them in breach of the Official Secrets Act.

The *Ashenden* stories closely follow Maugham's undercover operations in 1916 and 1917, the exception a brilliantly entertaining sequence narrated in three episodes, 'The Hairless Mexican', 'The Dark Woman' and 'The Greek', which was based on a mission described to him by Gerald Kelly, who had undertaken similar work in Spain. Ashenden himself is an engaging character, in almost all respects the exact reflection of his creator – he even gives his address as Chesterfield Street, Mayfair – a solitary man, rather shy, private, detached, but also incurably inquisitive. Unlike other story-book spies of his era, Ashenden is a very fallible human being, fond of his creature comforts, at times irritable, sometimes scared, and although an experienced traveller an inveterate sufferer from train fever: 'He was not happy unless he was settled in his corner, his things on the rack above him, with a good half-hour to spare. Sometimes by arriving at the station too soon he had caught an earlier train than the one he had meant to, but that was nerve-racking and caused him all the anguish of very nearly missing it.' When dispatched by Col. R. (a.k.a. Major Wallinger) to Lucerne to investigate a suspected traitor, Ashenden, like Maugham, enjoys the opportunity of acting a part: 'He was travelling with a brand-new passport in his pocket, under a borrowed name, and this gave him an agreeable sense of owning a new personality. He was often slightly tired of himself and it diverted him for a while to be merely a creature of R.'s facile invention.' While in Switzerland most of his time is spent in Geneva, where Ashenden dutifully carries out his instructions, interviewing agents, crossing the lake once a week into France, picking up his secret message from the butter-woman in the market, and at all times taking care to avoid the attentions of the Swiss authorities.

As he not infrequently remarks, much of his work is routine, even boring, and yet there are moments of high drama, when another side is shown of this amateur secret agent, who is discovered to be not only courageous but ruthless. In 'Giulia Lazzari', for instance, Ashenden's job is to get hold of an Indian called Chandra Lal, leader of a group of dangerous agitators controlled from Berlin. Col. R. has discovered that Chandra Lal is currently in neutral Switzerland, and Ashenden's mission is to lure him into France, where he can be arrested and taken back to be dealt with, harshly, in England. The instrument to be used in this operation is the eponymous Giulia, an ageing, third-rate music-hall dancer. She and the Indian are lovers, and it is up to Ashenden to force her, by means of a little blackmail, to write to Lal in Lausanne begging him to come and see her in France. Giulia is distraught: deeply in love with Lal, she knows only too well the fate that awaits him if the ruse succeeds, and over a period of days she implores Ashenden not to compel her to betray her lover; he, however, remains impassive, apparently unmoved by her desperation.

> [Giulia] staggered. She put her hand to her heart. Then without a word she reached for pen and paper. But the letter was not to Ashenden's liking and he made her write it again. When she had finished she flung herself on the bed and burst once more into passionate weeping. Her grief was real, but there was something theatrical in the expression of it that prevented it from being peculiarly moving to Ashenden. He felt his relation to her as impersonal as a doctor's in the presence of a pain that he cannot alleviate.

Of the stories that survive, six derive from Maugham's stay in Petrograd, and in these he largely ignores the political negotiating with which he had been involved with Kerensky, concentrating instead on his more personal relationships. The stickiest of these was with the British Ambassador, Sir George Buchanan, here appearing as Sir Herbert Witherspoon in a disguise that is thin to the point of transparency. When Ashenden pays his first official call on the Ambassador, he is received 'with a politeness to which no exception could be taken, but with a frigidity that would have sent a little shiver down the spine of a polar bear'. The finest of the Russian tales is 'Mr Harrington's Washing', a small masterpiece of tragi-comedy, telling the true story of the American banker who befriended Maugham on the trans-Siberian train journey from Vladivostok. As they rattle across Russia Mr Harrington, garrulous, kind-hearted and absurd, drives Ashenden mad. 'Mr Harrington was a bore. He exasperated Ashenden, and enraged him; he got on his nerves, and drove him to frenzy.' In their railway carriage, even when Ashenden tries to stem the relentless flow of conversation by opening his book, there is still no escape.

> When Ashenden himself was reading and felt on a sudden that Mr Harrington . . . was looking at him with his large pale eyes he began to have violent palpitations of the heart. He dared not look up, he dared not even turn the page, for he knew that Mr Harrington would regard this as ample excuse to break into a discourse, but remained with his eyes fixed desperately on a single word, like a chicken with its beak to a chalk line, and only ventured to breathe when he realised that Mr Harrington, having given up the attempt, had resumed his reading.

But for all this there is something very endearing about Mr Harrington. 'He was so well-meaning, so thoughtful, so deferential, so polite that though Ashenden would willingly have killed him he could not but own that in that short while he had conceived for Mr Harrington something very like affection.' The two men continue to see each other while in Petrograd, Ashenden helping the American by finding him an interpreter, Anastasia Alexandrovna, in reality Maugham's old friend Sasha Lebedev. It was perhaps also through Maugham that the banker met the Czech activist Emanuel Voska, for it was Voska who actually witnessed 'Mr Harrington's' pathetic demise, and his account of this vividly reveals how closely Maugham in his story keeps to the facts. According to Voska, there had been an outbreak of violence in the district and guests had been advised to evacuate the hotel. The American had foolishly insisted on first retrieving his laundry, which had not been returned to his room, setting out in search of it accompanied by Sasha. As Voska tells it in his memoir,

> A half-hour later I heard firing down the street and paid little attention to it. It stopped. Then the interpreter, considerably agitated, came into the lobby. On the way back from the laundry they had run into a street skirmish. In scurrying to cover, they had become separated . . . I ran to the scene of the fight. I found him dead in the gutter, with his bundle of washing under him.

Whether Maugham, too, was present and saw the body in the gutter or whether he was only told about it by Voska it is impossible to know. In the story, Ashenden and Anastasia search for Mr Harrington in the empty streets after the shooting is over. 'He lay on his face in a pool of blood, his bald head, with its prominent bones, very white; his neat black coat smeared and muddy. But his hand was clenched tight on the parcel that contained four shirts, two union suits, a pair of pyjamas and four collars.'

Some years after Maugham's death his friend the art historian Kenneth Clark recalled that Maugham 'often spoke about the Intelligence Service, which he greatly enjoyed. I suppose he liked the light that it shed on human nature.' The truth of this remark is emphatically borne out by *Ashenden*. Maugham was fascinated not so much by action and adventure as by the effect of these unusual situations on the people involved. He was never tempted to glamorise his assignments, never lost the cool clinical eye which rested so dispassionately on his surroundings. In his depiction of Wallinger as Col. R., for instance, he makes clear his admiration for the spy-master's wily intelligence, his resource, courage and determination; at the same time he notes how surprisingly unsophisticated the man is, unexpectedly inept when in a smart restaurant.

> It was true that he was an important person, with power to make or mar quite a large number of his fellows . . . but he could never face the business of tipping a waiter without an embarrassment that was obvious in his demeanour. He was tortured by the fear of making a fool of himself by giving too much or of exciting the waiter's icy scorn by giving too little.

Similarly, although a committed patriot unquestioningly dedicated to his country's cause, Maugham was well aware of the moral double standards involved. In 'The Flip of a Coin', he describes a mission of Ashenden's which if successful will result in the deaths of a number of innocent men; it is he, the man on the ground, who will have to do the deed, obeying the instructions of superiors who choose not to know how the deed is done. He reflects with disgust on their hypocrisy.

> They desired the end, but hesitated at the means . . . Though ready enough to profit by the activities of obscure agents of whom they had never heard, they shut their eyes to dirty work so that they could put their clean hands on their hearts and congratulate themselves that they had never done anything that was unbecoming to men of honour.

It is this clear-eyed vision that largely accounts for the extraordinary impact that *Ashenden* made on the writing of espionage fiction. The spy story as a genre had emerged at the beginning of the twentieth century, with Erskine Childers's 1903 novel, *The Riddle of the Sands*, still standing as one of the supreme examples of its class. Among the most popular practitioners were John Buchan with *The Thirty-Nine Steps* and the hugely best-selling William Le Queux and E. Phillips Oppenheim, both of whom specialised in tales that were unashamedly escapist and melodramatic. Their protagonists are superman-heroes, invariably engaged in missions of terrifying importance, foiling political assassination or delivering international spy-rings to London, frequently dodging violent death in their desperate struggles against the diabolical enemies of King and Country, whom they always brilliantly outwit. These are highly charged adventure stories with no interest at all in representing reality, and the contrast with *Ashenden* could hardly be greater. With the possible exception of Joseph Conrad's *The Secret Agent*, which is more a political than a spy novel, Maugham was the first to write about the business of espionage as it actually was. He was also joint-first, with his fellow novelist Compton Mackenzie, in having worked as a spy himself; but whereas Mackenzie recycled his Secret Service experiences in Greece as unalloyed farce,* Maugham depicted the world of undercover intelligence as not only morally dubious but frequently monotonous and dull.

Although this approach came as a shock to many readers, Maugham set the tone for an entirely new generation of British spy fiction. 'The modern spy story began with Somerset Maugham's *Ashenden*,' wrote the critic and crime writer Julian Symons, a statement with which many distinguished followers of the genre agreed, writers such as Eric Ambler, Graham Greene, who described *Ashenden* as 'that witty and realistic fiction', Len Deighton and John le Carré. Ambler stated that he was 'strongly influenced by the *Ashenden* ethos', while le Carré wrote, 'The Ashenden stories were certainly an influence in my work,' adding, 'I suppose that Maugham was the first person to write about espionage in a mood of disenchantment and almost prosaic reality.' Across the Atlantic, too, Maugham's unflinching realism attracted admirers. In 1950 the crime-writer Raymond Chandler, creator of Philip Marlowe, wrote to Maugham,

> *Ashenden* is unique . . . There are no other great spy stories – none at all. I have been searching and I know . . . There are a few good tales of adventure with a spying element . . . but they always overplay their hand. Too much bravura, the tenor sings too loud. They are as much like *Ashenden* as the opera *Carmen* is like the deadly little tale that Merimée wrote.

*Ashenden: or The British Agent* was eventually published in 1928, by Heinemann in England and Doubleday, Doran in the United States.

---

* Mackenzie's book, *Greek Memories*, was withdrawn after publication in 1932, and he was prosecuted under the Official Secrets Act.

Dedicated to Maugham's fellow spy Gerald Kelly, the book was slow in winning the acclaim it was eventually to achieve; this was partly due to the fact that for a war-weary public interest in the war was slow to revive (Erich Maria Remarque's *All Quiet on the Western Front*, Robert Graves's *Goodbye to All That* and R. C. Sherriff's play *Journey's End* were not to appear till the following year); and also because at that time few aficionados of the genre were prepared for such a low-key treatment. Most critics agreed with the *New York Times*, whose reviewer judged *Ashenden* to be 'a specimen of Somerset Maugham writing in second gear', although there were one or two more forthright expressions of disapproval. The least charitable notice appeared in *Vogue*, written by D. H. Lawrence. Maugham's characters, if well observed, are fakes, Lawrence wrote. 'We find they are nothing but puppets, instruments of the author's pet prejudice. The author's pet prejudice being "humour", it would be hard to find a bunch of more ill-humoured stories, in which the humour has gone more rancid.' Despite such lack of enthusiasm at its first appearance, *Ashenden* has gone on to flourish: it has been published in numerous editions, translated into many languages; it has provided the basis of a play (to date unproduced) and a film, *The Secret Agent*, by Alfred Hitchcock, with John Gielgud, Peter Lorre and Madeleine Carroll; most intriguingly, it was used as a handbook by the intelligence services, for several years required reading for entrants into MI5 and MI6, as well as apparently inspiring a study of British spy fiction on the part of Soviet military intelligence: as its author remarked, 'a strange outcome for a series of tales that were written *merely* to entertain'. But perhaps the ultimate accolade was awarded during the Second World War when the stories were referred to in a broadcast by Dr Goebbels, the German Minister for Propaganda, who cited them as a typical example of British cynicism and brutality.

Meanwhile as the long Scottish winter gave way to spring Maugham gradually felt his health improve, and to his great delight was given leave by his doctors to go south for the summer, on condition that he return in the autumn for further treatment. 'Madame', as Maugham referred to Syrie, came up to Banchory to visit him, full of the news that she had taken a house in the country for three months. Charles Hill Court was handsome and spacious, with a large garden and a pleasant study in which Maugham could work undisturbed. The house was near Hindhead in Surrey, an attractive area of woods and heath and gentle hills, within easy reach of London. But there was another reason why the location had been chosen: the fifteen-year-old Mounteney, Syrie's son by Wellcome, was at school in Hindhead, and his mother, who continued to suffer acute anguish at the separation imposed by her ex-husband, hoped that being so near might give her an opportunity of seeing him. She had continued to petition for increased access but her requests were always refused, even though Wellcome himself was continuously abroad and Mounteney obliged to spend his holidays with one of the masters. As before Syrie continued to be restricted to the occasional brief interview conducted in the presence of a third party, usually in the public lounge of the Langham Hotel. Great emphasis was laid by Wellcome's solicitors on the importance of ensuring that Mounteney should never in any circumstances come into contact with Maugham, a prohibition that achieved little except to make circumstances even more difficult for Syrie. At least she now had her daughter, three-year-old Liza, whom she adored. Maugham, too, was fond of the little girl, despite his disappointment that she had not been born a boy, and during their summer in the country the three of them managed to enjoy a relatively amicable time together, Syrie happy to have her husband returned to her, he delighted to be released from the sanatorium. Privately, however, he saw little to look forward to in his marital situation. 'What will happen in the future I cannot tell,' he wrote resignedly. 'I can only hope for the best & leave it at that.'

Although he was still weak and tended to tire easily, Maugham was pleased to discover one or two congenial Surrey neighbours, in particular the writer Robert Hichens, whom he had come across previously in London. Hichens, novelist, playwright and music critic, was a friend of Max Beerbohm and had known Henry James and Oscar Wilde; *The Green Carnation*, his novel satirising Wilde and the aesthetes of the 1890s, had been a great *succès de scandale*, although he had made his fortune with a bestselling romance, *The Garden of Allah*. Recently Hichens had set up house with a Swiss novelist, John Knittel; Knittel had a wife and children, but to Hichens this was no obstacle, and like a number of confirmed bachelors of the period, E. M. Forster for one, Hugh Walpole for another, he was content for his emotional and domestic life to revolve around a married man whose wife and offspring became part of the extended family. Maugham was delighted to see Hichens, and he, Hichens and John Knittel rode together almost every day, often calling in at the Frensham Ponds Hotel for tea. They played tennis and croquet, with Syrie making up a four, and in the evenings the two couples dined together, cheerfully animated after drinking John Knittel's terrifyingly strong cocktails. One evening the composer Maude Valérie White dined at Hichens's house, and Maugham, knowing of her travels in North Africa, told her he was thinking of writing a play set in Cairo and asked her to compose some suitable music. 'He and Maude spent a long time together at the piano,' Hichens recalled, 'and Maude played to him music which had been suggested to her by a sojourn in Egypt.'

Now and again visitors came down from London, including Hugh Walpole, who spent a couple of nights at Charles Hill. After getting to know Maugham in Petrograd, Walpole was surprised to see what kind of a woman he had married. She was nice enough, Hugh recorded in his diary, but it was difficult to understand what Maugham saw in her, as 'I should have thought that she was over-sentimental for his cynicism.' What interested him more on this occasion, however, was the fact that his friend was hard at work on a novel.

*The Moon and Sixpence*, the novel inspired by the life of Paul Gauguin, was written between May and August 1918. The similarities between Gauguin and Charles Strickland, the artist in the book, are marked: like Gauguin, Strickland is a respectable stockbroker with wife and children who abandons his family to live in poverty for the sake of artistic freedom; both painters settle in Tahiti, remaining in the South Seas for the rest of their lives; Gauguin, ravaged by syphilis and drug-addiction, was eventually killed by a heart-attack, while Strickland dies from leprosy. To tell his story Maugham employs a first-person narrator, a device not used since *The Making of a Saint* twenty years earlier, but one on which he was increasingly to rely, especially in his short stories. Here the unnamed 'I' has only a minor part in the action, his main function to comment and observe. A young writer closely modelled on Maugham himself, with the same youthful priggishness, dry humour and enjoyable streak of malice, he is taken up by Mrs Strickland, an ordinary woman of limited means with ambitions as a literary hostess. It is at her modest salon in Ashley Gardens that he eventually meets her stockbroker husband, a dull, rather commonplace chap, who reads *Punch* and the *Sporting Times* and has a picture of Lily Langtry on his mantelpiece. When to everyone's astonishment Strickland suddenly abandons his family and career to live as an impoverished artist in Paris, it is the narrator to whom Mrs Strickland appeals for help.

Arrived in Paris, he finds a very different Strickland from the man he had met in London, ruthless and irascible, unmovably set on his course and with no interest whatever in the life he has left behind.

> 'Has it occurred to you that your wife is frightfully unhappy?'
> 'She'll get over it.' [Strickland replies] . . .

The narrator has an artist friend in Paris, Dirk Stroeve, a foolish fellow and an abominable painter, but generous and kind-hearted. Just as the penniless Gauguin was selflessly cared for by his friend Emile Schuffenecker and repaid him by seducing his wife, so Strickland is cosseted by Stroeve, whom he similarly traduces. Blanche runs off with Strickland, and when he abandons her kills herself. Time passes, and the narrator, still in Paris, encounters Strickland, who evinces only indifference on the subject of Blanche. However, he is eventually persuaded to show the narrator his work, grudgingly allowing him into his studio in a scene strongly reminiscent of Maugham's visit to the studio of the surly Roderic O'Conor.

'You don't want me to talk, I suppose,' I said.
'No, blast you, I want you to hold your tongue.'

Some years later the narrator travels to Tahiti, and it is here on the island he learns that the painter has recently died; in the South Seas Charles Strickland had at last found fulfilment, living with a native girl and creating the disturbing but glorious masterpieces for which he was to become posthumously famous. Back in London, meanwhile, Mrs Strickland enjoys her role as keeper of the flame, since her husband's death living comfortably on the sale of his pictures while tastefully displaying a few coloured reproductions of his work on her sitting-room wall. 'They must be very pleasant to live with,' says one of her guests politely. 'Yes; they're so essentially decorative,' she complacently replies. (Understandably, this depiction of the artist's wife caused some distress to Mme Gauguin when she read it.)

The phrase 'essentially decorative' was a dig at Gerald Kelly, whom Maugham used to tease by declaring that his, Maugham's, prime interest in art was decorative. Indeed the novel owes a great deal to Kelly, as it was Kelly who had introduced Maugham to Gauguin's work, and it was with Kelly that he had first met Roderic O'Conor, who had known Gauguin well and whose snarling aggressiveness is faithfully reproduced in the character of Strickland.* Kelly suspected that he himself had served as the inspiration for Stroeve, the chocolate-box painter. 'I am always sure', as he cheerfully admitted, 'that all Willie's bad painters are portraits of myself.' But in this he was wrong: the character of Stroeve is modelled on Maugham's fellow novelist Hugh Walpole. This fact was fortunately

---

* It was also Kelly who persuaded Maugham to make a minor correction in the text: there is a scene in which Stroeve, driven beyond endurance by Strickland, makes to destroy one of his canvases by slashing it with a palette knife. 'I pointed out', said Kelly, 'that nobody could possibly slash a canvas with a palette knife . . . since a palette knife bends and will not cut . . . I suggested that he should indicate a "scraper" instead, for a scraper is sharp and pointed.'

undetected by Hugh, who failed to recognise himself in the plump, silly creature who with his bald head and pink cheeks was 'one of those unlucky persons whose most sincere emotions are ridiculous', whose work was 'hackneyed and vulgar beyond belief', and whose manner reminded the narrator of nothing so much as 'an agitated guinea-pig'. Had Walpole discovered his contribution no doubt there would have been a squeal of anguish, if nothing like the anguish suffered later when coming face to face with himself as Alroy Kear in *Cakes and Ale*.

*The Moon and Sixpence*, a minor novel that has always found greater favour with the general reader than with the critics, was published by Heinemann in April 1919. The exotic Tahitian setting made an obvious appeal to a world only recently emerged from war, and the theme was an interesting one, that of the nature of genius, of the conflict between the ruthlessness of the creative artist and the bourgeois society he escapes. In the book this society is portrayed with a delicately satirical touch, Maugham drawing on his own experience as a young unknown at Violet Hunt's salon on Campden Hill. His portrait of Violet as the novelist Rose Waterford is essentially affectionate, which is not something that could be said of his portrayal of Mrs Strickland, depicted with a subtle venom that betrays much about the author's own feelings of entrapment by marriage and the conventions of society. Mrs Strickland, we are told, 'had the true instinct of the nice woman that it is only really decent for her to live on other people's money', while the misogynistic anger in many of Strickland's outbursts lie close to strong buried feelings in Maugham. This being so it is disappointing that the novel's greatest flaw lies in the portrayal of Charles Strickland himself, who comes over not only as a brute but as a bore, and in whose sudden transformation from dutiful paterfamilias to blazing, foul-mouthed genius it is difficult to believe. As Katherine Mansfield wrote in the *Athenaeum*, 'We must be shown something of the workings of his mind; we must have some comment of his upon what he feels, fuller and more exhaustive than his perpetual: "Go to hell."' Despite such reservations, when in July the book came out in America its success was immediate and overwhelming: with an initial print-run of only 5,000 copies, it had sold close to 100,000 by the end of the year, its success resulting also in a huge and unexpected revival of interest in Maugham's earlier work, *Of Human Bondage*.

After leaving Hindhead at the end of August, the Maughams spent a couple of months in Chesterfield Street, Maugham's old friend Walter Payne having moved out at the end of the summer to make room for the family. He and Maugham continued to keep closely in touch, however, and when

Payne took a house in Regent's Park Maugham gave him some paintings, including one of his portraits by Gerald Kelly. Payne was to marry twice, his first wife much liked by Maugham, but the second, a Hungarian divorcée, was loathed. The friendship survived, nonetheless, and Payne until his death in 1949 continued to advise Maugham on his financial affairs.

In November Maugham returned for further treatment at Nordrach-on-Dee. Although still under par, he felt invigorated and full of plans for the future. With the war finally over, he could hardly wait once more to go on his travels. 'I am making my plans to conquer the Far East,' he told Kelly. 'How splendid it will be to set off, with adequate funds in one's pocket & what time one needs, for God knows where.' During his previous stay in the sanatorium he had been too ill to write, but now he could hardly bear to stop, composing four plays in eighteen months, *Caesar's Wife*,★ *Home and Beauty*, *The Circle* and *The Unknown*.

By the time the first of these, *Caesar's Wife*, went into rehearsal in February 1919, Maugham was back in London and able to attend. His presence in the dimly lit auditorium, however, was found somewhat daunting by the play's leading lady, Fay Compton, who was having trouble remembering her lines. 'He wasn't nasty about it,' she said, 'but he would stop and say, "We *must* have the correct words!" This was frightening to anybody as young as me, playing my big, straight part for the first time.' In the event it was Miss Compton, after the piece opened at the Royalty on 27 March, who was recognised as being largely responsible for the success of a production which otherwise had few memorable qualities. Inspired by Mme de Lafayette's famous novel *La Princesse de Clèves*, about a married woman's renunciation of illicit love, *Caesar's Wife* is set in contemporary Cairo, where the beautiful young wife of the British Consul develops a passion for her husband's attaché. Everyone concerned behaves with the utmost virtue and nobility and the situation is eventually saved with honour all round. As Maugham explained in his introduction to the published version, he had so often been reproached for concentrating on unpleasant people that he wanted to write a work 'in which all the characters were estimable'. This, perhaps predictably, is what makes the result so bland. Yet it did well enough at the time: the reviews were polite ('a triumphantly tactful evening', said *The Times*); the play enjoyed a good run in London, followed by a shorter run in New York, with Billie Burke in the lead; it was filmed in America in 1925 under the title *Infatuation*, making a final appearance in an adaptation on British television in 1951.

★ Originally entitled 'The Keys to Heaven'.

Shortly after the first night of *Caesar's Wife*, Maugham again fell ill. In April, the month which saw the publication of *The Moon and Sixpence*, he went to Capri for three weeks to stay at the Villa Cercola, without his wife, and by the time he returned to London in May his recovery was complete.

During the previous summer at Hindhead, he and Syrie had held long discussions about their future. Their marriage was an incontrovertible fact; it was far from ideal, but considered calmly the arrangement held advantages for both sides: for Syrie propriety and financial security, for Maugham the façade of respectability which one side of his nature craved; also, as parents there were important responsibilities which had to be shouldered together. Surely the two of them could work out a tolerable *modus vivendi*? Syrie had wanted them to live in her house in Regent's Park originally paid for by Gordon Selfridge, but Maugham, squeamish about the association, insisted that they settle in Chesterfield Street. However, what had provided a commodious bachelor establishment for himself and Walter Payne now seemed uncomfortably cramped. The house was five-storeyed but narrow, and in order to make space for a nursery Maugham had had to give up his airy top-floor study, instead making do with a small parlour on the first floor overlooking the street; this was not perfect and he was vulnerable to interruption, but at least there was just enough space for the big writing-table to which its owner was so attached.

It was here in the house in Mayfair that the Maughams' married life properly began, and at first it appeared that the couple were making a success of it: they were seen together at parties, galleries and first nights – including, in 1919, the first nights of two of Maugham's own plays – and they frequently entertained at home. The Maughams 'gave dinner parties to end all', recalled one of their friends, while another remembered these occasions as 'very jolly and merry'. Naturally enough, Maugham's brother F.H. and his wife Nellie were delighted to see him settle down, the last of the surviving brothers to marry, and Syrie was made warmly welcome in Rutland Gate. The three nieces, Kate, Honor and Diana, had always felt fond of their uncle Willie, who was kind, talked to them as equals and tipped a generous half-sovereign at every meeting, and now they were fascinated by their aunt and dazzled by her chic. The girls' clothes were bought off the peg at Bourne & Hollingsworth, whereas Syrie's were made in Paris by Lanvin and Chanel, and it was thrilling when she gave them her barely worn cast-offs and taught them about style. 'I had naturally bad taste, running to pleats, bows, frills and rosebuds,' Kate recalled, '[and] Syrie tried to train my eye.' Even F.H., usually so chilly and remote, had a soft spot for his sister-in-law. Frigidly polite towards his wife and a forbidding figure to his children, F.H. was a different character altogether with Syrie, gallant and charming. The two of them sometimes lunched together, and when Maugham was abroad F.H. would sometimes dine with Syrie at Chesterfield Street.

Yet if in public the Maughams behaved as though on the best of terms, in private all was not so serene. The basic problem was two-fold: the couple had almost nothing in common, and Syrie had made the mistake of falling in love with her husband. This complicated everything, for it placed an added strain on the relationship which it was quite unable to bear. Maugham was shy, reticent, highly disciplined and shrank from any form of emotional demonstration; Syrie by contrast was emotional, volatile, self-indulgent and enjoyed nothing more than making dramatic scenes, preferably last thing at night. '*Don't* make me a scene!' became a familiar plea of Maugham's. Extravagantly sociable, she adored parties and hated being alone, completely insensitive to her husband's desire for periods of silence and solitude. 'Syrie simply didn't understand how important his writing was to Maugham,' said a woman friend of hers. 'She would try to get him to take her to Henley or some such place when he wanted the morning completely to himself.' Nor did she realise how taxing a day's work could be: sometimes after Maugham had been writing all day he would come down to dinner dead tired, only to find a noisy group of his wife's friends, none of whom he knew, who had been invited in for the evening. Once the guests had gone, the rows would begin, sometimes continuing till two or three in the morning, Maugham eventually retreating to bed exhausted, before having to get up early the next day to write amusing dialogue for the current play, while Syrie, if she chose, could lie in until luncheon. With her remarkable eye for décor and design, Syrie loved buying pretty things for the house, and she spent a fortune on clothes, two subjects about which she was happy to chatter for hours. 'You have driven me to talk to you practically about nothing but frocks and furniture,' her husband exploded in one of his many fits of exasperation, 'and if you knew how sick I am of both these subjects!'

She loved smart, rather raffish society, and was ill at ease with many of her husband's old friends, Gerald Kelly chief among her dislikes. When she moved into Chesterfield Street she had insisted on the removal of *The Jester*, Kelly's glorious portrait of Maugham as a young man, which had hung over the fireplace in the drawing-room;★ she had the painting returned to the artist, and made no secret of the fact that she found the man himself a fearful bore: when Kelly came to dine Syrie often slipped away in search

---

★ In 1933 it was bought for the Tate by the Chantry Bequest.

of more amusing company elsewhere. And indeed, when in the company of her husband's fellow authors she tried to join in the literary talk, faking her way with all-purpose expressions of enthusiasm, it set Maugham's teeth on edge, irritating him beyond measure when he heard her gushing about books which he knew perfectly well she had never opened. He found it infuriating that she neither could nor would leave him in peace, and seemed stubbornly to resist every attempt on his part to find something to occupy her time: she never read, had no interest in cards, quickly gave up on the notion of charity work, and the traditional feminine occupations of knitting and needlework held no appeal for her whatsoever.

What Syrie wanted was her husband's approval and attention, and one of the few areas in which she got it was the theatre. This was an interest shared, and here Syrie briefly came into her own. When at work on a play Maugham often read aloud passages of dialogue to her, and was pleased when she occasionally attended rehearsals, more than once taking her with him when he had productions opening in New York. He particularly valued her advice on sets and costumes: during the preparations for *Caesar's Wife*, for example, it was Syrie who took Fay Compton shopping for her costumes. 'I didn't have a voice in it at all,' the actress recalled. 'Syrie took over and that was that. Maugham had perfect faith in her taste in dress and he was quite right.' Before an opening, Maugham was always in an acute state of nervous tension, leaving it to Syrie to make final arrangements for the cast party after the performance. And it was she who took pity on the first-night queues, sending down sandwiches and thermoses of soup to people waiting for long hours to buy cheap tickets in the pit and gallery.

The frequent scenes Syrie staged, the endless reproaches, the daily testing and questioning of Maugham's feelings for her, maddening to him, were all symptoms of her emotional insecurity, her huge desire to be loved. As a friend of Maugham's later remarked, 'I think that if Syrie hadn't fallen in love with him, the marriage would have lasted.' The fact that she was in love made her desperate for any show of affection. It also made her physically demanding, demands which her husband found increasingly difficult to satisfy. For Syrie, Maugham was the best lover she had ever known, but she had long lost any attractiveness for him. His wife's sexual demands, he told a man friend, 'were insatiable, intolerable', and to another he confided that he found physical relations with Syrie a great effort and when in bed with her was obliged to draw heavily on his imagination. Faced with his wife's increasingly bitter reproaches, which were undoubtedly fuelled by intense sexual frustration, Maugham was driven to lay some uncomfortable facts before her. 'I was forty-three when we married . . . [and] you were not very young either,' he bleakly reminded her. 'You cannot forget the circumstances under which we married. I think under these circumstances you should be very well satisfied if you get from your husband courtesy and consideration, kindness and affection; but really you cannot expect passionate love.'

Underlying all these scenes and arguments was of course the absent figure of Gerald Haxton. In February 1919 Haxton, released from his POW camp in Germany, had illicitly arrived in London hoping to see Maugham, but he had been quickly picked up by the authorities and deported before the two men could meet. He was never to set foot in the country again. Haxton was nonetheless an enormous, and profoundly threatening, presence in the Maugham marriage, the true basis of all their rows. Where Sue Jones had known about Maugham's homosexuality and tolerated it, Syrie knew and was tormentedly jealous. Had the object of her husband's affections been a woman she might have found a way of dealing with her; had he been a gentle, effeminate young man, she might have befriended him; but as Syrie sensed long before she met Gerald, this charismatic young cad, by whom her husband was so obsessed, was a dangerous enemy, and one whom she had small chance of defeating.

While recuperating in his Scottish sanatorium, Maugham had spent much time planning a voyage with Gerald to the Far East, and now that the war was over he was increasingly impatient to be off. His lucrative theatrical business, however, kept him in London throughout most of 1919, with the first night of *Caesar's Wife* in March, *Home and Beauty* opening in August in both London and New York,* and *The Unknown* soon to go into rehearsal.

In addition there was the upheaval of moving house. The confined quarters of Chesterfield Street had been exchanged for a much larger house, 2 Wyndham Place in Marylebone. Wyndham Place is a quiet, broad street leading north out of Bryanston Square, and number 2 is a handsome, four-storeyed Regency mansion, with three elegant, balconied windows on the first floor and an imposing porticoed entrance. Here at last Syrie was able to give free rein to her restless energy and decorative talents, overseeing the furnishing of a house primarily intended as a setting for an ambitious programme of high-level entertaining. Maugham did his best to keep out of the way, spending much of his time at the Garrick, when not

---

* In the States the play was known as *Too Many Husbands*. The line, 'England, Home and Beauty', from which Maugham took his title, came from 'The Death of Nelson', a popular song commemorating the Battle of Trafalgar, a subject which, it was decided, had rather less resonance in New York than it did in London.

writing or at rehearsal, or wandering round the auction houses looking at pictures; occasionally he brought an old friend, such as Sutro or Walpole, back to the house for dinner. One such evening was noted by Walpole in his diary. The evening had been pleasant, he wrote, but '[Willie] looks ill and bored. I'm afraid the marriage is not a great success.'

Away from the domestic arena, however, Maugham was riding high, much in the news with the opening at the end of August of his new play. A fast, frivolous and brilliantly funny farce, *Home and Beauty* turns on its head a particularly unhappy aspect of the time, that of women deprived of husbands by four years of war. Set in the present, the plot focuses first on Victoria, a delectably pretty but ruthlessly self-centred young woman, whose husband, William, was reported killed three years earlier at the Battle of Ypres. But William is not dead, indeed is on his way to London for a reunion with his wife, unaware of the fact that she is now married to his best friend, Freddie. This promising situation is complicated further by the discovery that the avaricious Victoria already has a third husband in view, a rich entrepreneur, for whom she eventually plans to dump both Freddie and William, feeling that she has made sacrifice enough for the war effort. 'I flatter myself there are not many women who've been married to two D.S.O.s,' she says smugly. 'I think I've done my bit.' Far from dismayed, the two men leap at the chance of liberty, both of them thoroughly tired of Victoria's egotism. 'I confess that sometimes I've thought it hard', complains Freddie, 'that when I wanted a thing it was selfishness, and when she wanted it, it was only her due,' a state of affairs well known to William, who 'couldn't quite understand why my engagements were made to be broken, while nothing in the world must interfere with hers'. At once they begin hotly competing to be the one to make the sacrifice, vying for the chance to be divorced by Victoria. In a wonderfully comic third act two new characters are introduced, a fashionable divorce lawyer and his colleague Miss Montmorency, a straitlaced spinster who earns her pin-money by acting as a professional co-respondent; and it is through their ingenuity that the two friends finally win their freedom, and Victoria her wealthy third husband.

*Home and Beauty* was precisely the right play to entertain a war-weary public, hungry for frivolity and fun. The topical themes – rationing, the black market, the scarcity of servants – the glorious silliness of the farcical situations, and the wit and rapidity of the repartee delighted London audiences;* even the cynicism implicit in the absolute refusal to take

---

* New Yorkers, on the other hand, less affected by the war and its aftermath, saw little to amuse them in the play, which was taken off after only two weeks.

anything seriously was accepted as a tremendous joke. This was just as
the author intended, any darker, more personal relevance a matter for
himself alone. 'The difference between men and women', says Victoria's
mother, 'is that men are not naturally addicted to matrimony. With patience,
firmness, and occasional rewards you can train them to it just as you can
train a dog to walk on its hind legs. But a dog would rather walk on all
fours and a man would rather be free.'

'A delightful entertainment' was the critical consensus, a play of 'style,
wit, elegance . . . a little masterpiece of polite merriment'. *Home and Beauty*
ran for seven months at the Playhouse Theatre, its success due in no small
part to an accomplished cast led by the incomparable Charles Hawtrey,
who also directed. The role of Victoria was taken by Gladys Cooper, a
thirty-year-old actress whose cool, classical beauty concealed a sterling
commonsense and an excellent head for business. Although she had been
on the stage since she was seventeen, she had no great natural talent; as
one of her colleagues put it, for Gladys acting was simply something she
did for a living; she worked hard at it, however, was utterly reliable, and
eventually, as Maugham wrote later, 'succeeded in turning herself from an
indifferent actress into an extremely accomplished one'. It was during the
war that she had gone into the administrative side of the business, joining
Frank Curzon in the management of the Playhouse. *Home and Beauty* was
their fourth venture together, the production marking the beginning not
only of a rewarding association between the Playhouse and Maugham, but
between Maugham and Gladys Cooper, who was to portray three further
Maugham heroines, in *The Letter*, *The Sacred Flame* and *The Painted Veil*.
The two became firm friends, Maugham a great admirer of Gladys's self-
discipline and determination, as well as of her luminous blonde beauty. The
role of Leslie Crosbie in *The Letter* and of Stella in *The Sacred Flame* were
both written with Gladys in mind, and as Maugham himself admitted the
knowledge that she would be playing these parts 'more or less unconsciously' coloured his depiction of them.*

Once the play was settled into its run Maugham felt able at last to depart
for the long-planned expedition to the Far East. The journey, of which he
kept detailed notes, later published as *On a Chinese Screen*, was to take over
six months. Leaving from Liverpool in August 1919, he went to New York,
then by train across country, collecting Gerald in Chicago before continuing to the west coast for embarkation. They sailed first to Hong Kong,

---

* When the very camp actor Ernest Thesiger asked Maugham why he never wrote
parts for *him*, Maugham replied, 'I do; but Gladys Cooper always plays them.'

after which they travelled on to Shanghai and Peking, and finally to Mukden in the north, returning home by way of Japan and the Suez Canal.

China was fascinating territory for Maugham, a country that 'gives you everything', as he was later to declare. At the time of his visit the nascent republic was in a state of flux: since the overthrow of the imperial dynasty in 1912 most of the country had fallen into the hands of feuding warlords, with a deep division opening up between on the one hand an almost medieval feudal economy and on the other a rebellious student movement committed to modernisation and reform. The government in Peking was precarious and ineffective, largely ignored at home although officially recognised abroad, with all the major powers maintaining embassies in the capital. For Maugham this was his first experience of being in a foreign country unable to speak the language, and outside the major cities he was largely dependent on the services of an interpreter, a restriction of minimal importance in his case as his consuming interest was in the expatriate milieu, in the behaviour of Westerners living uprooted within Chinese society. As before in Polynesia, the Americans and Europeans he encountered, the lives of doctors, diplomats, traders, missionaries and their women, were the subject of his closest scrutiny, and his notes are full of their stories: the consul; the taipan; the desperate-to-be-married spinster; the missionary who had come to hate his calling; the agent of British-American Tobacco driven half mad by homesickness; the saintly Mother Superior in her white-walled convent who talked nostalgically of her family home in the south of France. One of the few exceptions was an interview with a Chinese, a renowned scholar and expert on Confucius. Long retired, this ancient gentleman with grey pigtail and discoloured teeth had for many years been secretary to one of the Empress Dowager's greatest viceroys; educated at Oxford and Berlin, he spoke fluent English, and he sufficiently unbent, after some lavish flattery, to discourse on history, on philosophy and with considerable fervour on the relationship between his country and the West. 'You have thrust your hideous inventions upon us,' he fiercely harangued his somewhat startled visitor, '[but] do you not know that we have a genius for mechanics?. . . What will become of your superiority when the yellow man can make as good guns as the white?'*

Although travel within the country was often cumbersome and slow Maugham and Haxton covered vast distances. Accompanied by a team of bearers, blue-clad coolies in big straw hats carrying their luggage

---

* The old scholar's outburst as recorded in the notebook is given almost word for word to the character Lee Tai Cheng in the 1922 play *East of Suez*.

balanced on poles over the shoulder, they experienced a wide variety of transport. Sometimes they were carried by litter, or jogged along astride tough little ponies; for days at a time they walked, at night putting up in rough country inns, sometimes sleeping on the bare earth floor; and for 1,500 miles they sailed by sampan along the upper reaches of the Yangtse, on as far as Chengdu, from whose crenellated walls could be seen the snowy mountains of Tibet. Maugham was entranced by the beauty of the country, by the vivid green of the paddy fields, the little tree-covered hills, the graceful bamboo thickets that lined the side of the road; there were wide plains and narrow mountain passes, networks of narrow canals, pagodas and temples, and clusters of walled farmhouses with their tiled roofs tip-tilted in the Chinese fashion. He transcribed his impressions while they were still fresh in his mind, often while actually on the move, scribbling his notes while being carried in a chair or moving downriver in a sampan. On their way the two men visited shrines and temples, they sat in tea-houses and opium dens; they watched peasants in the fields ploughing with lumbering water buffalo, passed women on the road tottering along on tiny bound feet; by the river at night they saw fleets of junks, their sails ghostly in the moonlight; and once in remote country a group of Mongol tribesmen clattered by, dressed in black silk coats and trousers and boots with turned-up toes. On occasion the sight was less picturesque. Walking up to inspect a hillside graveyard they came upon a little tower, gruesome evidence of the Chinese custom of disposing of unwanted baby girls. 'At its foot were a number of rough baskets thrown about in disorder,' Maugham wrote.

> I walked round and on one side saw an oblong hole, eighteen inches by eight, perhaps, from which hung a stout string. From the hole there came a very strange, nauseating odour . . . It was a baby tower. The baskets were the baskets in which the babies had been brought . . . let down gently by means of the string. The odour was the odour of putrefaction. A lively little boy came up to me while I stood there and made me understand that four babes had been brought to the tower that morning.

The contrast between rural China and the great cities of Peking, Shanghai and Hong Kong could hardly have more marked. Hong Kong, the first port of call for Maugham and Haxton, was emphatically British, clean, efficient and redolent of home, with its clubs, racecourse, tennis-courts and comfortable, chintz-covered sitting-rooms where white-coated servants brought in cocktails and olives on the dot of six. Shanghai, commercial and cosmopolitan, was very different in character, with the great banks and businesses lining the Bund, streets jammed with motor traffic, with a busy night-life centred around the restaurants and night-clubs run mainly by a glamorous White Russian population in flight from the recent revolution. Here, as in the other major metropolises, every kind of sexual delicacy was provided, the famous boy brothels in particular popular with Europeans. The ancient walled capital, Peking, was yet another world altogether, 'an experience that really enriches the soul', as Maugham testified, 'one of the pleasantest places in the world to spend the rest of one's life'. Here there were cities within cities, the Forbidden City, the Imperial City, the Chinese City, each enclosed by its own massive wall surrounding temples and palaces, lakes, gardens, pagodas and a rabbit-warren of houses. In each the broad tree-lined streets and imperial palaces were surrounded by an infinite network of tiny *hutungs*, or alleyways; a doorway in a blank wall might open on to a series of cool courtyards fragrant with flowering shrubs, or on to an overcrowded slum stinking of rotting refuse. As Maugham remarked, 'very nasty smells' were often overwhelming: sewers were a rare luxury, instead open drains in the street and the night-soil wheeled out every morning to be spread outside the city walls and used as fertiliser. Unlike noisy Shanghai, there were few cars in Peking, the most common form of transport the rickshaw, silent on its pneumatic tyres and the soft-shod feet of its runner. Most foreigners lived within the Legation Compound, where there were clubs and a couple of European-style hotels. Expatriate social life was frenetic, with racing at Pa-Ma-Chung, day-long picnics in the Western Hills, dances, luncheons, as well as diplomatic dinner-parties, to many of which, as a distinguished visitor, Maugham was naturally invited, their pomposities and protocol meticulously transcribed. More to his taste was strolling unimpeded through the city, exploring the markets, for jade, for gold, and observing the crowds, women and children, and the old men with their pet songbirds attached to a long thread of silk.

Shortly before returning home Maugham wrote to his agent Golding Bright, 'I have got a good deal of material in one way and another (besides having a very good time).' The material referred to was to provide the basis for three works, a play, *East of Suez*, a novel, *The Painted Veil*, and the sketches in *On a Chinese Screen*. The latter was the first to be ready for publication, and when in typescript Maugham sent it for expert appraisal to H. I. Harding, a well-known sinologist and Second Secretary at the British Embassy in Peking. Harding read the typescript with care and made a number of corrections.

p. 124 I am inclined to criticize the epithet 'familiar'. I do not know that the habit of poisoning relatives one dislikes is commoner in China than in England . . .

p. 126 may I object to the epithet *singular*? The Chinese may strike us as singular, weird, funny, curious, strange, mysterious, etc, but at the same time we strike the inexperienced Chinese in just the same way . . .

Maugham was grateful, even if he did not agree with all the emendations. 'Your suggestions are most helpful & of the forty-one you made I am taking thirty-six,' he told Harding. '[But] once or twice I think you have misapprehended my meaning: for instance I did not call the Chinese singular because they are Chinese but because of artistic capacities which do surely distinguish them from other peoples . . .'

With the dedication 'For Syrie', as a nod to convention, *On a Chinese Screen* appeared in 1922, received with acclaim on both sides of the Atlantic. 'A fascinating volume', wrote Louise Maunsell Field in the *New York Times*. 'One feels that one is coming into contact with an unusually interesting mind, keenly intelligent, sensitive and sympathetic, quick to perceive and to understand.' Her opinion was echoed in London by Gerald Gould in the *Saturday Review*, who congratulated the author on the subtlety of his observation. 'His descriptions are not so much natural as psychological . . . he shows us the actual effect of China on minds with preconceptions similar to ours; and thus we learn the "feel" of that ancient and alien civilization.' Gould also makes an interesting comment on Maugham's uncompromising outlook, reacting to it in much the same way as those critics of his fiction who habitually accused him of cynicism. 'The cold violence of his method suggests cruelty,' said Gould, '[although] the philosophy underlying it is kind.'

The second work to come out of the Chinese experience was the novel *The Painted Veil*; although not published till 1925, the idea for it, as so often with Maugham, lay maturing in his mind for several years before he felt ready to set it down on paper. The theme was inspired both by an episode from Dante's *Purgatorio*,\* remembered from his first visit to Italy, and by a notorious scandal concerning an Englishwoman in Hong Kong that he was told while on his travels. It was, he said, 'the only novel I have written in which I started from a story rather than from a character . . . [The characters], constructed from persons I had long known in different circumstances . . . were chosen to fit the story I gradually evolved.'

---

\* In Book V, there is the story of the gentlewoman from Siena whose husband, suspecting her of adultery, takes her to his castle in the Maremma, hoping that the noxious vapours from the marshes will kill her.

The plot concerns the marriage of the ill-matched Walter and Kitty Fane. The couple first meet in London when Walter comes home on leave from his job as a government bacteriologist in China. Shy, scholarly and introspective, Walter is not at all Kitty's type, but at twenty-five and still unmarried pretty, frivolous Kitty has begun to grow anxious: as her ambitious mother disagreeably makes clear, she is in danger of being left on the shelf, and so in a panic she agrees to marry the besotted Walter, who proudly takes his new wife back to Hong Kong. Here, to Kitty's relief, life among the British colony turns out to be tremendously good fun. True, her husband is a dull stick and his eager and incompetent love-making is boring in the extreme, but there are compensations, chief among them the handsome Assistant Colonial Secretary, Charles Townsend, charming, gregarious and devilishly flirtatious.

Soon Kitty and Townsend are embarked on a thrilling affair, she as obsessed with the vain, charismatic Charlie as she foolishly assumes he is with her; she lives for their secret assignations, which take place mainly at the Fanes' house when Walter is safely at work in his laboratory. One afternoon while lying in bed they see to their horror the handle of the locked bedroom-door slowly turn. It must be Walter, unexpectedly come home. From this moment Kitty's life is irrevocably changed. Her husband, up to now slavishly devoted, shows an almost sadistic side to his character, turning hostile and uncommunicative. Coldly, he presents her with a murderous ultimatum: either she accompany him up-country to distant Mei-tan-fu, a town in the grip of a deadly cholera epidemic, or he will divorce her, citing Charlie Townsend as co-respondent. Initially Kitty seizes on the latter alternative: Charlie is as madly in love with her as she with him, and surely will jump at the chance of ditching his dull wife and marrying her. But in a mortifying scene in Townsend's office she is made to see that she has been horribly mistaken, and that her lover has not the least intention of involving himself in such a damaging scandal. She must be a sensible girl, pull herself together and go along with Walter to Mei-tan-fu. 'As far as I can make out your husband is behaving very generously,' Townsend pompously tells her. 'From his point of view you've been rather a naughty little thing . . . I don't pretend that Mei-tan-fu is a health resort . . . but there's no need to get the wind up.'

It is during the bleak and terrible weeks spent in the devastated little town, where a hundred people a day are dying of the disease, that Kitty finally comes to understand the reality of her situation. The love Walter had for her has turned to unrelenting hatred, the love she thought she had from Townsend was worthless, her own existence selfish and shallow.

Gradually, as she sees Walter's heroic work fighting to save lives, she begins to look outward, even volunteering to work among the orphans cared for in a convent run by French nuns. Although she still cannot bring herself to feel fond of her husband, she pities him, her greatest hope that he should be persuaded to forgive her, not for her sake but for his. But Walter is implacable: even the news that she is pregnant leaves him cold – 'Am I the father?' he acidly enquires. Finally Walter succumbs to cholera and dies, apparently unreconciled, leaving Kitty to return a much wiser woman to Hong Kong. Yet Maugham has her measure and is too much of a realist to leave it at that; despite herself his weak-willed heroine succumbs for the second time to Townsend's casual seduction, eventually departing for England humiliated and full of self-loathing.

The portrait of Kitty Fane is one of Maugham's finest fictional achievements. As with Bertha Craddock over twenty years before, he displays an extraordinary empathy, an ability to create a woman as seen not from a man's perspective but from that of the woman herself; he completely inhabits and possesses Kitty, knows her from the inside, down to the very nerves and fibre of her being. Apart from her prettiness, she is an ordinary little thing, silly, self-absorbed and not over-endowed with intelligence. And yet Maugham shows sympathy for her, for her loveless upbringing under the iron hand of a snobbish mother, for her terror at ending up a penurious spinster; and he understands completely her feelings for her awkward husband, towards whom she genuinely tries to behave well. Kitty is grateful to Walter for having rescued her, amused by his adoration, if bored to tears by his solemnity and inhibition. His manner changes only in bed, where, to Kitty's infinite tedium, Walter becomes embarrassingly passionate, 'fierce, oddly hysterical too, and sentimental . . . It seemed to her faintly contemptible that when she lay in his arms, his desire appeased, he who was so timid of saying absurd things, who so feared to be ridiculous, should use baby talk.' No wonder Townsend's confident love-making overwhelms her; and there is no doubt at all that the author knows precisely what he is talking about when he describes the almost physical pain Kitty suffers in her craving for sex with big, bad Charlie Townsend. ('One may doubt whether it is strictly necessary,' wrote the reviewer in the *Times Literary Supplement*, 'that purely lustful episodes should be described so conscientiously.')

Intriguingly, there is a great deal of the author himself in Walter Fane. Maugham once said that he had based the character largely on that of his brother F.H., and it is true that in appearance and in manner there are strong similarities. But so there are to Maugham. Here is Maugham describing Walter: 'He was self-conscious. When there was a party and everyone started singing Walter could never bring himself to join in. He sat there smiling to show that he was pleased and amused, but his smile was forced . . . You could not help feeling that he thought all those people enjoying themselves a pack of fools.' And here is Maugham on himself: 'Convivial amusement has always somewhat bored me. When people sit in an ale-house or, drifting down the river in a boat start singing I am silent . . . I do not much like being touched, and I have always to make a slight effort over myself not to draw away when someone links his arm in mine.' He is certainly drawing on his own experience in his account of Walter's emotional and over-eager love-making, which irresistibly recalls the youthful Maugham's clumsy affair years ago with Violet Hunt ('He is a fearfully emotional man, sexually,' Violet had said). There are, too, visible parallels between the home life of the Fanes and that of the Maughams, with both husbands, taciturn by nature, married to chatter-boxes. Like Syrie, Kitty was 'willing to chatter all day long'.

> [Walter's] silence disconcerted her. He had a way which exasperated her of returning no answer to some casual remark of hers. It was true that it needed no answer, but an answer all the same would have been pleasant. If it was raining and she said: 'It's raining cats and dogs', she would have liked him to say: 'Yes, isn't it?' He remained silent.

As in so much of Maugham's work at this period, a persistent leit-motiv is the misery of the married state. In *The Painted Veil* it is not only the Fanes' marriage that is unsatisfactory; Townsend is compulsively unfaithful to his loyal wife, with Kitty only the latest in a long line of 'little flirtations'; and Kitty's parents, too, exist within an utterly wretched relationship, Mrs Garstin a cruel, stupid woman driven by social ambition, her husband (a judge, like F.H.) a lonely and unhappy man despised by his wife and daughters. Much to be relished are the minutely calibrated snobberies of Mrs Garstin's South Kensington, as are the equivalent gradations among the British community in Hong Kong. 'There's hardly anyone here that one would bother about for five minutes at home,' Kitty tells her husband crossly, smarting from the realisation that as the wife of a medical man her social standing is considerably lower than that she had enjoyed at home as the daughter of a judge. '"I don't know that it exactly amuses me to be taken in to dinner by the agent of the P. and O," she said, laughing in order that what she said might not seem snobbish.' Admittedly the pace slows when the story moves to Mei-tan-fu, and the reader can quickly have enough of the smiling nuns and their pious, aristocratic Mother Superior. But the rest is enthralling, with the adulterous love triangle unfolding with hypnotic intensity, largely thanks to Maugham's two greatest strengths, his dramatist's infallible ear for dialogue and his instinct for psychological truth.

Maugham arrived home on 18 April 1920, his luggage filled with treasures, porcelain, Ming figures, Chinese silks, for Syrie a gold and jade necklace and a heap of chinchilla to make a cloak, and a white squirrel fur-coat and little blue coolie suit for Liza. But although he was immediately caught up in the busy demands of his London life, his overriding desire was to leave again as early as possible. For the previous half-year he had been living at close quarters with Gerald, and the abrupt change to marital domesticity was unpalatable in the extreme. Maugham still believed that every effort should be made to retain at least a veneer of harmony, that it was important to keep up appearances, and that he and Syrie should do their utmost to make the relationship work, as much for Liza's sake as for their own; and while he was at a safe distance of 9,000 miles he was able to view the prospect of cohabiting with his wife in a mood of relative equanimity. From Shanghai he had written to a woman friend,

> In married life there are times when one feels things are so hateful that it is worth while doing anything to get out of it, but one goes on – for one reason or another – & somehow they settle down more or less, & one becomes resigned or makes allowances or what not, & time goes on & eventually things seem not so bad as they might have been.

Yet when faced with the reality of life in Wyndham Place resignation seemed more difficult. Syrie, craving love, yearning for openness and warmth, was made miserable by her husband's emotional detachment, indeed his apparent inability to show any interest in her at all; he was civil but remote, and the more desperately she tried to provoke a reaction from him, the further he withdrew; when she tried to embrace him, he flinched. Inevitably she resorted to tears and reproaches, made scenes and gave way to wild accusations and bouts of furious temper, to such a degree that sometimes Maugham dreaded coming home. 'I seem to live in an atmosphere of complaints which I have never been used to and which I cannot think are reasonable,' he told her.

> Do you know that no one in all my life has said the things you have said to me? No one has ever complained of me and nagged me and harassed me as you have. How can you expect me to preserve my affection for you? You have terrorized me . . . Just think that at the age of forty-six, a

strong, healthy enough man, I should often have to go and have a cocktail in order to face you . . . You have lived all your life among people
who say the most awful things to one another, but I haven't. It humili-
ates me. It makes me miserable.

Syrie felt excluded from her husband's life, and understandably resented
the fact that he went abroad so often, for so long, and chose to travel
with a companion other than his wife. She longed to go with him, she
told him, longed to explore the remote regions of the world. But here
again Maugham was adamant. He was not a globe-trotter, he said, moving
from one luxury hotel to another. Reminding her how bored she had
been when travelling with Henry Wellcome, he pointed out that he, too,
travelled with a specific intention, and, like Wellcome, frequently in
dangerous and primitive conditions. 'You are very pleasant to travel with,'
he conceded, 'but I go with a special object . . . and you unfortunately
get between me and the impressions I am gathering. I go to seek ideas
and when I am with you I get none. I am very sorry, but that is the
brutal fact.'

Behind closed doors the quarrels continued, although as before the
two of them put on a good face in public. Syrie was a gifted and imaginative hostess, a quality much appreciated by Maugham who also
enjoyed social life, if on a rather less exuberant level. In the mornings
the two of them were often seen riding in the Row,* Syrie exquisitely
turned out in black habit, black hat and veil, and friends were frequently
brought back to breakfast afterwards. There were luncheon parties and
small dinners for old acquaintance, such as Walpole, Robbie Ross, H. G.
Wells and the very camp Eddie Knoblock, who on at least one occasion
turned up dressed as a woman. And there were big evening receptions,
notable for their lavishness and glamour, with marvellous food and copious
quantities of champagne. The writer Osbert Sitwell was one who fondly
remembered the gorgeous soirées at Wyndham Place. The Maughams
'were always particularly kind to the young and gifted', he recalled, '[and
there] in the large beige-painted, barrel-vaulted drawing-room of this
eighteenth-century mansion, their friends were privileged to meet all the
most interesting figures connected with the world of art, literature, and
the theatre in both England and America'. Here Syrie was in her element,
although not all Maugham's friends found her entirely sympathetic. 'Syrie
had a very heartless side,' said one; 'it was easy to be fascinated by
Syrie, less easy to love her', wrote another; 'her sparkling eyes could be

* Rotten Row in Hyde Park, a fashionable place to ride.

sharp, and the pert expression and staccato, high-pitched voice was not to everyone's liking'; while a third was even critical of her love of entertaining. 'Her hospitality did not spring from warmth of heart, but from an inability to be long alone,' he wrote not wholly inaccurately. 'Left to herself, she soon grew bad-tempered.'

On 9 August, four months after Maugham returned from China, his play *The Unknown* opened at the Aldwych. A curiously unsatisfactory work, it returns to territory covered in the 1901 novel *The Hero*. The characters are the same, with John, the young man home on leave from the war, and his pious fiancée Sylvia; but instead of the struggle between sex and duty, here John's struggle is with his religious faith: while at the front he has lost his belief in God, and now the question is, will he agree to take Communion in order to please his dying father? After much agonising he refuses to betray his conscience, but is eventually tricked into doing so by Sylvia, thus destroying the relationship between them. In spite of a strong cast headed by Basil Rathbone, *The Unknown* was taken off after less than two months, the general opinion concurring with that of the critic in *The Times*, who wrote that the argument was shallow and the play itself 'a little dull and lacking in drama'. After seeing it played before an audience Maugham recognised that it was flawed. 'The third act does not come off,' he wrote to Gerald Kelly. 'And now that I have discovered this I have ceased to be greatly interested. I do not want to sound pretentious but it is perfection (of a certain, limited sort of course) that I aim at; & having missed it I want to put the attempt out of my mind.'

Maugham, meanwhile, was absorbed in new projects, his head full of his impressions of China. When his study door was closed, between the hours of nine and twelve, the household knew he was not to be disturbed, a frustrating time for five-year-old Liza, who was excited to have her father home and longed for his attention. 'I was a little frightened of him as a forbidding father,' she recalled, 'but also I always loved his being back.' Maugham was fond of children, with a particular weakness for babies and the very young, with whom he was unusually patient and gentle. His daughter was a touching little figure, small and slight with a sweet, pale face and huge dark eyes; he loved her, wanted to do the best for her, and yet his feelings were painfully complicated by the fact that she was so much her mother's creature. (Significantly, Maugham for years insisted on referring to his daughter as Elizabeth, whereas Syrie, and everybody else, called her Liza.) Syrie doted on Liza and spoilt her shamelessly, indulging her with expensive clothes and toys, and keeping her with her as much as she could. The little girl naturally enjoyed this cosseting, infinitely preferring to be with her mother than with her nurse or governess, and in the nursery she made it her business to get rid of each new incumbent as quickly as possible. But whereas she knew she could depend on her mother, her father was the fascinating unknown, and his rare presence in her life was greatly prized. Maugham's own early life had been singularly lacking a father-figure: he had scarcely known his own father and his uncle the Vicar was unloving and remote; without a role model he found himself awkward in that role, well intentioned but not quite knowing what to do. 'I think he must have had a picture of what fathers should be like,' said Liza later, '[but] it was all a bit studied.' Unlike Syrie, her father was not a great provider of treats, never took her to the pantomime, for instance, or the circus, or even for an ice at Gunter's in nearby Berkeley Square; but there were trips to the zoo, and sometimes he rode with her, or let her accompany him on a walk, when he would tell her stories, though he never talked to her on a personal level, never told her anything about himself or his own childhood. Most enjoyable to both was the 'happy ritual', as Liza described it, of his coming upstairs in the evening to read aloud to her once she was tucked up in bed. Maugham was charmed by the sight of the little girl in her pyjamas, pink from her bath, her hair in two tight plaits, eagerly waiting for his visit. 'He never stammered when he read,' said Liza, 'which was really extraordinary.'

Young though she was, Liza could not but be aware, however subconsciously, of the tensions in the house when her parents were in residence together. Sometimes she heard sounds of fearful rows, sounds which terrified her, and she would creep away afterwards to hide so that no one should ask why she was crying. One symptom of anxiety manifested itself in the child's reluctance to eat: fussy and difficult at mealtimes, she often drove her governess to distraction by refusing to finish whatever was on her plate. During the whole of one cold winter when Maugham was abroad Liza was given her breakfast by herself in his study, the warmest room in the house. Filled with despair at the sight of the sausage and bacon in front of her, she waited till the maid had left the room, then quietly hid every last scrap of the fatty food behind the rows of books on the shelves. This subterfuge continued undetected for weeks, until her father eventually returned to find a disgusting smell and dozens of his precious volumes covered in putrefying grease and ruined beyond repair. Not unnaturally he was extremely angry. On another occasion when threatened with paternal retribution, she was so terrified of what he might do that she rushed into his study, snatched up a bundle of papers from his desk, threw open the window and screamed, 'If you come near me I'll drop them all out!' Maugham was so surprised that for several moments he just stood there. 'I held him at bay,' said Liza, 'but I remember the panic of it and wondering how I was going to get out of the situation eventually . . . [In the end] I was punished but nothing very severe.'

Throughout the summer of 1920 Maugham had dutifully played the part of husband and father, but now he was planning to escape. The relationship with Syrie had become so wretched that it was imperative a serious decision should be made about the future. The couple were hopelessly incompatible and deeply unhappy. Maugham had recently begun to feel suicidal, and this had shocked him into realising that something must be done. It was after all he who had the upper hand, as was made very clear during the debate he held with his wife on the subject. 'There are only two courses open to us now,' he told Syrie flatly, when a couple of weeks later he put in writing the points made in their discussion. 'You must either accept the claim I made then for freedom and go and come when I like, for as long as I like and as often as I like in peace and without scenes; or else separation . . . I have said little enough of Elizabeth,' he continued, 'but you know how constantly she is in my thoughts . . . For her sake, as well as for yours and mine, I should like us to continue to live together if you can only bring yourself to a willing compromise.'

Syrie had little option but to agree, however much she may have disliked the terms. Certainly she had plenty of time to think them over, as shortly after delivering his ultimatum her husband again left for abroad, this time remaining away for over a year.

# 9

## 'A World of Veranda and Prahu'

Unlike many of his peers, Maugham for most of his long life retained an unusual ability to move with the times. As he told his friend Eddie Knoblock, 'In all production that has anything to do with the arts, to stand still is to go back.' As a playwright Maugham was finely attuned to his audience, alert to new movements and quick to supply what a changing market demanded. 'A play is very like a suit of clothes,' he once explained. 'The tailor must make it fit or the client will not wear it, & it must be the sort of thing that people are wearing at the time or he will feel a fool.' In 1925, when he was over fifty, he noted that 'the drama is in a state of unrest', a state he himself intended to explore by looking at the work of young dramatists in France and Germany 'so that I can find out what they are aiming at'. As a writer of fiction he stayed surprisingly up to date both in his choice of themes and in the sometimes startling modernity of his approach; and with his short stories he became in commercial terms a global phenomenon, translated into almost every language. Yet even more remarkable for a writer born in the mid-Victorian era, Maugham early became established as a valuable property in the motion-picture industry. His own attempts at writing scenarios were undistinguished, his personal interest in the medium limited, and he found most of the people involved in the business antipathetic, yet it was through film that his work became famous to millions, many of whom knew nothing at all about his books. Throughout the 1920s and 1930s and during the Second World War Maugham spent considerable time in Hollywood, rarely with pleasure, and although personally involved in the process on a number of occasions he never cared for the film versions of his fiction. When invited to watch Garbo in *The Painted Veil*, he recoiled in horror. 'I cannot *imagine* that anything is likely to take me to see the film. I cannot bear seeing my works when they are made into pictures.' Nonetheless he was canny enough to realise that here was a fabulous source of income, to be exploited at every opportunity.

The first call to California came in 1920, from the pioneering film producer Jesse L. Lasky, who during a recent swoop on London had signed up a number of well-known authors, including Eddie Knoblock, Henry Arthur Jones (father of Sue Jones), Arnold Bennett and Elinor Glyn. Lasky had started his company in 1912 in partnership with his brother-in-law Samuel Goldwyn, their first employee Cecil B. DeMille, who was then a little-known stage director. In 1916 Lasky had joined forces with the newly formed Paramount Pictures, the most powerful studio of the silent era, which dominated the industry with a stable of stars such as Douglas Fairbanks, Mary Pickford, Gloria Swanson and Rudolph Valentino. Although the talkies were still some way off (the first talking picture, *The Jazz Singer*, was not released till 1927), Lasky and Goldwyn were convinced that distinguished writers were essential to their enterprise, and they spent vast sums bringing in eminent authors from Europe and America, assuming they could easily be taught how to create plot and delineate character in terms of the silent cinema. The experiment, although costly, was a failure: the writers, whose skills were verbal, not visual, were baffled by the new medium and most were wholly unable to adapt. Eddie Knoblock, for example, in a screenplay for DeMille went down in Hollywood legend for the unhelpful line, 'Words fail to describe the scene that follows.'

Maugham, although accustomed to writing dialogue for the stage, did little better. With Gerald Haxton he arrived in Hollywood in November 1920, and immediately found himself part of a group effort, obliged to listen to director, producer, other writers and even the actors themselves, for none of whom he had much respect: 'the obscene Cecil', as he privately referred to DeMille. Assuming he would be delivering stories for $15,000 to $20,000 a time he was disappointed that the only deals he was able to make were the sale of the rights to his 1918 play *Love in a Cottage*,\* and a $15,000 commission for a script which in the event was never used. 'I look back on my connection with the cinema world with horror mitigated only by the fifteen thousand dollars,' he told Knoblock shortly after leaving Los Angeles. Despite several attempts, Maugham never made a success of writing for the pictures. 'I am sure it is not difficult,' he said in 1937, 'but it happens to be a knack that I do not possess.' He was nonetheless one of the few writers coming in from outside who from the first understood the nature of what was required. As he explained in an article published the following year, 1921, 'The technique of writing for the pictures is not that of writing for the stage

---

\* Altered almost beyond recognition it was released in 1922 under the title *The Ordeal*.

nor that of writing a novel. It is something betwixt and between ... a technique of its own, with its own conventions, its own limitations, and its own effects.' Ironically, although Maugham himself was never to master this technique, during his lifetime he was to have more works adapted for film than any writer in the language.*

If dealing with the studio was frustrating, outside working hours there were considerable compensations. Even during Prohibition, Southern California was an agreeable place in which to pass a few weeks. In the early 1920s Hollywood still had something of the atmosphere of a sub-tropical village, with small farms, lemon and orange groves, and here and there empty plots of land overgrown with sagebrush and wild flowers. As now, the big avenues were lined with tall fan palms, the side streets overhung with pepper trees and bougainvillaea, but few of the houses were more than two storeys high and private swimming-pools were almost unknown. Then as now there was something surreal about the film world, about the illusion and artificiality that pervaded even everyday life, as Maugham discovered when walking down Sunset Boulevard and finding himself suddenly surrounded by cowboys and Indians, or ladies from the harem. Even more bizarre was an incident that resulted in his first-ever appearance on celluloid. When out for a stroll one morning he joined a small crowd that had gathered to watch the shooting of a scene for a movie. Suddenly, 'I was shoved roughly into the front of a crowd by a bullying assistant director, who yelled at me: "Look excited!" A pack of oddly garbed American bobbies were rushing pell-mell down the street. I think they called them "The Keystone Cops". So I became an actor, but without pay.' Maugham, staying at the Spanish-style Hollywood Hotel, was delighted to link up with some old friends, John Barrymore, who had starred in *Jack Straw* on Broadway; Eddie Knoblock, currently working on an adaptation of *The Three Musketeers* for Douglas Fairbanks and Mary Pickford; and the playwright Ned Sheldon, who had come down from New York in the hope that the Californian sun would help the arthritis that was soon to paralyse him completely. On New Year's Eve 1921 Knoblock took Haxton and Maugham to a seedy dance-hall, Dreamland, where they listened to a black jazz band and drank illicit whisky out of teacups.

Among the many members of the film colony to whom Maugham was introduced was the comedian Charlie Chaplin, a great figure in

---

* At the time of writing there have been ninety-eight versions, for film and television, of works by Somerset Maugham. His nearest rival is Conan Doyle, with ninety-three film adaptations of the Sherlock Holmes stories.

Hollywood and one of the highest-paid, and most famous, men in the world. Chaplin was in the process of making his first independent feature, *The Kid*, a semi-autobiographical story drawing on his childhood experience of extreme poverty in the tenements and workhouses of Walworth and Lambeth. This was an area Maugham knew well from his time at St Thomas's, and the two men formed an immediate bond, Maugham entranced by Chaplin's knockabout humour and genius for mimicry, especially of languages like French and Spanish of which he knew not a word; but behind the exuberant clowning Maugham sensed a profound melancholy, a nostalgia for the life of the London slums, for a warmth and liveliness unknown in the affluent avenues of Los Angeles. One night the pair took a long walk together, two short Englishmen, dapper and dark-haired, strolling in a haze of tobacco smoke and talking, talking, as they made their way towards the poorest quarter of the city; here, among squalid row-houses and dingy little shops, the streets were strewn with rubbish and noisy with children playing, watched over by their shabbily dressed, gossiping mothers. Looking around, Chaplin's face lit up and he exclaimed in a cheerful voice, with its curious half-cockney intonation, 'Say, this is the real life, isn't it? All the rest is just sham.' When Sam Goldwyn gave a dinner for the first private screening of *The Kid*, Maugham was one of the guests, delighted to join in the tremendous ovation that greeted Chaplin's poignant work.

It was purely by chance that Maugham before he left Hollywood struck one of the most lucrative deals of his career. A fellow guest at the Hollywood Hotel was John Colton, a young American playwright, who one evening asked if he might borrow something to read. Maugham offered him the galley proofs of his South Seas story, 'Miss Thompson', as yet unpublished, and next morning Colton came down to breakfast in a great state of excitement, saying he had been enthralled by the story and please might he adapt it for the stage. As the piece had been rejected by a number of periodicals before its eventual acceptance by the *Smart Set*, Maugham had no great hopes for it and equally agreed to Colton's proposal: nothing to be paid for the rights as Colton was hard up, but a fifty–fifty split on any profit. They shook hands and Maugham thought little more about it, until a few weeks later when the story appeared and made an enormous splash, with offers coming in for film and play rights worth thousands of dollars. Whatever his private regrets, Maugham stuck by his agreement, and the following year saw Colton's play produced in New York, retitled *Rain* and with the popular star Jeanne Eagels in the lead. *Rain* was an outstanding success, running for the best part of a year on Broadway, followed by a long tour and further productions throughout the States, eventually grossing more than $3 million. The extraordinary trajectory continued, with film rights sold for $150,000 and the play staged in England in 1925 by Basil Dean at the Garrick Theatre. Dean's first choice for leading lady had been the beautiful but volatile Tallulah Bankhead, who had pursued the part with some avidity, but when Maugham attended the first two days of rehearsal he was so disappointed by Miss Bankhead's performance that he insisted she be replaced. Humiliated and furious, the actress threw a volcanic tantrum in Basil Dean's office, then flounced out of the theatre, went straight back to her flat, wrote a histrionic suicide note and swallowed a very small handful of aspirin. Fortunately she awoke next morning with no ill effects, while leaving an exhausted author and director in her wake. Tallulah caused 'more bother than you can imagine', Maugham reported. 'She used every scrap of influence she had to sway me and when finally I put my foot down I was the object of the obloquy of all her friends.' The production continued, with the less well-known Olga Lindo as Sadie, who gave a performance which, if reliable, was fatally lacking in sex appeal, a quality possessed in abundance by the husky-voiced Miss Bankhead. Some years later Maugham admitted that the greatest mistake of his professional life had been preventing Tallulah from appearing in *Rain*.★

Maugham and Gerald Haxton left Los Angeles in February 1921, going first to San Francisco, where they spent a few days with the financier Bert Alanson, first encountered en route to Hawaii in 1916. On 21 February they sailed for Honolulu, and from there to Australia, before setting out on the final leg of the voyage to Singapore.

To the vast majority of his readers Somerset Maugham has come to be associated with the latter days of the British Empire, and in particular with the British Empire in the Far East. Just as Kipling is identified with India and the Raj, so is Maugham identified with the Malayan archipelago. Those famous tales of his set on rubber estates, on remote outstations, in the card-rooms of the local club, those stories of incest and adultery, of sex-starved missionaries and alcoholic planters, of footsteps in the jungle and murder on the verandah are what remain in the minds of many as the very image and epitome of Maugham's fictional territory. As Cyril Connolly once wrote, 'If all else perish, there will remain a

★ Immediately after her well-publicised dismissal by Basil Dean the actress was cast in Noël Coward's play *Fallen Angels*: on the first night she changed her line, 'Oh dear, rain' to 'My God, RAIN!', which predictably brought the house down. Tallulah did finally get to play Sadie, to great acclaim, in the 1935 revival in New York.

story-teller's world from Singapore to the Marquesas that is exclusively and forever Maugham, a world of veranda and prahu which we enter, as we do that of Conan Doyle's Baker Street, with a sense of happy and eternal homecoming.' Connolly explained: 'He tells us – and it had not been said before – exactly what the British in the Far East were like, the judges and planters and civil servants and their womenfolk at home.' In fact Maugham spent relatively little time there, six months in 1921 and four months in 1925; but from these journeys came a couple of short-story collections, *The Casuarina Tree* and *Ah King*, which contain some of Maugham's most accomplished work, written during the years when he was roaming the world with Gerald Haxton and at his most fecund and creative.

The world which Maugham portrays in these two books is that of a still extensive empire, but an empire that had been substantially weak-ened by the First World War. Up to 1914 the 12 million square miles of the land on which the sun never set seemed almost impregnable, the confidence of the British in their innate superiority by and large accepted as unquestioningly by the ruled as by the rulers. As one colonial admin-istrator put it, 'Most English households of the day took it for granted that nobody could be always right, or ever quite right, except an Englishman. The Almighty was beyond doubt Anglo-Saxon . . . [and] dominion over palm and pine . . . was the heaven-conferred privilege of the Bulldog Breed.' The colonial possessions were to be administered first and foremost for the benefit of Britain, but kindly administered, naturally: 'nobody but the most frightful bounder could possibly question our sincerity about that – but firmly too, my boy, firmly too, lest the school-children of Empire forget who were the prefects and who the fags'. During the war, however, this image of imperial infallibility was badly cracked, and the fags were treated to the unedifying spectacle of the prefects being killed in their hundreds of thousands, indeed coming close to humiliating defeat. At the same time the prestige of the white man, of paramount importance in governing territories far too extensive to be controlled by force, was further undermined by the arrival of the cinema, revealing to audiences throughout the pink part of the globe a view of the master-race as variously licentious, criminal or clownish. In an attempt to counter these regrettable influences it was decided by the governing elite that a tightening of regulations, with an increased emphasis on moral rectitude, was essential. As George Orwell, employed in the colonial Civil Service in Burma, wrote of this period, 'A sahib has got to act like a sahib . . . it is the condition of his rule that he shall spend his life in trying to impress the "natives".' Inevitably such a policy resulted in strains and stresses in certain areas of expatriate society. And it was this society that provided such a fertile field for the novelist who at the end of March 1921 landed in its midst.

At the time of Maugham's and Haxton's arrival in Malaya the country was going through a period of relative prosperity, mainly due to the pre-war rubber boom occasioned by the expansion of the motor industry in America. There was a general air of confidence and stability throughout the region, comprising the three Straits Settlements of Singapore, Penang and Malacca, which were directly under British rule, as well as the four Federated Malay States administered by Britain, the sultanates of Selangor, Perak, Negeri Sembilan and Pahang, with Kuala Lumpur the capital. Despite the upheavals caused by the war, there was still a general belief that British rule would last indefinitely, with the daily round continuing much as before and a standard of living improving all the time. Even the poorest planter now ran a car in place of a pony and trap, a cold-storage company had opened in Singapore, and two big modern hotels had recently gone up in KL, where there were a railway station, some good shops, a cinema, tea-room, golf-course, polo-ground and racetrack. The British presence was divided into two groups, the Malayan Civil Service on the one hand and the professional and technical departments on the other, with the former in social terms considering itself a definite cut above the latter: a large proportion of the MCS, which in the upper echelons provided the ruling class of Residents and District Officers, were products of the major public schools and universities, whereas most of the rest, planters, tin-miners, doctors, engineers, were not. Maugham in his notebook described the attitude of planters towards government officials as 'a combination of awe, envy, contempt and petulance. They sneer at them behind their backs, but look upon a garden party or a dinner at the Resident's house as an event in their lives. You would have to go far to find among the planters a man of culture, reading or distinction.' Such a situation naturally gave rise to a certain amount of divisiveness and insecurity, and there was a good deal of competitive talk about which school one had gone to, one's regiment and one's holiday home on the Isle of Wight; a titled family connection, however distant, was universally accepted as the trump card.

The European settlement of the FMS, predominantly British, was extremely sparse: on some of the more isolated rubber estates a planter could go for months, years even, without seeing another white face. The mail arrived by river once a month, bringing letters and books, as well as magazines and newspapers which were at least six weeks out of date. To some, like Mr Warburton in 'The Outstation', it was a matter of vital importance that despite his solitude standards should be rigidly maintained.

> Most people living in out-of-the-way places when the mail comes tear open impatiently their papers and taking the last ones first glance at the latest news from home. Not so Mr Warburton. His newsagent had instructions to write on the outside of the wrapper the date of each paper he dispatched, and when the great bundle arrived Mr Warburton looked at these dates and with his blue pencil numbered them. His head-boy's orders were to place one on the table every morning in the veranda with the early cup of tea and it was Mr Warburton's especial delight to break the wrapper as he sipped his tea, and read the morning paper. It gave him the illusion of living at home. Every Monday morning he read the Monday *Times* of six weeks back, and so went through the week. On Sunday he read the *Observer*. Like his habit of dressing for dinner it was a tie to civilization.

Even in the towns the expatriate population was small, which intensified the strong sense of community, the conscious desire to stick together and to reproduce as nearly as possible the way of life as it had been lived back home. Nearly every little town boasted its Anglican church, its cricket-pitch and mock-Tudor tavern, and the wives, the memsahibs, went to great lengths to teach their Chinese cooks how to make bread sauce, parsley stuffing, Welsh rarebit and steak-and-kidney pie. However hot and steamy the weather, in bungalows throughout the colony breakfast was tea, porridge, bacon and eggs or kippers, followed by toast and marmalade; a typical dinner consisted of tomato soup, cold asparagus smothered in bottled salad dressing, roast chicken (invariably overcooked), mashed potatoes and tinned peas, with tinned fruit salad for dessert.

At the heart of all expatriate social life was the club. It was here that the locals gathered in the cool of the evening to talk and play tennis and generally relax among themselves, relieved of the effort of maintaining the dignified demeanour the white man was expected to adopt in his dealings with the native. Offices closed at 4.00 pm, which allowed for a couple of hours of golf or tennis before the sun set, after which the men, changed out of their sports clothes or their shorts and sun-helmets, congregated in the bar. Here, served by white-coated servants in scarlet sashes, they downed a few stiff drinks, a couple of pahits (gin and bitters) or two or three good stengahs (whisky and soda), while on the verandah their mems smoked, gossiped, complained about the heat and their servants, and leafed through newly arrived issues of *Punch*, the

*Lady* and the *Illustrated London News*. A perennial topic was 'home' and where to live when the time came to retire. Home leave was granted every five or six years, passionately looked forward to but often a disappointment in the event. For months people excitedly planned what they were going to do: London, with its shops, theatres, restaurants: they were going to have the time of their lives! But frequently after a couple of weeks, 'they were more lonely than in the jungle. It was a relief when at a theatre they ran across someone they had known in the East . . . and they could fix up an evening together and have a good laugh and tell one another what a grand time they were having.'

No such dissatisfactions would be admitted, of course, once back at the club. In Kuala Lumpur there were three clubs, the biggest, the Selangor, possessing a billiard-room, card-room (almost everybody played bridge), reading and tiffin (luncheon) rooms, a hairdresser and barber, and two bars, from one of which women were excluded. There were weekly dances to music provided by a wind-up gramophone, occasional fancy-dress balls, and jolly amateur dramatics and smoking concerts, with classical music on the whole avoided but lots of songs from the current West End shows enthusiastically performed by fellows who had recently returned from London on leave. Most evenings the Resident dropped in for a game of cards, and at regular intervals gave an official dinner party at the Residency, where in tropical temperatures the men in stiff shirts and tails and the women in long dresses ate their roast beef and Yorkshire pudding to the strains of a medley from Gilbert and Sullivan played by a regimental band on the verandah. 'They are bored with themselves, bored with one another,' was Maugham's impression. 'They look forward to their freedom from bondage and yet the future fills them with dismay.'

Although the colony prided itself on maintaining a high level of racial harmony, there was on the whole little interest in indigenous customs or culture. As that tireless traveller Alec Waugh wrote of the English in the 1920s, 'They make no attempt to assimilate into the character of the countries that they occupy . . . An Englishman living in Penang is as little affected by the presence round him of the Malays, the Tamils, and the Chinese as is his elder brother in South Kensington by the slums that are west of Hammersmith.' In the FMS members of the non-European population were generally referred to as 'natives' or 'Asiatics', usually in a tone of vague contempt, although any incident of maltreatment of a native by a white man was severely frowned upon. Social interaction was rare, except with the local sultans, who were treated with due deference as their willing co-operation was essential to the imperial purpose. In his

notebook Maugham describes being taken by the Resident to meet the
Sultan of Tenggarah, to the east of Java. The palace, built in the Moorish
style,

> was like a very big doll's house and it was painted bright yellow, which is
> the royal colour. We were led into a spacious room, furnished with the
> sort of furniture you would find in an English lodging-house at the seaside,
> but the chairs were covered with yellow silk . . . In a cabinet was a large
> collection of all kinds of fruit done entirely in crochet work.

For people of mixed race the situation was especially tricky. Whereas
a blind eye was turned to white men visiting brothels and using native
prostitutes, it was very definitely not done to appear in public with a
Eurasian or Asian woman on your arm. Interracial marriages were vigorously discouraged and half-castes had a difficult time of it, accepted as
equals by neither one side nor the other. Eurasians spoke English with
an accent known as 'chee-chee', regarded as comical by Europeans, and
many went to considerable lengths to conceal their racial origins. Such
a one is Izzart in 'The Yellow Streak'. An old Harrovian, handsome and
stylish, member of a distinguished regiment during the war, Izzart has a
shameful secret: his mother is of mixed blood. His insecurity on this
account and his desperate anxiety to conceal his origins, brilliantly delineated by Maugham, make him thin-skinned and snobbish, quick to put
down anyone whose background is less than pukka, so frightened is he
of exposure.

> [Izzart] wondered whether by any chance the men at Kuala Solor with
> whom he was so hail fellow well met suspected that he had native blood
> in him. He knew very well what to expect if they ever found out. They
> wouldn't say he was gay and friendly then, they would say he was damned
> familiar; and they would say he was inefficient and careless, as the half-
> castes were, and when he talked of marrying a white woman they would
> snigger.

If it was tacitly accepted that white men consorted with native women,
the subject, if not the practice, of interracial homosexuality was taboo,
this despite the fact that a career in the colonies attracted an unusually
high proportion of men who had good reason for wishing to avoid
marriage at home. It was unspoken but well known that opportunities
for a wide variety of casual sex were far greater overseas than in Britain,
and the Far East in particular was seen as offering unparalleled largesse.
As soon as an Englishman was east of Suez a new world opened before
him, from the *terrassiers*, the boys working the hotel terraces in Cairo and

Port Said, to the all-male brothels of Karachi and Tientsin, the easy acceptance of homosexual practices in Siam, and the willing youth of Peshawar
on the north-west frontier, where it was said that 'to get a boy was easier
than to pick flowers by the wayside'. Much the same liberal sexual climate
existed in the FMS, and Maugham always maintained that the most
memorable sexual experience of his life had been a moonlit night on a
sampan with a boy in Malaya.

Within the British administration of the Malay States a notable
exception to the policy of racial separateness had existed before the
war in the custom of concubinage, of white men living with Malay or
Chinese mistresses, a custom that had of necessity been widely accepted
as so few European women had been prepared to endure the hardships
of life in the East. But with post-war prosperity the situation began to
change, with more and more men bringing wives out from home. These
were often sheltered and unsophisticated young women who were
profoundly ignorant of the world into which they were now introduced. For some the discovery that their husbands had had an Asian
mistress, and sometimes children, came as a profound shock. According
to one of the many articles on the subject in the *Malay Mail*, 'brides
coming out from England often learned the truth about their husbands
only after arriving in Malaya . . . [and] only if girls insisted that their
potential husbands had led equally blameless lives before marriage would
the problem cease'.

Naturally such a state of affairs was meat and drink to Maugham,
always intensely interested in sexual relationships, and he describes exactly
such an instance in his story 'The Force of Circumstance'. Doris, newly
wed and only recently arrived in Malaya, is blissfully happy with her
husband Guy and entranced by the exotic surroundings in which she
finds herself on their remote outstation. The best part of the day is when
Guy returns from his work in the court-house, and after a game of tennis
they sit companionably together looking out at the peaceful river and at
the palm trees on the opposite bank.

> The blinds on the verandah were raised now and on the table between
> their two long chairs were bottles and soda-water. This was the hour at
> which they had the first drink of the day and Guy mixed a couple of gin
> slings . . . He took her hand and pressed it.
> 'Are you happy here, darling?'
> 'Desperately.'
> She looked very cool and fresh in her linen frock.

Gradually, however, Doris begins to be disturbed by the vaguely menacing presence of one of the native women from the kampong, who with her three half-caste children has taken to hanging around outside the bungalow. When she asks Guy about her he at first prevaricates, before finally admitting that the woman for ten years had been his mistress and that the children are his. Doris is appalled. 'I think of those thin black arms of hers round you and it fills me with a physical nausea. I think of you holding those little black babies in your arms. Oh, it's loathsome. The touch of you is odious to me.' Unable to overcome her revulsion, she tells Guy the marriage is over and that she must return to England. Guy pleads with her, but as nothing he says has any effect he has no choice but to agree, while knowing that Doris's departure will break his heart. And yet he is not to be left entirely unconsoled. As he sits alone after seeing his wife off to Singapore a small boy sidles into the room.

> It was the elder of his two sons.
> 'What do you want?' said Guy . . .
> 'My mother sent me. She says, do you want anything?'
> Guy looked at the boy intently . . .
> 'Tell your mother to pack up her things and yours. She can come back.'
> 'When?' asked the boy impassively . . .
> 'To-night.'

Yet if the men were fallible, so, too, were the women. Men who brought wives with them to the tropics 'had real trouble on their hands', according to Maugham. 'White women were scarce, and bachelors were fair game to the neglected wives of overworked civil servants or planters.' Part of the trouble was boredom. With their husbands out all day, the mems had almost nothing to do, unless they were among the few prepared to interest themselves in local charities or community work. Many found themselves enjoying a far higher standard of living than they had been used to at home, with even the lowest-grade civil servant allotted a spacious bungalow of five or six rooms where he was looked after by a cook, one or two 'boys', a syce or chauffeur, an amah if there were children, a gardener, and a dhobi to do the laundry. Thus domestic responsibilities were few, and as it was not done for a mem to go to market herself almost her only duty was to order the meals, leaving hours to fill until her husband came home. As a handbook of the period explained,

> The chief disadvantage for ladies is often the lack of interesting occupa-
> tion during the day. In the larger towns, where there are European stores,
> it is possible for a lady to go shopping during the morning, or to visit

friends, but in the smaller stations or on estates or mines, life is apt to be monotonous. The climate is unsuited to housework, and too much sewing or reading may have its effect on the eyesight. A lady will therefore often find that time hangs heavily on her hands in the morning. The afternoon is usually devoted to a siesta, which most ladies find necessary in a hot and somewhat enervating climate.

Not unnaturally love affairs were regarded by some as a welcome diversion – if few ended as badly as that of poor Mrs Proudlock, wife of a schoolmaster in Kuala Lumpur. In 1911 Ethel Proudlock was charged with murder, having shot dead William Steward, manager of a tin mine in Salak, who she claimed had turned up one evening when her husband was out and tried to rape her. The court, however, was unpersuaded by her account, concluding that Steward had been her lover whom she had killed in a jealous rage after discovering he was living with a Chinese mistress. Mrs Proudlock was sentenced to hang, but after an impassioned petition had been signed by friends and supporters she was eventually granted a free pardon by the Sultan.

It was Mrs Proudlock's lawyer, E. A. S. Wagner, who in Kuala Lumpur ten years later described the case to Maugham. Immediately alert to its possibilities, Maugham constructed a fictional version, 'The Letter', in which he keeps fairly closely to the framework of events as described in court, with the wife, whom he calls Mrs Crosbie, shooting the would-be rapist, Hammond, and being arrested and sent to trial. It is at this point that the novelist adds an ingredient of his own. In the real case no concrete evidence was found of an intimate relationship between Mrs Proudlock and Steward, but in the story a letter is produced written by Leslie Crosbie that leaves little room for doubt that Hammond was her lover. Up to that moment her lawyer had been convinced she had nothing to worry about and that he would have no trouble in establishing her innocence. But the letter changes all that: she is guilty, and unless this damning evidence is destroyed she will be convicted. The incriminating document is in the hands of Hammond's Chinese mistress, whose recently discovered existence was the cause of Mrs Crosbie's frenzy; the Chinese woman is prepared to sell but only for an outrageous sum, and the lawyer has no choice but to ask for the money from Leslie's nice, stupid, utterly trusting husband, who has never for one moment doubted his wife's virtue. When he hears the sum required a terrible realisation begins to take hold.

Crosbie grew very red. His mouth sagged strangely.

'But . . .' he could not find the words, his face now was purple. 'But I don't understand . . . You don't mean to say they'd find her guilty?' . . .

Then something seemed to dawn in that slow intelligence of his.

'The Letter', which first appeared in *Hearst's International* in 1924 before its publication two years later in *The Casuarina Tree*, was to become one of Maugham's best-known short stories, mainly thanks to its stage and screen adaptations: he himself dramatised it for a production at the Playhouse in 1927, with Gladys Cooper playing Leslie Crosbie; in 1929 there was a silent-screen version with Jeanne Eagels; and in 1940 the famous Warner Brothers film directed by William Wyler with Bette Davis in the lead. Ironically the one part of the world where it was not popular at all was in Malaya. A member of the Malayan Civil Service who arrived in the country shortly afterwards wrote of Maugham's passage through the FMS that it 'was clearly marked by a trail of angry people. The indignation aroused by his play, *The Letter* . . . was still being voiced in emotional terms when I came by. It was also charged against him that he abused hospitality by ferreting out the family skeletons of his hosts and putting them into his books.' Other, similar accusations followed, and Maugham was so stung by them that for the American edition of *The Casuarina Tree* he added a tetchy postscript in self-defence.

> Some of the smaller communities in the countries washed by the China Sea are very sensitive, and their members are much agitated if, in a work of fiction, a hint is given that the circumstances of their lives are not always such as would meet the approval of the suburban circles in which contentedly dwell their cousins and their aunts . . . Living, with all the East about them, as narrowly as in a market-town, they have the market-town's faults and foibles; and seem to take a malicious pleasure in looking for the originals of the characters, especially if they are mean, foolish or vicious, which the author has chosen for the persons of his stories. They have small acquaintance with arts and letters and do not understand that the disposition and appearance of a person in a short story are dictated by the exigencies of the intrigue . . . Because a reader, unprofitably employing a useless leisure, recognises in a character one trait, mental or physical, of someone he knows and is aware the author has met, it is silly to put the name of this person to the character described and say: here is a portrait.

Such a surly tone was unlikely to soothe hurt feelings, and more than a decade later resentment at Maugham's depiction of the colony was still rumbling round the FMS. 'It is interesting to try to analyze the prejudice against Somerset Maugham which is so intense and widespread in this part of the world,' began an article in the *Straits Budget* in June 1938.

> The usual explanation is that Mr Maugham picks up some local scandal at an out-station and dishes it up as a short story . . . The second cause is disgust at the way Mr Maugham has explained the worst and least representative aspects of European life in Malaysia – murder, cowardice, drink, seduction, adultery . . . always the same cynical emphasis on the same unpleasant things. No wonder that white men and women who are living normal lives in Malaysia wish that Mr Maugham would look for local colour elsewhere.

At first taken aback, in time Maugham grew relatively indifferent to such accusations, to local fury over those 'masterpieces of disloyalty and betrayal', as they were regarded by many decent, uxorious, well-meaning servants of Empire. These stories of Maugham's, wrote the critic Logan Pearsall Smith with a certain amount of relish, 'are all ghastly betrayals of confidences the publication of which has ruined the lives of the hosts who kindly entertained him in the East and confided in him the sad secrets of their frustrated lives'. Maugham never denied that he travelled in order to find stories or that the stories he found formed the foundation of his tales. Most of his characters were based on real people, as he admitted.

> I tried to make use of them, and their problems, as capably as I knew how. That I didn't portray them, or their emotional circumstances, as attractively as they imagined them to be, earned me, of course, considerable criticism and hatred. On my return visits to many of those places a lot of doors were rudely slammed in my face, I was publicly insulted, and some even threatened to do me bodily harm. But I learned to accept all that . . . If they didn't like the way I honestly thought them to be, then to hell with them.

Both he and Gerald were good listeners, adept at drawing people out, and time and again discovered for themselves the truth of the observation that people talk to strangers in a way they never would to family and friends. 'I made acquaintance with them with just the degree of intimacy that suited me,' Maugham wrote in *The Summing Up*. 'It was an intimacy born on their side of ennui or loneliness . . . [an intimacy] that separation irrevocably broke.' While in a bar, or on a club verandah, or staying up-country with some lonely District Officer, Maugham heard the extraordinary dramas in these seemingly ordinary lives: '[when] sitting over a siphon or two and a bottle of whisky . . . [within] the radius of an acetylene lamp . . . a man has told me stories about himself that I was sure he had never told to a living soul . . . I have in this way learned more about men in a night than I could have if I had known them for ten years.' It was thus he learned of the incestuous affair between brother and sister that he describes in 'The Book-Bag'; the case of the alcoholic husband murdered by his wife in 'Before the Party' was inspired by a couple he met at dinner one evening in Singapore; the basis of 'The Force of Circumstance', of a wife's discovery of her husband's illegitimate half-caste children, was told him by a trader staying in the same up-country rest-house; while it was Gerald who heard about the scandal that was to reappear as 'Footprints in the Jungle'. The two men were in Sumatra, and Maugham had arranged to meet Haxton for dinner, but as usual Gerald had lingered in the bar drinking, and Maugham, tired of being kept waiting, began eating on his own. Just as he was finishing, Gerald lurched into the dining-room. 'I'm sorry, I'm sorry,' he said. 'I know I'm drunk, but I've got a corking good story for you,' and out came the shocking sequence of events surrounding 'the Cartwrights', as they appear in the story, who on the face of it had seemed just another nice, elderly couple innocently enjoying a few rubbers of bridge during their evening at the club.

It is at the end of the postscript to *The Casuarina Tree*, while he was still smarting from the first accusations of betrayal, that Maugham, with a bold disregard for the facts, states that of the six stories in the collection only one, 'The Yellow Streak', was based on an actual incident, and that, he says pointedly, 'was suggested by a misadventure of my own'. 'Misadventure' is putting it mildly, for what happened very nearly cost him his life.

In March 1921 Maugham and Haxton had arrived in Singapore, where they collected their mail ('Do write to me,' Maugham had asked Eddie Knoblock, 'and tell me all the secret history of London'), explored the city and made the most of their letters of introduction. Singapore, one of the great ports of the East and seat of the governor of the Straits Settlements, was very different in character to the rest of the country, crowded, noisy, exotic and morally lax. The harbour was spectacular, with the great sweep of the bay crowded with gunboats, passenger liners, junks and sampans, the quay a muddle of naval and passenger launches landing and disembarking, of goods being unloaded into godowns (warehouses), gharries and motor taxis waiting for trade, touts and guides competing to offer services of every imaginable variety. The city was half oriental – largely Chinese – and half European – predominantly

British. The Asian city with its bustling street life, its open-air work-shops, its markets and food stalls, temples, tea-houses and opium dens stood in close proximity to the European district of luxury hotels, including the famous Raffles, of department stores, restaurants and nightclubs, of huge imperial buildings housing government offices, of parks and public gardens, and of the expensive residential areas inhabited by rich Westerners and by even richer Chinese, who controlled most of the more profitable businesses. It was here in Singapore that Maugham smoked his first pipe of opium, the immediate effect a feeling of great peace and clarity of mind, unfortunately followed next morning by a cracking headache and hours of noisy retching.

From Singapore Maugham and Haxton travelled the length and breadth of the Peninsula, staying sometimes in hotels and rest-houses, sometimes with a Resident or DO, or, less comfortably, on remote outstations or rubber estates: compared to the relative luxury of official residencies, planters' houses, Maugham noted, were 'a bit dreary, a lot of gimcrack furniture and silver ornaments and tiger skins. And the food's uneatable.' They sailed widely about the islands of the archipelago and beyond, often taking passage on board the pearling luggers that plied their trade throughout the South Pacific, voyaging to Merauke in New Guinea, to Banda and the Kai Islands, to Mobiag and Thursday Island in the Torres Straits. Particularly memorable was their visit to Sarawak, on the north coast of Borneo. Here in the kingdom of the White Rajahs, the only oriental kingdom in world history to be ruled by an English dynasty, they were entertained by the Rajah himself, the very handsome, very English Vyner Brooke, whose wife was the lively, eccentric Sylvia Brett, sister of the painter Dorothy Brett, a close friend of D. H. Lawrence. Anxious to explore, Maugham and Haxton set off on an expedition up the Skrang river, travelling by canoe with a crew of Dayak boatmen. They themselves reclined comfortably beneath an awning, enjoying the peace and beauty of the scene, of white egrets flying low over the dark-green water, of the sandy banks lined with feathery casuarinas, and beyond, sloping uphill, the jungle dense with acacia and coconut palms. Every evening they tied up by a Dayak village, spending the night in one of the thatched long-houses, each inhabited by several families, twenty to thirty people, all intensely, exhaustingly hospitable. At night the two men were entertained to feasting and dancing that continued into the small hours, and even then there was little chance of sleep as babies cried, cocks crowed, chickens and dogs wandered freely around, and under the house pigs rooted noisily through the garbage.

One day while slowly moving upriver they suddenly saw approaching an enormous tidal wave, a bore, roaring towards them and rapidly increasing in volume until with a rush a great wall of water eight feet high burst over them, capsizing the canoe and throwing them into the water. Desperately Maugham and Haxton tried to hang on to the side of the boat but it was impossible to get a grip, and with the wave surging and storming around them, they were repeatedly submerged. Before long, Maugham, bruised, exhausted and gasping for air, felt his strength go and knew he was in imminent danger of drowning. 'I thought the best thing was to make a dash for the bank, but Gerald begged me to try to hold on . . . I swallowed a good deal of water . . . Gerald stayed near me and two or three times gave me a hand.' After several further minutes of struggle, they heard a shout from one of the crew who had caught hold of a thin mattress as it floated past, and with this to support them they managed to reach land. Their feet sinking into thick mud, they pulled themselves ashore and somehow succeeded in scrambling up the bank, collapsing into the tall grass at the top. Here they lay motionless for quite a while, covered in mud and too exhausted to move, until Maugham eventually summoned the strength to get up and strip off his filthy clothes, making a loincloth out of his shirt. It was then he saw to his horror that Gerald in attempting to rise had collapsed and appeared to be in the throes of a heart-attack. 'I thought he was going to die,' Maugham recalled. There was no help at hand and nothing to be done. For what seemed like hours Maugham sat beside his lover, soothing him and talking to him, telling him that the pain would pass and everything would be all right. Eventually help arrived, and the two exhausted men were taken by canoe to a long-house, where slowly they recovered. In retrospect Maugham was surprised that he had felt no fear, although he was intensely glad to find himself still alive. 'Later in the evening when I was sitting in a dry sarong in the Dayak house and from it saw the yellow moon lying on her back it gave me a keen, almost a sensual pleasure.'

For the first day or two Maugham and Haxton felt so happy at their escape that nothing else seemed to matter. But soon they began to fret for all those personal possessions that had gone to the bottom of the river, and decided to return to Singapore to refit. From here in mid-August they set out again, this time to Java, where the intention was to stay for a few weeks before starting on the long voyage home. But weeks turned into months, for it was on Java that Gerald, still weak after his near-drowning, fell seriously ill with typhoid and had to be moved to a sanatorium at Garoet on the south coast. Maugham, too, was unwell, with an attack of colitis, and so they remained in the pleasant little hill town while Gerald underwent his treatment, Maugham perfectly happy as long as he could spend hours a day reading. Throughout his life Maugham referred to his love of reading as an addiction; it was, he explained, 'a necessity, and if I am deprived of it for a little while I find myself as irritable as the addict deprived of his drug'; wherever he was he took care to be well supplied with books, on his travels always taking a trunkful with him. But now, staying on so much longer than planned, he found to his dismay that he had nothing left, and that the only literature locally available which was not in Dutch were school textbook copies of Goethe, La Fontaine and Racine. 'I have the greatest admiration for Racine,' he wrote later, 'but I admit that to read his plays one after the other requires a certain effort.' It was as a result of this experience that Maugham resolved never again to risk running out: he purchased a book-bag, a large canvas sack with a leather base, cumbersome but capacious, which from then on, filled to the brim, accompanied him on all his travels.

This experience of being stranded with nothing rewarding to read clearly marked Maugham, for on his return to England he wrote to the Society of Authors with a scheme devised as a direct consequence of his deprivation. He wished to set up a bequest, he said, to fund an annual award that would encourage the English writer to 'have the opportunity of living for a while out of his own village'. During his extensive travels in the Far East, he continued,

> I have been very much struck by seeing what sort of English books are read by the English who live out of England, and by the large number of foreigners who read English.
>
> The members of your Society would be very much surprised if they knew what books the Dutch, for instance, read in the Malay Archipelago . . .
>
> On the whole I think it may be said that the better English writers are not read at all . . . This has appeared very strange to me and the only reason I have been able to discover for such a lamentable state of things is that the best English writers of the present day are so provincial . . . They have nothing much to say to readers who by the circumstances of their lives have acquired a broader outlook on the world in general.

In years to come Maugham was to pursue this theme, which was eventually to result in the setting up of a travelling scholarship for young writers, known as the Somerset Maugham Award.

In contrast to the cramped quarters of pearl luggers and Dayak canoes, the final leg of the long journey back to Britain was aboard the *Aquitania*, not only the largest liner in the world but the most luxurious. Among the passengers sailing from New York was a twenty-year-old American, Dwight Taylor, who had been provided with an introduction to Maugham by his mother, the actress Laurette Taylor. Maugham invited the young man to join him for a cocktail, talking to him affably about Europe, where Taylor had never been, and also describing his unchanging daily routine while at sea: reading or writing all morning until twelve when he emerged for a single martini before taking a brisk walk around the deck until luncheon at a quarter to one; after lunch he again retired to his cabin where he remained incommunicado until it was time for dinner. Taylor was impressed by the writer's discipline and by his immaculate appearance, both in marked contrast to those of his 'secretary', Gerald Haxton, who, his fair hair *en brosse*, slouched around scruffily dressed, rarely appearing on deck but spending most of his time smoking, drinking and playing cards for high stakes. His devil-may-care attitude rather shocked Taylor. 'It seemed strange to me', he primly remarked, 'that Maugham should allow his secretary to go around looking like a scarecrow.'

It was while still in Java, shortly before setting off for home, that Maugham received some bad news. His broker in New York, Trippe & Co., had suddenly failed, with the loss of a considerable portion of his savings. 'I am dreadfully put out about it,' he complained, 'because I had been saving all I could so as to put myself in such a position that I would never write for money again.' He turned to his friend Bert Alanson, asking if he could recommend a reliable stockbroking firm in the United States, and Alanson at once offered to manage the portfolio himself: he had already made a few investments on Maugham's behalf and now suggested that he should take on the rest, working without commission as an expression of his admiration and affection. Alanson was in Maugham's debt, also, for a favour he had done him while he was in Russia in 1917, cabling a coded warning about the fall of the rouble ('AUNTIE RACHEL VERY ILL') which had saved Alanson a small fortune. Maugham for his part was grateful for Alanson's offer, although he had little idea how grateful he would have cause to be. For the next thirty-six years, from 1922 until his death in 1958, Alanson made Maugham a very rich man, turning the dividend cheques that were regularly sent him into a substantial fortune. For Maugham as he grew older money, and amassing vast quantities of it, was to become increasingly important on a number of levels: it gave him personal and artistic freedom, it allowed him to be generous when he chose, to buy silence when necessary, and the knowledge that he could afford the best of everything compensated him, up to a point, for other, less material deprivations in his youth. Money was a highly emotive area of his life in which Bert Alanson was intimately involved, giving their friendship a depth and texture it might not otherwise have possessed. Alanson was one of the few people in whom Maugham had complete trust and his gratitude and reliance never wavered. 'You are a wonderful friend,' he told him in February 1921 after staying with him on his way to the Far East, and nearly thirty years later the theme was much the same. 'You were as ever wonderfully good to me,' Maugham wrote in 1949, '& I can never hope to repay all the care you have taken of me for so many years except by giving you my deep & sincere affection.'

In the event the failure of Trippe & Co. was not as disastrous as first appeared, and by the following year Maugham had recovered about two-thirds of his original losses. In addition, during his absence abroad a new comedy had been produced which was proving an impressive money-spinner. *The Circle*, opening on 3 March 1921 at the Haymarket, had run for nearly six months, doing excellent business, before being staged in New York in September, where it was bringing in $20,000 a week* and collecting a sheaf of adulatory reviews from some highly influential critics. 'One delicious situation follows another just as fast as the characters can get on and off the stage,' wrote Robert Benchley in *Life*, while Arthur Hornblow in *Theatre Magazine* judged it 'the best English comedy since Pinero's days'. Well received at the time, its popularity continued to grow on both sides of the Atlantic throughout the playwright's lifetime, the American Louis Kronenberger in 1952 describing *The Circle* as 'one of the very few creditable high comedies written in English in the 20th century', while the British critic James Agate wrote of 'this brilliant play-wright' that 'his technique is flawless and *The Circle* is his best play'.

*The Circle* is a highly polished, expertly structured piece, which deals with the difficulties of the survival of love within marriage, with the pressures of society and with the triumph of character over circumstance. The action takes place in a large house in Dorset, where Arnold Champion-Cheney and his pretty young wife Elizabeth are expecting the arrival of Arnold's mother and her lover. Thirty years ago Lady Kitty scandalised society by running off to Italy with Lord Porteous, a married man, with whom she has been living in sin ever since. Arnold is apprehensive, still resentful at his mother's abandoning him, but Elizabeth is thrilled by the romantic love-story of lovely Lady Kitty and the glamorous peer and can hardly wait to meet them. All are taken aback when the couple walk in,

---

* Approximately 10 per cent of this sum would go to the playwright.

she an idiotic chatterbox with heavily painted face and dyed hair, he a bald, bad-tempered old man complaining about his rheumatism; it is quite clear the two are badly on each other's nerves and hardly able to exchange a civil word. Their example is not lost on Elizabeth, who had herself been intending to leave her husband and run off with her lover. Lady Kitty, when she learns of the plan, makes an impassioned speech imploring Elizabeth to stay, describing her own unhappy experience of life outside the pale. 'One sacrifices one's life for love and then one finds that love doesn't last. The tragedy of love isn't death or separation . . . The tragedy of love is indifference.' In the end, however, the young lovers remain resolute and succeed in making their escape, aided in a surprising reversal by Kitty and Porteous, who underneath all the snapping and snarling are shown still to have a true fondness for each other.

In many ways *The Circle* offers a curious premise for a comedy, a fusion of romance and reality, with a bleak message underneath the frequently very funny dialogue. There is real cruelty, particularly in the exchanges between Porteous and Kitty, and little comfort to be found in any of it: the adulterous lovers are by and large miserable, unfaithful to each other and bored by idleness and exile; and yet marriage is hardly a satisfactory answer, certainly not for Elizabeth and Arnold, who live together in a state best described as amiable indifference. 'You can't expect a man to go on making love to his wife after three years,' Arnold asserts. 'After all, a man marries to have a home, but also because he doesn't want to be bothered with sex and all that sort of thing.' (That Arnold is not by nature a marrying man is delicately indicated throughout: not only by his lack of interest in his attractive wife but also by an unmanly passion for décor and furniture.) When the young lovers go off together in the final scene the audience is left not knowing if they are looking at a happy ending or not, a lack of resolution that on the first night attracted some boos from the gallery and which encouraged several critics to accuse the author of cynicism, an accusation with which Maugham was to grow wearily familiar. In reviewing the play both Frank Swinnerton and St John Ervine described the cynical tendency as a flaw, although the more perceptive Desmond MacCarthy recognised it as the vital driving force behind Maugham's comedic gift, a 'gift [that] sprang from a clear-sighted, hard-edged cynicism, rare in English writers'. Indeed, '*The Circle* is one of the best plays he has yet written . . . [and] it is one of the most cynical.'

Despite a few critical reservations, the play was a huge hit, and Maugham was relieved to be able to tell his agent Golding Bright that *The Circle*'s popularity had restored his financial independence. Maugham's reputation had been further enhanced while abroad by the publication in Britain and America of the short stories inspired by his travels in Polynesia, collected under the title *The Trembling of a Leaf*. Predictably, 'Rain' was singled out as the most remarkable, but as the *Saturday Review* put it, 'each separate tale is begun by inspiration and completed by artistic perfection'. It was an age in which the form was popular and the author was gratified by his enormous sales. 'My short stories have been a very great success here & everyone is being very nice to me,' he wrote to Bert Alanson, admitting that he was enjoying being lionised. Maugham found it a strange experience to return after such a long absence, away from England for over a year, and find everyone doing and saying much the same as when he had left. The first time he dropped in at the Garrick one of the members greeted him with, '"Hulloa, Maugham, have you been away?" "Yes," I said, "I've been to Brighton for the week-end." "Ah," he answered, "I thought I hadn't seen you about lately."'

Not everything had stayed the same, however, and there were two major changes, one occasioned by the death of Maugham's publisher William Heinemann, the other by the death of his agent, J. B. Pinker. Heinemann at only fifty-seven had died of a heart attack in October 1920, less than three weeks after Maugham had left England. With no obvious successor in line, the firm had been stranded until Heinemann's associate director had managed to do a deal with the New York publisher F. N. Doubleday, persuading him to buy a controlling interest in the business while leaving the English company intact. Doubleday, a powerful, charismatic figure, with many prominent English writers on his list, Kipling among them, had taken his son Nelson into the company – when Nelson was a baby Kipling had dedicated to him his famous poem 'If' – and it was Nelson Doubleday, a big, energetic, sporty young man, who was to form not only a close professional connection but a lifetime's friendship with Maugham. Pinker also died unexpectedly, in February 1922 while on a business trip to the States. He had done well for his client in the early days of their association, but as Maugham now was at least as well known in America as in Britain he decided to put his business in the hands of an American agent, Charles Hanson Towne. Towne, regarded by Maugham as 'one of the most agreeable persons I know in New York', was a very different type, an engaging, sophisticated man of letters, novelist, poet, magazine editor and columnist, a considerable celebrity in bookish circles in Manhattan.

Very much in the public eye, Maugham was immediately swept up in an energetic round of entertaining and being entertained, catching up with old friends like Walpole, Knoblock and Kelly as well as making new acquaintance, among them the American novelist Sinclair Lewis, over from the States on a visit to London. Lewis, lean and lanky, with red hair and a gaunt, pale face, had become famous with the publication two years earlier of his novel *Main Street*, a work which had fascinated Maugham with its detailed depiction of small-town life in the Middle West. During his frequent train journeys across America Maugham had seen men of exactly this background lounging about the smoking-car, 'in their ill-fitting, ready-made clothes, gaudy shirts and showy ties, rather too stout, clean-shaven . . . with a soft hat on the back of their heads, chewing a cigar, [but] they were as strange to me as the Chinese and more impenetrable'. Now having read *Main Street* he felt he understood something about them and was eager to talk to the author, inviting him to dinner at Wyndham Place. 'Maugham seems to fancy me,' Lewis delightedly reported to his wife, '[and] invites me to dinner for both the tenth and the 22nd of this month.' The first of these occasions turned out to be a somewhat uncomfortable occasion. To meet Lewis, Maugham had asked Eddie Knoblock, the painters Ambrose McEvoy★ and Christopher Nevinson, the playwright and critic St John Ervine, Osbert Sitwell, Hugh Walpole and that exquisitely refined connoisseur and patron of the arts Eddie Marsh. Syrie as hostess was the only woman, but even her presence failed to restrain Lewis, the guest of honour, from becoming wildly over-excited, in the words of Nevinson,

> restless, clownish, and intense . . . Never have I met a man so sensitive and yet with such a gift of putting his foot in it . . . After dinner, Sinclair Lewis took Eddie Marsh's monocle, stuck it in his own eye, and began parading up and down with Eddie Marsh following like a dog on a string. Then, to amuse himself, he parodied high-brow conversation in the best Oxford manner, at times imitating McEvoy's cracked voice . . . All of us were embarrassed, as the parody was grotesquely realistic.

Eventually, to Maugham's relief, Nevinson rescued the situation by taking Lewis off to a nightclub.

Among the old friends assembled at Wyndham Place that February evening there was one notable absentee, Gerald Kelly, perhaps away on one of his sojourns in Spain, or perhaps vetoed by Syrie who had never liked him. Kelly was making a good living in fashionable portraiture, 'the

★ In the account of the dinner party in Nevinson's diary no first name is given for McEvoy: the probability is that it was Ambrose McEvoy, though it could have been the playwright Charles McEvoy.

most reliable portrait painter of his time', as Kenneth Clark rather tepidly described him, and he had recently married, his wife Lilian (always known as Jane), a blonde and beautiful working-class girl who had been one of his models. Maugham had been delighted by the match. 'I think you have done a very clever thing & I am sure you will make a great success of it, & be very happy,' he had told him, recognising that Jane's gentleness and calm would provide the necessary counterbalance to Kelly's high-strung, restless nature. Next to Kelly, Knoblock and Walpole were the friends to whom Maugham was closest. Eddie Knoblock, sweet-natured and gregarious, was recklessly spending far too much money buying antique furniture for his pretty house in Brighton, where Maugham sometimes stayed, and when penury threatened, as it frequently did, he returned to Hollywood to write film scripts and recoup. Walpole, on the other hand, was going from strength to strength, popular as a novelist, a distinguished member of the literary establishment, living in an expensive flat in Piccadilly and revelling in a glamorous, if frustrating, affair with the Danish tenor Lauritz Melchior. Bluff and boyish, an indefatigable self-promoter, he was by and large a popular fellow, despite a deplorable habit of dropping with a bland indifference anyone no longer useful to him. Although extremely pleased with himself, Hugh was desperate for approval and at heart insecure; nervous of his friend's slightly barbed teasing, he nevertheless admired Maugham and craved his good opinion. The two met frequently, with Hugh eagerly noting in his diary any words of praise let drop by the older man. 'Willie Maugham came to tea and warmed my heart by speaking well of my work . . . actually praising my "urbane humour" which everyone else denies me.'

A relative newcomer in the group at Wyndham Place was Eddie Marsh, who in years to come was to play a unique role in Maugham's career. Only two years older than Maugham, Marsh, once described as a cross between Puck and Mme de Maintenon, was a man of impressive erudition, with a double first in Classics at Cambridge and an extraordinarily retentive memory, particularly for poetry, of which given the slightest encouragement he would recite reams in his thin, slightly squeaky voice. Editor of the much admired five-volume anthology *Georgian Poetry*, he was also a connoisseur of contemporary painting, and although of modest means had assembled an important collection of works by artists such as Mark Gertler, Duncan Grant, Stanley Spencer and Paul Nash. By profession Marsh was a civil servant and for nearly twenty years held the post of private secretary to Winston Churchill. The first letter extant from Maugham to Marsh, written in 1919, is a note of thanks for services unspecified –

'My dear Marsh,' Maugham had written, 'Thank you very much *indeed*. I am very grateful indeed for what you have done for me' – but most probably a reference to Marsh using his influence with Churchill in obtaining an imprimatur for the *Ashenden* stories. Nattily dressed and insatiably social, Marsh led an impeccable bachelor existence, much given to romantic attachments to gifted and beautiful young men, Rupert Brooke being one, the actor and composer Ivor Novello another. It was through following Novello's career that Marsh had developed a passion for the theatre, present at every first night, madly enthusiastic no matter how terrible the play. 'Heavens!' exclaimed James Agate one evening when Marsh had loudly clapped a player's exit only minutes after the rise of the curtain, 'you *can't* be enjoying it *already!*' With his scholar's mind and sharp eye for error Marsh as a hobby had started correcting proofs for writer friends, most notably for Churchill himself, as well as for Desmond MacCarthy, Harold Nicolson, Walter de la Mare, Dorothy Sayers, A. A. Milne and eventually Somerset Maugham.

At home Maugham was relieved to find that relations with Syrie were calmer and more amicable than at any time during the marriage so far. There was good reason for this: Syrie had found something to do. Bored and restless while her husband was away, she had decided to follow a bent for interior decoration, with the aim of eventually establishing herself in business. She was fortunate in her timing: up until 1914 it was almost unheard of for a respectable lady to go into retail, with interior design the preserve of the big stores such as Fortnum & Mason, Liberty's, Whiteley's and Waring & Gillow. But with the post-war economic decline a number of ladies had set up in trade, opening smart little shops selling hats or dresses or ornamental knick-knacks, thus bringing about an important change in attitude. (An article in *Vogue* commenting on this trend began, 'Someone once said that a woman is either happily married or an Interior Decorator . . .') When installed by Gordon Selfridge in York Terrace, Syrie had employed a designer, Ernest Thornton-Smith, head of the antiques department at Fortnum's, and it was Thornton-Smith to whom she now turned, asking him to take her on as an unpaid apprentice to teach her about furniture and restoration, how to deal with customers, and all the invaluable little tricks of the trade. It quickly became apparent that Syrie had found her vocation, not only in décor but as a businesswoman, tough, tenacious and with a keen eye for a bargain; and in 1922 with borrowed capital of £400 she opened a shop, Syrie Ltd, at 85 Baker Street. Stocked initially with the contents of the house in Regent's Park, Syrie Ltd was an immediate success, its proprietor delighting in the process of buying and selling, of attending auctions and picking up cheaply pieces which could be cleaned up, cleverly embellished and sold on at a handsome profit.

Over the next two decades the name Syrie Maugham was to become synonymous with elegant modernity. Her artistry and sense of style were to make a considerable impact on interior decoration in both Britain and the United States, with her famous all-white rooms copied widely, from Mayfair to Manhattan. 'With the strength of a typhoon,' wrote the photographer Cecil Beaton, '[Syrie] blew all colour before her . . . turning the world white . . . White sheepskin rugs were strewn on the eggshell-surface floors, huge white sofas were flanked with white crackled-paint tables, white peacock feathers were put in white vases against a white wall.' Syrie was even paid the compliment of being caricatured by Evelyn Waugh: in *A Handful of Dust* there are undeniable similarities between Syrie and the ruthless Mrs Beaver who desecrates the Gothic gloom of Hetton Abbey with natural sheepskin and white chromium plating. Syrie's emphasis on neutral colour and the importance of space was regarded as exciting and new, especially in England where the prevailing taste tended towards violently contrasting schemes in black and orange, or else tea-cosy travesties of Tudor design, complete with bogus beams and inglenooks. Influential though Syrie was, however, she was not original in her use of white, coming across it first in a house at Sandgate in Kent belonging to a Mrs Ralph Philipson, one of her main investors. It was Mrs Philipson who persuaded her away from her early rather florid taste, a penchant for oak tables and copper pots filled with Cape gooseberries, to something more startling and innovative. Syrie made a workshop for herself in one of Liza's nurseries where she could practise her techniques, and soon she was pickling and bleaching tables and chairs and stripping the black lacquer off Coromandel screens with a gusto that delighted her clients and provoked shocked accusations of vandalism from the more traditional sections of the trade.

If not altogether pleased to find his wife running a shop, Maugham was relieved that Syrie's formidable energies had found an outlet other than in marital rows. And he had always admired her flair for colour and design. 'She has exquisite taste,' he wrote in his notebook in 1922, before going on to list further good qualities.

> She is clever. She has charm . . . She is generous and will spend her own money, to the last penny, as freely as she will spend other people's. She is hospitable . . . In sickness she will show herself an admirable and devoted nurse. She is a gay and pleasant talker. Her greatest gift is her capacity for

sympathy. She will listen to your troubles with genuine commiseration and with unfeigned kindliness will do everything she can to relieve them . . . There is real goodness in her.

But on the other side of the coin, 'She is not only a liar, she is a mythomaniac . . . She is grasping and will hesitate at no dishonesty to get what she wants. She is a snob . . . She is vindictive, jealous and envious. She is a quarrelsome bully. She is vain, vulgar and ostentatious. There is real badness in her.'

At this period, however, the good appeared to outweigh the bad, and while he did not entirely approve, Maugham did nothing to stop his wife's new venture. It is telling that Syrie had not turned to her wealthy husband for the capital to fund it, preferring instead to borrow from friends, less as a statement of independence than from a conviction that he would almost certainly refuse her. For when it came to his wife Maugham kept a tight hand on the purse-strings; her wilful extravagance infuriated him, and refusing her money was an effective method of punishment and control. He gave her a generous annual allowance of £3,000 for clothes and personal expenses, which she was always exceeding, and her profligacy in housekeeping drove him to distraction, the gallons of cream, the case upon case of champagne, the enormous numbers of dishes prepared, never eaten and then ordered by Syrie to be thrown away. One summer having rented a house for a family holiday in Brittany, Maugham became so enraged by the food bills Syrie was running up that he refused to pay them, even though there were guests staying at the time, and Syrie was forced to borrow in order to settle the accounts. Nonetheless there were periods of harmony: it suited Maugham to appear with Syrie on his arm in public and he was grateful for the seamless skill with which she ran the household and for her expertise as a hostess. With regard to Liza, now seven, the fact that the little girl was so wrapped up in her mother eased his conscience, protected him from feeling that he might be failing in his duties as a father; he himself in childhood had had only a tenuous relationship with his father, which may go some way to explaining a curious statement made later that year that 'I have a notion that children are all the better for not being burdened with too much parental love.'

While thankful that the atmosphere at Wyndham Place was less turbulent Maugham still was not prepared to spend much time there, and at Easter he left for Italy to meet Gerald Haxton, who had been parked in Florence while awaiting the next departure for the Far East. On his return from Java Maugham had written to his old friend Reggie Turner, who had been long settled in an apartment on the Viale Milton, asking him to take the young man under his wing. Haxton, 'my constant companion on all my travels . . . [is] a very dear friend of mine for whom I hope you will do everything you can . . . Particularly I should be grateful if you can tell him of some rooms where he can live inexpensively . . . & also I hope you will introduce him to as many people as you can so that he may not feel lonely.' When Maugham arrived he and Haxton joined a group containing Turner, Hugh Walpole, Eddie Knoblock and the Italian publisher Giuseppe ('Pino') Orioli, who at the time was living with that crusty, charismatic figure Norman Douglas. Douglas, admired as the author of *South Wind*, notorious as an unregenerate paedophile, was now in his fifties and after many years on Capri and then in England had settled in Florence in an attempt to recoup his fortunes after a long period of poverty and several run-ins with the law for molesting young boys. 'I left England under a cloud no bigger than a boy's hand,' he used to quip. His financial situation had recently become so desperate that a secret appeal had been launched by Rebecca West; when she approached Maugham he told her he would assume total responsibility, depositing enough money to provide a roof over Douglas's head for life on condition that his identity as benefactor was never revealed: Douglas, he joked, had a habit 'of attaching himself to the hand that feeds him'. With such dazzling conversationalists as Douglas and Reggie Turner, the three weeks in Florence passed swiftly; the weather was beautiful, and it was immensely agreeable meeting for cocktails at Doney's, lunching, dining and going to the opera with such a congenial band of fellow travellers. Turner in particular was delighted to see Maugham again, his only criticism that his old friend could be 'a little arid' when it came to tipping. Haxton, the new boy, was liked by all, Walpole recording in his diary that Maugham's chum was 'charming, full of kindness and shrewdness mixed'.

There was no question of Maugham staying away long as his presence was required in London for rehearsals of his new play, *East of Suez*, a prospect regarded without much enthusiasm. 'You cannot think how impatient I am to be on the wander again,' Alanson was told. 'London is very nice to come back to, but to my mind flat & unprofitable to live in . . . It is like an artificial comedy, amusing enough to sit through for a period, but apt to grow tedious if it lasts too long. I am feeling very much as though it were time for the curtain to fall.' Far from falling, the curtain was about to go up on a costly extravaganza, a show which despite critical disdain was to prove a notable success, embellished with all kinds of expensive novelty, including a spectacular Peking street scene with shops, rickshaws, sixty Chinese extras, a real Ford motor-car and an orchestra on stage playing some twangy 'Chinese' music especially commissioned from Eugene Goossens. The play, in some respects a looking-glass version of *The Painted Veil*, is set among the British colony in Peking, and in an undeniably melodramatic tone offers a rich mix of adultery, racism, suicide and attempted murder. Produced by Basil Dean at His Majesty's, with a cast headed by Basil Rathbone and Meggie Albanesi, *East of Suez* opened on 2 September 1922 in London and almost simultaneously in New York, derided by reviewers on both sides of the pond: 'insincere' said Agate, 'archaic and conventional' according to Heywood Broun in the *New York World*, while the *Spectator* described *East of Suez* as crude and pretentious, shocked that Mr Maugham could have written anything so amateurish. 'Another piece of work like this and his reputation as a serious playwright will be gone!'

Fortunately for his peace of mind Maugham had left London a few days before these notices appeared. He narrowly escaped another unpleasant press report, of a very different nature, when shortly after his departure Syrie was involved in a fatal accident. Driving down Park Lane one evening she knocked down a woman cyclist, who subsequently died of a fractured skull. Giving evidence at the inquest Syrie swore she had never seen the cyclist, and to her enormous relief it was ruled that the death was not her fault.

By this time Maugham was thousands of miles away, again headed for the Orient. His destination this time was Burma, a British dominion rather less docile in mood than the Federated Malay States: Burma was administered not as a separate colony but as a province of India, thus relegated to second-class status in the imperial order, a fact much resented by the Burmese. Maugham had been warned to expect trouble, from head-hunters, tigers and snakes as well as from native insurgents. 'We have got quite an arsenal with us,' he wrote to Bert Alanson, although as it turned out the expedition, if arduous, passed off without threat. In his account of the journey, published under the title *The Gentleman in the Parlour*, Maugham makes no mention of any political issue, an omission for which he has been censured by some. By contrast George Orwell, who was in Burma at exactly the same period, working in the Burmese police, was intensely alive to the seething resentments around him, coming to loathe what he regarded as the despotism of British rule. Orwell portrayed the colonial oppressors as at worst vicious, at best stupid and dull: a dull people, 'cherishing and fortifying their dullness behind a quarter of a million bayonets'. He clearly foresaw the end of Empire, while Maugham appeared not so much unaware of as indifferent to the subject. In his introduction to *The Gentleman in the Parlour* he introduces the matter in a tone of slightly awkward facetiousness. 'I cock a snook at the historian of the Decline and Fall of the British Empire,' he writes, after rehearsing the arguments he supposes lined up against him: 'Did he go through Burmah and not see how the British power was tottering?' he imagines his critics asking. 'Was there no matter for his derision in the spectacle of a horde of officials who held their positions only by force of the guns behind them?' To such detractors, though, the reply is simple: the fall of Empire was not his topic. Much of the enormous popularity of Maugham's stories stems from the fact that he knew his limitations, perfectly understood the range of his engagement: it was not the big picture that appealed to his imagination but the small lives of unremarkable individuals struggling to create the reassuringly ordinary out of an extravagantly exotic environment.

Maugham and Haxton arrived in Rangoon from Colombo in Ceylon, sailing up the Irrawaddy on a hot, bright morning, dazzled by the sight of the great golden spire of the ancient Shwedagon Pagoda glinting in the sunlight. The plan was to journey from Rangoon to Mandalay, then up north into Siam and from there to Bangkok, going on into Indo-China, and finally to Hanoi and Haiphong, whence they could board a ship to Hong Kong from where they would sail home. Rangoon, Mandalay, Bangkok, their names so full of mystery and promise, turned out to be disappointing, hot and dusty, all three noisy modern cities with European restaurants and hotels, their crowded streets jammed with traffic, with trams, cars, gharries and rickshaws, and little sign of the mysterious East, of the 'narrow alleys . . . [and] devious ways down which the imagination may wander'. Once out into the country, however, the modern world disappeared, as they slowly progressed north and into the Shan States. Here the going was hard, as they travelled through jungle and up mountain passes, riding, or trudging along on foot, sometimes rowed upriver on ramshackle rafts, or jolting uncomfortably along mud-rutted roads in the back of a bullock-cart. Only rarely was there respite in the form of passage by car, or on occasion in a wood-fuelled train puffing its leisurely way across a vast, parched plateau, past villages and groves of teak, past paddy fields and white pagodas.

The most difficult part of the journey was from Taunggyi, capital of the Shan States, to Keng Tung on the border with Siam, a distance of nearly 700 miles, which was to take twenty-six days to cover, Maugham and Haxton astride sure-footed Shan ponies at the head of a caravan of mules transporting the luggage and equipment. As well as the team of porters, there were two Indian servants, a Ghurka manservant, Rang Lal, and a Telugu cook. Rang Lal was well trained and efficient, but the cook proved to be a problem, dirty, frequently drunk and his cooking inept and monotonous: dinner, preceded by gin and bitters, was either curry, tinned sardines or a stringy bird shot by one of the two white men, inevitably followed by trifle or cabinet pudding, 'the staple sweets of the East'. After a while, desperate for change, Maugham took matters into his own hands and showed the cook how to make corned-beef hash. 'I trusted that after he left me he would pass on the precious recipe to other cooks and that eventually one more dish would be added to the scanty repertory of Anglo-Eastern cuisine.' Progress was slow, especially when it came to persuading the mule train across a river, the Salween or Mekong, or pushing through dense thickets of bamboo, or on foot while pulling their ponies knee-deep in mud along a forest trail. Sometimes it was suffocatingly hot and steamy, while high in the mountains it was misty and cold. Nights were spent either in circuit-houses, one indistinguishable from the other with their shabby teak furniture and years-old copies of the *Strand* magazine; or in monasteries, their camp beds and mosquito nets placed among golden Buddhas brooding on their great lotus leaves in the gloaming; or in little temporary shelters, two rooms and a verandah made of freshly cut bamboo and constructed within hours for the travellers' convenience. The journey was exhausting and occasional rest days were a necessity, instead of rising at dawn a late lie-in with tea and a cigarette, peaceful hours spent lounging in pyjamas, playing patience and reading. A favourite work which Maugham had brought with him was *Du côté de Guermantes*, and for fear of finishing it too quickly he rationed himself to thirty pages a day. 'A great deal of course was exquisitely boring . . . [but] I would sooner be bored by Proust than amused by anybody else.'

Once they had crossed the small stream that marked the boundary with Siam the landscape changed completely, and they found themselves in open agricultural country, with rice fields on either side of the road, neat little villages, and gentle hills covered with well-husbanded teak forests. Then riding into a village at noon Maugham suddenly felt a familiar perfumed warmth, 'the harsh, the impetuous, the flamboyant' air of the south, and realised with a shock of delight that he was in the tropics. Once in Siam everything was easy: they were welcomed by a polite village official who insisted they stay in his own spacious house, putting at their disposal a bright red Ford motor-car in which they drove off at what seemed a vertiginous speed of eight miles an hour to the nearest station to catch the train to Bangkok.

The heat in the capital was overwhelming, and soon after settling into his hotel Maugham succumbed to a bad attack of malaria, recurrences of which would dog him for many years. A doctor was called who immediately administered quinine, but at first this had no effect and Maugham's temperature soared dangerously to over 105 degrees.

> Neither wet sheets nor ice packs brought it down. I lay there, panting and sleepless . . . Those wooden rooms, with their verandahs, made every sound frightfully audible to my tortured ears . . . One morning I heard the manageress of the hotel, an amiable creature but a good woman of business . . . say to the doctor: 'I can't have him die here, you know.' And the doctor replied: 'All right. But we'll wait a day or two yet.' 'Well, don't leave it too long,' she replied.

Eventually the crisis came, and drenched in sweat the patient began to recover: soon he could breathe easily, his head ached no longer and he was free from pain. 'I felt extraordinarily happy,' he recalled.

From Bangkok the two travellers continued by sea to Kep on the Cambodian coast, and from there to Phnom Penh and Angkor, where the ruined, overgrown Khmer temples deep in the forest, 'looming gigantic and black in the moonshine', made a powerful impression. One of the last cities on the itinerary was Saigon in French Indo-China, a charming place with the air of a little provincial town in the south of France, its hotel terraces crowded with bearded, gesticulating Frenchmen drinking Dubonnet and talking nineteen to the dozen in the rolling accents of the Midi. From Saigon their route took them to the royal city of Hué, where they had an audience with the Emperor, then to Hanoi, and finally to the big French naval base at Haiphong, where they boarded a steamer to Hong Kong, from there making their way via Shanghai, Yokohama and Vancouver to New York and the welcome comfort of the *Aquitania*.

*The Gentleman in the Parlour*, Maugham's account of his adventure, is notable for the author's obvious enjoyment, his high spirits – 'Whoops, dearie!' is the somewhat surprising end to one sequence – and the exuberance with which in a prose both lucid and relaxed he writes of his experiences. The title is taken from an essay of William Hazlitt's, 'On Going a Journey', in which Hazlitt describes his delight in travel, and particularly in the opportunity it provides 'to shake off the trammels of the world and of public opinion – to lose our importunate, tormenting, everlasting personal identity in the elements of nature, and become the creature of the moment, clear of all ties . . . to be known by no other title than The Gentleman in the Parlour!' With such a sentiment Maugham whole-heartedly concurred: he loved to explore, loved to be on the move, and always found in travel not only a source of inspiration for his writing but an enormous sense of freedom, freedom from social, domestic and moral constraints, and freedom as well from the limitations of his own sometimes suffocating sense of self. 'I am often tired of myself,' he wrote, 'and I have a notion that by travel I can add to my personality and so change myself a little. I do not bring back from a journey quite the same self that I took.'

On this occasion he returned with copious notes on which to base his book, the result an attractive mix of simple yet vivid descriptions of the land and the people, with a number of intriguing histories gleaned from characters met on the road, among them a saintly Italian priest living in a remote jungle village, a degenerate figure who had been a fellow student of Maugham's at St Thomas's, and an eccentric American couple, the Wilkinses, proprietors of a tiny travelling circus. The Wilkinses, whom Maugham years later still remembered as the oddest people he had ever encountered, were fellow passengers aboard a squalid little steamer plying along the Cambodian coast between Bangkok and Kep, and during the long hot hours on deck they tell Maugham about their animals, all of whom they regard as family.

> 'I guess Egbert would like a sip of your lemonade, my dear,' said Mr Wilkins.
> Mrs Wilkins slightly turned her head and looked at the monkey sitting on her lap.
> 'Would you like a sip of mother's lemonade, Egbert?'
> The monkey gave a little squeak and putting her arm round him she handed him a straw . . .
> 'Mrs Wilkins thinks the world of Egbert,' said her husband. 'You can't wonder at it. He's her youngest.'
> Mrs Wilkins took another straw and thoughtfully drank her lemonade.
> 'Egbert's all right,' she remarked. 'There's nothing wrong with Egbert.'

There are also some mild philosophical reflections and literary musings, a few brief passages of autobiography, and as always in Maugham's accounts of his travel abroad there flows a small subterranean stream of nostalgia for the Kentish countryside of his boyhood: in Petrograd he was moved by the resemblance of the Lavra monastery to Canterbury Cathedral; in China, 'the bamboos, the Chinese bamboos, transformed by some magic of the mist, look just like the hops of Kentish fields'; while in Burma a distant tributary of the Mekong recalls the little stream where as a child he used 'to catch minnows and put them in a jam-pot'. On its publication in 1930 *The Gentleman in the Parlour* was widely acclaimed. 'Never was Mr Maugham more readable or so wholly delightful as in this,' declared the *New York Herald Tribune*, while Desmond MacCarthy in an essay on Maugham described the work as 'sombre and beautiful, entertaining and sincere'.

The one overwhelmingly significant absence in the account of this long journey is that of Gerald Haxton. From first page to last, both in *The Gentleman in the Parlour* and in the published notebooks, there is rarely the smallest indication that the author is not travelling alone. Yet Gerald was there every step of the way, his presence a crucial component of Maugham's emotional and physical wellbeing. Like another of his fictional counterparts, Tom Ramsay in 'The Ant and the Grasshopper', Haxton 'was a most amusing companion and though you knew he was perfectly worthless you could not but enjoy his society. He had high spirits, an unfailing gaiety and incredible charm.' In a memoir Maugham wrote of him, 'He was fearless. He was always ready for an adventure and could turn his hand to anything, whether it was to persuade a stubborn car to behave reasonably or in the wilderness to cook a savoury dinner.' Even those who disliked and distrusted Gerald – and there were quite a few – were captivated by his vitality and charm: it was Gerald who was the Master of Ceremonies, said one, '[Gerald] who set the pace, and lit the stage . . . There was charm in abundance, an endless supply of the loose change of charm, which he flicked with a sort of gay disdain across the table cloth as though he were over-tipping a young waiter who had attracted him.' In more practical terms it was Gerald who supervised the details of Maugham's journeys, Gerald who acted as photographer, as secretary, typing Maugham's letters on a machine laboriously lugged all the way from London; and it must have been Gerald who nursed Maugham during his life-threatening attack of malaria in Bangkok. But of what he thought, what he said, how he conducted himself there is left no trace. When on the last day of the voyage the *Aquitania* docked briefly at Cherbourg, the two men took their leave of each other, Gerald disembarking in France while Maugham sailed on to Southampton and his alternative identity as respectable family man. That Haxton was much on his mind, however, is made clear in a letter written while still in mid-Atlantic to Bert Alanson. 'Will you invest $5,000 in the name of

Gerald Haxton,' Maugham asked him. 'I am making him a present of this . . . He has been very faithful & devoted to me for many years. Of course he has not been able to save anything & I should like this to be a nucleus of some provision for him in case I die.'

# IO

## Separation

When Maugham returned to England from the Far East in 1923 he was in his fiftieth year, rich, famous, outwardly confident and composed. In an article that year in *Vanity Fair*, he wrote, 'Middle age has its compensations . . . you feel no need to do what you do not like. You are no longer ashamed of yourself. You are reconciled to being what you are, and you do not much mind what people think of you.' As prolific as ever, his by-line on a playbill or magazine cover was a guarantee of big sales; everyone wanted to know him, and in the relatively small society of 1920s London, almost everyone did. Yet in private the strain of maintaining a double life, of dividing himself between Syrie, who increasingly bored and repelled him, and Gerald Haxton, to whom he was wholly in thrall, was beginning to seem untenable. Maugham still looked on London as his base: it was his home, the centre of his social and professional life; and yet it was also where he felt most repressed and confined. Gerald, representing freedom and adventure, remained on the other side of the Channel, and it was not possible for Maugham to endure his absence for long.

Arriving in London at the end of May Maugham was gone again by October. The four intervening months were spent in the usual industrious activity, including overseeing rehearsals for *Our Betters*, the play which had been banned during the war for its alleged anti-Americanism. Opening on 12 September with Margaret Bannerman in the lead as the dissolute Lady Grayston, it proved an immense success and ran for well over a year. Maugham was also occupied with completing a couple of short stories, writing a new farce, *The Camel's Back*, and starting his Chinese novel, *The Painted Veil*. To add to the pressure, there was the upheaval of again moving house, leaving Wyndham Place for a bigger, even grander establishment barely 100 yards south at 43 Bryanston Square. 'It is simply magnif,' Arnold Bennett reported after being invited to a dinner-party there with Charles Towne, H. G. Wells and Virginia Woolf, adding enviously, 'The fellow's study is larger than my drawing room.' In the embittered memoir of his old age, Maugham attributed the move to Syrie's 'social aspirations': she was no longer satisfied with Wyndham Place, he said, because she wished to entertain on a more ambitious and lavish scale. In fact it was Maugham, not Syrie, who initiated the move, although it was true she found considerable advantages in it, not only for entertaining but as a showcase for her business, a beautiful backdrop for the bibelots and 'restored' pieces of furniture that were her stock in trade. It took Maugham some time to realise what was going on, why the sofa he sat on one evening would be gone the following morning, that the price of tables and chairs could be quoted on enquiry. Yet at the beginning Maugham was pleased with the move to Bryanston Square and enjoyed his handsome new house, 'so roomy and spacious', as he told Bert Alanson, 'and I bless "Rain" which made it possible.'

'Rain' had also helped pay for a small flat in Paris for Gerald, at 65 rue la Fontaine, off the Avenue Mozart in the 16th arrondissement, a nearer and more convenient location than Florence in which to pass the time during the inevitable periods of separation. By now the relationship had lasted almost ten years, and in the homosexual circles in which Maugham moved it was looked upon as something of a model. When Eddie Knoblock, for instance, wanted to bring his working-class boyfriend from America to live with him in England it was to Maugham that he turned for advice. Maugham gave careful consideration to his reply. 'For your own sake as well as his,' he wrote, 'I think you should reflect carefully before you take him away from the life & the future which he is used to . . . The standards in America are so entirely other than our standards here that I think you may have a great shock unless your affection for Bruce is so great that nothing else much matters.' With Gerald the situation was different in that social class was not an issue, and there was never any question of his coming to London. But there were problems nonetheless, and Maugham was never easy about leaving Gerald to cope on his own.

Haxton at thirty was fast developing into an accomplished wastrel. In childhood he had been spoilt and adored by his mother, just as now he was spoilt and adored by Maugham. He was an intelligent man, well read in both English and French, yet except briefly during the war he had never worked for his living. Unmotivated and lacking in discipline, left for long periods with nothing to do, it was all too easy to slide into dissipation. For a long time now Gerald had been a heavy drinker; he was also dangerously addicted to gambling, regularly running up enormous debts, all silently settled by his patron; as Maugham pragmatically phrased it, 'You must expect to pay something for the amusement you get out of knowing wrong 'uns.' Sexually, too, Gerald could be wildly irresponsible: 'charming but *very* naughty', according to that old reprobate Norman Douglas, who might be expected to know. When in Paris he was often to be found in the shady bars and clubs of the rue de Lappe, well known as a homosexual market-place of unusual variety and sophistication.★ With a natural preference for adolescent boys, Haxton was also more than ready to prey on any available female, housemaids, debutantes, married women – once even attempting to seduce Gerald Kelly's wife Jane – and sometimes very young girls: it was one of his boasts that while in Siam he had bought a twelve-year-old girl for a tin of condensed milk. 'He was a naughty boy and he grew into a wicked man,' said one of Maugham's homosexual acquaintance, '[and] he took off his trousers far more frequently than most of us, in the most unlikely bedrooms.'

To Maugham, Gerald was irresistible. With his vitality and daring, he alone had the power 'to unlock a door inside Maugham's shut-away secret wall'. Maugham was charmed by Gerald, invigorated by his company, and he also valued his intelligence, very much relying on the younger man's critical opinion of his work. According to Rebecca West, who shrewdly observed the couple over a number of years, Haxton 'was probably the only person he really felt at home with, and from that point of view I think Willie had a right to him . . . Gerald was exactly . . . his cup [of tea].' The relationship was complex, and not always clear to the casual witness. Those who saw them together were sometimes shocked by the insolent manner in which the younger man behaved towards the older: Gerald waving his long cigarette-holder, imperiously summoning Maugham from across the room to replenish his cocktail; 'the handsome young man, lolling in his arm-chair, with one bare leg thrown over the arm, holding up his glass, demanding his poison. The ageing genius . . . pouring out the libation, as if he were making a sacrifice to a young god.' Yet what such onlookers failed to grasp was the complicity, the nature of the bond, the elaborate rules of the sexual power games played out between them. And there was more to it than that: while Maugham was frequently exasperated by Gerald's behaviour, there was a protective, paternal element in his feelings, aware as he was of the young man's vulnerability, a vulnerability which was deeply buried and invisible to most; he was bewitched, too, by his extraordinary charm; and he was touched by an unexpected gentleness

★In his novel *The Razor's Edge* Maugham was to describe the rue de Lappe as 'a dingy, narrow street . . . [where] men danced with podgy boys with made-up eyes'.

that surfaced when Maugham was ill or depressed, when his lover offered those little attentions so often learned by an only child living with an ailing parent. Most of all, though, Maugham was fascinated by Haxton's dangerous edge, by the bad-boy aura that surrounded him. Gerald's world in the 1920s was much as described by Evelyn Waugh in *Vile Bodies*, a world of 'ambiguous telephone calls and the visits of menacing young men who wanted new suits or tickets to America, or a fiver to go on with'. In a sense Gerald was the Mr Hyde to Maugham's Dr Jekyll: it was Gerald who let rip, gave full rein to a sensuality and subversiveness that in the older man were in the main strictly held in check.

Compared to Haxton's appetite for risk and debauchery, Maugham's tastes seem almost prim: he liked sex and he liked a lot of it – few good-looking young men who crossed his path were left unpropositioned – but his preferred practice tended towards the straightforward and conventional. 'Willie's sex life was not necessarily virtuous but it was extremely simple,' remarked a homosexual friend, the writer Glenway Wescott. Once when he and Maugham were contemplating a nude painting of a man and woman making love in the missionary position, Maugham observed that it was a pity two males could not perform like that. 'I didn't have the heart to tell him,' said Wescott. Gerald's physical presence had a potent effect on Maugham, and if they were no longer, or not often, sexual partners, they continued to be intricately involved in each other's sexual activities. In the same way that Maugham when abroad relied on Gerald to go out and make contact with strangers in order to discover their stories, so he relied on him to go out and find boys to bring back to his bed. Maugham was fastidious in his tastes, recoiling from the actuality of the decadent and shady, as Haxton well understood. 'Gerald Haxton was wonderful for Willie,' said the film director George Cukor. 'He kept him in touch with the gutter.' Thus it was Haxton who cruised the streets and bars, Haxton who made the choice and struck the deal – as he did one night in Mexico City, returning to the hotel with a young boy who knelt down to pray and make the sign of the cross before readying himself for service.

On 9 August 1923 Haxton's invalid mother Sara died. She had not seen Gerald for nearly ten years, although Maugham, like a dutiful son-in-law, had always kept in touch, visiting her in St John's Wood whenever he was in England. The writer Clemence Dane was later to say of 'her dear friend Sally Haxton' that she 'worshipped' Maugham because of what he had done for her son. 'I personally had much affection for her,' Maugham told Bert Alanson, '[but] it was a dreadful life she led . . . [and]

I am thankful that she is dead at last.' Gerald, overwhelmed by feelings of grief and guilt, was deeply distressed, mourning his mother and wretched at the thought of the miserable existence she had led, isolated, ill and permanently deprived of the presence of her adored only child.

The departure for the United States at the end of September thus came as a timely distraction, and during the two-and-a-half months in New York Maugham and Haxton enjoyed themselves, despite the fact that Maugham's new play was a failure. *The Camel's Back*,★ about an overbearing domestic tyrant whose family takes revenge by treating him as a lunatic, opened at the Vanderbilt Theater on 13 November and closed again after only fifteen performances, doing only slightly better the following year in London. Maugham remained unperturbed by this minor setback, however, much more interested in the signing of a contract with Ray Long, editor-in-chief of Hearst magazines, including *Cosmopolitan*, *Good Housekeeping*, *Harper's Bazaar* and *Town and Country*, for a series of short stories for $2,500 each, 'a very substantial, comfortable sum', as he remarked. He and Haxton saw a number of plays, including a hit farce, *The Nervous Wreck*, which, Maugham reported, 'kept me laughing wildly for nearly three hours'. They also went to the theatre with Charlie Chaplin, and Maugham was impressed by the enthusiastic reception the star received.

> It was quite an experience to see that huge audience get up and applaud him, and when we came out through a side door in order to avoid the mob we had to fight our way through a couple of thousand people . . . [Charlie] was frankly delighted, and I could not help thinking it must be an intoxicating experience thus to receive face to face the acclamation of the people.

Returning to Europe at the end of December, Maugham spent a few days with Gerald in Paris, the two of them attending a rackety New Year's Eve party from which they crawled home at five o'clock in the morning.

The next few months were spent by Maugham in London, his main objective the writing of his novel *The Painted Veil*, which was due to be published the following spring. The only fiction of his in book form to appear in 1924 was a short story, 'The Princess and the

---

★ The title refers not to the straw breaking the camel's back but to Hamlet's teasing of Polonius:

HAMLET: Do you see yonder cloud that's almost in shape of a camel?
POLONIUS: By the mass, and 'tis like a camel, indeed.
(*Hamlet*, Act III, Scene 2)

Nightingale'. This was Maugham's contribution to a collection of 200 miniature manuscripts by famous writers commissioned to furnish the library of Queen Mary's Dolls' House, designed by Sir Edwin Lutyens and on show that year at the British Empire Exhibition at Wembley. The contents of each little book, an inch and a half high and bound in yellow calf with the Queen's bookplate inside, were transcribed in tiny writing by its author, among whom were Thomas Hardy, Barrie, Kipling, Hilaire Belloc and Conan Doyle. Maugham's minuscule opus is a pretty fairy-tale about a young princess befriended by a nightingale whom she comes to love so much she puts him in a golden cage so he may not fly away; but kept a prisoner the little bird can neither eat nor sing, and the Princess realises that unless she releases him he will die. 'Take your freedom,' she tells him at last. 'I love you enough to let you be happy in your own way,' a message of peculiarly personal relevance to the story's author.

With *The Painted Veil* completed, Maugham, as restless and energetic as ever, now planned a long journey to Central America in search of new material. He wrote to Bert Alanson who had recently married, congratulating him on his new status and asking also for some introductions for Mexico. 'I cannot tell you how much I am looking forward to breaking into a new hunting ground,' he told him. In the event this particular hunting ground was to prove disappointing, yet it was with high hopes that in September 1924 Maugham and Haxton yet again crossed the Atlantic. On board the *Majestic* they found a number of friends, among them the young playwright Noël Coward, whom Maugham had first met at the end of the war. Despite a mutual liking and a genuine respect for each other's work, the two men were never to become close, mainly because Coward was too fond of Syrie ever to be on intimate terms with Maugham. Also among the passengers were Eugene Goossens, who had composed the music for *East of Suez*, and Basil Dean, who had directed it. Goossens, a formidable poker player, spent much of his time in the card-room with Gerald, while Dean kept himself occupied reading play-scripts. 'I steered clear of Haxton as much as possible,' he later wrote meaningfully in his autobiography. In New York Maugham was introduced to the writer and photographer Carl Van Vechten, who was to remain a friend for life. Van Vechten, a big, burly man only six years younger than Maugham, was extraordinarily versatile, a ballet critic, opera-lover, jazz enthusiast, one of the great promoters of the Harlem Renaissance of black music, a novelist, an essayist and a prominent figure in artistic and intellectual social circles.

Although twice married, 'Carlo', as he always signed himself, was homosexual, a dandy by nature if not in physique, specialising in a camp jokiness that Maugham found amusing. The two men met the day before Maugham and Haxton left town, and Van Vechten took them to a whore-house in Harlem before presenting Maugham with a copy of his latest novel, *The Tattooed Countess*. Three days later Van Vechten was thrilled to receive from New Orleans 'a perfectly amazing letter' from his new friend saying how much he had enjoyed it.

After a brief stay in New Orleans Maugham and Haxton crossed the border into Mexico. 'I must confess that I am disappointed with Mexico,' Maugham wrote to Eddie Knoblock after a couple of cold, rainy weeks in the capital.

> I cannot find very much that's interesting except the civilisation that the Spaniards brought and if one is willing to be excited about that one is after all better off in Spain. Mexico City is not thrilling and I do not think that we shall stay here long. My chief object of course was to find material for stories and so far as I can see there is not the smallest likelihood of it . . . It is exasperating to have come so far and feel that one is wasting one's time, but I suppose that is a chance which one always takes and it cannot be helped.

In fact the time was not entirely wasted and material was unearthed for a couple of stories with Mexican themes, 'The Man with a Scar', about a brave rebel saved at the last moment from death by firing squad, and 'The Closed Shop', regarding the good business sense of the madam of a local brothel, although in both the author's lack of engagement is evident in the telling. Unlike China and Malaya, the country had no dominant expatriate community, and the foreign residents, though numerous, were too internationally varied to provide that particular colonial ambience that so fascinated Maugham.

The reaction of another English writer in Mexico at exactly this time was different. D. H. Lawrence, who was to be powerfully inspired both by the country and by the people, had recently arrived in Mexico City with his wife Frieda and their friend the painter Dorothy Brett, sister of Sylvia Brett, Ranee of Sarawak. Lawrence had never met Maugham, but hearing he was in town dispatched a civil note from his modest hotel. 'Dear Somerset Maugham,' he wrote, 'I feel that two such literary Englishmen as you and I ought not to pass as ships in the night, with a piece of wide sea in between. Would you care to come to lunch at this little place? If so, you might ring up, or leave a message.' Maugham sent a telegram refusing as he was on the point of leaving for Cuernavaca to write, a reply that upset the famously thin-skinned Lawrence, who felt he had been snubbed. 'Damn his eyes and his work,' he exclaimed crossly on 25 October, while four days later, still brooding over the imagined slight, he wrote to a friend that Somerset Maugham, 'a narrow-gutted "artist" with a stutter', was apparently 'no loss: a bit sour and full of nerves and fidgets lest he shouldn't produce a Maughnum opus with a Mexican background before Christmas', adding enviously, 'As if he could fail!!' The following month, when Maugham returned to Mexico City for a few days before leaving for Yucatán, the meeting finally took place. He and Haxton, Dorothy Brett and the Lawrences were invited to lunch by the distinguished American anthropologist Zelia Nuttall★ at Casa Alvarado, her sixteenth-century house in the suburb of Coyoacán. The scholarly Mrs Nuttall, elegant in a black silk dress, warmly welcomed her guests, showing them round her beautiful garden, with its great falls of white roses, bougainvillaea and scarlet hibiscus. Yet what should have been a pleasurable occasion quickly turned sour. Something Gerald said offended his hostess; Dorothy Brett was predisposed against both Haxton and Maugham having received unfavourable reports from her sister in Sarawak; Maugham was in a sullen mood; and Lawrence, tense and aggressive, was infuriated by what he took to be the older writer's lack of interest in himself. As they sat down at table, Frieda Lawrence, placed next to Maugham, asked him how he liked Mexico. 'He answered crossly: "Do you want me to admire men in big hats?" I said: "I don't care what you admire."And then the lunch was drowned in acidity all around.'Afterwards Lawrence described Maugham as 'sehr unsympatisch'; 'I didn't like him,' he concluded, 'a bit rancid', an adjective that obviously struck him as apposite as he used it again four years later in a carping review of *Ashenden*.'It would be hard to find a bunch of more ill-humoured stories, in which the humour has gone more rancid,' he wrote. Maugham returned the compliment by describing Lawrence in print as 'a sick man of abnormal irritability . . . warped by poverty and cankered with a rankling envy'.

The Mexican trip continued to Yucatán, Cuba ('just like Atlantic City'), Jamaica, British Honduras, where they made an expedition by mule into the bush, and finally Guatemala; from Guatemala City they sailed to Hué in Indo-China, continuing from there to Saigon, where they boarded a Messageries Maritimes ship for Marseilles. During these travels Maugham as far as possible maintained his daily writing routine, adapting 'The Letter'

★ The model for Mrs Norris in Lawrence's novel *The Plumed Serpent*.

for the stage, and firing off instructions, typed up by Gerald, to his hard-worked agents in London and New York about his business affairs, about the sale of moving-picture rights, about new theatre productions and about the placing of his stories in various magazines. Shortly before sailing home, Maugham gave Eddie Knoblock a summary of his professional position.

> We are drawing near to the end of this trip and although it has not given me anything like so much as I expected I have at least got out of it one or two very useful things. I have met several people curious enough to work up eventually into characters that amuse me and I have been told of one story which I am making the central incident of my next novel. I have also arrived at the conclusion which I think is not without use that I am reaching the end of my exotic material. I have of course notes for a good many stories which I have not yet written but shall write, but I have not the capacity to assimilate much more. I have no doubt there is here and in the East a great deal which another writer could make stories of and plays, but not much that I can. I have reached the end of the vein and I must leave to others the making of any further diggings. It will at all events take me four or five years to get finished with the material I now have collected.

Maugham arrived back in London at the end of March 1925 in time for the publication of *The Painted Veil*.* This, the story of Walter and Kitty Fane and of Kitty's affair with the caddish Townsend, had already run into trouble. It had first appeared in Britain serialised in *Nash's* magazine, when the two protagonists had been called not Fane, but Lane, with the unfortunate consequence of bringing a libel action from an unknown Mr Lane, which was settled for £250, the author agreeing to the change of name. But there was further trouble when *The Painted Veil* was published in book form, and an objection was made by the Hong Kong government over the adulterous role ascribed to the colony's Assistant Colonial Secretary; uneasy that awkward conclusions might be drawn, they insisted that the location of the story be altered. Thus Maugham was obliged to turn Hong Kong into the imaginary Tching-Yen, Happy Valley into Pleasant Valley, The Peak into The Mount, Kowloon into Lushan, with all references to neighbouring Canton removed (the original place names were restored in later editions). As bad luck would have it, by the time these corrections were made two printings of 4,000 copies each had

---

* The title is taken from a sonnet by Shelley beginning,
>   Lift not the painted veil which those who live
>     Call Life . . .

already been run off and a large number distributed to the press, all of which had to be recalled. There was a further annoyance. Despite the book's immediate jump into the bestseller-list in the United States, with sales of over 100,000 and a number of good reviews, Maugham felt that his American publisher George Doran had been remiss in promoting it. For once it was not a question of finance. As Maugham explained to his agent Charles Towne, 'I am not so anxious to make a large sum of money out of a book as to have it as widely read as possible. I seek distinction rather than lucre.' Yet with *The Painted Veil* Doran seemed to have been culpably inactive. 'He just sent it out like a parcel of tea and let it sell on its own merits, without anything more than a perfectly mechanical and useless advertising,' he complained. 'I do not wish Doran to look upon me as a goose which lays regularly a golden egg,' he continued, suggesting that after his contract expired,

> we go to Doran and unless he is prepared to guarantee success for my next books (which will consist of a volume or two of short stories, a travel book, and, last, a novel) make arrangements elsewhere. There is only one way I know in which a Publisher can guarantee success, and that is by giving so large an advance that it is necessary for him to do everything he can for the book in order to get his money back.

One element in *The Painted Veil* recognisable only to Maugham's inner circle is that of the portrait of his brother F.H. Maugham admitted that he took much of the character of Walter Fane from F.H., his shyness and superciliousness, his coldness and steely self-control; but he is also visible in the person of Kitty's father, Bernard Garstin. Like F.H., Garstin is a barrister, a KC, a reticent, lonely figure, given to depression. Pathos surrounds Garstin, a man despised by his selfish, ambitious family, and largely ignored. 'It never occurred to them to ask themselves what were the feelings of the subdued little man who went out early in the morning and came home at night only in time to dress for dinner. He was a stranger to them, but because he was their father they took it for granted that he should love and cherish them.' F.H., too, dwelt at home in a state of self-imposed isolation, after his return from Chambers working late every evening alone in his study, emerging only at dinner. But unlike Garstin, who is looked down on by his two daughters, F.H. was a figure of fear to his children, cold, captious and remote; he never came near the nursery or school-room, and during meals his few utterances were invariably words of rebuke, his censoriousness rendered all the more cutting by the haughty manner in which while speaking he raised his monocle to his eye. In fact the tragedy of F.H. was that his icy manner hid a craving for affection which within the family he was unable to express. Outside the house he could be lively company: at his club, the Savile, he was regarded as genial and amusing, within his profession many a young barrister had cause to recall his kindness, and for some years he conducted a secret love affair with a woman with whom presumably he was more forthcoming than with his wife.* Yet with Nellie he was distant and fractious, and with his children he found it impossible to unbend. Maugham was never close to F.H., but that this cold, difficult man was to be pitied was a fact which the novelist, with his extraordinary insight into the hidden loneliness in others, at a deep level understood; and his sense of the sadness inherent in his brother's situation is movingly indicated in his portrait of Garstin.

If the sisters were lacking in love from their father, it was more than made up for by their mother's passionate involvement in every aspect of their lives. Nellie adored her daughters and played with them, read to them, heard their prayers and organised jolly family holidays at their seaside house at Littlestone on the Romney Marshes, where F.H. liked to play golf. Sometimes Maugham played with him, coming down to spend a night or two at Littlestone in conditions rather more rough and ready than he was accustomed to at home. Nellie's idea of bliss, he teased her after one of these visits, 'is to eat cold mutton in a howling draught'. Kate, Honor and Diana, born at the beginning of the century, were approaching adulthood when in 1916, twenty years after their parents had married, Nellie to everyone's astonishment gave birth to a boy. As the son of the house, Robert Cecil Romer, always known as Robin, might have been expected to engender some feeling of affection in his father, but in fact he was treated with an even greater frigidity than his sisters. 'My father was fifty years old when I was born,' Robin wrote later, 'and the half century that separated us was certainly one of the factors that made our relationship difficult.' But it went further than this, and for years the boy received at his father's hands nothing but callous rejection. He was an unwanted child: even his mother, who came to love him, treated him severely, believing that boys, unlike girls, needed to be toughened up and denied any form of indulgence. As a result Robin had a miserable childhood, spending much of his time away from the rest of the family, looked after by a series of nurses and governesses. He was almost exactly a year younger than his cousin Liza and sometimes Syrie

* According to admittedly sketchy evidence in F.H.'s pocket appointment diary, this affair seems to have come to an end in 1923.

would bring Liza to have tea with him in the nursery at Cadogan Square while she talked to Nellie downstairs.

The sisters-in-law had become good friends, and sitting on the drawing-room sofa with the door closed they confided in each other, comparing the difficulties both had with their husbands. In each case, the couples were disastrously mismatched, two lively, sociable women married to clever men who were exceptionally controlled and controlling – and whose affections were engaged elsewhere. If Nellie remained in ignorance of her husband's mistress, Syrie was only too well aware of the danger represented by her long-term rival Gerald Haxton. For several years before her marriage to Maugham Haxton had been in the picture, but she had yet to set eyes upon him, a situation that was now about to change.

During the six months that her husband was abroad Syrie's career had continued to prosper, so much so that she had been able to move her shop, Syrie Ltd, from Baker Street to fashionable Mayfair premises, 87 Duke Street, at the corner of Grosvenor Square. From here she not only continued to sell her decorative furniture but ran a successful design business, taking on commissions to decorate rooms, apartments and even entire houses. Recently she had built herself a house at fashionable Le Touquet on the Normandy coast, a destination that was fast becoming popular with the rich British, who could fly from Croydon Aerodrome, or take the Channel ferry over to Boulogne, or stop off while motoring to or from the Riviera, for a weekend of gambling, golf, polo, tennis and sea-bathing. The Villa Eliza, among pine trees and set some way back from the beach, provided a perfect backdrop for Syrie's modernistic décor, cool and airy, with the emphasis on beige and white: the spacious drawing-room, opening out through French windows on to a wide lawn, was painted in beige and white, the big fireplace was white, the floor carpeted in beige sheepskin, the chairs, which had been stripped and pickled, and the massive sofas were all in beige, while the dining-room was white, with white china and cutlery, white silk curtains and natural oak chairs upholstered in white leather.

As Syrie correctly calculated the Villa Eliza provided a valuable showcase for her work, as well as giving her easy access to the junk- and antique-shops of the Seine valley. However, the project had been expensive, and with ready money not always available Syrie had to do what she could to raise it. Thus, shortly before he sailed from Hué, Maugham to his extreme annoyance learned that Syrie had let his house in Bryanston Square for the summer; she was planning to move into rented accommodation in Chelsea, he was informed, where a bed-sitting room would be prepared for his use. 'Needless to say I could not work in a bed-sitting room in the King's Road,' he exploded to Golding Bright, '& in any case I am too old to pig it!' Fortunately it then transpired that the tenants were postponing their arrival till July, and as Maugham had no intention of staying in London for more than two or three months there was no reason why his plans should be affected, no reason why he should be cut off from his 'papers & books & accustomed surroundings'. As the ship neared Marseilles, his thoughts increasingly focused on his homecoming and the reunion with his wife. 'I do not of course know', he wrote to Eddie Knoblock, 'whether it is to be war or peace; but I shall when I arrive.'

In the event the summer of 1925 was a combination of the two. As before husband and wife assumed a convincing appearance of harmony. The artistic young men who had begun to gather around Syrie, such as Glyn Philpot, Rex Whistler, Cecil Beaton, Oliver Messel, mixed well with the literary young men, novelists and playwrights, who clustered around Maugham. Once again the house in Bryanston Square was the location for some glamorous parties, where theatre people, writers, publishers, painters, designers, met the more cultured members of high society; George Doran, Eddie Marsh, Jeanne Eagels, Gladys Cooper, Ivor Novello, H. G. Wells, Rebecca West, Noël Coward and Michael Arlen mingled with the eccentric Lord Berners, with Sir John and Lady Lavery, with the theatrical peer Ned Lathom, with Sitwells and Guinnesses. On a couple of occasions the gaunt figure of D. H. Lawrence could be seen going up the steps of number 43, a fragile reconciliation between himself and Maugham having been effected by Reggie Turner. 'Don't expect us to be two roses on one stem,' Lawrence had warned Turner. 'But perhaps he's nice, I don't pretend I know him. And if he'd like to see me, I should like to see him. Honi soit etc.' Sometimes friends from abroad came to stay, one of whom was the novelist Theodore Dreiser; it had been Dreiser's review of *Of Human Bondage* that had first won the novel serious attention, and Maugham put himself out to entertain his American guest, every evening concocting the martinis fashionable in New York if still something of a novelty in London. When talking about it later, Dreiser said that he had enjoyed everything about his visit except for the awful cocktails.

But it was when the guests had gone that the rows started. Always, always the figure of Gerald Haxton loomed over their increasingly fer-ocious fighting. Syrie, still craving her husband's affection, was venomously jealous, tormented by the reality of Maugham's sexual relationship with the hated Haxton ('she did desperately mind . . . about the sex part', said her daughter later). She was unable stop herself nagging and reproaching him, her high-pitched voice growing ever more staccato as she worked herself up into screaming, shouting rages which Maugham countered either by icy withdrawal or, when driven beyond endurance, by shouting back at her himself; more than once he hit her. These frightful quarrels* left Maugham drained and depressed, usually with a splitting head, 'sweating at every pore . . . harassed and miserable and haggard and broken'. Extremely self-disciplined, a private, undemonstrative man who found it difficult to show emotion, he was profoundly shaken by being provoked to such violent outbursts, bitterly humiliated by his loss of control. Syrie on the other hand recovered much more rapidly: quick-tempered by nature, she had always thrived on confrontation – as her employees both at home and in the shop knew only too well – and she relished the daily drama of her volatile emotions, a pattern of behaviour with which Maugham was by now wearyingly familiar. In depicting a character partly based on Syrie in one of his short stories, he wrote, 'Resistance only exasperated her. If she did not immediately get what she wanted she would go almost insane with rage. Fortunately she lost interest in a thing with the same suddenness with which she hankered for it, and if you could distract her attention for a minute she forgot all about it.'

From Maugham's point of view the marriage was effectively over. He and Syrie had little in common, her chic, frivolous world was not his, her aggressive acquisitiveness anathema to him, and only traces remained of the youthful prettiness he had once so admired. Now in her late forties Syrie despite rigorous efforts (sugarless tea and an Energen roll for breakfast) was growing plump; she still retained her flawless complexion but it was heavily powdered, her square chin and big nose were more prominent, and her hair, styled in a modish Eton crop, was cut unbecomingly short.† It was now common knowledge that relations between the Maughams were strained to breaking point, a topic which Syrie, with a level of vituperation which sometimes shocked her listeners, had little compunction in airing. 'I realized', said one, 'that what she was chiefly concerned about was doing Willie damage.' Some of the couple's close

---

* To be vividly described a few years later in *The Constant Wife*.

† In his short story 'A Man with a Conscience', Maugham describes a husband's feelings of revulsion towards the wife he is about to murder. 'Marie-Louise had started a little while before having her hair cut differently, quite short, and I thought it repulsive . . . the stubble of cropped hair on her neck made me feel rather sick.'

friends, like Eddie Knoblock, Noël Coward and Gladys Cooper, tried to intervene, to lower the temperature between them, but it soon became distressingly clear that nothing could be done. According to H. G. Wells, Syrie 'was incapable of realising Maugham's distaste for her . . . [and] always expected a reconciliation to take place. This was impossible, as Maugham's writing about her showed.'

The one area where the couple might have found some accord was in regard to their daughter; instead the subject of Liza became one of the bitterest battlegrounds of all, and she herself described her parents' quarrels over her upbringing as 'volcanic'. Although doted on by her mother and in many ways over-indulged, the little girl was also neglected, often lonely and sometimes wretchedly unhappy. Apart from a couple of cousins, Robin Maugham and a little Barnardo cousin, Eilidh, who some-times came to play, she had few friends of her own age, and now that Syrie was so immersed in her business she often appeared to forget about Liza for days at a time, leaving her in the care of one of the maids. On the first day of a seaside holiday in Dinard, Syrie, anxious to prepare the rented house for the arrival of guests, deposited her daughter on the beach and was astonished when at the end of the day a policeman turned up to deliver her child, weeping and distraught. '"Did you have a nice day, darling?" she asked, then she saw how upset I was and was very sorry,' Liza recalled. 'She had been completely absorbed in what she was doing. And she was very absent-minded.' It was during this same holiday that Liza for the first time witnessed a series of violent fights between her parents, including one that so frightened her she was physically sick; on other occasions their rows reduced her to hysterical crying, once covering her face with greasepaint in an attempt to disguise her tears. 'I had a great feeling of insecurity,' she said of this period of her life, 'quite the reverse of a happy childhood.'

Liza was now ten, and Syrie wanted to keep her at home, doing her lessons in a relaxed fashion with a series of governesses. At the age of eight Liza had contracted tuberculosis, forced to spend several months confined to a spinal carriage, and this had made her mother even more determined to keep her closely under her wing; her father, however, was adamant that the child should be sent away to school. He was determined she should be properly educated, and saw it as essential that she should be removed from her mother's influence and allowed to make friends of her own age. So Syrie was overruled and the child dispatched to a boarding school in the country, a decision that caused great wretchedness to both, with Syrie constantly on the telephone with anxious instructions regarding

Liza's comfort and care. One Sunday evening a group of dinner guests at Bryanston Square were embarrassed to witness their hostess provoked to such exasperation over some matter to do with Liza's schooling that she threw the receiver on the floor. When she returned to the table, her husband tauntingly remarked, 'S-S-Syrie d-d-didn't really imp-p-prove matters by l-losing her t-t-temper with that wretched woman,' at which Syrie, white with rage, retaliated with icy distinctness, 'You said you wanted a child, but you lied. You didn't want a child, you only wanted to be a father.' Rebecca West, a close ally of Syrie's who was present at this exchange, recalled, 'Willie took this without protest. It was quite obvious that she was alluding to something which was understood between them.' Meanwhile Liza at school was so miserably homesick that she went on hunger strike, eventually making herself ill enough to be sent to the sanatorium. From here she ran away, caught a train to London and turned up at the house, imploring her parents not to send her back. There was an emotional scene, but Maugham refused to be swayed and insisted that she return to school; again Liza escaped, was again returned; but when she escaped a third time Syrie could bear it no longer and resorted to trickery. She took Liza to the oculist and asked the man to put drops in her eyes temporarily to obscure her vision: unable to see, she was unable to go to school.

At this point Maugham admitted defeat and made little further attempt to influence his daughter's education, other than by opening an account in her name at Bumpus' bookshop in Oxford Street, where she was allowed to buy as many books as she pleased. Under her mother's regime Liza's schooling remained haphazard, sometimes lessons with a temporary governess, or occasionally a few weeks in a school in London, Chicago, Nassau, New York or wherever else Syrie's expanding business and peripatetic way of life happened to take her. Even in adulthood Liza's handwriting remained childish and she never learned to spell, a fact that exasperated her father, who accused her of 'writing like a chambermaid'. On the other hand, well dressed, well travelled and accustomed to the company of her mother's sophisticated social set, in a curious way the child appeared much older than her years. 'She had a miniature, rather touching dignity,' in the view of one contemporary. 'She seemed already to have entered into "society", and to exist there like a waif, waiting to be a few years older.'

While Maugham admired Syrie's taste and flair, he loathed her ruthless commercialism. Embarrassed enough by the notion of his wife running a shop, he found it abhorrent when she conducted business at home, frequently bringing in complete strangers to sell them a table or looking-glass practically from under his nose. (After waiting for his guests to be seated at a luncheon party one day, he drily announced, 'I think I should warn you, l-l-ladies and gentlemen, to hold tight to your chairs. They are almost certainly for s-s-sale.') Publicly he dealt with it by pretending it was all a great joke, that they were so hard up Syrie had been forced to go to work selling bits of old junk, but inwardly he hated the situation, hated the flow of people in and out of the house and the disruption of his working routine. The actress Cathleen Nesbitt, who stayed for a few days in Bryanston Square, saw for herself the effect it had on him. '[Syrie] for a time used her own house as a show place for precious pieces which were always being snapped up and removed by eager clients,' the actress recalled. 'I confess I was rather astonished by the courtesy with which he [Maugham] accepted the constant change of surroundings!' But there came a day when Syrie went too far. One evening when Maugham came downstairs before dinner, 'he found that his sacred writing desk was gone from his study, and all his papers and manuscripts laid out on a table . . . When Syrie said cheerfully, "There's a magnificent new desk coming tomorrow, darling," I almost expected him to knock her down but he merely said, "I see," with a tight face and closed the door.' The discarded writing table was the one Maugham had used for over twenty years, bought when he moved into his house in Chesterfield Street; it suited him perfectly, an integral part of his working life, and to him Syrie's removing it was an outrage, a brutal act, insensitive in the extreme. 'He appeared to take it calmly,' said Cathleen Nesbitt, 'but I sensed a rage of fury coldly controlled.' Later he was to say it was the selling of his desk that finally determined him to end his marriage, and his anger about it remained unassuaged until eventually finding vitriolic expression in his 1930 novel *Cakes and Ale*.

Increasingly, Maugham was growing uneasy about his wife's methods: there was in Syrie's character a lack of moral fibre, a coarseness that shocked her fastidious husband. It was one thing to charge outrageous prices – she was hardly unique in the trade for that – but there were more serious suspicions about her conduct. 'Some of Syrie's activities made me nervous,' Maugham wrote. 'She was none too scrupulous in her dealings with customers.' Already there had been a couple of lawyers' letters demanding reimbursement for a fake passed off as an antique, and she was beginning to earn a bad reputation among her colleagues to whom she presented a hard, self-assured, opinionated surface. 'She was tricky in business,' an American decorator remembered; 'I knew Syrie slightly and hated her as did anyone who had business dealings with her:

she was dishonest,' said another; while a third remarked of her that Syrie was 'a tough old rogue who never paid for anything unless she had to; she was a schemer, hard as nails'. Needless to say, Maugham distanced himself as far as possible from his wife's business transactions, but there was one occasion when her lack of integrity was forcefully brought home to him. The magnificent jade and gold necklace he had brought back for Syrie from China in 1920 had become a great favourite and she wore it often, having first insured it for a considerable sum. One evening she returned to the house from a buying trip to Paris and immediately burst into tears. 'I don't know how to tell you,' she sobbed. 'I've lost my jade string.' It appeared that she had been in the Louvre, absorbed in matching silks, and in the crowd some clever thief must have slipped it off her neck. Maugham consoled her as best he could, Syrie put in a claim and the insurance company paid up. A few months later one of the company's employees walking down the rue de la Paix spotted the very same necklace on display in a jeweller's window, and on enquiry learned that it had been sold to the shop by a Mme Maugham. Fortunately Syrie escaped prosecution as the company, having been reimbursed, was persuaded not to pursue the matter further.

At about the same time as the affair of the necklace, Maugham began to have suspicions of further duplicity on Syrie's part, suspicions that were confirmed by one of her girlfriends. This was almost certainly Barbara Back, wife of the surgeon Ivor Back. Barbara, a slim, smartly dressed blonde with literary ambitions, had originally been a supporter of Syrie's, but she had been shocked by the way Syrie talked about her husband, spreading scandalous gossip about his private life, and so she had come more and more to sympathise with Maugham. When Barbara warned him that Syrie had taken not one but two lovers, he was unsurprised. 'I knew them both,' he wrote sourly, 'and had a very poor opinion of either.' In fact Maugham cared very little how his wife conducted herself; if anything, he was pleased, recognising that her adultery strengthened his position: she could hardly make such a fuss about his relationship with Gerald if she were in much the same position herself. But the discovery of her unfaithfulness coming so soon after the attempted fraud over the necklace fired his imagination, and on three separate occasions in his writing he was to use a necklace, in each case of pearls rather than jade, to stand as a symbol of sexual licentiousness and betrayal. The theme first appeared in 1925 – at exactly the period when the topics of the false insurance claim and of marital infidelity were high on the domestic agenda – in a short story, 'Mr Know-All', published in *Cosmopolitan*. The narrator on board an ocean liner finds himself sharing a cabin with a Mr Kelada, a bossy, boastful, irrepressibly self-satisfied businessman who has to know best about everything. 'We called him Mr Know-All, even to his face. He took it as a compliment.' For all his insufferable vanity, however, Max Kelada turns out to be a man of honour. One evening at dinner the conversation turns to pearls, on which of course 'Mr Know-All' is an expert, showing off his expertise by giving an instant valuation of the necklace worn by one of the ladies at the table, worth, he says, many thousands of dollars. Nonsense, her husband protests: it's a cheap string she bought at a department store just before leaving New York, and to prove his point he tells his wife to hand the necklace to Mr Kelada to see for himself.

> [Mr Kelada] took a magnifying glass from his pocket and closely examined it. A smile of triumph spread over his smooth and swarthy face . . . Suddenly he caught sight of Mrs Ramsay's face. It was so white that she looked as though she were about to faint. She was staring at him with wide and terrified eyes . . .
>
> Mr Kelada stopped with his mouth open. He flushed deeply. You could almost *see* the effort he was making over himself.
>
> 'I was mistaken,' he said. 'It's a very good imitation, but of course as soon as I looked through my glass I saw that it wasn't real.'

Nearly twenty years later in the story 'A String of Beads' the career of a humble and apparently virtuous governess takes off in a very different direction after she is spotted at a lunch party wearing a fabulously expensive string of pearls for which she insists she paid only a few shillings. And in the 1932 play *For Services Rendered* the suspicious wife of a philandering husband has her suspicions confirmed when she notices the very good pearls worn by the pretty but impoverished young daughter of near neighbours.

The subject of divorce was now being seriously discussed between the Maughams. From Maugham's point of view there was no future in the marriage and the sooner they effected a clean break the better: he had made it clear there was to be no question of his separating from Gerald, and that he was more than happy for Syrie to divorce him, after which they could both go their separate ways. But Syrie did not wish to divorce. She enjoyed the prestige of being Mrs Somerset Maugham, she still loved her husband, and she still hoped that somehow an amicable compromise might be found. With this in mind it was decided that the next step was for Syrie and Haxton to meet, a suggestion she had previously refused to consider. Thus it was arranged that in August the two men should spend a week with Syrie at her house in Le Touquet. The child Liza, who was to be a silent witness of this momentous encounter, recalled it as 'a disaster from the start. I shall never forget the terrible atmosphere of those few days . . . Syrie and my father were completely and tragically incompatible in every way and that Le Touquet episode was the real beginning of the end.'

The arrangements having been made, Maugham did his best to feel optimistic about the proposal. Le Touquet 'is really a very charming little place with golf links, tennis, bathing and a Casino; and all kinds of amusing people go there for the summer so that I think we ought to have a very pleasant time', he wrote tentatively to Bert Alanson. Meanwhile he fortified himself for the ordeal by taking Gerald off for a couple of weeks' holiday on Capri to stay at the Villa Cercola with John Ellingham Brooks. The island was as seductive as ever, and Maugham, not for the first time, was much taken with the idea of buying a house there, a refuge to which he could retreat to work in peace; he asked Brooks to look for one in his absence, arranging access to his bank for any necessary deposit. From Capri he and Haxton went on to a spa at Brides-les-Bains in the French Alps, where they followed a strict teetotal regime and took vigorous exercise on the golf-course and tennis-court.

Fit and rested, Maugham and Haxton arrived at the Villa Eliza in the second week of August 1925 to find a house party in progress: Noël Coward and his handsome American lover Jack Wilson; the former musical-comedy star Gertie Millar, now Countess of Dudley; Barbara Back; the glamorous Delavignes, brother and sister; Frankie Levesson, a Danish decorator whom Syrie was shortly to take on as manager of her shop; and Beverley Nichols, a good-looking young man with literary ambitions, very much on the make. As soon as the two newcomers entered the house the tension in the air became almost tangible. Syrie, dressed in white and heavily made up, was over-vivacious, trying to conceal her nervousness by gushing embarrassingly – '*Darlings!*' she cried on greeting the couple, dramatically flinging up her arms. Maugham, in blue blazer and pale-blue trousers, remained courteous but remote, while Gerald in open shirt and shorts made a point of being elaborately relaxed, lounging about smoking and picking his teeth or hovering absorbedly over the cocktail tray. 'Gerald makes the *best* sidecars in the *world*!' Syrie complimented him anxiously, blowing him a kiss which he ostentatiously disregarded. Some of the guests walked down to Paris-Plage to swim, others gossiped, read or played backgammon on the terrace; Coward, slender and elegant in white flannels, took Gertie Dudley off for a game of tennis; Liza wandered about, alternately petted and ignored. After tea Syrie accompanied by Beverley Nichols, Haxton and Liza drove off to see an *antiquaire* who had a Provençal armoire she had her eye on. 'She'll pickle it before you can say knife,' Noël joked. Arriving back at the house Haxton, accidentally-on-purpose, gave Liza a sharp push as she climbed out of the car, causing her to fall and graze her knee.

In the evening several people came in for dinner, including the Swedish multi-millionaire industrialist Ivar Kreuger, who had founded his vast fortune on matches. Watching Kreuger fumble with his lighter, Maugham made everyone laugh by saying as he proffered a matchbox, 'Mon cher ami, it paraît qu'il vous manque une allumette?'* After dinner Noël, much relied on to make the party go, entertained at the piano, then at around midnight Haxton, already fairly drunk, took the younger guests off to the nearby Casino, among them Beverley Nichols, who later described the scene. Gerald at the tables was 'still very decorative', though his cheeks were flushed, his eyes glazed, and there was cigar ash all down his dinner-jacket. 'He caught my eye and shouted, "Come over here, you pretty boy, and bring me luck." Which', Beverley added prissily, 'is not how I cared to be addressed.' It was after three in the morning when Nichols returned to the villa, but no sooner had he crept into bed than he was joined there by Coward's boyfriend, Jack Wilson, their lovemaking terrifyingly interrupted by Coward himself crashing open the door, a furious figure in a green silk dressing-gown, looking, Nichols recalled, 'like the wrath of 49,000 Chinese gods'. Next day Nichols felt so humiliated by what had happened that he told Syrie he had to return home at once, and to his surprise she promptly decided to leave with him, pouring out while on the boat train to London her feelings of fear and loathing for Gerald Haxton. Haxton, she said, was poisoning her husband's mind against her; he was a liar, a forger and a cheat; he had no morals at all, and 'if he thought it would be of the faintest advantage to him he'd jump into bed with a hyena'.

This is Nichols's version, produced more than forty years later. By that time all three principals, Maugham, Syrie and Haxton, were safely dead and Nichols was focused on revenging himself on Maugham, with whom at the end of the old man's life he had fallen out. His book, entitled *A Case of Human Bondage* and purportedly an analysis of the Maugham marriage, nonetheless gives some telling detail of the week at Le Touquet

---

* 'It seems you need a match, old boy.'

and of Syrie's emotional state: she and Beverley were fond of each other and he was undoubtedly one of the many in whom she confided. In essence, however, the book is untrustworthy, fuelled by spite and warped by deliberate distortion: for instance, Nichols in his book asserts that it was Haxton, not Wilson, who came into his room, and Maugham, not Coward, who caught them at it, a falsification he later admitted in a letter to Coward's secretary, Cole Lesley. Certainly his is a more coloratura rendition than that given at the time by Maugham, who clearly believed that the visit, despite the tense atmosphere and numerous unspoken anxieties, had been not unsuccessful. 'I went over to Le Touquet & spent a week there; Syrie was as nice as nice could be & is evidently eager to turn over a new leaf,' he wrote to Eddie Knoblock. It appears that Maugham noticed nothing odd in Syrie's early departure with Nichols; it is plain there had been some serious talks between husband and wife, and equally plain that Maugham was determined not to move one inch from his stated position. 'I hope', the letter continued, '[Syrie] will cease her complaining about me to all her friends . . . but if she complains to you, you will do me a service by reminding her that she has only to say the word & I am willing to let myself be divorced. I cannot change & she must either bear with me as I am, or take her courage in both hands & make the break.'

By the time this letter was written, in October 1925, Maugham and Haxton were on their way back to the Far East. 'I am so thrilled at getting off that I can think of nothing much else,' Maugham had written to John Ellingham Brooks on the eve of departure. They arrived in Singapore at the beginning of November, where they stayed for over three weeks before travelling on to Bangkok, then to Borneo and Brunei, Maugham en route giving courteous interviews to the local press, which respectfully kept track of his progress. 'Mr Somerset Maugham and his secretary Mr Gerald Haxton have been paying North Borneo a visit,' the *Malay Mail* reported. 'They went from Brunei by launch to Weston and thence by train on January 19 to Jesselton where they were guests of His Excellency the Governor and Mrs Pearson at Government House. They left on January 23 by the "Darvel" for Sandakan en route to Manila and Hong Kong.' To accompany them on their travels Maugham had employed a servant supplied by an agency in Singapore. Ah King, a sweet-natured young man of twenty, turned out to be a marvel.* 'He could cook, he could valet, he could pack, he could wait at table. He was quick, neat

---

* Ah King makes a further appearance as the devoted servant in the 1932 novel *The Narrow Corner.*

and silent . . . Nothing surprised him, no catastrophe dismayed him, no hardship ruffled him, no novelty took him unawares. It was impossible to tire him. He smiled all day long. I have never met anyone so good-humoured.' There was only one drawback: although Ah King was able to speak some English he understood hardly a word, which made communication difficult. When at the end of six months Maugham paid him off, he saw to his astonishment that Ah King was crying.

> I stared at him with amazement . . . he had always seemed to me strangely detached . . . as indifferent to my praise as he was unconcerned at my reproofs . . . That he had any feeling for me had never entered my head . . . I felt a little uncomfortable. I knew that I had often been impatient with him, tiresome and exacting. I had never thought of him as a human being. He wept because he was leaving me. It is for these tears that I now give his name to this collection of stories that I invented while he was travelling with me.

The two collections of Far Eastern stories garnered during Maugham's expeditions in the 1920s, *The Casuarina Tree* published in 1926 and *Ah King* in 1933,* contain some of his finest work in the genre at which he remains an acknowledged master. Maugham himself recognised that the short story, of approximately 12,000 words in length, was a form that ideally suited him. 'It was very agreeable to live with the personages of my fancy for two or three weeks and then be done with them,' he wrote in *The Summing Up*. '[The length] gave me ample room to develop my theme, but forced upon me a concision that my practice as a dramatist had made grateful to me.' Fluent in style and apparently effortless, the stories are tightly constructed and minutely observed, amply demonstrating the three virtues which he himself prized highest, of lucidity, simplicity and euphony. As a writer of fiction, Maugham was a realist: his imagination needed actual people and events to work on, and these his travels amply furnished, enabling him to explore the imperial theme from an intimately personal and domestic standpoint. During those months spent listening to strangers telling him their private dramas, 'I seemed', he said, 'to develop the sensitiveness of a photographic plate.' Shrewd and uncompromising, he is finely attuned to nuance in speech and gesture; he is also compassionate, often funny, and almost never passes judgment on the frequently appalling behaviour of his usually far from estimable characters. He wrote about ordinary, fallible people, the kind

---

* Like most of Maugham's short stories, the seven in *The Casuarina Tree* and the six in *Ah King* appeared first in magazines.

of people he knew and understood, the white professional middle classes, and when challenged about why he never attempted to depict native life, he replied that it was because he did not believe any European could get to the inside of it.

> I felt that all the depictions that had been made of either Chinese, Indians, or Malays were merely superficial impressions combined with a lot of conventional prejudices. It is very nearly impossible for an English author to create a French character so that French readers would accept him as real. How much more difficult then would it be for an English writer to create a Chinese the Chinese would accept as plausible.

It is his oriental tales that many readers most associate with Maugham, and they were and are widely admired, in his day by such distinguished literary figures as George Orwell, Evelyn Waugh, Graham Greene, Christopher Isherwood, Angus Wilson and Anthony Burgess. Burgess, describing these two collections as containing some of the finest examples in the language, wrote, 'The width of observation was something new in English fiction, as was the willingness to explore moral regions then regarded as taboo'; the novelist L. P. Hartley in a review of *The Casuarina Tree* concluded that within its limits 'Mr Maugham's work is nearly perfect'; while Cyril Connolly, who selected *The Casuarina Tree* for his influential compilation *100 Key Books of the Modern Movement*,★ particularly praised the author for 'his mastery of form', going on to say that 'Maugham achieves an unspoken ferocity, a controlled ruthlessness . . . He tells us – and it had not been said before – exactly what the British in the Far East were like, the judges and planters and civil servants and their womenfolk at home . . .'

Permeating the lives of the British colonists in the East is a sense of loneliness and exile, a theme well understood by Maugham. Nowhere is this better demonstrated than in 'The Outstation', described by the poet Edwin Muir as 'surely one of the best short stories written in our time'. 'The Outstation' tells of the deadly hostility between two men forced into close proximity on a remote outpost in Borneo. Mr Warburton is the long-established Resident of the district, his character, stiff, snobbish, honourable and brave, based on that of Edward Johnston, the British Consul Maugham had known as a young man in Seville. Although he is the only white man for hundreds of miles, Mr Warburton prides himself

---

★ *The Casuarina Tree* was listed under 'The Twenties', with *Ulysses*, *A Passage to India*, *The Great Gatsby*, *The Sun Also Rises*, *To the Lighthouse* and *Decline and Fall*.

on keeping up the standards, despite the heat dressing for his solitary dinner every evening in dinner-jacket, boiled shirt and black patent-leather shoes. Accustomed to solitude, it is with some apprehension that he awaits the arrival of an assistant, and when Cooper appears it instantly becomes apparent that he is everything Mr Warburton dislikes. Cooper is rude, loutish and worst of all behaves bullyingly to the natives. 'I don't think there's much about niggers that I don't know,' he boasts. 'We were not talking of them,' Mr Warburton acidly responds.

> 'We were talking of Malays.'
> 'Aren't they niggers?'
> 'You are very ignorant,' replied Mr Warburton.

Cooper sneers at what he regards as Mr Warburton's fussy pretentious-ness, the elaborately folded napkins, the menus written out in French, and he brutally destroys his superior's pleasure in his treasured reminis-cences of titled acquaintance with whom he had so proudly hobnobbed back home. 'Don't you know that you're the laughing stock of the whole country?' Cooper taunts him. 'I could hardly help bursting into a roar of laughter when you told your celebrated story about the Prince of Wales. My God, how they shouted at the club when they told it.'

Before long the hatred between the two men is so intense that they can barely speak to each other, eating their meals separately and com-municating mainly in writing, a state of affairs ended when Cooper is mysteriously murdered, a shockingly violent death officially regretted if privately unmourned by Mr Warburton. The story, narrated with a delicate irony and with perfect balance and control, is given an added dimension by the author's sympathy for both his protagonists: not only for Mr Warburton's decency and foolishness, but for Cooper, who underneath his bumptiousness is lonely and insecure.

> In the bungalow, two hundred yards away, Cooper was eating a filthy meal clad only in a sarong and a baju [a short jacket]. His feet were bare and while he ate he probably read a detective story . . . In his bitter loneliness on a sudden [he] lost all control of himself. Painful sobs tore his chest and heavy tears rolled down his thin cheeks.

In a very different vein is 'The Vessel of Wrath' in *Ah King*, set in the remote Alas Islands east of Java. A slyly comic plot involves a couple of middle-aged missionaries, the Joneses, brother and sister, he dogmatic and austere, she thin, sallow and flat-chested. The islands are administered by a Dutch controller, a stout, self-indulgent fellow whose favourite drinking-companion is a dissolute remittance man known locally as Ginger Ted. Ted is always getting into trouble, frequently drunk, brawling in bars, behaving disgracefully to women, for whom despite his foul mouth and rumpled appearance he has an irresistible magnetism. As the result of a complicated series of events, Ginger Ted and Miss Jones find themselves fellow passengers, together with two native crew, on a shabby launch whose broken propeller forces them to beach for the night on a small uninhabited island. The virginal Miss Jones is convinced she will be ravished by Ted, and she determines to stay awake in order to defend herself. But Ted and the others settle down comfortably by the fire, ignoring Miss Jones who watches them avidly from a distance. 'Ginger Ted would rape her. She knew his character. He was mad about women . . . She bit her lip. She watched them, like a tiger watching his prey; no, not like that, like a lamb watching three hungry wolves.' The next thing she knows it is morning and Ted, who, as he later phrases it, wouldn't touch such a desiccated old hag 'with the fag-end of a barge-pole', has come to wake her. 'She could not look at him, but she felt herself as red as a turkey cock. "Have a banana," he said.' The rest of the story follows Miss Jones's determined pursuit of Ted and his eventual capture, the comedy lying in the reversal of expectation, of the nice juxtaposition of the unadmitted lust of the respectable spinster and the surprising conversion to sobriety and domesticity of the bum.

It is also in this collection, in *Ah King*, that there appears one of the earliest examples of Maugham's use of the first-person narrator,* a device on which he came increasingly to rely, developing it and building on it and making it peculiarly his own. The 'I' in these first-person stories is almost, if not quite, Maugham himself, a genial, clubbable character fond of reading and bridge, and insatiably curious about other people's lives. Typically a tale will begin in an informal tone of voice, with plenty of autobiographical detail proffered, so that the reader is effortlessly drawn in, the story becoming as immediate as an anecdote related by a friend. In 'The Book-Bag', for instance, about an incestuous love affair, the unnamed narrator begins in a leisurely manner apparently going nowhere in particular, until suddenly and seamlessly we find ourselves in the middle of the story. In the first few pages the writer amiably discusses his addiction to reading, the terrible experience of running out of books once while staying in Java, and his purchase in consequence of a special travelling book-bag. This precious bag accompanies him in his wanderings

* *The Moon and Sixpence* was the earliest of Maugham's substantial exercises in first-person narrative.

round Malaya, and much impresses a local Resident by whom he has been invited to stay.

> 'Should you be ready for a gin pahit in ten minutes?'
> 'Easily,' I said . . .
> 'I suppose you haven't any books with you,' he said . . .
> 'Books?' I cried . . . 'Look for yourself.'
> Featherstone's boys had unlocked the bag, but quailing before the sight that then discovered itself had done no more. I knew from long experience how to unpack it. I threw it over on its side, seized its leather bottom and, walking backwards, dragged the sack away from its contents. A river of books poured on to the floor. A look of stupefaction came upon Featherstone's face.

The first evening Featherstone takes his guest down to the club where they are joined by a couple of members for a rubber of bridge. The following day the narrator idly remarks that one of the two played a remarkably good game. 'That was Hardy,' says Featherstone. 'He doesn't come to the club very often.'

> 'I hope he will to-night.'
> 'I wouldn't bank on it. He has an estate about thirty miles away. It's a longish ride to come just for a rubber of bridge.'
> 'Is he married?'
> 'No. Well, yes. But his wife is in England.'
> 'It must be awfully lonely for those men who live by themselves on those estates,' I said.
> 'Oh, he's not so badly off as some. I don't think he much cares about seeing people. I think he'd be just as lonely in London.'
> There was something in the way Featherstone spoke that struck me as a little strange. His voice had what I can only describe as a shuttered tone . . .

The moment passes and the two men casually begin to talk of other matters, yet the reader is hooked, knowing that now the real story is about to unfold.

Maugham returned to Europe in March 1926, having spent most of the voyage confined to his cabin with a recurrence of the malaria from which he had been so ill during his first visit to Bangkok. 'The journey on a French boat from Saigon to Marseilles, over thirty days, has seemed terribly long,' he wrote to Alanson, '& I am thankful as I write to you to see out of the window of the smoking-room the shining, sunny coast of Corsica.' A letter from Syrie had just reached him, containing the information that she was currently on business in New York and had again let the house in Bryanston Square, news that left him feeling both angry and depressed. 'I am tired of wandering about & would gladly remain quietly at home, but at present I have no home,' he told Alanson; 'a domestic disturbance, whether permanent or temporary I do not yet know, has left me without a roof to my head.' Still feeling unwell, Maugham with Haxton retired to a comfortable hotel in Aix en Provence to recuperate, but the more he brooded on the situation, the more intolerable it seemed that he should be denied access to his own home, that Syrie was treating Bryanston Square as hers, to do with entirely as she pleased regardless of his wishes. The plan to purchase a property abroad now became a priority, a house where he could live with Gerald and to which Syrie would have access only by invitation. Reading between the lines, he was even cautiously optimistic that his wife was beginning to come round to the possibility of a judicial separation. 'I cannot but think that she has at last determined on a break,' Maugham wrote hopefully to Knoblock, 'though I cannot imagine what has made her reverse her very definite desire to have nothing of the sort with which I left her last autumn. If you hear anything of interest to me I am sure that you will let me know.'

Maugham's arrival in London on 3 May 1926 coincided with the beginning of the General Strike, ten days which provided a once-in-a-lifetime opportunity for the educated classes to play at being train drivers, bus drivers, newspaper editors and policemen. Even to those of a left-wing bent the chance was irresistible, and Maugham, through a friend in the Public Prosecutions Department, landed a job in Scotland Yard, 'sleuthing', as he described it to Arnold Bennett. With the strike ended, the house vacated by its tenants and Syrie returned from New York, negotiations between husband and wife began in earnest, and for once appeared to result in an agreement acceptable to both: Bryanston Square would be sold, and with the proceeds Syrie would buy a house of her own, while Maugham would look for a permanent base abroad: not on Capri, which on reflection was too difficult to reach, but in the south of France. 'I have made a very agreeable arrangement with my wife,' Maugham wrote to Alanson. 'She is to have her house in London & I my house on the Riviera & we are going to stay with one another as guests when it suits our mutual pleasure and convenience. I think this is the best thing for both of us & it will give me the opportunity which I need to work in pleasant surroundings & without interruption.'

But instead of house-hunting he was first caught up in a series of professional projects. There were talks in progress about a film version of 'Rain', a revival of *Caroline* had just opened at the Playhouse, and Maugham had a new play, *The Constant Wife*, which he was anxious to see staged; there were as well constant requests from Ray Long for stories for Hearst magazines, and there was also some complicated business to sort out with his New York publisher George Doran. While Maugham was abroad, Charles Towne had arranged a new contract with Doran which, to his client's irritation, not only appeared to tie him to the company for life but on much less advantageous terms than before. 'I will not conceal from you that I am extremely vexed at your having signed an agreement with Doran which gives me nothing that I wanted but on the contrary takes away what I value most dearly, my freedom of action,' Maugham crossly complained.

> You seem now to have bound me hand and foot for the rest of my career as a novelist . . . [nor] is the contract you have signed so good as the offer which Doran made me himself by letter several months ago. In this he proposed to give me an advance of twenty five hundred dollars on all books other than novels which I submitted to him and five thousand dollars on novels. From your letter I judge that he has only made a contract for one volume of short stories beside *The Casuarina Tree*, so that for future volumes of short stories, or for anything else I may write such as travel books, I am left at the mercy of his generosity. I do not know exactly what advantage I get in receiving an advance of five thousand dollars on a novel. It is to be presumed that with such a reputation as I have any novel I write will earn that sum in royalties without any effort on the part of the publishers; and what I particularly aimed at was to force the publisher to do a little more than his best for me.

Within months, however, the cause of the quarrel became academic: Doran's firm was absorbed by Doubleday and Towne resigned his agency to take on the editorship of *Harper's Bazaar*, a move regarded by Maugham with approval. 'I am sure you will make an excellent editor and bring the greatest possible success to the magazine,' he told Towne. 'Though I consider you too arbitrary to be an agent I continue to think you a charming and an amiable companion.'

With the house in Bryanston Square up for sale, Maugham felt disinclined to remain in London, going first to Brides-les-Bains, then to Capri, then to Salzburg for a few days to meet Syrie for the festival. He returned to London in August, but only for a brief interval, leaving at the end of September for the States in order to be present at the opening of *The Constant Wife*. On arrival in New York he wrote to Bert Alanson with some exciting news. After looking at a number of houses on the Riviera he had finally found one that he liked on Cap Ferrat, a rather dilapidated property which had long been left vacant as so much money was needed for its restoration. An early-twentieth-century house near the top of the Cap, it had been curiously embellished by a series of pseudo-Moorish architectural features, thus accounting for its name, the Villa Mauresque. 'Twenty minutes before starting for the station to take the train to Southampton and the ship for New York,' Alanson was told, 'the agents of the owner of the house I have been haggling over for the last six months came to see me and accepted my last offer; so that I am now the possessor of nine acres of land and a villa half way between Nice and Monte Carlo.'

# 11

# The Villa Mauresque

The Villa Mauresque and Somerset Maugham, Somerset Maugham and the Villa Mauresque, for nearly forty years the two were inextricably linked, the house the richest thread in the fabric of the legend – visited, photographed, filmed, described in countless articles, regarded with awe as the glamorous and exotic backdrop for one of the most famous writers in the world. If the villa itself were of no great architectural merit, its location was superb, overlooking the sea and hidden among trees at the top of Cap Ferrat, a thickly wooded promontory jutting out into the Mediterranean. To the west are Nice, Cannes and the wide sweep of the Baie des Anges, while to the east lie Beaulieu, Monte Carlo and the Italian Riviera; behind are the snow-covered peaks of the Alpes Maritimes, while before stretches the wide blue expanse of the ocean, where on a clear day the misty outline of Corsica can be glimpsed on the horizon. Here was the south, here was warmth, light, vibrant colour, white houses with terracotta roofs and a luxuriant vegetation reminiscent of the tropics, mimosa and oleander, yucca and bougainvillaea, olive and palm trees. Most of the land on Cap Ferrat had been bought in the early years of the century by King Leopold II of the Belgians, who had built himself a palace there, in 1906 adding a house near by for his elderly confessor. This gentleman, a Monseigneur Charmeton, had spent much of his life in Algeria and understandably wished to end his days in the Moorish style to which he had become accustomed; thus, the square, white-washed villa had had imposed upon it horseshoe windows, a Moorish archway, a large cupola on the roof and tacked on to one side a grandiose Venetian portico.

Maugham was entranced by his new acquisition, and considered the £7,000 he paid for it a very fair price. 'I have at last found a place that pleases me more than Capri,' he wrote to Gerald Kelly. 'Of course at present everything is upside down and one requires the eye of faith to see what the house and garden will be like when the place is shipshape.' A local architect, Henri Delmotte, was engaged to restore the house to its original shape, a fairly straightforward job as the Arabian ornamentation of lath and plaster was easy to remove. Indoors a courtyard was constructed, spacious and quiet, and leading from it was a dining-room and a long, high-ceilinged drawing-room, in summer its tall windows kept cool and shuttered from the glare outside. From the large hall a white marble staircase ascended to a gallery around which were the bedrooms and bathrooms: as well as apartments for Maugham and Haxton, there were big double bedrooms with dressing-rooms for guests, with two bachelor bedrooms on the ground floor. At the very top of the building, reached by a wooden stair leading on to the flat roof, was Maugham's study, a private chamber apart from the rest of the house; entered through French windows, the room was airy and spacious, with wide views over the tops of pine trees to mountains and the sea. Alone in his eyrie on days when the mistral was blowing, Maugham used to say it was like being on the deck of a ship.

While the builders were painting and hammering in the house, Maugham turned his attention to the steep, overgrown hillside on which it stood. He had never had a plot of his own to cultivate before, he wrote, and 'I hadn't reckoned on the temptation that is afforded by a great neglected garden.' When he first saw it, the land was a dense jungle of foliage, pine trees, mimosa, aloes, with the ground beneath a tangle of wild rosemary and thyme. Once this had been cleared and cut back the garden was properly stepped and levelled, and flowering shrubs were planted, camellias, hibiscus and bougainvillaea, a lily pond was scooped out, and orange and lemon trees set in a formal pattern on the terraces immediately outside the house. Thousands of spring bulbs were dug in and, extremely rare for the Mediterranean, turf was laid for a grass lawn, readily admitted by Maugham to be a rich man's folly. 'The great luxury on the Riviera is grass, for it will not bear the long heat of summer and must be dug up at the end of every spring and replanted every fall'; yet he had an inextinguishable nostalgia for the smooth green swards of English country houses and wished to have something of the same himself. 'I made lawns on each side of the drive that led to my front door, and I made a broad green pathway that meandered under the pine trees to the end of the garden.' Away from and above the house were glasshouses and a kitchen garden, and just below these a tennis-court, reached by a flight of stone steps and hidden by a hedge; a long marble swimming-pool was installed, at each corner a handsome lead pine-cone from Italy, with at one end a diving board, at the other, gushing water, a magnificent mask of Neptune carved by Bernini which Maugham had found in Florence. 'The swimming pool is a great success,' Maugham wrote to Bert Alanson in the midst of the construction work in August 1927. 'We go in four or five times a day and lie about in the heavenly sunshine.' With the arrival of his furniture and other possessions from Bryanston Square, his books, theatrical pictures and the various ornaments and objets d'art collected in the East, the Villa Mauresque soon began to feel very much like home.

There was little time to enjoy his new property, however, as Maugham's professional commitments required his presence in London, where he was involved in the preparation of two new dramatic works, *The Constant Wife* and *The Letter*, the second an adaptation he had made of his Malayan short story about Mrs Crosbie's shooting of her lover and her subsequent trial. From the first Maugham had been determined that Gladys Cooper should take the part of Leslie Crosbie, and her performance more than fulfilled his expectation, so impressing him that he offered her the option on his next three plays. Directed by Gerald du Maurier, *The Letter* opened on 24 February 1927, rapturously received both by audiences and in the press. 'Miss Cooper's acting . . . was superb, and could certainly not have been bettered by any living English actress,' wrote the critic in the *Sunday Times*, who judged of the play itself that 'it would be impossible to speak too highly. It is perfect theatre of its kind.' In September *The Letter* opened at the Morosco in New York, produced by the well-respected Messmore Kendall and with Katherine Cornell in the lead, where again it proved a triumph, a success repeated eighteen months later with a French version at the Théâtre de l'Athénée in Paris.

Maugham was a great admirer of Gladys Cooper: he admired her beauty, her professionalism and her no-nonsense attitude towards life in general, while she for her part had the greatest esteem for him. 'I place Somerset Maugham as our finest writer for the stage,' she stated in her autobiography. It was during rehearsals for *The Letter*, of which she was also co-producer, that Gladys properly came to appreciate Maugham's method, impressed by how accommodating he was with regard to making changes to his text. 'The majority of authors', she wrote, 'are terribly sensitive and jealous of their work, regarding every word they have written as almost a pearl beyond price . . . Not so Somerset Maugham.' He would sit in the stalls, ready with his blue pencil to cross out or rewrite whatever she or du Maurier wished. In large part this relaxed attitude derived from the detached view Maugham took of his dramatic work: it was the private process of composition that engaged him, not the play's evolution on stage; once the work was in the hands of the actors and director, it became something else, with which he no longer felt closely concerned.

For this reason the theatre was ultimately regarded as an unsatisfactory medium for a writer, as Maugham explained in a letter to Noël Coward.

> [We] have to content ourselves with at the best an approximation of what we see in the mind's eye. After one has got over the glamour of the stage and the excitement, I do not myself think the theatre has much to offer the writer compared with the other mediums in which he has complete independence and need consider no one.

For Maugham rehearsing had become dull work, attended to more from a sense of duty than because he felt crucially involved in the interpretation of his script. This attitude, verging almost on indifference, had been noted by the director Basil Dean, who during preparations for *East of Suez* had concluded, rightly, that it sprang from the fact that 'Maugham lacked genuine enthusiasm for the theatre . . . Throughout the rehearsals, he remained withdrawn, neither helpful nor obstructive, never offering advice unless it was asked for. I think he found the whole business tiresome and the actors' arguments rather petty. Yet, when appealed to, he was always ready with the unconvincing response: "Oh, ex-excellent!" Once I asked him whether I might cut certain lines: "Wh-wh-why not?" he spluttered. "The st-st-stage is a w-w-workshop."'

With *The Letter* doing so well on both sides of the Atlantic, and with a sell-out production of *Pluie* (*Rain*) at the Théâtre de la Madeleine in Paris, Maugham's theatrical reputation had never been higher, and much was expected of the new work, due to open in London in April 1927. But with *The Constant Wife* almost everything went wrong from the start.

In much the same format as a number of Maugham's earlier drawing-room comedies, plays like *Penelope* and *Caroline*, *The Constant Wife* tells the story of a husband and wife, John and Constance Middleton, who are the best of friends but no longer in love. John is currently engaged in what he fondly imagines is a secret affair with a married woman, Marie-Louise, an affair Constance privately knows all about and equably accepts, although she has no wish either to confront John or to allow her girlfriends to tell her about it, as they are dying to do. Then Bernard arrives on the scene, returned from fifteen years in the Far East and as much in love with Constance as he was before he left, his devotion providing Constance with the perfect instrument with which to teach her husband a lesson, should the need arise. This happens when Marie-Louise's husband becomes suspicious about his wife's affair, and Constance skilfully rescues the situation, in so doing finally revealing that she had known about John's adultery all along. John, grateful but humiliated, barely has the chance to take in what is happening before Constance announces she is leaving for a holiday with Bernard; not only that but she intends to pay for it with money she has earned herself, thus declaring herself a free woman.

In the guise of a smart little comedy of manners, *The Constant Wife* is in fact ablaze with anger, anger about the injustices and constraints of the married state, with just below the surface Maugham's feelings of bitterness about Syrie. 'I'm tired of being the modern wife,' says Constance. 'What do you mean by the modern wife?' her sister asks, to which Constance bleakly replies, 'A prostitute who doesn't deliver the goods.' It is for this reason that Constance makes up her mind to earn her own money – by working as an interior decorator, interestingly enough. She harangues her husband on the subject of the meretriciousness of her previous position.

> CONSTANCE: Are you as great a fool as the average man, who falls for the average woman's stupendous bluff that just because he's married her he must provide for her wants and her luxuries, sacrifice his pleasures and comfort and convenience, and that he must look upon it as a privilege that she allows him to be her slave and bondman? . . . What is a wife in our class? . . . no more than the mistress of a man of whose desire she has taken advantage of to insist on a legal ceremony that will prevent him from discarding her when his desire has ceased . . .
>
> JOHN: You were the mother of my child.
>
> CONSTANCE: Let us not exaggerate the importance of that, John. I performed a natural and healthy function of my sex . . . Let us face it, I was only a parasite in your house . . .

Even more venomous is the advice Constance gives Marie-Louise on how to punish her husband, in words which derive directly from the author's own miserable experience.

> Refuse to speak to him, but never let him get a word of defence in edge-ways. Cry enough to make him feel what a brute he is, but not enough to make your eyes swell. Say you'll leave him and run sobbing to the door, but take care to let him stop you before you open it. Repeat yourself. Say the same thing over and over again . . . and if he answers you take no notice, but just say it again . . . [until] at last . . . you've reduced him to desperation, when his head is aching as though it would split, when he's sweating at every pore, when he's harassed and miserable and haggard and broken . . .

*The Constant Wife* was produced in 1926 in America, with Ethel Barrymore in the lead, the first time she had played in a piece by

Maugham since *Lady Frederick* twenty years before. Opening in Cleveland, Ohio, on 1 November, the play suffered a bad start because the actress, stricken with stage-fright, repeatedly forgot her lines, obliging the assistant stage manager, George Cukor, to hide in the fireplace on stage in order to prompt her. Maugham was in the audience. 'I suffered agonies,' he later admitted to Cukor. 'When the curtain came down for the last time I went on to the stage. Ethel flung her arms round my neck and kissed me on both cheeks. "Darling," she said. "I've ruined your play, but don't worry; it'll run for two years." And it did.'

But if the play recovered after its poor beginning in the States, it was given no such chance in London. The production was booked to go into the handsome Theatre Royal, Haymarket, with a cast led by Leon Quartermaine and Fay Compton. To direct, Maugham approached Basil Dean, 'vain as a peacock' in the playwright's opinion, yet who knew very well what he was about. Dean accepted, although with reservations as he was unhappy with the choice of the two stars. 'Quite early in rehearsals I discovered they were not well suited to their parts,' he recalled. 'Maugham's cynical comedy called for the lightest of treatment. Fay's comedy style was too arch and Leo was too pedantic.' Then came the news that the Haymarket was no longer available and the Strand was taken instead, a much smaller theatre with a stage unsuited for any but the broadest effects. But most damaging of all was the disastrous opening on 6 April 1927, when a managerial blunder succeeded in totally disrupting the performance. In those days rope barriers cordoned off the main, expensive section of the stalls from the cheaper seats at the back, known as the pit, with the barriers moved according to demand. As always for a Maugham first night booking had been heavy, but by some mishap instructions to move back the barriers had not been given. As a consequence violent rows broke out between the fashionably dressed gentry, with their numbered tickets, and the rougher element of 'pitites', who were already in place and refusing to budge, peace being restored only when the theatre manager went up on stage to appeal for order. 'Maugham and his wife sat in a stage-box, dismayed, while the argument was going on,' Dean recalled. '[And] the effect on the actors can well be imagined. Already suffering from the usual first-night nerves they were put completely out of countenance by the fracas.' More disruption was to follow when at the end of the play Fay Compton came forward to make the traditional speech of thanks and, mistaking a cry of 'shut up!' from the gallery as intended for her, pointedly thanked the 'civil' members of the audience, which immediately provoked loud booing from the upper regions.

Unsurprisingly, the production never recovered, and the critical consensus, that 'Mr Maugham was out of form when he wrote *The Constant Wife*,' kept audiences away.

Maugham had already left the theatre by the time Miss Compton made her speech, as Syrie was giving a combined first-night and house-warming party at her new address, 213 King's Road, Chelsea. The property comprised a four-storey, early-Georgian house of great beauty with a smaller house linked by a wide indoor passage round the corner in Glebe Place. On the first floor of the King's Road house Syrie had made a large and spectacular drawing-room decorated wholly in white, with white sofas, off-white satin curtains, white velvet lampshades, a white carpet by Marion Dorn, and behind a white brocade sofa a huge folding screen made of narrow pieces of mirror reflecting great sprays of white flowers, roses, lilies, peonies, lilac, supplied on a regular basis by a recent associate of Syrie's, the florist Constance Spry. Above this were apart-ments for herself and Liza, and on the top floor a bedroom for her husband – 'nice enough', he granted, 'but it had the disadvantage of being also the "gentlemen's cloakroom", so that when there was a party I had to put away my writing materials.' Displeased by such a constraint, Maugham soon moved his quarters from the main house to the Glebe Place annexe, which was quieter and more private; with this arrangement he and Syrie were in effect living apart while still appearing to be under one roof. Certainly they were regarded as joint hosts for the glamorous first-night party for *The Constant Wife*, attended by almost everyone who was anyone in theatrical and literary circles. 'Crowds and crowds at the party,' Arnold Bennett reported, with major stars such as Marie Tempest and Tallulah Bankhead much in evidence; altogether the evening was deemed 'a great success . . . Only Maugham and wife were a bit gloomy . . . I hear the play is rotten.'

If it was hardly surprising that Maugham was gloomy following the débâcle earlier in the evening, nonetheless at this point it was Syrie whose state was the more precarious. With her husband's purchase of the Villa Mauresque she had been finally forced to accept that he had chosen a way of life in which she would have little part. Unable to conceal her despair, she poured out her misery to any sympathetic friend who would listen; Rebecca West was one who spent several long afternoons sitting in a darkened room while Syrie wept over what she considered her cruel desertion; another friend, Cecil Beaton, was shocked by Syrie telling him that during a visit to New York she had been so distraught over the prospect of her marriage ending that she had 'spent three whole nights in Central Park too miserable to go home'. Despite a possible element of exaggeration, there is no doubt that Syrie was wretchedly unhappy and on the point of collapse. 'My mother had a very bad nervous break-down,' Liza recalled of this period, a breakdown which reached its nadir during a business trip to the States. While in New York Syrie became so frantic that she decided to go to Bermuda to try and find peace, but once there could hardly wait to leave, insisting on boarding the first ship out of the harbour, a tramp steamer with no passenger accommodation, she and Liza sleeping in chairs on the open deck as far as Nassau. Here in the Bahamas the two of them stayed for several weeks and here at last Syrie began to recover, Liza attending a little open-air school run by nuns, 'the nicest of my collection of schools', as she remembered it.

Upon returning to England it seems that Syrie made one final attempt to persuade Maugham not to leave her. She asked him to come once more to Le Touquet, in the hope that between them they might find some form of resolution less drastic than divorce. Little came of the meeting, except for a shocking incident involving Liza and Gerald Haxton. 'I always hated Gerald Haxton and he always hated me,' said Liza. Their first encounter the previous summer had been uncomfort-able, the child wary of this strangely powerful friend of her father's, and he no doubt irritated by the spoilt little miss he saw being cosseted by her mother. On this second occasion Barbara Back was again staying with them, and she, Haxton and Liza went for a drive, Liza taking with her an adored puppy she had recently been given. Suddenly in an act of possibly drunken, seemingly inexplicable cruelty Gerald at the wheel scooped up the dog and hurled it out of the window. 'I was hysterical,' said Liza, 'and tried to throw myself out of the car after it but was held back.' Months later the dog was found and returned, but the damage was done: the enmity between Haxton and the two women was irreparable, and Syrie made sure that while in her care Liza would never set eyes on Gerald again.

It was after these few days in Le Touquet that Syrie finally acknow-ledged that her marriage was over. Now her friends were told that it was she who was pressing for a divorce, mainly for her daughter's sake, it appeared: it was painfully obvious, said Syrie, that Gerald was going through her husband's money at a terrifying rate and soon there would be nothing left for Liza. Sitting on the beach at La Garoupe in the south of France, Syrie told the actress Ruth Gordon that '[Willie] watches Gerald losing thousands on the Juan-les-Pins gaming tables. To insure Liza's inheritance I *must* divorce.' During that summer, the summer of 1928, Syrie was staying on the Riviera with her old friend and rival, the flamboyant Elsie Mendl. Lady Mendl, now in her sixties and recently married to the diplomat Sir Charles Mendl, had had a long and successful career in America as Elsie de Wolfe, the first woman interior decorator, much admired for her knowledge of French art and culture. In this she had been educated by her long-term lesbian lover Elisabeth Marbury, who, coincidentally, was well known to Maugham as a leading theatrical agent in New York. While Syrie was staying with the Mendls at Antibes Maugham was near by at the Villa Mauresque. According to his version of events, he invited Syrie to lunch with no other purpose than to show her his house, sending his car to collect her and take her back. 'We lunched tête à tête,' he recalled,

> and after lunch I took her over the premises. She was becomingly appre-
> ciative. After she had seen everything . . . I put her in my car. An hour or
> two later the car came back with a letter. In it she said that she wished
> to divorce me and hoped I would put no obstacles in the way. It took me
> by surprise. I thought the matter over for a day and then wrote to say I
> would do what she wished if she would be satisfied with a French divorce . . .
> because divorce in France is a simple matter and there is no publicity
> attached to it. Syrie agreed and the lawyers went to work.

The lawyers must have had their hands full, with a multitude of complex negotiations to be carried out on both sides. According to the Maugham family record, pressure had to be put on Syrie not to cite Haxton as co-respondent, and there are other indications that she was prepared to use his homosexuality against him ('Your mother dragged me through the mud when she divorced me,' Maugham later told Liza). Eventually Syrie was persuaded to drop any such charge, a charge which would have had a devastating effect on Maugham, with the potential to ruin him professionally and socially and to prevent him from ever setting foot in England again. Evidence of his wife's adultery may well have helped his case, but as Maugham knew very well his most effective bargaining tool was financial, and he was willing to pay a substantial price for his liberty, making over to Syrie the house in the King's Road with all its contents, the house in Glebe Place, which was put in Liza's name, and the car, a Rolls-Royce, as well as a generous annuity of £2,400, with £600 a year for Liza. Syrie filed suit in Nice in the autumn of 1928, and the decree was granted, on grounds of incompatibility, on 11 May 1929, quietly and without publicity. 'Everything is absolutely finished,' Maugham wrote to Barbara Back, 'and all there is for me to do is to hand over twelve thousand pounds and resign myself to paying six hundred pounds a quarter free of income-tax until Syrie marries again.'

Maugham was finally freed from a union he had come to detest. 'I made a mistake when I married her,' he wrote. 'We, she and I, had nothing in common and by doing what was considered "the right thing", I brought happiness neither to her nor to myself.' As the years went by, instead of fading into indifference Maugham's feelings for Syrie grew increasingly corrosive; he hated her for the large sums of money she had cost and would continue to cost him, and he could not forgive her for the misery and humiliation she had inflicted. For a man who enjoyed the company of women, who in his fiction and his friendships was so understanding and compassionate towards them, his attitude towards his ex-wife is startling, indicative of a very deep wound indeed. Although after the divorce he seldom saw her, his distaste for Syrie turned into an active and visceral loathing. 'She made my life utter hell,' he would say, bitterly referring to Syrie as an 'abandoned liar' and the 'tart who ruined my life', and describing her as '[opening] her mouth as wide as a brothel door' in her constant demands for money. His great hope was that she would marry again and thus relieve him of the pecuniary burden, and many joking references were made to this prospect in letters to friends. 'I have learned from the papers', he wrote to Barbara Back, 'that [the homosexual decorator] Mr Johnnie McMullen is spending the summer with her [Syrie] at her house in London and have a strong hope that at the end of the season when debutantes settle these matters she will make an honest woman of him.' But Syrie never remarried, remaining financially dependent on her ex-husband till the day she died. The two of them communicated mainly through lawyers, they rarely met, and Maugham made it clear to interviewers that he disliked talking about his marriage; if questioned he testily dismissed the subject as a 'very unimportant detail'.

Once the divorce had gone through, the Maughams closed ranks and shut their doors to Syrie; she was no longer welcomed by F.H. and Nellie at Cadogan Square and Liza lost touch with her cousins. Yet, if seldom discussed within the family, the Maugham divorce was a subject of intense fascination to their friends, especially among the homosexual coterie. 'For those who seek a moral, one stands clear: / Don't marry if you happen to be queer,' giggled the aesthete Harold Acton, while a number of other young men began jockeying for position, hoping that if they played their cards right the famous writer's patronage would help their careers. One of the first in the field was Beverley Nichols. Originally a friend of Syrie's,

Beverley was pretty, intelligent, highly sexed and drivingly ambitious. He had already begun to make quite a name as a journalist, had written a couple of novels, had big plans for himself as a dramatist, and in 1926 at the age of only twenty-five had published an autobiography, appropriately entitled *Twenty-Five*. This he had persuaded Maugham to praise in the *Sunday Times*, a considerable achievement as Maugham almost never wrote book-reviews. 'He wrote it at my request after a very lavish dinner at the Café Royal and gave it to me as a birthday present,' Beverley recalled with satisfaction. Beverley, vain and unscrupulous, was more than ready to make himself sexually available in exchange for favours such as these; there was no reason why men like Maugham should not 'help one up one's little ladder', as he whimsically phrased it. 'Struggling to make a living from letters, one would be a fool to ignore the kindly attentions of the literary lions, particularly if they happen also to be extremely rich . . . [and] Willie's attentions were very kindly indeed.' Naturally Beverley was unable to resist boasting of his conquests, to, among others, Cecil Beaton, who was frankly shocked by his revelations. 'With drink Beverley's tongue was wildly lubricated & I heard more that staggered me that evening than I have during the past few years,' Beaton confided to his diary.

> I, who have not been to bed with anyone but myself since I was at school, had come to think that the amount of people who actually went to bed together was very small . . . but Beverley disproved my beliefs with the most hair-raising stories of the unceasing lusts of nearly all my friends . . . [he] assured me, at first hand knowledge, of the homosexuality of Noël (Coward), Somerset Maugham, Avery Hopwood, Sydney [sic] Howard,★ Edward Knoblock — a most disturbing evening & a great eye opener.

Another 'tarty' young man who caught the eye of Willie Maugham at this period was a friend and colleague of Beverley's, Godfrey Winn. Similarly ambitious, Godfrey, too, was making a career in journalism, specialising in cosy pieces for women's magazines about his cottage in Esher, his dog 'Mr Sponge' and such important topics as 'The Girl I Hope to Marry', 'Why I like Working with Women' and 'Should Wives have a Career?' He, too, had brought out a novel and, as luck would have it, it was exactly at this moment that he met Maugham, introduced over a game of bridge, Winn being a player of championship standard. 'I have been very fortunate in my life in regard to the sponsors whom I encountered at a crucial

---

★ Avery Hopwood (1882–1928) was a successful playwright of the American jazz age; Sidney Howard (1894–1946) was an English film actor.

moment,' he wrote in his autobiography. 'Soon after my first novel was published, I had the good fortune to come under the literary influence of Somerset Maugham.' Godfrey, like Beverley, was sexy and attractive, equally willing to oblige the great man, and equally unable to resist boasting about it afterwards. Unwisely he chose to brag of his triumph during a stay at the Villa Mauresque, while at a party at the house of a neighbour of Maugham's, the beautiful Lady Kenmare, whose guests found Godfrey's claim, 'that Willie had fallen for him in a big way and chased him all over London', distasteful in the extreme. It may be that ultimately Maugham came to hear of the betrayal: for some years he regarded Winn as a friend, invited him to stay, advised him on his writing and brought his work to the attention of well-disposed critics. But then something happened to sour the relationship, and in *Strictly Personal*, a wartime memoir published in 1941, Maugham drew a contemptuous portrait of Godfrey.★ In the relevant passage, excised from the British edition, Godfrey Winn appears as George Potter, who when first encountered seems 'an attractive young person', with a first novel that shows definite signs of promise. But then a few years later Maugham comes across the gossip column which Potter, now highly paid and famous, writes for one of the tabloids: 'it was sentimental slush . . . vulgar, snobbish, shatteringly moral and blatantly religious'. That Potter should waste his talent on such rubbish is bad enough, but what really shocks Maugham is that the young man believes every word of it. '[If] you were laughing up your sleeve all the time . . . I should think you a rogue, but it would make me laugh,' he tells him. 'But the tragic thing is that you write straight from the heart.'

Yet, if men like Nichols and Winn were taking advantage of Maugham, he was far too shrewd not to understand what they were after. He liked young people, liked to be surrounded by good-looking boys and was more than prepared to help them when he could. And he for his part was hardly hesitant in making his own wishes known: Constance Spry's brother, Gordon, remembered being taken aback by the unvarnished nature of the older man's approach; while the ballet-dancer Anton Dolin had great trouble with him at a party of Ivor Novello's at the Savoy. 'Don't be a fool,' said Novello as Dolin was trying to escape. 'It will mean a gold Cartier cigarette case tomorrow.' The famously charming, famously charismatic young peer Napier Alington was another of Maugham's conquests, 'a delicious creature', as Maugham described him after their

---

★ The unfortunate Godfrey was to be pilloried in print again, this time under his own name, when the following year he was skewered by Evelyn Waugh in *Put Out More Flags*.

night together. Beverley Nichols, who might be assumed to know what he was talking about, said of Maugham, 'He was the most sexually voracious man I've ever known'; and Hugh Walpole, himself no laggard on the homosexual scene, told Virginia Woolf that in his view Maugham was lucky not to have been 'jugged [imprisoned]. You don't know the kind of life that Willie has led. I do.' As Maugham was recognised wherever he went, his behaviour inevitably became the subject of gossip, and not only within the queer world. It was at about this time that some disquieting information on the matter came to the attention of none other than the Commissioner of the Metropolitan Police at Scotland Yard; alarmed by its content the Commissioner felt obliged to convey a message to F. H. Maugham, discreetly indicating that he should issue a warning to his younger brother. F.H., who was now a High Court judge and had recently been knighted, was extremely embarrassed by the situation; revolted by the whole subject of homosexuality, for years deliberately ignoring this aspect of his brother's nature, he found himself in the distasteful position of having to tell Willie straight that if he did not curtail his activities while in London he would almost certainly be arrested.

And in the main Maugham made his contacts discreetly, ideally in safe houses belonging to like-minded friends. It was in one of these, at a stag-dinner in George Street given by a wealthy collector, Robert Tritton, that in 1928 Maugham met a young man who was to become of crucial importance in his life. Alan Searle was a very youthful-looking twenty-three, a working-class boy from Bermondsey, the son of a Dutch tailor and cockney mother. With his dark eyes and thick curly black hair, Alan was well known in certain circles as 'a modified version of rough trade', a common, sexy boy who was also quick-witted, good-natured and eager to better himself. 'I was quite a dish,' as he himself said. His taste was for older men, and already he had an enthusiastic following among a number of distinguished figures. 'He was wonderful with elderly gentlemen,' the critic Raymond Mortimer recalled. Lytton Strachey was mad about Alan, called him his 'Bronzino boy',\* and wrote him a series of erotic letters; Reggie Turner fell for him, as later did the composer Lennox Berkeley and also Guy Little, a friend of Osbert Sitwell's, who was besotted by 'my starry eyed little friend . . . the darlingest pet in the world', as he dotingly addressed him. Alan was currently working at a picture gallery

---

\* A similar comparison is made in Proust's novel by the homosexual Baron de Charlus about the object of his infatuation, the violinist Morel: 'he has become so beautiful, he looks just like a Bronzino . . .' (*Remembrance of Things Past: The Captive* part 2, trans. C. K. Scott Moncrieff (Chatto & Windus 1941) p. 16).

in Brook Street, which is probably where he had met Bob Tritton. When on the day of the dinner one of Tritton's guests failed at the last moment, Alan had been whistled in to take his place, seated next to Maugham, the guest of honour. Maugham was immediately attracted by the cheeky cockney, and as was his custom began to question him about his life and ambitions. Alan told him he longed to travel, which naturally struck a chord with Maugham, who at once offered to take him on a continental tour, and suggested they leave the party together to discuss further plans. But Alan had already made an arrangement with another guest, Ivor Novello, and to Maugham's frustration it was with Novello that he went off that night. Next day Maugham sent a wire claiming to have been very upset by Alan's treatment of him, 'but if you'll have dinner with me tonight all is forgiven'. They dined at Quaglino's, an evening which, said Alan, 'changed the whole course of my life'. Not only did the two men become lovers ('Willie was the most marvellous lover I ever had') but that night saw the start of an association of supreme importance to them both, one which was to endure for nearly forty years.

At this stage there was no question of Alan taking Haxton's place. Maugham frequently had reason to make short trips within Europe, some-times to see one of his plays, more often just to wander round picture-galleries, neither occupation of particular interest to Gerald. Alan, on the other hand, was the most enthusiastic travelling companion and he had a passion for paintings. As he was also extremely practical, Maugham engaged Alan to act as his secretary, to deal with his correspondence in London when he was in the south of France, and to act as gentleman's gentleman on his visits to England. Before the divorce from Syrie, whenever Maugham stayed at Glebe Place it was Alan who accompanied him. The two men kept very much to themselves: 'the less Syrie knows about you the better,' Maugham had told him; but the King's Road housekeeper remembered Searle, remembered remarking how young he was, and that 'Mr Maugham wouldn't have anyone else to valet him and look after him.' Fascinated by Alan's background and history, Maugham questioned him about them in detail, anxious also to meet Alan's mother. But this proved impossible: she knew the kind of man who wants to take a young boy on a trip to Europe, she said, and declined the opportunity. Maugham was curious, too, about Searle's lovers, and expressed a particular wish to meet Lytton Strachey. Alan Pryce-Jones, a mutual friend, arranged a dinner for the four of them, far from successful as it turned out. Strachey was in a sour mood from the start, Searle remained silent, while Maugham failed to engage his audience with long-winded stories about Augustus Hare.

It was shortly after this awkward occasion that Maugham went to New York to oversee the production of a new play, *The Sacred Flame*. The idea for it had come from a situation within the family: the eldest of the Maugham brothers, Charles, had a nineteen-year-old son who at the age of twelve had fallen while climbing a tree and been semi-paralysed ever since, looked after by his mother Beldy with a devotion that had touched her brother-in-law. In *The Sacred Flame* the plot involves a young man badly wounded in the war and now confined to a wheelchair. Maurice, knowing that his condition is hopeless, is profoundly depressed and wishes only to die, although bravely determined to conceal his depression, especially from his adored wife Stella, whose life he feels he has ruined. Stella, no longer in love though loving her husband, has secretly been having an affair with Maurice's brother Colin, by whom she has become pregnant. Suddenly her carefully concealed condition is brutally revealed by Maurice's austere nurse, Nurse Wayland, who announces it to the family early in the morning, having just discovered that her patient has died during the night from an overdose of chloral. To everyone's horror, Nurse Wayland then charges Stella with having administered the drug. Although Stella continues to insist on her innocence, in the face of Nurse Wayland's vehement accusations her position begins to look increasingly untenable, until finally Maurice's mother, Mrs Tabret, admits it was she who gave her son the sleeping draught, honouring a private promise to help him die when his life became unendurable. It then appears that she had known all along of Stella's affair with Colin, for both of whom she has the greatest sympathy. 'Perhaps we should all look upon these matters very differently,' says Mrs Tabret, 'if our moral rules hadn't been made by persons who had forgotten the passion and the high spirits of youth. Do you think it so very wicked if two young things surrender to the instincts that nature has planted in them?'

*The Sacred Flame* is a strong and compelling drama, particularly noteworthy for the broad scope of the author's emotional intelligence. As ever Maugham is on the side of love,★ sexual, romantic and maternal, and against the narrow-minded morality of conventional society. Quietly subversive, he demonstrates his belief in the supreme importance of tolerance, even if its exercise goes against the accepted rules. Each member of the family loves and is concerned for the others, and ironically it is only the professional carer, the nurse, with her steely adherence to 'duty', who shows herself to

---

★ The title is taken from Coleridge's poem 'Love': 'All thoughts, all passions, all delights, / Whatever stirs this mortal frame, / All are but ministers of Love, / And feed his sacred flame.'

be narrow, vindictive and lacking in compassion. For Maugham himself a large part of his interest in the play was technical, experimenting with a move away from a naturalistic style and towards a more formal dialogue. 'Stage dialogue has been simplified out of all relation with life but that of the cocktail bar,' he wrote with a sideways swipe at the rising star Noël Coward.* It was his wish to redress the balance, 'to make my characters use not the words and expressions that they would have used in real life on the spur of the moment . . . but words and expressions that they might have used if they had had time to set their thoughts in order.' In the event this proved largely unworkable; at a time when Coward was delighting audiences with the brittle colloquialism of *The Vortex* and *Hay Fever*, the actors found Maugham's style ponderous and declamatory and he was obliged to make substantial revisions.

The play, co-produced by Messmore Kendall and Gilbert Miller, opened in New York on 19 November 1928, where, largely due to the last-minute substitution of an understudy in the part of Stella, it was given a poor reception: according to the *New York Times*, it was no more than 'another of Mr Maugham's highly cultivated shilling shockers'. Maugham was taken aback, and more than usually apprehensive about its staging in London. 'I know that I am for it,' he wrote to Alfred Sutro a couple of days before the first night at the Playhouse. 'There is nothing to do but set one's teeth & bear it. But it isn't pleasant.' However, on the evening of 8 February 1929, well before the final curtain it was clear that he had another hit on his hands. Gladys Cooper excelled herself as Stella, while Mary Jerrold and Clare Eames as Mrs Tabret and Nurse Wayland, reprising the parts they had played in New York, reached new heights under Raymond Massey's direction. 'Isn't it grand that *The Sacred Flame* should have turned out a success?' Maugham wrote to his niece Kate. 'After New York my heart was in my boots & I was trying to steel myself to accepting failure in London too: I could hardly believe my eyes when I opened the papers . . . next morning & found one laudatory notice after another.' After several weeks of sold-out performances, *Flame* was given a further boost when the Bishop of London denounced it as shockingly immoral, thus ensuring, as Gladys Cooper delightedly recalled, that 'our business went up by leaps and bounds, people besieging the box office for seats, and instead of the play coming off it got a new lease of life'.†

---

* 'Everyone but Somerset Maugham said that I was a second Somerset Maugham,' wrote Coward in his autobiography, *Present Indicative*. (Methuen 2004) p. 196.

† The same happened the following year when the play opened in Rome and was denounced by the Vatican on the front page of its official organ, *L'Osservatore Romano*.

It was to be a year before Maugham set himself to writing another play, a year spent mainly in travel – Denmark, Germany, Austria, Greece, Cyprus and Egypt – and in enjoying a long summer on the Riviera. It was only since the mid-1920s that the Riviera had become fashionable in the warmer months. For over fifty years the British, in the footsteps of Queen Victoria, had regarded the south of France as a winter resort, but recently, following the example set by a high-profile American contingent, people like Scott and Zelda Fitzgerald, the Cole Porters, Gerald and Sara Murphy, growing numbers of the smart set had begun to colonise the Côte d'Azur during July and August. The grand hotels in Nice and Cannes were now staying open all year, and at the end of 1922 a new fast train service was launched, the Calais–Méditerranée express, universally known as Le Train Bleu, after its smartly painted blue coaches.★ Richly panelled, velvet upholstered, famous for its luxury and haute cuisine, the first-class-only Blue Train left from Calais, stopped in Paris, then speeding through the night arrived the following morning in the south, letting off passengers at stations along the coast, Juan-les-Pins, Antibes, Monaco, before reaching its final destination at Menton near the Italian border. Maugham was often on the Blue Train, disembarking at Beaulieu, only a short drive from Cap Ferrat. In September 1928, at the end of his first full summer at the Mauresque, he described to Bert Alanson the busy social season just ended.

> For some reason (chiefly I suppose the wretched climate of the north of Europe) the Riviera has suddenly become the fashion; the hotels have been packed & the casinos making money hand over fist. There have been parties every day & everywhere, & it really looked as though all the world were assembled here. It has been amusing, but a trifle tiring. Now it is over; the smart world vanished as though by magic on the 1st of September & betook themselves in a vast body, with their motor-cars, maids & valets, to Biarritz. Sheep!

If hardly one of the great showplaces, like the Fiorentina at Saint-Hospice or the Château de l'Horizon near Cannes, the Villa Mauresque had nonetheless been transformed into a dwelling of impressive luxury. Approached along a narrow road bordered by pine trees and winding up to the top of the Cap, the Mauresque stood within gates on whose white plaster posts the familiar sign against the Evil Eye was picked out in red.

---

★ In 1924 there was a Diaghilev ballet inspired by the train. Based on a story by Cocteau, *Le Train Bleu* had a front-curtain by Picasso, music by Milhaud and costumes by Coco Chanel.

A short drive led up through terraced gardens to the white-painted house with its green shutters and tall green double doors. Immediately inside the front door was a black-floored, high-ceilinged hall, dominated by a Chinese figure of the goddess Kuan-Yin, brought back by Maugham from Peking. A large dark-green drawing-room was given a somewhat Baroque flavour by heavy Spanish furniture, blackamoor figures, gilded wooden chandeliers and Savonnerie carpets; over the fireplace was a magnificent gold eagle, wings outspread, and against the walls a pair of black lacquer cabinets containing oriental porcelain and four narrow book-cases decoratively carved; there were comfortable chairs, a couple of sofas, and a round table piled high with new books. The white-washed dining-room was comparatively small, with a Louis XVI table surrounded by small Directoire armchairs, and on the walls four paintings of white-skinned, coal-eyed girls by Marie Laurencin. Up the marble stairs with their white-and-yellow walls were the bedrooms and dressing-rooms, these plainly but beautifully appointed, with muslin curtains, white silk bedspreads and Chinese prints on the walls; each had a desk with a good supply of sharpened pencils, as well as books, fruit and flowers, bottles of mineral water, and a carved glass box of biscuits beside the bed. The bath-rooms were modern and luxurious, well stocked with piles of thick towels and with new soaps, oils and essences from Floris.

Maugham's own quarters were simple to the point of austerity. In his bedroom a narrow bed jutted out crossways from a corner near the window so that he could see the garden from his pillow; behind it stood the effigy of a Spanish saint, and built into one wall was a bookcase filled with the works of favourite authors such as Hazlitt, Samuel Butler and Henry James; there were also Grimms' *Fairy Tales*, the journals of Gide, Edward Lear's letters, poems by Yeats and the sonnets of Shakespeare. On the bureau beside his bed, next to the books, lacquered cigarette-box, matches, paper-knife and spectacles, there was a photograph of his mother. Above the bedroom floor was the flat roof reached by a wooden stair, and here, a structure standing alone, was Maugham's study. A large square room full of light, with windows on all sides, it had an open fireplace, bookcases, a comfortable sofa on which to read, and for a desk a big seventeenth-century Spanish refectory table, lowered by several inches to accommodate the writer's short stature; the window immediately above it, looking towards Nice and the Mediterranean, had been blocked up so that there would be no distraction from the view. There were only two paintings in the room, a head of Sue Jones by Gerald Kelly, and forming the middle panel of a triple window Gauguin's beautiful Tahitian Eve.

Maugham was pleased with this secluded refuge, as he was pleased with the whole house, which was at last exactly as he had envisaged it. 'I was prepared to spend the rest of my life there,' he wrote, 'and I was prepared to die in the painted bedstead in my bedroom. I sometimes crossed my hands and closed my eyes to imagine how I should look when at last I lay there dead.'

From the very beginning, Maugham was the most hospitable of hosts. Among the earliest visitors to the Villa Mauresque were Max Beerbohm, now living in Rapallo, an ageing dandy still speaking in the accents of the 1890s; H. G. Wells, who also had a house in the south of France; Arnold Bennett, sailing along the coast on his luxurious yacht; Walter Payne and his first wife Phil, Desmond MacCarthy, the Gerald Kellys, Maugham's American publisher Nelson Doubleday and his play-agent Golding Bright. It was Bright's wife, Mary Chavelita Bright, who described the experience of staying at the villa as 'the raffinement de luxe . . . [with] perfect unfussed service', an opinion endorsed by many others, that the Mauresque was 'a haven of comfort, good food, beauty and entertaining talk'. And indeed Maugham knew exactly how he wanted his household run and was prepared to go to considerable trouble and expense to achieve the highest standards. With a well-trained staff of thirteen, a butler, two footmen, a *femme de chambre* to look after the ladies, a chef, kitchen maid, chauffeur and six gardeners, the attention to detail was immaculate, the impression of ease and informality maintained by means of a discreet but tightly disciplined order behind the scenes. If guests arrived, as most of them did, by train, they were met at Beaulieu by Jean with the limousine and driven the short distance to the house. As the car drew up on the gravel, the front doors were opened by Ernest, the butler, and there in the hall would be Maugham, in open-necked shirt, white linen trousers and espadrilles, smiling, his arms outstretched in greeting. 'The arms would drop back again to the sides without contact,' as one of his neighbours, Rory Cameron, shrewdly observed, 'but it was meant as a welcoming gesture.' The new arrivals were then led out to the terrace for tea or a drink while their bags were unpacked and evening clothes laid out upstairs.

For visitors the days were leisurely and relaxed. Ladies breakfasted in bed, awakened by the light filtering through the mosquito net and a cooing voice – 'Bonjour, Madame. Madame a bien dormi?' – which accompanied the arrival of an exquisitely arranged breakfast tray, with coffee, croissant, fruit and fresh orange juice. Downstairs the men enjoyed a more substantial meal in the dining-room, often preceded by an early swim or game of tennis. Mornings were spent reading on the terrace, the air fragrant with the scent of orange and lemon blossom, or strolling in the garden, or basking on linen mattresses by the pool while watching the brilliant blue dragonflies skim the surface. The pool on one side was backed by a thick hedge of pink and white oleanders behind which was a dense screen of rock and pine trees, and on the other gave on to a glorious view over Villefranche Bay. It was here that most people congregated and where much of the day was spent, swimming and sunbathing, or if the sun became too hot lying in the shade provided by a little natural grotto formed in the rock. Near by was a bronze gong brought back from the East which was sounded twice a day to announce the hour of pre-prandial cocktails – an ice-cold Gibson, perhaps, or a very dry mint-flavoured martini. During the summer lunch and dinner were usually on the terrace, both rather formal meals of several courses served by the white-coated footmen supervised by Ernest. Wines and champagne were always plentiful and excellent, and the food delicious, classic French with an interesting American accent, most of the salads and vegetables grown in the garden. Lunch might be a clear white tomato broth, followed by Chicken Maryland and Pêche Melba; for dinner there might be eggs in aspic, a fillet of beef with sauce béarnaise, an exquisite brie *en gêlée*, followed by fresh figs, peaches or *fraises du bois*. One of Maugham's favourite dishes was corn-beef hash, the same corn-beef hash he had taught to his drunken cook when in Burma; and in later years a great *specialité de la maison* was an avocado ice-cream, a rich concoction of crushed avocado, Barbados rum, sugar and cream, the pears picked from trees grown from cuttings which Maugham had smuggled back in his golf-bag from California, reputedly the first avocados to be grown in France. With such cuisine, it is no wonder Maugham's guests enjoyed themselves. 'I am silent with pleasure at almost *every* dish that is put before me,' Desmond MacCarthy wrote to his wife during a stay at the Mauresque.

The infrastructure required to maintain such levels of comfort and efficiency demanded constant supervision; Maugham was the overseer, with Gerald responsible on a day-to-day basis for the smooth running of the house. It was Maugham who interviewed the cook after dinner every evening and ordered the meals for next day. Although he ate sparingly himself, he enjoyed and was interested in culinary matters and knew precisely how a dish should be. '[Willie] always had a genius for food,' said the very social Christabel Aberconway. The French chef at the Mauresque was superb, but after it was discovered that he was supplementing his salary by selling surplus produce from the kitchen, he was sacked and the Italian kitchen-maid, Annette Chiaramello, promoted to his place. Annette turned out to be an inspirational cook, and she and her employer made an ideal team, he bringing back descriptions of dishes encountered elsewhere, she delighting him by her perfectionism as well as by her invention and flair. This area apart, it was Haxton, 'the faithful watchdog', who was the majordomo: like Syrie, he was an excellent organiser and knew precisely what was wanted. As Maugham's secretary, part of the day was spent in his office immediately below Maugham's study, deciphering his employer's not always legible hand and typing up manuscript, as well as taking dictation for letters; he also dealt with the servants and made sure that the house-guests had everything they desired, ready to chat for hours by the pool, play billiards or tennis, arrange a shopping expedition to Cannes or Beaulieu, or at night a trip to the casinos in Nice and Monte Carlo. During the siesta hour Gerald, tall, angular, square-headed, in candy-pink shirt and shorts, would sit peacefully playing patience on the shady side of the terrace. Sometimes if the weather were fine he took the house-party out on the *Sara*, a comfortably converted old fishing-trawler kept anchored at Villefranche; after a couple of hours sailing the anchor was dropped so that everyone could swim before eating the delicious picnic loaded in hampers on board. A few of Maugham's friends privately detested Gerald ('He had about him an aura of corruption,' said one), but most found him a great asset. 'Haxton was a most amiable creature,' the director George Cukor recalled. '[He] was very charming and sociable and he made things easy for Maugham.' As long as he was sober he was an engaging, high-spirited companion, 'very jolly and delightful, the life and soul of the party', according to Raymond Mortimer, while another Mauresque regular, Arthur Marshall, thought that Gerald 'charmed the birds from the trees'. 'It was Gerald Haxton', wrote Maugham's nephew Robin, 'who was largely responsible for the atmosphere of happiness and comfort' at the Villa Mauresque.

Maugham was a genial host, a benign presence whose formidable discipline was carefully concealed beneath an apparent ease of manner. In a sense, the way of life at the Mauresque summed up the two sides of his nature, on one side *luxe* and warmth and sensuousness, on the other the austerity of the artist and a rigorous self-control. While his guests slept late and idled by the pool, for Maugham the daily routine was strict and unvarying, and nothing was allowed to disarrange it. Every morning he awoke early and spent the first hour or so reading before his breakfast was brought to him in bed, with the newspaper which he read while smoking his one pipe of the day. At 8.30 he had his bath, shaving while doing so, and dressed. At about 9.00, he retired to his roof-top retreat, silent, solitary and safe, and there he remained until just after 12.30 when he came downstairs to join his guests for a cocktail, never more than one, on the terrace before lunch. After lunch he retired for a nap and more reading, reappearing again about four to suggest tennis or golf, a swim or a game of cards before tea. He loved to walk along the grassy, tree-shaded paths accompanied by his beloved dachshunds, all given the names of characters in Wagnerian opera, the first called Elsa after the heroine of Lohengrin; it always upset Maugham, a great animal-lover, when preparing to leave for London* to see the little dogs climb into his empty suitcases, hoping not to be left behind. At some point there would be a session with Gerald, dictating replies to his copious correspondence, although much of this he answered himself, scrupulously replying in long-hand to his often enormous fan mail. Dinner was preceded by more cocktails, with everyone in evening dress, unless he and Haxton were alone or with one or two close friends when Maugham sometimes favoured more unconventional garb, for instance a black Mandarin's robe brought back from China, a costume in which to some he appeared curiously simian, his diminutive figure swamped by the swathes of heavy silk. Conversation was usually lively thanks to quantities of pink champagne and the host's skill at encouraging others to talk. 'Fundamentally,' said Rory Cameron, 'Maugham was a formal man and not given to confidences'; he could tell a good personal anecdote when required, but it was usually a polished performance, rarely the result of spontaneous expression. After dinner there was a rubber or two of bridge over a cigar, following which Gerald would take a group off for some serious gambling. Maugham rarely accompanied them, retiring to bed by 11.00 in order to be on form for the next morning's work.

For Maugham writing was not just what he did: it was where he lived. 'I have never been able to persuade myself that anything else mattered,' he wrote in The Summing Up. While at work he was completely in control, in a world of his own making, and in extreme old age he stated that the happiest hours of his life had been experienced while seated at his desk when his writing was going well, '[and] word followed word till the luncheon gong forced me to put an end to the day's work'. His strict adherence to only three hours a day, no more, no less, derived, rather curiously, from the example set by Charles Darwin. '[As Darwin] never worked more than three hours a day and yet proceeded to revolutionise

* Britain imposed strict quarantine laws, which made it impracticable to bring animals into the country for short visits.

biological science,' Maugham explained, 'I decided I could probably achieve what I wanted to achieve by the same amount of labour.' The tools of his trade were simple, a fountain-pen specially designed with a thick collar to give added weight, a bottle of black ink and white unlined paper purchased from the Times Bookshop, of which there was always a neat stack on his desk. He wore horn-rimmed reading spectacles, and chain-smoked as he worked; in later years he took to wearing a pink elastic mitten with zip fasteners designed to protect against repetitive strain and poor circulation. While Maugham's productivity was unceasing, he always made a point of differentiating between invention and imagination. 'I have always had more stories in my head than I ever had time to write,' he said,

> [but] though I have had variety of invention . . . I have had small power
> of imagination. I have taken living people and put them into the situ-
> ations, tragic or comic, that their characters suggested. I might well say
> that they invented their own stories. I have been incapable of those great,
> sustained flights that carry the author on broad pinions into a celestial
> sphere. My fancy, never very strong, has been hampered by my sense of
> probability.

The countless stories in his head meant he was never at a loss for a subject; indeed most of his life was passed in a state of possession, with ideas for plays, novels and stories dominating his thoughts, not letting him rest till he had written them down. Because he lived with his themes and characters for months beforehand, sometimes years, there was never any need for an outline, and when eventually he was ready to begin he wrote fast, not stopping for anything. While in the middle of a novel, Maugham said, his characters were more real to him than the characters of real life; he inhabited a different dimension, more vivid and more meaningful than the physical world outside.

With the first draft complete, the work of revision followed. 'Then I go over very carefully all I have written & get order into the thing, look for the right words, bother myself with euphony, shorten, make what was obscure clear.' The words did not always flow and sometimes a single page had to be written and rewritten, but, however difficult, the experience never failed to be wholly absorbing. Yet in the final analysis the actual process of creation, for Maugham 'the most enthralling of human activities', was impossible to pin down. As many writers have attested, the precise moment of alchemical reaction remains a mystery, explicable only as the work of the subconscious, of 'the useful little imp that dwells in your fountain pen and does for you all your best writing'. Once he had rid himself of the story by putting it on paper, once the text was revised, the proofs corrected, the final version edited and approved, there was the excitement of seeing the work in print – a brief excitement, however, as by the time the book was published and in the shops, 'I am no longer interested in it and I don't really care what people say about it.'

After the intense mental activity of the morning's writing, Maugham often found the world outside his workroom rather colourless by comparison, and 'anything you do in the remaining hours of the day seems a little pale and flat'. Sometimes when he came downstairs to join the others for lunch it was evident his mind was elsewhere; always punctilious in making the proper enquiries about how everyone had slept and breakfasted, and what plans had been made for the afternoon, yet he could seem preoccupied, and his habit of encouraging others to talk was as much to provide himself with space for private reflection as to fulfil his duties as host.

It was not long after moving into the Villa Mauresque that Maugham in 1929 began work on a novel, his first since *The Painted Veil* four years before. At last in possession of his own domain, free after years of a miserable marriage, Maugham found that his imagination was all at once thronged with the places and people of his distant childhood: sitting in his study overlooking the Mediterranean his mind's eye rested on the Kentish countryside of his boyhood and the wind-blown streets of Whitstable; his thoughts were full of his uncle and aunt and the vicarage and, finally released from the compulsion to write about Syrie, he returned to memories of the lovely, loving, promiscuous Sue Jones, 'who had lingered in my mind for the last fifteen years and whom I could never till now find a way of disposing of'. In this new work, to be entitled *Cakes and Ale*,★ Sue appears as Rosie, the first wife of a famous novelist, Edward Driffield, who, once a simple countryman, is now a greatly revered national figure. On the book's publication, the inspiration for Driffield was immediately identified as Thomas Hardy, a fact at the time energetically denied by the author. 'I swear I never thought of Hardy at all when

---

★ From *Twelfth Night*, Act II, scene 3:
  SIR TOBY BELCH: Dost thou think, because thou art virtuous, there shall be no
    more cakes and ale?
In a letter to the critic Paul Dottin written shortly after the novel's publication Maugham explained, 'the title is supposed to suggest the gaiety of life which my heroine's attitude at all events exemplified. If I had thought of it I might very well have called it "Beer and Skittles"' (1.1.31 HRHRC).

writing the book,' Maugham told the *Daily Telegraph*, although later he became more equivocal when questioned on the subject. 'Oh, I don't know. I've denied it and admitted it and denied it . . . [There] might have been some small thread of him [Hardy] in the fabric. In any case, what does it matter?'

Like most novelists Maugham was irritated by attempts to identify the 'real' people behind his fictional characters; he was ready to admit that of course his characters were drawn from life – where else? – but insisted on making the point that 'by the time I have finished with them little remains of the persons who served as my models'. Yet in Maugham's case this is less than completely accurate: far more than most writers he made use of actual people with little alteration, putting them on to the page very much as they were in life, with small attempt at disguise. And nowhere in his work is this practice of verisimilitude more striking, indeed more notorious, than in *Cakes and Ale*. With the character of Edward Driffield, the parallels with Hardy (who, significantly, had died in January 1928, not long before Maugham began writing his novel) are too conspicuous to be convincingly denied: both men came from humble backgrounds, both wrote novels about simple folk, both had lower-middle-class, socially ambitious second wives,\* both in old age retired to their native counties, Hardy to Dorset, Driffield to Kent. Driffield at Ferne Court, like Hardy at Max Gate, became an object of pilgrimage to the literary, fashionable world; both were awarded the Order of Merit.

By early summer the book was almost done, Maugham on 30 May writing cheerfully to Gerald Kelly that 'I am just finishing a novel y-clept *Cakes & Ale* or *The Skeleton in the Cupboard*.' His high spirits were justified for here Maugham is at the height of his powers, the novel a masterly work, technically dextrous and written in a sinuous, silky prose ideally adapted to the author's sardonic view of the world. Cleverly constructed, the characterisation is vivid, the dialogue flawless, the whole shot through with a ruthlessness and wit that is irresistibly enjoyable. Except for a couple of short passages of self-conscious jocularity which slightly impede the flow, this is Maugham at his most seamless and seductive

---

\* In 1944 Logan Pearsall Smith discussing *Cakes and Ale* with Hugh Trevor-Roper wrote, 'The second Mrs Driffield is a photo straight from life. Shortly after the book was published I sat by a "Mrs Thomas Hardy" at a luncheon party in Lady Noble's palace and this female's talk about social life in Dorsetshire seemed to come so directly word for word out of *Cakes and Ale* that I honestly believe that she was a sham Mrs Hardy acting the part for fun' (Edwin Tribble (ed.) *A Chime of Words: The Letters of Logan Pearsall Smith* (Ticknor & Fields 1984) p. 86).

best. From the very first sentence, written in that familiar conversational style, with its air of urbane detachment, the reader is caught. 'I have noticed that when someone asks for you on the telephone and, finding you out, leaves a message begging you to call him up the moment you come in, as it's important, the matter is more often important to him than to you,' he begins in a deliberately casual manner. 'So when I got back to my lodgings with just enough time to have a drink, a cigarette, and to read my paper before dressing for dinner, and was told by Miss Fellows, my landlady, that Mr Alroy Kear wished me to ring him up at once, I felt that I could safely ignore his request.'

The story is told in the first person, the narrator once again William ('Willie') Ashenden, a literary gentleman, to all intents and purposes the author himself. Ashenden is invited to lunch by an old friend and fellow writer, Alroy Kear, a boastful, bumptious, self-satisfied fellow who has made a successful career out of his second-rate novels by assiduously sucking up to critics and cultivating the prominent. Kear has just been commissioned to write the life of the famous novelist, the late Edward Driffield, whom Ashenden knew when he was a boy living with his uncle and aunt at Blackstable in Kent. Kear is anxious for details, and his questioning takes Ashenden back to memories of his early life, of his boyhood at the vicarage with his uncle Henry and aunt Sophie, and of his friendship with Driffield and his much younger wife, Rosie. They first meet after Willie Ashenden is given a bicycle: unsuccessfully trying to master it, he runs, literally, into the Driffields. Driffield kindly offers to teach him how to ride, and Willie, a priggish boy, accepts with some reluctance, aware that the couple are socially beneath him, Driffield the son of a local bailiff and Rosie an ex-barmaid known to have been no better than she should be. It is not long, however, before Willie is won over by Driffield's amiability and by Mrs Driffield's sweet nature and sensual beauty, and he soon becomes a regular at the hearty teas and sing-songs held at their cosy cottage. Idolising Rosie, he loyally dismisses the ill-natured gossip he hears about her, and it is thus a shock when he comes across her making love in a hedgerow with the Blackstable coal-merchant, a colourful, swaggering character known in the neighbourhood as 'Lord' George Kemp.* It is soon after this that the Driffields, heavily in debt, do a moonlight flit and disappear from Blackstable.

Some years later Ashenden, now a medical student in London, by chance meets Rosie in the street. Driffield is beginning to earn a considerable

---

* Mr F. Kemp and Mr C. M. Driffield had both been members of the Whitstable parish council under the Rev. Henry Maugham.

reputation as a novelist, and it is in the Driffields' modest lodgings off the Vauxhall Bridge Road that Ashenden meets an interesting group of young writers, actors and musicians, as well as a lady highly regarded in society as a distinguished literary patron. Mrs Barton Trafford, it appears, has marked Edward Driffield out for great things, promoting him vigorously to the critics, showing him off to her fashionable friends. Rosie, so sexy, so common, is a problem, of course (the skeleton in the cupboard), but a problem with which Mrs Trafford knows exactly how to cope. '[Her] manner with Mrs Driffield was perfect . . . She was cordial, playful, and gently determined to put her at her ease. It was strange that Rosie could not bear her.' Ashenden becomes infatuated with Rosie, and they enjoy a brief affair, important to Ashenden if not to Rosie who, generous as ever, sleeps with him out of kindness. By now Ashenden has come to accept Rosie's promiscuity, but he is nonetheless stunned when Rosie suddenly disappears, running off with none other than the Blackstable coal-merchant Lord George. Abandoned by his wife, Driffield, frail and elderly, allows himself to be wholly taken over by the energetic Mrs Trafford, who engineers his reputation to ever greater heights, even continuing her support after he moves back to Kent and, shockingly, marries his nurse. It is Amy, the second Mrs Driffield, a tireless keeper of the flame, who after her husband's death, and assuming that Rosie, too, has died, commissions Alroy Kear to write the biography. Kear, smugly satisfied to have landed such a plum job, takes Ashenden down to Ferne Court, the Driffields' house outside Blackstable, where the widow proudly displays the great writer's study, no longer a workroom but a showplace. Harking back to a scarring incident with Syrie, Maugham has Kear explain how Amy had had to replace with new all the awful old furniture Driffield brought with him.

> 'She told me the hardest job she had was with his writing-desk. I don't know whether you've noticed the one there is in his study now. It's a very good period piece . . . Well, he had a horrible American roll-top desk. He'd had it for years, and he'd written a dozen books on it, and he simply wouldn't part with it . . . You must get Amy to tell you the story how she managed to get rid of it in the end. It's really priceless. She's a remarkable woman, you know; she generally gets her own way.'
>
> 'I've noticed,' I said.

Shortly afterwards Ashenden leaves for New York to oversee the production of a new play, and it is here that he meets Rosie for the last time, a contented widow in her seventies, stout, red-faced, white-haired, but with the same sweet smile. That she is alive and in full possession of the facts about her first husband's life is information unlikely to be passed on to Alroy Kear.

In a preface to a later edition of *Cakes and Ale*, Maugham wrote, 'I had long had in mind the character of Rosie. I had wanted for years to write about her, but the opportunity never presented itself.' There is no doubt that he had continued to think about Sue after she refused his proposal all those years ago in Chicago; and there is even a small but crucial indication that they met at least once after this, by which time Sue, married to Angus McDonnell, had turned into the stout, red-faced woman described in the novel. In half a sentence in *The Gentleman in the Parlour* Maugham writes that while riding through the Shan States his thoughts turned to 'the yellow hair of a girl with a sweet smile, hair now grey and shingled'. Now, in this intensely autobiographical novel, Maugham distils the essence of his affair with Sue, reproducing on the page, as Gerald Kelly had done on canvas, her voluptuous blonde beauty, as well as her amorousness and calm good nature. The scene in which Willie Ashenden for the first time makes love to Rosie and breaks down in tears, overwhelmed by emotion, has all the signs of having been drawn from life, even down to such details as Rosie wrapping her corsets in newspaper before slipping out of the house at dawn the next morning. Willie's childhood and adolescence in Blackstable, his love of the Kentish countryside, his relations with his uncle and aunt, all cover much the same ground as *Of Human Bondage*, although here the mood is softer and more benevolent, the Vicar and his wife drawn with humour and something almost amounting to affection. The portrait of Willie himself is enormously engaging, a touching young man, conventional, slightly snobbish, very conscious of his dignity and of the dashing figure he believes himself to cut in his smart new clothes. Like Maugham, Ashenden goes to London to study medicine, lodging in Vincent Square with a warmhearted landlady, going on, like Maugham, to become a writer, and eventually achieving considerable distinction.

It is in his delineation of the London literary world that Maugham as social satirist shows himself at his most lethal and incisive. Ashenden's entry on to the scene compares closely with that of the author's, when as a very young man he was invited to literary teas in South Kensington, to Edmund Gosse's 'at homes' in Hanover Terrace, and under the wing of Augustus Hare to dinner with hostesses such as Lady St Helier: it was while dining with Lady St Helier in Portland Place that in 1908 he had met Thomas Hardy. In *Cakes and Ale* there is more than a vestige of the indefatigable Lady St Helier in the character of Lady Hodmarsh, 'who neither read the books nor looked at the pictures of the people to whom she offered hospitality, but she liked their company and enjoyed the feeling it gave her of being in the artistic know'. Gosse and Hare combine in the person of the influential critic Allgood Newton, who 'was very amiable to the authors he met . . . and said charming and flattering things to them, but when they were gone he was very amusing at their expense . . . no one could with more point tell a malicious story about a friend'. Recalling the time when Hare rebuked him for his vulgarity in referring to an omnibus as a bus, Maugham has this exchange between Ashenden and Allgood Newton. 'I'm going to take a bus,' says Ashenden on leaving a tea-party at the Barton Traffords'. 'Oh?' replies Newton. 'Had you proposed to go by hansom I was going to ask you to be good enough to drop me on your way, but if you are going to use the homely conveyance which I, in my old-fashioned manner, still prefer to call an omnibus, I shall hoist my unwieldy carcase into a four-wheeler.'

The queen of the metropolitan literati is the influential Mrs Trafford, wife of an exquisitely scholarly civil servant; she is regarded with deference, in particular for her close friendship with a very famous writer indeed, whose letters to her after his demise Mrs Trafford had graciously allowed to be published, her husband following up with an elegant biography, 'in which he showed quite definitely how great a part of the writer's genius was due to his wife's influence'. The originals of the Barton Traffords were a prominent pair, the Sidney Colvins, he the director of the Fitzwilliam Museum in Cambridge, she an intimate friend of Robert Louis Stevenson; as in the novel, after Stevenson's death Colvin produced an edition of his letters, and in such manner as to shed the most flattering light upon his wife.

The Colvins, together with Gosse, Hare and Lady St Helier, had all been leading members of the cultural establishment, and as such tempting targets to the irreverent streak in Maugham's nature. And yet his treatment of them is positively benign compared to that meted out to a fellow writer, his old friend Hugh Walpole. By 1930 Walpole, too, was a member of the literary elite, the self-appointed 'viceroy of the literary world'. Bluff, self-important, phenomenally industrious, he was the author of numerous popular novels, chairman of the Book Society, an indefatigable lecturer in Britain and the United States, busy on numerous boards and committees, a devoted friend to the famous (who, however, quickly found themselves dropped if their reputations declined), and above all an assiduous promoter of his own career. Maugham, who had known him well since their time in Petrograd during the war, had grown quite fond of old Hugh, while at the same time regarding him as eminently ridiculous (an attitude clearly conveyed in his portrayal of Walpole as Dirk Stroeve in *The Moon and Sixpence*). In recent years, however, the ruthlessness of Walpole's self-promotion coupled with a lack of generosity – 'he was mean as cat's meat', said Maugham – had begun to repel him. Hugh, it seems, had behaved badly to a couple of good friends of Maugham's, Gerald Kelly being one; he had also, in the course of a recent and prestigious Cambridge lecture, omitted Maugham's name from a list of well-regarded contemporary novelists; and yet in none of these instances does the offence seem sufficient to inspire such a deadly attack: there must, surely, have been something more at the bottom of it. Perhaps a clue lies in a brief reference to the subject by the thriller-writer Eric Ambler, describing a dinner-party given by the publisher A. S. Frere in Albany. Maugham was present, and so were Noël Coward and J. B. Priestley. In the course of the evening somebody mentioned Walpole. 'I knew Hugh Walpole for a great many years,' said Maugham.

> 'I can tell you from my own knowledge that he behaved disgracefully to several talented young writers, one of whom I knew personally. Hugh Walpole ruined his life.'
> He glowered at us. His meaning was plain. We all knew perfectly well that what he was really talking about was not a talented writer but a stolen boyfriend, an unrequited love and an old canker of jealousy . . .

Maugham's depiction of Walpole as the self-serving Alroy Kear, hearty, humourless and vain, is devastatingly true to life. '[I had] a considerable affection for Roy,' Ashenden begins innocently enough, before going on to describe with relish the man in all his glorious fatuity.

> Than Roy no one could show a more genuine cordiality to a fellow novelist whose name was on everybody's lips, but no one could more genially turn a cold shoulder on him when idleness, failure, or someone else's success had cast a shade on his notoriety . . . I could think of no one among my contemporaries who had achieved so considerable a position on so little talent.

Like Walpole, Alroy Kear is desperate to be liked, anxious to be a friend to all the world so that nothing will threaten his standing as a good fellow. When he describes the important biography he plans about Driffield, Ashenden can see all too clearly the sort of oleaginous hagiography it will turn out to be. 'I'll tell you the sort of book I want to write,' says Roy, 'a sort of intimate life, with a lot of those little details that make people feel warm inside, you know, and then woven in with this a really exhaustive criticism of his literary work, not ponderous, of course, but although sympathetic, searching . . .' Would it not be more interesting to draw the man warts and all, Ashenden asks?

> 'Oh, I couldn't . . . I must behave like a gentleman.'
>
> 'It's very hard to be a gentleman and a writer.'
>
> 'I don't see why . . . Of course I don't deny that if I were thoroughly unscrupulous I could make a sensation . . . [but] they'd only say I was imitating Lytton Strachey. No. I think I shall do much better to be allusive and charming and rather subtle, you know the sort of thing, and tender.'

Of Alroy Kear's private life Ashenden is comparatively discreet, although there was a great deal more he could have said as Walpole was as boastful about his sexual conquests as about everything else. After a vigorously active young manhood Hugh in middle age had contentedly settled down with a married policeman; in the past, however, Maugham had had to listen to a great deal about Hugh's affairs, in particular about his frustrating passion for the famous, and very handsome, Danish tenor Lauritz Melchior, an episode obliquely referred to in the novel thus:

> [Alroy Kear's] views on marriage were abstract, for he had successfully evaded the state which so many artists have found difficult to reconcile with the arduous pursuit of their calling. It was generally known that he had for some years cherished a hopeless passion for a married woman of rank, and though he never spoke of her but with chivalrous admiration, it was understood that she had treated him with harshness.

To readers who had no personal acquaintance with Hugh Walpole this would have meant very little, but to Hugh himself it was an outrageous betrayal of confidence, proof positive of the deliberate nature of Maugham's calumny.

*Cakes and Ale*, ranked by Maugham as the favourite among his novels, was published by Heinemann on 29 September 1930, and four days later by Doubleday, Doran in New York. A new novel by Somerset Maugham was naturally a noteworthy event; no one, however, could have foreseen the brouhaha that broke out among the cognoscenti over the caricature of Walpole as Alroy Kear, described by one commentator as 'one of the most memorable literary dissections since Dickens's treatment of Leigh Hunt as Mr Skimpole in *Bleak House*'. Hugh himself, completely unaware, had received an advance copy a few days before publication. On 25 September, he had come back in the morning in a very happy mood from a visit to Cambridge, attended a meeting of the Book Society, then dined with a friend with whom he had gone to the theatre. Returning home after midnight, he had started to undress when he caught sight of Maugham's book on his bedside table. Sitting on the edge of his bed in his pyjamas he idly picked it up and began to read. 'Read on with increasing horror,' he recorded in his diary. 'Unmistakable portrait of myself. Never slept!' At 4.00 a.m., by now in a frenzy, he telephoned Maugham's publisher, A. S. Frere, imploring him to stop publication, which Frere told him he was unable to do. 'I can't see any resemblance to you in any of the characters,' he assured him. All the next day, 'dreadfully upset', Walpole spent calling on his friends, desperate to know what was being said. Most did their best to persuade him he was imagining it, while others swore that Maugham was already strenuously denying the rumour. 'But how can he,' wailed Hugh, 'when there are in one conversation the very accents of my voice? . . . He has used so many little friendly things and twisted them round.'

Having exposed his wounds so publicly, Walpole had to suffer the further torment of knowing that everyone was talking about it, that there was much gloating, by friend and enemy alike, over his distress. *Cakes and Ale* 'contains a most envenomed portrait of Hugh Walpole, who is out of his mind with agitation and horror', wrote Lytton Strachey to his sister, Dorothy Bussy, adding delightedly, 'It is a very amusing book'; E. M. Forster in a letter to Maugham himself admitted that 'your laudable fiendishness fascinates me more than I can say'; Eddie Marsh gleefully observed that 'I hear poor Hugh says it has finished him'; Logan Pearsall Smith, in a wickedly apt metaphor, described the novel as 'the red-hot poker that killed Hugh Walpole', while Arnold Bennett made matters even worse by insisting that the portrait was not malicious at all, but 'thoroughly just, accurate and benevolent'. The general view was that that ass Walpole had had it coming – he 'cried aloud to be caricatured', said Beverley Nichols – and few blamed Maugham for succumbing to temptation. In the words of the philosopher Isaiah Berlin, 'I can see why Maugham, why any sharp toothed person, could not resist the temptation of getting his teeth into flesh so pink & innocent, so obviously made for cannibals.'

During October numbers of reviews appeared on both sides of the Atlantic, most of them adulatory, even if several critics claimed to be taken aback by the author's blatant subjectivity. 'No English writer is more transparently, more unblushingly autobiographic than Somerset Maugham,' wrote Leslie A. Marchand in the *New York Times*. In the *Graphic* Evelyn Waugh (whose *Vile Bodies* appeared the same year) praised Maugham for his 'supreme adroitness and ease . . . I do not know of any living writer who seems to have his work so much *under control*.' Although he had one significant reservation – Maugham's 'diplomatic polish', he said, 'makes impossible for him any of those sudden transcendent flashes of passion and beauty which less competent novelists occasionally attain' – Waugh nonetheless applauds his extraordinary technical dexterity: 'he is a master for creating the appetite for information, of withholding it until the right moment, and then providing it surprisingly'. As time passed admiration for the novel continued to grow. Desmond MacCarthy writing in 1934 called *Cakes and Ale* 'a model of construction', and the character of Rosie a great artistic achievement. In the second half of the century Gore Vidal regarded it as a 'perfect novel', while Anthony Burgess described the work as 'superb . . . [as well as] a textbook of literary criticism'.

In print no one was so tactless as to notice any possible similarity between Hugh Walpole and Alroy Kear: nearly everyone, however, remarked, mostly with disapproval, on the strong resemblance between Edward Driffield and the late, great Thomas Hardy. Disgracefully, Ashenden in the novel shows little admiration for Driffield's oeuvre, which shows some striking similarities with that of Hardy. '[Driffield] gave you the impression of writing with the stub of a blunt pencil,' says Ashenden. '[My] heart sank when he led me into the forecastle of a sailing ship or the taproom of a public-house, and I knew I was in for half a dozen pages in dialect of facetious comment on life, ethics, and immortality.' Such unreverent opinion was considered an outrage, and 'Trampling on Thomas Hardy's Grave', 'Hitting Below the Shroud' and 'Grave Profaned by Literary Ghoul' were typical of some of the headlines in the press. When Walpole finally got up the courage to write to Maugham, complaining of the cruel treatment he had received at his old friend's hands, Maugham was able to use Hardy as a decoy. 'I am really very unlucky,' his letter began.

> As you may have seen I have been attacked in the papers because they think my old man is intended to be a portrait of Hardy. It is absurd. The only grounds are that both died old, received the O.M. & were married twice. *You* know that for my story I needed this & that there is nothing of Hardy in my character. Now I have your letter. I cannot say I was surprised to receive it because I had heard from Charlie Evans [at Heinemann] . . . it had never occurred to him that there was any resemblance between the Alroy Kear of my novel & you; and when he spoke to me about it I was able very honestly to assure him that nothing had been further from my thoughts than to describe you . . .
>     . . . Alroy Kear . . . is made up of a dozen people and the greater part of him is myself. There is more of me in him than of any writer I know.

I suggest that if there is anything in him that you recognise it is because to a great or less extent we are all the same . . .

In his reply to this deeply disingenuous explanation,* Walpole wrote that of course he accepted Maugham's word on the matter, although in truth he did nothing of the sort. He continued to agonise over the subject, rehearsing it again and again to anyone who would listen. The following month he went to tea with Virginia Woolf, who described Hugh as 'piteous, writhing & wincing & ridiculous' in her diary. 'Indeed it was a clever piece of torture,' she wrote of his 'flaying alive' in *Cakes and Ale*.

Hugh palpably exposed as the hypocritical booming thick skinned popular novelist . . . who is thick fingered & insensitive in every department. But said Hugh, turning round on his bed of thorns again & yet again, & pressing them further & further in, 'That's not what I mind so much. What I mind are a few little things – little things that Willie & I had together – only he and I knew – those he has put into print. That's what I cant get over . . . And he wrote to me & said he could not believe that I could be hurt. He said he had written without a thought of me. But that letter is almost worse than the book.'

By the end of the year the fuss had largely died down, to the relief of both parties. The relationship between the two men continued amicable, at least on the surface: when Hugh's new novel, *Judith Paris*, came out the following summer Maugham sent him a jokey telegram of congratulation signed, 'ALROY MAUGHAM'. But then the affair blew up again in May 1931 with the publication in America of a scurrilous piece of fiction, *Gin and Bitters*, which was an overt attack on Maugham. The author, disguised under the pseudonym 'A. Riposte', was at first assumed to be Walpole, but in fact was a prolific if little-known writer, Elinor Mordaunt, née Evelyn Clowes. A friend of the second Mrs Hardy, who had been bitterly hurt by *Cakes and Ale*,† Mordaunt had decided to retaliate by drawing an instantly recognisable, deeply offensive portrait of Somerset Maugham in the guise of the famous novelist, Leverson Hurle. Mordaunt had travelled widely in the Far East, which gave some measure

---

* 'Hugh was a ridiculous creature and I certainly had him in mind when I wrote *Cakes and Ale*,' Maugham admitted in a letter written in 1961, long after Walpole's death (to Myrick Land 6.9.61 Berg). And in a preface to the 1950 edition of *Cakes and Ale* (Random House), he states, 'It was true that I had had Hugh Walpole in mind when I devised the character to whom I gave the name of Alroy Kear.'

† Maugham had been supplied with quantities of accurate detail about the Hardys and about the social and domestic life at Max Gate by several visitors to the house, among them Desmond MacCarthy and Siegfried Sassoon.

of credibility to an otherwise feeble story, but as she had never met Maugham and clearly knew nothing about him that was not in the public domain, he at first took little interest in the matter. But then it appeared that the book, under the title *Full Circle*, was now to be published in England, and not only that but by Maugham's publisher Heinemann. Understandably reluctant to offend their bestselling author, Heinemann offered to suppress it; Walpole, too, appalled by the prospect of the whole affair being given a new airing, begged Maugham to take out an injunction; but it was not until F. H. Maugham, alarmed by the libellous nature of the text, strongly advised his brother to take action that Maugham decided to issue a writ. By this time the book had been taken over by another firm, Martin Secker, who found themselves in the unfortunate position of having to withdraw it from circulation shortly after publication following the receipt of a threatening letter from Maugham's solicitors.

Within a surprisingly short time Walpole succeeded in convincing himself that after all there was little similarity between himself and Alroy Kear, although of course he could understand how a popular and successful figure such as himself might appear 'to a cynic and an uneasy unhappy man like Willie'. Yet despite these consoling arguments his standing in the eyes of the world never recovered from Maugham's portrayal, and after the publication of *Cakes and Ale* there were few in literary London who regarded either the man or his work with much respect: when in 1937 Walpole finally received his longed-for knighthood the wits all said it was a consolation prize for *Cakes and Ale*. Admiration for the novel, however, continued to spread. '[After *Cakes and Ale*] Maugham's reputation as a novelist had no immediate parallel,' wrote the critic Frank Swinnerton. 'Within a few months of its publication all active novel-writers were considerably his juniors.'

# 12

# Master Hacky

*Cakes and Ale* was published in 1930 at the start of a decade that was to bring turmoil to the Western world, but for Maugham it was a period of ever increasing fame and prosperity. On 25 October 1929, subsequently known as Black Thursday, the American stock market crashed, heralding the start of the Great Depression, during which millions lost their livelihoods. Maugham, however, came through relatively unscathed, his investments carefully tended by Bert Alanson. 'As what I have was invested in gilt-edged securities,' he told Messmore Kendall, 'I do not care and am prepared to wait till things right themselves again.' Everywhere there were signs of retrenchment, with theatre audiences falling off and book and magazine sales disastrously in decline; and yet Maugham, as though he possessed some magic amulet, remained almost unaffected. His plays continued to be produced, not only in Britain and America but globally, and for his stories he was now paid by *Cosmopolitan* and *Nash's* the astronomical sum of a dollar a word. With his publishers, too, he was exceptionally fortunate. The Depression created a crisis in the publishing industry, and yet on both sides of the Atlantic Maugham's publishers were among the few who continued to flourish. Heinemann, under the joint directorship of Charles Evans and A. S. Frere, remained profitable and strong, while in the States the merger in 1927 of Doubleday with George Doran had resulted in the creation of one of the most distinguished imprints in America. In 1928 Nelson Doubleday, son of the firm's founder, had been elected president, and under his dynamic leadership Doubleday, Doran by the early 1930s had grown into the largest publishing company in the English-speaking world.

Both Frere and Nelson Doubleday became personal friends of Maugham. Frere, small, energetic, in some ways a mysterious man, evasive about his early years, had great charm as well as a genuine love and wide knowledge of literature; he was sociable and counted many writers among his close acquaintance. 'He was warm, affectionate, generous and stimulating,' said Frere of his famous author. 'All he asked was that one should repay

him with a similar loyalty and affection.' On a professional level Frere
was a shrewd judge, clear-sighted in assessing his most valuable property.
Maugham 'had an inestimable gift of story-telling', he said once in an
interview. 'His strength . . . was integrity (to his art) based on an unshake-
able humility. He knew he wasn't a great writer but set out to make a
living by whatever ability he had.' Both men understood perfectly the
rules and limits of their professional relationship, the writer's job to deliver
a manuscript, the publisher's to publish it, with no question of editorial
interference. 'In all the years I was associated with Willie I never had a
cross word with him about anything connected with his work,' Frere
recalled. 'When I got a manuscript from Willie it went straight to the
printer. I'd send him proofs and get them back within ten days and that
was that. We didn't alter a comma. He used to say, when I finish the
proofs I don't want anything more to do with it. He never commented
on the jackets.'

Nelson Doubleday enjoyed a similarly untroubled working relationship with Maugham, if in character he was very different from his English
counterpart. A big, hearty, cigar-chomping heavy drinker, keen on outdoor
sports, Nelson was ill at ease in society, although generous and affectionate towards his family and intimates, among whom Maugham was
considered one. 'Willie to me is the most interesting character I have ever
met in all my life,' Nelson stated. Always a reluctant reader, Nelson was
first and foremost a businessman, known to be a tough operator and one
of the shrewdest men in the trade. 'I don't *read* books,' he used to boast,
'I sell 'em.' He prided himself on driving a hard bargain, 'but Willie', said
one of Doubleday's colleagues, 'can back Nelson into a corner every
time'. It used to amuse the editorial staff when Maugham visited the
office on Long Island to watch Nelson towering over the short Englishman,
'as a St Bernard towers over a beagle . . . "Of course I know nothing
about business,"' Maugham always began, 'but before the conversation is
over he will have got from Nelson everything he wants – which, incidentally,
is plenty.'

With his enormous sales, Maugham had become one of the most
famous authors alive, translated into almost every language. He was also
attracting some serious critical attention, most of it, perhaps surprisingly,
away from his home ground. Like his fellow novelists Charles Morgan
and Rosamond Lehmann, Maugham came to be held in far greater esteem
in France than in England, where it was not done in highbrow circles
to take his writing seriously. In France a professor at the University of
Toulouse was one of the first in the field: in 1926 Paul Dottin published

an essay on Maugham, 'Le Réalisme de Somerset Maugham', which two years later was expanded into a full-length study, *Somerset Maugham et ses romans*, followed in 1937 by *Le Théâtre de Somerset Maugham*. In 1935 Maugham was made an *officier* of the Légion d'Honneur for his services to literature. Soon there were other scholars eager to pay their respects, not only in France but in Germany and the United States. In Britain by contrast Maugham was largely disregarded by the intelligentsia. His picture was included in the Famous Writers series on the Wills cigarette cards, and yet the three most influential literary surveys published in 1930 almost wholly ignored him: *The History of English Literature* by Emile Legouis and Louis Cazamian hardly mentions his name, A. C. Ward's *Twentieth-Century Literature* refers only to the plays, while the same author's *The Nineteen Twenties* does not notice Maugham at all.\* Extraordinarily for such a popular and prolific author, *The Oxford Dictionary of Quotations* included not a single entry for Maugham, until the 1953 edition when he was permitted one. It was left to a more renegade group of critics, serious intellectually but ranging outside the walls of academe, to give Maugham his due, critics such as Raymond Mortimer, Richard Aldington and Cyril Connolly, who in *Enemies of Promise* categorised him as 'last of the great professional writers'.

The critique that meant most to Maugham himself was written by his old friend Desmond MacCarthy. Published as a pamphlet by Heinemann in 1934, *William Somerset Maugham: The English Maupassant* was part critical assessment, part memoir, recalling MacCarthy's first meeting with Maugham in France in 1914. Of the writer's similarity to Maupassant, MacCarthy says this: 'He has a sense of what is widely interesting, because, like Maupassant, he is as much a man of the world as he is an artist . . . while at his best he can tell a story as well as any man alive or dead.' Such a testimony was gratifying not only because MacCarthy was respected as a critic but also because he was a member of the Bloomsbury group, an elite by whom Maugham felt he had been unfairly cold-shouldered. Typical of their attitude was a remark of David Garnett's. 'I can tell you nothing about Maugham's reputation in the Bloomsbury group,' Garnett loftily told an enquirer, 'because I never heard him discussed.' Such dismissiveness rankled. It was not that Maugham was deluded about his professional status: 'I know just where I stand,' he said more than once,

---

\* Nearly half a century later little had changed: in Valentine Cunningham's monumental *British Writers of the Thirties* (1988), published by Oxford University Press, the only work of Maugham's to be mentioned – briefly, inaccurately and in parenthesis – is the short story 'Rain'.

'in the very front row of the second rate'; but it irked him that a writer as successful as he, one moreover who, like Bloomsbury, had consistently defied public attitudes towards religion, class and sexual morality, should be so ignominiously ignored. And yet as much as his middle-brow reputation it was his success, and the affluence that came with that success, which in the eyes of Bloomsbury placed him beyond the pale. Somerset Maugham with his villa, his swimming-pool, his chauffeur-driven limousine was the ultimate anti-bohemian, his luxurious style of living organically antipathetic to the high-minded inhabitants of Charleston and Gordon Square.

Three years before MacCarthy's article was published, the first bibliographical record of Maugham's work appeared, from a somewhat unexpected quarter. Fred Bason was a working-class lad from Walworth, who in 1931 brought out *A Bibliography of the Writings of William Somerset Maugham*,* with a preface contributed by Maugham himself. From a very poor family but an avid reader, Bason from boyhood had pursued his literary heroes with vigour, hanging around outside theatres and fashionable restaurants in the hope of collecting an autograph. With Maugham he went further, and when only nineteen wrote to propose compiling a bibliography. Maugham was intrigued. 'If you have a snap-shot of yourself you might send me that . . . so that I may know to what sort of boy I am writing,' he told him, adding, 'I hope we shall meet when next I come to London.' They did meet and the friendship flourished, despite Bason's making clear from the start that sex was not on offer (after receiving some expensive presents from Maugham, Fred wrote in a private memorandum, 'We Cockneys try to repay. But not in the way he really wants – that Never Never'). At the older man's request Bason showed him round Walworth, the neighbouring borough to Lambeth and thus a nostalgic experience for Maugham; they went greyhound racing, to a boxing match, for tea with Bason's parents (Mrs Bason knitted Maugham a cardigan for Christmas), and to the music-hall at the Elephant and Castle, Maugham conspicuous in his expensive black overcoat which he was too cold to take off. He was touched by this young man from the slums with a passion for books and the theatre, and over the next few years sent him tickets for his plays, as well as occasional sums of money when times were hard, and for a while gave advice on Bason's own attempts at writing, until the prolific young author grew too exigent. 'No, I do not think I want to read your new play,' Maugham told him

* An amateurish effort, described by the scholarly Ben Abramson of the Argus Bookshop in Chicago, as a 'dreadful work . . . full of errors' (Bason to Maugham n.d. HRHRC).

in November 1931. 'I read one of yours earlier in the year. Remember that there are a great many people who want my opinion on their unpublished works and in the last fortnight I have had to cope with no less than five different authors. I think you have had your fair share for the present.'

Bason's ambition was to set up his own antiquarian book business, and it was Maugham who made this possible by giving him manuscripts and signed first editions to sell on a 10 per cent commission. 'This was my *Glorious* chance,' Bason recalled. 'The one chance in my Life either to get a freehold Bookshop or a nice house.' To begin with, all went well, until Bason overstepped the mark. First, there was a 'misunderstanding' over money that should have been paid to Maugham but was spent by Fred. 'You know quite well that you should not have done this,' Maugham wrote in a tone of paternal reproof. 'I daresay it was a temptation to you to make use of this money which did not belong to you . . . but it was not the right thing to do.' No sooner was this mishap behind them than Fred earned himself a more serious rebuke, discovered selling for inflated prices to American dealers signed copies which he had assured Maugham were for personal customers only. The final break came after one of Maugham's visits to Bason's mother: here he was not only made to spend the entire time signing dozens of books but inscribing in them fulsome messages at Fred's dictation, solely to enhance their value. It was at this point that Maugham brought the association to an end: there would be no more autographed copies, the young man was told, although 'you are at perfect liberty to sell the postcards I sent you or my letters to you if you can find anybody silly enough to buy them'.

Approaching sixty, Maugham showed no sign of slowing down, with a planned schedule of work stretching far into the future. It was now that he set himself to complete what he had determined would be his four last plays, with *The Sacred Flame* the first of the quartet. As all four treated with 'difficult' subjects – euthanasia, for instance, in *The Sacred Flame* – Maugham suspected they were unlikely to be popular: the success of *The Sacred Flame* had come as a surprise. But at this stage he was unconcerned with writing to please: he had spent nearly thirty years in the theatre, had written over thirty plays, he felt he had almost exhausted the medium and that there was little enjoyment to be had out of any of it. Describing in an interview the sheer effort, 'the toil and struggle', of writing a play, he went on to complain of the 'awful' business of having to co-operate with actors and director. 'I haven't the desire, the time, nor the physical ability to watch rehearsals, to quarrel with performers, and to cut and rewrite,' he said. With a play 'you cannot have that intimate relation there is between the writer of a book and his reader'. There was also a growing conviction that he was out of touch. 'Play-writing is a young man's job,' he stated in the preface to the final volume of his collected plays. 'Fashions change in the theatre much more radically and more swiftly than they do in other forms of art,' and younger writers, 'led by the brisk but determined form of Mr Noël Coward', were now in vogue. To underline this last point he sent Coward a photograph of himself under which he had written 'a picture of a gentleman on the shelf'.

At the end of March 1930 Maugham delivered the script of a new play, *The Breadwinner*, which began a five-month run at the Vaudeville on 30 September, with Ronald Squire, Marie Löhr, Jack Hawkins and Peggy Ashcroft. *The Breadwinner*, a lively, if ultimately unsatisfactory piece, tells the story of Charles Battle, a stockbroker, who suddenly decides he is bored by his job, bored by his family and comfortable domesticity in Golders Green, and is no longer prepared to satisfy the greedy material demands of his wife and children. In a somewhat pallid replay of Charles Strickland's dramatic exit in *The Moon and Sixpence*, Battle walks out on the lot of them, not, like Strickland, to dedicate himself to his art but simply to start an unspecified new life on his own. Dutifully Maugham put in time at rehearsals, and he also attended the out-of-town previews prior to the play's coming in to the West End. Yet, if he found the companionship of actors unrewarding, he was by no means inattentive to his cast, as an incident during the run of *The Breadwinner* shows. After the first night's performance in Eastbourne the leading man, Ronald Squire, lost his temper with a young actress whom he successfully reduced to tears. When the company assembled at the restaurant where Maugham was giving them dinner, the playwright immediately noticed Miss Hood's absence and dispatched his chauffeur to collect her, insisting he be told exactly what had happened. Somewhat shamefacedly Squire admitted he had 'given her a roasting', as he put it, whereupon Maugham coldly made clear that if the actor bullied any member of the cast again the management would lose the performing rights to the play. The nineteen-year-old Jack Hawkins, who with the others had been watching the scene open-mouthed, recalled that when Maggie Hood finally arrived, she was 'red-eyed and miserable, but Willie placed her on his right at the dinner table, and spent the rest of the evening treating her as though she was the leading lady'.

Since the divorce from Syrie, Maugham when in London stayed in lodgings at various locations in or near the West End. His first rented apartment was at 18 Half Moon Street, off Piccadilly, his landlady a most respectable woman, 'businesslike, quiet, coolly cynical, and very expensive'. Maugham's rooms were on the ground floor, the parlour was decorated with potted ferns, there were antimacassars on the chairs, and romantic scenes of knights and ladies hung on the walls. One journalist who came to interview him was struck by how odd it was 'to see the brilliant castigator of modern morals against a background of Victorian plush and lace curtains'. Maugham enjoyed his London life. 'I dote really on the smell & the crowds & the colour of London,' he wrote to Osbert Sitwell's companion David Horner. 'I know no place where I feel more myself; & then, it's one of the few places in the world in which you can idle with complete satisfaction.' At Half Moon Street he was within walking distance of everything he needed: the theatres in Shaftesbury Avenue and the Strand; his tailor, Lesley & Roberts, in Old Burlington Street; his barber, Trumper's in Curzon Street; the London Library in St James's Square; bookshops, Hatchard's in Piccadilly, Bumpus' in Oxford Street. Also within easy reach were the Bond Street galleries, the Royal Academy, the salerooms of Sotheby's and Christie's, and close by, too, was his club, the Garrick, where Maugham called in often for a drink and a hand of cards. Sundays he always kept free for a round of golf, either with his brother, F.H., or with Barbara Back; this was usually followed by an evening of bridge with Barbara and her husband at their house near Regent's Park. Here Maugham was completely content, sitting bespectacled in a cloud of cigarette smoke at the card-table, with the Backs and whoever else had been invited to play, H. G. Wells sometimes, or Gerald Kelly, or Basil Bartlett, a good-looking young actor who lived near by. A large part of his pleasure lay in the lack of social effort required, minimal conversation, the company of old friends, and a simple supper of cold beef and baked potatoes.

Since he was a young man Maugham had had a passion for bridge, which he considered 'the most entertaining game that the art of man has devised'. He enjoyed all card games, was often to be seen amusing himself, particularly on his travels, with various forms of patience, he was a good poker-player and he liked a hand of whist; but it was bridge he preferred above all else. Inevitably his stammer was a handicap. 'I've lost hundreds because of that stammer,' he complained. 'I may have a perfectly legitimate slam in my hand, but I can't bid it – the "s" just won't come out.' Nonetheless he loved the intellectual exercise of the game, the ruthlessness, the quick decisions and the need for intuition and balanced judgment;

and he relished the opportunity it gave him to study his partner and opponents. 'The student of human nature can find endless matter for observation in the behaviour of his fellow card-players,' he once wrote. 'Few are so deep that you do not know the essential facts about them after a few rubbers of bridge.' Just as he rated himself as a writer in the top rank of the second class, so he judged himself as a bridge-player. 'I do not flatter myself that I am in the first flight,' he wrote to a fellow enthusiast, 'although I think, without any undue vanity, that I might describe myself as fairly well-up in the second class.' Maugham's hero was the American World Champion Charles Goren, and he collected all Goren's books on the subject, regarding his *Better Bridge for Better Players* as his bible. 'I wish I could make a novel as absorbing as you make your books on bridge,' he told Goren, with whom he occasionally played when in New York, once to his incredulous delight winning $12 off him at the end of an evening's play. In 1944 Goren asked Maugham to contribute an introduction to his *Standard Book of Bidding*, and his own work is full of references to bridge, in plays, such as *Smith* and *The Circle*, in novels and in many of the short stories ('Footprints in the Jungle', 'The Book-Bag', 'The Three Fat Women of Antibes'), as well as in non-fiction, as in *The Gentleman in the Parlour*.

With his time in London limited, Maugham rarely found himself with a free evening. He entertained generously, usually at the Caprice, the Savoy or the Café Royal, and was much sought after by fashionable host-esses, among them those two forceful leaders of the pack, Sibyl Colefax and Emerald Cunard. Lady Colefax and her husband lived at Argyll House in the King's Road, immediately next door to Syrie; the two women disliked each other, in competition professionally – Sibyl Colefax was also an interior decorator – and at odds with each other as neighbours, the Colefaxes' dog driving Syrie mad with its barking, while the late-night slamming of taxi doors after Syrie's parties annoyed Lady Colefax. Naturally this was of no consequence to Maugham, who liked the celebrity-chasing 'Coalbox'. He saw her for the good-hearted woman she was and liked being one of her 'lions', enjoyed mixing with the other celebrities at her salon. Here he met the Cole Porters, the Gershwins, Artur Rubinstein, H. G. Wells, Max Beerbohm, Noël Coward, as well as figures from public life, Winston Churchill, Chips Channon, Harold Nicolson, and the more glamorous members of the aristocracy, such as Lady Diana Cooper and the Prince of Wales. Sibyl Colefax had a famous Birthday Book in which she asked favoured friends to write, Maugham contributing a typically quizzical quotation from the symbolist poet Henri de Régnier: 'Qu'importe sa vie a qui peut par son rêve / Disposer de l'espace et disposer du temps?'[*]

Many of the same people were also regular guests of Lady Cunard in Grosvenor Square, but here the atmosphere was very different. Emerald Cunard, the American widow of the shipping magnate Sir Bache Cunard, was small, exquisite, clever and extremely chic; 'light as thistledown', with blue eyes and the head of a Nymphenburg shepherdess, according to one admirer. Birdlike was an adjective often applied – 'she was like a little parrot', said one of her friends. Yet although Emerald might appear feather-headed in fact she was widely read, profoundly musical and politically astute. She was also very witty: 'it was impossible to be bored in her house', recalled Harold Acton, while Cecil Beaton said of her that her sometimes devastatingly frank observations 'were delivered with the artistry of a great actress'. Her intricately orchestrated luncheon- and dinner-parties were brilliantly entertaining, with the hostess acting as conductor, rapping her tiny talons on the table before pointing to one of her guests – Anna Pavlova, it might be, or Sir Thomas Beecham, the Duke of Westminster or some promising young playwright – with the announcement that he or she was going to address the company on a subject of Emerald's choosing. Not unnaturally some participants found the prospect daunting – Maugham was not the only one to be seen taking a turn or two round Grosvenor Square before summoning the nerve to ring the doorbell – but the results could be enthralling. 'The talk goes rocketing round,' as one friend described it, 'and Emerald herself . . . [with her] shock-tactics manages to get something out of everyone.' Maugham became extremely fond of Emerald; it was a real friendship, and she was one of the few who could tease him with impunity. Once when he got up to leave an evening party unusually early, he jokingly proffered the excuse, 'I have to keep my youth.' 'Then why don't you bring him with you?' Emerald archly enquired.

During these London visits Maugham maintained minimal contact with his ex-wife, whose recently expanded business had been badly hit by the slump. With branches in Chicago, Palm Beach and Los Angeles as well as her showroom in New York, Syrie had been forced to close down almost all her American operations: a timely exit perhaps, as there had been some awkward confrontations with United States Customs

[*] 'What does life matter to him who in his dreams has space and time at his disposal?' From 'Au pays Musulman'.

regarding the bringing in and taking out of the country items which turned out to be not quite as they were described on the manifest. There was also a US Treasury investigation which uncovered two sets of books and some highly creative accounting. Fortunately for Maugham, such embarrassments were no longer his concern: his sole reason for communicating with Syrie was to arrange a couple of times a year to see his daughter. Liza, now in her mid-teens, was prettier than ever but painfully ill at ease, and these rather formal encounters – lunch or dinner in Claridge's restaurant – were agonising for both: years later, when an American friend invited Maugham to dine at Claridge's he begged off on the grounds that it would bring back too many painful memories. Maugham, unused to the company of adolescent girls, was not always tactful with his choice of topic, as Liza recalled. 'I remember being terribly hurt when he said to me when I was about 14 that he had been bitterly disappointed that I was born a girl . . . I was frightfully upset.' On a couple of occasions Maugham took Liza to the theatre, which made the time pass more easily, but both were relieved when the ordeal was over and Maugham could tip Liza half a crown and put her in a taxi home. In 1931 when she was sixteen he gave her a car, which thrilled her, enabling her for the first time in her life to have some independence from her mother. It was around this time that Liza found out about her father's homosexuality, of which until then she had known nothing. 'It was the most terrible shock,' she recalled. 'Lord Wharncliffe, a horrible man, said to me one day, point blank, "Did you know your father's a queer?" And my father always, always believed that it was my mother who had told me. She never did but he couldn't believe it, and it was another source of great bitterness between them.'

On returning from London to the south of France Maugham was returning to his vocation, his writing, and yet the pace of his social life hardly abated. In his late fifties Maugham had the physique of a much younger man. Although his face, with its neatly trimmed moustache, was beginning to look lined and his dark eyes had shadows under them, his hair, brushed straight back, was thick and without a trace of grey, and his figure slim. He took vigorous physical exercise every day, went for long walks over the Cap, swam, water-skied, played golf and tennis. He was invited everywhere and entertained lavishly himself, his guests ranging from the raffish to the extremely grand. Maugham was not a snob in the sense of rating people solely by social status, yet he did love dining with a duke: he was impressed by titles and by the old-established aristocracy, discreetly thrilled when in the presence of royalty. At a luncheon party of Emerald Cunard's, Chips Channon, possessor of the most sensitive social antennae in Europe, observed Maugham's attitude towards that grand old courtier Sir Harry Stonor. 'There was a trace of subservience in Maugham's manner to the supercilious Stonor,' Channon acutely noted, 'and a touch of contempt in Sir Harry's condescension to Somerset Maugham.' Soon after moving to the south of France, Maugham was a guest of the Duke of Connaught, one of the sons of Queen Victoria, at a dinner given by His Royal Highness at his villa on Cap Ferrat. On another occasion the thriller-writer E. Phillips Oppenheim, arriving at the Mauresque for tea, found to his surprise Maugham in smart white ducks and Gerald in his best pale pink entertaining the King and Queen of Siam. 'A strange little gathering,' Oppenheim remarked. 'Our host was chiefly occupied with the Queen, a circumstance not to be wondered at, for Her Majesty, although diminutive, is charming in face, figure and conversation. She plays tennis, too, in quite a pleasant fashion.'

Within his own rules of engagement Maugham was hospitable and he thrived on intelligent talk, not always easily available in the expatriate circles of the Côte d'Azur. There were some interesting local residents, however, writers such as F. Tennyson Jesse, whose Burmese novel, *The Lacquer Lady*, naturally appealed to Maugham; there was the amusing and malicious Elizabeth Russell, author of *Elizabeth and her German Garden*; and Michael Arlen, who after making a fortune from his bestseller *The Green Hat* had bought a property outside Cannes. Among Maugham's French friends one of the cleverest and most entertaining was Horace de Carbuccia, a fat, jolly, bald-headed Corsican who had a house along the coast at Sainte-Maxime. Founder of the publishing house Editions de France and editor of the violently right-wing journal *Gringoire*, Carbuccia was a brilliant, intemperate, charming and unscrupulous man, with a profound knowledge and love of literature. He and Maugham had first met in London after the war and had become friends, Carbuccia publishing a number of Maugham's stories in *Gringoire*; more importantly, he was instrumental in promoting Maugham on the Paris stage, arranging for the translation of four of the plays, *Rain*, *The Circle*, *The Letter* and *The Sacred Flame*. The translator, Mme Blanchet, was a girlfriend of Carbuccia's, and as Maugham had no need of the money and Carbuccia wished to do something for his 'petite amie' it was arranged that the royalties should be divided between her and Gerald. 'J'ai un secrétaire que j'aime beaucoup,'★ Maugham had told him. Carbuccia was delighted when Maugham moved

★ 'I have a secretary of whom I am very fond.'

to France, relishing the dryness of the Englishman's wit. 'Et puis, vous aimez bien la France,' Carbuccia said to him one day. '"J'aime vivre en France," répliqua-t-il avec son sens exquis des nuances.'* Maugham for his part respected Carbuccia as an editor and was enormously entertained by him, while disliking his politics and knowing perfectly well that the man was a rogue. 'He was a gangster who had the gangster's code of honour . . . [but] he was a wonderful raconteur of droll, bitter stories . . . [with] a cynical effrontery that I could not but find fascinating.'

Just as clever, if very different, was the infinitely genial H. G. Wells, who had recently built a house for himself at Grasse. Since those early years before the war, when Maugham had first met Wells with Max Beerbohm and Reggie Turner, an agreeable friendship had developed between the two, Maugham fascinated by Wells's huge intelligence and mesmerising conversation, if not whole-hearted an admirer of his fiction. In Maugham's view Wells failed as a novelist because he was more interested in the type than in the individual; as a result, 'The people he puts before you are not individuals, but lively and talkative marionettes whose function it is to express the ideas he was out to attack or to defend.' Now they were neighbours the two men saw each other often, Wells initially in the company of his attractive but tiresome mistress Odette Keun. Recently, however, H.G. had fallen in love with a beautiful Russian, Moura Budberg, and was trying to disentangle himself from Odette, while she, ferociously jealous, was doing everything in her power to stymie his new affair. Finding in Maugham a sympathetic listener, Odette poured out her hurt feelings, crucially mistaking his courteous attentiveness for partisanship. In gratitude, she inserted a fulsome dedication 'To W. Somerset Maugham' in a little book she had written on England and the English. 'My dear William . . . During a time of great bewilderment, you showed me a fearless, wise and steadfast friendship for which I do not cease to be grateful . . . I love and admire in you a genuineness of spirit and a sensitive kindness of heart which set you apart from the men and women I have known.' Shortly after the book was published, however, Odette discovered that in her absence Maugham, unforgivably, had entertained H.G. with the hated Moura at the Mauresque, an act which so enraged her that she immediately instructed her publisher to remove the dedication in future editions, writing a bitterly hurt letter to 'William darling' telling him what a treacherous brute he had been.

---

* '"So you like France?" "I like living in France," he replied with his exquisite sense of nuance.'

It is not true that you are exceptionally kind; it is not true that you are exceptionally sensitive . . . I cannot bear what I have written [in the dedication], because it is so extravagantly *false* . . . Oh, William! Oh, William! . . . Do not answer this letter. I never want to hear from or of you again. Finished, this shallow and brittle friendship . . .

Needless to say, such an eruption made no difference whatever to relations between the two men, with Maugham growing almost as fond of the mysterious Moura as he was of Wells himself.

The numbers of expatriates enormously increased during the summer, when crowds of exotic imports arrived on the Riviera and there was no shortage of lively company: Eugene O'Neill, for instance, the opera singer Mary Garden, Charlie Chaplin and Alexander Woollcott, who was found to be a great addition when he rented a villa for the season at Antibes. It was Woollcott who introduced Maugham to the actress Ruth Gordon, and to Harpo Marx, of the Marx Brothers, both of whom became friends. Some years later Maugham was amused to learn that in Harpo's 'library' in his house in California there were only two books, both inscribed by their authors: a copy of *Saint Joan* given him by Shaw, and *Of Human Bondage*.

By and large friends invited to stay at the Villa Mauresque fell into two categories, the first composed mainly of married couples, the other of what one observer later described as 'cosmopolitan gay'. In the first group were friends like the Kellys, the Brights, Frere and his wife Pat, Alan and Poppy Pryce-Jones, Desmond MacCarthy, Jacques Raindre, a wealthy financier from Paris, and Nelson Doubleday, who had just divorced his first wife and was shortly to marry his second. Barbara Back, closest to Maugham of all his women friends, was frequently called upon to play the part of hostess, her brassy blonde elegance, love of gossip and especially her expertise at the bridge-table much admired by Maugham: presenting her with one of his novels he inscribed it, 'For Barbara, because she never calls on his diamonds to the Queen, from her appreciative partner the author'. Barbara came often to the Mauresque, usually on her own as her flamboyant and far from faithful husband, Ivor Back, the fashionable surgeon,* was rarely able to accompany her; this suited Maugham, who liked to have Barbara to himself. He enjoyed indulging her and once on an impulse gave her a mink coat. She for her part knew exactly how to handle him, with a combination of mischief and respect; he loved her earthiness, her 'guttersnipe humour', and relied on her long chatty letters to provide him with all the most indiscreet gossip of the

* There is a devastating portrait of Ivor Back as the smooth, self-serving Mr Ivory in A. J. Cronin's novel *The Citadel*.

town. 'Your letters are a boon & a blessing,' he told her. 'They bring a whiff of London down to the Riviera.' Another member of the Mauresque inner circle was the novelist G. B. (Gladys Bronwen) Stern, always known as Peter. Enormously fat with a round face and Skye-terrier fringe, Peter Stern was no beauty, but her entertaining conversation and general jolliness were considered great assets, even though Maugham was dismayed by her greed at table and not over-keen, aesthetically, on her habit of sunbathing naked. She was, however, a good sort and he respected her critical opinion. 'She is the least self-centred writer I know,' he wrote to his niece Kate, '& the more one knows her the more delightful one finds her.' Also included on the regular guest-list were Maugham's nephew and nieces, sometimes accompanied by their father F.H. 'I think they all enjoyed themselves,' Maugham wrote to Barbara Back after a family visit in June 1931. 'I know the girls did. F.H. as you know would rather die than let a word of appreciation pass his austere lips.'

The second group of visitors were men only, some with partners, some alone, some near Maugham's generation in age, others considerably younger. There was Osbert Sitwell who came with his lover David Horner, an attractive man by whom Maugham for a while was very taken; there were Harold Nicolson ('so nice, gay & easy to please'), Harold Acton, Raymond Mortimer, Noël Coward, Cecil Beaton. (A story that gleefully went the rounds was of the poet Edna St Vincent Millay arriving at the Mauresque to find Maugham sitting on the terrace with Haxton, Beaton and Coward. 'Oh, Mr Maugham,' cried Miss Millay, clapping her hands. 'This is fairyland!') Those two ambitious young men, Godfrey Winn and Beverley Nichols, were regularly invited, Winn recalling with mortification his first visit to the villa when he arrived wearing a grey flannel suit. 'This is the South of France in August, not Finals Day at Wimbledon,' said Maugham severely and sent him off in the car with Gerald to buy linen shirts and trousers and a pair of espadrilles. Another good-looking young writer, Keith Winter, was reeled in after being spotted in Villefranche with the Waugh brothers, Alec and Evelyn, who were staying with their parents at the Welcome Hotel. The three young men were asked to dine. Alec with his beautiful manners made an excellent impression, while Evelyn – ingeniously affecting ignorance of Maugham's literary reputation, addressing him throughout as 'Dr' Maugham – was dismissed as 'odious'.*

---

* Evelyn's relations with Maugham remained tricky. Some years later he was taken to stay at the Villa Mauresque by Diana Cooper, an old friend of Maugham's. Describing the occasion to Harold Acton, Waugh told him he made 'a great gaffe. The first evening he [Maugham] asked me what someone was like and I said: "A pansy with a stammer." All the Picassos on the walls blanched' (Mark Amory (ed.) *The Letters of Evelyn Waugh* (Ticknor & Fields 1980) p. 372).

The Waughs left after dinner but Winter stayed the night, returning to Villefranche the next morning, very pleased with himself, said Alec. 'Willie had told him how well he used his fingers, which made me think of Strickland in *The Moon and Sixpence*, who often despised the people he was enjoying.' Later that year Alec saw Maugham with Winter at a cocktail party in London. 'Keith was getting a drink and he touched Willie's hand and I saw a look of real lust cross Willie's face.'

On a rather different level was the friendship Maugham formed with a brilliant young don from King's College, Cambridge, George ('Dadie') Rylands. Rylands with his schoolteacher friend Arthur Marshall and another young Cambridge academic, Victor Rothschild, had come on holiday to Monte Carlo, where they encountered Maugham. Invited to the Mauresque, Rothschild, the only heterosexual member of the party, was somewhat taken aback by their reception. 'Somerset Maugham', he wrote, 'may have misunderstood the purpose of our visit, at least a stroll in the garden with Gerald Haxton led me to that conclusion.' Rylands and Marshall meanwhile were duly propositioned by their host, but once that was out of the way the pair, and Rylands in particular, soon became part of Maugham's circle. Blond, blue-eyed, pink-cheeked and enchanting, Dadie Rylands was an ebullient, magnetic personality. A member of the Apostles at Cambridge and an habitué of Bloomsbury, he was already recognised as a leading Shakespearean scholar; he had, too, a passion for live theatre, for directing and acting (his performance as the Duchess of Malfi was talked about for years); and he was an inspired teacher. Although Rylands was so much younger, Maugham was soon looking to him to correct his writing – 'his taste appeared to me faultless', Maugham wrote in *The Summing Up* – and requiring him to give what amounted to a series of tutorials in English literature. These, as Marshall recalled, usually took place over meals.

> Lunch would have been going for about five minutes when a tentative, stammering voice would say, 'D-D-D-Dadie, I have a notion that when George Eliot says in *Adam Bede* "Our deeds determine us, as much as we determine our deeds", what she really meant to say was . . .' and there would follow some additional thought or comment of his own. Dadie would pause and cogitate and then reply, but if Willie's remark was something of a bromide (and bromides from his lips were by no means unknown . . .), Dadie would just smile and nod and say 'Yes, Willie,' upon which Willie would give me a sideways glance and just whisper 'I've b-b-b-been reproved.'

Maugham grew devoted to the two young men: they were quick-witted, they made him laugh and, significantly, they were among the few who had no ulterior motive: they wanted nothing from him.

Rylands and Marshall were both struck by Maugham's benevolence and generosity, and also by how 'marvellously entertaining' he was. They adored his jokes, 'which were more frequent and funnier than some may imagine', and were both perfectly in tune with his astringent sense of humour: 'he loved to make one laugh aloud', said Dadie. 'He loved to *tease*.' This is far from the image more commonly purveyed of the formidable figure with a bitingly sarcastic tongue. Maugham could be caustic – as Rebecca West remarked, 'it would be idle to deny that a great many people feel a certain alarm at the sight and thought of Mr Maugham' – but he could also be very funny, even if his wit were sometimes so dry it came over as more wounding than witty. Occasionally he was enveloped in a strange melancholy, which inevitably cast a gloom over the company. 'It is exasperating that with everything to induce content I have not been able to get rid of an almost constant depression,' he wrote to the pianist Harriet Cohen in 1933. 'I take it hardly because in general I have high spirits and none of the misfortunes of daily life has power to affect me for more than a day or so.' Maugham's shyness, too, was hardly conducive to putting guests at their ease; his stammer was disconcerting, and he flinched from personal contact. 'Willie hated to be touched except by arrangement,' said the American writer Glenway Wescott. 'If you touched him by surprise, he was like a shellfish quivering when you pour lemon juice over it.' When relaxed, however, he could be marvellous company. Alan Pryce-Jones while staying at the Mauresque in July 1932 remarked on how charming Maugham was. This stammer could be alarming, it was true, but when at ease his gentle malice was most seductive and the famous cynicism little more than a writer's pose.

Yet the benevolent mood could disappear very quickly, for Maugham's temper was largely dependent on the ups and downs of his daily relations with Gerald. This particular fact of life was impressed upon Glenway Wescott, who as a young man was brought to the villa to meet Maugham. Blond, boyish, bookish, charming, Wescott was all that should have been found appealing, and yet everything he said was snubbed or crossly contradicted by his host, who was 'carping at everyone, his eyes blazing . . . [pulling] his mouth down like a snapping turtle's . . . "You're another one of those young Americans who think they know everything because they've read Proust,"' Maugham tetchily remarked. The reason for Maugham's bad temper on this occasion, as Wescott later discovered, was that he had just had a fight with Haxton.

Such quarrels were becoming more and more frequent, and were beginning seriously to disrupt the *luxe, calme et volupté* that had been so carefully created at the Mauresque. For Maugham it was essential that he should be in absolute control of his environment: everything must be regulated, disciplined, running on time, and it was Gerald whose job it was to keep the system in order. This, when sober, he did very well. On a personal level, too, his 'naturally happy temper' acted as an effective antidote to Maugham's occasional depressions. Gerald animated the household, his vitality and exuberance a welcome counterbalance to his employer's cautious, sometimes chilly reserve. As Alec Waugh put it, Haxton was 'debonair and dashing, good company and a good mixer, everything that Maugham was not'. Gerald was ebulliently, irrepressibly friendly; he was outgoing, articulate, amusing, and he provided a much needed element of fun and frivolity, especially during the morning sessions round the pool, where he loved to show off his athletic figure in graceful dives into the deep end – in all-male company there was a rule at the Mauresque that everyone swam in the nude. After dinner, too, he was always ready for fun. 'I lead a peculiarly quiet life, having made a vow not to go out in the evening,' Maugham warned Gerald Kelly who was arriving to stay, 'but Gerald tears about from end to end of the Riviera and he will give you all the gaiety you require.' Some of the pretty boys, like Nichols and Winn, were wary of Gerald, the alpha male – 'no mincer of words, he said what he thought in the bluntest terms', Harold Acton recalled – but most of Maugham's guests found him delightful. Both Barbara Back and Peter Stern adored him, and Gerald Kelly's wife Jane said of him, 'He was a delightful creature . . . You couldn't help loving him.'

The balance of the relationship was plain, with Maugham much the more devoted, cajoling and wooing the younger man. 'The mental domination exercised over Somerset Maugham by his friend Gerald Haxton was total and unbreakable,' said Beverley Nichols, an impression also received by Arthur Marshall. 'No matter how badly he behaved, Willie was always enraptured by him.' Marshall recalled one afternoon when he, Rylands and Maugham, waiting for Haxton to make up a four at tennis, suddenly saw him sauntering towards them through the trees. 'Oh, here's Master Hacky now,' said Maugham softly, and the expression on his face and his tone of voice showed 'such affection and love, as if about a child'. Almost paternal, too, was the way in which Maugham put up with behaviour from Gerald that would not have been tolerated for one second from anyone else. But then that, too, was, or had been, part of the appeal, part of the delinquent type, the cocky, handsome rogue with sex-appeal and charm to which Maugham had always been attracted. That canny witness Horace de Carbuccia understood exactly what it was about, having often seen the two together in Paris as well as in the south. In Paris, Carbuccia observed,

> [Maugham] venait généralement accompagné de son sécretaire, un garçon d'une grande beauté, sportif, intelligent et sympathique ... Ce jeune homme était aussi dissipé, fantaisiste, gaspilleur et intempérant que mon ami paraissait sérieux, économe, sobre et discipliné. Ils s'entendaient parfaitement.★

Was this what was going on between them, an echo of some old playfulness mutually acknowledged, when sometimes Maugham, astonishingly, failed to react to what appeared to be outrageous provocation? One day when Wells, Moura Budberg and Elizabeth Russell had come to lunch, Maugham inconsequentially remarked that he had just had 'a most h-h-h-heavenly hot bath'. 'And did you masturbate?' demanded Gerald, staring at him challengingly. The others were horror-struck, not knowing what to do or say; but Maugham seemed unperturbed. Taking his time, he continued calmly scooping out his avocado. 'As it h-h-happens,' he replied, 'n-n-n-n-no.'

There were other old-established patterns deeply embedded in the relationship. As during their travels in the Far East and elsewhere when Gerald had acted as pander for Maugham, so now in the south of France he fulfilled much the same role, cruising the sea front, hanging out in bars, picking up young men to be sneaked into the villa. A favourite hunting ground was the Welcome Hotel. Villefranche was a naval base and, when the fleet was in, the quiet family hotel overlooking the harbour was transformed into a noisy bar and brothel, where to the sound of loud jazz sailors danced, drank, fought and got as much sex as they could before their shore-leave expired. As one of its homosexual patrons appreciatively remarked, 'What a place that is – when the white-caps are in port!' Such a location was a magnet to Gerald. One night he brought back to the Mauresque a couple of ratings from the American Sixth Fleet, one of whom while being shown round the house pocketed a pen from Maugham's study, and afterwards cheekily sent his host a letter telling him it had been written with his own pen. Such goings-on were relatively straightforward and above board: the sailors knew what they were in for and were well paid for their services. But there were rumours that

★ '[Maugham] was usually accompanied by his secretary, a young man of great beauty, athletic, intelligent and nice ... This youth was as extravagant, capricious, wasteful and over-indulgent as my friend appeared serious, frugal, sober and controlled. They got on perfectly.'

Gerald sometimes went further than this, talk of involvement with a procurer in Nice, of underage boys, which if true was a potentially dangerous situation, and a serious anxiety for Maugham. He knew only too well how fatally attracted Gerald was to trouble: 'just this side of being a crook', in the opinion of some.

A further anxiety lay in Gerald's addiction to gambling. From Cap Ferrat it was only a short drive to the famous casino at Monte Carlo, as well as the casinos at Nice and Beaulieu. Night after night Haxton, far from sober, would take the car and either alone or with a group of guests drive along the coast and install himself at the tables until the small hours, face flushed, cigar in hand, a glass of whisky and a pile of chips at his elbow. After a good night's play, he was wildly generous and would turn up at the villa laden with gifts; once he came home with a Great Dane, and on another occasion presented Maugham with a two-seater sports car bought with a single night's winnings; Maugham loved it and drove it for years. More often than not, however, there were appalling losses, and these inevitably were a cause of contention, although in the end his patron always paid up. 'I'm p-p-perfectly aware that Gerald is both a drunkard and a gambler,' Maugham would say, 'but he does have great qualities.' Yet there were some debts so large, amounting to several thousand pounds, that Gerald dared not confess them, and on more than one occasion was forced to apply to Bert Alanson for rescue. 'Thank you again for your kindness in so quickly responding to my signals of distress,' Gerald wrote after a particularly bad run. 'I had a most awful winter in the various casinos along the coast never getting a win at all. Fortunately this summer has smiled upon me and I have made nearly ten thousand dollars. I have decided that that is enough and will gamble no more till winter.'

Promises made were easily broken, especially when alcohol played such a large part in driving Gerald's behaviour. He had long been a heavy drinker, but now his drinking was frequently out of control. 'He was a bad, bad, loud drunk, a big martini drinker,' said one of the regulars at the Mauresque. Habitually now Haxton appeared in the morning with his eyes bloodshot, his face grey beneath his tan, sometimes wearing make-up to give himself a better colour; his breath reeked of alcohol, despite copious quantities of peppermint mouthwash, and his hands shook while holding his cards at the bridge-table. By the evening his speech was blurred, his mood on that dangerous edge between gaiety and rage which so easily explodes into violence. '*Why* do you have to drink so much?' Maugham would despairingly ask. 'Because it makes life look rosier,' was the defiant reply. Drunken scenes were a frequent occurrence, both depressing and enraging Maugham, who was appalled by the transformation of his beloved companion into a creator of chaos, a manic Lord of Misrule set on destroying the balance and control so essential to the writer's existence. 'You do not know what it is like, and I hope you never will, to be married to someone who is married to drink,' Maugham remarked feelingly to Godfrey Winn. It had become impossible to conceal Gerald's condition, and there were some appallingly embarrassing incidents. One such occurred when the Duke of Connaught arrived for an elaborately arranged luncheon, accompanied by his sister Princess Louise and an ADC. To Maugham's fury, Gerald, who had been out all night, staggered in late, sweating and unshaven, and sat at the table glassy-eyed, unable to eat or speak. Sometimes he would emerge from his disgrace contrite and hung over, promising never to touch a drop again, but as soon as Maugham's back was turned he was at the drinks tray pouring himself a full tumbler of gin to be knocked back in a single gulp.

There was no doubt that the relationship between Maugham and Haxton was under severe strain, but it was only years later and in retrospect that Maugham fully confronted the complexities involved. In a number of ways Gerald's life was full of frustration. A generation younger than Maugham (Gerald turned forty in 1932, Maugham sixty just two years later), he was a man of energy and resource who had very little to do, and no outside interests to keep him amused. Except for a small legacy from his mother, he was dependent on his patron for everything, for his salary of $2,000 a year and for his board and lodging, provided in return for duties as secretary and majordomo; every year he was allowed a holiday on his own, usually spent in Austria or Italy. Yet keeping an eye on the servants and writing letters to dictation were hardly the most rewarding occupations for an intelligent man, and there were long periods when he was by himself while his employer was in London. He could have left, but under Maugham's protection there was guaranteed security, and by now Gerald was fatally accustomed to a life of wealth and ease, to first-class travel and luxury hotels, to the company of clever, glamorous, famous people. On his own there would be nothing like that; and yet part of him resented his subservient position, perhaps even despised the person he had become. He was fond of Maugham, he enormously admired him, and at the same time he felt rebellious and penned in. 'At times when I'm shut up there in that great villa all alone with him I feel I could scream,' he confessed. There were days and weeks, especially during the winter, when there was little social life, no guests came to stay, it was cold, it rained, an icy mistral blew for days on end, and Maugham was completely wrapped up in his writing. 'Gerald couldn't help resenting the fact that he played only a peripheral part in Willie's life,' said Maugham's nephew Robin. 'Although Willie loved him desperately, he couldn't give all of himself to Gerald because he felt he had to reserve the most important part for his work.' Sometimes, too, Maugham was submerged in a black melancholy that rendered him silent and remote. 'He has moods when he gets depressed,' said Gerald, recalling the loneliness of these desolate periods, 'but then he'll say something to make me smile, or to fascinate me, and I'll forgive him everything.'

Up to a point Maugham was sympathetic about Gerald's situation. 'What's wrong?' he would gently enquire. 'I'm getting bored: that's what's wrong,' was the sullen response. Occasionally Maugham tried to do something about it: he bought a fast motor-boat, for instance, which Haxton loved, roaring out to sea at full throttle and spending hours tinkering with it in the harbour at Villefranche. But there seemed no solution to the drinking, which was fast destroying all signs of the vital, attractive man Maugham had met nearly twenty years before. To Dadie Rylands Maugham confided his unhappiness. 'Gerald now likes the bottle more than he likes me,' he told him. And in the notebook of this period there are lines of verse that almost certainly refer to his state of wretchedness over Gerald.

> I could not bear the thought that I should ever lose you
> Or that our lives might ever be disjoined,
> But yet I knew that in your wanton heart
> There was for me nor love nor tenderness . . .
> Humbly I thanked you when you feigned to love me.
> I bought your grudging lips for gold.
> And now the love I thought would last till death is dead . . .
> In weariness, and not in death or parting, is
> The bitterness of love. Spent is my passion . . .
> I look into my empty heart and shrink dismayed . . .
> . . . I regret
> My pain, my rapture, my anguish and my bliss.

The sheer tedium of living with an alcoholic weighed almost as heavily on Maugham as the private misery of his deteriorating relationship; his despair over Gerald's bad behaviour temporarily obscured much deeper feelings, leading him to believe, mistakenly, that his love for Haxton was exhausted. Every day was dominated by Gerald's drinking and destructiveness, and he refused to consider a cure. But then something happened which seemed to change everything. In the early autumn of 1930 Gerald, drunk, dived into a half-empty swimming-pool and broke his neck. The accident took place during a party at the house of a rich American neighbour, Charlotte Boissevain, and Gerald as usual had become quickly inebriated. 'I don't know about you, ducky,' he had declared to his hostess, 'but I'm going to have a swim.' Tearing off his clothes he had lurched off to the pool before anyone could stop him. Gerald came very near to death: his life was despaired of, but miraculously he survived. Badly damaged, with cracked vertebrae and a dislocated spine, he was rushed to Paris to be operated on. While there, encased in plaster and immobile in his hospital bed, Gerald for many weeks had no access to drink, and when he finally returned to the Mauresque it looked for quite a while as though the bad times might be over. '[Gerald] is getting more peaceful, sleeping without drugs & looking astonishingly well,' Maugham wrote cheerfully to Barbara Back. 'He carries his head a bit askew . . . & he cannot brush his hair yet. But there is no great harm in that. He looks like a rough & there are people who fancy that.' Months passed, and still there was no sign of the bad old ways returning. 'It is really very pleasant here,' Barbara was told. 'For the first time since I bought the house I am leading an entirely peaceful life . . . Gerald seems to like it & to be very happy. The house is running smoothly & the garden . . . is ravishing.'

During all his difficult dealings with Gerald, Maugham found immense comfort in the soothing contrast of his continuing relationship with Alan Searle. The young man was rarely out of his thoughts, Maugham writing to him from the Mauresque every two or three days, affectionate letters addressed to 'Alan my lamb', 'dearest Alan', 'Alan my sweet', letters full of longing for his presence, of eager anticipation of the next meeting, and of concern for the boy's health and wellbeing. If more than a few days passed without a reply, Maugham would dispatch a teasingly reproachful note. 'Wretched creature, Why don't you write to me? Your last note was brief & you sounded ill. Were you? If so, what is the matter with you? Or is it that you just love another? . . . I'm not going to write to a filthy little beast who doesn't write to me . . .' Alan, much given to hypochondria and self-pity, was frequently under the weather, complaining of a hundred-and-one minor ailments, from acne to 'nerves' and chronic exhaustion, about all of which Maugham sympathised and advised, even offering to pay all Alan's medical bills. After receiving a letter in which a rare period of good health was reported, Maugham wrote, 'I am so very glad to think that you are well & strong & spotless. I hope you will remain so. Has it occurred to you that not a bad way to achieve so desirable an object is not to tear about too much, to get a proper amount of sleep & not to fill your greedy belly with masses of rich food?'

At Christmas and on his birthday Alan received expensive presents, silk pyjamas from Hawes & Curtis, a dinner-jacket from Anderson & Shepherd. Alan's old admirer Lytton Strachey reported to a friend that it was quite clear Mr Somerset Maugham was 'entiché [besotted]' with Searle, which probably 'makes his relations with H[axton] easier . . . Perhaps he will find happiness in that direction – why not?. . . It would be shattering for me at first, no doubt, but if it was really a solution of his difficulties one couldn't complain.' Alan had been pressingly invited to stay at the Villa Mauresque, but his occasional visits were inclined to be tense as he was terrified of Gerald – needlessly so, as Gerald never perceived Alan as a threat, and his manner towards him remained one of benign contempt. Much more rewarding were the sojourns in London, when Alan for the duration of Maugham's stay moved in to his rented chambers. It was Searle's responsibility to find the accommodation. 'You know what I want,' Maugham wrote to him, 'two bedrooms, a bathroom, a sitting-room & my own front door . . . & a bed large enough for me to turn over in.' By now Alan had left his job at the Mayfair picture gallery for employment which his compassionate nature found infinitely more rewarding. Through the good offices of Guy Little, another of his old gentlemen, Alan had been taken on as an official prison visitor at Wormwood Scrubs and Pentonville; he was also working for the Discharged Prisoners' Aid Society and, on a voluntary basis, for the Salvation Army in his native Bermondsey. He earned a small supplementary income by running errands for Maugham, making travel arrangements, booking theatre tickets, sending parcels of cigarettes, cigars and tobacco from Dunhill, and for Gerald ordering corduroy trousers from Simpson's and his favourite White Hyacinth eau de toilette from Floris.

Whatever his emotional state, Maugham allowed nothing to get in the way of his work. 'The artist should never allow his happiness to interfere with his work,' he wrote once, 'for his work is more important than his happiness.' During the summer of 1931 his main undertaking was an adaptation for Gladys Cooper of *The Painted Veil*, on which he collaborated with an American dramatist, Bartlett Cormack. Maugham came over to London for the first night at the Playhouse on 19 September, congratulating Gladys on her 'marvellous performance' as Kitty Fane. 'I have never seen you act so naturally, with so much variety, care & command of your medium,' he told her. 'There is no one in Europe who can hold a candle end to you.' Two weeks later, after a short visit to Paris to oversee the staging of *Le Cyclone* (*The Sacred Flame*), he was back in London for the publication of *Six Stories Written in the First Person Singular*, the first collection of his to appear since *Ashenden* in 1928.

As a compilation, *First Person Singular* is typically Maugham in style and content, even if a couple ('The Round Dozen' and 'The Creative Impulse') can hardly be considered Maugham at his best. There are two outstanding stories, however, 'The Human Element' and 'The Alien Corn'. The first tells with sly humour of Betty, a beautiful divorcée, who abandons her smart social circle in England for the island of Rhodes in order to live, very discreetly, with her chauffeur, a situation familiar to Maugham in the homosexual world and here efficiently transposed. The shocking truth of Betty's domestic arrangements is discovered by an old suitor of hers, who has come to stay.

> One morning when he had been in Rhodes a little over a week, he happened to be coming upstairs as Betty was walking along the passage.
> 'You've never shown me your room, Betty,' he said.
> 'Haven't I? Come in and have a look now. It's rather nice.' . . .
> His eye took in the bed-table . . . there were two or three books on it, a box of cigarettes, and on an ash-tray a briar pipe. Funny! What on earth had Betty got a pipe by her bed for?

In 'The Alien Corn'* George Bland is a young man who seems to have everything, good-looking, clever and adored by his wealthy father, who proudly expects him to take over the family estate and eventually stand for Parliament. But George is uninterested, set on making a career as a concert pianist. After much debate a deal is struck by which George is allowed to study in Munich on condition that if after two years his playing is judged to lack promise he will give up. When the time comes, the judgment is unfavourable, and George shoots himself. Here the plot, as the title of the collection implies, is told by a first-person narrator, one who usefully involves himself in the story, as a friend of the family, visiting George in Munich, and so on; but in this instance plot is secondary to context, which is crucial. For George is Jewish. His family name, Bland, was until recently Bleikogel, and his parents, Adolph and Miriam, have determinedly translated themselves into Freddy and Muriel. At heart the struggle between George and his parents is a racial and cultural conflict, the son in order to return to

---

* From Keats's 'Ode to a Nightingale:' 'the sad heart of Ruth, when, sick for home, / She stood in tears amid the alien corn'.

his roots rejecting the hearty philistinism of the English shires so slavishly adopted by his parents.* Finely and with precision, Maugham reveals the infinite complexities of English anti-Semitism: the casual, snobbish anti-Semitism of the upper classes, who regard Jews as somehow, well, slightly *common*; then the Jewish anti-Semitism of those who, like George's parents, are desperate to disguise their alien origins: Muriel, for instance, is a Catholic convert, and with utmost delicacy makes clear her distaste for her own people. 'I think some of them are very nice,' she tells the narrator,

> 'They're so artistic. I don't go so far as to say Freddy and I deliberately avoid them, of course I wouldn't do that, but it just happens that we don't really know any of them very well . . .'
>
> I could not but admire the convincing manner in which she spoke.

Finally, there is the brilliantly observed portrait of Ferdy Rabenstein, Freddy Bland's uncle, the perfect type of English society's token Jew. Rich, handsome, scholarly, charming, he is received everywhere, cleverly making himself acceptable by playing up his Jewishness, telling funny Jewish stories and flashing the big diamond rings on his fingers. 'After all, I am an Oriental,' says Ferdy. 'I can carry a certain barbaric magnificence.' Yet at the same time and at some profound level Ferdy despises the world in which he moves. 'Though he spoke facetiously, there was in his tone the faintest possible derision and I felt, hardly felt even, the sensation was so shadowy . . . [that] there was in the depth of his impenetrable heart a cynical contempt for the Gentiles he had conquered.'

Over the next couple of years the high rate of production continued, with more short stories, two plays and a full-length work of fiction. In the latter, *The Narrow Corner*, published in November 1932, Maugham returns under full sail to the Pacific, to the islands of the Dutch East Indies in the Malay Archipelago. *The Narrow Corner*,† clearly influenced by Conrad, is heavily imbued with mystery, with all the favourite ingredients of lust, guilt and disillusion; it is cynical, witty, written in a graceful, lucid style, and of all Maugham's novels it evokes the most powerful sense of place. Here delineated with simplicity and restraint are a series of unforgettable impressions of the heat, the sounds, the squalor and the

* In 1939 an article was published in Germany entitled 'Die Rassenfrage [The Race Question] in W. S. Maughams "The Alien Corn"' (*Zeitschrift für Neusprachlichen Unterricht*, XXXVIII) in which the story was used to support the Nazi thesis that racial barriers are natural and that the Jews will always remain the alien corn in any country.

† The title is taken from *The Meditations of Marcus Aurelius*: 'Short, therefore, is man's life; and narrow is the corner of the earth wherein he dwells.'

lush, numinous beauty of the tropics. Much of the action takes place in and around a dilapidated bungalow in Kanda-Meria* that had once belonged to a Dutch *perkenier*, a nutmeg planter.

> It was a large, square building not on piles, but on a foundation of masonry, covered with an attap [palm-leaf] roof and surrounded by a neglected garden . . . In the cool of the evening the air was limpid. The kanari trees, in the shade of which grew the portly and profitable nutmeg trees, were enormously tall . . . You heard the boom of great pigeons and saw them flying about with a heavy whirr of wings.

There are, too, several sequences at sea, magnificently conveyed, with a description of a terrifying sunlit storm worthy of Conrad himself. One of the chief protagonists is a medical man, and in the picture of Dr Saunders as a passenger on board a yacht sailing between the islands there is a clear reflection of Maugham himself in similar circumstances in the past.

> Mainsail and foresail were hoisted, the anchor weighed, and they slipped out of the lagoon. There was not a cloud in the sky, and the sun beat down on the shining sea. The monsoon was blowing, but with no great force, and there was a slight swell. Two or three gulls flew round them in wide circles. Now and then a flying-fish pierced the surface of the water, made a long dart over it and dived down with a tiny splash. Dr Saunders read, smoked cigarettes, and when he was tired of reading looked at the sea and the green islands they passed.

Of the three main characters, all outcasts, two have made brief appearances in earlier works, Dr Saunders in *On a Chinese Screen* and Captain Nichols in *The Moon and Sixpence*. Dr Saunders, returning home to China after treating a rich patient on an outlying island, takes passage in Captain Nichols's shabby old lugger, currently conveying Fred Blake, a beautiful but sullen young Australian whose circumstances are tantalisingly obscure. After several days' sailing they put in at Kanda-Meria, and it is here, in and around the nutmeg plantation, that the crux of the drama takes place, with sexual passion and betrayal, suicide and the revelation that Fred is on the run having murdered a man in Sydney. The plot is taut and heavy with sexual tension, predominantly between Fred and the lovely young daughter of the plantation-owner; Fred casually seduces her, whereupon her dull but decent fiancé, Erik, shoots himself. But with characteristic contrariness Maugham reveals the girl, Louise, to be as unmoved by her

* In reality Bandanaira, a settlement on one of the Banda Islands, Indonesia, once part of the Dutch East Indies.

deflowering as Fred himself. 'She was just aching for it,' Fred tells
Dr Saunders, while Louise coolly admits that 'I wanted him simply frightfully . . . And afterwards I didn't regret it . . . I didn't really care if I never
saw him again.' There are further, deeper sexual currents covertly running
through what Gore Vidal described as 'Maugham's one and only crypto-
fag novel'. Fred himself, whose girlish beauty is much dwelt upon,
develops a strong emotional attachment to Louise's fiancé, the manly Erik:
he had been unaware that the two were engaged when he seduced Louise
and is appalled when he hears of Erik's death. 'Oh God. If I'd known I
wouldn't have touched her,' Fred bursts out. 'Erik was worth ten of her.
He meant all the world to me.' And Dr Saunders, through whose eyes
the drama is viewed, has a close, if unspoken attachment to his Chinese
servant, Ah Kay, who brings him tea in the morning and prepares his
pipes of opium last thing at night. 'He was a slim, comely youth with
large black eyes and a skin as smooth as a girl's . . . Dr Saunders sometimes flattered himself with the thought that Ah Kay regarded him with
affection.'

If not without flaws, *The Narrow Corner* is a remarkable novel, one
that has been consistently underrated by critics. There is an occasional
clumsiness in design and there are a couple of typically Maughamian
*longueurs*; but on the whole it shows an impressive mastery of technique,
in the beautifully controlled, understated style, and in the careful withholding of information, so that the reader is all the time kept in a state
of pleasurable suspense. Above all, and dominating the story, there are two
of Maugham's most complex and fascinating characters, Dr Saunders and
the rascally Captain Nichols. Saunders, a medical man and a Buddhist by
belief, has seen everything and nothing surprises him. 'Under his bushy
grey eyebrows his green eyes gleamed bright, amusing, and clever . . . his
expression was charged with an extreme but not ill-natured malice . . .
He was an agreeable companion, but neither sought intimacy nor gave
it.' Captain Nichols is an out-and-out scoundrel, unashamedly amoral, but
at the same time courageous, amusing and possessed of a devilish charm.

Returning from London to the south of France at the end of November
1931 Maugham had immediately begun work on his next project, one
to which he had inadvertently drawn a great deal of attention. In a newspaper interview he had casually remarked that he was approaching the
end of his career as a dramatist and intended to write only two more
plays. 'This matter, which I supposed of concern only to myself, aroused
nearly as much interest as though a well-known prize-fighter had
announced his intention of retiring from the ring.' For this reason the

atmosphere on the first night of *For Services Rendered*, on 1 November 1932, was more than usually electric, although the audience that crowded into the Globe full of anticipation was to leave the theatre sharply divided on the merits of what it had seen.

*For Services Rendered* has its roots in Maugham's loathing of war, a loathing intensified by an acute awareness of the ominous deterioration in international relations. Although at a distance from the centres of power, Maugham was intensely alert to developments in the political arena and often very perceptive about them. 'I live on the Continent,' he told a reporter, 'and every moment I see the countries of Europe arming themselves to the teeth as hard as they can go, and that is why I wrote my play . . . to try to protect the new youth of today from dying in the trenches or losing five years of their lives in a war that seems almost imminent.'

The play, set in 1930, paints a bleak picture of post-war chaos and disillusion as symbolised by the Ardsleys, the family of a country solicitor living in a small village in Kent. The son, Sydney, awarded the MC, was blinded in action; a daughter, Eva, lost her fiancé and now faces a frustrated middle age as the family drudge; another daughter married beneath her to a heavy-drinking farmer; while the youngest girl, Lois, already twenty-six, regards her prospects as bleak. Only the head of the family, old Ardsley, is convinced that all is well, stupidly unaware of the misery that surrounds him. In the course of the action, played out against an ordinary domestic background of tennis, card games and tea, the family fractures: there is madness, suicide and a heartless seduction, with Lois agreeing to run off with a rich neighbour – a red-faced roué with a wretchedly unhappy wife – in a desperate bid to escape. Harsh, bitter and uncompromising, *For Services Rendered* is a powerful work, at one level dealing with the destructiveness of war, and at another with the devastating results of self-delusion and of the failure to take responsibility. In the Ardsley family it is the blind brother, Sydney, who sees the situation most clearly. 'She wants a man, that's all,' he states bluntly after a hysterical outburst from his spinster sister Eva; and he understands his own position only too well.

> The day's long past since I was a wounded hero for whom nothing was good enough. Fifteen years is a long time . . . They say suffering ennobles. It hasn't ennobled me. It's made me sly and cunning. Evie says I'm selfish. I am. But I'm damned artful. I know how to make people do things for me by working on their sympathy.

Maugham had no great expectations for his new work's reception, which in the event was much as he had anticipated: despite a first-rate cast, with Cedric Hardwicke, Flora Robson, Ralph Richardson and Marda Vanne, the play closed after barely two months.* Decades later *For Services Rendered* was to be recognised as one of Maugham's finest dramas, but for the middle and upper classes of the 1930s such radical pessimism was unpalatable; at a time of political instability and acute economic depression audiences were angry at what they saw as a lack of patriotism and they were made uncomfortable by the author's dismal prediction for the future. 'We were the dupes of the incompetent fools who ruled the nations,' Sydney rages at his smug old father. 'They muddle on, muddle on, and one of these days they'll muddle us all into another war . . . It's all bunk what they're saying to you, about honour and patriotism and glory, bunk, bunk, bunk.'

Typical of the outrage the play provoked was an article by the journalist Cecil Roberts, who gave full vent to his fury in an editorial in the *Daily Express* headed, 'Should Maugham Get Away with It?' 'I was stirred to indignation by the nature of this play,' Roberts wrote, '[by] its bitter, jaundiced outlook on human affairs, by its sheer determination to stress human misery, cowardice, selfishness, greed, and bestiality . . . It is a play of malevolent propaganda against those who live with courage and hope.' There were others, too, who considered the author's pacifism reprehensible, his patriotism in doubt, although the play did have its supporters, among them Desmond MacCarthy and James Agate, who in the *Sunday Times* concluded that *For Services Rendered* was 'the work of a man possessed of something like genius'. But controversy continued, with the contradictory opinions about the play neatly distilled in an exchange of letters between two literary acquaintance of Maugham's, Louis Marlow and Llewellyn Powys. 'My dear Lulu,' wrote Marlow.

> Somerset Maugham's new play is remarkably fine . . . *Incomparably* his best play . . . I was moved to tears and, for some hours afterwards, the area of my liver, spleen, kidneys and whatever else is thus affectible, remained disturbed & exhausted. I wish I could take you to see it. I have more free tickets for next Saturday – and long to see it again. Your loving Louis

To this Powys replied,

> My dear Louis, *For Services Rendered* obviously has a grip of a kind but good heavens Louis I was astonished that you can think so highly of it . . . God! I think it is a thoroughly banal and commonplace piece of work –

* It fared even worse in New York, where it lasted only three weeks.

utterly lacking in imagination, platitudinous, popular, melodramatic and without any distinction except a rather obvious Movie House Grip. If this is your idea of the tragic impact Good Luck to you! Yours Lulu

Unruffled by the reaction Maugham continued calmly to carry out his plan, his last play, *Sheppey*, unlike any other in the Maugham repertoire. The plot tells of a simple man, a barber, a contented husband and father, who dreams of retiring one day to a little cottage near the sea in Kent. The first act opens with Sheppey in the barber's shop in Jermyn Street, where we see him enjoying his usual lively banter with his colleagues, his clients, the manicurist and the girl behind the cash-desk. But although all looks normal two events make the day unusual: Sheppey has just returned from giving evidence in court against a thief, and the sight of the poor, half-starved creature in the dock has upset him; then he learns that he has won an enormous sum on the Irish Sweepstake. In Act Two, set in Sheppey's modest home in Camberwell, his wife and daughter are brought up short in their pleasant plans for the future: instead of spending his winnings on improving their own lives, Sheppey tells them, he intends to follow Jesus's teaching and give everything away to the poor. Underlining his point he brings into the house the same thief he had faced earlier in court as well as a local prostitute down on her luck. Clearly there is nothing for it but to have the man declared insane, which the family doctor is more than happy to do.

Up to this point the play follows closely a short story, 'A Bad Example', that Maugham wrote nearly forty years earlier, published in his first collection, *Orientations*, in 1899. In 'A Bad Example' the plot is similar, with the hero, a clerk in the City, declared insane when he decides to give everything away after witnessing some harrowing examples of poverty and starvation at a coroner's inquest. If it is extraordinary that this particular theme should have remained alive for so long in Maugham's imagination, even more extraordinary is what he now chose to do with it. The short story ends with Mr Clinton about to be carted off to an asylum. In the last act of the play, Sheppey, who we know is about to be certified, is left alone on stage, the thief and the prostitute having returned, with considerable relief, to their respective occupations. It is evening, the lights are dim, and Sheppey is dozing in his wing-chair. Silently the door opens and Bessie, the prostitute, reappears; but is it Bessie?

SHEPPEY: You are Bessie Legros, aren't you? You're just like 'er. And yet there's something different. You're not Bessie Legros.

WOMAN: No.
SHEPPEY: Who are you?
WOMAN: Death.

A surreal dialogue then takes place between the two, in which the reluctant Sheppey is gently but implacably prepared for his imminent demise.

SHEPPEY: To tell you the truth, I'm feeling rather tired. I don't feel like making a journey to-night.

DEATH: It's an easy one . . .

SHEPPEY: You know, I don't feel at all well. I think I ought to see the doctor.

DEATH: You'll feel better presently.

*Sheppey* opened at Wyndham's Theatre on 14 September 1933, to a somewhat bemused response. Nobody had expected anything like this. To its author it was 'a perfectly straightforward sardonic comedy . . . I cannot for the life of me', he wrote, 'see why it should puzzle because the theme is Jesus rather than adultery.' Yet puzzle it did, and it was not only the critics who were unsure what to make of it: both the producer, Bronson Albery, and the director, John Gielgud, admitted to a degree of bewilderment. During rehearsals Albery had tried and failed to persuade the author to change the last scene, 'so as to make it more palatable to the audience', while Gielgud admitted he was confused by the play's generic identity. 'It seemed to be conceived in an extraordinary mixture of styles,' he wrote, 'with a first act of Pinero-esque comedy, a second of almost Shavian cynicism and drama, and a third of tragic fantasy.' Gielgud's job was made more difficult by the fact that Maugham was out of the country for the first two weeks of rehearsal, and when he did appear was prepared to offer little in the way of criticism or guidance. 'I was very nervous when I approached him first,' Gielgud recalled.

> He was charming, but seemed oddly devoid of enthusiasm. He made some practical and useful suggestions, but he did not comment at all on the work that I had done. I could not tell whether or not he was excited that a play of his was in rehearsal and that the first night was drawing near. He seemed dispassionate, quite untouched by the expectant atmosphere in the theatre.

Matters were made worse by problems over casting, and in the title role the choice of Ralph Richardson, an actor who had played mainly in Shakespeare, turned out to be far from ideal. Agate wrote of him that

'Shakespeare will out ... [and] the player's whole manner of speech, including his respect for intonation, was never heard in a Jermyn Street saloon,' an opinion shared by Noël Coward, who in a heartfelt letter to Maugham described Richardson's performance as 'extremely false and theatrical'.

> I almost bowed in acknowledgement when he occasionally condescended to drop an aitch just to show he was of humble origin ... his ringing, beautifully modulated voice was so dreadfully incongruous ... Oh Willie Willie how very very naughty of you to write a play filled with subtle implications and exquisite satire and then cheerfully allow dull witted lunatics to cast it!

*Sheppey* ran for only eighty-three performances, a fact which perturbed its author not at all. '[It] was the last play I ever intended to write ... [and] I was perfectly indifferent to its success or failure,' he explained some years later. 'Since then I have never had the smallest inclination to write a play. That they continue to be acted from time to time in various parts of the world, shows, I suppose, that I had some natural gift for the theatre.' So it was that after a phenomenally successful career spanning more than thirty years, during which he wrote twenty-seven original plays and three adaptations, Maugham with a sigh of relief shut up shop and left the whole business behind him. Shortly after *Sheppey* closed he wrote to Coward, 'I cannot tell you how I loathe the theatre,' a view he continued to hold for the rest of his life. 'With all its glamour, I found it a frustrating and maddening world, full of childish people' and 'I can never get over my astonishment that people remain enraptured with it till ripe old age.' (In a sentence deleted from his 1938 memoir *The Summing Up* he wrote, 'I have never been able to look upon actors as human beings.') Maugham made a great deal of money from his dramatic work, which would continue to be produced, translated, adapted for cinema and television, but now he could turn his attention elsewhere. 'I want to write novels & stories & essays,' he told Bert Alanson. '[They give] one so much more scope to say what one wants to, & though of course the financial result can never be as great, it is surer; and after all no one but an idiot would at my time of life do anything but what he wants.'

Interestingly, Maugham once referred to the fact that only in his playwriting had he knowingly compromised, deliberately designed his work to meet the demands of a specific audience at a specific period of time. Now, released from any such obligation he could do precisely as he pleased, and during the next decade and beyond, far from a slowing down he was to experience a surge of creative energy which was to take him in some unexpected directions. There would be an immensely ambitious novel dealing with a realm of experience of crucial significance to its author; there would be essays and criticism, emanating from a lifetime's attentive reading; and, perhaps most surprising from this most private of men, there would be works of autobiography, one of which in the eyes of many was to place him firmly and for ever beyond the pale.

# 13

# The Teller of Tales

With his career as a dramatist behind him, Maugham's working life temporarily took on a more leisurely pace. His name was constantly kept before the public, but as a result of relatively little effort on his part. During the 1930s several short-story collections were published, including *First Person Singular* and *Ah King, Cosmopolitans*, an omnibus edition of very short pieces written for *Cosmopolitan* magazine, and *Altogether*,* a compendium of reprinted longer stories. There was a Tauchnitz edition of Maugham's works, and a Pocket Edition brought out by Heinemann, who between 1931 and 1934 also published the selected plays in six volumes. At the end of the decade *The Circle* was being filmed in London for the new medium of television, which would have introduced Maugham to yet another audience had it not been for the order to close down the service on the outbreak of war. In 1933 Nelson Doubleday, excited by his world-famous author's phenomenal sales, commissioned a massive anthology of English prose and poetry, *The Travellers' Library*,† with Maugham choosing the entries and writing a brief introduction to each section. Nelson's hunch that this was just what the market required proved correct, and less than a year after publication Maugham reported with satisfaction that 'seven hundred colleges in America have already adopted *The Travellers Library* for compulsory reading . . . I am tickled at finding myself in the unexpected rôle of an educationist.' Eager to repeat the success, Doubleday suggested a similar exercise with an anthology of short stories, *Tellers of Tales*, which appeared in 1939.

But it was Maugham himself as a teller of tales, as a writer of short stories, that he was most widely known and admired. With one single exception,‡ all his 122 stories appeared first in magazines, easily accessible

* Entitled *East and West* in America.

† Reissued as *Fifty Modern English Writers*, 'a stupid title not of my invention' Maugham told Desmond MacCarthy (Raymond Toole Stott *A Bibliography of the Works of W. Somerset Maugham* p. 187).

‡ 'The Book-Bag' was rejected by Ray Long for *Cosmopolitan* because of the shocking nature of its content, an incestuous affair between brother and sister.

on newspaper-stands and station bookstalls even to people who would never dream of entering a library or bookshop. 'Beloved by unliterary, unofficial, unacademic humanity', as Glenway Wescott put it, Maugham, 'the mahatma of middlebrow culture', exerted a hold over the popular imagination matched by few of his contemporaries. 'Mr Maugham's short stories are among the best now being written,' wrote William Plomer in a review of *Ah King*. There was something infinitely seductive in the persona he frequently adopted as narrator, a narrator who both is and yet is not part of the story, a man of the world with a clear eye and sardonic sense of humour, who in a leisurely manner over a drink and a cigar settles down to confide in the reader something pretty fascinating about the kind of ordinary chap encountered any day of the week in a bar or club. 'His extraordinary knowledge of human beings is like that of an experienced confessor,' said Raymond Mortimer, and like a confessor 'he is never shocked'. The deceptive simplicity of Maugham's method conceals a well-honed technique, as anyone who has tried to imitate it will know: in the opinion of the novelist John Fowles it is as necessary for a writer to have mastered the 'Maughamesque short story . . . as it is for an artist to have mastered the art of drawing'. His hallmarks were the plain style, the absolute verisimilitude, the dramatist's deftness with dialogue and often the provision of the unexpected denouement, the twist in the tail, that leaves the reader shocked and delighted. 'His plots are cool and deadly and his timing is absolutely flawless,' said Raymond Chandler, himself an expert in the genre. Naturally there were critics quick to condemn him for what he was not: his stories were not remarkably profound; he was never particularly inventive; and he lacked the vision, the genius, 'the transforming passion', in V. S. Pritchett's words, of a Conrad or Chekhov; and yet what he did he did superbly well, and occasionally he approached perfection.

It was with the short story that Maugham found his true métier. 'I have never pretended to be anything but a story-teller,' as he stated more than once. He enjoyed the form, worked hard at it, and was always on the look-out for new characters and plots. Just as he had done all those years before in the East, he continued to encourage strangers and familiars alike to describe their experiences, even if there were sometimes a high price to be paid for the process. 'I find it often a very tedious business,' he wrote in his notebook. 'It requires a good deal of patience . . . [and] you must be ready to listen for hours to the retailing of second-hand information in order at last to catch the hint or the casual remark that betrays.' Knowing his method, friends were helpful in putting material his way. Rebecca West, for instance, wrote to recommend her sister, Letitia

Fairfield, who was coming to the Côte d'Azur on holiday. 'She is not mondaine, she doesn't play bridge, and she is a devout Roman Catholic,' Rebecca warned him. '[But] she is a doctor and a lawyer, and has worked on the L.C.C. for twenty years, and has some good prison and asylum yarns, which she tells very well.'

Curiously, Maugham never seemed to find in the south of France the wealth of inspiration he uncovered elsewhere. The Riviera, that 'sunny place for shady people', as he once memorably described it, serves as a background for only a handful of tales, among them 'Gigolo and Gigolette', 'The Lion's Skin' and the exquisitely comic 'The Three Fat Women of Antibes'. Perhaps he was wary of raising hackles so near home, as otherwise it is difficult to believe he would not have been tempted by the richly rewarding cast of characters dotted along the coast from Cannes to Monte Carlo. 'He had a certain dreadful circle along the Riviera,' said Dadie Rylands, '[a] group of very trivial, rich expatriates . . . [but] after work he wanted some light entertainment and he enjoyed the spectacle of people's silliness.' Dadie, dyed-in-the-wool Bloomsbury, had nothing but contempt for such a breed, yet there was a side of Maugham that revelled in the trappings of luxury and wealth, that enjoyed being lionised by a transatlantic millionairess with a fabulous villa and a famous chef. Among his regular hostesses, almost all American, were Charlotte Boissevain, Marion, Lady Bateman, Emily Sherfesee, daughter of a meat-packing king from Chicago, Daisy Fellowes, the Singer sewing-machine heiress, the sharp-tongued Princess Ottoboni – she and her homosexual husband were known as Péderaste et Médisance – and the notorious Lady Kenmare, who was popularly supposed to have murdered four of her five husbands ('Lady Killmore' was Maugham's nickname for her). 'He was too much impressed by money, and by being able to associate with millionaires as a millionaire,' remarked Cyril Connolly with his customary perspicuity, '[but] he gave the Riviera point, so that it became more than just a rest-camp for Philistines.'

During the winter many of the villas were closed and their owners departed to London, Paris or New York, but during the summer social life became frenetic; the harbours were crammed with large yachts, the hotels were full, and chic-looking crowds – the women in beach pyjamas, the men *en matelot* – shopped, strolled, sunbathed on the sand and met each other for cocktails at the crowded little bars along the Croisette. With guests staying most of the summer, Maugham was glad to be able to take them to lunch and dinner in private houses or at smart local restaurants, at Caramello's overlooking the harbour at Saint-Jean, at the outrageously expensive La Réserve at Beaulieu or, grandest of all, on the terrace of the Casino in Monte Carlo, where there was dancing every night and a spectacular cabaret on the stage overlooking the sea. Although he rarely played at the tables himself (he left that to Gerald), Maugham dined at the Casino, attended the galas and was on excellent terms with the father of the Principality's ruler, the handsome, half-Mexican Prince Pierre. It was at the Casino one evening that Maugham saw the terrifying stunt which he later made the basis of his story 'Gigolo and Gigolette'. In this he gives a decidedly sour impression of the clientele, so bored and blasé they turn up night after night in the hope of seeing the cabaret artist killed while performing her dangerous act. The group's hostess is Eva Barrett, a wealthy American.

> It was a representative Riviera party. There was an English Lord and his Lady . . . who were prepared to dine with anyone who would give them a free meal . . . There was an Italian countess who was neither Italian nor a countess . . . and there was a Russian prince who was ready to make Mrs Barrett a princess and in the meantime sold champagne, motor-cars and Old Masters on commission.
>
> While they were standing at the bar Paco Espinel passed through and stopped to shake hands with Eva Barrett . . . It was his duty to be civil to the rich and the great . . .
>
> 'Got a good table for me, Paco?' said Eva Barrett.
>
> 'The best.' His eyes, fine, dark Argentine eyes, expressed his admiration of Mrs Barrett's opulent, ageing charms. This also was business.

A more charitable picture is given in 'The Three Fat Women of Antibes', an affectionate send-up of feminine silliness and rivalry among a trio of middle-aged ladies who take a villa together one summer in order to diet and play bridge. 'It was their fat that had brought them together and bridge that had cemented their alliance.' Beatrice, Arrow and Frances (known as Frank) are very much at home on the coast, either on the beach mixing with French, Italians and 'the long-limbed English', or at the Monkey House at Eden Roc,★ 'an enclosure covered with glass overlooking the sea, with a bar at the back . . . it was crowded with chattering people in bathing costumes, pyjamas, or dressing-gowns, who were seated at the tables having drinks'. It is here that the friends finally face defeat: after nobly supporting each other through a tormenting fortnight of nothing but rusks, tomatoes and hard-boiled eggs, their resolve

★ The Hôtel Eden Roc was the inspiration for the Hôtel des Etrangers in Scott Fitzgerald's *Tender is the Night.*

is fatally undermined by the delicious breakfasts served every morning at the Monkey House.

> In front of Beatrice was a plate of croissants and a plate of butter, a pot of strawberry jam, coffee, and a jug of cream . . .
>
> 'You'll kill yourself,' said Frank.
>
> 'I don't care,' mumbled Beatrice with her mouth full.

Never able to stay in one place for long, Maugham had established a pleasant annual routine, spending several weeks in London every autumn and spring,* and with Gerald travelling on the Continent for part of the summer. Venice and Florence were favourite destinations, as were Munich and Vienna, but the two unchanging fixtures each year were Salzburg in August for the music festival and Badgastein for its spa. Maugham always took care of his health, susceptible to chest complaints and dogged by recurrences of malaria, and over the years he had been a frequent visitor to spas in France and Italy, to Vichy, Abano and Brides-les-Bains, taking Gerald with him as often as possible in order to dry him out for a few weeks. But it was Badgastein in the Austrian Tyrol that became the favourite. Lodged at the luxurious Kaiserhof the two of them ate sparingly, submerged themselves in the thermal waters and took long walks along the Gastein Valley. Maugham liked the discipline of the spa routine, enjoyed the fresh air and bracing hikes through the mountains, and as long as he could play bridge in the evening was perfectly prepared to put up with the monotony. 'The cure at Bad Gastein . . . is amazing,' he told Sibyl Colefax. 'The place is unbelievably dull & staggeringly expensive . . . [but] I never felt so well in my life.'

From Badgastein to Salzburg was an easy drive, but here the pace was very different, the town thronged with a fashionable international society for whom the festival was an unmissable event. Under its two leading conductors, Toscanini and Bruno Walter, the Salzburg festival during the 1930s was at its most brilliant, with the Vienna Philharmonic and the Vienna State Opera performing throughout the day, from morning to late at night. Music meant a great deal to Maugham; he was not trained, had never played an instrument and to professional friends, such as the pianist Harriet Cohen, he described himself as 'very ignorant', yet he derived enormous pleasure from listening to music, his tastes were catholic and he was always interested in exploring new experience. When in Paris or London, Munich or Vienna, he went regularly to concerts and the

* For Maugham to retain his non-resident tax status he could spend no more than ninety days a year in Britain.

opera, to Wagner in particular; but Salzburg was the great highlight in his calendar. 'We went to a lovely performance of *Rosenkavalier*,' he reported to Alan Searle in August 1934. 'I have never heard the trio in the last act more beautifully sung; & last night *The Magic Flute* . . . We leave here tomorrow immediately after the *Verdi Requiem*.' In between performances there was a demanding social schedule, with English, French, Germans, Italians – many of them dolled up in peasant costume, the women in dirndls, the men in shorts and feathered hats – meeting each other in restaurants and cafés, for picnics and for excursions on the lakes. 'I am pretty well tired out,' Alan was told. 'Four or five hours music every day since we arrived, lunch parties & supper parties . . . [But] for a wonder the weather is quite lovely & all the bits & pieces are strutting about in their new Tyrolean costumes.' Even Gerald had succumbed and bought a pair of lederhosen, '[and] expects to make a great sensation with them on the Riviera'.

Gerald of course was left behind when Maugham went to England, and in London it was Alan Searle in whose company the writer was most often seen. The young man was generally popular with Maugham's old friends: Barbara Back was fond of him, as was Peter Stern, who invited him to dine in her chambers in Albany. When in October 1934 Maugham was asked for the first time to stay at Renishaw, Osbert Sitwell's family seat in Derbyshire, Searle was included in the invitation, welcomed by Osbert and David Horner and cosseted by Osbert's sister Edith. Yet Maugham was careful never to cross the line by taking his lover into company that was likely to be censorious. With Gerald it was different: socially he was of the same class, he spoke with an educated accent, and his position as Maugham's secretary provided the perfect cover. But Alan was a cockney straight out of the East End. There was no question, for instance, of introducing him into the family, towards whose members Maugham had always behaved with the utmost decorum, looked up to by his nephew and nieces as an eminently respectable figure.

Of the three surviving brothers, Maugham, the youngest, was by far the richest and most famous, a fact resolutely unacknowledged by his nearest in age, F.H., who rarely referred to any of Willie's books or plays. This was despite the fact that he himself was near the top in his own profession: in 1928 F.H. had been knighted, and in 1935 was honoured further when he was appointed a lord of appeal as Baron Maugham. The eldest brother, Charles, had been much less fortunate in life. A quiet, modest man, with 'easily the nicest character of the four of us' according to Maugham, Charles had retired from his legal practice in Paris and moved to London with his wife and only son, Ormond, the boy who had been paralysed in a childhood accident. In January 1935, Ormond died, aged only twenty-five, followed six months later by his father, at seventy. In the British press Charles Maugham's death was only briefly reported, of interest solely on account of his family connections. 'Judge and Author Bereaved' was the heading over three very short paragraphs in the *Daily Telegraph*. 'Charley's death was expected,' Maugham told Gerald Kelly, 'but was nevertheless a shock to me since it brought back to me recollections of my earliest childhood & youth. He was a very good man, I think the best I have ever known, & wonderfully kind & unselfish & unenvious.'

Charles's death made little change to the barbed relationship between the two remaining brothers; there was an unspoken mutual respect but the wariness and hostility remained, although it never had any bearing on Maugham's feelings for F.H.'s children. All three girls were married, and Kate and Diana had both published novels, their uncle taking trouble to comment helpfully on their work, if privately he had little opinion of their ability. The third sister, Honor Earl, was a painter, and for some reason she and Maugham never hit it off, he dismissing her work as 'quite negligible' and making no secret of the fact that she bored him. The only time she got his attention, Honor recalled, was when she became a visitor at Holloway women's prison. One of the inmates there was Ruby, a prostitute, who specialised in '"kinky clients" . . . [and] the only time I ever managed to interest my uncle, Somerset Maugham, in anything I said was when I told him of some of Ruby's experiences'.

But of all F.H.'s children the one to whom Maugham became most attached was the youngest, Robin. Born in 1916, with almost a generation between himself and his sisters, Robin endured a miserable childhood, frightened of his father and badly bullied at Eton. After his sisters left home, Robin was brought up as an only child, his holidays spent living 'alone with my parents in a cold, grey world of loneliness'. During those early years he retained only vague recollections of his uncle, 'a well-dressed attractive man with a skin the colour of parchment, who came to visit my mother'; but from the time Robin left school at seventeen Maugham began to take an interest in him. He was a well-mannered boy, eager to please and, despite a short upper lip and a long, pointy nose like a shrew's, nice-looking. Maugham had always wanted a son, and up till now his paternal instincts, so wretchedly warped in his relations with Liza, had emerged mainly in the protective feelings he showed towards his male lovers, not only Haxton and Searle, but towards young men like

Beverley Nichols and Godfrey Winn. Now there was Robin, and for this nephew Maugham began to feel a strong fatherly affection, an affection, however, in which there was a strong, if subliminal, element of sexuality. This undercurrent of erotic attraction was remarked upon over the years by a number of Maugham's homosexual friends, among them Harold Nicolson and Glenway Wescott. 'I'm not saying I think there was incest,' said Wescott, who saw both men at close quarters, 'but Willie was infatuated with Robin, and told everyone how extraordinary he was.' There was so much in Robin's situation to provoke Maugham's sympathy: he pitied his position at home, which reminded him of his own unhappy childhood, and understood very well the boy's problems with his father. F.H. was determined his son should read for the Bar, but Robin wanted to be a writer, and on this he naturally turned to his uncle for advice. And there was another, more sensitive subject on which Maugham was able to help. Robin was struggling with the problem of his sexual identity, desperately trying to persuade himself he was 'normal', terrified of his father's reaction should he admit to being queer.

In the summer of 1934, after Robin's last term at school, F.H. arranged for him to go to Vienna for a couple of weeks, chaperoned by his sister Kate. Hearing of this, Maugham wrote Robin a letter that any youth might dream of receiving from a rich and worldly uncle.

> This is only to say that if you find yourself in straitened circumstances, for I imagine that life in the great city may prove a little more expensive than your sainted parents imagine, you can write to me & I will come to the rescue. Also if you get into any hole, trouble or jamb [sic], I recommend you to communicate with me rather than with the above-mentioned sainted parents. Having led a vicious but not unpleasant life for a vast number of years I am conscious that there are difficulties which even the best brought-up young men cannot always avoid and being as you know a hardened cynic I have a great tolerance for the follies of the human race.

Maugham mischievously let drop to F.H. that as it happened Gerald was going to be in Vienna at the same time and would be pleased to keep an eye on the young people. F.H. was furious – 'the man's a drunkard and worse' – and forbade either of his children to have any contact with the infamous Haxton. 'But, of course, we did – quite by chance,' said Robin.

> We met him the first night we went to the opera, and I was extremely disappointed, for he didn't look wicked at all: he was a smart, dapper, lean man of forty with a small moustache, a cheerful laugh and an innocent

smile . . . But a week later, when Gerald got blind drunk in a weinstube,
I began to appreciate that he wasn't quite as innocent as he seemed.

Nor, by the time he returned home, was Robin. 'I learned many things
in Vienna at the age of seventeen,' he wrote later. Gerald offered to take
him to Venice for a couple of days on his own, driving there and back
in Maugham's big Voisin coupé. They shared a twin-bedded room at the
Danieli, and it was here that Gerald made his intentions plain. Robin,
shocked, pushed him off, whereupon Gerald crossly returned to his own
bed. 'I should have known,' he grumbled, before turning out the light
and falling asleep. The next day to the boy's relief no reference was made
to the previous night; on the contrary, 'he was very kind to me . . . [and]
took me sightseeing around Venice'.

Robin was only a year younger than Liza, but since the Maughams'
divorce the cousins, close in childhood, had been kept apart. When Liza
was seventeen Syrie arranged for her to be presented at Court, and during
her first season had thrown a memorable dance, paid for by Maugham, at
the house in the King's Road. The ballroom was banked with white
flowers, a parquet-floor had been laid in the garden, and a coffee-stall set
up in Glebe Place. 'I had a lovely party and enjoyed everything very, very
much,' said Liza, who had looked ravishing in pink-and-white tulle. 'All
the friends and all the contacts and what seemed to me the wide world,
everything was ready for me. It was a very happy time.' From the moment
of Liza's debut, Syrie focused on her daughter with a new intensity. To all
intents and purposes Liza was an only child, her half-brother Mounteney
having been consigned to the past. Judged to be backward, after leaving
school he had been put in the care of a farming couple in Essex, and his
mother was either denied access or of her own volition gave up trying
to see him. Liza was now the centre of her life, and the socially ambitious Syrie was determined not only that Liza should marry soon but that
she should marry well. Nothing was considered too good for Liza, and
her mother with her formidable energy oversaw every detail, every moment
of her day. 'She was wrapped up in cotton-wool,' said one of Liza's friends.
'She and Syrie were *very*, *very* close . . . far too much so.' Liza adored her
mother, but some commentators remarked on the way the young woman
appeared to be too much under her mother's thumb, one gossip-columnist
going so far as to describe her as puppet-like, with an 'almost mechanical correctness in speech and deportment. It seemed as if an inner voice
were continually saying, "On the command one – smile. On the command
two – say how much you are enjoying the party."'

Needless to say Maugham had not attended his daughter's dance, and he continued to keep as much distance between himself and his ex-wife as possible. From time to time, however, he was reluctantly involved in her affairs, as when Syrie, up to her old tricks, was again found to be engaging in some fancy footwork with the Inland Revenue. 'What do you think,' he wrote to Barbara Back in March 1934, 'I have to appear before the income tax authorities who are claiming two thousand pounds from me for Syrie's income tax: she is swearing that during the first four years I was at the Villa Mauresque she & I were living together. A bit thick, eh?'

This letter was written from Spain, from the Alhambra Palace Hotel in Granada. For some time Maugham had felt drawn to return to the subject of Spain, which since his year in Seville in the 1890s had continued to exert a powerful fascination. At ease in the language and widely read, especially in the writers of the Golden Age, his first idea had been a novel set in the sixteenth century, but now this was put aside in favour of a highly personal travel book. In February 1934 he and Gerald set off on a six-week tour in the Voisin, taking in Barcelona, Granada, Malaga, Seville, Córdoba, Toledo and Madrid. In Córdoba they were pleased to run into Alan Pryce-Jones, 'gay, fantastic & amusing', in Maugham's words, who joined them on a couple of expeditions into the spectacular mountains above Granada. Pryce-Jones was surprised by Maugham's practicality: after stopping for lunch at a small inn, he was impressed to see Maugham go into the kitchen and in fluent Spanish order an excellent luncheon of raw ham, a tortilla, fish and a good bottle of manzanilla sherry. Nonetheless the older man's company proved something of a strain, and returning to their hotel in the evening Alan found it a relief to have a cocktail alone in the bar with Gerald, that 'odious charmer', as he referred to him, who regaled him with a funny story about taking the writer J. B. Priestley to a brothel in Nice.

*Don Fernando*, the work resulting from the expedition, is an agreeable ramble through fifteenth- and sixteenth-century Spain, an idiosyncratic introduction to Spanish history and culture interspersed with recollections of Maugham's own travels in the country as a young man. In an easy, discursive manner he considers the work of the great novelists and dramatists, of Cervantes, Calderón, Lope de Vega, as well as the religious writers and mystics, like St Teresa, St Ignatius Loyola and Fray Luis de León. Interspersed with this are descriptions of the Spanish character and way of life, and an account of the work of the great painters, Velázquez, El Greco and Zurbarán. From a biographical point of view the most interesting section is on El Greco, in which Maugham in discussing the painter's putative homosexuality revealingly sets out his own view of the characteristics of the homosexual artist.

> a distinctive trait of the homosexual is a lack of deep seriousness over certain things that normal men take seriously. This ranges from an inane flippancy to a sardonic humour. He has a wilfulness that attaches importance to things that most men find trivial and on the other hand regards cynically the subjects which the common opinion of mankind has held essential to its spiritual welfare . . . He has small power of invention, but a wonderful gift for delightful embroidery . . . He stands on the bank, aloof and ironical, and watches the river of life flow on.

Published in 1935, *Don Fernando* received on the whole an indifferent reception, most critics treating it with little more than polite interest. 'St John of the Cross is not everyone's cup of tea,' as Raymond Mortimer in the *New Statesman* remarked. The exception was Graham Greene, whose Catholic sensibilities were finely attuned to this account of the country of the Catholic kings: 'This is Mr Maugham's best book . . . I have never', said Greene, 'read a book with more excitement and amusement . . . Mr Maugham is here at the peak of his achievement as an artist.'

The trip to Spain had been a success, and Gerald since recovering from his accident had been much more like his charming old self, 'kind, very considerate & easy to get on with', Maugham told Barbara. He was drinking less and concentrating more on his duties towards his employer, and as a result the quality of domestic life at the Mauresque had greatly improved. 'I have been playing golf today, a lovely day, & came back very tired,' Maugham wrote one evening to Alan Searle.

> Now I am writing to you after a long soak in a pine bath. Gerald has just given me a Baccardi cocktail & I am breaking off this little letter to drink it in peace. It was delicious, made with fresh limes from the garden . . . Here is Ernest to announce dinner . . . The fleet is in [he subsequently continued] & I went down the other night to have a look see; but it was lateish, & there was nothing much to reward me . . . We are rather thinking of going down again this evening . . .

So encouraged was Maugham by Gerald's good behaviour that he began planning a journey to Central America and the Caribbean, the first long voyage since the two of them had returned from the South Pacific in 1926. However, it was at this point that matters started to deteriorate fast, and Maugham was soon confiding to Searle and Barbara his intense anxiety about Haxton: the situation was worse than ever, it appeared, with Gerald back on the bottle and suffering fits of delirium tremens. 'Things are going very badly here & I do not know exactly what is going to happen,' Maugham wrote to Searle in April 1935. 'I am restless & miserable & do not know what to do.' By July little had changed and Maugham admitted to feeling deeply depressed, writing to Searle in August that circumstances were desperate and that he was left with no choice but to issue Gerald with an ultimatum.

> The doctor tells me that G. is so unbalanced that I must take no notice of anything he says, but in another week he (the doctor) assures me he will be in a state sufficiently normal for me to be able to discuss the position reasonably with him. I dread those sort of explanations, they make me wretched & nervous, but I realise that they now cannot be avoided, & I hope it will settle things for good & all. I am afraid it won't, however, & that not much will come of it. At present G. tells his friends that he will *not* come to America, but heaven knows whether that is a definite decision. If it does [sic] it will change my own plans very completely, & when he discovers how much this change must affect him he will very likely reverse his decision. Anyhow, even if the worst comes to the worst, & I don't really know what *is* the worst, the air will to some extent be cleared.

In the event the plan seemed to work: Gerald swore he would go on the wagon, and on 3 November they finally set sail for New York on the SS *Europa*, en route for the West Indies.

The crossing was agreeable, Maugham pleased to have been allotted a large and luxurious suite, and Gerald in excellent form. 'He has got off [had sex] twice during the journey & is very much pleased at having such a success,' Maugham reported to Alan. Each morning a sheaf of radio telegrams was delivered with invitations to events in New York, and on arrival a swarm of journalists and photographers came on board to question Maugham about his plans. Hoping for a quiet few days with Nelson Doubleday and his new wife Ellen at their house on Long Island he was slightly dismayed by the succession of large parties the Doubledays had arranged in his honour. Returning to Manhattan, comfortably installed at the Ritz-Carlton, Maugham was immediately caught up in a whirl of more parties, of theatres, newspaper interviews, photograph sessions, book signings, and insistent telephone calls from studio heads in Hollywood offering 'fantastic contracts', which, he said, 'it gives me singular pleasure to turn . . . down'. Maugham was a celebrity, recognised everywhere he went. The biographer Leon Edel remembers his excitement at catching sight of this famous man simply strolling down Madison Avenue like

anyone else, 'small, neat, impeccably dressed, wearing a soft hat he sometimes had to hang on to while his other hand controlled the straining
leashes of his dachshunds'. One of the few genuinely enjoyable social
occasions was a small luncheon with Maugham's old friend the novelist
and photographer Carl Van Vechten, who had taken the opportunity of
this visit to make a remarkable series of photographs of Maugham and
Haxton together. Alec Waugh was also at the lunch and he remembered
looking up to see Maugham deep in conversation with Van Vechten.
'Maugham was leaning forward talking with an absorbed concentration
that I had never seen before and was not to see again. "That's the real
man," I thought.' Even with so much hospitality pressed upon them,
Haxton remained resolutely abstemious. 'Gerald', Maugham reported, 'has
been behaving with great prudence & I have no complaints to make
whatever.'

The three-month voyage in the Caribbean, sailing from island to island
aboard a series of tramp steamers, had been looked forward to by Maugham,
who was counting on it to provide him with interesting new material
for his fiction: Rudyard Kipling, who had been there five years earlier,
had recommended its potential. The reality was uninspiring. Haiti was
the first stop, but the island whose exoticism and decadence was later to
enthral Graham Greene★ had little to offer Maugham. 'The place is picturesque enough,' he told Alan, '[but] there are no amusements of any kind.'
The next port of call, Martinique, was no better – 'I see no sign of any
material that I can make use of' – with Dominica and Trinidad equally
barren. 'The traders & planters can think & talk of nothing but rum
which is their sole source of revenue . . . [and] the wives are dull, dull,
dull & have nothing in the world to talk about . . . I ask you, what material can a novelist possibly hope to find in circumstances like these,'
Maugham wondered, gloomily concluding that 'There is not the romance
& excitement in the life in these islands that there is in the South Seas
& in Malaya.'

A longer and more considered account of the voyage was sent to a
relatively new friend, Lady Juliet Duff, at whose house in Wiltshire
Maugham had stayed on his last visit to England. Tall, handsome, angular,
aquiline, Lady Juliet, now in her fifties, was the daughter of the Earl of
Lonsdale and a noted patron of the arts, with a wide circle of friends in
the theatre and ballet worlds. Maugham was proud of his acquaintance
with Lady Juliet: 'You can't go higher in English society than [that],' he

★ Greene's novel about Haiti, *The Comedians*, was published in 1966.

used to boast; and wishing to make a good impression he took care in composing his letter, which is worth quoting from at length for the picture it gives of Maugham at work. 'The West Indies are disappointing,' he begins.

> They are very pretty of course, though not nearly so pretty as the islands of the South Seas, & the people who live in them are in too close touch with England or the US to have acquired the oddness which makes them when they live in places out of the beaten track so fascinating . . . I expected Martinique to be very romantic . . . [but] I found only mean little French fonctionnaires whose only idea was to save as much money as they could so that they could get back to France & planters whose sole conversation was the sugar out of which they make their living. They were immensely kind to me. They asked me night after night to dinner parties of twenty people, when I was placed between the women . . . who were completely silent; I started a topic of conversation, it dropped, I started another, it dropped; by the time we had finished the fish I had run dry & could think of nothing more to say. And when dinner was over the women sat round in a huge circle quite silent while the men stood alone in the other parts of the room & discussed sugar. And then there were the champagnes d'honneur . . . I hate champagne anyway because it gives me urticaria, & I especially hate sweet champagne; but I had to go through with it & pretend I was terribly flattered, though I knew I should not sleep a wink all night, & it lasted from six in the evening till dinner time or from half past eleven in the morning till one; & all the time I said polite things to the people round me & they said polite things to me, & as each bottle was brought along & my glass refilled my heart sank. Mais voyons donc, cher maître, videz votre verre, on ne bois pas le champagne tous les jours.*

During these dull weeks among the islands there was one brief period of absorbing interest. While staying on the South American mainland at Cayenne, the capital of French Guiana, Maugham obtained permission to visit the great penal colony at Saint-Laurent-de-Maroni. This was much more to his taste. Saint-Laurent, more like a town than a prison, had a population of over 6,000 entirely made up of convicts and their guards; all shipped out from France, a few were en route to far harsher conditions offshore, to one of the Îles de Salut, of which the Île de Diable (Devil's Island) was the most notorious; the majority, however, had remained at Saint-Laurent for years, considered too passive and harmless to attempt escape. The Governor lent Maugham a bungalow in which to stay for a

* 'Come on, my dear sir, empty your glass, we don't drink champagne every day.'

few days, '& gave me a couple of murderers serving their sentence to look after me', he told Juliet Duff. 'The director of the gaol said to me, you know, they're perfectly honest, you can leave anything about; but all the same I locked my door & my shutters when I went to bed at night.' At Saint-Laurent Maugham had 'a wonderful time', conducted all over the camp and allowed to talk to the inmates. In his notebook he describes the lay-out of the settlement in some detail, including the sinister execution cell. 'The guillotine is in a small room within the prison . . . To make sure that it will work well a banana stem is used for practice because it is of the same thickness as a man's neck. From the time a man is strapped up to the time his head is off, it takes only thirty seconds. The executioner gets a hundred francs for each execution.' In his interviews with the convicts, many of them murderers, the subject that interested him most was remorse, but 'of all the men I questioned', he said, 'I only found one who regretted his crime'. Saint-Laurent-de-Maroni was undoubtedly the highlight of the trip. 'I got one very good story★ out of my visit,' he told Alan. 'Grim naturally, but I think uncommon. I must be one of the few Englishmen who have seen that place.'

From Cayenne Maugham and Haxton began the long journey home, first by banana boat up the Mexican coast to California, staying for a few days in Hollywood, where Maugham was much fêted, then with Bert Alanson in San Francisco, before taking the train, the *Twentieth Century Limited*, to New York, sailing from there at the beginning of April 1936. At Cherbourg, as so often before, the two men parted, Gerald and the heavy luggage returning to the Mauresque, Maugham going on to London.

Uppermost in his mind was reunion with Alan Searle. 'I have been thinking much of you lately, more than usual in fact,' he had written from New York, '& I have got suggestions to make to you which I hope will please you.' During the previous five months Maugham had written every few days to Alan in England, describing the voyage ('My happiness would be complete if you were only here to share it with me') but also and at length discussing plans for Alan's future, offering advice on everything from his finances and his love affairs to his work in the prison service, and chivvying him about his health. Every page of this correspondence is permeated with Maugham's own deep feelings for the young man, while at the same time and in a fatherly fashion he is careful to put Searle's interests first, debating with scrupulous objectivity the pros and cons of Alan's various plans and ambitions. There was, for instance,

---

★ 'An Official Position' tells the story of Louis Remire, a policeman from Lyons, who is serving a twelve-year sentence at Saint-Laurent for murdering his wife.

a marriage proposal made to Alan by a rich older woman. 'I can quite see that the prospect of unlimited money & all possible luxury . . . must be exciting & tempting,' Maugham allowed, '[but] remember that to be a rich woman's husband is a whole time job. No woman that I have ever known fails to exact her money's worth . . . Further of course you must be prepared to give up your friends . . .' And this last point revealed the crux of the matter. 'So far as I am concerned I should regret it if you did a thing which must necessarily separate me from you. We have been so intimate for so many years that I have got into the habit of looking upon you as a fixture in my life or what remains of it; but that is a purely selfish & personal view.'

The truth was that Maugham now looked longingly upon Alan as the ideal companion. He was attractive, efficient and sweet-natured; he enjoyed travel, was musical, knew about and had a very good eye for pictures; unlike Gerald, Alan never got drunk, never made scenes; above all he was biddable. First and foremost Maugham was a writer, and about his writing he was ruthlessly self-protective. He needed to guard his privacy, to keep the outside world at bay. For years the role of guardian and administrator had been Gerald's, but Gerald could no longer be relied upon. Not only was his behaviour destroying the essential solitude and calm but it was often he who had to be looked after, requiring an expenditure of time and emotional energy on Maugham's part that was profoundly resented. For the moment all was well, but Maugham was sceptical of any lasting reform, and he dreaded a return to the horrific experiences of the recent past. It was Gerald whom he loved, Gerald who was in his blood, but Alan whom he needed. There was no question of Maugham abandoning Gerald, but he felt that Searle was essential to his work, and it was this strong instinct for artistic survival that was largely driving him now.

Maugham arrived in London on 10 April 1936. 'I am only coming to see you,' he had written to Alan before setting out on his transatlantic crossing. The most important topic to be discussed was that of the young man's future. Alan loved his work with the Salvation Army in Bermondsey and for the Discharged Prisoners' Aid Society at Wormwood Scrubs, and kept Maugham well supplied with stories.* On several occasions he took him to see for himself the mean streets of the East End, and once even arranged for him to visit the prison, warning him that to save embarrassment if he saw anyone he knew among the inmates he was to make no sign of recognition. The Scrubs, a first offenders' prison, Maugham

---

* The plots of 'Episode', 'The Kite' and 'The Round Dozen' were all supplied by Alan.

described as 'grim and cold . . . I had goose-flesh as the gates were unlocked for us and we went in.' There was no immediate possibility of Alan working full time for Maugham, but they talked about various schemes which in the future might allow Searle to come more often to the Mauresque. 'Of course what I should like is that you should spend at least several months, a year if you thought you could, with me & making the Mauresque your headquarters . . . It would be grand to have you there for an indefinite time & be able to go on long trips here & there with you.' In the meantime, Maugham had to content himself with seeing Alan on his visits to London and for occasional holidays on the Riviera.

On his way south Maugham stopped in Paris, partly at the request of Marie Laurencin, who had asked to paint his portrait. Mlle Laurencin had been to the Mauresque several years earlier to see the four pictures of hers, of graceful, pale-faced young girls, frivolous and sugary, which hung in the dining-room. 'Ses Laurencins étaient jolis,' she said approvingly. This amicability was furthered when in 1934 Maugham wrote an enthusiastic preface for the catalogue to a Laurencin exhibition at the Mayor Gallery in London, for which no doubt she felt indebted. He for his part was flattered by her suggestion that he should sit for her, 'but felt it only right to remind her that I was not a young thing with a complexion of milk and roses . . . but an elderly gentleman with a sallow, wrinkled skin and tired eyes'. He posed in her studio during four afternoons, during which she told him the story of her life. 'She was very frank and I enjoyed myself,' said Maugham.* When she had finished she put down her brushes and looked analytically at the canvas. 'Vous savez', she said, 'on se plaint toujours que mes portraits ne sont pas ressemblants. Je ne peux pas vous dire à quel point je m'en fou.'† With that, she lifted the canvas off the easel and handed it to her sitter as a present. Maugham expressed his gratitude but privately he considered his portrait was indeed a poor likeness, 'lousy' as he privately described it. Later his admiration for her work diminished further and he sold his Laurencins, causing the painter considerable pique when she heard of it: he had become 'trop mondain' ('too worldly'), she said crossly. 'J'ai dû être remplacée par un autre snobisme.'‡

Back on the Riviera, Maugham spent only a few weeks at home before

* In his 1944 novel *The Razor's Edge*, Maugham used parts of Marie Laurencin's story, she herself bearing marked similarities to the character of Suzanne Rouvier.

† 'People complain that my portraits are not a good likeness. I should tell you I don't give a damn.'

‡ 'I had to be replaced by another snobbery.'

he returned to England. In April Liza's engagement had been announced, her fiancé Lieutenant-Colonel Vincent Paravicini, son of the Swiss Minister to the Court of St James's. Paravicini was delightful, a sweet-natured man of notable elegance and charm, but Syrie was furiously disappointed in her daughter's choice and had 'fought like a steer' against the match. In Syrie's view Vincent was just another young man about town, and with neither money nor title was certainly not good enough for her daughter. On this occasion, however, Liza defied her: she loved Vincent, was determined to marry him, and Syrie had no choice but to give in. The wedding, a sumptuous society occasion, took place on 20 July 1936, at fashionable St Margaret's, Westminster, Liza, aged twenty-one, looking pale but beautiful in a white brocade dress designed by Schiaparelli. For the first time in years her parents appeared together, walking down the aisle arm in arm, Maugham in top hat and tails to give his daughter away. At the large reception afterwards at the Swiss Legation Maugham behaved towards his ex-wife with an immaculate courtesy. 'I found myself posi-tively in danger of falling in love with him again!' Syrie gushed. 'It was the first time since our courtship that I ever knew Willie to be so wonder-fully thoughtful towards me.' As a wedding present Maugham had bought the young couple a house in Wilton Street, off Belgrave Square, and for her contribution Syrie had decorated it. 'A perfect decorator's house,' Maugham dismissively remarked when he saw the finished result. 'Nothing personal about it!' For their honeymoon the Paravicinis were lent the Villa Mauresque, the first time Liza had been there, Maugham and Haxton moving out to give 'the young things' a chance to be on their own. At first Maugham had been slightly contemptuous of Paravicini, referring to him as 'Liza's Swiss waiter', but Vincent soon won him over by his charm and by a simple sense of humour that tickled Maugham immensely; it amused him, too, that his son-in-law was not remotely bookish, his preferred reading two magazines, *Farmer & Stockbreeder* and the *Connoisseur*.

Returning at the beginning of September from a tour that had taken in Badgastein, Salzburg, Budapest and Vienna, Maugham settled down at the Mauresque for a brief period of intensive work before returning to London in October. His most immediate concern was to put the finishing touches to a novel, *Theatre*, the only one of his fictional works to deal with the world in which he had been intimately involved for more than thirty years. Employing the favourite plot-line of the older woman in love with a worthless and much younger man, *Theatre* tells the story of Julia Lambert, a celebrated actress married to a successful theatre manager, who in middle age falls for a boy scarcely older than her schoolboy son.

Tom Fennell is an accountancy clerk brought in to look over the theatre's books, and Julia's husband Michael, amused to see that the boy is stage-struck, invites him to lunch to meet his famous wife. The affair begins, with Julia at first rather condescending towards Tom, flattered by his passion; but soon she falls helplessly and humiliatingly in love, despite the fact that Tom is revealed to be a common little snob, regarding Julia, with all her grand friends, as a useful means of forwarding his career. The climax comes when he asks her to give a part in her new play to a girl-friend of his, a pretty but over-confident young woman who, Julia quickly realises, is nothing like as talented as she believes. During a glittering first night it is Julia's cunning upstaging of Avice, in the most literal sense, that effects the denouement and brings the story to a satisfactory end.

There is nothing bohemian in the theatrical world that Maugham depicts, which is solidly entrenched in the upper echelons of the West End. Julia has her clothes made in Paris, she dines in the most expensive nightclubs and restaurants, and is much sought after in elevated social circles. As might be expected, the theatrical milieu is faultlessly drawn, with Maugham giving a particularly well-observed portrait of his leading lady, always performing whether on stage or off, and endowed with a number of characteristics drawn from actresses such as Ethel Barrymore, Irene Vanbrugh and Marie Tempest. Julia is endearingly foolish and vain, and yet once in the theatre we are left in no doubt that she is a star. There are some diverting scenes which would play marvellously well on stage,* and some excellent parts among the supporting cast, in particular Julia's husband Michael, handsome, complacent and sexually lazy, far more interested in his good figure and his game of golf than in worrying what his wife might be up to. *Theatre* is not one of Maugham's finest novels – he was perhaps too little engaged with the world he was depicting – but it is highly accomplished, and after its publication in March 1937 it sold well (in Britain over 22,000 copies in the first two months), despite a tepid reception by the critics, many of whom applauded the technical expertise while complaining of an emotional superficiality. 'Mr Maugham anatomises emotion without emotion,' wrote Elizabeth Bowen in the *New Statesman*, '[but] what a writer he is!'

With *Theatre* finished, Maugham in October went again to London, where as usual his diary was crammed with appointments. He spent a

---

* The novel was dramatised by Guy Bolton and produced in New York in 1941, staged in England, under the title *Larger than Life*, in 1950. *Theatre* has also been filmed twice, in France in 1962, as *Adorable Julia*, with Charles Boyer and Lilli Palmer, and in 2004 as *Being Julia*, with Annette Bening and Jeremy Irons, with a screenplay by Ronald Harwood.

weekend at Renishaw with Osbert Sitwell and David Horner, and another at Bulbridge in Wiltshire with Juliet Duff, where H. G. Wells was also staying. On 13 October he attended a dinner at the Savoy, organised by PEN,\* to celebrate H.G.'s seventieth birthday, the toast proposed by Bernard Shaw, who 'with his puckish humour said many things highly embarrassing to the guest of the evening', Maugham recalled. 'It was a most amusing discourse.' At the end of the month he attended a large dinner-party given by the recently widowed Sibyl Colefax, her last before moving out of Argyll House. The guests were old friends, among them the Winston Churchills, the Duff Coopers, Artur Rubinstein, Harold Nicolson and Desmond MacCarthy, and the talk was all of 'the great Simpson question', as Harold Nicolson called it, and the 'very serious rumours that the King will make her Duchess of Edinburgh and marry.' The Prince of Wales's affair with the American Mrs Simpson had been the subject of scandalised gossip in upper-class circles for the past couple of years, although not at first reported in the British press; but since the death of George V in January, the matter had become of immense constitutional importance, and with the coronation of Edward VIII only weeks away the status of the relationship was suddenly a matter of passionate debate throughout the nation. Maugham had known Wallis Simpson for years – she and her husband had had a flat off Bryanston Square – and he was distressed by the violent hostility provoked by the King's decision to give up his throne for the woman he loved. 'I am a writer & it is my instinct to put myself in other people's shoes,' he told Juliet Duff,

> & I have been strangely harassed by the thought of that wretched man, unshaven, unwashed, unkempt, kicking the doors & beating his head against the walls, that people who have seen him describe; & I am shocked by the suddenness of that fall, from such an amazing popularity to such a universal contempt. Now the man in the street, who worshipped him, calls him a mess & says, a good riddance to bad rubbish.

On 11 December, in a corner of the public lounge at Claridge's, Maugham with Eddie Marsh, Osbert Sitwell and Graham Greene listened to the Abdication broadcast on a radio borrowed from one of the porters. By this time Wallis Simpson had left the country, fleeing to the south of France, where she would wait out the stressful months before her divorce was finalised and she and the Duke of Windsor, as he now became, could marry. On Christmas Day Maugham, who had returned to the Mauresque, invited Wallis and her aunt, Bessie Merryman, to lunch, together with Bob Boothby,

---

\* A writers' society founded in 1921 to promote literature.

a slightly raffish, slightly renegade member of Parliament. Despite the obvious tensions, it was a cheerful occasion, and in the afternoon there was a game of bridge, with Maugham partnering Wallis. 'I'm afraid I am not a very good partner,' he said putting down his hand. 'I've only got a couple of k-k-kings.' 'What's the use of them?'Wallis wisecracked. 'They only abdicate.' Throughout the following weeks, Maugham, sensitive to the pressures and problems of her situation, continued to be attentive, inviting Wallis to meals and to stay for a weekend. 'I think she had a very difficult role to play,' he said, 'and I doubt whether any woman could have played it successfully.' Finally in March Wallis prepared to leave Cannes to be reunited with the Duke at the Château de Candé in Tours, where they would marry. 'I am leaving Cannes tomorrow,' she wrote to Maugham, 'and I wanted to tell you again how very much I have appreciated your kindness to me since I have been here.' 'What many people did not understand', she said later, 'was that Willie was at heart a very kind man. That Christmas I felt in the wilderness, and I have never forgotten his sympathetic understanding in those especially difficult, lonely days.'

Perhaps fortunately, Gerald had not been in evidence on Christmas Day. 'Gerald is in bed with a bad attack of malaria, which is awkward since there is . . . [my lunch party] tomorrow,' Maugham with a certain irritation had written to Alan Searle on Christmas Eve. 'But still I shall manage, & in a day or two more he should be quite well.' Yet Gerald did not get well, indeed became so desperately ill that a nurse was employed, a specialist called in and the local doctor obliged to drive over three times a day. For a while it was feared he might die, but then the crisis was reached and survived, and very gradually Gerald began to grow stronger. Maugham, despite his frequent fury and exasperation, had been desperately worried, and was grateful to be consoled by Alan, who came out to stay for a couple of weeks. Searle's presence at the Mauresque impressed on Maugham the contrast between the young man's gentle, if somewhat colourless personality and Haxton's. '[Alan] is being very sweet,' Maugham told David Horner, '[but] he is never what you could call the life & soul of a party; so there is no one for me to be funny about – or with – & I wander about the garden & long to laugh.' In Alan, dependable and comforting, he missed the wickedness and wit, the sheer excitement of being with Gerald. 'Searle was more pussy-cat,' said one friend who knew them both, 'whereas Haxton was bristlingly abrasive, like a bulldog about to break his lead.'

One beneficent result of Gerald's illness was a renewed resolution on his part to keep his drinking under control. 'So far as I am concerned I can do no more,' Maugham told Barbara Back in a letter whose tough stance is belied by the tenderness of the final sentence:

> I have told him, & he knows it himself that if he starts drinking again he will kill himself; & if he does, it will mean that he has come to the conclusion that he would rather drink & die than not drink & live. If he really comes to that conclusion that is the end of it, I shall pension him off & resume my domicile in England; I cannot spend the few remaining years of my life acting as nurse & keeper to an old drunk. But, I have no need to tell you, I hope with all my heart that it will not come to that.

In order to keep himself busy and amused Gerald bought a boat, a small yacht with just enough room below decks for a couple of bunks. The weather was beautiful, and Gerald spent nearly every day sailing, entranced by his new toy. Equally entrancing was the young cabin boy who regularly accompanied him. Louis Legrand, known as Loulou, was a ravishing sixteen-year-old male whore, slender, blond, tanned, with a soft mouth and a sweet smile; he wore gold bangles on both wrists and spent most of the day dressed only in a minute pair of faded swimming-trunks. Gerald was infatuated with him, and when not on the boat Loulou passed much of his time at the Mauresque, at the disposal not only of Haxton and Maugham, who grew very fond of the charming boy, but of any male guest who desired his services, Gerald afterwards discreetly settling the bill. Both Harolds, Nicolson and Acton, became appreciative customers ('Mon cher Lulu,' wrote Nicolson from Paris, 'merci pour la soirée délicieuse'); and so, in the course of the summer, did Maugham's nephew Robin.

Under pressure from his father, Robin had gone up to Cambridge to read law, but in his spare time continued to write, sending his compositions to his uncle for criticism. Maugham saw little evidence of talent – 'quite the worst play I have ever had to look at' was his opinion of a dramatic sketch – but he was determined nonetheless to help Robin and instil in him as much as he could of his own philosophy. The play, he told him on this occasion,

> is a ghastly mess . . . [and] I think you should prepare your mind for the possibility that it will be a failure. You are so monstrously conceited that I am afraid you will find failure very difficult to bear . . . [but] to bear failure with courage is the best proof of character that anyone can give . . . My last piece of advice is not to let anyone see your mortification.

Robin, fascinated by what he had heard of the high life at the Mauresque, had asked if he might come and stay during his long vacation, ostensibly in order to concentrate on his writing. But when he arrived he found himself alone with his uncle, Gerald having left for Paris to collect a new car, and any hopes he might have had of plunging into a glamorous Riviera society soon disappeared in the actuality of the daily routine, with Maugham, intent on his work, spending all morning in his study, in the afternoon walking round the garden with the dogs, and disappearing to bed fairly soon after dinner. There was plenty of opportunity for some frank discussion, however, with Robin particularly anxious for reassurance about his homosexuality. His uncle was both practical and bracing, advising him to accept what he was and to have as much fun as he could. 'You are quite attractive,' he told him. 'Don't waste your assets. Your charm won't last for long.' That having been said it was important that Robin should bear in mind that being queer was no impediment to marriage, and as the only son it was his duty to marry and propagate.

This was a theme that Maugham returned to repeatedly, impressing on Robin that of the next generation it was only he who bore the family name, a responsibility that became of crucial importance when in 1938 Robin's father was appointed lord chancellor. Maugham, who for all his socialist beliefs was far from impervious to the benefits of rank, was delighted. He was intensely gratified by the prestige conferred on the family, and impressed that F.H. entirely by his own efforts should have achieved such an exalted position. 'It is very wonderful, if you come to think of it,' he wrote to Bert Alanson, 'that an obscure young man, without money or influence to help him should by sheer merit in his profession achieve . . . the highest office in the British Empire that any lawyer can attain.' As a law lord F.H. could not pass his title on to his descendants, but as lord chancellor he was sure to be offered a hereditary peerage, an offer that Maugham was anxious he should accept, his visions for Robin's ermined future as the second Viscount Maugham revealing a profound reverence for the old aristocratic order. 'There is no reason why your father should not live another ten or fifteen years,' he wrote to Robin,

> & in that time you might easily have gained a considerable experience as a member of parliament & then, as a peer, would have . . . a great chance to get office or a governorship. I can't imagine a more agreeable position than to be governor of Bengal with the likelihood, if one does well, of becoming Viceroy of India. Remember also that while your father is one of the most distinguished men in the country, he is distinguished by reason

*Right:* The Villa
Mauresque

*Below:* Maugham
with (*clockwise from
left*) Dadie Rylands,
Raymond Mortimer,
Paul Hyslop, Gerald
Haxton, Barbara Back
and Arthur Marshall
(*front*)

The elegant Barbara Back, witty and indiscreet

Beverley Nichols, a young man on the make

The writer Glenway Wescott had much in common with Maugham

Maugham with G. B. Stern, a cheerful presence at the Mauresque

*Right:* Alan Searle, the Bronzino boy

*Below:* By the pool: (*left to right*) Gerald, Raymond Mortimer, Maugham, Paul Hyslop and Godfrey Winn

*Left:* Maughan on the terrace with Winston Churchill and H. G. Wells

*Below:* Breakfast in bed at the Mauresque

*Above:* Maugham and Haxton in Central Park, New York

*Right:* Robin Maugham, well-mannered and eager to please

*Above:* Haxton and Maugham riding with friends in South Carolina

*Left:* Liza with her father and Bert Alanson in California

*Above:* A slightly tense
evening on the Riviera:
Searle (*back view*), Liza,
Maugham and Camilla

*Right:* Bridge, 'the most
entertaining game that the
art of man has devised'

*Above:* Robin was very attentive to his aged uncle

*Left:* Alan, the perfect nanny of Maugham's second childhood

of his office; to be the son of a deceased Lord Chancellor is to be very small fry, to be a peer is always to be something.

Towards the end of Robin's stay, Gerald arrived back from Paris. By chance he and Robin had run into each other in Salzburg earlier in the summer and renewed their friendship. Cheerful and relaxed, the older man had made an irresistible impression. 'Well-dressed, attractive and slim,' Robin recorded, 'very European though he was an American . . . Gerald exuded vitality and charm and money.' Friendly as ever, Haxton had taken Robin to the opera, and afterwards to a *Bierstube*. Here they drank schnapps while Gerald gave him a knowledgeable summary of the local rent-boys lined up along the bar, before disappearing with his personal favourite, 'mein lieber Felix, mein Schatz', a winning fourteen-year-old always available for 'Onkel Gerald'. Now returned to the Mauresque Gerald generously determined to give Robin a night to remember before he returned home. Beginning the evening at the casino in Nice, the two of them went on to a couple of back-street bars, where they got pleasantly drunk, and then on to a brothel, where Gerald paid for the young man to be expertly entertained. Finally in the early hours of the morning it was decided to drive over to Villefranche to look at the boat. Here they found Loulou on board, lying on one of the bunks, 'his hair tousled, his limbs sprawled out in sleep, his lips slightly parted'. Gerald immediately saw that Robin was smitten. 'Have a good time,' he winked at him, and lurching up the gangplank he left. 'Goodnight, ducks,' he called out. 'See you both in the morning.'

Gerald continued, just, to keep his drinking within limits, his employer having made plain that if he wished to retain his position he would have to make some radical reforms. The situation was not a happy one, however, and the tensions and uncertainties now inherent in the relationship made Maugham restless and uneasy, so much so that for a while he even contemplated giving up the Mauresque. 'If I can sell without loss I shall get rid of the place,' he wrote to Barbara in June 1937. 'I shall live in England much more, at least five months a year, & I shall take a flat in London.' But for the moment such drastic plans were shelved as he concentrated on preparing for a Far Eastern journey, this time to India, proposing to depart at the end of the year, returning the following spring. 'I am tired & want a change,' he told Charles Towne, '& besides, I want to get some material for a novel I have in mind to write in the future.' Meanwhile, the summer passed in trips abroad – the usual visits to Munich, Salzburg and Badgastein, as well as a disappointing excursion with Peter Stern to Scandinavia ('Sweden . . . such a boring place') – and in entertaining at home. Barbara came down as usual, as did Dadie Rylands and Arthur Marshall, and their old friend from Cambridge, Victor Rothschild, now with a wife, Barbara Hutchinson. Maugham thoroughly enjoyed such clever company, and was pleased to welcome other members of the Cambridge network. 'Yesterday Anthony Blunt & a friend Burgess came over to lunch & are coming for the week-end,' Maugham reported to Searle. 'Do you remember Anthony? You met him once or twice at Cambridge. He is (or was) a fellow of Trinity & is an authority on baroque.'

Before leaving for India Maugham was determined to finish a book of great personal importance to him, a form of memoir on which he had been working intermittently for some time. 'I have put into it all I know,' he told Charles Towne; but if his readers were hoping for details of a personal nature then they were to be disappointed. In its author's own words *The Summing Up* 'is not an autobiography nor is it a book of recollections': rather it is an overview of his professional career and intellectual development, and of 'the subjects that have chiefly interested me during the course of my life'. The first half of this personal credo deals with his boyhood and youth, and, at greater length, with his development as a writer. Here he argues for the three favourite tenets, lucidity, simplicity and euphony, and discusses some of the authors whom he most admires, Dryden, Swift, Dr Johnson, Hazlitt, Voltaire, Stendhal, Colette and Maupassant, the last of whom exercised such influence over his own style of short story. Like Maupassant, 'I preferred to end my short stories with a full-stop rather than with a straggle of dots. It is this, I imagine, that has led to their being better appreciated in France than in England.' Maugham also addresses his career in the theatre – 'I caught the collo-quial note by instinct' – paying his respects to his fellow playwrights, in particular Ibsen ('the greatest dramatist the last hundred years have seen'), Chekhov and Shaw. And with admirable detachment he analyses his own strengths and weaknesses as a practitioner of the art to which he had dedicated his life. 'I am a made writer,' he states unequivocally. 'I do not write as I want to; I write as I can . . . I have had small power of im-agination . . . no lyrical quality . . . little gift of metaphor . . . [but] I had an acute power of observation, and it seemed to me that I could see a great many things that other people missed.' Clear-sighted about his abil-ities, he yet shows a certain sensitivity to the fact that he has been largely ignored by serious critics. 'There are but two important critics in my own country [Desmond MacCarthy and Cyril Connolly] who have troubled to take me seriously,' he complains; the rest by contrast have either ignored or dismissed him. 'In my twenties the critics said I was brutal, in my thirties they said I was flippant, in my forties they said I was cynical, in my fifties they said I was competent, and now in my sixties they say I am superficial.'

The second large theme in *The Summing Up* is the author's lifelong exploration of philosophy and religion, which had absorbed him since boyhood. Always curious, always searching, ever eager to find a pattern or purpose to his life, Maugham for years had read diligently in the works of the great philosophers, from Plato to Bertrand Russell, from the Christian mystics to the *Upanishads*, looking for but never finding the certainty that would bring consolation. Here Maugham the autodidact is to the fore, the intelligent enquirer, hopeful of enlightenment on the great questions that have preoccupied man through the ages: 'what is the value of life, how he should live and what sense he can ascribe to the universe'. Unable to regain the faith he lost in boyhood, he yet remains unsatisfied, puzzled by the frustration experienced by his rational self in failing to take comfort in religion. 'It may be that my heart, having found rest nowhere, had some deep ancestral craving for God and immortality which my reason would have no truck with.' Unable to integrate his perceptions in an all-inclusive creed, he states his conviction, in characteristically uncompromising terms, that 'There is no reason for life and life has no meaning.'

Although the author is at pains to remain at a dignified distance – 'I have no desire to lay bare my heart, and I put limits to the intimacy that I wish the reader to enter upon with me' – *The Summing Up* is shot through with a sometimes startling candour. Of his experience of love he says, 'Though I have been in love a good many times I have never experienced the bliss of requited love . . . I am incapable of complete surrender'; and 'I have most loved people who cared little or nothing for me, and when people have loved me I have been embarrassed'; and 'there are few things that cause greater wretchedness than to love with all your heart someone who you know is unworthy of love'. Writing of sex, enthusiastically described as 'the keenest pleasure to which the body is susceptible', he states it is his great regret that because of 'a native fastidiousness' he never indulged enough, a surprising admission from one who was so deeply interested in the subject, wrote about it with such feeling and was so tireless in its pursuit. Throughout the writer is revealed, not always consciously, as a sensitive, vulnerable, passionate man, aloof, unillusioned, a realist rather than the cynic he was so often taken to be; he is solitary by choice ('I find social intercourse fatiguing . . . It is a relief to me when I can get away and read a book'); a depressive capable of some happiness and much enjoyment. As one of his critics was to write, in this book there is revealed 'an injured and defensive heart behind the fluent mind of the impervious man of the world'.

Anxious that *The Summing Up* should be as good as he could make it Maugham sent proofs to both Eddie Marsh and Dadie Rylands for criticism. Eddie Marsh was particularly relied upon for detailed textual editing. Recently retired from the Civil Service, he had made a speciality of correcting the work of well-known authors, Winston Churchill among them. Referred to as his 'diabolization', it was a process this pernickety, scholarly, kind-hearted character relished; there was no question of payment, for it flattered his vanity to be consulted by famous writers ('There's glory for me!' Marsh noted in his diary after he was first approached by Maugham), and he was proud of what he called 'my morbid eye for detail', loved showing off his exhaustive knowledge of grammar, derivation and the finer points of style. Maugham's first meeting with Marsh had been during the war at a luncheon★ of the Winston Churchills', but the first books of his to be diabolized were *Don Fernando* and *Theatre*. 'I think you must know grammar better than anyone in England,' Maugham had written gratefully after receiving back the corrected scripts. 'I can't tell you how wonderfully useful I've found your notes, but, my word, some of them have made me sweat.' On *The Summing Up* Marsh went to work with gusto: 'p. 28 Has "massivity" any advantage over the usual "massiveness"? . . . p. 110 Surely three infinitives are too many? . . . p. 113 Your argument here is tantalizingly incomplete . . .' Not all his suggestions were accepted, but most of them were, and his sharp eye demonstrably saved Maugham from error, inelegance and some impossibly tangled lines of argument. In gratitude Maugham made a present to Marsh of some beautiful eighteenth-century emerald buttons from India to use as cufflinks. 'I like to think they may have adorned the sleeve of one of the Moghuls' page boys,' he told him.

---

★ The word 'luncheon' was something of a stumbling-block between Marsh and Maugham. 'Whenever I wrote *lunch*, he changed it to *luncheon*. I protested that the word was obsolete . . . It was natural to say, I urged, "Will you come and have lunch with me," and so why shouldn't you use it in a book. "But it isn't natural to me," Eddie cried in his shrill voice, "I won't come and have lunch with you. I will, however, if I am disengaged be pleased to come and have luncheon with you"' (*Eddie Marsh: Sketches for a Composite Literary Portrait* compiled by Christopher Hassall and Denis Mathews (Lund Humphries 1953) p. 29).

While a few of Maugham's friends, hoping for personal revelations, were disappointed – 'Never have I read an autobiography which contains so little auto,' complained Peter Stern – by the majority of his readers *The Summing Up* was respectfully received. After publication in January 1938 (two months later in the United States) most opinion praised the work for its intellectual and emotional honesty, and for its illuminating reflections on the writer and writing, if politely dismissive of the more metaphysical passages. Typical of the consensus the critic in the *Criterion* wrote that it is in the discussion of Maugham's literary life 'that both the main interest and the importance of the book lie. The concluding sections on truth, beauty, and goodness, and also on God and immortality, are negligible.' Nonetheless it was generally perceived to be 'immensely read-able' (V. S. Pritchett) and 'continuously entertaining' (Graham Greene), and sales figures were excellent, quickly reaching 100,000 in the United States, to Nelson Doubleday's satisfaction.

Meanwhile, with the book completed by the end of summer 1937, Maugham returned to planning his expedition to India, arranging to let the Mauresque for the four months he and Haxton would be away the following year. As usual the autumn was spent in London, where he gave a party to celebrate the birth of Liza's first child, a boy, to Maugham's delight, Nicolas Vincent Somerset. The reception, at Claridge's on 8 December, was a glamorous occasion. 'Never before were so many celeb-rities gathered together under one roof,' Hugh Walpole observed, with Syrie much in evidence among them. 'Willie [had] hoped she wouldn't come'; she was easy enough to avoid, however, as Maugham had taken care to surround himself with old friends, Wells, Barbara, Sibyl Colefax, Osbert Sitwell, Harold Nicolson, Juliet Duff and Desmond MacCarthy. Once this ordeal was over, Maugham concentrated on finalising the details of his journey, his intention to leave just before Christmas, embarking from Genoa for the five-week voyage to Bombay. Maugham had already been furnished with letters of prestigious introduction from friends, including his Riviera neighbour the Aga Khan, and naturally expected while in Delhi to be received by the Viceroy, the Marquess of Linlithgow. But then came an unexpected hitch which threw everything into confu-sion: the India Office refused to issue Gerald with a visa. Maugham was furious: it was humiliating and outrageous. How could this be happening, when his trunks were packed, it was too late to revise his plans, and how could he possibly cope without Gerald, who had 'been to pretty well every British colony with me for the last umpteen years'? Discreet approaches were hastily made, strings pulled, and fortunately at the last minute the ban was rescinded, although it was made very clear that there would be no official recognition of Mr Maugham's presence on the sub-continent. In practical terms this hardly mattered, as it was Maugham's intention to concentrate not on British but on Hindu India and on the states ruled by the Indian princes.* Nonetheless the slight rankled and was not forgotten.

It may seem curious that Maugham, with his passion for travel and for the Far East, should have waited so long to visit India: by his own account the blame lay with Rudyard Kipling. He had long believed that 'so far as stories were concerned Kipling had written all the good ones', a belief he now saw was baseless: in a letter sent to E. M. Forster from Calcutta he wrote, '[I] only regret that the shadow of Kipling lurking over the country in my imagination prevented me from coming twenty years ago.' Kipling had died only two years before, but in fact his world had long been gone; the British hold on India, for over 100 years the jewel in the crown, the symbolic centre of the imperial structure, was weakening by the day; the Government of India Act of 1935 was a virtual guarantee of independence in the near future, and movements for nation-alisation were rapidly, in some states violently, gaining ground. Yet it was not this complex political situation that concerned Maugham, nor this time was he on the prowl for stories; his main objective was to explore Hindu philosophy and religion, to meet religious leaders and teachers, and to learn what he could at first hand of a subject of passionate personal interest, one which he intended to use as the foundation for a novel, eventually to be published as *The Razor's Edge*.

After a calm and comfortable voyage Maugham and Haxton arrived in Bombay at the beginning of January 1938, and left from there exactly three months later. Their itinerary took them first to Goa, to Trivandrum and Madura on the southernmost tip of India, then north to Madras on the east coast, to Hyderabad, up to Bidar and Nagpur in the interior, then to Calcutta and Benares, and finally to Agra, Jaipur, Delhi, where Maugham, but not Haxton, was invited by Lord Linlithgow to lunch at Viceregal Lodge; the invitation was declined. From Delhi they returned to Bombay to board a ship bound for Naples on 31 March. Despite all he had read and been told, Maugham was unprepared for the impact of India. The endless travelling was exhausting, the trains slow, the heat frequently oppressive, the social demands enervating in the extreme, yet

* The British Raj, or Indian Empire, was divided into two regions, British India, which was administered directly by the British Government, and the Princely or Native States, governed by individual rulers under the paramountcy of the British Crown.

he was fascinated by all of it, and pages of his notebook are filled with detailed descriptions of the country, the white beaches and empty churches of Goa, the Black Pagoda in Orissa, sunset on the Ganges at Benares, the noise and bustle of Calcutta, and in Agra the astonishing beauty of the Taj Mahal, his own reaction to which Maugham observed with interest. 'I can understand that when people say something takes their breath away it is not an idle metaphor. I really did feel shortness of breath. I had a queer, delightful feeling in my heart, as though it were dilated. I felt surprise and joy and, I think, a sense of liberation.'

For Gerald, on the other hand, sightseeing was all very well, but far more exciting were the couple of days spent driving through the jungle, where he was able to get some shooting. He had hoped for a tiger, and they waited for hours up a fifteen-foot bamboo platform in the trees, but none appeared; he shot a crocodile, however, and a peacock, which they ate that same evening for dinner. Maugham, distressed by the incident, described it in his notebook.

> We were driving through the jungle. It was not thick and presently we caught sight of a peacock among the trees with its beautiful tail outspread . . . I have seldom seen a sight more thrilling than that peacock threading its solitary way through the jungle. My companion told the driver to stop and seized his gun.
>
> 'I'm going to have a shot at it.'
>
> My heart stopped still. He fired, and I hoped he'd miss, but he didn't. The driver jumped out of the car and brought back the dead bird which a moment before had been so exultantly alive. It was a cruel sight.

There was no question now, as there had been in the past, of roughing it, and wherever they went the two men were entertained in magnificent style. '[We] are living in the lap of luxury,' Maugham wrote to Searle from Trivandrum, where he was a guest of the Maharajah of Travancore. He and Haxton had been given a house in the palace grounds, 'where we have a bed-room, dressing-room & bathroom each, a dining-room & two sitting-rooms; we are looked after by a butler & two footmen, & a large yellow car stands at the door all day with a chauffeur & a footman'. And from Cochin he wrote to Juliet Duff, 'we are on our way to Madras & then we go to stay with the Maharajah of Mysore & the Nizam [of Hyderabad]. I am inclined to think that I am getting a little above myself.' The only drawback to this regal level of hospitality was that there was little opportunity for more private activities. 'Of course no larks,' Maugham regretfully told Searle, '& we are being as good as gold.' Throughout the princely states they visited, Maugham's Indian hosts were discovered to be infinitely courteous, learned, charming and generous; 'as soon as the maharajas realized that I didn't want to go on tiger hunts but that I was interested in seeing poets and philosophers, they were very helpful.' This was in marked contrast to the British, whom Maugham found philistine and narrow-minded. 'Oh the doddering old fools who are running this country!' he lamented to Barbara from Bombay. 'It is a wonder India hasn't been lost long ago.' He was repelled by the instances he witnessed of the colonists' insufferably superior attitude towards Indians, particularly on the part of the women, the memsahibs, few of whom seemed to have any interest in the people, customs or culture that surrounded them. At a tea-party given by the wife of a minor official, his hostess asked him about his trip, 'and when I told her that I had spent most of my time in the Indian States, she said: "You know, we don't have anything more to do with Indians than we can help. One has to keep them at arm's length." The rest of the company agreed with her.'

Such an attitude may well have accounted for Maugham's grumpy mood while staying at the magnificent British Residency in Hyderabad. Here his fellow guest was M. M. Kaye, then a young woman of thirty, later to become well known for her novel about India, *The Far Pavilions*. 'I was enthralled to meet him,' she recalled, 'but disappointed to find him a sour and unfriendly old gentleman who stumped off fairly early to bed.' By next morning, however, Maugham's mood had improved, and 'we got on like a house on fire.' Encouraged, Mollie Kaye mentioned that she had just written a novel,

> but that I was afraid I would never make a writer. He asked why, in a distinctly bored voice, and I said because I wrote much too slowly and would stick for hours on end over a sentence that I couldn't get right . . . The old boy peered at me over the top of his spectacles exactly like an elderly tortoise, and said: 'My dear young woman, that is the only thing I have heard you say that makes me think you may be a writer one day.'

Maugham's quest in coming to India was to investigate the vast subject of Hindu religion in the hope of gaining an insight into a spiritual side of life that had always intrigued and at the same time eluded him. In preparation he had read widely, Charles Eliot's *Hinduism and Buddhism*, Radhakrishnan's *History of Indian Philosophy*, L. D. Barnett's *Brahma-Knowledge* and his translation of the *Upanishads*, Krishnaswami Iyer's *Vedanta* and much more. Armed with a sheaf of introductions, Maugham met and talked to numbers of scholars and priests, but try though he might was unable to make very much of what they told him. The experience frustrated and tantalised him. 'As for getting any insight into the intense spiritual life that one finds here, there & everywhere,' he wrote when halfway through his tour, 'well, it is like seeing the Himalayas at night only in one flash of lightning.' Doggedly he persevered. Under instruction from a yogi he tried for himself the benefits of meditation, sitting cross-legged on the floor in a darkened room and making his mind a blank. 'I remained in that state for so long that I thought I must have by far exceeded the quarter of an hour he [the yogi] had prescribed. I looked at my watch. Three minutes had passed.' Travelling the length and breadth of the country he interviewed swamis and sadhus; he watched fakirs gouging out their eyeballs and sticking skewers through their cheeks; in Hyderabad, through the good offices of Sir Akbar Hydari, the Finance Minister and a friend of Morgan Forster's, he talked to an immensely distinguished Hindu holy man, but '[he only] said the things I had heard from others twenty times before'. It was the same when he met a Sufi, from whom he hoped to gain some different perspective, only to find that the Muslim mystic spoke 'of the self and the supreme self in the same strain as the Hindu teachers speak'. To Maugham this was the crux of the problem, that all the Indian thinkers relayed the same doctrines in the same words.

> And though you feel that it should not make you restive, for if they possess the truth, as they are convinced they do, and if the truth is one and indivisible, it is natural enough that they should repeat it like parrots, there is no denying the fact that it is irksome to listen interminably to the same statements. You wish at least they could think of other metaphors, similes, illustrations than those of the Upanishads. Your heart sinks when you hear again the one about the snake and the rope.*

At Tiruvannamalai near Madras Maugham visited the ashram of the famous sage Sri Ramana Maharshi, where he enjoyed the unique opportunity of talking to an English sadhu. Major A.W. Chadwick, a retired British army officer, currently incarnated as Sadhu Arunachala, had lived in the ashram for years, and was more than happy to discourse at length about karma and reincarnation and to describe his personal efforts 'to realise the self in him in communion with the universal self, to separate

---

* 'The world is illusory, judged from the standpoint of Reality, but it is not an illusion. It is a fact of consciousness,' Maugham explains. 'The wise men of India are fond of using the following illustration: you see on a dark night what you take to be a snake and you run away from it; but when a light is brought, you see that what you took for a snake is in fact a rope. It was an illusion that what you saw was a snake, but it *was* a rope . . .' (*Points of View* p. 58).

the I that thinks from the self, for that is the infinite.' But even with a fellow Englishman Maugham was left little the wiser, and by the end of the interview still 'could not get from him exactly what he meant'. The Maharshi received visitors at an audience every afternoon, and Maugham and Haxton having arrived at midday were halfway through their picnic lunch on the verandah outside Chadwick's room when Maugham suddenly fainted. Chadwick carried him indoors and laid him on his bed, where he stayed for some time, feeling too unwell to join the crowd in the central hall. The Maharshi, informed of what had happened, graciously consented to come and see him, and 'Bhagavan [the Maharshi] and Somerset Maugham sat opposite to each other for about half-an-hour without uttering a word,' Chadwick recalled. 'At the end of which Somerset Maugham looked nervously across in my direction and said, "Is there any need to say anything?" "No," replied Bhagavan. "Silence is best. Silence is itself conversation."'

He may have failed to achieve enlightenment but so intrigued was Maugham by this first visit to India that before embarking from Bombay on the voyage home he had already determined to return the following year, a project that events far outside his control were to render impracticable. While still at sea, on board the *Conte Biancomano*, the gravity of the situation in Europe was forcefully impressed upon the passengers, as news reports arrived daily over the ship's radio of Franco and the Civil War in Spain, of the Fascist imperialism of Mussolini in Italy, and now on 14 March of the Anschluss, of Hitler's invasion of Austria. 'We have been much disturbed over the Austrian business . . . [and] Gerald has been much in the dumps over it all because so many of his friends are affected,' Maugham wrote to Alan Searle. 'For a moment I was terribly afraid that it might mean a general war; but that seems now not to be the case.'

Docking at Naples, they were met by Jean the chauffeur and by Alan, who was to join them on the leisurely drive back to the south of France. 'It isn't really necessary for me to tell you, is it?' Maugham had written while still at sea, 'that I am looking forward very, very much to seeing you.' From Naples they went to Rome and then Florence, where the three of them were hospitably received by Harold Acton and his parents at the family villa, La Pietra. During their stay, Harold remembered, 'while Gerald painted the town red, Willie sat glued to the bridge-table'. Maugham also called on his old friend Reggie Turner, whom he found in a state of deep depression. The city was festooned with Fascist banners in preparation for a triumphal visit by Hitler and Mussolini, and Reggie was appalled by what he saw happening to his beloved Italy. He was also a

very sick man, his famous wit and brilliant conversation almost extin-
guished by a cancer of the tongue, which was shortly to kill him. He
was, however, able to accompany the party to Montegufoni, the Sitwells'
massive medieval castle just outside Florence, where Edith was staying
with her father.

Maugham finally arrived back at the Mauresque in May 1938, to enjoy
what appeared in prospect another idyllic summer on the Riviera. The
weather was flawless; he was already making good progress on his new
novel; Gerald was happy, having bought another, bigger boat, which he
and Loulou were planning to sail to Sicily; and there were relays of friends
coming out from England to stay: Barbara, Robin, Beverley Nichols,
Raymond Mortimer and his lover Paul Hyslop, the Paravicinis, the Actons
and Harold Nicolson. It was Nicolson that summer who captured the
essence of the Mauresque magic. 'It really is the perfect holiday,' he told
his wife, Vita Sackville-West, 'the heat is intense, the garden lovely, the
chair long and cool, the lime-juice at hand, a bathing pool there if one
wishes to splash, scenery, books, gramophones, pretty people.' At the end
of one day he describes himself alone in the garden after everyone else
had gone inside to dress.

> There was a lovely soft warm evening, that marvellous pink light among
> the pines. I went up and sat alone with Tacitus by the swimming-pool. It
> is surrounded by great massifs of red and white oleanders. The sun set over
> Cap d'Antibes. The lighthouses began to wink across a still purple sea. I
> stayed there until the red oleanders became invisible and only the white
> oleanders shone in the moon.

But then he suddenly realised the time, closed his book, descended the
steps, walked across the terrace and into the house to shave, bathe and
put on a black tie as the newly married Duke and Duchess of Windsor
were expected that night to dine. This was a slightly tense occasion as
Wallis to her husband's fury had been denied the title of Royal Highness,
and there was thus a slight unease among the group waiting in the drawing-
room as to how she should be addressed. When the car was heard drawing
up on the gravel, Maugham, accompanied by Liza, went into the hall to
receive them. A few seconds later the Duke walked into the room. 'I'm
sorry we were a little late,' he said cheerfully, 'but Her Royal Highness
couldn't drag herself away.' 'He had said it,' Nicolson recorded. 'The three
words fell into the circle like three stones into a pool . . . and not one
eye dared to meet another.'

The Mauresque may have provided a haven of beauty and tranquillity, yet all around events were unfolding of the most sinister nature. With the threatened German invasion of Czechoslovakia there was no question of the usual expedition to Salzburg and Badgastein. 'I do not think there is any danger of war,' Maugham wrote to Bert Alanson, 'but the Austrians have a little lost their heads just now and are behaving in such a manner that it is better for foreigners to keep out of the country.' Maugham was already doing what he could to help the flood of Jewish refugees pouring into Britain and France, using his influence to find work and accommodation, as well as giving substantial sums of money to Jewish charities. When approached for a donation by Herman Ould, the secretary of PEN, he sent a fairly brisk reply. 'I have not waited until I received your letter to do what I could for the Austrian Jews of my acquaintance who have had to leave their country,' he wrote, 'and so I must ask Mr Frischauer to be content with a cheque for ten guineas and to look upon it more as a mark of my sympathy than as a reasonable contribution to so worthy a fund.'

In the third week of September, while Nazi troops were massing on the Czech border, Maugham left the Côte d'Azur for London, driven by Jean. Near Auxerre, south of Paris, the car hit a tree and overturned, leaving both occupants badly shaken, Maugham the worse off, very bruised and with a broken rib. Determined not to enter a nursing home, he insisted on being taken to a Paris hotel, the France et Choiseul, where they knew him and where Alan came out to nurse him. 'Alan has been an angel,' Maugham told Barbara. 'For two or three days I couldn't move in bed without help. Fortunately the surgeon who was looking after me was merciful enough to keep me under morphia.' After a couple of weeks he was well enough to complete his journey, arriving in London at the beginning of October just as reports were coming in of Hitler's annexation of the Sudetenland. The talk everywhere was of the crisis, and of Neville Chamberlain's triumphant return from Munich, waving his piece of paper with its declaration of 'peace for our time'. On 1 November 1938 Maugham felt well enough to attend a dinner-party of Sibyl Colefax's, among his fellow guests Max Beerbohm, Virginia Woolf and the talented young novelist Christopher Isherwood. 'That young man holds the future of the English novel in his hands,' Maugham told Virginia. She, perhaps not knowing of his accident, was privately appalled by his appearance, 'like a dead man', she wrote in her diary. 'And his lips are drawn back like a dead mans [sic] . . . A look of suffering . . . A mechanical voice as if he had to raise a lever at each word . . . Sat like an animal in a trap: or like a steel trap. And I could not say anything that loosed his dead man's jaw.'

In fact, while still in physical pain, Maugham was feeling more cheerful than he had for some time. During the past few years he had grown increasingly pessimistic about the likelihood of a lasting peace, a pessimism given full expression in his recently completed novel *Christmas Holiday*. But now, with the signing of the Anglo-German pact confirming the two countries' stated desire 'never to go to war with one another again', there was room for cautious hope. 'Well, we've escaped war, & (I think) for many years,' Maugham wrote to Alanson. 'Things should go better now at least for a bit.'

# 14

## An Exercise in Propaganda

Maugham always claimed not to care for the novel of ideas, the novel as polemic. 'I think it an abuse to use the novel as a pulpit or a platform,' he stated more than once. 'If readers wish to inform themselves of the pressing problems of the day, they will do better to read, not novels but the books that specifically deal with them.' As he used to remark, in his view H. G. Wells's novels had failed in the end because Wells's characters were not individuals but 'marionettes', activated to represent the various ideas the author was currently intent on conveying. Yet now Maugham in his new work of fiction was attempting something very similar himself. In *Christmas Holiday*, written during 1938, the story is not driven by character but is constructed primarily to carry a message, an impassioned denunciation of the malevolent forces developing within Europe, of the powerful dictatorships in Germany, Italy and Spain. Since the beginning of the decade Maugham had been pessimistic about the possibility of maintaining a viable peace, as he had made plain six years earlier in *For Services Rendered*. Since then he had watched with acute apprehension the increasingly bitter conflict between left and right – the rise of Fascism, the widening divisions between rich and poor – and the terrifying threat which they presented, a threat that in his opinion blinkered Britain appeared dangerously slow to understand.

*Christmas Holiday* begins with the departure for Paris of a naive young Englishman, Charley Mason, looking forward to a few days' holiday before starting work in his father's office. A likeable, intelligent boy, Charley has been well brought up by middle-class parents who pride themselves on their cultural sophistication, both more than a little smug about their mildly avant-garde taste in music and painting. For Charley the high point of his holiday is a reunion with his best friend from childhood, Simon, now working in Paris, with whom he expects to enjoy a ripping time. But the Paris he finds himself in is unfamiliar, a shabby, uneasy city, rank with poverty and corruption, and Simon, too, is almost unrecognisable, transformed into a raging, power-hungry fanatic, full of hatred and contempt as much for the workers as for the bourgeoisie. A dictator in the making, harsh, cynical and unscrupulous, Simon rants relentlessly on, determined to disrupt his friend's instinctive tolerance and mildly socialist values. With this in mind, Simon takes Charley to a clip-joint nightclub and introduces him to one of the girls, Lydia, a gloomy Russian forced by poverty into prostitution. Purely out of pity Charley asks Lydia back to his dingy hotel, and for the next three days listens appalled to her story: her father was killed by the Bolsheviks, while her husband, Robert, an amoral crook to whom she is slavishly devoted, is currently serving fifteen years in South America for a particularly nasty murder.★ When Charley finally returns to England, to his warm, self-satisfied family, he feels he has been living in a nightmare, but one which 'had a fearful reality which rendered all else illusory . . . Only one thing had happened to him . . . and he didn't just then know what to do about it: the bottom had fallen out of his world.'

*Christmas Holiday* is first and foremost a political allegory, in which the author employs three of the main characters, Simon, Lydia and Robert, to illustrate the ideological struggles in Europe, using them to personify the nature of Fascism and the totalitarian states, and the fatal malleability of the oppressed. Unfortunately, all three of these characters are two-dimensional, and the lengthy relating of their various stories at second hand grows monotonous. The only human aspect of Simon, carefully left unexplored by the author, is a strong impression that he is and always has been hopelessly in love with handsome, heterosexual Charley (thus refuting Gore Vidal's assertion that *The Narrow Corner* is Maugham's only 'crypto-fag' novel). Ironically, the scenes that at once spring vividly to life are those concerning Charley and his comically complacent family snugly at home in Porchester Close. The Masons, like the Maughams, have only recently moved up from working-class status, a fact of which they are not in the least ashamed; and indeed in many aspects Leslie and Venetia Mason represent a sympathetic view of England: they are a little too pleased with themselves and are nowhere near as cultured and sophisticated as they fondly believe, but they are decent, liberal, tolerant people, their chief failing, in common with most of the rest of the country, a refusal to take seriously the threat of the imminent destruction of their comfortable way of life.

---

★ Here Maugham used the details of an actual case: in 1932 he had attended the trial in Paris of Guy Davin, convicted of the murder of his friend, Richard Wall. Davin was sentenced to fifteen years at the penal settlement of Saint-Laurent-de-Maroni, where by chance Maugham met and talked to him in 1936.

At the time of its publication in 1939, *Christmas Holiday* attracted some discouraging reviews: 'maladroitly handled', wrote Graham Greene in the *London Mercury*, while others homed in on the lack of balance between 'the completely normal Charley and the three who are made foils for him'. The novel had its admirers, however, among them Evelyn Waugh, who expressed the view that, 'For pure technical felicity I think his new novel is his best.' Certainly sales figures were everything Maugham's publishers could wish; in Britain 25,000 copies had been sold by the end of the first month.*

In February 1939, when *Christmas Holiday* was published, Maugham was on business in the United States (where the novel appeared in October), visiting Chicago and New York, staying with Bert Alanson in San Francisco and, also in California, with Eugene O'Neill and his wife Carlotta, whom Maugham had met previously on the Riviera. As before, he was inundated with requests to broadcast – he was paid $500 for one two-minute radio talk – for interviews, articles and short stories, and with the usual pressing offers from Hollywood. 'I am now advised that Maugham will not, under any circumstances, consider a picture assignment,' wrote the producer David O. Selznick. 'There is no indication that he may change his mind in the future.' By the time he returned to Europe, sailing from New York on the *Queen Mary*, Maugham was exhausted, eager for his annual restorative retreat. As there was no question at the present of visiting Austria and Badgastein, the spa at Montecatini was chosen instead. 'Here in Italy everyone seems convinced that there will be no war,' he wrote to Alanson in June, 'so unless the Germans do something idiotic I think we are safe.'

Back at the Villa Mauresque by July Maugham saw no reason to alter his plans or to cancel his guests for the summer. Among them were Liza and her husband, who with a group of young friends were whirling from tennis-parties to picnic-lunches to evenings dining and dancing at the Sporting Club in Monte Carlo. It was a particularly gay season on the Riviera, with a plethora of theatres, open-air concerts, horse shows, fireworks, balls and, keenly anticipated, the inauguration of the first-ever Cannes film festival, due to open on 1 September. But by the beginning of August it was ominously apparent that no such festivity would be taking place. On 23 August, with the signing of the Nazi–Soviet Non-Aggression Pact, the atmosphere grew darker and more tense. All at once soldiers were everywhere, their tented camps erected among the trees;

* The following year Maugham donated the manuscript of *Christmas Holiday* to a sale for raising money to help European writers made homeless by the Fascist regimes.

Cap Ferrat was converted into a highly fortified military zone, with machine-gun emplacements installed along the cliffs and an anti-aircraft battery at one end of the road that ran below the Mauresque. Suddenly everyone seemed to be on the move, with holidaymakers rushing to return home – there was not a place to be had on the Blue Train – and the roads jammed with traffic as heavily laden cars and trucks full of troops heading north met hordes of refugees fleeing south. Within one twenty-four-hour period during the last week in August the Mauresque was virtually evacuated, the guests suddenly packed and gone and most of the servants departed: the kitchen-maid, the footman and his wife, all Italian, returned to Italy, Jean the chauffeur was called up, as were a couple of gardeners, while the butler, Ernest, a Swiss, was recalled to Switzerland; only Annette, the cook, and a housemaid, Nina, remained in the house. At the same time an order was posted that all private yachts must immediately leave the harbour at Villefranche. With the decision to move forced upon them, Maugham made up his mind to take the *Sara* west to Cassis, a port too small to be of interest to the navy. He and Gerald drove hurriedly into Nice to stock up on provisions, and with these stowed on board they set sail, taking with them as crew a couple of Italian boatmen too old for conscription.

The weather was perfect and at first, Maugham recalled, 'there was a feeling of gentle excitement at the notion of getting away from the danger zone . . . I read and slept and smoked . . . enjoying the quiet after those harassing days'. Registered in Gerald's name, the *Sara* at forty-five tons was roomy, with a saloon, two berths, a bathroom and kitchen, as well as quarters for the crew; the Stars and Stripes floating from the stern ensured her safety. With coastal waters heavily mined, they were obliged to navigate a circuitous route and by the third day had sailed only as far as Bandol, a pretty fishing village halfway between Toulon and Marseilles; as there seemed little point in going further, here they resolved to stay until the furore had died down and it was safe to return. At Bandol a routine was quickly established, with Maugham every morning rising early to go ashore and visit the market, an experience entirely new to him. 'I bought chickens with trepidation because I could never tell if that dead, featherless creature was young and tender or old and tough; I tried to pretend I knew what I was doing by poking a timid finger into its breast but the cold and clammy skin gave me goose flesh.'

As the days passed, news of the international situation grew increasingly grim, with the invasion of Poland on 1 September, France officially mobilised on the 2nd, and on the 3rd Britain and France declaring war on Germany. With little to do, time moved slowly, the fine weather turned cold and cloudy, and Maugham grew restless, anxious to return home and discover if any reply had arrived to the letter he had sent the Ministry of Information offering his services. With his country prepared for war Maugham once again was eager to participate. 'I am hoping . . . [to] get some sort of work in the department I was in during the last war,' he confided to Desmond MacCarthy on the *Sara*'s elegant writing-paper (canary yellow, with the name of the yacht in dark blue).

> It may be that the authorities will think me useless: in that case I don't quite know what I shall do . . . I have four novels in my head that I should like to write before I finish & if I can do nothing else I suppose the sensible thing would be to sit down & write them, but at present I am too distraught to give them a thought; I spend my time devouring such papers as I can get hold of & turning on the radio whenever there is news.

Finally after nearly a month away he and Gerald decided to decamp, abandoning the boat at Bandol and ignoring the stringent restrictions recently imposed on movement between one *département* and another. Brazenly the two of them climbed into a taxi and ordered the astonished driver to take them to Cap Ferrat, a journey which, miraculously, they completed without a hitch.

Arriving unannounced, they found the house shuttered and airless, and apart from the obvious comforts of being at home, the atmosphere was melancholy. It was difficult to settle, not knowing what was to happen. 'I much fear that I shall be left to twiddle my thumbs indefinitely,' Maugham wrote to his nephew, while Gerald told Robin, 'Willie and I are . . . feeling very aged and on the shelf – nobody seems to want our services. He is very low and gloomy about it. I am trying to take it easily but only succeeding at times.' Then finally a message came through from the Ministry with a definite offer of work. 'This raised my spirits,' said Maugham, 'for it looked as though I were at last going to be given something to do.'

In 1939 the Ministry of Information was in a state of some confusion, vaguely aware that well-known writers should be useful, but unsure exactly how to deploy them, much time being wasted in the forming and dissolving of committees and the sending out of impractical statements of intent. Yet amid the muddle the almost unique usefulness of Somerset Maugham in respect of Anglo-French relations had been noted: not only had the man lived in France for over a decade, but he was widely known there and held in high regard – as recently as August 1939 he had been raised to the rank of *commandeur* of the Légion d'Honneur – and consequently would have access to people and information available to few outsiders. Thus he was asked, first, if he would compile a private report for the Ministry on the attitude of the French towards their British allies; and secondly, if he would write a series of articles to be published in Britain extolling France and the French war effort.

Immediately galvanised, Maugham packed his bags and left for Paris. Here he made arrangements for visiting the front, paying calls on Jean Giraudoux, dramatist and diplomat, currently head of the Bureau of Information, and Raoul Dautry, Minister for Armaments, who provided him with the necessary introductions and laissez-passer. It was from these highly placed contacts, too, that he gleaned such information as might be discreetly transmitted to London, 'private reports', as he termed them, 'upon such matters as it behoved the government to be informed'. Much of this information was gathered when he dined out in the evening after his day's work was done, and frequently he came away appalled by the pro-German sentiments he heard expressed. Many of the more prosperous sections of society had loathed Léon Blum and his socialist government and were terrified by the threat of Communism, openly admitting that they believed they would do better under German domination. Patriotism was regarded as a notion a civilised man should have outgrown. 'What difference will it make to us if Hitler does conquer France?' they asked. 'We shan't be any worse off.' Others were more circumspect and took care what they said in front of the quiet, well-mannered Englishman with the dark, watchful eyes. The vehemently pro-Fascist Horace de Carbuccia, Maugham's Riviera neighbour, was one who had a shrewd idea what his old friend was up to. 'Méfiez-vous de cet Anglais,' he claimed to have been warned. 'Il est de l'Intelligence Service . . . Soyez assuré que s'il tire de vous un renseignement de quelque intérêt, le deuxième étage de Downing Street en sera informé le lendemain.'*

During the following month Maugham made an extensive tour. Beginning at Nancy in the east, he went first to the headquarters of General de Lattre de Tassigny, commander of the Fifth Army, where 'I was entertained by generals whose composure terrified me.' From there he moved up to the Maginot line, 'driving through a fog at night with no lights in a military car with a driver who doesn't know the way and goes at fifty miles an hour', as he told Juliet Duff. Here he was shown

---

* 'Beware of that Englishman. He's in the Intelligence Service. You can be sure that any interesting information he gets out of you will be known in Downing Street the next day.'

over one of the massive, and reputedly impregnable, fortresses that stretched along France's border with Germany. It was an impressive sight. 'The officer in command told me he could hold out for six months if he were besieged,' Maugham reported. 'It came as something of a shock to me to see in the paper some months later that this particular fortress had been captured after four days.' He was taken down a coal mine at Lens, and was conducted round several munitions factories, both in the east and near Paris; during the third week he travelled to the Charente, in the south-west, to inspect the resettlement there of half a million evacuees, French nationals, from Alsace and Lorraine. The final week was spent at sea on board two naval vessels based at Toulon. Privately, Maugham was horrified by much of what he witnessed, by the innate corruption, the lack of morale, the deep and bitter divisions between the social classes, and he found it an enormous struggle to conceal his personal reactions while for propaganda purposes presenting as positive a picture as he could. 'I was determined to write nothing that was untrue,' he said later, '[and] it would have caused a useless scandal to relate the facts as I saw them.' To his masters at the Ministry, however, the facts were sent back unvarnished, one of the subjects of most concern the resentful attitude of the French towards British forces on French soil, regarded as insufficient in number and shockingly licentious in behaviour.

> The impression I received [Maugham wrote] was that there was widespread dissatisfaction with the inadequacy of British support and with the behaviour of British troops, and that such cordiality as the French thought fit to display to their allies was due to policy rather than to friendliness . . . There was a lot to be done in the direction of improving the feeling between the B.E.F. [British Expeditionary Force] and the French.

It was as a step in this direction that Maugham wrote a series of newspaper articles, later published as a pamphlet, *France at War,*★ specifically designed to foster in Britain respect and fellow feeling for her ally across the Channel. In a tone of heartfelt admiration, these articles present an unstintingly heroic picture – a picture that was to be devastatingly undermined when less than two years later Maugham in his book *Strictly Personal* produced his true impressions, written to set the record straight. Considered together, *France at War* and *Strictly Personal* make an interesting study in contrasts. After touring a munitions works, for instance, Maugham in his article reverently exclaims, 'I cannot attempt

★ *France at War* sold more than 100,000 copies between publication in March 1940 and the fall of France in May and June, when it was withdrawn.

to describe the wonderful things I saw . . . the pains that are taken . . . every part is quite exquisitely finished. The machines that are used for the manufacture of all these lethal weapons are miracles of ingenuity'; whereas in the book he makes plain how disturbing it was to find signs in every factory of seething dissatisfaction, attempted sabotage and frequent incidents of revolt. Similarly, he reveals two very different perspectives in his visit to the Charente, where he witnessed the meanness and hostility shown to French families who had been living near the German border and were now forcibly removed and resettled. Arriving in a strange part of the country with almost nothing, these people were deeply resented and given little help by the locals, their fellow countrymen. Straining to shine as favourable a light as possible, Maugham concentrates in his article on the industry and courage shown by the displaced persons. 'There are plenty of empty houses and abandoned cottages . . . in a sad state of dilapidation . . . [but] the refugees set to with a will to make them habitable. It is wonderful with what spirit these people, snatched away from comfortable homes, bear their lot.' In fact the conditions were disgraceful.

> These wretched people had been hustled out of their houses at two hours' notice . . . put in cattle trucks and had spent three days and sometimes more, in the heat of day, in the cold of night, till they reached Poitiers and Angoulême . . . Some fell dangerously ill on the way and not a few died . . . They learnt after a few weeks that their houses had been looted by the soldiers who had been entrusted with their care . . . They were miserably housed . . . in broken-down hovels in which you wouldn't have put a pig.

For the last leg of his tour Maugham visited the naval base at Toulon, where he was invited to witness routine exercises at sea. Dividing his time between two vessels, a warship and a torpedo boat, he was struck by the casual attitude displayed by both officers and crew. In the article this relaxed deportment is tactfully described as 'pleasantly democratic . . . Orders are given in a less peremptory fashion than in our own ships . . . [and] officers and men smoke where and when they please on board, during working hours and out of them'; in *Strictly Personal*, however, Maugham confesses himself shocked: 'I had not been able to help noticing the slovenliness of the men's appearance, which contrasted in so marked a manner with the trim cleanliness so conspicuous in British and American vessels, and I had been taken aback by something that looked very like lack of discipline.'

Having completed his tour of inspection, Maugham returned to the Mauresque shortly before Christmas to write his articles, which were so well received that he was immediately recalled to London to discuss a parallel series, about the Home Front, to be translated into French. On this occasion and for the first time in his life Maugham made the journey by air, flying in extremely bad weather from Le Bourget, outside Paris, on an RAF transport plane. After long delays they finally took off, keeping low over the Channel so as not to be mistaken for an enemy aircraft, finally landing at a military aerodrome somewhere in Sussex. From here he was driven by truck to the nearest town, where he managed to hire a car as there were no trains, and 'arrived in London cold, tired and hungry, but in time for late dinner at the Café Royal'.

During the next three months, the spring of 1940, Maugham was forced to endure the hanging about and time-wasting that was an inevitable part of the wartime experience, with the men at the Ministry unable to make up their minds exactly how to employ him. 'I was like a performing dog in a circus,' he wrote, 'whose tricks the public would probably like, but who somehow couldn't be quite fitted into the programme.' During this period two books were published, *Books and You*, a gathering together of three essays on favourite classics, and a collection of short stories, *The Mixture as Before* (the phrase used by doctors when writing a repeat prescription). This included some vintage Maugham – 'The Three Fat Women of Antibes', 'The Lion's Skin', 'The Facts of Life' – so dismay was expressed at the author's pronouncement in his preface. 'I have now written between eighty and ninety stories,' Maugham states. 'I shall not write any more.' In fact, as he was later to make clear, the typesetter had left out an 'm' and the line should have read, 'I shall not write many more.'

Meanwhile, his diary was filled with the usual social engagements, with weekends in the country, with the Sitwells at Renishaw and Juliet Duff at Bulbridge, and in town catching up with the family: Syrie had closed down her business and was temporarily living in Paris; Liza was spending as much time as she could with Vincent before he was sent overseas; and F.H. had finally been awarded the hereditary peerage for which Maugham had so fervently hoped (F.H. had enjoyed only a brief period on the woolsack however, as to his bitter disappointment Chamberlain had replaced him as lord chancellor the day after war was declared). 'I am glad that your father has been made a Viscount,' Maugham wrote to his niece Kate. 'I was thrilled when I read about it in the paper.' Now Robin would inherit the title, and Maugham, anxious to make appropriate provision for his beloved nephew, arranged with Bert Alanson for a generous allowance to be paid him – 'It means that the second Viscount will be able to pursue the political career on which he has set his heart,' he told Alanson – as well as leaving him a large sum in his will. Regarding the latter, Maugham wrote,

> Robin dear, I am settling $25000 on you which will be paid you immediately & without further formalities on my death. But I very strongly advise you to leave it in the care of Bert, who is both clever & honest . . . If you die without issue I should like you, if you will, to leave the money (if you have not already squandered it) in some way that may be to the advantage of English literature; but of course I shall turn in my grave if you don't have issue . . .

Recently Robin had been the subject of some concern to his uncle, who had heard worrying reports of the young man's heavy drinking, destructive bouts which had obliged the family doctor to forbid any alcohol at all for a while. 'I am very glad,' Maugham scolded him. 'You were quite obviously drinking a great deal too much . . . [and] I have had too much to do with soaks not to look with dismay upon the prospects of anyone I know becoming one.' But on the outbreak of war Robin had redeemed himself by immediately enlisting, joining the Inns of Court Regiment, news which pleased Maugham, who wrote fondly, 'I am told on all sides . . . that your buttons are brighter than any buttons in the British Army.'

At the beginning of May Maugham returned to the south of France, less than a week before the German invasion of the Low Countries. 'It was very quiet on the Riviera,' he recalled. Permission was received to bring the *Sara* back from Bandol to her old berth at Villefranche, but no yachts were allowed outside the harbour. There were shortages of food, of coffee in particular, a black-out was enforced, and petrol was severely rationed, which drastically curtailed the opportunities for social life. As the Phoney War, the *drôle de guerre*, continued people grew restless and resentful. 'Everyone is bored & more or less irritable,' Maugham told Ellen Doubleday. 'Not me! I am delighted that it is impossible to go out to dinner & if only I could afford the gas to go & play golf two or three times a week I should have nothing to complain of.' But then the end came with startling suddenness. On 28 May Belgium surrendered, and in northern France the BEF was routed and forced to flee, the remnant rescued from the beaches at Dunkirk during the first few days of June. On 10 June Italy entered the war, four days before the Germans marched into Paris. Immediately the entire Côte d'Azur was thrown into turmoil: within a few hours 50 per cent of the population of Monaco had fled and Menton and the area around it was evacuated. If, as seemed probable, the Italians occupied the Riviera, all British residents would be interned, a fate that Maugham was not prepared to contemplate: as a last resort he would kill himself with the sleeping pills he kept by him for just such an emergency. In order to find out what was happening he drove into Nice, where he found the Consul General surrounded by a panicking crowd begging for information. After an anxious wait a message came through from the British Embassy, hastily relocated to Bordeaux, that all British subjects were advised to leave the country as quickly as possible, and that two ships, now at Cannes, had been requisitioned to take them off. Passengers were to be on the quay at eight o'clock the following morning, each person permitted one small bag of personal belongings, a blanket and enough food for three days.

That evening over a hurried dinner plans were made for the immediate future. It was decided that Gerald, protected by the immunity conferred by his American passport, should stay on at the villa for a few days to save what he could of the pictures and the most valuable possessions, including Maugham's notebooks and the unfinished manuscript of his new novel. Annette and Nina, both Italian, would remain where they were for as long as it was safe to do so, Maugham giving instructions that if the house had to be abandoned his favourite dachshund, Erda, should be killed. Reckoning that the roads would be impassable by morning, he decided to leave at midnight, hurriedly packing a few clothes, three books, a blanket and a pillow, and filling a basket with lump sugar, tea, a couple of packets of macaroni, a jar of marmalade and a loaf of bread. 'It never struck any of us that I should want a tin opener, a plate, a knife and fork, a glass and a cup.' Having said goodbye to the maids, he and Gerald left the Mauresque. 'We drove in silence. I was unhappy,' Maugham wrote. 'Every few miles a lantern was waved at us and we stopped to have our papers examined by a picket of soldiers.' In Cannes Gerald dropped Maugham at the Carlton Hotel on the Croisette, and the two men took leave of each other; as in the first war, neither knew how or when they would meet again.

The Carlton, one of the grandest hotels on the Riviera, was thronged with people, most of them in evening clothes, many of them drunk, a few hysterical. Sleep was out of the question. Early next morning, Sunday 23 June, Maugham walked down to the harbour where he found a scene of indescribable chaos. On the quay a dense mass of over 3,000 people, all laden with luggage, was pushing forward towards a counter where a couple of customs officers were inspecting bags. There were all types and classes, men, women and children, some invalids come straight out of hospital, even a few on stretchers who, refused entry, were forced to turn back. From time to time a large car would drive up and the well-dressed occupants alight to join the queue, the driver having no choice but to abandon his vehicle and toss the keys into the little crowd of locals looking on. The sun blazed overhead and the heat grew intense. In the harbour the two ships could be seen moored to bollards, not the spacious vessels envisaged but a couple of small colliers, the *Saltersgate* and the *Ashcrest*, en route to Algeria after discharging their cargoes of coal at Marseilles. It was four hours before Maugham was directed on board the *Saltersgate*, where he was told to join eighty others allotted a small space in the hold. When that evening they were finally ready to sail, there were 500 passengers, many of them wealthy, owners of fine villas, accustomed to first-class hotels, now jammed into accommodation intended for a crew of thirty-eight. Every surface was covered in coal-dust, there was hardly room to move, and Maugham finding unbearable the crowding and stuffiness below decks decided to sleep in the open; but the iron deck was painfully hard and it grew cold before dawn, so on the following night and thereafter he slept below.

The next morning the two ships reached Marseilles, where after waiting all day they received instructions to join a French convoy headed for Oran. They were at sea for a week and the conditions on board were frightful. It was very hot, water was in short supply, the few lavatories were filthy and hopelessly inadequate, and rations were extremely limited; most of the day was spent queueing in the sun either for food (four sweet biscuits and a cube of bully beef) or for the chance of a quick wash in a bucket in which fifty people had washed before; everyone was covered in a thick paste of sweat and coal-dust. Ill equipped, Maugham was grateful when a kind lady gave him a scrap of towel and someone else a jam-jar to hold his drinking-water. As the days passed fear of attack by torpedo and the misery caused by over-crowding intensified: four people went out of their minds and one elderly woman died. As there were neither rafts nor lifebelts and U-boats were known to be in the area, it occurred to Maugham to ask one of his neighbours, a retired doctor, how best to drown quickly; ever since his experience in Burma when he had nearly lost his life in a tidal wave he had had a horror of drowning. 'Don't struggle,' was the advice. 'Open your mouth, and the water pouring into your throat will bring on unconsciousness in less than a minute.'

Spirits rose as the coast of Algeria came into view: word had gone round that a liner would be waiting to take everyone on to England. But after they docked at Oran a wireless message was received that there was no liner and that the captain should quickly take on what stores he could and proceed immediately under escort to Gibraltar.

Accordingly, the *Saltersgate* left that night, a Sunday, arriving in Gibraltar the following Tuesday. Rations had slightly improved as bread, fruit and cigarettes had been brought on board, and the prospect of disembarking on British soil, of a bath, a drink, a good meal before transferring to more comfortable accommodation for the last leg of the voyage, cheered everybody up. Hopes were dashed, however, when after reaching port they were refused permission to land: thousands of refugees were already on the Rock and there was no room for more; nor was there another vessel: they would have to sail to England in the ship they were in. 'Many broke down then,' Maugham wrote, '[for] it was a cruel disappointment.' The *Saltersgate* remained in port for three days, and eventually passengers were allowed ashore, in parties of fifty for two hours at a time. Maugham was in the last batch, and he hurried off to buy a quilt, sardines, tinned fruit, whisky and rum. Conditions had improved by the time they were ready to leave as more than 200 passengers, children, the sick and the over-seventies, had been taken off, and Maugham was able to move out of the hold and into the slightly more spacious fo'c'sle, where in a corner he constructed a bed for himself by laying a couple of planks over three baskets and covering it with his quilt.

In a convoy of twelve ships, *Saltersgate* and *Ashcrest* left Gibraltar on 28 June, finally reaching Liverpool on 8 July. With the ship less crowded Maugham had been able to pass the time in relative ease. Sitting cross-legged on the hard iron deck he read Plato in the morning, and in the afternoon played patience and continued with one of the two novels he had brought with him, Thackeray's *Esmond* and Charlotte Brontë's *Villette*; after a meagre supper at seven he told stories, despite his stammer, to anyone who cared to listen. Eventually the convoy came in sight of the coast of Lancashire and the mouth of the Mersey, 'the blessed shores of England'. After twenty days on the ship Maugham was haggard, dirty, weak and exhausted. Arriving by train that night in London he was surprised to learn that his whereabouts had been a matter of some concern to the British press. 'Among well-known people still missing in France are Mr Somerset Maugham,' the *Daily Telegraph* had reported on 24 June, thus causing considerable disquiet to his family. 'The telephone went all day from reporters about Willie, who has disappeared,' Nellie

Maugham wrote anxiously in her diary, adding on the following day, 25 June, 'Still no news of Willie and I do hate not knowing. The American embassy say they can't get any news from Paris, nor can the Red Cross.' She was therefore relieved to read in the *Daily Mail* on 2 July that at last he had been sighted. 'Somerset Maugham's countless admirers will be happy to hear that he has appeared in Gibraltar . . . E. Phillips Oppenheim, too, has escaped . . . Only P. G. Wodehouse of our leading authors remains, as far as one can assume, in German hands.' Finally on the night of 8 July Maugham himself telephoned from the Dorchester Hotel. 'Willie got home!' Nellie wrote. 'He is coming to dinner tomorrow, but is too tired to speak tonight, poor darling.' And on the evening following, 'Willie dined here. He looks terribly tired & thin but not so bad as might be expected after his awful experiences . . . He didn't take off his clothes for 3 weeks . . .!'

Maugham's immediate concern, after a few days' necessary respite, was to return to work. He made a series of propaganda broadcasts, both for home and overseas transmission, their purpose to bolster Anglo-French relations. He was also commissioned by the Ministry of Information and by *Redbook* magazine in America to write a series of articles about the war effort and life on the Home Front. To this end he toured the arsenal at Woolwich, and he conducted a number of interviews, among them with General Sir Alan Brooke, commander in chief of the Home Forces, with A. V. Alexander, First Lord of the Admiralty, as well as with Lord Beaverbrook, Minister of Aircraft Production, and Ernest Bevin, Minister of Labour. On at least one occasion he took the opportunity to combine duty with pleasure by visiting Alan Searle, currently based at a military camp in Strenshall in Yorkshire; here his job was to help run a forces' 'hut' set up by the YMCA to provide a canteen and leisure facilities for troops off duty. 'Would it be possible for me to visit a naffy (is that how you spell it),' Maugham had written to Alan, sensing a good subject for an article. Alan, with his good nature, saucy humour and talent for administration, was proving a success, 'a first-class Hut-Leader' in the words of the Colonel in command, while one of the men was moved to express his appreciation in verse.

> In Alan Searle it seemeth me
> The flower of rarest courtesie
> Blossoms with such a fragrance rare
> As disinfects the foulest air –
> Long may he live, & never cut
> His good companions of the Hut.

'I can't tell you how much I enjoyed my little stay in the North & how much I was interested in the canteen & the camp,' Maugham told him after his visit.

It was now that Maugham for the first and only time in his life tried to find a cure for his stammer. Realising that he would be increasingly called upon to speak in public and on the radio he consulted a Dr Leahy, a hypnotist to whom he had been referred by his old acquaintance Christabel Aberconway. After several sessions with Dr Leahy, in which he was taught a method of self-hypnosis, he was surprised to find that up to a point the treatment worked: he continued to stammer in private conversation, but when performing in public he was able to speak on the whole without stumbling. Unfortunately the Leahy effect wore off after a while, but nonetheless it gave Maugham confidence and from this time on he spoke far more fluently before an audience than when at home with his friends.

Meanwhile in London daily life carried on as near normally as possible under wartime conditions. Barrage balloons floated high overhead, Hyde Park was scarred with trenches, sandbags were piled against shop-fronts and round the statue of Eros in Piccadilly, and pillar-boxes, lamp-posts and trees had been striped with white paint to help pedestrians find their way in the black-out. Maugham had booked a suite on the top floor of the Dorchester Hotel on Park Lane, a conveniently central location. Over the last few months this modern hotel had been experiencing a boom: built of reinforced concrete and boasting a gas-proof shelter in the basement, it was popularly supposed to be indestructible; several Cabinet ministers had taken up residence and rooms were much in demand by people coming up from the country or returning from abroad, or by Londoners too nervous to remain at home. '[There is] practically no night-life in London now,' the *Daily Express* reported. 'Of early-evening "life" . . . the Dorchester has almost a monopoly. Its bar is to London what the Ritz bar used to be to Paris – crowded with business men, socialite women, diplomats, spies.' Maugham was constantly running into old friends in the busy lobby, and a couple of days after disembarking in Liverpool he found himself face to face with Syrie. 'Willie!' she cried, rushing up to him. 'Thank God you're safe! I've been so worried!' 'So I should hope,' Maugham drily responded. Syrie, too, it turned out, was staying at the hotel, having left Paris shortly before the Germans arrived. News of this public encounter between the famously embattled Maughams was naturally seized upon by the gossips, who came up with any number of hilarious versions of the frightful snubs and insults that had been traded.* But in fact during this one short period at the beginning of the war the two were on genuinely friendly terms. They met almost every afternoon for tea, where they were often joined by Liza, she and her mother fervently hoping that this is how it would be from now on. 'But it didn't work that way at all,' Liza sadly recalled.

At the beginning of September the air-raids began, at first by day and then night after night, often starting at dusk and continuing until dawn. For the first two nights of the Blitz, Maugham stayed on the top floor, but the pounding of the anti-aircraft batteries only yards away in Hyde Park became unendurable, and so from the third night he went down to the basement after dinner, joining the other residents who were camping out in pyjamas and dressing-gowns, huddled together on the floor with pillows and eiderdowns, sleeping as best they could until the all-clear sounded between five and six in the morning. 'After my three weeks on an iron deck on the *Saltersgate* this was luxury and I slept like a child,' Maugham wrote. During the day, as he walked along the familiar streets of the West End, he saw the 'grim sight' of the bomb damage, the pavements covered in broken glass, the gaping, smoking holes where a house or row of houses had stood, including the building in Portland Place where previously he had stayed with Alan. One afternoon with Nellie and F.H. he went to look at the mangled remains of a Messerschmitt that had crashed down into the forecourt of Victoria Station. When other duties permitted Maugham arranged to meet friends, eagerly seized upon by that dedicated hostess, Sibyl Colefax, who invited him to lunch together with Diana Cooper, Robert Bruce Lockhart, Moura Budberg and H. G. Wells. Wells was garrulous, delivering a tedious monologue on the subject of God. 'Willie Maugham was palpably bored and chewed the string of his eyeglass cord most of the time,' Bruce Lockhart noted in his diary. One night returning after a dinner-party in Westminster, Maugham with Virginia Woolf was walking up Whitehall when a couple of bombers came over. '[I] shouted at her [Virginia] to take cover but in the noise she couldn't hear,' Maugham recalled. 'She made no attempt to take cover but stood in the middle of the road and threw her arms into the air. She appeared to be worshipping the flashing sky. It was a most

* The most widely repeated anecdote draws on Maugham's account of the advice he was given by the doctor on board the *Saltersgate*. In the most popular version Syrie tells her husband she is planning to cross to the States and is terrified of being torpedoed. 'Well, S-S-Syrie,' Maugham is supposed to have replied, 'I am assured that when you find yourself in the water, if you open your m-m-mouth wide, it's all over much more quickly' (Godfrey Winn, *The Infirm Glory*, p. 253).

weird sight to watch her there, lit up now and then by the flashes from the guns.' Yet on the whole dinner engagements were rare: few cared to venture out in the evening, and the bar and restaurant at the Dorchester were always packed, everyone steadying their nerves with stiff drinks, the resulting party atmosphere providing a welcome insulation from the constant raids. 'You know we've had some air raid warnings here,' Maugham told Alan Searle. 'The Dorchester is very gay while they last . . . [I] spent such a nice evening, with Diana & Duff [Cooper] & Juliet [Duff] & Alf [the novelist A. E. W.] Mason.'

Duff Cooper had recently been appointed Minister of Information and it was he, shortly after Maugham arrived in London, who had proposed a propaganda mission to the United States, a mission which by its nature had to be very hush-hush. For Britain it was a matter of paramount importance to win American support for the war, a tough proposition as the majority of the population was isolationist and Anglophobic and nursed a deep suspicion of anything that smacked of foreign propaganda. Memories remained vivid of the last European conflict and most Americans were darned sure they wanted nothing to do with this one. Clearly it would be a hard task to convert an essentially unsym-pathetic nation into a loyal and active ally, and in furthering their cause the British government had to step extremely carefully as any overt attempts at propaganda would be deeply resented and deleterious: since the signing in 1935 of the Neutrality Act, it had become illegal for foreign agents to conduct propaganda within the United States. In order to avoid the appearance of any suspicious activity, Lord Lothian, the Ambassador in Washington, had urged the use of well-known authors on the lecture circuit; and for this a writer such as Maugham, with a long-established reputation in the States, was considered ideal, likely to be regarded with deference by audiences and, crucially, viewed as a private individual inde-pendent of government control. During the nearly two-and-a-half years before America entered the war numbers of well-known British writers toured the country, many to great effect, but few worked harder, made more of an impact or proved as invaluable as Somerset Maugham.

Maugham agreed with alacrity to Duff Cooper's proposal. To provide himself with cover, he contacted Nelson Doubleday, who sent him a letter stating that he was urgently required in New York to arrange for the publication of his next book, a ruse that in the event deceived nobody: 'W. Somerset Maugham is in this country as a British agent,' blithely begins an interview in the New York Times which appeared soon after his arrival. Maugham left London one afternoon at the very end of September, spent the night in Bristol, and next morning caught the plane for Lisbon, taking off with an escort of Spitfires. Capital of a neutral country, Lisbon was imbued with an almost holiday atmosphere, warm and sunny, crowded with people of all nationalities, the shops stocked with food and other merchandise long unobtainable elsewhere. None of this was much enjoyed by Maugham, who found himself billeted in a filthy little pension, obliged to spend hours queueing to have his papers examined and passport stamped prior to his departure for the United States. Finally on 7 October after several frustrating days he was free to go, boarding the Pan-Am Clipper, a luxurious flying-boat, for the sixteen-hour flight, via the Azores and Bermuda, to New York.

As on previous occasions Maugham stayed at the Ritz-Carlton Hotel, on 64th and Madison, where he proposed to remain until Gerald, now making his way to Portugal, was able to join him. Currency restrictions imposed on British subjects abroad were extremely tight, but as Maugham was in America to promote the British cause it had been discreetly arranged with the Treasury that he be allowed to draw on a portion of his American royalties, thus enabling him to enjoy a rather higher standard of living than would otherwise have been the case. Almost immediately he was put to work, writing articles, making speeches, giving interviews, attending fund-raising dinners and helping sell books for the British War Relief Bookshop. He also made a number of radio broadcasts, his first with Edward Weeks on NBC, during which, in answer to a question about great war novels, Maugham said, 'Just as the best novel about the First World War, *All Quiet on the Western Front*, came out of Germany's defeat, so I hope and believe that the best book about this war will come from the same source, and for the same reason.' It was an emotive reply and it received an outburst of applause from the studio audience. During the first month Maugham addressed gatherings which varied in size from 3,000 in a flag-draped hotel ballroom to 100 ladies at tea in a private house. Sometimes he was the sole speaker, at other times part of a panel with other writers, among them Louis MacNeice, Robert Sherwood, Thomas Mann and the Austrian novelist Franz Werfel. Whatever the occasion, Maugham was careful to emphasise the ineradicable links between Britain and America. 'When, in this war, we British are defending our culture, the rich and fertile culture of the English-speaking peoples, we are defending, not only what is ours but what is yours,' he told a large audience one night at the Waldorf-Astoria. Another reiterated theme, carefully chosen to counter the New World's dislike of the Old with all its arrogance and imperialism, was the future partnership of the two great democratic countries. The war, Maugham repeatedly stressed, was having a democratising effect: 'the crisis was destroying the class consciousness which has been one of the evils of English life . . . [after the war] the country shall be much more democratic than ever before. Some accept it with resignation, some with joy. I myself accept it with joy.' Such sentiments, genuinely held, were also directly in line with the briefings Maugham regularly received both from the Embassy in Washington and from the British Information Services in New York. His masters were pleased with him. 'On his arrival Maugham was given widespread and favourable publicity,' it was reported to the Foreign Office in London. 'He is apparently well-liked by the Press . . . [and] is widely quoted in out of town papers.'

In his free time and while waiting for Gerald, currently kicking his heels in Lisbon while trying to get a seat on the flying-boat, Maugham saw friends, news of them retailed in long letters to Alan Searle, to whom he wrote devotedly every week. There were the Doubledays, Alexander Woollcott, Dorothy Parker, George S. Kaufman, Carl Van Vechten, H. G. Wells, 'looking old, tired and shrivelled', and the playwright Ned Sheldon, now paralysed and blind but as saintly and charming as ever. A fellow guest at the Ritz was Emerald Cunard, 'my girl Emerald', as Maugham affectionately referred to her; she had a suite five floors above his, where 'she managed to create the nearest thing to a salon that New York has ever had'; every afternoon he went up to take tea with her, '& hobnobbed with all the fantastic people she gathered about her'.

It was with Emerald one day that Maugham met again the writer Glenway Wescott, first encountered in 1928 when Wescott had been brought to lunch at the Mauresque. On that occasion Maugham in a surly temper had snubbed the young man, but now he was enchanted by him, much taken by his blond, youthful good looks and quickly finding large areas in common: like Maugham, Wescott was intensely interested in sex and literature and in other people's lives; he was a novelist; he had lived in France, and with his lover, Monroe Wheeler, a director at the Museum of Modern Art, knew everyone in literary and artistic circles in Paris and New York. For his part Wescott enormously admired Maugham and the two men soon became close friends, developing an almost father–son relationship. Wescott sensed that Maugham would have liked something more, and he was grateful for the elder man's tact in not making this an issue: 'though frequently complimenting me on my youthfulness, etc., he has never felt, at least never let me feel the least strain in this way. His discretion never fails.' Glenway invited Maugham to spend a weekend at Stone-blossom, the country house in New Jersey he and Monroe shared, and here they had long discussions about books, and about Glenway's writing – Maugham had reservations about Wescott's first novel, *The Pilgrim Hawk* – and Maugham encouraged Glenway to describe his sex life. 'I said that for my part I am never as eager to have intercourse with a new lover as with one I have already enjoyed, again and again and again. Somewhat to my surprise Willie said that oh, indeed, it was so for him as well.'

Also in New York were Liza with her little son, and Syrie. With Vincent away in the army, Liza, newly pregnant, had come over in July and almost immediately fallen ill, for a time so ill that her hostess, Nelson Doubleday's sister, had panicked and cabled for her mother. Immediately all the old bitterness flared up between Maugham and his ex-wife: he thought his daughter should live quietly, preferably in the country, at least until after the baby was born; Syrie on the other hand was determined that Liza should be with her in Manhattan, and saw no reason, once she was well again, why she should not lead as active a social life as she chose. At the back of her mind was the thought that Liza, so chic and pretty, might meet a rich man who would eventually take the place of the impecunious Vincent. Liza felt torn apart. She was touched by her father's concern: 'I had the feeling that he wanted to be and to remain friends with me'; but she hated the position of being yet again the cause of quarrels between her parents. 'It was a very painful situation,' she said. 'In the end I chose to share an apartment with my mother at the Sulgrave Hotel . . . though I must say there were times when I would have preferred to be independent and on my own.'

Finally at the beginning of December 1940 Gerald arrived in New York; after several weeks in Lisbon he had eventually made the crossing by sea, having despaired of obtaining a passage on the Clipper. Maugham was relieved to see him safe, but his heart sank when it immediately became obvious that Gerald was back to his bad old alcoholic ways. 'I can't bear this,' Maugham declared, pacing up and down. 'Haven't I done enough for him? Why do I have to go through more?' If only Alan could come over and take his place; but there was no chance of that with the world in its present state.

Within a couple of weeks of Gerald's arrival he and Maugham left for Chicago, where there were further propaganda talks to be given, and before audiences that were notably less sympathetic, with Chicago a bastion of the non-interventionist America First Committee. During the month that they spent in Illinois the two men took off a couple of days to go to Oregon to visit a handsome, hard-drinking ex-lover of Gerald's, Tom Seyster. They took with them on the trip a thirteen-year-old English boy, Daniel Farson,★ a godson of Seyster's, who had been entrusted to their care by his aunt, with whom he was staying in Chicago as an evacuee. Farson remembered the occasion vividly: he had no idea that Maugham was a famous author and chattered brightly to him all the way on the train, Maugham listening politely, Haxton palpably bored by the child's presence. Both men seemed at a low ebb, Farson said later, and it was plain that Haxton was drinking heavily, the impression that lingered of Gerald 'a large ginger moustache and violent temper when he was not mute from hangover'. During their stay in Oregon Seyster and Haxton quarrelled furiously, Seyster still besotted by Gerald, who was permanently intoxicated, while Maugham remained silent and detached. Dutifully the three adults bought the boy popcorn, took him bowling and to the cinema, a strange little group to be wandering the streets, as Farson remarked: 'in this small midwestern town our appearance must have been disconcerting to the point of shame'. When they finally returned to Chicago Maugham drew Farson's aunt aside and warned her that Seyster was not a suitable companion for a boy of Dan's age.

From Chicago Maugham and Haxton travelled to California, staying with the Alansons in a rain-soaked San Francisco for three weeks, where Maugham dutifully continued his lecturing. Here on the west coast he skilfully played up the German threat, not to distant Europe but to territories much nearer home. 'If by any chance we are beaten, then your danger will be great. It isn't a ruined Europe that Hitler wants, it isn't an unproductive Africa; it's those great undeveloped territories of South America, with their inexhaustible stores of raw material that he hankers after.' He also made a point of distancing indomitable Britain from her fallen ally, France. Describing the collapse of France as the most tragic event of the war, he laid much of the blame on the climate of corruption that had long permeated the country. 'In France there were many thousands of men of the highest integrity. There were not enough. They were swamped by men who were greedy, dishonest, selfish, and immoral . . . The Germans have been saying for years that the French were a decadent people; they were right.'† Effective as propaganda, this was also something of which Maugham himself was bitterly convinced; his awareness

★ Farson later became a noted writer, photographer and television journalist.

† Needless to say such sentiments were ill received among the French community in California. When the director René Clair met Maugham in Hollywood the encounter was frigid in the extreme.

of the atmosphere of moral decay seeps on to almost every page of *Christmas Holiday*, and the degeneracy of the French national character is a subject examined at length in *Strictly Personal*: 'If a nation values anything more than freedom, it will lose its freedom, and the irony of it is that if it is comfort or money that it values more, it will lose that too.' When Glenway Wescott asked Maugham what he thought France would be like after the war, he replied 'in his hardest, narrowest voice . . . "They will have eaten so much shit they will stink of it."'

Exhausted after a bout of influenza, Maugham was finding public speaking a strain, and it was a relief finally to reach Los Angeles, where he and Gerald stayed at the Beverly Hills Hotel and they could spend at least some of the day relaxing in the sun by the pool. Where Chicago had been defiantly isolationist, in California the general attitude was more difficult to define. It was 'a jittery population', Maugham told F.H.

> The vast majority are ready to give all aid to Britain, but the vast majority also are very much afraid of being forced into the war . . . [having] been frankly terrified by the stories of the bombing of London & the pictures of destruction that have been sent over . . .
>
> [There are also] vast numbers of Republicans who cannot forgive Roosevelt his victory in November & are prepared to oppose any measure, regardless of its merits, merely because he proposes it. I wouldn't go so far as to say they would like a British defeat, but it hasn't escaped them that it would be a smack in the eye for the President . . . Of course this is confidential; I don't let a hint of this escape me when I talk.

Committed to promoting his country's cause, Maugham in Los Angeles suddenly found himself cornered, faced with an offer he felt honour-bound to accept. Over the years he had persistently turned down all offers of film work, uninterested in the medium and knowing full well he lacked the requisite skills; now, however, he found himself obliged to give in. At the instigation of Brendan Bracken, the dynamic new Minister of Information in London, Maugham was approached by David O. Selznick with a proposal for a propaganda film about an English family in wartime. Selznick, one of the most successful producers in the business – two of his films, *Gone with the Wind* and *Rebecca*, had recently won Best Picture Oscars – was excited at the prospect of at last signing up the world-famous author, so much of whose work was already on celluloid. With this particular new property Selznick was aware that he would have to tread carefully, not wishing to estrange either the film industry itself or potential audiences, for whom any hint of propaganda was something alien and sinister. 'Naturally we should keep confidential from everybody other than the British authorities the fact that . . . [the film] will have a propaganda value,' he wrote in an internal memo.

Reluctantly Maugham agreed to the deal, and by the beginning of March 1941, when he returned to New York, he had already completed the first thirty pages of *The Hour Before the Dawn*. But then followed several weeks of interruption, with lectures to be given in Chicago, Philadelphia and Lafayette, Indiana. On 15 March, Liza's baby was born, a daughter, christened Camilla. 'So far I have only been allowed to see the infant through a sheet of glass,' Maugham reported after visiting mother and child in New York City Hospital. '[She] has bright red hair at present & the most lovely little hands you ever saw.'

At the beginning of April Maugham went to Washington for the first night of a dramatised version of *Theatre* ('poor & poorly acted'), and that same month a novella, *Up at the Villa*, was published by Doubleday. Set in Florence, *Up at the Villa* tells the story of Mary, a beautiful widow romantically inclined, who one night picks up a young man, a refugee on the run, and takes him to bed, thinking to give him an idyllic experience to treasure for the rest of his life. But humiliated by her motive the young man shoots himself in front of her, and faced with having to dispose of the body, she turns in her panic to Rowley Flint, a sexy, slippery fellow whose morals and character she had hitherto despised. As a result, and in a typically Maughamian conclusion, it is Rowley Flint to whom Mary becomes inextricably linked, rather than to the successful, honourable, stiff-upper-lip British diplomat whom everyone had expected her to marry. A slight work, with some unusually wooden dialogue, *Up at the Villa* nonetheless maintains an exciting tension, and the almost universal panning it received – 'fictional drivel', his 'worst novel', must have been 'talking in his sleep' – is difficult to justify. In later years Maugham came to hate *Up at the Villa* and flinched when it was mentioned. 'I don't want to hear a word about it!' he would angrily exclaim. 'I'm ashamed ever to have done it!', a curious response from one who was famously impervious to critical censure. But his reaction may have had more to do with a feeling of guilt: the cad Rowley Flint – 'an unscrupulous scamp . . . a waster' – is in all major respects a portrait of Gerald Haxton; and there are telling similarities, too, between Gerald and Mary's dead husband, a charmer but a soak. 'He had immense vitality. He was so kind and gentle and sweet – when he was sober. When he was drunk he was noisy and boastful and vulgar and quarrelsome . . . He was a dreadful gambler and when he was drunk he'd lose hundred of pounds.' 'Why didn't you leave him?' Mary is asked. 'How could I leave him?' she replies.

'He was so dependent on me.' These were portrayals Maugham may have bitterly come to regret, given the harrowing sequence of events that was shortly to unfold.

By the end of May, despite constant distraction, *The Hour Before the Dawn* was finally finished, and Maugham and Haxton returned to Hollywood. The story, about an upper-middle-class English family, with one son a pacifist, one in intelligence, and complete with a beautiful Nazi spy, appeared first in *Redbook* magazine, for which Maugham was paid $25,000; the plan was then to rework it as a film-script before finally processing it into a full-length novel – by which time its author was heartily sick of the whole project: 'the most tedious job I have ever done in my life'.

As he had agreed to make himself available during shooting, Maugham rented a house, complete with a couple of servants, at 732 South Beverly Glen Boulevard, in the leafy residential area of Beverly Hills. 'It is two miles from the sea & so gets the cool breeze,' he told Ellen Doubleday.

> It has a very nice garden & a swimming pool. It is furnished in Hollywood Italian, but quite unobjectionably & has a studio in the garden for me to work in, a drawing room, a bridge room with a bar, a dining-room & a little breakfast room looking on to the garden; four nice bedrooms, each with bath, & an upstairs sitting room.

Relieved to be settled, Maugham started work on the screenplay, for which he had been paid $15,000, with an additional $5,000 for every week he spent on it. He was in a relatively contented frame of mind, following much the same daily routine he had established at the Mauresque: writing all morning, swimming and golf after a sleep in the afternoon, followed by an evening entertaining or being entertained. Gerald, too, was delighted to be back in California, full of good resolutions to curb his drinking while at the same time determined to enjoy himself to the full. Soon after they moved in Liza, the children and a nanny arrived for an extended visit. At first Liza had been nervous about accepting the invitation as she was frightened of Haxton and apprehensive about staying in the same house, but her father had assured her that Gerald was hardly drinking now and was 'so good and sweet'. That this was not entirely the case Liza immediately realised. 'Of course it wasn't true about his not drinking: he just did it secretly,' she said. 'There was a bar in the living room and he would have glasses full of drink for himself lined up under there while he served everyone else and kept a soft drink in full view.' Yet there seemed to be a tacit agreement not to mention the problem.

On one occasion when Liza and Maugham went with the Alansons to Lake Tahoe for a few days, they returned to find Haxton in the grip of delirium tremens. 'My father seemed to accept even this from him,' she resignedly remarked. Soon, however, she too ceased to worry, quickly swept up in a glamorous social life, out most of the day and rarely coming home till the small hours, with a constant stream of handsome young actors calling at the house to take her to parties and screenings.

Whether drunk or sober, Gerald, too, was loving the life, detailed accounts of which he sent back in affectionate letters to Louis Legrand in France. Loulou was painfully missed by Gerald, who worried about his health and situation, and whenever possible sent him parcels of provisions through the good offices of a friend in the Red Cross. To Loulou he described the wonderful time he was having, taking advantage of everything southern California had to offer, sex, swimming, gambling, shopping for clothes, driving a big car and, rather worryingly given the alcoholic intake, learning how to fly. Most exciting of all, as he knew Loulou would appreciate, was actually meeting the stars. 'J'étais dans une grande soirée hier ou il y avait tout le monde de Hollywood,' he boasted, 'Chaplin, [Ronald] Colman, [Herbert] Marshall et toutes les plus jolies femmes de cette terre. Hedy Lamarr était la plus ravissante, mais j'ai trouvé plus à mon gout Rosalind Russell et Loretta Young.'* In another letter he described a lunch-party Maugham had given where both Douglas Fairbanks and Bette Davis were present, the latter 'charmante mais très laide'† in Gerald's opinion. In the circumstances Miss Davis had reason to be charming, as it was the film of *Of Human Bondage* that in 1934 had turned round what she herself described as a 'fast-disappearing career . . . I had been wandering aimlessly until *Of Human Bondage* came along and brought me out of the fog,' she said in an interview. 'We have such reverence for the chance this picture gave [me] . . . that everything in our family dates BB (Before *Bondage*) and AB (After *Bondage*).'

Predictably, Maugham was considerably less enamoured of Hollywood than Gerald and Liza, regarding the film colony with much the same weary indifference with which he had regarded theatre folk in London. 'I see something of the stars; I cannot say they greatly excite me,' he languidly admitted to his niece Kate, while to Osbert Sitwell he complained of the almost total lack of culture of most actors: 'one little ray of sunshine

---

* 'I was at a big party yesterday with the whole of Hollywood, Chaplin, Colman, Marshall and all the prettiest women in the industry. Hedy Lamarr was the loveliest but I preferred Rosalind Russell and Loretta Young.'

† 'charming but very ugly'.

was when Mr Cary Grant told me he didn't really think much of Cézanne', he added sardonically. To Peter Stern he elaborated on the tedium of Hollywood parties. 'I went to my last the other day. There were eighty people to dinner. I had a moment's conversation with my host & I asked him if he knew any of the people there. No, he said, do you?' To this most disciplined of men the relaxed atmosphere, the lack of regard for punctuality was frustrating in the extreme: it maddened him when he arrived for dinner precisely on time to find his hostess had just drifted upstairs to have a bath. The stupidity and self-regard within the acting profession, the suffocating parochialism of the industry bored him intensely. 'I meet few people who interest me,' he complained. 'They are cordial & hospitable . . . but I can find no one who is willing to talk to me of the things I like talking about. It is like having nothing to eat but candy.' Typical of this kind of experience was an evening when that well-known actor Errol Flynn called at the house to collect Liza. For once there had been a rare Allied victory widely reported that day in the papers, and Maugham asked the star if he had seen the wonderful news. 'You mean about Mickey Rooney?' came the guileless response. Occasionally Maugham tried to enliven proceedings for himself, as on the day he was taken to see Spencer Tracy filming *Dr Jekyll and Mr Hyde*. The star came on set costumed as Dr Jekyll, formally dressed, very elegant and dapper, and began his scene. 'Which one is he supposed to be now?' asked Maugham in a carrying whisper, provoking a loud guffaw from the camera crew for which Tracy never forgave him.*

Much more to Maugham's taste was the company of fellow writers, Dorothy Parker for instance, whom he was pleased to find next to him at a dinner-party, 'demure in black silk, but with a demureness fraught with peril to the unwary'. Among the English contingent were Aldous Huxley, the playwright John Van Druten, Gerald Heard, mystic and polymath, and Christopher Isherwood. Isherwood, now living in Los Angeles, was delighted by the reunion. 'I was so pleased to see Willie again,' he noted in his diary, 'that old, old parrot, with his flat black eyes, blinking and attentive, his courtly politeness and his hypnotic stammer.' Maugham was as much a mystery to him as he was to Maugham. In a letter to E. M. Forster, Isherwood compared the sixty-seven-year-old writer to 'an old Gladstone bag covered with labels. God only knows what is inside,' while Maugham referred to the lively, boyish Christopher as 'that delightful,

---

* Twelve years later when Spencer Tracy was in the south of France with Maugham's old friend Garson Kanin, he was adamant in refusing an invitation to dine at the Mauresque.

strange man whom you could never really know'. The two of them had a good deal in common and relished each other's company, Maugham finding in Christopher and his compatriots the restless intelligence, the subversive wit and wide culture he had failed to find elsewhere in California. Isherwood one day invited Maugham to visit him at the MGM studios where he was working. The Marx Brothers were also there, and Harpo, excited to see his old acquaintance, rushed at Maugham, the whole gang following, 'screaming like devils', Christopher recalled, '[climbing] all over him, hugging and kissing him, as Willie submitted to their embraces with shy pleased smiles'. At Isherwood's house in the Hollywood hills, he, Maugham and Gerald Heard had long conversations about the *Upanishads* and the Hindu scriptures, about Vedanta and the eighth-century philosopher Shankara, all of absorbing interest to Isherwood and Heard, both disciples of the influential California guru Swami Prabhavananda. Maugham told them that his great ambition was to return to India and write a serious book about Shankara and his teaching. 'I was much moved on hearing this,' Isherwood recorded, 'until the news reached us, through van Druten and others, that Willie had made fun of Gerald [Heard], albeit quite affectionately, at a cocktail party next day, and deplored my wasting my time with mysticism when I ought to be writing novels.'

Expecting at any moment to be called in for the filming of *The Hour Before the Dawn*, Maugham was beginning to feel frustrated, sick to death of writing propaganda and longing to start on a novel that had nothing to do with the war. As he had told Isherwood, a return to India was uppermost in his mind, his plans yearningly elaborated in letters to Alan Searle. As soon as the war ended and they could travel again, he told him, Gerald would return to France to put the house in order, while Alan would come out to California and from there the two of them would sail for India. 'I am afraid this is no more than wishful thinking . . . but how grand it would be if it were so! No more propaganda writing for me & a lovely journey ahead . . . & peace, peace, peace for a generation at least.'

Maugham was abruptly awakened from these pleasant day-dreams by a communication from David O. Selznick Productions: the screenplay of *The Hour Before the Dawn* had been judged wholly unacceptable. 'I have read scripts and reviewed fiction since 1932 but never have I felt so speechless,' began one internal memorandum.

> It is impossible to credit Maugham with this formless, maundering, illiterate rubbish. It is so trite and dead; the characters are stock of the worst

novelette type. I just do not know what to say or how to say it, except that for his own sake Mr Maugham had better just tear this up and forget what must have been a bad dream.

The author was consequently informed that his services would no longer be required, a dismissal to which he reacted partly with relief and partly with extreme irritation that so much time had been wasted. 'I loathe the people I am working for,' he told his niece Kate, and 'I will never again have anything to do with pictures.' A film of *The Hour Before the Dawn* eventually appeared in 1944, with Veronica Lake and Franchot Tone, and disappeared again shortly afterwards, while the novel was brought out only in the United States, Maugham having refused to let it be published in Britain. 'I know very well it was poor & I was miserable about it,' he confessed to Eddie Marsh. 'I tried to console myself by looking upon it as my contribution to the war effort, but that did not help much and I prefer to think now that it will be unread in England and forgotten in America.'

In mid-September Liza and the children left California to return to New York, followed a week later by Maugham and Haxton, who completed the first part of the journey by car, driving through Texas to South Carolina. The purpose of the detour was to visit Bonny Hall, a property near Charleston belonging to Nelson Doubleday, who had offered to build Maugham a bungalow there, to be paid for out of future royalties, where his author could live and work in peace for the duration. Maugham had been delighted by the suggestion, and pleased by the look of the little house already almost finished. On arrival in New York he enjoyed shopping for furniture to fill it, a welcome diversion, as the weeks passed, from the almost ceaseless drudgery of the propaganda treadmill. 'Writing, writing, writing all the time,' he complained to Searle. 'No sooner do I get through with one job than I have to get started on another.' He was gratified, however, to be invited to join the Pulitzer Prize Committee as a judge of the drama section, the first time an Englishman had been asked to take part; however, 'the result so far is that I have seen as lousy a lot of plays as it has been my misfortune to see for many years . . . the only halfway good one being Noël's [*Blithe Spirit*] . . . [and] he not being American is not eligible'.

But then suddenly everything changed. On 7 December 1941 the Japanese bombed Pearl Harbor and the United States entered the war. Maugham, who had just returned to the south, felt as though an enormous weight had been lifted off his shoulders. 'Now that America is in the war my job has come to an end,' he wrote with relief to Glenway Wescott. 'I can't be any use in further trying to persuade the Americans that the English are not so bad after all since you've got to put up with us now if you like us or not.'

It was at Yemassee in South Carolina that Maugham was to be based for the rest of the war. His little house, Parker's Ferry, was situated in the middle of marshland, on the banks of the Combahee River, less than an hour's drive from the Atlantic coast. It was a rural, sparsely populated region, with the nearest town, Beaufort, twenty-six miles away and Charleston more than fifty. The landscape was flat, the marshes intersected by rivers and narrow canals, which cut through rice fields interspersed with patches of forest and with areas of open pasture grazed by small red cattle. The trees were magnificent, tall pines, eucalyptus, glossy-leaved magnolia and ancient live-oaks festooned with heavy swathes of Spanish moss; in spring the dogwood burst briefly into flower and the woods were carpeted with lilies and wild azalea. 'The countryside [is] wild, lonely, monotonous & lovely,' Maugham wrote. 'I like it very much indeed & find myself happy here.'

The Doubledays' handsome house, Bonny Hall, recently rebuilt but on the old plantation pattern, was at the centre of an estate now turned over to the cultivation of azaleas and camellias. Two miles from the Hall and set in its own garden was Maugham's white-painted bungalow, simple in design, yet spacious and comfortable: there were three bedrooms, each with a bathroom, a small sitting-room, a large living-room with doors leading on to a verandah, a dining-room, a kitchen and a wide entrance hall; reproductions of pictures from the Villa Mauresque hung on the walls. A short distance from the house were servants' quarters and a separate small cottage which served as a study, with a large desk, bookshelves and an open fireplace. To look after him there was a black cook and housemaid, Nora and Mary, and a gardener, Sunday, who was helped out on an irregular basis by his nephew, Religious. Maugham's innate courtesy impressed the two women, and he in turn was very taken by them. '[They] have captured my sympathy because they find me the funniest man they have ever known,' he reported. 'They simply bellow with laughter at my smallest joke.' Nora was an excellent cook, with a repertoire of southern dishes which Maugham found much to his taste – gumbo, fried chicken, corn fritters – though she refused to cook any Yankee food, such as his favourite Boston baked beans. As he had done with Annette at the Mauresque, Maugham immediately began to teach Nora some basic French cuisine. Shortly after his arrival the

Doubledays, invited to dine for the first time at Parker's Ferry, were astonished to be offered *soupe à l'oignon, truite au bleu, canard à l'orange* and a perfect almond soufflé, all expertly served, under their host's watchful eye, by Mary and Sunday.

During the winter Nelson ran his publishing business from Bonny Hall, returning to Oyster Bay in the spring when it began to grow hot. While the Doubledays were in residence there was a great deal of coming and going of editorial staff and their wives from Garden City, resulting in a busy social programme of bridge, cocktails and dinner-parties, in which Maugham on occasion joined. On the whole, however, he preferred it when the couple were on their own, when he could go up for a game of cards with Ellen in the afternoon and in the evening join Nelson for a drink before returning to his own house for dinner. Husband and wife could hardly have been more different. Nelson was a buccaneer, a big, beefy man, moody and flamboyant, an outdoorsman who loved duck-shooting and churning down the river in his powerful motor-boat; 'a bluffer and a boaster', according to Maugham, he was also a prodigious drinker, rarely without a glass of Bourbon in his hand, unattractively referred to as his 'phlegm-cutter'. Ellen, 'dramatically rich', was 'quite nice, a little shy & not very amusing but anxious to please'; she was a sweet, nervous woman, completely overwhelmed by her noisy, dominating husband, hopelessly untidy and disorganised, her domestic affairs always on the brink of chaos. 'Ellen ran the worst household in America,' said Jerry Zipkin, a New York friend of Maugham's who visited him at Parker's Ferry. 'The roast never went round, [and] if you were sitting on her left you starved. Nelson roared about what a rotten housekeeper she was, and she'd come in tears to see Willie and ask him how to run a house, since his cottage was so well organised.'

As fuel was severely rationed, there was little opportunity for driving about the countryside, and when calling at Bonny Hall Maugham and Haxton usually walked the couple of miles up to the house; otherwise they rode nearly every day, exploring the area on a couple of horses provided by Nelson, a form of exercise which Maugham had always enjoyed. 'I have grand gallops through the country,' he wrote in April 1942. 'The woods just now are lovely, all the young green of the green trees very gay against the dark green of the live oaks & the gray of the Spanish moss; and here and there, in great patches, white lilies, & on the canal banks, iris.' For Gerald this was all very well, and for a while he amused himself fishing from the river and shooting duck, but the nearest tavern, the Golden Eagle in Beaufort, was miles away, and with

Maugham as usual absorbed in his writing he soon grew restless and bored. He was also unwell – he had recently had a bout of heart trouble – and so he decided to return to New York for treatment. Here his condition turned out to be more serious than anticipated, necessitating a three-week stay in hospital followed by a month's convalescence in Florida.

With the United States' entry into the war Maugham had assumed that his usefulness would end and he could devote himself to the novel which he had had in mind for over three years. But in this he was mistaken, and to his dismay he found his services constantly called upon, 'roped in', as he put it, 'to do stuff for America'. The Maugham name was known to have a powerful effect: *Great Modern Reading*, a poetry and prose anthology he compiled with the ordinary reader in mind, sold nearly a million copies within the first twelve months of publication in 1943. Again he was asked to broadcast and write articles, to promote Defence Bonds and report on the local leisure facilities provided by the USO (United Services Organisation) for the armed forces; one of his lowest points was reached when he was faced with having to come up with an inspiring article to encourage Americans to send vegetable seeds to Britain. 'It's no good your telling me that Dean Swift wrote a very pretty piece about a broomstick,' he grumbled to Eddie Marsh. 'I know he did.' Briefly there was even talk of sending him on a propaganda tour of Brazil, a country honeycombed with pro-German organisations, but after a brief flurry this particular project was abandoned.

Once the Doubledays had left, Maugham spent a great deal of time on his own at Yemassee, very contentedly for the most part. Except for the occasional weekend Gerald did not return after his convalescence in Florida, having decided to go to Washington to try to find some war work of his own, a plan of which Maugham whole-heartedly approved, even though it would leave him without a secretary. 'Of course I should miss him,' he told Alan, 'but I think he will be happier doing some such work & I think it will keep him out of mischief.' Sometimes friends visited, Glenway Wescott and Monroe Wheeler among the most welcome. Maugham was impressed by Monroe's standing and scholarship, his knowledge of the art world, but he was closest to Glenway, who often came on his own and with whom Maugham felt he could talk about anything, writing, philosophy, psychology, literature and life, and with whom he relished dissecting their mutual friends. It was Glenway who picked up on the fact that Maugham was still involved in some way with 'government business': 'I know that people used to come to see him in Yemassee and I'd have to go out of the room,' Wescott recalled, and once Maugham told him, 'The day doesn't pass that I don't send some poor [pro-German] Englishman back home.'★

Dorothy Parker was another visitor. She came for three weeks, 'three long, long, long weeks', during which she suffered hours of tedium. Expecting to join an amusing house-party, she was dismayed to find herself alone with Maugham, who offered little in the way of entertainment except endless games of bridge. 'That old lady', as she described her host, 'is a crashing bore.' Occasionally people were asked in to cocktails, but they turned out for the most part to be 'various handsome young men who were not interested in ladies but who were interested in Mr Maugham', and thus of no use to Mrs Parker. Presumably she managed to conceal her ennui, however, as a couple of years later Maugham contributed an admiring preface to a collected edition of her stories and verse.

A far more appreciative guest was Eleanor Roosevelt, who stayed at Yemassee after visiting the State University in North Carolina. Mrs Roosevelt had been a fan of Maugham's since the late 1920s; they had met more recently on one of Maugham's visits to Washington and had taken a great liking to each other, Maugham admiring the remarkable First Lady for her courage, tenacity and strong social conscience. In 1941 when Maugham was in Washington for a production of *Theatre*, Mrs Roosevelt had given a dinner in his honour, which was followed by a party thrown for him by her niece, Alice Longworth. The two also shared an interest in food, and the small correspondence that survives is mainly on this subject. 'Dear Eleanor,' begins a jocular note from Maugham, 'Thank you very much for the recipe. We are going to try it immediately and if you see that my whole household has died suddenly, you will know the reason.' Mrs Roosevelt also sent Maugham the photographs she had taken during her stay at Parker's Ferry. 'What a distinguished profile you have given me,' he wrote appreciatively. 'You are indeed a marvellous photographer & I feel that you have wasted your time being a wife & mother. You should have been a great artist & led a life of sin.'

In May when the heat in South Carolina became unbearable, Maugham

---

★ Maugham's involvement was obliquely acknowledged years later by Sir William Stephenson, code name 'Intrepid', who was head of British Security Co-ordination in the United States during the war. 'Intrepid had a variety of friends and contacts working for him . . . [and there] were those who subsequently made it plain that they were not opposed to being acknowledged publicly. I don't think Somerset Maugham ever made this feeling known' (Ted Morgan *Maugham* p. 467).

went to New York, but as the temperature there was hardly less ferocious – 'too hot to do anything', he complained to Alan from his suite at the Ritz, 'too hot to work, too hot to play' – he moved to Martha's Vineyard, off the coast of Massachusetts, and stayed at the Colonial Inn in Edgartown. Here he was able to be quiet and cool and, most importantly, to work undisturbed on his novel; he saw almost no one and was able to write when he wanted, sunbathe, swim off the beach at Chappaquiddick, eat clams, go to the movies and every day walk for miles along the empty shore. His sole appearance in public was at a showing of the film version of *The Moon and Sixpence*, which, as Maugham's presence on the island had become known, was given its premiere at the local movie-house in Edgartown. After a couple of months he felt much restored, able to face the demanding schedule of broadcasts and lectures that awaited him during the coming autumn. One of his lectures was on the subject of Political Obligation, which he delivered at Columbia and Yale, both given extempore, without a note. He described the occasion at Yale to Barbara Back.

> The hall was packed, undergraduates were standing in the open doorways & jammed in the aisles. Well, all right, I held them for fifty minutes & reached the last sentence; & I started: The price of freedom is . . . then a black shutter came down in the middle of my head & I couldn't, I simply couldn't remember what in hell the price of freedom was. Three words only & I couldn't have thought of them if I'd been offered a thousand pounds.

Constantly weighing on Maugham's mind was the progress of the war. As an Englishman, he could not but be aware how disastrous in effect throughout 1942 was the lowering of Britain's prestige, defeat following defeat, the fall of Singapore, the loss of Malaya and Burma, and the fiasco of the Eighth Army's performance in Libya. 'Our stock is falling lower & lower in this country,' he told Searle. 'At present you hear nothing but that the English are stupid & incompetent & that all Winston has to offer is fine speeches. It is terribly discouraging & one doesn't know what to answer.' Since the previous winter, both Robin and Vincent had been fighting in North Africa. '[Willie] does not mind so much about his son-in-law,' Wescott recorded, 'but his nephew, Robin, is there, too, and the possibility of losing him makes his heart ache.' Terrible reports were coming through of casualties in the Western Desert as the Eighth Army engaged with the Panzer divisions of Rommel's Afrika Korps. Then in July came the news that Captain the Honourable Robin Maugham had been wounded and shipped out to hospital in Egypt. Robin, it appeared, in command of a Crusader tank had been knocked over by a piece of shrapnel,

> & next day when he was being taken back to hospital – I suppose at Alexandria – the car he was in was machine gunned by a Stuka, his batman was killed by his side & he was hit on the head & on the arm. Nellie was naturally very anxious but at last she heard that he was doing well & was to go to Kenya to recoup as soon as he could get out of hospital. So he will be out of danger for some weeks & that at least is something to the good.

Eventually Robin returned to England and was invalided out of the army, registered unfit for active service.

After an autumn in New York Maugham returned to South Carolina for the winter and spring. From there at the beginning of May 1943 he finally finished the first draft of his novel, *The Razor's Edge*. 'The book has been a great pleasure to me to write & I do not care if people on the whole think it good or poor. I have got it off my chest & that is all that matters to me.' This letter was addressed to Karl G. Pfeiffer, a teacher of English at Washington State University, whom Maugham had first met in 1923. Pfeiffer, an ardent fan, had attached himself to Maugham, wrote to him frequently, even visited him at the Mauresque; for his part Maugham had liked the man, found him intelligent company and had answered his endless questions with considerable patience and candour: a candour he came to regret when in 1959 Pfeiffer published an invasive and inaccurate 'portrait' of him. Now, however, he needed Pfeiffer's help, asking him to correct infelicities in the writing, and also, with a largely American cast of characters and much of the action set in the States, to point out any fact or phrase that rang untrue. 'Any other criticisms you make will likewise be well received,' he added. 'You know me well enough to know that it is impossible to hurt my feelings in a matter of this sort.'

*The Razor's Edge*★ is undoubtedly one of the most interesting of all Maugham's novels. In it he engages with the three topics that always most fascinated him, sexual passion, the mores of society and the nature of goodness, in this case as illustrated in the division between the material and spiritual worlds. The story opens in Chicago in 1919, with the narrator, 'Maugham', passing a few weeks in the city on his way to the Far East, just as the real Maugham had done that same year on his way

---

★ The title refers to a quotation from the *Katha Upanishad*: 'The sharp edge of a razor is difficult to pass over; thus the wise say the path to Salvation is hard.'

to China. A wealthy acquaintance from Paris, Elliott Templeton, tele-phones out of the blue, explaining that he is staying with his widowed sister and inviting him to luncheon at her house. Here, as well as his hostess, Mrs Bradley, Maugham meets her plump, pretty daughter Isabel and Isabel's fiancé Larry Darrell. It is clear that Isabel, a bouncy, self-confident young woman, is passionately in love with handsome Larry, although to Maugham's experienced eye Larry seems curiously unin-volved, a quiet, smiling figure, amiable but remote. It transpires that Larry, an aviator in the war, had been badly shaken when his greatest friend was killed, shot down during a dogfight, leaving Larry obscurely troubled ever afterwards, unable to connect with normal life. Reluctantly Isabel agrees to his suggestion that he should go on his own to Paris, on the understanding that he will use the time to pull himself together so that they may begin on the richly upholstered married life to which she avidly looks forward. Elliott Templeton, an exquisite, snobbish old queen who lives for his rarefied social life, generously offers to launch Larry in Paris – 'Believe me, my dear fellow, the average American can get into the kingdom of heaven much more easily that he can get into the Boulevard St Germain' – but to Elliott's astonishment Larry rebuffs him, instead disappearing to a shabby hotel room to pursue some mysterious course of study of his own. When eventually Mrs Bradley and Isabel, alarmed at the absence of news, follow Larry to Paris, he in as kindly a way as possible breaks off the engagement.

Ten years pass before Maugham runs into any of them again. By this time Isabel has married a prosperous banker, Gray Maturin, with whom she leads a lavishly materialistic life in Chicago, while Larry in Paris is encountered one day in the street, thin, bearded, sunburnt, dressed like a tramp. Invited by Maugham to tell his story, he launches into a lengthy description of his journey towards spiritual enlightenment, his reading of the great philosophers and religious teachers, his work as a manual labourer first in a coal mine,[*] then on a farm, the months studying in a monastery in Alsace, then five years with a swami at an ashram in India. At the same time the Maturins, too, return to Paris. They have suffered badly in the crash of 1929, Gray's business completely wiped out, and are

---

[*] On his official tour in France in 1939 Maugham had been taken down a coal mine. '[I] got just the material I wanted,' he wrote to Barbara Back. 'I simply *couldn't* get the coal dust out of my eyebrows & eyelashes afterwards & I went about looking like a broken down film-star.' In *The Razor's Edge*, he describes one of the miners thus: 'His eyes were blue and because he hadn't been able to wash the coal dust off his eyebrows and eyelashes he looked as if he was made up.'

now living entirely off Isabel's Uncle Elliott, who cannily managed to keep his fortune intact. Elliott, in whom family feeling is strong, has given them his splendid apartment on the Left Bank, while he spends most of the year on the Riviera. 'I dare say I shall go to Paris now and then,' he tells the narrator, 'but when I do, I don't in the least mind pigging it at the Ritz.' Maugham is pleased to see that the hoydenish Isabel has fined down, become a slim and extremely chic young woman; her husband, on the other hand, looks far older than his years, red-faced and over-weight, lost without his professional occupation. It is Maugham who brings Larry back into their lives, to Isabel's particular delight – until she learns that he is about to be married, to Sophie, a girlfriend of hers from Chicago. Sophie is a drug-addicted dipsomaniac who will sleep with anyone for the price of a drink, and Larry, hooked on sacrifice and salva-tion, believes he can save her by making her his wife. This Isabel cannot allow: passionately possessive of Larry, she ruthlessly determines to scuttle his plan, which she does by means of a cruel trick.

Elliott, meanwhile, having magnificently held court on the Côte d'Azur, is now beginning to fail, to find himself out of date, no longer in demand. Old and ill, his passion for society is yet undimmed, and thus it is a near-mortal blow when he finds he is not invited to the great ball of the season, given by the Princess Novemali, a rich American.* Maugham, realising his old friend is dying, schemes to purloin the longed-for card, his description of his encounter with the odious Edna Novemali providing an effective counterpoint to the genuinely moving scenes surrounding Elliott's death. By this time, the end of the story is in sight: Larry, divested of all earthly possessions, is happy at last and leaves for America where he plans to earn his living as a taxi-driver; Isabel, well provided for by her uncle Elliott's bequest, goes back to Chicago with Gray, who is reju-venated by the prospect of returning to work. In the final paragraph the author writes that, to his surprise, 'I had written nothing more or less than a success story. For all the persons with whom I have been concerned got what they wanted: Elliott social eminence, Isabel an assured position backed by a substantial fortune . . . Gray a steady and lucrative job . . . and Larry happiness.'

In answer to a question put to him about *The Razor's Edge*, Maugham said that he had had the character of Larry Darrell in his mind for over

---

* Princess Novemali is a portrait of Maugham's Riviera neighbour, the sharp-tongued Princess Ottoboni. 'Ottoboni' in Italian means 'eight good things', here changed by Maugham to 'Novemali', 'nine evils'. The Princess was not pleased by her appearance in *The Razor's Edge* and for some while there was a rift in the relationship.

twenty years, and that it was the experience of India in 1938 that revived his interest and determined him to write his story. In fact Maugham had already used a version of the theme twice before, in 'The Road Uphill', an unpublished play, now lost, written in 1920, which has close similarities to the novel, and in the short story 'The Fall of Edward Barnard', written in 1921. Ironically, in *The Razor's Edge* it is Larry and his self-centred search for salvation that constitutes the book's flaw, while everything else, construction, characterisation, setting, narrative tone, shows Maugham at his most supremely accomplished. In pursuing the theme that had always intrigued him, that of freedom, of the anti-materialist, the man who turns his back on the world, the author shows himself to be inextricably a part of that world: while strongly attracted by the spiritual, his feet remain firmly planted on the ground. He knows from the inside out the society he portrays, that of the nouveaux-riches Americans, intelligent, ambitious, far from uncultured, the sort of people painted by Sargent on both sides of the Atlantic. And it is not saintly Larry who holds our attention but the ultramondain figure of Elliott Templeton; for in vain, snobbish, kind-hearted Elliott, Maugham achieves one of his most brilliant creations, so vital and ridiculous with all his fuss and furbelows that he comes near to stealing the novel. Inevitably after the book came out, there was much busy speculation about Elliott's original: the aesthete and art-dealer 'Bogey' Harris, according to Logan Pearsall Smith; Maugham's Riviera neighbour the art-collector Henry May, according to others; while that ultra-Europeanised American, Chips Channon, socialite and super-snob, knew for a fact that the character was based on him: Maugham had told him so at dinner one night, but then had teasingly added that he was also the model for Larry Darrell, a statement which must have left poor Chips somewhat bewildered. In the end it was Maugham's publisher who revealed that the prototype was one Henry Chalmers Roberts, a retired American diplomat. Roberts had made his first appearance in *Our Betters* as Thornton Clay, who 'calls more countesses by their Christian names than any other man in London'. '[Willie] was fascinated by him,' said Frere. '[Roberts] was a pederast, knew Henry James, and was as crashing a snob as an expatriate American could be.'

In contrast to such a vivid flesh-and-blood figure as Elliott, indeed in contrast to Isabel, Gray or any of the others, Larry comes over as something of a cardboard character, vacuous, dull and a little smug, with his long-windedness and his refusal to engage, a beautiful symbol rather than a real man. On two occasions the earnest accounts of his spiritual pilgrimage bring the novel almost to a halt, and it is with relief that the reader is returned to Elliott agonising over whether to wear a pearl or an emerald pin in his new silk tie from Charvet. The problem is that Larry's picaresque path to enlightenment is unconvincing, a mystical goal that in effect eludes him just as it had always eluded Maugham. When in India the Swami tells Larry, 'By meditation on the formless one, I found rest in the Absolute,' Larry comments, 'I didn't know what to think'; nor does the reader, and nor does Maugham. In fact the key to Larry, whether consciously intended by his author or not, is his sexlessness: prepared, just, to go through the motions when absolutely necessary, he appears devoid of any sexual feeling. His single strong emotion is that expressed for the dead airman who was his comrade in arms during the war, subliminally suggesting an element of suppressed homosexuality. Certainly his anaemic behaviour is in marked contrast to that of the hot-blooded Isabel, whose physical passion for Larry she is unable to conceal.\* Maugham, the narrator, describes an occasion when he, Gray, Larry and Isabel are driving back to Paris after a day's sightseeing. Maugham and Isabel are in the back of the car, Gray at the wheel with Larry beside him.

> Larry sat with his arm stretched out along the top of the front seat. His shirt-cuff was pulled back by his position and displayed his slim, strong wrist and the lower part of his brown arm lightly covered with fine hairs . . . Something in Isabel's immobility attracted my attention . . . Her breath was hurried. Her eyes were fixed on the sinewy wrist with its little golden hairs and on that long, delicate but powerful hand, and I have never seen on a human countenance such a hungry concupiscence . . . It was a mask of lust.

From the moment of its publication on 18 April 1944,† *The Razor's Edge* made an enormous impact. There were many adulatory reviews – 'sheer delight', said Cyril Connolly, 'Mr Maugham's best novel since *Cakes and Ale*' – and sales were immense, in the States over a half a million copies sold by the end of the first month. Maugham expressed himself gratified by such an appreciative response to a work that was of tremendous personal importance to him. 'I will not pretend that I am not staggered,' he admitted to Eddie Marsh, while in October he wrote to

---

\* Maugham, who wrote about sexual passion so often and so well, was appreciative when he found it convincingly done by other writers. 'Passion is one of the most difficult things to get into a novel & the most thrilling,' he told Frank Swinnerton when congratulating him on his 1938 novel *Nocturne*. 'What gives *Nocturne* its peculiar savour is that it has a cockstand in it & there are very few novelists who can get that on to a printed page.'

† The British publication date was 17 July 1944.

his niece Diana, 'It has given me a lot of satisfaction to have produced a novel in my old age which has had such a great success. In this country the publisher has already sold not far from three quarters of a million copies & before he is finished expects to sell between a million & a quarter & a million & a half.* The book is in process of being translated into nine languages.'

Maugham was in New York when *The Razor's Edge* came out, its success providing him with a brief respite from a long period of anxiety, as usual over Gerald. In the autumn of 1943 Gerald, tired of working for almost nothing at a local radio station in Washington, had accepted instead an offer of employment from Nelson Doubleday, overseeing a staff of nearly fifty in the firm's commissary on Long Island. 'Gerald is working very hard providing food for three thousand people,' Maugham reported to Robin. 'It is a marvel to see him getting up at six thirty to go to work and getting home just before eight . . . He is happier than he has been for many years.' But shortly afterwards a more interesting prospect came Haxton's way, which led to his returning to Washington to take up a minor post in intelligence, at the Office for Strategic Services in the State Department.

This was work Gerald thoroughly enjoyed, and he had been in the highest spirits when he came up to New York on business in November, full of talk about his new job. Maugham was struck by the extraordinary change in him. Poignantly he saw for the first time the man Gerald might have been had he not been tied all those years to his dependency on Maugham: in a way Maugham had made Gerald's life and in a way had ruined it, too. Once and for all Maugham made up his mind that there must be no question of Haxton returning to his old employment and that he must be persuaded to remain in America for good. '[He] is delighted really to be on his own & absolutely independent of me,' Maugham told Alan, '[and] it is a wonderful relief to me to be free of that responsibility & of the constant worry & anxiety.' Now within weeks of his seventieth birthday Maugham was anxious about the future: he wanted to write at least one more novel and had several non-fiction projects in mind, but he felt he had become an old man. He had begun to refer to himself as 'the old party', and believed he might not have very much longer to live. He needed calm and routine, needed to be sure that what remained of his life should be free of the constant crises created by Gerald. Thus, after thirty years together, the two men agreed to separate, Maugham arranging

* In fact Doubleday sold more than 3 million by the end of the decade.

with Bert Alanson for a sum of $35,000 to be settled on Haxton, which would provide him with a generous annual income. As soon as the war was over Maugham would return to France, and Gerald's place as secretary and factotum at the Mauresque would be taken by Alan, dear Alan,

> who will give me, I think, a happiness I have not known with Gerald for ten years . . . He has neither Gerald's vitality . . . [nor] energy, but is sober, modest, affectionate & of a great sweetness of nature . . . I must expect to grow progressively frailer & less active; I want someone kind, unselfish & considerate who will look after me till my death & that I think my little Alan will be only too glad to do.

With these plans afoot and Gerald settled contentedly in Washington, Maugham at Yemassee continued his industrious output. His seventieth birthday on 25 January 1944 he spent alone, perfectly serene in his own company.

> I worked as usual in the morning and in the afternoon went for a walk in the solitary woods . . . after which I went back to my house, made myself a cup of tea and read till dinner time. After dinner I read again, played two or three games of patience, listened to the news on the radio and took a detective story to bed with me. I finished it and went to sleep. Except for a few words to my coloured maids I had not spoken to a soul all day.

He had decided to prepare for publication his writer's notebooks, and these had to be carefully perused and edited. There was also a revival of his last play, *Sheppey*, due to open in New York in April, for which Maugham had made some crucial alterations to the last act. Attending rehearsals, he was vividly reminded of his reasons for abandoning the theatre: the director, Cedric Hardwicke, was suddenly called to Hollywood in the middle of rehearsals, then after the Boston opening two actors had to be let go and two more found to fill their places, with only days before the first night in New York. The fact that *Sheppey* was as great a failure in New York in 1944 as it had been in London eleven years earlier left its author relatively unmoved. 'I was disappointed, but not distressed,' he told Eddie Marsh, 'for the play was written long ago & I have long ceased to be interested in the theatre.' And by the time of its opening there was another, far more serious matter on his mind.

'I have been in great trouble,' begins a letter to Barbara Back. At the end of April Gerald in Washington had suffered an attack of pleurisy so severe that Maugham, alarmed, had brought him to New York where he could be looked after at Doctors Hospital, regarded as one of the best nursing-homes in the country. Here an X-ray revealed that his lungs were badly infected with tuberculosis, the dangerous disease that had haunted Maugham since his mother died of it when he was eight. Now Gerald's condition began to deteriorate with terrifying rapidity: he was feverish and suffered an intense pain that could be controlled only with morphine; he had a racking cough and found it difficult to swallow; he was fast losing weight and every movement hurt him. 'It was agonizing to watch him,' Maugham told Barbara. Although he had been told it was unlikely Gerald would survive, Maugham believed that if he could get him out of the heat and humidity of New York and into the dry, pure air of Colorado he just might have a chance. But the doctors refused to allow it, saying that Gerald was far too ill to be moved and was expected to die within weeks, information that was carefully kept from the patient. Maugham, who sat by his bed for hours a day, was distraught. The detachment of a short time earlier, the calm and optimism with which he had been looking forward to a future without Gerald at the Mauresque, vanished in an instant as all his old feelings of love and protectiveness came flooding back. 'Though I have long known that the life he led must kill him now that he is dying I am shattered,' Maugham confessed to Ellen Doubleday.

> He made life impossible for me & I was thankful when he left me, he brought shame & disgrace on me, but now I can forget all that. I only remember how devoted he was to me & how he trusted me & depended on me & how eager he was to help me. I can only think of those years when his vitality & his gift for making friends were of so much service to me. Without him I should never have written those stories which did so much for my reputation in the world of letters & it was he who helped me to get out of the commonplace life of the ordinary humdrum writer & put me in the way of gaining that wider experience of life which has made me what I am today. I can never forget that he was mixed in with some of my happiest & most fruitful years & now that it is finished, or so nearly, I cannot but weep because his long end has been so miserable & so worthless. I don't know how much I am to blame. If I had been firmer, if I had not tried to force a kind of life on him for which he was temperamentally unsuited, it may be that he would have made less of a hash of things than he has. Of course I shall get over it, one gets over everything, but just at the moment I am broken.

At last in July there was a very small improvement in Gerald's condition, and Maugham was advised that he could after all risk a journey.

It was decided not to go as far as Colorado but to take him by ambulance to Saranac in upstate New York, to the famous Adirondack Cottage Sanitarium where Robert Louis Stevenson had been treated. Here in the fresh mountain air Gerald, to Maugham's enormous relief, began 'to breathe a little better & is in less pain'; he was still very weak and emaciated but seemed in fairly good spirits on the whole, and, Maugham was anxious to emphasise, so uncomplaining of his lot and grateful for everything that was being done. Maugham had set great hopes on Saranac. 'If we can only get through the next two or three weeks it won't be so bad,' he wrote to Barbara. He was tireless in his attendance on Gerald, could not bear to think of him left to the mercy of strangers, prepared to stay in Saranac for months if necessary, despite the fact that his hotel was comfortless, the food awful and the only people he could find with whom to play bridge were 'coughing & spitting convalescents . . . I can't remember that I've ever hated a place more.' Morning and afternoon he went to the hospital, where he did his best to keep Gerald's spirits up. 'I think going to see him twice a day & encouraging him cheers him & helps him to make a fight for it,' he wrote to Barbara. 'The attitude I take is that of course he is very ill, but that lots of people have had T.B., myself included & have completely recovered & I see no reason why he should not be as strong as ever in a year.'

But Saranac had little beneficial effect, and every day Gerald grew more frighteningly feeble, although there were occasions when he seemed briefly possessed by a frenzied energy, raging against his dying and hurling obscenities at Maugham, screaming that he had ruined his life, had kept him a prisoner, that he hated him; once while in a drugged delirium he laughed wildly at the thought of the fun he would have after Maugham himself was dead. In desperation Maugham decided to move him once more, this time to the New England Baptist Hospital in Boston, where he could be seen by specialists at the Leahy Institute. Here he was told the only chance that remained was a risky operation to remove a couple of ribs, which could best be carried out in New York. The four-hour train journey was undertaken with Gerald, heavily drugged, on a stretcher. 'I am afraid he is growing weaker & weaker & I am beginning to lose hope,' Maugham wrote to Eddie Knoblock from Manhattan at the beginning of October. 'They say as one grows old one feels less; I wish it were true.' By now Gerald was barely conscious, always in pain, on some days too ill to see even Maugham, who was in a state of tormenting indecision. 'I have to face the prospect that the operation will kill him,' he told his niece Diana; he was unable to make up his mind 'whether to let him die by inches or to risk all on this final attempt . . . I can hardly help wishing that he would die one night quietly in his sleep without knowing that he was in danger of death.' Finally on 2 November the operation was carried out. To everyone's surprise Gerald survived it, and although very weak and in great pain seemed to be holding on. 'There is a slight hope that he may make a recovery after a fashion,' Maugham reported to Alan, 'but will still be very ill for a long, long time.' For three days Gerald remained in a drugged semi-coma, knowing nobody, with Maugham allowed to see him only for a few minutes at a time. Then on the morning of 7 November, aged fifty-two, Gerald Haxton died.

Maugham was inconsolable, beside himself with grief and tormented by remorse. At the funeral on 9 November 1944 at the Episcopal Church of St James on Madison Avenue he broke down and wept. In response to the many letters of condolence he poured out his overwhelming unhappiness, his anguish at losing the love of his life. 'Gerald's death has been a bitter blow to me & I am finding it very hard to cope with life without him. I am lost & hopeless & lonely,' he told George Cukor, while to Charles Towne he wrote, 'Please don't write & sympathize, letters like that just tear me to pieces. You see, I'm too old to cope with so much grief.' Towards the end of December he described to Alan 'the tempestuous grief that tore me to pieces . . . the last few weeks have been very hard to get through . . . [and] I have been terribly depressed'. The writer Cecil Roberts, wishing to offer his sympathy in person, was taken aback by the agony in Maugham's voice when he answered the telephone. '"I don't want to see you! I don't want to see anyone! I want to die!" he cried in a distressed voice, and put down the telephone.' Another friend, the playwright Sam Behrman, was also shocked to see how near Maugham was to complete breakdown. Behrman, who had been working on a dramatisation of one of Maugham's short stories, had arranged to lunch with him in his suite at the Ritz; he naturally expected to see some sign of distress, but to his surprise there was none. 'He had his habitual composed and impassive expression,' Behrman recalled, as they chatted about people they knew and Maugham asked Behrman about his latest production. Finally Behrman thought he must mention Gerald. 'Willie, you haven't told me,' he began.

> 'How was it with Gerald – at the end?' I was instantly sorry.
> 'Please,' he said in a broken voice, 'don't ask me that.' He began to cry and left the room. It was the sudden demolition of a carefully built image.

After the funeral all that remained was for Maugham to carry out the instructions Gerald had made in his will, a simple document in which his personal effects were left to Maugham, his money to Robin, who had become almost an honorary younger brother, and the proceeds from the sale of the flat in Paris, which had been in Gerald's name, to Louis Legrand. 'Mon pauvre Loulou,' Maugham wrote sadly, 'Sois heureux, mon petit, et tache de ne pas te tracasser avec des souvenirs tristes. Ça ne sert à rien et tu es trop jeune. Oublies.'* As soon as the will was proved Maugham left New York for South Carolina. With the end of the war at last in sight he was faced with returning to France, to the Villa Mauresque, a prospect he now dreaded, he told David Horner.

> I suppose I shall give it a trial, but if Gerald dead is all over the place, wandering about the garden, sitting at the card table playing patience, I couldn't stand it; & so I would sell it for what I could get & buy myself a little house somewhere in the English country, Wiltshire perhaps, & settle down there for the rest of my life. That would not be for very long, for by now I am a very old party.

* 'My poor Loulou, be happy, my little one, and try not to torment yourself with sad memories. There's no point and you are too young. Forget.'

# 15

# The Bronzino Boy

Maugham's desolation in the months following Gerald Haxton's death was impenetrable and profound. 'For thirty years he has been my pleasure and my anxiety and without him I am lost and lonely and hopeless,' he wrote to Noël Coward in February 1945. 'It is three months since he died now and I cannot get used to it. I try to forget and a dozen times a day something I come across, something I read, a stray word reminds me of him and I am overcome with my first grief . . . I am too old to endure so much grief. I have lived too long.'* To Gerald's beloved Loulou he also wrote most poignantly of his unhappiness: 'Tout me le rappelle et je le revois souvent, trop souvent pour ma paix, dans mes rêves, ou il est toujours gai et vivace et délicieux.'† Maugham was in mourning for his dead lover, but in mourning, too, for his own past, for the years of travel and adventure he had shared with Haxton, and, crucially, in mourning for his powers as a writer, for the artistic impulse and inspiration that wrought those experiences into novels and stories. 'The best years of my life, those in which we were wandering about the world, are inextricably connected with him, & in one way & another, however indirectly, all I have written during the last thirty has something to do with him, if only that he typed my manuscripts.' It was almost as if Gerald had possessed some talismanic power and that without him he would no longer be able to write. And in a sense this was true: none of the work Maugham produced after Gerald's death would amount to very much.

After the funeral Maugham had been relieved to leave New York and return to Parker's Ferry, his little house at Yemassee, but once there he was tormented by loneliness and yearned more than ever for the solace of Alan Searle's company. Yet Alan was in England and unable to leave his army canteen in Yorkshire. Maugham's plight was desperate, however,

---

* It was this letter that gave Coward the idea for his 1966 play *Song at Twilight*, which he admitted was based on Maugham.

† 'Everything reminds me of him, and I see him often, too often for my peace of mind, in my dreams, where he is always cheerful and steadfast and delightful.'

and his friends realised he could not be left to continue without companionship. Discreet approaches were made to the Foreign Office, with the result that Brendan Bracken at the Ministry of Information arranged with his opposite number in Washington to obtain permission for Maugham's nephew Robin to visit the States for a few months, officially to launch a magazine, *Convoy*, he had just started in Britain. It was an arrangement that was of benefit to both: Maugham was delighted to see his beloved nephew, and Robin, still very jittery and unwell after his experiences in North Africa, was grateful for a period of convalescence. He arrived just before Christmas 1944, and the two men supported each other through the somewhat rumbustious seasonal celebrations under way at Bonny Hall. 'I found Willie overwhelmed with misery,' Robin recalled, shocked when Maugham more than once broke down in tears in front of him. He was shocked, too, to see how much his uncle had aged, still physically fit, clean-shaven now, but with his face very lined, his dark eyes hooded, and heavy creases pulling his mouth downward, giving him the appearance of an old and melancholy tortoise.

Even at his most wretched, Maugham had never stopped working, continuing to fulfil the programme he had mapped out for himself. His daily stint of writing was the one reliable escape, the one drug that never failed in its effect. Just as ten years earlier he had decided to bring his career in the theatre to an end with four last plays, so now he planned to write four last novels. The first of these was *The Razor's Edge*, to be followed by two historical works of fiction, and finally by a novel about a working-class family in Bermondsey, thus coming full circle with a return to the territory treated in *Liza of Lambeth* fifty years before. In the event this last was never written, but already by February 1945 *Then and Now*, the first of the two historical novels, was completed and sent off to Eddie Marsh for editing.

*Then and Now* describes an embassy of Machiavelli to the court of Cesare Borgia, and although it conscientiously conveys the background of Renaissance Italy and the elaborate dealings and counter-dealings between the two men it is a pedestrian work; a few scenes, concerning Machiavelli's attempted seduction of a beautiful young woman, flicker briefly into life, but all too clearly it reflects the despondent state of mind of its author. When the book was published in 1946, however, it won some admiring reviews on both sides of the Atlantic, and Nelson Doubleday, who had printed 2½ million copies, saw more than 750,000 sold in the first fortnight, while film rights were bought for $200,000. And there the matter might satisfactorily have rested had it not been for a long article in the *New Yorker* by America's most influential critic, Edmund Wilson. Unluckily, *Then and Now* was the first fiction by Maugham that Wilson had read: he had long been irritated by some of Maugham's critical judgments, particularly pertaining to Henry James, and considered his reputation as a writer ludicrously overrated; yet by his own admission he knew nothing of any of the novels, plays or short stories. 'It has happened to me from time to time to run into some person of taste who tells me that I ought to take Somerset Maugham seriously, yet I have never been able to convince myself that he was anything but second-rate,' he begins. *Then and Now* 'seemed to me . . . one of the most tasteless and unreadable books from which I had ever hoped to derive enjoyment, and nothing but the necessity of supplying this review could ever have taken me through it . . .' And so on. Maugham, who had always admired Wilson,★ describing him in one of his wartime articles as 'the most acute critic now writing in America', reacted to this devastating attack with almost superhuman sang-froid. 'He has always disliked me,' he told Ellen Doubleday. '[But] nobody can be liked by everyone and I bear Edmund Wilson's dislike with good humour.'

On 8 May 1945, VE Day, the war in Europe was finally declared at an end, a cause of wild celebrations elsewhere but Maugham at Yemassee was unable to feel any great exhilaration. 'Everyone here is of course very much relieved & I am too,' he wrote to Alan, 'but my chief feeling, I think, is one of sadness for all the death & misery it has caused, so that I haven't been able to be as cheery about the surrender as most people.' At the front of his mind was the prospect of a return to the freedom he had known before the war. 'I am hoping restrictions upon travel will be lifted soon & that we shall all be able to go wherever we want to & when we like.' He longed for Alan to come to him, and he longed to return to France, but neither was a possibility at the present.

Instead, with Robin having left to promote his journal in New York, Maugham was obliged to return to Hollywood on his own, his presence required for the filming of *The Razor's Edge*. As the screenplay commissioned by the studio had been judged unsatisfactory and jettisoned, Maugham had been asked if he would write it, a job he took on with uncharacteristic enthusiasm because his old friend George Cukor was to direct. The two men had first met in 1923 when Cukor was a young stage-manager on the American production of *The Camel's Back*; six years later Cukor had abandoned the theatre for the film industry, where he

★ It was Maugham's recommendation that persuaded Nelson Doubleday in 1946 to publish Edmund Wilson's short-story collection, *Memoirs of Hecate County*.

had enjoyed some notable successes, among them directing Katharine Hepburn in *Little Women* and Greta Garbo in *Camille*. One of his few failures had been the film of *Our Betters* in 1933, about which Maugham had been most understanding. '[Willie] was very, very kind to me and took it philosophically, just as he did most things,' Cukor recalled. Now Cukor invited Maugham to stay with him at his house off Sunset Strip, ideal for Maugham as not only was Cukor charming and intelligent but, homosexual himself, he knew all the reliable pimps and whores, and was generally recognised as master of revels throughout the Hollywood fraternity. Cukor's poolside parties were particularly popular: glamorous female stars were invited to join the company for lunch, but after they left a gang of good-looking young men – actors, waiters, motor-mechanics – would arrive for an afternoon of all-male entertainment; as the wags put it, when the ladies departed the naughty boys came by to eat the leftovers. On Maugham's previous visits to Hollywood both he and Gerald had enjoyed Cukor's hospitality, and it was an additional pleasure for Maugham that he could talk about Haxton, whom Cukor had liked. Cukor for his part was fond of Maugham personally, admired him for his inimitable stagecraft, and as he said once in an interview always regarded it as to Maugham's credit that 'Willie liked Jews.'

The film rights to *The Razor's Edge* had been bought for Twentieth Century-Fox by Darryl Zanuck for the very large sum of $250,000. Understandably, Zanuck was reluctant to spend more on having the script rewritten, but when Cukor explained the situation to Maugham the author immediately offered to do it for nothing. '[His] script was wonderful,' Cukor recalled, and Zanuck, delighted, suggested the studio should buy Maugham a painting, worth anything up to $15,000. 'I'd never bought a picture at such a price before and I was thrilled,' said Maugham. Nervous about spending such a sum on his own, he asked Monroe Wheeler to advise him, and the two men spent several agreeable mornings visiting dealers in New York. Eventually Maugham chose a Camille Pissarro, a view of the harbour at Rouen (*Quai Saint-Sever à Rouen*) which moved him because it was the view Flaubert must often have looked at when at work on *Madame Bovary*; Monroe, however, persuaded him instead to buy a Matisse, a snow scene, which he said was a much better picture. 'But I could not get the Pissarro out of my mind,' Maugham wrote later. 'I thought I should always regret it if I did not have it, so I exchanged the Matisse for it.' Few projects in the film world run smoothly, and inevitably there were problems with the shooting schedule, the actor chosen to play Larry was suddenly unavailable, and Cukor, by this time committed elsewhere, had to be replaced as director; in the end Maugham's script was abandoned, the film finally going into production in 1946, with Tyrone Power as Larry, Gene Tierney as Isabel, and some frightful painted backdrops of the Himalayas.

Throughout his stay in California Maugham continued to press for Alan to join him: he missed the comfort of his company and he was finding it increasingly difficult to cope without a secretary. But civilian travel between Europe and America was still difficult and exit permits hard to obtain. Maugham appealed to everyone he could think of who might have influence, asking Frere to approach the Foreign Secretary, Ernest Bevin, on his behalf, and himself writing to Lord Halifax, the British Ambassador in Washington. As a graceful gesture, Maugham had offered to present to the Library of Congress the manuscript of his most famous novel, *Of Human Bondage*, 'in grateful acknowledgement of the kindness and hospitality shown by the people of this country', and who could better be entrusted with it than Alan Searle? 'You would be doing me a great favour,' Maugham told Halifax, 'if you would ask the Foreign Office to give my secretary . . . now released from war work, the exit permit which will enable him to bring the bulky package over.' Fortunately for Maugham his request was favourably regarded behind the scenes, his contribution to the British war effort standing him in good stead in Whitehall. 'I know that at one time he was working privately and unofficially as a propagandist for us in the US,' a Foreign Office memorandum noted. 'The national interest requires us to regard Mr Maugham as in a special category . . . and do whatever we reasonably can to help him. I think that Mr Searle should be granted an exit permit and that we should give him a moderate degree of priority in obtaining a sea passage.'

This was written in September 1945, yet it was not until December that Alan succeeded in making the crossing, docking at Hoboken, New Jersey, on Christmas Day. From there he made his way by train to South Carolina where Maugham was waiting for him at the station. The two men had not seen each other for over five years, during which time Maugham had written to Alan every week, had thought of him constantly, and had yearned for the presence of his sweet, sexy Bronzino boy. The first sight was something of a shock: during the war at his army canteen Alan had done himself well, and the figure that stepped down on to the platform was no longer that of the slender youth Maugham remembered but of a stout, round-faced, middle-aged man. 'Alan arrived, very heavy with his chipmunk cheeks,' Glenway Wescott recalled, '[and] William was grief-stricken at the loss of his looks. "You may have looked like a

Bronzino once, but now you look like a depraved Franz Hals," ' Maugham commented sourly. Nonetheless Maugham was happy and relieved to be reunited with Searle, who was to be his devoted companion for the rest of his life. Alan immediately took over all Gerald's duties and more, writing letters, telephoning, shopping, dealing with the maids; unlike Gerald, he was endlessly good-natured and happy to serve, eager to fulfil his employer's every whim. '[Alan] is a great comfort to me,' Bert Alanson was told. 'He is falling into the work very easily & is taking a lot of tiresome chores off my shoulders. I think he will be a great help, & he is so happy to be here, & with me, that it is heart-warming.'

With the war over and Alan restored to him, all Maugham's energies were concentrated on his return to France. At the end of March he and Searle went to New York, and then to Washington for a few days, where on 20 April Maugham presented his manuscript of *Of Human Bondage* to the Library of Congress. It was a prestigious occasion, every seat in the Coolidge Auditorium filled for Maugham's address, in which he talked about literature, about his own career as a novelist, and about writing *Of Human Bondage*, revealing that recently when making a recording of it he had broken down and wept while reading the passage describing the death of Philip Carey's mother: 'it recalled a pain that the passage of more than sixty years has not dispelled'. The main purpose of his speech, however, was to record his gratitude to the people of the United States, in particular 'for the kindness and the generosity with which you received the women and children of my country when in fear of a German invasion they came to America'.

At last, on 29 May, Maugham and Alan sailed from New York, arriving in Marseilles in the second week of June. Looking back Maugham used to say that the day he set foot again in France was one of the happiest of his life. When later in the summer Ellen Doubleday pressingly invited him to return to South Carolina he was firm in his refusal. 'I am very grateful to you and Nelson for having given me Parkers to live in during the war,' he wrote, 'but as you know I only looked upon it as a temporary residence, and though I am pleased that you should want me to come back I think it much better to tell you that I never shall. I hope occasionally to come to New York on brief visits during the rest of my life, but when all is said and done Europe is where I belong.'

He and Alan took rooms at a small hotel, the Voile d'Or, overlooking the harbour at Saint-Jean, a short distance from the Villa Mauresque. Although he had received occasional reports about the state of the house, Maugham had no real idea what to expect, but to his relief the depredations were less serious than he had feared. The villa had been occupied first by the Italians, then by the Germans, who had mined the garden but otherwise done little harm; the only significant damage had been caused by the Royal Navy while attempting to shell a semaphore positioned at the top of the Cap. By paying some heavy bribes Maugham soon assembled a team of workmen to repair the holes in the roof and to replace the shattered windows; indoors there was much repainting to be done, as well as the replacing of moth-eaten carpets and almost all the fixtures and fittings: after the Germans left, the local French, it appeared, had taken everything they could lay hands on, including crockery, cutlery and even the bolts from the bathroom doors. Soon the work was sufficiently advanced for furniture and pictures to be brought out of store, and to Maugham's great gratification most of the staff returned, with Annette, who had remained at the villa throughout the war, rejoined by Ernest the butler, who reappeared from Switzerland accompanied by a wife and two small children, by Jean the chauffeur, and by Louis, one of the gardeners. 'My old servants are back & they seem as delighted to be back as I am . . . Oh you can't think how pleasant it is here, the sea, & the blue sky & the quiet (when the workmen have done their day's work) & the flowers & the general feel of the place.'

One of Maugham's most immediate concerns was to fulfil Gerald's bequest to Louis Legrand. Loulou had escaped conscription because of a tubercular infection, and had spent the first couple of years of the war running in and out of the Mauresque, where he had made himself not altogether popular with Annette. Now he had gone to Paris, Maugham having given him permission to live in Gerald's flat until it was sold, when the proceeds would be made over to him. Maugham had felt very tender towards Loulou, the boy so adored by Haxton, but now he found to his extreme annoyance that the young man had been up to some distinctly underhand behaviour. In compiling a list of losses incurred during the war Maugham had included the contents of his substantial wine cellar, which had been emptied, he assumed, by the Italians. Now he learned from Annette that it was Loulou who had sold the lot to a local wine merchant. And not only that: Loulou had pocketed some personal items of Maugham's, including two favourite wristwatches. These, Maugham told him sternly, must be returned. With his confidence in Loulou shaken, Maugham felt uneasy about leaving him unsupervised in the Paris apartment; and with reason, as it turned out: the enterprising Louis was already carrying on a brisk trade. 'Cher Lulu,' begins a besotted letter, postmarked London, from an American army officer, 'Voila votre Colonel d'Amerique votre grand ami . . . TRES TRISTE – car son Louis est à Paris bien loin d'Angleterre . . .'\* That autumn Maugham himself was in London, and from there wrote to Loulou informing him that David Posner, a young student friend from the States, would shortly be arriving in Paris and would stay in the flat until he found a place of his own. For his part Posner had been well briefed. '[I lived] in Maugham's Paris apartment,' he recalled, 'ostensibly to have digs when I first arrived in France; but actually to "spy" upon the boy who was living there, Gerald Haxton's former pickup, whose activities Maugham was afraid of (rightly, as it turned out).'

David Posner was an extraordinary episode in Maugham's life. In the spring of 1943 Posner, then a seventeen-year-old schoolboy at Lawrenceville, New Jersey, had written Maugham a letter describing himself as a poet and expressing an ardent admiration for *Of Human Bondage*. Intrigued, Maugham had invited the boy to call on him at the Ritz in New York, where he instantly found himself overwhelmed by a tidal wave of emotion, a powerful mixture of fascination and lust. David Posner was sensual and swarthy, tall, very handsome, with thick lips, olive skin and dark curly black hair. He frankly set out to seduce the older man and Maugham succumbed utterly, later delightedly boasting that he had been raped by this 'gigantic Jewish poet . . . a sort of satyr'. Glenway Wescott, an interested observer of the relationship, said Maugham had believed he was finished with love affairs and then 'along came this little storm and he rode it in . . . Willie was very proud of himself because this great poet violently booted sprang on him.' Maugham invited Posner to stay at Yemassee, and Posner, infinitely ambitious, eagerly accepted. 'I was starry-eyed,' he later recalled. 'I was hoping this would happen.' Maugham as a lover 'wasn't particularly virile', he recalled, and 'was rather businesslike about sex, but it's equally true that there were occasions when we would spend a long time just fondling . . . When we were alone he could be the world's most enchanting conversationalist.' Maugham was so taken by the young man, and so impressed by his love and knowledge of literature, that he offered to pay part of his tuition fee at Harvard. They continued to see each other, and after the war Posner, in France to study at the Sorbonne, visited the Mauresque on several occasions, until Maugham eventually became irritated by the

---

\* 'Here's your American Colonel, your great friend – VERY SAD – because his Louis is in Paris so far from England . . .'

young man's pushiness and self-regard, and turned against him. 'Willie just cut his head off,' said Wescott. '[Posner] came and stayed at the Villa and Willie couldn't stand him.'*

When Maugham arrived in London in September 1946 he found a city seemingly drained of all vitality. Buildings stood unpainted and unrepaired, windows covered with plywood, stucco blackened and peeling; the streets were full of pot-holes, and bomb-sites, thickly overgrown with rosebay and willow-herb, were everywhere. Life in the capital was grim, he reported to Nelson Doubleday. 'People are strangely apathetic and do not seem very much interested in anything . . . [and] the food is awful.' However, most of his old friends had survived, the happiest among them Barbara Back, whose son, whom she had feared dead, having just returned from a Japanese prisoner-of-war camp. The family, too, was intact, Robin much improved in health, F.H. visibly aged but as dry and withering as ever: he and Maugham had had some sharp exchanges after Labour's landslide victory the year before, with F.H., an entrenched Tory, vehemently opposed to his brother's socialist views. Liza had been reunited with Vincent, who had left the army as a full colonel, awarded the DSO for bravery under fire in North Africa; however, after such a long separation relations between husband and wife had been strained, and now they had decided to divorce. 'I hope I shall like her next husband as much as I liked the last,' her father told Bert Alanson. 'She pretends that she will never marry again, but I don't for a moment believe her.' Liza meanwhile had gone to Switzerland to install her mother in a sanatorium, 'said mother, aged 67, having contracted T.B.', Maugham wrote unfeelingly. 'I am told that to get it when you are as old as that gives little hope of recovery, but my own impression is that said mother is indestructible.'

Even with the punitive rates of post-war taxation Maugham was by any standards a rich man, widely regarded as the wealthiest writer in the world – 'even richer than Shaw . . .!' exclaimed the *Daily Herald* excitedly. Since his first success as a playwright Maugham, an honorary member of PEN since 1933, had been generous to writers, young and old, who were down on their luck, often helping anonymously when appealed to for funds; and he nearly always responded to requests from impecunious friends with a sizeable cheque – unless, as happened on occasion, he felt

---

* Posner later added W. H. Auden, Thomas Mann and André Gide, among others, to his literary conquests. He studied at the Sorbonne and at Oxford, published seven books of poetry and taught at New York State University and the University of California. He married, fathered two sons and died of AIDS in Florida in 1985.

they were taking advantage when a sharp snub would be administered instead. The appeals were constant and increased in size and number as his celebrity grew. 'In the last week I have had requests for loans amounting to £36000,' he complained in 1960, and a few months later, 'By every post demands come by the dozen for gifts, loans, guarantees and financial assistance of every kind. I am bewildered and harassed by it all.' Now that he was growing old money was much on his mind. He had provided liberally for Liza and her children and for Robin, and when Peter Stern and then a widowed Barbara Back fell on hard times he provided for them, too. Nonetheless Maugham was complicated about money. He loved talking about it, would boast about how much he himself made, and he was acutely aware of the effect his wealth had on other people. Money gave him freedom and privacy and the ability to do as he pleased, but it also gave him considerable power, power which towards the end of his life he was to wield with devastating effect.

It was now, shortly after the war, that Maugham finalised arrangements for the establishment of a literary prize, the idea for which had first occurred to him while on Java twenty-five years before. 'Millionaires & such like are always ready to give money to universities [and] hospitals . . . but will never do anything for the arts,' he explained. 'I was disappointed that neither Kipling nor Barrie did anything, & I suppose Shaw will leave his fortune in the same foolish way as his wife did.[*] So I think I should do what I can, but not after I am dead, now.' Worth £500 and administered by the Society of Authors, the Somerset Maugham Award was to be presented annually for a work of fiction, non-fiction or poetry written by a British subject under the age of thirty-five, the money to be spent on travel. In 1947 the first announcement of this glittering prize attracted the attention of Evelyn Waugh. Mr Maugham's proposal 'of giving £500 yearly to a young writer to be spent in foreign travel' was cruelly tantalising, Waugh complained in a letter to the *Daily Telegraph*.

> Does Mr Maugham realize what a huge temptation he is putting before elderly writers? To have £500 of our own – let alone of Mr Maugham's – to spend abroad is beyond our dreams . . . What will we not do to qualify for Mr Maugham's munificence? What forging of birth certificates, dyeing of whiskers, and lifting of faces! To what parodies of experimental styles will we not push our experienced pens!

[*] Charlotte Shaw directed that the bulk of her fortune be employed in improving the manners and deportment of the Irish people, a scheme described by Shaw's biographer Michael Holroyd as 'Charlotte's version of the *Pygmalion* experiment' (*Bernard Shaw* vol. III: *1918–1950: The Lure of Fantasy* (Chatto & Windus 1991) p. 499).

The first year's judges were V. S. Pritchett, the historian C. V. Wedgwood and the poet Cecil Day Lewis, who chose as the winner for 1947 A. L. Barker with her short-story collection, *Innocents*. Although he took no part in the judging, Maugham followed the process and the subsequent careers of the winners with attention, among them, during his lifetime, Doris Lessing (1954), Kingsley Amis (1955),★ Ted Hughes (1960), V. S. Naipaul (1961) and John le Carré (1964).

Another venture close to his heart was the founding of a national theatre, to the planning of which over the years he had contributed both time and money, only to see the project postponed again and again, 'overcome [by] the indifference of governments and the apathy of the public'. But in the post-war period it looked as though the scheme might prove practicable at last, and Maugham redoubled his efforts to involve his fellow playwrights in the cause. 'I wish I could enlist your help in interesting the British people in a National Theatre,' he wrote to J. B. Priestley in 1948. 'It seems to me a scandal that England should be the only European country that does not possess one.' The following year the National Theatre Bill was finally passed by Parliament, a significant step forward which Maugham recognised by giving to the Trustees his eighty theatrical pictures. Maugham's collection was impressive, second in importance only to that owned by the Garrick Club, and it included three oils by Zoffany, fifteen by De Wilde and a fine version of Reynolds's famous portrait of David Garrick. The paintings were removed from the Mauresque in 1951, but have been seen only infrequently since in the building for which they were intended.†

Of all Maugham's charitable bequests, that made to his old school, King's School, Canterbury, might be regarded as the most unexpected, given his wretchedness while a pupil there. And yet Maugham had always

---

★ When Maugham picked Amis's award-winning novel *Lucky Jim* for his 1955 book of the year in the *Sunday Times*, he caused something of a rumpus by referring to its characters as 'scum', a remark he later qualified. 'I very much admire Amis's book . . . The people he wrote about are scum, but there is nothing wrong with that. Many of the people I have written about are scum, too' (interview with Godfrey Smith *Encore II* 1957).

† When the National Theatre finally opened in 1976, eleven years after Maugham's death, plans for the hanging of his collection met with vigorous resistance from the architect, Denys Lasdun, who felt the paintings did not accord with the architectural style of his building. Maugham would not have been surprised. 'The theatres that they build now are severely functional,' he had written in 1955. 'They are apt to make you feel you have come to the playhouse to undergo an ordeal rather than to enjoy an entertainment. It seemed to me that my pictures in the foyer and on the stairs of a new theatre would a trifle mitigate the austerity of the architect's design' (Raymond Mander and Joe Mitchenson *The Artist and the Theatre* (Heinemann 1955) introduction).

felt a nostalgia for the place, for the grounds and the ancient buildings magnificently overshadowed by the great grey cathedral; he had, too, always felt rooted in the Kentish countryside, and on a number of occasions had returned to wander round Whitstable, where more than once he was spotted tending the graves of his uncle and aunt in the churchyard. The notorious account of his schooldays in *Of Human Bondage* had hardly endeared him to KSC, but since his day the school had fallen on hard times and shortly before the war the then headmaster, Canon Shirley, a vigorous and resourceful character, had written to Maugham soliciting a donation, to which Maugham had generously responded. Encouraged, Shirley took trouble to cultivate the connection, writing regularly, extending invitations to visit the school, and eventually enrolling Maugham on the governing body. His attentiveness paid off, and over the years Maugham gave thousands of pounds, for new buildings, for tennis-courts, for pictures and furniture, and for the construction of a library which would eventually hold a proportion of his books, 1,800 volumes, from the Villa Mauresque. He also presented the school with his portrait, especially commissioned from Gerald Kelly, and with the manuscripts of his first and last novels, *Liza of Lambeth* and *Catalina*. In 1952 he surprised Canon Shirley with a request that he should be buried within the precincts of the school.

When Maugham returned to Cap Ferrat from London at the end of 1946, his chief concern was to finish his novel *Catalina*, begun earlier in the year. It was to be his last full-length work of fiction and he was particularly anxious that Eddie Marsh should work on it, if a little taken aback, when the manuscript was returned to him, by the extent of Marsh's diabolization. 'I think you have been harsher than I have ever known you before, but I kiss the rod & I have accepted all your emendations,' Maugham told him gratefully. Ten years earlier in *The Summing Up* Maugham had stated that 'The novelist should turn to the historical novel towards the end of his career,' advice which he himself had taken, with his previous work about Machiavelli and now with *Catalina*. Set in sixteenth-century Spain, the story follows the adventures of a crippled peasant girl cured by a miraculous Virgin, and while it is firmly founded in Maugham's lifelong study of Spanish history and literature it shows a substantial falling off from the energy and invention of *The Razor's Edge*, reading less like the work of an experienced novelist and more like a good school essay written by a diligent pupil who has clearly done all his homework. He himself was not at all sure how *Catalina* would be received, but both Frere and Nelson Doubleday professed themselves delighted, and with reason, for on publication in 1948 it was chosen as Book of the Month in America and in Britain had sold 93,000 copies by the end of the first week. 'I cannot tell you what a relief to me it is to think that I have written my last, my very last novel,' Maugham confessed to Glenway Wescott.

By Christmas 1946, when Maugham was once more in residence, the Villa Mauresque had been almost completely restored to its luxurious pre-war standard. The number of indoor staff had been slightly reduced, but under the sharp eye of Ernest the butler and of Germaine the house-keeper the same high levels of immaculate efficiency were maintained. In the kitchen Annette was once more producing delicious menus, despite the continuing shortages: 'rice, oil, bacon, sausages, corned beef, parmesan cheese, tagliatelli . . . and a pot or two of Keillers marmalade' were some of the supplies Maugham solicited from friends in the States. Pictures were rehung, the silver and china unpacked, and the statue of the Chinese goddess Kuan-Yin returned to the hall. The dachshunds, rumoured to have been roasted and eaten during the occupation, were replaced by three pekinese, Ching, Li and a miniature, Kiki, to which were added a couple of pedigree poodles, Luke and Mark, a present from Lady Kenmare. The garden statues, which had had their ears and noses broken off, were repaired, the lily-pool restocked with goldfish and the garden itself, badly damaged by shellfire and completely over-grown, was carefully replanted; already some of the spring bulbs which Maugham in a moment of optimism had put in just before leaving in 1940 were beginning to show. The cars had been seized by the Italians but in the garage now were a Citroën and a big new Buick shipped over from America. Altogether, as Maugham wrote to Ellen Doubleday, he was 'very much pleased with it all. It is on the whole a much more beautiful house than it was before.'

The one great change was the absence of Gerald. It was now Alan Searle who was running the house, Alan who sat opposite Maugham at the dining-table, Alan typing and telephoning in the little room under-neath Maugham's roof-top study. In no time at all it seemed as if Alan had been there for years, and, despite a failure to learn French, his friendly manner and talent for organisation ensured that the staff were happy and their duties smoothly carried out. With Searle, Maugham had no need to dread rows or to worry that he would be embarrassed in front of his guests: Alan was obedient, even-tempered and polite, his overwhelming desire at all times to please his employer. And indeed Maugham had soon grown completely dependent on him; he trusted him, was fond of him, and the two enjoyed a sexual compatibility that was unusually long lasting, Alan now sleeping in Gerald's bedroom, divided only by a bathroom from Maugham's. Not everything was perfect: Alan had none of Gerald's wit, charm or sophistication, none of his daring,* certainly none of his elegance or style. In summer Searle trotted about the house in garishly patterned shirts, his plump thighs bulging out of a pair of tiny white shorts, and in winter he wore thick double-breasted suits which with his crinkly dark hair and red face gave him a curiously aldermanic appearance. Nor was Alan as intelligent as Gerald; he knew something about pictures but about little else, and had no interest in reading, except for pornographic magazines which he ordered by the box-load from America; he did, however, have a camp humour and a repertoire of comic imitations that Maugham on occasion found amusing. But if Alan's opinions were of limited interest, Maugham nonetheless needed and relied on him, and if Alan were sometimes irritating and a bore it was a small price to pay for equanimity and peace of mind.

Although in theory Alan's position in the household was the same as Gerald's, in fact it was not: Gerald had been accepted everywhere as Maugham's social equal; Alan was working class, he spoke with a cockney accent, his manner was ingratiating, and this inevitably put him on a different footing. But it was not only, or even mainly, the fact that he dropped his aitches: Maugham's friends took their cue from the master of the house, and because Maugham showed Alan little respect, ordered him about and sometimes angrily rebuked him in public, he was inevitably regarded more as a favoured employee than as a friend. Most visitors to the Mauresque liked Alan, and they were glad to see Maugham so well settled. Searle was clearly the ideal companion for his later years, 'as right as rain for William', said Glenway Wescott, '[the perfect] nanny of his second childhood', another friend remarked. But how did Alan regard his situation? His devotion to Maugham was never in question: 'I loved him with all my heart & being,' he wrote later in a private memorandum. 'I didn't care about his faults & vices, I loved every facet of him.' And yet all was not quite as serene as appeared on the surface. 'I am, I think, very happy, sometimes I am not sure,' Alan wrote to Ellen Doubleday as early as December 1946. 'Life can be very difficult, and people too.'

This oblique mention of 'people', carefully left unspecified, referred to

---

* When Daphne du Maurier once asked Alan to bring some jewellery over to New York, a Customs officer found it when searching his suitcase and charged him duty. 'Such a thing would never have happened to Gerald!' Maugham contemptuously exclaimed.

members of the Maugham family, for whom Alan nursed a covert but profound hostility. Liza, quite unknowingly, was the object of his most intense hatred, and from the very beginning of Alan's residence at the Mauresque there is expressed in some of his correspondence an under-current of venom towards her and her children of which he gave not the smallest hint when in their company. 'I'm so glad you're here, dear,' he would say to Liza as she arrived, 'give me a little squeeze.' As far as Liza was concerned, Searle seemed perfect for her father, a huge improve-ment on the terrifying Gerald, and she was grateful to him for his devotion; her children, too, Nicolas and Camilla, loved Alan's company, loved running up to his office where he would tell them jokes and outra-geous stories in funny voices which made them laugh. 'The family were all fond of Alan,' said Nic. None of them had any inkling of the bitter resentments that lay beneath the surface, for the moment expressed only in letters to a few trusted correspondents. 'Liza and the children are here,' Alan wrote to Bert Alanson in the summer of 1947. 'I find it a very disturbing element and do not like it at all.'

In July 1948 Liza remarried, as her father had predicted she would, her new husband a Conservative member of Parliament, Lord John Hope, younger son of the Marquess of Linlithgow. It was Linlithgow who as viceroy in India in 1938 had snubbed Maugham by refusing to receive Gerald Haxton, a slight neither forgotten nor forgiven by Maugham, and as a result John Hope was regarded with disfavour from the start. 'He is a pompous donkey,' he told Ellen Doubleday, 'but Liza dotes on him.' For the time being, however, he put a good face on it, courteously writing to his future son-in-law to welcome him into the family and sending the couple a cheque for 100,000 francs as a present. He went over to London for the wedding, where with professional ease he acted the part of proud father, managed to be civil to Syrie and made a creditable speech at the reception at Claridge's afterwards. For the second time Liza spent her honeymoon at the Mauresque, bringing with her a lavish trousseau designed by Mainbocher, which her mother had arranged to have smug-gled over from New York. As John was anxious to return to Scotland for the grouse shooting, Liza left Nic and Camilla with their grandfather for the rest of the summer, 'which adds greatly to the gaiety of the proceed-ings', Maugham told Nelson Doubleday. 'I must say they are very good, but now and then rather hard work. They eat like wolves, sleep like dormice, swim like fish, and in the interval run helter-skelter about the garden like hares.'

This letter was written partly in response to some ominous news from

Ellen about her husband's health. Nelson had recently been diagnosed with alcoholic neuritis, his prodigious consumption of 'phlegm-cutters' having finally caught up with him, although he himself was refusing to acknowledge the problem. The depressing details, poured out in letters from Ellen, were all too familiar to Maugham. 'Ostensibly, he is cutting down on the consumption of alcohol, only takes at most two cocktails, fairly weak before dinner and lunch, but actually he spends his time sneaking out to the pantry drinking great tremendous hookers of straight whiskey . . .' The situation grew so bad that eventually Nelson was obliged to relinquish the presidency of Doubleday, his place in the company taken by Douglas M. Black, Nelson's lawyer and long-serving employee for whom Maugham had considerable respect. Ever a shrewd businessman and alert to the many changes taking place in the post-war world, Maugham ventured to offer Doug Black some advice.

> Nelson has created a vast empire & the time has now arrived when, rather than seek to enlarge its frontiers, common sense suggests that the acquisitions already won should be firmly consolidated . . . I believe the future is fraught with peril . . . [and] I do not believe you will ever see again books bought in such quantities as they have even during these last years when people had nothing much else to do with their money.

Meanwhile Nelson's condition continued to deteriorate: he was found to have advanced lung cancer, and despite an apparently successful operation he died on 11 January 1949, five days before his sixtieth birthday. Maugham had been genuinely fond of Nelson, despite his drunkenness; he went to see him before he died, and in his letter of condolence told Ellen how much he owed both to her husband's friendship and to his acumen. 'I am not so foolish as not to be aware that I should not hold the position I do in America except for his confidence in me & his constant effort to make me better & better known. I shall always be grateful to him for that, but also, even more, for the affection he bestowed upon me.'

As Nelson's involvement in the business over the last couple of years had been minimal, Maugham experienced little change in his dealings with Doubleday. Somerset Maugham was the firm's most valuable property and he was treated accordingly. It was disappointing there were to be no more novels, but there was no question of Maugham retiring, and his name on fiction and non-fiction alike was a guarantee of sales often in the hundreds of thousands. The quality may not have been quite what it was, but if the critics were caustic nobody cared: reviews had long

ceased to matter when marketing Maugham. In 1947 a short-story collection, *Creatures of Circumstance*, was published, which included Maugham's
only Second World War story, a chilling tale set in occupied France
describing the tortured relationship between a German soldier and the
young Frenchwoman he has raped. The following year saw the publication of *Great Novelists and their Novels*,★ introductions to ten world-class
novels – such as *Pride and Prejudice, Moby-Dick, War and Peace* – accompanying shortened versions of the works, abridged by Maugham. The
*Sunday Times*, in the person of the paper's Foreign Manager, Ian Fleming,
bought the serial rights for £3,000, Fleming flying down to Nice to
negotiate personally with the author; the serialisation ran for fifteen weeks,
resulting in a weekly increase of up to 50,000 copies, 10 per cent of the
paper's circulation. In 1949 Maugham published *A Writer's Notebook*, a
selection from the fifteen volumes of notes and memoranda he had kept
since he was eighteen, including descriptive accounts of his travels, with
the dedication, 'In Loving Memory of My Friend Frederick Gerald
Haxton'. And in the 1950s there were two collections of essays, *The
Vagrant Mood* (1952) and *Points of View* (1958). In *The Vagrant Mood* are
recollections of writers Maugham had known, including a lively portrait
of his old mentor, Augustus Hare, as well as of Henry James, Arnold
Bennett and H. G. Wells. There is also an essay on 'The Decline and Fall
of the Detective Story': originally intended for Cyril Connolly's magazine *Horizon*, it had been rejected after some lengthy pondering on the
part of the editor. 'It's good enough to be accepted for *Horizon*,' Connolly
had finally pronounced, 'but not quite good enough for me.' *Points of
View* contains a lengthy survey of 'The Short Story' as well as essays on
Goethe, the Goncourts, Jules Renard and the Hindu holy man the Bhagavan
Maharshi, who had made such an impression on Maugham when he had
encountered him in India in 1938.

Far from trailing off during his seventies and eighties, Maugham's career
grew ever more phenomenally successful. In his old age he was regarded
even in Britain as one of the Grand Old Men of English letters, every
birthday marked by newspaper articles and interviews, and the arrival of
literally hundreds of letters and telegrams at the Mauresque. He was the
recipient of honours both at home and abroad, including honorary
doctorates from the universities of Oxford, Heidelberg and Toulouse. In
1954 at Winston Churchill's suggestion he was appointed a Companion
of Honour by the Queen, who received him in a private audience at

★ In Britain published by Heinemann as *Ten Novels and their Authors*.

Buckingham Palace. '[The Queen] was very nicely dressed & looked extremely pretty,' Maugham told Bert Alanson. 'She asked me to sit down & we sat & talked for a quarter of an hour, after which she said, It's been very nice to see you, Mr Maugham; so I got up & she got up, we shook hands again, I bowed & retreated backwards for about three steps, then turned to reach for the door & walked out. It was all very easy & cosy.' In 1961 the Royal Society of Literature elected Maugham a Companion of Literature, his fellow CLs that year Churchill, E. M. Forster, John Masefield and the historian G. M. Trevelyan. Such recognition was gratifying, if late in arriving and in Maugham's view inadequate. After going to Buckingham Palace to receive his CH Maugham had lunched at the Garrick with Dadie Rylands and Arthur Marshall, who congratulated him warmly on his award. 'But don't you see what the C.H. means for somebody like me?' he asked them. 'It means "well done, but . . .".' In Maugham's inner circle it was understood that he had refused a knighthood (it would be ridiculous, he used to say, to be Sir Somerset Maugham while Bernard Shaw was still a mister), hoping instead for one of the most distinguished awards of all, the Order of Merit: it rankled that both Hardy and Galsworthy, inferior novelists in his opinion, had been awarded the OM, and as 'I am the greatest living writer of English, they ought to give it to me.' Undeniably there was a tacit understanding in establishment circles that Maugham's homosexuality had damaged his reputation. The nature of the relationship with Gerald Haxton had been widely known, whereas other homosexual writers, Hugh Walpole, for instance, had been far more successful in keeping their private lives private: Walpole had been knighted as long ago as 1937.

Astonishingly, Maugham, who was born in the year Disraeli succeeded Gladstone as prime minister, now found a large new audience through the medium of television. In 1948 four stories were filmed, 'The Facts of Life', 'The Alien Corn', 'The Kite' and 'The Colonel's Lady', all scripted by R. C. Sherriff, author of *Journey's End*, the famous play about the First World War. Maugham himself appears on screen to introduce *Quartet*, his study at the Villa Mauresque painstakingly recreated at J. Arthur Rank's Gainsborough Studios in Shepherd's Bush. 'You will remember how astonished I was to find the set an exact reproduction of my writing-room on Cap Ferrat,' he told the director, Antony Darnborough. 'When I sat down at the desk & noticed the paper knife . . . I said to myself: "the dirty dogs, they've sneaked my paper-knife" & when I took it up I was staggered to find by its weight that it was made of, I suppose, papier mâché.' By today's more naturalistic standards, Maugham gives a stilted performance. With his gentle Edwardian enunciation ('looking beck'), he is plainly struggling to remember his lines and there is some frantic fiddling with the said paper-knife. Nevertheless, he claimed to have enjoyed the experience of 'being a movie star for a couple of days', and *Quartet* was such a success that it was followed by *Trio* ('The Verger', 'Mr Know-All' and' Sanatorium'), and then by *Encore* ('The Ant and the Grasshopper', 'Winter Cruise' and 'Gigolo and Gigolette'), the latter nominated for the Grand Prix at the 1952 Cannes Film Festival.

There was no doubt that Maugham relished his celebrity, partly because it brought him a great deal of money, and also it went a long way towards soothing his sense of grievance over what he considered a lack of critical acclaim. Since his television appearances he could go nowhere without being recognised, pursued by journalists and photographers, by fans and students of literature, by would-be writers asking for advice, and by literary ladies, 'soulful damsels', as Maugham described them, who expected him to be 'terribly sinister & cynical'. When he went to the United States in 1950 for the showing on CBS of *Trio*, dinners were given in his honour by the Society of Arts and Letters, which elected him an honorary member, by the Pierpont Morgan Library and by the Library of Congress in Washington. And in 1956 at the wedding of Prince Rainier and Grace Kelly in Monte Carlo, it was Somerset Maugham whose presence among the prominent guests was among the most widely reported, his photograph one of the biggest in *Life* magazine's coverage of the event. Such recognition brought with it practical advantages, too: special rates at hotels, a swift passage through Customs at Calais, Dover and New York, and always the best table and most unctuously mannered maîtres d'hôtel at restaurants everywhere. Not all the appurtenances of fame were agreeable, of course, and Maugham grew increasingly resentful of the numbers of people who on the merest acquaintance made tiresome demands on his time. 'People I haven't seen in thirty years write letters saying "darling Willie we must meet",' he complained. 'They don't care a fuck about me . . . [they] simply want to show me off.' He hated being used, and exploded once when he found a couple of young men, who claimed to know one of the family, hanging about outside the Mauresque expecting an invitation to stay. 'I am not a monkey in the zoo for people to come & stare at & I very much resent being treated as such,' Maugham wrote furiously to his niece Kate Bruce.

> I was not here when the young men came & they waited at my gate till the dinner hour when they presented themselves again with their luggage

apparently expecting me to be so flattered by their condescension in visiting me that I should ask them to stay. They were very rude to my secretary when he would not admit them. I do not know your son in law & I think he took a most impertinent liberty in telling his friends to "look me up". I shall be obliged that you see that he does not repeat a proceeding which is highly offensive to me.

Such a demanding way of life would have exhausted many a younger man but Maugham remained exceptionally limber, lusty and fit. 'When he emerges [from the pool] . . . and lies down to sun himself,' wrote the film director Garson Kanin, 'I see an old body but a firm one, wrinkled but unblemished.' Always abstemious, Maugham continued to restrict himself to no more than two courses at lunch and dinner, with, at the most, a couple of cocktails beforehand. The results of such self-discipline were rewarding. Robert Bruce Lockhart at a dinner in London described the seventy-four-year-old Maugham's appearance with admiration. 'Willie arrived punctually at eight looking very dapper in a double-breasted coat of light navy-blue, black silk socks and a monocle. The figure is wonderful. He has no spare flesh, but quite a good calf for a man of his age. He sat on the sofa with his legs tucked up and revealed an expansive stretch of calf and sock-suspenders.'

There was to be more to it than self-discipline, however. In 1954, shortly after his eightieth birthday, Maugham spent ten days at a clinic in Switzerland run by a Dr Paul Niehans. Overlooking Lake Geneva just outside Vevey, La Prairie offered an expensive and apparently revolutionary method of rejuvenation known as 'fresh-cell therapy', in which the patient was injected with a solution made from cells taken from the foetus of a freshly killed sheep. Dr Niehans had always declined to publish details of his research, and thus was deeply distrusted by the scientific community, which was highly critical of 'the whole air of hanky-panky, instant cookery, and big money' that surrounded him. But to his patients the charismatic Niehans was a genius, a saviour, consulted by large numbers of famous people who had complete faith in his treatment as well as in his absolute discretion. Among the many clients who booked into La Prairie in search of a lost youth were Noël Coward, Gloria Swanson, Marlene Dietrich, Konrad Adenauer, Thomas Mann, the Aga Khan, Wilhelm Furtwängler, Christian Dior and Charlie Chaplin. By far the most important of Niehans's patients was Pope Pius XII, who was treated under conditions of great secrecy in the Vatican, Niehans flying to Rome for the first consultation, it was said, accompanied by two heavily pregnant ewes. When Maugham arrived in Switzerland with Alan, who was also to undergo the treatment, he received the red-carpet reception from Niehans, who invited them to dine at his house and gave them a tour of the clinic, the abattoir and the laboratories. He explained the procedure in detail, that in the short space of an hour the sheep was slaughtered, the foetus removed and the tissue sliced, minced, mixed with saline solution and injected by means of a large horse-syringe into the patient's buttocks. A three-week stay was the norm, but after only ten days Maugham announced he had had enough and returned to France, with strict instructions not to smoke or drink for the following three months. 'I feel strange,' he reported after returning to the Mauresque. 'Not ill, nor especially well, simply − strange.'* Alan on the other hand was delighted to notice an immense surge in his virility, an effect to which he drew attention on every possible occasion. 'We had Willie Maugham and his catamite Searle to lunch,' Diana Cooper told Evelyn Waugh. 'They both had the "cell" treatment in Switzerland . . . [and] Searle has become a garrulous Tom Cat . . . I heard him say . . . in a cockney-pansy voice, "My dear you can't imagine what it's like − I wake up to find myself under a *tent*" − here an obscene gesture was made, denoting a fabulous erection.'

The visit to Niehans's clinic was repeated in 1958 when Maugham was eighty-four, but in all other respects the pattern of Maugham's life remained much the same as before the war: winter and spring at the Mauresque, a few weeks of foreign travel (Austria, Italy, Spain), with a stay at a spa (Vichy, Abano or Vevey), an intensely social summer on the Riviera, followed by the autumn in London in his regular suite at the Dorchester Hotel. On the Riviera Maugham was a generous host − 'It may interest you to know', he wrote to Frere in 1950, 'that in three months, exclusive of breakfasts, we served 1060 meals' − and he enjoyed having people to stay, particularly if they were prepared to entertain themselves and not disturb his highly structured daily routine. Over the years he had encountered in his guests every type of delinquency, and now in old age he was fiercely intolerant of the slightest infringement of house rules. Like an experienced hotelier, he listed the offences that annoyed him the most, the worst

---

* Maugham's French doctor, Georges Rosanoff, strongly disapproved of the Niehans treatment, which he believed had had a deleterious effect on his patient. 'Une cure de cellules fraîches, très à la mode, qu'il avait suivie en Suisse . . . avait été très mal supportée . . .' he wrote in his memoirs. 'J'eus beaucoup de difficultés à réparer les dégâts' ('He had not reacted well to a fresh-cell treatment, very fashionable, that he had undertaken in Switzerland. I had much difficulty in repairing the damage') (Rosanoff *Racontez Docteur* (Guy le Prat 1977) p.145).

offenders treating his house 'as though they were gauleiters in a conquered province'. These marauders left lights on, made cigarette burns in the sheets, borrowed books and never returned them, borrowed money that was never paid back, and sometimes arrived with three weeks' dirty laundry expecting it all to be washed and ironed before they went home.

From the guests' perspective, Maugham could be a daunting host. 'One could never be quite certain of the reception one was going to get,' his daughter recalled. 'He might be kindness itself or he could on occasion be very crushing.' Unpunctuality was the greatest sin, and he refused to wait a single second for anyone who was late arriving for a meal. Liza, for example, suffered agonies of nerves when staying with the children in case Camilla or Nic should delay proceedings and incur her father's displeasure; and the writer Peter Quennell, whose experience was typical of many, was not the only one to describe Maugham as a martinet. 'He imposed a régime and demanded a standard of behaviour that his guests neglected at their peril; and a single ill-judged remark or minor mis-step might plunge them into permanent disgrace.' Such a mis-step was taken by the producer Peter Daubeny, who as a young man, recently engaged to be married, was invited to spend a week at the Mauresque. On the first afternoon Maugham took him for a walk along the Corniche, and as they rounded a corner a car roared by, loaded with small children, a pram strapped to the roof.

> 'That's what you'll be doing a year from now,' commented Maugham, chuckling and slipping his hand into mine . . . There was something faintly suggestive in his tone of voice, and in a reflex I pulled my hand away. I immediately sensed that I had done something foolish and gave him an uneasy smile. It was met by a face of freezing scorn and hostility. The walk continued in ominous silence . . . From then on the week was pure disaster. At dinner, and every subsequent meal, Maugham made desultory conversation, but with an icy, withering malice, bitingly disparaging of anything I had done in the theatre.

Despite the risks involved and the many traps for the unwary, invitations were much sought after, with the Mauresque one of the prized landmarks of the Riviera. Maugham became accustomed not only to friends asking themselves to stay, but friends of friends, or children of friends, and especially during the summer he sometimes found he had only a slight acquaintance with the people seated round his table. Inevitably stories of bad behaviour and frightful gaffes were much prized and widely circulated, increasingly embellished as they did the rounds. There was the story of the 'well-known peer' caught attempting to leave with a suit-case full of Maugham first editions, his bag conveniently 'bursting open' at the bottom of the stairs as he was about to scuttle to safety through the front door. Then there was the story of Cyril Connolly famously caught filching three avocados from the orchard, an anecdote much relished and endlessly repeated, to Connolly's considerable annoyance, when 'all I had done', as he plaintively explained, 'was to bring him [Maugham] in an unripe windfall from the garden'. Most famous of all was the story of Patrick Leigh Fermor and the stammer, which became one of the great setpieces, sure to be retold in certain circles whenever Maugham's name was mentioned. In the original version, the travel-writer Paddy Leigh Fermor was taken to stay for a few days at the Mauresque by Ann Fleming, a great favourite of Maugham's. Lunch on the first day 'went like a marriage bell', but at dinner an exuberantly tipsy Leigh Fermor found himself telling a funny story about a man with a stammer. Afterwards when 'we were enjoying a nightcap, Mr Maugham got up, shuffled across the Aubusson, and with a limp handshake said . . . "Well, I will say good-night now and perhaps I should say goodbye too, as I expect that I will be in bed tomorrow when you leave," and then ambled off.' Leigh Fermor was instantly mortified, convinced he had been humiliatingly dismissed as a direct consequence of his lack of tact. Over the years he worked up this brief incident into an ornate melodrama, in which Maugham is trans-formed into a Gothic monster – 'his face is the wickedest tangle of cruel wrinkles . . . alligator's eyes peer from folds of pleated hide and below them an agonizing snarl is beset with discoloured and truncated fangs' – who, mortally offended, brutally banishes the defenceless hero from his house. The fact that Maugham, by then more than a little deaf, may not even have heard the stammer story, nor cared very much if he had, seems never to have occurred to Leigh Fermor; nor the fact that, with so many people brought to the villa, Maugham probably had only the vaguest idea who he was or how long he intended to stay and genuinely believed him to be leaving the next morning.★

Ann Fleming, who had married the writer Ian Fleming in 1952, provided exactly the kind of feminine company Maugham most enjoyed: like

★ In 2001 Leigh Fermor was interviewed by the *Paris Review*. At the interviewer's request, he produced a photocopy of a letter written by him to Deborah Devonshire on 26 August 1956, immediately after his visit to the Mauresque, in which he describes what happened. This was quoted extensively in the article [*Paris Review* no. 165 pp. 205–8]. A second, even more ornate version of the same letter was published seven years later in a collection of the correspondence between Leigh Fermor and Deborah Devonshire, *In Tearing Haste* [John Murray 2008].

Barbara Back, she was chic and amusing, and wrote witty, gossipy letters full of scabrous comment about their mutual friends; like Barbara, she was not in the least daunted by Maugham. Her husband Ian on the other hand adopted a slightly deferential manner when in the presence of the older man, whom he much admired. When Fleming wrote his first novel, *Casino Royale*, he sent it to Maugham and was delighted to receive an enthusiastic letter in return: Maugham had been so absorbed by James Bond's adventures he had read into the early hours, he said. 'It goes with a swing from the first page to the last & is really thrilling all through.' Eager to make the most of such a valuable opinion, Fleming asked if he might use a quote from the letter to promote the book. 'No,' came the answer. '[It's] not that I didn't mean what I said, but that I am asked all the time to write something that can be used in such a way . . . & have always refused . . . I would not do it even for the author of the Book of Genesis.' Soon after their wedding the Flemings came to stay at the Mauresque and Maugham was touched to see how deeply the couple were in love. He was puzzled, however, by the large number of towels they used, upwards of nine a day left in a damp pile on the bathroom floor. It later transpired that Fleming during sessions of highly inventive sex liked to whip his wife with a wet towel, then use another to wrap her in and soothe the smart.

With Fleming tied to his job at the *Sunday Times*, Annie often came to the Mauresque on her own, joining that group of old friends in whose company Maugham was happiest, including Desmond MacCarthy, the Freres, Juliet Duff, Raymond Mortimer and the charming and irascible Gerald Kelly. In 1948 Kelly had been elected to succeed Sir Alfred Munnings as president of the Royal Academy, and in writing to congratulate him Maugham recalled the old days. 'Do you remember Paris in 1904?' he asked him nostalgically. 'We did not imagine then that either of us would come to the point we have.' When Elizabeth II paid an official visit to the Academy, Kelly arranged for Maugham to be seated on her right at dinner. 'I had wanted the Queen to be amused,' Kelly explained to Bert Alanson, 'and I asked her whether I could put Willie to sit next to her, and she said she would be too frightened, and I had to reassure her that he could, if he chooses, be the nicest company, and she agreed to take the risk.' One of the less congenial figures to be found sitting on the terrace at the Mauresque was that of F.H. Unlike his son and daughters F.H. was a rare visitor to Cap Ferrat, but although very frail he was there on the occasion of his brother's seventy-sixth birthday in 1950. Throughout his stay he irritated Maugham by addressing him as 'my boy', and true to form gave little sign of enjoying the celebrations.'Your father', Maugham reported to Robin, 'bore with grim disapproval the various festivities which my friends & neighbours had arranged.' The antagonism between the pair was real, and when in 1954 F.H. published an autobiography, *At the End of the Day*, he made in 600 pages only three brief references to his younger brother, the longest comprising the book's last sentence: 'I need not describe the works of my brother William Somerset Maugham.' And yet at some deep level there was affection, too, and in their written exchanges there is often a dry wit, mutually relished and understood. Once when F.H. received a letter intended for Maugham and forwarded it on, Maugham jokingly wrote back that it was 'Shakespeare and Bacon all over again', that posterity will find that the Lord Chancellor had published his plays and novels 'under the insignificant name' of his younger brother.'You may well be right in thinking that you write like Shakespeare,' F.H. replied. 'But one word of brotherly advice. *Do not attempt the sonnets.*'

More cheerful company was provided by some of the regular visitors from America, George Cukor for instance, Garson Kanin and his actress wife Ruth Gordon, the playwright Sam Behrman and a rich, amusing man about town, Jerry Zipkin. Zipkin, who divided his time between escorting prominent ladies to fashionable soirées and pursuing a hedonistic homosexual career undercover, had met Maugham at the bridge-table in New York. Like Maugham, he was addicted to the game, and when on the Riviera played regularly with Maugham and his coterie of wealthy widows, his bunch of 'old baguettes', as Zipkin unchivalrously called them, ladies like Leslie Doverdale, Charlotte Boissevain and the brightly painted, heavily bejewelled Marion Bateman, who had her maid brush her white hair with cornflour every night to make it shine. Lady Bateman liked to add tone to her table with blue blood, the aura of *anciens régimes*, and she was proud of her biggest catch, the exiled Queen of Spain, who as a friend of Prince Rainier was a frequent visitor to Monte Carlo from her home in Lausanne. A granddaughter of Queen Victoria, Queen Ena was accustomed to homage, and enjoyed being kowtowed to by the rich and snobbish on the Riviera. Maugham, who had met her with the Duke of Connaught in the late 1920s, often entertained her, inviting her to lunch to meet Charlie Chaplin and arranging bridge-parties for her. Ena loved to play, although she was no good at the game and drove Maugham and other serious players frantic by her habit of looking at her cards and giving away what was in her hand by absent-mindedly muttering to herself, 'only two hearts', or 'quite a nice lot of spades'.

Since the war the Sporting Club in Monte Carlo had more than regained its international lustre, and with Princess Grace as patron there was every summer a programme packed with world-famous performers. In June 1958 Maugham attended a gala dinner at the Sporting Club at which Frank Sinatra was to sing, with Noël Coward as compère. Both Coward and Garson Kanin were staying at the Mauresque for the occasion, and both left descriptions of the event. On the night, Maugham and his party sat at a table with the New York columnist Leonard Lyons and his wife. According to Kanin, Sinatra stopped by on his way from the stage, and Noël introduced him to Maugham. 'Frank says, "Hiya, baby!" Maugham replies, "Very well, indeed, but hardly a b-b-baby." I have never seen Maugham in circumstances as strange as these,' Kanin continued. 'There are too many people, too much noise . . . But he takes it all in good part and sees to it that he has a good time. He has a positive gift for enjoying himself. He stays as long as he wants to, then takes his leave, making certain to stop at the main table in the middle of the room on his way out to pay his respects to the Prince and Princess.' The more observant Coward gives a slightly different version, unlike Kanin alert to Maugham's impatience underneath the bonhomous veneer. The evening was chaotic, he noted in his diary.

Far too many people and suffocating . . . Willie was getting more and more fractious as the evening wore on . . . Finally I went on and introduced Frankie in French and English, then he hopped up on to the stage and sang for an hour, enchantingly. Willie was off home like a shot the moment Frankie's last note had died away. I don't think he enjoyed it much, or that either he or Alan really saw why and how Frankie is such a superb performer.

Naturally such society was anathema to the more cultural among Maugham's friends, among them the historian and diarist James Lees-Milne, whose wife Alvilde had a house at Roquebrune; Christopher Isherwood, who with his very young lover Don Bachardy had an open invitation to stay at Cap Ferrat; and that exquisite bird-of-paradise Jean Cocteau, who with his fabulously good-looking boyfriend 'Doudou' stayed often at the Villa Saint-Sospir, only a short distance down the road from the Mauresque. An artist as well as a writer, a close friend of Picasso, a celebrity in literary and theatrical circles in Paris, Cocteau should have had a great deal to offer Maugham; and yet although they continued to meet from time to time it was clear from the first that the friendship would never prosper. Cocteau had little regard for 'Somerset', as he always addressed him, regarding his work as facile and populist, while Maugham was highly resistant to the flamboyant Frenchman's dazzling conversational flights of fancy, irritated by what he dismissively described as his 'long-winded insincerity' and by his determination always to hold centre-stage. 'M. Cocteau talks for the benefit of the servants,' Maugham remarked in a grumpy sotto voce; Cocteau overheard and taking it as a compliment redoubled his efforts. Maugham had recently bought two fine Picassos, *La Mort d'Harlequin* and *La Grec*, and Cocteau as he was leaving one day stopped to admire them. He asked Maugham if he knew Picasso, and when Maugham said he did not, offered to arrange a meeting. 'D-d-does he play b-b-bridge?' came the quizzical response.

During the 1940s and 1950s Maugham added substantially to his picture collection. 'It has always been an ambition of mine . . . to make a small collection of Impressionist pictures,' he wrote to Bert Alanson while on a post-war shopping spree in New York. It was here that he bought some of his most important works, the *Femme assise dans un fauteuil jaune* by Matisse,★ *Bateaux à Argenteuil* by Renoir, Rouault's powerful *Christ crucifié*, as well as a small Pissarro, a Bonnard, a Monet and a Utrillo. Maugham has been condemned by much of the art establishment for his pedestrian taste in painting, marked down for his primarily literary approach to the visual arts. 'He liked a picture for what he could read into it and write out of it rather than for any aesthetic reason,' commented Harold Acton, an opinion which Maugham's own writing on the subject undeniably supports. 'I do not think Utrillo is a great painter,' he stated in a magazine article in 1941, 'but I have occasionally seen a picture of what is called his white period that has wrung my heart. To someone who knows Paris, those street scenes of sordid suburbs, with their air of desolation and their hostile silence, are of an infinite sadness.' During this same period further purchases were made in Paris and London, *La Neige à Louveciennes* by Camille Pissarro, *Femme à l'ombrelle verte* by Matisse, Sisley's *Le Loing à Moret* and a luscious nude by Renoir, 'rather buxom & a bright tomato colour, not very big, but very beautiful', as Maugham delightedly described it. The last painting Maugham bought was a river scene, *La Seine à Paris*, by Lépine. He and Alan were passing a well-known gallery in Bond Street when they saw two men carrying in a picture covered by a sheet. Following them, they watched while the canvas, dirty

★ Maugham used occasionally to visit Matisse, a neighbour of his on the Riviera. 'J'achète des tableaux pour fleurir ma maison' (I buy pictures to make my house blossom) he once told him, echoing the attitude he had expressed years before to Gerald Kelly. In response Matisse gave a snort of disgust. 'Ça, c'est la decoration!' (That's mere decoration) (*Purely for My Pleasure* p. 6).

and unframed, was unwrapped. 'It was the picture I had been looking for in vain for years,' Maugham wrote. He asked the price, and a formidable sum was named. '"All right," I said. "I'll buy it."' Another favourite work was by Toulouse-Lautrec, *Le Polisseur*, a painting of a nude man on his hands and knees polishing a stone floor. The dealer told Maugham he could have asked three times the price had it been a naked woman, but 'buyers jibbed at a male nude and I was able to buy it for a very reasonable sum'. Raw, brutal and disturbing, *Le Polisseur* is untypical Lautrec, far removed from his courtesans and can-can dancers, and it amused Maugham to ask visitors to the villa to guess the artist: only once was the correct answer given.

Much as he loved the visual arts, Maugham knew he was an amateur with a comparatively uninformed taste, and when spending large sums of money he looked to others to advise him. In the early days he had been guided by Gerald Kelly and Hugh Lane; he had also consulted the great Parisian collector and connoisseur Alphonse Kahn. It was Kahn who introduced him to Fernand Léger, from whom he bought the abstract *Les Toits de Paris*, which Léger had painted in homage to Cézanne. Subsequently Maugham turned for advice to Monroe Wheeler, to Jean Cocteau and to one of the greatest of British art-historians, Sir Kenneth Clark. Before the war a pupil of Bernard Berenson, Surveyor of the King's Pictures, Director of the National Gallery, 'K' Clark was recognised in his field as one of the foremost scholars of the age, admired as much for his lucid, lapidary style of writing as for his formidable intellect. He and Maugham formed a firm friendship, Maugham much appreciating Clark's dry wit, his fastidiousness and urbanity, and becoming fond, too, of his elegant wife Jane. The first time the Clarks came to the Mauresque, Maugham, as usual, challenged his guest to name the painter of *Le Polisseur*. 'Toulouse-Lautrec,' Clark replied with barely a moment's hesitation. Unlike his mentor Berenson, Clark respected Maugham's response to painting. Berenson, on the one occasion on which Maugham visited him at I Tatti, remarked afterwards that the writer had displayed 'a fantastic absence of feeling for visual art. In so far as he praised anything here, it was the poorest stopgap paintings.' Clark, on the other hand, thought that Maugham 'was remarkably perceptive of excellence in all the arts', including painting.

> In the big sitting-room were pictures by Renoir and Monet in richly carved frames; on the staircase pictures by Matisse; but if one showed him reproductions of work by a painter unknown to him, like Paul Klee, his response was surprisingly quick and just. I once tried him to the limit with a Mondrian. To my astonishment he said 'Yes, it is very fine.'

The Clarks stayed several times at Cap Ferrat, yet despite a genuine affection for their host their pleasure was not unalloyed. 'Mr Maugham was exceedingly kind to us,' Clark recorded in his memoirs,

> but staying there was rather a strain . . . The evenings were a problem. We had exhausted our conversation by the end of dinner, and the sitting-room was too big for comfortable talk . . . What he really liked was a game of bridge, but Jane cannot play, and I pretend that I cannot. We were always relieved when he was invited out to play bridge, but it happened too seldom. Sometimes he took us to call on his neighbours, who lived in large houses of unspeakable vulgarity . . .

It was through an introduction from Monroe Wheeler that Maugham met a protégé of Clark's, the painter Graham Sutherland. In 1947 Sutherland and his wife while staying in the south of France were invited to the Mauresque, where Sutherland, like many before him,★ was immediately struck by the 'paintability' of Maugham. He had never attempted a portrait before but Maugham agreed to sit, and the Sutherlands moved into the villa for a week so that the painter could give himself over to his work, making pencil studies of his sitter's head, sketching his arms, hands, legs, and making notes about his clothes, a brown velvet smoking-jacket, a rose-coloured silk foulard, grey flannels, a pair of suede slippers. On a tall, narrow canvas, the now famous picture, creating the image by which Maugham is most widely identified, shows the subject seated on a bamboo stool, the figure set against a thickly painted yellow background, with a few palm fronds above his head making a delicate reference to the Orient. The posture is slightly hunched, the eyes are melancholy, the mouth down-turned, and yet there is a glimmer of sardonic amusement, an impression of a detached observer quietly enjoying the spectacle of human frailty. 'The first time I saw it I was shocked,' Maugham said in an interview, 'and then I began to realize that here was far more of me than I ever saw myself.' Others, too, claimed to see in the portrait a different side to the man they thought they knew. Gerald Kelly joked that Sutherland had made his old friend look like the madam of a brothel in Shanghai, while Max Beerbohm was revolted by the painting and thought the subject appeared to have been tortured. Although he had

---

★ As well as eighteen portraits by Gerald Kelly, Maugham was depicted by Philip Steegman, Marie Laurencin, H. A. Freeth, B. E. Wendkos, Edouard McEvoy, in a silverpoint by Bernard Perlin and sculpted by, among others, Sir Jacob Epstein and Sarah Ryan. Of the Perlin Maugham said, 'It is the only portrait ever made of me which shows how handsome I was in my youth' (Robert Phelps (ed.) *Continual Lessons* p. 168).

often attempted it, Max had never succeeded in drawing a caricature of Maugham, but in his view this was what Sutherland had done, had 'carried caricature as far as it could go'. Maugham himself, however, was so taken with the work that he offered to buy it, agreeing with Sutherland a price of £500. The next day Alan turned up with £300 in his hand, explaining that as the payment was in cash a £200 discount was expected, a cut which the disgruntled artist felt forced to accept. Sutherland did well from the portrait, nevertheless: *Time* magazine carried a photograph of it, with other publications quickly following suit, and the picture was exhibited at the Tate, with the result that the painter found himself much in demand, commissioned to portray, among others, the press baron Lord Beaverbrook and Winston Churchill.

As became widely known, when Churchill saw his portrait, which had been commissioned by Parliament and destined eventually to hang in the House of Commons, he was appalled by the image represented, by the sadness and sense of defeat, and the canvas was destroyed on his wife's orders. Interestingly Maugham, too, grew to dislike his Sutherland portrait, and before long found an excuse to have it moved out of the villa. 'Although I wouldn't like Graham to know it for worlds, I found it a terribly difficult picture to hang,' he explained to Clark. 'It is a museum picture rather than a picture for a private house.' But the truth was he came to be haunted by it, haunted by its merciless vision and by the terrifying vista it revealed of an inexorably approaching and miserable old age.

# 16

## Betrayal

On the day after his seventieth birthday in January 1944, Maugham wrote in his notebook, 'On the continent of Europe they have an amiable custom when a man who has achieved some distinction reaches that age. His friends, his colleagues, his disciples . . . join together to write a volume of essays in his honour.' But when Maugham reached seventy the war was on and he was in America and there was no opportunity for any such act of homage; and so it was not until ten years later, when he reached eighty, that just such a plan was put into action. Heinemann commissioned the novelist Jocelyn Brooke to put together a Festschrift, a collection of essays on Maugham by fellow writers to be presented to him as a birthday tribute. Brooke solicited contributions from many of the most distinguished literary figures of the day, from poets, publishers, novelists, critics. These included Elizabeth Bowen, Angus Wilson, Rosamond Lehmann, Anthony Powell, William Plomer, Rose Macaulay, Rupert Hart-Davis, William Sansom, Raymond Mortimer, Peter Quennell, J. R. Ackerley, Noël Coward. One after the other the polite excuses came flowing in: 'not a great fan of his . . . obliged to decline' (William Plomer), 'don't think I'm at all the person to write about [him]' (Angus Wilson), 'May I be excused?' (William Sansom), '[cannot] because of the novel which I *MUST* finish' (Elizabeth Bowen), 'truly and deeply sorry to say that I cannot contribute' (Noël Coward). The only two acceptances came from Anthony Powell and Raymond Mortimer. '[I] shall produce 2000 words for you if I possibly can,' wrote Mortimer, '[but] I don't myself think that there is a great variety of things to say about Maugham . . . [and] a devastating paper could be written on the limitations of his taste . . . I am the last person, however, to emphasise such deficiencies . . . for he is a very old friend whom I regard with grateful affection.' But two contributions were not enough, and in the face of this fastidious flinching, of this general lack of respect for Maugham's work, Brooke had no option but to abandon the project.

The birthday did not pass unnoticed, however: it was given extensive coverage in the press, and *Punch* ran a caricature of the writer by Ronald Searle accompanying a ditty by the magazine's assistant editor B. A. Young.

> I bask in Antibes and in honour, and consider the works of my pen
> That have made me in one full lifetime all things to all literate men:
> The rich man's MARIE CORELLI, the poor man's ANDRE GIDE,
> A STEVENSON told of the facts of life, a KIPLING shorn of his creed.
> O, I was TERENCE RATTIGAN when TERENCE was still in his cot,
> And the films and TV will call on me when USTINOV'S long forgot.
> Though the Ale I brewed was bitter, my Cakes were as sweet as sin,
> And they brought me the Moon I sighed for, with a bit over Sixpence thrown in.
> The world's most delectable secrets turned to Ashenden in my mouth,
> And the fetters of Human Bondage hold me fast in the suns of the south.

Among the most generous accolades was one from Maugham's old friend Compton Mackenzie, who wrote an open letter in the *Author*, the journal of the Society of Authors, speaking not only on behalf of Maugham's fellow writers but also for 'those thousands of readers and playgoers all over the world whom you are still entertaining as you entertained their fathers . . . [and] grandfathers'. Mackenzie referred to his lifelong admiration for Maugham, which, he said, dated back to 1897 and his first reading of *Liza of Lambeth*, when 'I regarded you with reverence as one of those fearless spirits who were liberating us from the shackles of Victorianism.' As well as this, there was an exhibition of Maugham's manuscripts and first editions at the Times Bookshop in Wigmore Street, and a dinner given for him at the Garrick, during which a toast was proposed by the playwright St John Ervine, followed by a speech from Maugham himself. This turned out to be a harrowing experience. Maugham gave a most impressive performance, Ervine recalled, his speech, which he had learned by heart, 'full of wit, humour, well-turned phrases, and, surprisingly to some people, but not to me, full of feeling'. But then towards the end he suddenly dried up.

> Anybody else would have sat down in confusion . . . But Maugham stood perfectly still, though his fingers were trembling. After a few moments, he said, 'I'm just thinking of what I shall say next!' Then he lapsed into silence again. A little later, he said, 'I'm sorry to keep you waiting!' and became silent once more. Then, suddenly the machine of his mind moved again, and he finished the speech finely. He must have had a dry-up for about

a couple of minutes, rather more than that, I should say, but remained imperturbable apparently, throughout what must have been a dreadful ordeal. And the company sat absolutely still.

Inevitably with such a world-renowned writer Maugham had long been targeted by would-be biographers. Since the late 1920s there had appeared a number of critical studies of his work, and to those who wrote to him for information he was unfailingly helpful and courteous; for such a reticent man he answered questions with surprising frankness and often at length: as Sam Behrman remarked, 'he will tell you everything, up to a point'. Maugham nevertheless made it clear to these authors that they must not expect him to read the results of their research. 'I really cannot stand reading about myself unless I am absolutely forced to do so,' he explained to an American academic, Richard Cordell, who published a critical study in 1961. 'It is a pathological defect . . . [but] it is as uncomfortable for me to read praise . . . as it is to read censure.' On biography, however, Maugham took a tougher stance, implacably opposed to any revelations about his personal life. In 1959 there had been one biographical work, *W. Somerset Maugham: A Candid Portrait*, by Maugham's old acquaintance Karl G. Pfeiffer, then a professor of English at New York University; it was gossipy, inaccurate, mildly malicious and on the whole harmless, but Maugham had disliked it exceedingly, not only because of the invasion of privacy but because he felt betrayed: he had known Pfeiffer, had even had him to stay at the Mauresque, and had had no idea that their conversations were being secretly recorded for a book.

Now in his old age there were frequent requests from writers known and unknown hoping that he would agree to co-operate, or at the very least not oppose the writing of the big biography. Such a man, such a life presented an irresistible subject, but Maugham was determined to allow none of it, and he went to great lengths to protect himself. He instructed his literary executors (Frere, until he retired from Heinemann in 1961 when his place was taken by the literary agent Spencer Curtis Brown) that after his death they should continue to refuse information and access to all applicants, deny permission for the publication of letters and where possible urge any person in possession of letters to destroy them. To cover his tracks further Maugham burned every scrap of documentary evidence he could lay his hands on. For years he had been ruthless with his own correspondence; Glenway Wescott remembered watching him answering letters at Yemassee, how 'he tears everything into small scraps with a kind of spiteful haste and energy; and now and then he calls our attention to the fact, and says that he trusts we all do likewise with whatever he may write us'. Now in a series of great bonfires at the Mauresque, Maugham threw into the flames every morsel he could find, including letters he had overlooked from long ago, letters from Arnold Bennett, Ada Leverson, H. G. Wells, Gerald Kelly, Desmond MacCarthy. Into the bonfire, too, at Maugham's insistence, went everything of Alan Searle's, including, to Alan's dismay, his love letters from Lytton Strachey. 'I had held on to those letters', he pathetically recalled, '[because] I thought if something happened to Willie I might sell them.'*

In the last years of Maugham's life, attitudes in England towards homosexuality were beginning to grow more tolerant, although the homosexual law reform bill was not to be passed until two years after his death. Yet Maugham was very much a product of his age, and his deviant sexuality, as it was then regarded, was an aspect of his life he strongly felt should be kept concealed. The outward appearance of respectability had always been of the utmost importance to him: when in 1954 Terence Rattigan asked for signatures to a petition supporting the young peer Edward Montagu, on trial for homosexual offences, Maugham and Noël Coward were the only two who refused. With the gate firmly barred against *bona fide* biographers, Maugham might have felt relatively secure, but he still had to deal with the threat of blackmail. The first such approach was fairly easy to brush off. It came from Gerald's boyfriend, Louis Legrand, who in middle age had gone out to Australia to seek his fortune. When he failed to prosper, it occurred to Loulou that he was in possession of some valuable property in the form of letters not only from Haxton and Maugham, but also from a number of distinguished gentlemen, such as Harold Nicolson, whose acquaintance Loulou had made at the Mauresque, and who might not be entirely overjoyed if the nature of that relationship were to be revealed. Loulou sent a series of misspelt letters to Maugham himself, to Alan, to Robin and to Liza ('Your kids of Paravicini & Lord Hope, will not be pleased when I shall give my memoires at the public [sic]'), but fortunately he was found to be open to reason and the matter was satisfactorily settled by a lawyer's letter and by a cheque.

But then a far more insidious threat materialised, this time from within the family, from none other than Maugham's nephew Robin. Of all Maugham's relations, it was only Robin whom Alan regarded as a friend. The two had always been close, Robin lending a sympathetic ear to Searle's grievances, while Alan acted as an invaluable mediator between

* Searle did, however, manage to keep back several dozen letters written to him by Maugham.

Robin and his uncle; he spoke up for him when Robin was in trouble and he kept him informed about what was going on at the villa. Naturally Alan was privy to all Maugham's affairs, affairs about which Robin increasingly began to show a lively curiosity. It was Alan one day, while the two of them were sitting by the pool, who indiscreetly revealed that the old man, disapproving of an increasing fecklessness and self-indulgence in Robin's behaviour, had substantially reduced the financial provision he had made for his nephew. Robin, who had long lived with the comforting prospect of inheriting a generous unearned income, had been appalled. 'I must tell you that this has come as a terrible blow . . . one of the greatest blows I've ever known,' he wrote to Searle after he returned to England.

> During all these long years, I have always been able to console myself with the thought that . . . I had a substantial amount to look forward to when I could no longer make much money from writing . . . Please, dear Alan, if you possibly get the chance, do put in a word for me so that I can get the settlement made back to me now.

Alan promised to do what he could, but it would have to wait for the right moment. Meanwhile he expressed his readiness to help forward a more immediately lucrative project, the writing of a full-scale biography, with no holds barred. Robin had first suggested the idea of a biography more than ten years before, but Maugham had rejected the proposal out of hand; now, however, with Alan as his backstage informant Robin had an immensely profitable proposition in view; and with his financial future suddenly diminished he could hardly be expected to let it go. With a certain amount of trepidation he wrote to Maugham. 'Dearest Willie,' his letter began,

> I've had an offer from the American publisher, Victor Weybright, of an advance of 50,000 dollars . . . Obviously I can't afford to turn down such a good offer. But equally obviously I don't want to write such a book behind your back. As you know, although I earn enough from my writing to keep me going each year, I haven't a penny of capital because the £9,000 that my father left me went to buying and furnishing my little house in London . . . So what I really need, if you will give it me, is first of all, your blessing that I should accept the offer to write a full-length biography, and secondly as much help as you could possibly give me . . . It does seem to me that with my deep admiration and affection for you I am at least likely to produce a better biography of you than anyone else.

Despite the undoubtedly genuine expression of affection, Maugham had no trouble in recognising blackmail when he saw it. He instantly paid up, sending Robin a cheque for the exact same sum he had been offered by Weybright, on the strict understanding that he drop all plans of writing about him. 'I promise you here and now that I will keep my part of the bargain,' Robin wrote with every appearance of sincerity.

> I give you my word that I shall not write any other biography about you – ever ... I can use part of the money to pay off my overdraft and I can use the rest to buy myself an annuity which will make all the difference to my life because it will give me security. I'm really awfully shy about all this, but I'm also very grateful.

When after his eightieth-birthday celebrations Maugham returned to the south of France he found over a thousand letters of congratulation awaiting him. This was in addition to the normal heavy volume of business and personal correspondence and of fan letters, often amounting to 500 a week, nearly all of which had to be dealt with by Alan Searle. There were also frequent telephone calls, invitations, requests for interviews, all filtered through Alan, who as Maugham's secretary revelled in his position as guardian of the gate, even if it sometimes left him feeling flustered and exhausted. '[Mr Maugham's] celebrity in Europe has reached its peak, and I am hard put to it to protect him from the Press and all and sundry,' he wrote to Bert Alanson. 'I get insulted most days by all the people I keep at bay, but its part of the job . . . [and] I rather enjoy the reflected glory.' Despite the stresses and strains, Alan relished the glamour and excitement, particularly when they were in London and staying in luxury at the Dorchester, meeting famous people and constantly petitioned by sycophantic journalists all dependent on Alan for their access to Maugham. Indeed, Searle was usually happier when away from Cap Ferrat, where he had the responsibility of the whole household on his shoulders, and where he often felt unwell. Alan suffered from a skin condition, psoriasis, which the heat in summer made worse; he was prone to haemorrhoids and also to frequent liver attacks: the food at the Mauresque was rich, Alan was very greedy, and as a result he frequently had to spend a day in bed overwhelmed by headaches and nausea. Against this, he loved the social life, the lunch-parties at neighbouring villas, the lavish dinners at the Château de Madrid and Rampoldi's, the constant arriving and departing of guests from England and America. With most of Maugham's friends he quickly adopted a manner of cosy intimacy, and in many cases, because they in return were genial towards him, he came to believe that he was held in much higher regard than was in fact the case.

Generally speaking, visitors to the Mauresque liked Alan well enough;

he appeared a dear fellow, always bustling busily about, 'smiling . . . heavily perfumed, plump, with his lovely black hair, pink cheeks and chubby appearance',[*] in the words of Maugham's physician, Dr Georges Rosanoff. His good humour and desire to please, above all his obvious devotion to his master, won respect; but most people, although naturally they concealed it, also found him silly and a bit of a bore. '[Alan] was not in himself very interesting company,' said Glenway Wescott, 'a namby-pamby' said Jerry Zipkin, 'muddle-headed . . . [and] not very bright' according to the art critic Douglas Cooper. Highly strung and emotional, Alan was quick to interpret a normal show of friendliness and good manners as a sign of deep and undying affection for himself, and for some it was faintly embarrassing when Searle, after typing a letter of his employer's, would add an effusive handwritten postscript of his own. On letters of Maugham's to Lady Clark, for instance, Alan nearly always wrote a sentimental, some-times rather bold, personal message – 'I think you are a darling, and I love you. XX [kisses] Get some nice chap to give you these for me' – while Jerry Zipkin was frequently and fervently told, '[you are] such a darling' or 'I have few friends I love as much as I love you . . .'

For Searle, the two greatest pleasures in life were sex and self-pity. He loved to wallow in self-pity, complaining about his health, his nerves, the pressure of work and above all his anxiety about what was to happen after his employer's death, when, he claimed, he would be turned out of the house with nothing and left to starve. He talked endlessly about his expectations, or lack of them, his voice breaking as he described the pathos of his situation, the fact that he believed Maugham was going to leave him penniless, that he would be thrown out on to the street when he was too old and frail to make a fresh start. That all this was nonsense, that Maugham had made it clear from the beginning that he had gener-ously provided for him, made not the slightest difference to the burden of Alan's song. Some of Maugham's old friends, like George Cukor, weary of the endless litany, tried to make him see reason; but Alan refused to listen. The truth was, as Jerry Zipkin soon realised, 'he enjoyed the complaining'. Every summer when Zipkin came to the Mauresque he would be treated yet again to 'Alan's annual speech of complaint about all the *objets* that were his or that Willie had promised him, and what would happen after Willie died'. Eventually, Zipkin suggested he draw up a list and get Maugham to sign it, which Maugham was perfectly willing to do, 'but Alan never would, preferring to complain'.

[*] 'souriant . . . très parfumé, grassouillet, de beaux cheveux noirs, les joues roses, l'air poupin'.

It was Zipkin who was central, also, to Alan's other hobby, as he arranged for regular supplies of pornographic material to be sent over from the States. Boxes of photographs and magazines (the parcels carefully disguised to avoid the attentions of French Customs) arrived at intervals from a specialist firm in Arizona, from which Alan, alone in his bedroom, derived many hours of vigorous pleasure. 'Thank you for all those wonderful picture books!' begins one enthusiastic letter. 'They've nearly driven me mad, and I am in a state of complete exhaustion, and almost too weak to turn the pages.' Any good-looking young man invited to the Mauresque was pounced on, and most nights after dinner Alan, like Gerald before him, would go over to Villefranche on the prowl. Searle was known along the Riviera for his proclivities; he tipped generously and so was always made welcome, his stout figure a familiar sight in back-street bars and on the quayside when the American fleet was in. Sometimes he brought his new friends back to the villa, giving them champagne, letting them swim in the pool, and when appropriate introducing them to Maugham. 'Oooh, you should have seen all those lovely boys,' he would giggle next morning at breakfast.

Yet, for all his foolishness and neuroses, it was Alan who made Maugham's highly structured routine possible, who protected him, cared for him and showed him infinite kindness and compassion. The two men were largely compatible and understood each other very well; '[Mr Maugham] was generous to me & loved me with all my faults,' wrote Alan in later life. Yet Maugham, irascible in his old age, was frequently impatient with Alan and, a master of the lethal barb, he would sometimes lash out at him with a ferocity that sent Searle rushing from the room in tears. This could annoy Maugham more, or alternatively overwhelm him with guilt so that he would treat Alan with particular tenderness for the following day or two. Occasionally the attack was physical, as on one afternoon when walking past the lily-pond Alan idly threw a stone at a frog and Maugham hit him so hard he almost knocked him over. Guests at the villa were often shocked at the treatment meted out to Alan. 'Alan Searle was a knight,' according to Liza, '[and] some of the crushing and cruel things my father said to him were devastating,' a perception shared by Christopher Isherwood, '[who] said in his entire life he's never known anyone so mistreated as Alan, so pissed on, kicked and shamed and disbelieved'. Yet it was also evident that Alan revelled in the drama of it: he loved to be petted and pitied, and Maugham's harshness provided him with ever richer material for his grievances.

There were, too, enormous advantages to living with Maugham, and among the most prized by Searle was the opportunity to travel. Every year they journeyed within Europe, to Germany, Austria, Italy, Portugal and Spain; in 1950 they went to Morocco, in 1953 to Greece and Turkey, and in 1956 to Egypt where they were sumptuously entertained by the Aga Khan. After the war Maugham went only twice more to the United States, in 1949 and in 1950, when he presented the manuscript of 'The Artistic Temperament of Stephen Carey' to the Library of Congress; but in 1959 at the age of eighty-five he returned to the Far East, to Japan, where he had long been enormously popular, revisiting en route many of the old ports of call, Singapore, Saigon, Manila, Hong Kong. On their arrival in Yokohama, a crowd of several thousand was waiting to greet the great English novelist, a scene that was repeated in Tokyo, to Alan's intense excitement. 'Mr M.'s popularity in Japan is quite fantastic, and we can't put our noses outside the door without being instantly recognised . . . it has been really staggering!' They were escorted during part of their stay by the English novelist Francis King, then living in Kyoto. King was impressed by Maugham's lively curiosity about Japanese life and culture. 'He still felt he had something important to learn . . . He was often almost dead from exhaustion but he was determined to see all that he could.'

Until well into his eighties, Maugham made little change to the schedule he had established as a young man, every morning retiring to his study to write as he had done all his life, although now he had to wear an elastic brace on his right hand. While no longer producing fiction, Maugham was still an immense bestseller, with nearly 80 million copies sold, his books used in schools abroad to teach English, his work translated into all European languages, as well as Russian, Turkish, Arabic, Japanese and several Indian dialects; his plays continued to be performed all over the world; and his novels and short stories were frequently reissued, their popularity substantially boosted by the three television series; in 1957 there was even an opera, with music by John Gardner, based on *The Moon and Sixpence*. Naturally enough, Maugham was much sought after to write introductions to the works of others, contributing to books about Robbie Ross, Eddie Marsh, Charlie Chaplin and Gladys Cooper; he wrote a foreword to the autobiography of the Aga Khan, and a preface to a translation of *The Letters of Madame de Sévigné* by his childhood friend from Paris, Violet Hammersley (née Williams-Freeman).

In 1951 Maugham brought out *A Choice of Kipling's Prose*, his personal selection of stories by a writer for whom his feelings had always been somewhat ambivalent. Maugham had known Kipling only slightly, meeting him first at a dinner-party in the 1890s, during which he remembered thinking that if Kipling said 'pukka sahib' one more time he would throw a decanter at him. During the 1930s Kipling was brought to lunch at the Mauresque, and Maugham was amused to find that little had changed. 'He's a white man,' Kipling declared of a chap he admired, and Maugham waited for the inevitable phrase to follow. 'He's a pukka sahib all right,' continued Kipling, exactly on cue. Maugham had been asked to do the book by the writer's daughter, Elsie Bambridge, and before making his choice he reread all the short stories, as he reported to Peter Stern. 'I have been reading Kipling, reading Kipling, reading Kipling (the repetition is designed to express endurance, constancy, perseverance, a will of iron, determination & bull-dog courage) & at his best I think he is grand (Caps); at his worst − O God!' Such facetiousness notwithstanding, Maugham's admiration was genuine, in particular for the Indian stories, and his appraisal is both generous and judicious. Kipling 'is our greatest story writer', he concludes, 'the only writer of short stories our country has produced who can stand comparison with Guy de Maupassant and Chekhov.'

In his eighties Maugham continued to write because in a sense he had no choice. 'The fact is that, like drinking, writing is a very easy habit to form & a devilish hard one to break,' as he explained to Bert Alanson. And yet now in old age his inspiration was failing him; his imagination had run dry, and he could no longer inhabit the vivid interior landscape in which he had lived with such intensity and absorption for well over half a century. '[My] fertile invention . . . is a thing of the past,' he ruefully admitted, '[and] I am well aware that I have lost any talent I may have had . . . Not being a creative writer anymore, is very lonely. Your characters don't exist with you anymore.' In a newspaper interview Maugham gave in 1958, he said sadly, 'Writing with me has been like a disease, but now I must be content with an hour a day, if my hand allows, of writing about books instead of people. It is not the same thing at all.' He sounded, said the reporter, 'like a man about to be divorced from a woman he really loves but cannot live with any longer . . . As he spoke he kept rubbing the muscle between the thumb and the first finger nervously. Then he said, seeing my interest: "That is where it hurts. The muscle has just given up after all these years."'

Increasingly, memories of the past began to haunt him, memories of his vigorous young manhood, of his childhood, and of his love for his mother, the only fully requited love he had ever known; his mind dwelt on Gerald and of their years together and their travels in the South Pacific and the Far East. To H. E. Bates, who in 1953 dedicated a book of stories to him, Maugham wrote poignantly that 'the last one "The Delicate Nature" took me a long way back & my memory fizzled with all my half-forgotten recollections of the East. I was thrilled & at the same time rather unhappy. Oh, the past!' By comparison Maugham found his daily life colourless; he grew increasingly restless and dissatisfied, and for a time he even considered selling the Mauresque and moving either to London or to Lausanne. 'I have good servants, good food, a beautiful house & a nice garden. But that does not prevent me from being bored,' he complained to his niece Kate. 'I could not stand the life for a month if I hadn't got a certain amount of work to do, but that occupies only my morning & I have the rest of the day to get through.'

There was plenty of society available, but many of his old friends were gone: Emerald Cunard had died in 1948, Desmond MacCarthy in 1952, Eddie Marsh in 1953, Max Beerbohm, whom Maugham had last visited in Rapallo only months before, in 1956, Bert Alanson, profoundly mourned, in 1958. Rather less regretted were a couple of deaths within the family. On 23 March 1958, F.H., after suffering a stroke, died at his house in Cadogan Square, aged ninety-one. A widower for eight years, he had been looked after by his eldest daughter, Kate, and his death was neither unexpected nor greatly grieved over. Yet if the death of his brother left Maugham largely unmoved, that of his ex-wife three years before had been a cause for positive rejoicing. Returning to London after the war, Syrie had moved into a flat on Park Lane, where she continued to conduct her business, although on a much smaller scale than before. In her seventies her formidable energy had begun to fail her, and she spent much of her day in bed, talking on the telephone and rapping out orders to her long-suffering maid and secretary. Since the bout of tuberculosis a few years earlier, her health had been precarious: she suffered from angina, and this coupled with a bad bout of bronchial pneumonia brought about her death, at the age of seventy-six, on 25 July 1955. Maugham learned of it in a telegram from a heartbroken Liza. 'It would be hypocrisy on my part to pretend that I am deeply grieved at Syrie's death,' he told Barbara Back. 'She had me every which way from the beginning & never ceased to give me hell.' Indeed his strongest emotion was one of relief that he would no longer have the financial burden of supporting a woman from whom he had been divorced for nearly thirty years. 'Tra la la, no more alimony, tra la la,' he would sing, tapping his fingers on the card-table. He attended neither the funeral nor the memorial service at the Grosvenor Chapel, nor did he contribute to the purchase of the sculpture presented in her memory to the Victoria & Albert Museum.

In his own last years Maugham thought constantly about death and about what form his end would take. 'I am like a passenger waiting for his ship at a war-time port,' he had written on the last page of *A Writer's Notebook*. 'I do not know on which day it will sail, but I am ready to embark at a moment's notice.' He became obsessed with his ageing appearance, standing in front of the looking-glass and deploring his hooded eyes and deeply lined face. And indeed there are many descriptions of Maugham in diaries and memoirs of this period in which the same saurian similes are repeated again and again, a crocodile, a tortoise, 'an iguana sunning itself on a rock'; the diarist Frances Partridge compared Maugham to a chameleon, 'with his pale deeply furrowed face, sunken glittering eyes and the mouth that opens deliberately and sometimes sticks there'; while Harold Nicolson was 'reminded of the lizards that creep slowly over the dry boulders of the Galapagos Islands'; Glenway Wescott conjured up a more cheerful image after seeing his host wearing nothing but a straw hat poised to jump into his swimming-pool: '[Willie] was shapely but tiny and with his little pot-belly he looked like the King of the Frogs in the fairy tale.' Yet Maugham in old age remained nimble and fit; he was still sexually active, not only with Alan but with boys brought by Searle to the villa: he saw sex as one of the physical appetites it was healthy to indulge, he told Wescott; and he still enjoyed his food and drink, looking forward to the pre-prandial cocktail (the martinis now made with a dash of absinthe) and continuing to take an informed interest in the ordering of menus for lunch and dinner.

As he neared the end of the 1950s, 'a seedy relic of the Edwardian era' as he wrily described himself, Maugham rarely invited his friends to stay. 'Things I could do with pleasure years ago now exhaust me,' he wrote aged eighty-five to Gerald Kelly. 'I am always (or nearly always) glad if people I like will come & lunch with me, but that is all the entertaining I can do.' Among his favourites as luncheon guests were two men also far from their first youth, Winston Churchill and the Canadian press baron Lord Beaverbrook, proprietor of the *Express* newspapers. Churchill was often on the Riviera, and as an exact contemporary Maugham could not resist remarking on how much fitter he was than his old friend, who, with his pink complexion and wispy white hair looked like 'a poor old celluloid doll', walking with great difficulty and taking in little of what was said. 'If you think I'm g-g-g-ga-ga,' Maugham would crow, 'you should see W-W-W-Winston.' Max Beaverbrook, on the other hand, five years younger, was still vigorous and spry, and when he was in residence at his villa on Cap d'Ail the two men regularly visited each other, in between sending their chauffeurs to ferry over little gifts of figs or pots of marmalade.

If few friends were invited to stay, an exception was always made for members of the family. Maugham was fond of Liza and the grandchildren, and of his nieces and, despite his sometimes questionable behaviour, of Robin, although it had long been clear that Robin's high-flying ambitions for himself were unlikely to be realised. In 1941 when Robin had stayed with his uncle in South Carolina, he had talked a great deal about his plans for the future and his desire to write. Maugham had been supportive, if uneasy about certain facets of Robin's character, in particular a lack of application and a tendency towards showing off. 'Robin's handicap has always been that he was not interested in people for their own sake but only for the impression he was making on them,' he told Kate Bruce. 'That's not the attitude that makes a good writer.' Since the war Robin had failed to make a success of anything: he had given up the law, had failed at farming, and despite a brief success with a novella, *The Servant*,★ later made into a film, his writing remained unremarkable, giving rise to a suspicion that it was not writing *per se* that attracted Robin so much as the lavish lifestyle with which a few practitioners, notably his uncle, were rewarded. '[Robin] is as frivolous & scatter-brained as he was as a boy,' Maugham complained as Robin approached his fortieth birthday.

> He has never grown up. He mixes with very disreputable people & throws his money around in the most reckless fashion. He has tried all sorts of ways of making a living . . . & hasn't made a success of any of them . . . It is all a terrible pity; he was a nice lad . . . [and] might have amounted to something if he hadn't been so self-satisfied and fond of the bottle.

For Maugham it was Robin's habitual heavy drinking that gave rise to the greatest anxiety, having seen at close quarters how effectively alcohol could wreck a career. 'It has been my ill-fortune to live much among drunkards,' he had written in his introduction to *A Choice of Kipling's Prose*, 'and for my part I have found them boring at their best and

---

★ It was Maugham who persuaded Robin to replace his relatively upbeat ending with a bleak, and truer, alternative. The film version of *The Servant* (1963) owes its enduring success to a screenplay by Harold Pinter, to Joseph Losey as director, and to a masterly performance by Dirk Bogarde in the title role.

disgusting at their worst.' When in his cups Robin could be both, and his uncle's tolerance was wearing thin. On his father's death Robin had inherited the viscountcy, and as the second Lord Maugham had immediately begun throwing his weight around, spending heavily to impress his attendant court of rent-boys and hangers-on, confident that on his uncle's death he would become a very rich man. However, his expectations in that direction were less secure than he knew. The trust that Maugham had set up for Robin before the war had increased considerably in value, but Maugham had grown so alarmed by his nephew's irresponsible behaviour that he decided to reduce it, siphoning off a substantial part into the settlement he had made for Liza and her children. Maugham saw no reason to inform his nephew of his action (it would be Alan who would take it upon himself to do that): Robin would still have a capital sum of $50,000, the interest on which, he considered, would yield a more than adequate annual income.

Liza's visits every summer were always an agreeable distraction. Maugham, who adored babies and young children, had been infinitely beguiled by Nic and Camilla when they were small, and was equally charmed by the two little boys of Liza's second marriage, Julian, born in 1950, and Jonathan two years later. With his son-in-law he had nothing in common: he and John maintained the civilities, but privately Maugham found the man a bore, a dry stick, and it was tacitly agreed that whenever possible Liza should come without him. Especially for the two elder children the Mauresque was a magical place: they knew they had to be on their best behaviour with their grandfather, whose patience might suddenly give way and whose temper could be terrifying, but there were the enormous garden, the tennis-court, the swimming-pool – and there was Alan. Alan had become a playmate, a confidant, ever ready with a giggle and a joke, making them collapse with laughter as he gave them a comic rendition of his exploits with the sailor-boys down at the port the night before. As Maugham in his old age grew increasingly unpredictable, it was good, devoted Alan to whom everyone turned, Alan who seemed so kind and capable, soothing his employer, reassuring the visitors, and making everything all right. None of the family, not the children, not Liza herself, had any inkling that he detested them and was determined to do them down. And yet with hindsight there are a few indications that all was not quite as it appeared. In retrospect both Nic and Camilla remembered occasions when Alan tried to coax them into naughty behaviour which would have got them into serious trouble; and several of Maugham's friends detected a more complex personality behind the cheeky-chappy façade, saw something unctuous and money-grubbing in his demeanour. 'Alan', wrote Christopher Isherwood's boyfriend Don Bachardy, 'is not nearly as simple and unimpressive as he pretends to be,' while Alan Pryce-Jones described Searle as 'an intriguer, a schemer with a keen eye to his own advantage, a troublemaker'.

The origins of Alan's vindictiveness towards Maugham's family are obscure. Alan Searle was a sweet-natured man who, as his previous career demonstrated, genuinely loved to do good;★ his devotion to Maugham was absolute; he had never been a gold-digger, out to amass a fortune; and yet from the moment he arrived at the Mauresque he became obsessed, dangerously and irrationally obsessed, by a conviction that Liza and John Hope were scheming to cheat him, to grab for themselves what rightly belonged to him. Maugham had always been generous with Alan. He had set up a trust, as he had in the past for Gerald, which would provide him with a comfortable income for life, and he frequently made him presents, not only of money and clothes – a mink-lined overcoat, on one occasion – but paintings and even his own manuscripts, which were fetching high prices at auction in London and New York.† And yet none of this reassured Searle. There must have been some profound insecurity embedded in his past that led him so bitterly to resent Liza's position as Maugham's only child. Perhaps a clue is to be found in a line written in an autobiographical memorandum discovered after his death: 'Parents subjected me to appalling mental cruelty.' Whatever the origins of his delusion, Alan over the years worked himself up into a state of bitter hatred for Liza, and by extension for her husband and children, a hatred he continually harped on to several of Maugham's closest friends. 'I'm always thinking about the future and getting scared as to what will happen to me after I no longer have Willie to care for me . . . his family, of course, are longing to cut my throat, so I am afraid . . . I am in for a pretty rough time.' Occasionally and in diluted form he expressed his anxieties to his employer, but Maugham bored by his companion's endless complaining was briskly dismissive. 'What will become of me when you die?' Alan would whine. 'You'll have to go into lodgings,' Maugham teased him, and when Alan's eyes welled with tears, he would snap at him, 'Oh, stop it, you silly cunt.'

---

★ Alan continued his prison work while in France, volunteering to sit with condemned men during their final hours.

† In 1960, for example, the University of Texas paid the then very high price of £1,200 for the manuscript of the novella *Up at the Villa*, which Maugham had donated to raise money for the London Library.

In his determination to defeat what he saw as the Hopes' wicked plans, Searle now determined do everything he could to turn Maugham against them. Yet here he had to tread carefully. Maugham was no fool, and it would be self-defeating openly to criticise Liza in front of him. But then by chance the ideal occasion presented itself, arising from a decision of Maugham's to sell his collection of Impressionist paintings. Now there fell into Alan's lap the perfect opportunity to make trouble, trouble that was eventually to grow, to dominate and wholly destroy not only the end of Maugham's life and his relationship with his daughter but his standing in the eyes of the world before and after his death and for years to come.

By the mid-1950s Maugham's picture collection had grown enormously in value. Of the thirty or so works of art bought since the beginning of the war nine had been purchased in Liza's name, including the Renoir nude and a Picasso: legally they were hers, but it was understood that they should remain at the villa for her father's lifetime. During Liza's visits in the summer Maugham enjoyed talking to her about her pictures and about his will, in which he had left her almost everything; since 1954 she had been the majority shareholder in the company that owned the Mauresque, formed in order to bypass death-duties, but he also wanted the villa's contents, his money and his royalties to go to her and the children. 'I want you to know that you are going to be extremely well off,' he would tell her. 'You are going to be an extremely rich woman.' Liza was a little embarrassed by these conversations, she said, but 'it was always a friendly atmosphere and I thought it was very generous, naturally'. Her father took care to go over with her every detail of her substantial inheritance, and it was during one of these conversations that he shocked her by revealing that she had been born before he married her mother, a fact of which she had been wholly unaware. Recounting the circumstances of her birth, he explained that in his will he had deliberately referred to her not only by name but specifically as 'my daughter', in case anyone should question her status after his death.

And there matters might have rested had it not been for Maugham's sudden decision to sell his collection. In 1960 there had been a series of well-organised art thefts along the Côte d'Azur, and these had alarmed him, his disquiet increased by the mayor of Saint-Jean who called on him one day to warn him that his paintings were bound to be targeted. Unwilling to put up with the nuisance of strong-rooms and burglar alarms, he contacted Sotheby's, the Bond Street auction house, and plans were put in place for a high-profile sale to be held in the spring of 1962;

this would be accompanied by a short essay by Maugham about his pictures, *Purely for My Pleasure*, handsomely bound and illustrated with colour plates. Everything was to go, including the Gauguin on the glass panel in Maugham's study, and further to increase the impact of the sale Maugham persuaded the Hopes to include Liza's nine pictures with the rest. 'It will also be very nice for you both,' he said, 'as you can have the money now and not wait for my death.' This was amicably agreed between them during his daughter's annual visit to the Mauresque in August 1961. After she had returned home, Liza wrote to thank him for her stay, as she always did, and she also confirmed her consent to the selling of her paintings with his.

In October Maugham as usual came to London, and Liza telephoned him at the Dorchester to arrange a meeting. But instead of her father, Alan answered, sounding strangely overwrought: he must come round and see her at once, he said, as there was something he needed urgently to discuss. On arrival at the Hopes' house in Chelsea, Alan abruptly informed Liza that her father had been made so angry by her 'aggressive' letter that he refused either to speak to her or to see her. She must on no account try to contact him, said Searle, but meanwhile he himself would try to calm the old man down and do his best to effect a reconciliation. Stunned, Liza at first agreed to do as she was told, but when after a week she had heard nothing she again telephoned the Dorchester. Again Alan answered, this time telling her that her father was beside himself with rage, still refused to see her, and was now insisting that she give up at least 50 per cent of her share of the proceeds of the sale. She must obey, said Alan, as Maugham was in a terrible state, his condition was fast deteriorating, and if there were any recalcitrance on her part he could not answer for the consequences. Appalled by Alan's account and seriously worried, Liza wrote to her father. 'Dearest Daddy, You really are making me quite miserable by refusing to see me,' she began.

> When I think how well we have got on, and what happy times we have had even as recently as six weeks ago when you were so sweet to the children, and we all had such fun at the Mauresque . . . How can you suddenly turn on me when I have done absolutely nothing? Please let me come and see you and don't let's have any more of this awful rift.

In reply she received a solicitor's letter insisting that it was not possible for Mr Maugham to meet Lady John while there were certain matters under dispute between them. Mystified and disturbed, Liza wrote a note to her father asking him please to explain what was going on. This note she attached to the lawyer's letter, giving both to Searle, who had again been round to see her and had again pressed her to take half the proceeds of the sale.

This second visit of Searle's was on a Friday. On Monday Liza was telephoned by Alan, who to her astonishment said that her father would like her to come to tea. Searle gave her strict instructions, however, not to mention the pictures. 'As far as he's concerned the whole thing is forgotten.'

Or could it be that Maugham knew nothing of the matter? Certainly the subject of the sale was never mentioned. Liza found her father 'very pleasant and friendly', and, extraordinarily, it was as though he were unaware that anything disagreeable had passed between them. A few days later he and Alan returned to the south of France.

The sale, which realised £592,200 ($1,466,864), took place at Sotheby's on 10 April 1962. Maugham remained at the Mauresque, but Searle, who had been much involved with the preparations, came over to London for the occasion. The night before the auction he called on Liza, and talked to her in a manner which both shocked and frightened her. Red in the face and highly emotional, he said her father was determined not to let her have a penny of the picture money, and that if she pressed for it he would disinherit her children. But Liza was not Syrie's daughter for nothing: by now furious, she told Searle that if any attempt were made to deprive her of what was rightly hers she would fight it in court, at which Alan shouted that she was 'a damn fool' and slammed out of the house.

From that moment open war was declared between Maugham and his only child, a source of profound unhappiness to them both. It was only after Maugham's death that Liza began to suspect how deeply implicated Alan Searle must have been in the traumatic breakdown of her relationship with her father; only later, she said, that she realised 'Alan must have had a hand in it.'[*] Now nearly ninety, Maugham was a very old man, his mind was deteriorating, his grip on reality becoming increasingly fragile. With Alan by his side, a podgy Iago constantly briefing against the family, it is hardly surprising that Maugham became convinced of their treachery and greed. Searle's letters to his cronies on the subject give a startling insight into the depth of his hostility. Liza, 'his vile so-called daughter',

---

[*] In a letter to *The Times* more than thirty years later Nicolas Paravicini recalled that 'my mother's repeated attempts to see or even speak to her father when he became ill were continually thwarted by Alan Searle, thus making any reconciliation impossible, to my mother's lasting sadness' (16.1.99).

was 'a scavenger . . . a bitch . . . [who] fills my heart with murder. She goes around saying "I love my daddy, and I want to be with him." I wonder she doesn't drop dead . . . she's only interested in what she can get out of him . . . The greed of these people and their callousness is beyond belief.' He told Maugham that Liza and her husband had been seen at the Mauresque counting the silver, making inventories and walking around as if they owned the place, that Liza was interested only in his money. As Alan knew, Maugham was vulnerable to such propaganda because of his past history – since his pre-war trip to India he had held a grudge against John Hope's family, but more crucial was his miserable marriage and his loathing of Syrie which was as virulently alive as ever: Liza was Syrie's daughter, and he saw too much of Syrie in her ever to forget the association.

By now there seemed little chance of resolution. 'Alan incites Willie against Liza, Willie loathes Lord John Hope, and poor Liza is ill at ease but a cautious, discreet, ambitious girl,' Ann Fleming reported to Evelyn Waugh. Maugham's niece Diana was another who saw faults on both sides, believing that Liza, too, was becoming unreachable by reason. 'There is something in her – perhaps a coldness . . . to do with money,' she observed, and she tried to persuade Liza to show more understanding towards her father. But any retraction was now out of the question. Liza was determined to sue, lawyers were called in, and Alan for one looked forward to his day in court. 'I only hope that he [Maugham] will say all the things that he has kept hidden all these years,' he wrote to Robin. 'It will ruin them [the Hopes] completely . . . and serve them right too.'

The 'hidden things' so ominously hinted at by Alan was a reference to a sensational revelation he had up his sleeve regarding Liza's true paternity: the scandal was not that she had been born out of wedlock, which she now knew, but that Maugham was not her father. Taking full advantage of Maugham's increasing senility, Alan easily convinced him that Syrie had deceived him, that it was not he but any one of half a dozen lovers who might have fathered the child. From there it was a small step to persuade the eighty-nine-year-old Maugham that he should disown Liza and adopt Frank Alan Searle, aged fifty-seven, as his son; and once the adoption had been made official, the obvious next step would be to disinherit Liza and make Alan his heir. On counsel's advice, and to simplify the paternity case, it was decided not to bring up the subject of several lovers, but to argue that because Syrie was still married to Henry Wellcome when Liza was born, and because Wellcome had never disclaimed her as his daughter, then legally Liza was his child, not Maugham's. To make doubly sure that Liza would be left with nothing, Maugham, who by now had been worked up into a state of fury against his daughter, intended also to sue for the return of all gifts made to her on the grounds that over the years she and her children had clearly demonstrated 'gross ingratitude'.

This complicated case was complicated further by the fact that with Maugham domiciled in France it involved both French and English law, with the opposing sides each obliged to hire two teams of lawyers. The process was lengthy, distressing and horrifyingly expensive; inevitably it attracted a great deal of media attention, with the press turning the whole affair into a freak show, a circus of scandal, gossip and sanctimonious morality, embellished by irreverent jokes and jocular cartoons. The French hearing took place *in camera* at the Palais de Justice in Nice, at the end of which on 3 July 1962 the court ruled in Liza's favour, declaring that there was no evidence to show Lady John Hope was not the daughter of Somerset Maugham; that under British law a child born out of wedlock becomes legitimate when the parents marry, and that in France a legitimate child cannot be disinherited; and that the attempted adoption of Alan Searle was invalid ('dire et declarer nul et de nul effet l'acte d'adoption passé entre Mr Somerset MAUGHAM et Mr SEARLE devant Me PASQUILINI, notaire'). In London after much wrangling the quarrel over the ownership of the villa and the proceeds of the Sotheby's sale was settled out of court: Maugham agreed to pay Liza 50 per cent (£229,500) of the money raised by the sale of her nine pictures, as well as her considerable court costs, and she would also retain her right of ownership of the Mauresque. Everything else, the contents of the house, money, royalties, which had always been destined for her and her children, Maugham was now free to leave to whomever he chose.

The legal hearings and accompanying publicity had imposed an enormous strain on Alan. ('I am peace-loving, so you can imagine what a torment all these dreadful law-suits are,' he unblushingly complained. 'None of the quarrels are mine, but I seem to get all the knocks and the odium.') Yet for Maugham it was much worse. Already half demented, he was plunged into a maelstrom of anger and fear, haunted by all the most sulphurous memories of the past and of the torment of his marriage to Syrie. Several of his friends were disturbed by his state of mind, Noël Coward among them. 'He is devoured by retrospective hate of poor Syrie and it has become an obsession,' Noël noted in his diary. The obsession was now to take a material form, following an innocent suggestion of Glenway Wescott's that Maugham should write an autobiography. At first dismissive of the idea, Maugham began to consider it, and during the period of the hostilities with Liza he set to work. Naturally enough, the project was vigorously encouraged by his publishers, and also by Maugham's neighbour, Max Beaverbrook, who scented a richly rewarding subject for serialisation in his newspaper the *Sunday Express*. When finished the book was everything Beaverbrook could have hoped for, but its content appalled Frere, who was the first to see a typescript of 'Looking Back'. It was quite clear to him that its central theme, a vitriolic account of the author's marriage, was the product of an unsound mind, that Maugham, in short, had taken leave of his senses, and that he must be protected from having his dotage exposed. Honourably, he refused to publish 'Looking Back', and persuaded Doubleday to do the same. But Beaverbrook had no such qualms. Working with the eager co-operation of Alan Searle, the work's dedicatee, Beaverbrook played his hand cleverly, persuading Maugham to add yet more revelations and organising a sensational publicity campaign. Alan, to whom the proceeds had been made over, was delighted to have done so well out of the deal, paid £35,000 for the serialisation by Beaverbrook Newspapers and $250,000 by *Show* magazine in America. 'I am thrilled,' he wrote to Beaverbrook. 'It is a very pleasant feeling to have something secure for the future.'

'Looking Back' is visibly the product of a failing intelligence, in which Maugham rambles over episodes of his life, describing fairly cursorily his childhood and education, his career as a dramatist, his travels, his work in espionage; he ponders on religion and philosophy, and talks a little of the visual arts; he fondly recalls his affair with Sue Jones; but it is the account he gives of his relationship with Syrie, unfettered and envenomed, that in the eyes of the world made the work both so fascinating and so shocking. His description of Syrie's relentless pursuit of him, of her giving birth in Rome under an assumed name, her attempted suicide in the face of his reluctance to marry her, the frightful quarrels during their time together, her dishonesty in her business dealings – all is retailed in a strangely bland and monotonous tone. At the end of the book Maugham, describing himself as 'a very imperfect and tormented creature', admits that 'I cut a very poor figure,' before adding his familiar mantra, inscribed so often before. 'If I have written it, it is to rid myself of recollections which too often have given me sleepless nights, for I have learned by experience that a sure way to free myself of haunting memories is to set them down in black and white.'

This time, however, the fail-safe formula failed. During the seven weeks that 'Looking Back' ran in the *Sunday Express*, in September and October 1962, 'All hell', as Frere remarked, 'was let loose.' Maugham was inundated by abusive letters, many of them anonymous. 'Everyone is fully aware of the stinking, filthy life you have led,' runs one typical example. 'You are a perfect disgrace to Britain and the sooner you leave this island of ours, the better, together with that boy-friend of yours.' But far more personally wounding was the reaction of many of his friends, to the fore those who had been also friends of Syrie's. 'Entirely contemptible,' said Noël Coward; 'a senile and scandalous work', Graham Greene wrote in a letter to the *Daily Telegraph*; Maugham was 'an obscene little toad', according to Rebecca West; while Garson Kanin described the work as 'shabby, sordid, embarrassing . . . [and] a wildly faggoty thing to have done'. In October, Maugham came over to London as usual, and as usual went to the Garrick. As he entered the bar on the first floor everyone stopped talking, and after a couple of seconds several members ostentatiously walked out. Maugham was devastated. It was borne in upon him that he was to be ostracised, that he had gravely offended, had broken the English gentleman's code of conduct, a code that no one understood better than he, which he had admired, analysed, sometimes mocked, and on the outward observance of which he had based his entire existence. With the writing of 'Looking Back', said Gore Vidal, 'the ancient Maugham mined his own monument; and blew it up'. Alone with Alan, he wept and wept, tortured by guilt, overcome with remorse. The two of them returned to the Mauresque in December, and Maugham never came to England again.

For a man who had achieved such success in life as Somerset Maugham, who had shown such wisdom, such perception in his understanding of human nature, few would have predicted an old age of almost unrelieved anguish. He began to suffer from nightmares from which he awoke terrified, and Searle now slept in Maugham's bedroom so he could comfort him when he awoke, getting up as many as six times in the night; during the day Maugham sat for hours at a time immobilised by despair, crying uncontrollably, refusing to be consoled. Wretchedly unhappy, he was unable to find relief in anything or anywhere. Towards the end of 'Looking Back' he states uncompromisingly that 'I believe neither in the existence of God nor in the immortality of the soul,' and yet the subject of religion, continued to attract and mystify him, while offering neither comfort nor conviction.*

---

* In 'Looking Back' Maugham describes a strange manifestation witnessed on one of his last visits to Venice. He had gone as usual to look at pictures in the Accademia and, feeling tired, had sat down in front of Veronese's *The Feast at the House of Levi*. In this painting Jesus is shown presiding over the banquet at the centre of a long table, his head in profile, in conversation with John the Baptist seated on his left. As Maugham gazed at it, he suddenly saw Jesus turn and look him full in the face, an optical illusion as later he tentatively explained it, but nonetheless an occurrence that left him profoundly moved.

As he neared his ninetieth year he grew more miserably restless, compelled to travel, as though searching for the safe haven which his own home no longer provided. 'The maps are out,' Alan would report with a sinking heart. 'He is very frail, but longs to be on the move. It is a great anxiety for me.' And indeed, with Maugham confused and increasingly incontinent, it was becoming impossible to cope, even in the grandest hotels. There had been some nightmarish incidents while staying at the Vier Jahreszeiten in Munich in October 1963, leading Alan to swear, 'Never again will I stir an inch without the valet and a male nurse'; and the following year a trip to Venice was such a disaster that 'we had to come home two weeks early. It has finally taught me that our travelling days are over.'

And yet returning to the Mauresque offered little respite. 'Rarely sensible, and in acute misery', as Searle described him, Maugham knew he was dying and he longed to depart. 'Poor, poor Willie,' Alan wrote to Robin. 'He takes his medicines with reluctance. ' "Don't try to keep me alive" he begs. "Just let me slip away." ' On his ninetieth birthday, 25 January 1964, he was photographed shuffling along the terrace well wrapped up, accompanied by his beloved dachshund George, a present from the Freres. In a birthday interview published in the *Sunday Express*, Maugham was quoted as saying that he still grieved for his mother: 'even today the pain of her passing is as keen as when it happened in our home in Paris'; and that he longed for death: 'I am drunk with the thought of it. It seems to me to offer me the final and absolute freedom.' Occasionally old friends dropped in to see him, among them Noël Coward, who was staying near by. 'I called on Willie Maugham,' he wrote in his diary on 25 August 1965, 'and I am glad I did because he was wretchedly, pathetically grateful. He is living out his last days in a desperate nightmare, poor beast. He barely makes sense and, of course, he *knows* his mind has gone. I managed to cheer him a bit and certainly helped poor Alan who is going through hell.'

Alan was indeed going through hell. Having cried wolf for so many years, he now had serious cause for complaint. Maugham, deaf and with failing eyesight, was helpless, hopeless, and entirely dependent on him for everything. To make matters worse, the old man was subject to violent changes of mood, sometimes tearful and whimpering for sex, on other occasions seemingly possessed by furies, physically attacking Searle with a strength that hardly seemed possible from such a frail and shrunken body. 'I have been shut up with a madman,' Alan wrote desperately to Robin. 'His beastliness is beyond endurance.' He told Jerry Zipkin, 'He lives in some terrifying world of his own which must be grim if his screams and terror are anything to go by.' It was Robin who came most often to the villa, an immense comfort to Searle who, unless there was someone prepared to sit with Maugham, was literally a prisoner in the house; the servants refused to be left alone with their master and would have nothing to do with any nursing, feeding, washing or cleaning up. 'I have a good many very unpleasant chores to perform,' Alan told Glenway Wescott. 'Poor old darling, how he would have hated and loathed it all in the old days.' The staff were also afraid of him: as the old man seemed physically to shrivel so his rages became more ferocious; he was 'like a malignant crab', said Robin, and even he had to summon all his courage to face his uncle at his most maniacal. Yet for Robin these last days at the Mauresque yielded their own rewards. During the hours when the old man was in his right mind, Robin questioned him industriously about his life and the people he had known, scurrying upstairs to his room afterwards to write down every word of the conversation for future use. He also carefully recorded details of the clothes Maugham wore, his moods, his appearance, and even the dishes that were served at meals: 'black double-breasted quilted smoking jacket with purple design. White silk shirt open at neck. Narrow black trousers. Black velvet shoes with his monogram on toes in gold braid . . . Lace table cloth. Pink champagne . . . pea soup, chicken in aspic and green salad, figs in strawberry sauce, cheese. Dates and nuts.' And after Maugham had been put to bed, Robin would interrogate Alan, who needed little persuading to reveal the secrets that over the years Maugham had confided in him, as well as the many episodes that he himself had witnessed.

Robin's last visit was in July 1965, and it was shortly after this that Alan reached the end of his tether. 'Willie is now completely out of his mind and is in a constant state of terror and misery,' he wrote to Ellen Doubleday. 'He rarely knows me now and wanders about the house muttering, muttering and muttering. Sometimes he talks for two or three days and nights without ceasing, and his energy is frightening.' It was now that Alan in desperation decided to make contact with Liza, begging her to come down to the Mauresque. Liza, who had not seen her father for more than four years, arrived on 3 November, met at the station by Searle, who warned her that she would find Maugham 'absolutely mad' and possibly violent. Despite the warning Liza was appalled by the sight of her father, a tiny, wizened figure, his face contorted as he constantly bared his teeth and growled at her, sometimes lunging towards her, his hands like claws. It was plain he had no idea who she was. Alan told her he could no longer go on, that he was at breaking point, and they agreed that Maugham should be brought to England where he could be certified as insane. That evening on the drive back to Beaulieu Alan burst into tears and was still crying as Liza's train drew out of the station.

Events moved swiftly after Liza's departure. At the beginning of December Maugham tripped on a corner of carpet, fell and cut his head, and shortly afterwards he developed pneumonia. An ambulance was called and he was taken to the Anglo-American Hospital in Nice, where he could be looked after by his personal physician, Dr Rosanoff. Here Maugham remained for over a week, lying semi-comatose in a ground-floor room whose French windows looked out on to a garden and a distant view of the Mediterranean. Camped outside the main entrance of the hospital was a growing crowd of reporters, photographers and cameramen, to whom a daily briefing was delivered with considerable élan by the flamboyant Dr Rosanoff, proud of his sudden celebrity status and enjoying every moment of his performance. Meanwhile in his hospital room Maugham grew restless, disturbed by the strong mistral blowing outside which rattled the windows. A young English nurse who came in to sit with him found her patient anxious and confused, desperately in need of comfort. When she tucked in his blankets, he asked her to get into bed with him. 'It wasn't sexual,' she said, 'he wanted comfort'; he wanted to be held as his mother had held him when he was a small child, and she fetched a soft bolster and laid it up against his back which seemed to soothe him. During the early hours of 16 December Maugham died, barely a month short of his ninety-second birthday. The doctor on duty was summoned. 'Il est mort,' he confirmed. Alan was telephoned and within the hour arrived from the Mauresque. Quickly and under cover of darkness Maugham's body was carried into the car and driven back to the villa, from where during the course of the morning it was announced to the world that Somerset Maugham had died in his bed at home, thus avoiding the autopsy that would otherwise have been required.

The body was laid out, and for several days neighbours came in to pay their respects and the press descended en masse. The cremation took place in Marseilles on 20 December, with only Alan present. In a stupor of weariness and grief he sat in a waiting-room at the crematorium for what seemed like hours, holding the small urn he had brought to receive the ashes. Eventually a man appeared carrying a tray covered by a linen cloth. Removing the cloth he revealed several long greyish-white bones, too big to have been consumed in the fire, and asked if he might break them up so that they would fit into the casket. Producing a hammer from his pocket he went to work with enthusiasm, at which point Searle, overcome, ran out into the street and vomited. Two days later, on 22 December, Maugham's ashes were interred outside the Maugham Library at the King's School, Canterbury, the ceremony presided over by the Headmaster and by the Dean of Canterbury, in the presence of boys from the school and a small group of mourners led by Liza, her husband and her four children.

When Maugham's will was read Alan Searle learned he was to be a very rich man. The Villa Mauresque went to Liza, who also kept the original financial settlements made for herself and her family. Robin, too, retained his trust fund, the income from which he supplemented by writing a series of memoirs of his uncle; within weeks of Maugham's death he had outed him as a homosexual in a mass-circulation Sunday newspaper, and continued to supply the market with more of the same, in *Conversations with Willie*, *Somerset and All the Maughams*, *Escape from the Shadows*, *Search for Nirvana* and so on. There were bequests of £2,000 each for Annette and for Jean the chauffeur, and Maugham's portrait by Edouard McEvoy was willed to the city of Nice. Everything else, the contents of the villa, all money, all investments, all royalties, all proceeds from the sale of manuscripts were left to Alan for his lifetime, the residue after his death to go to the Royal Literary Fund in London for the relief of impoverished writers. Yet, despite all his scheming, Alan derived little pleasure from his immense bequest. He moved into an expensive apartment in Monte Carlo which he filled with treasures from the Mauresque; as he had done with his master, he continued to travel, staying in luxurious suites at the Dorchester in London, the Gritti in Venice, the Plaza in New York, where he spent extravagantly on boys, clothes and enormous meals. And yet Alan was not happy: he was lonely, he missed Maugham and the glamorous life they had led together, and he soon succumbed to ill-health; he grew enormously fat, suffered painfully from arthritis and later from Parkinson's Disease. Shortly before he died in 1985, aged eighty, he confessed to Ann Fleming, one of the few of Maugham's friends who kept in touch, that he bitterly regretted having caused such trouble.

After his death the reputation of Somerset Maugham suffered the inevitable decline of renowned writers, the decline that especially follows a long career which has been lived much in the public eye and in tune with its times. In the 1960s the times were rapidly changing, and few cared to read then of the old order, of the days of Empire, of district officers in the jungle or the wiles of wives in repressive Edwardian marriages. Maugham would not have been surprised. 'The first little splutter of interest that follows a person's death in the case of a writer is followed by some years of neglect,' he wrote in 1946. 'Then if there is in his work anything of enduring value, interest in him is renewed. But the dead period may well last twenty or thirty years.' This was prescient, for the last couple of decades have seen a remarkable revival of the work of this extraordinary man. Maugham learned very young to be wary and secretive in his personal life, which was full of pain, but in his writing he found happiness and release. He described the act of creation as 'the most enthralling of human activities', the one place where the writer can find solace, 'can tell his secret yet not betray it'. His love for his art, his single-minded dedication made him one of the most popular and prolific writers who ever lived, and it is safe to say now that he will again hold generations in thrall, that his place is assured: Somerset Maugham, the great teller of tales.

# Acknowledgements

I am enormously grateful to the many people and institutions who have helped me during the writing of this biography. I would like in particular to express my gratitude to the Royal Literary Fund, holders of the copyright and executors of the literary estate of Somerset Maugham, and also to the Trustees of the literary estate, for allowing me freely to quote from Maugham's work and correspondence. Secondly, I would like to put on record my heartfelt thanks for the generosity of Neil and Reiden Jenman, who offered me the most warm-hearted hospitality while allowing me unrestricted access to their extensive Maugham collection. I would also like to thank Harry Frere for his kindness in making available the transcripts of his mother's conversations with Liza Maugham.

I owe sincere thanks to the following for their contributions to this book: Kate Amcott-Wilson, Mark Amory, Alan Anderson, Professor William Baker, Frith Banbury, Nicolas Barker, Jonathan Bates, Michael Bloch, Adrian Bridgewater, Katherine Bucknell, Michael Burn, Peter Burton, John Byrne, Comtesse Chandon de Briailles, Aleid Channing, Anne Channing, Colette Clark, John Clay, Lisa Cohen, John Coldstream, Sally Connely, Bryan Connon, Robert Conquest, Anthony Curtis, Caroline Cuthbert, Timothy D'Arch-Smith, Lady Daubeny, Richard Davenport-Hines, Mary Dawson, Winton Dean, Nelson Doubleday Jr, Charles Duff, Lord Dunluce, Sue Fox, David Freeman, Jean Frere, Lord Glendevon, the Earl of Gowrie, John Haffenden, Andrew Harvey, Nicholas Haslam, Doreen Hawkins, Peter Haxton, Tim Heald, Belinda Hollyer, Jonathan Hope, Glenn Horowitz, Barry Humphries, Bruce Hunter, Paul Hunter, Alan Judd, Zbigniew Kantorosinski, P. J. Kavanagh, H. K. Kelland, John Kenworthy-Browne, Alice Leader, Andrew Lycett, James McDonnell, Diana Marr-Johnson, Chris Maxse, Joan Morley, Patrick O'Connor, Nicolas Paravicini, June Pearson, Paul Pollak, Tom Sargant, Professor Lewis Sawin, Tony Scotland, David Shackleton, Stella Shawzin, Craig V. Showalter, Malcolm Sinclair, Tom Stacey, James Stourton, David Twiston Davies, Hugo Vickers, C. M. Vines, Michael Watkins, Vivienne Waugh, Christopher

Wilkinson, Lindy Woodhead, Howard Woolmer, David Worthington, Samantha Wyndham.

Among the following libraries and archives I would like to single out for especial thanks the Howard Gotlieb Archival Research Center at the University of Boston, and the Harry Ransom Humanities Research Center at the University of Texas at Austin. I would also like to thank: Bancroft Library, University of California; Barnardo's; Beinecke Rare Book and Manuscript Library, Yale; Berg Collection, New York Public Library; Bodleian Library, Oxford University; British Library; Cornell University, New York; University of Delaware Library; Eton College Library; Fales Library, New York University; Garrick Club; Jacob Rader Center of American Jewish Archives; Keble College, Oxford University; Kent County Council Centre for Kentish Studies; King's School, Canterbury; Library of Congress, Washington DC; Lilly Library, University of Indiana, Bloomington, Indiana; the London Library; McFarlin Library, University of Tulsa; Mander and Mitchenson Theatre Collection, Jerwood Library of the Performing Arts, Trinity College of Music, Greenwich; Margaret Herrick Library, Academy of Motion Picture Arts and Sciences, Beverly Hills, California; University of Maryland Library; National Trust; New York Public Library; Princeton University Library; Public Record Office, The National Archives, Kew; Random House Group Archive; St John's College Library, Cambridge University; Stanford University Library; University of Sussex Library; Texas A&M University; Victoria and Albert Museum Theatre Collections; Wake Forest University Library, North Carolina; Warburg Institute; Wellcome Library; Whitstable Museum; Z. Smith Reynolds Library, Wake Forest University, Winston-Salem, North Carolina.

I am immensely grateful to Julie Kavanagh for her kind support during the writing of this book and for her unfailing editorial eye. I would also like to give most sincere thanks to Professor T. F. Staley and Professor R. F. Foster for their invaluable criticism, encouragement and advice.

Every reasonable effort has been made to trace the holders of copyright and I very much regret if inadvertent omissions have been made: these can be rectified in any future editions.

# Notes

## CHAPTER 1: A BLACKSTABLE BOYHOOD

1. 'The lives of modern writers': *Sunday Express* 16.4.55
4. 'une femme charmante': *Gil Blas: Hebdomadaire Illustré* (Paris) 6.2.1882
5. 'Because he never': *The Summing Up* p.16
6. '[The servant] opened the door': *Of Human Bondage* p. 5
7. 'cher papa, chere maman': Jeffrey Meyers *Somerset Maugham* p. 10
8. 'well above the ordinary': Francis Oppenheimer *Stranger Within* (Faber 1960) p. 132
10. '[He] opened a large cupboard': *Of Human Bondage* p. 10
    'I can still remember': *The Summing Up* p. 19
11. My father was a stranger': Robin Maugham *Somerset and All the Maughams* p. 110
    'It was the end of a home': Viscount Maugham *At the End of the Day* p. 19
12. 'one link with all': Robin Maugham *Somerset and All the Maughams* p. 118
    'I shall never forget': ibid. p. 117
    'He had had so little love': *A Writer's Notebook* p. 261
    'he was very narrow-minded': Viscount Maugham *At the End of the Day* p. 19
13. 'the hall was paved': *Of Human Bondage* p. 15
    '*Of Human Bondage*': ibid. p. 3
14. 'The vicar, having said grace': ibid. p. 17
    '[Mr Carey] pointed out': ibid. p. 16
    'he was fond of children': Robin Maugham *Somerset and All the Maughams* p. 157
    'A parson is paid': *A Writer's Notebook* p. 2
15. 'I'll hear you say it': 'Looking Back' p. 10
    'His aunt was not sorry': *Of Human Bondage* p. 29
16. 'She was never ill': *Cakes and Ale* p. 56
    'in his secret soul': *Of Human Bondage* p. 30
17. 'His guardians would rigidly take care': letter of Hubert Collar to Robert Cordell 2.8.61 Texas A&M
    'The banker had a little boy': *Of Human Bondage* p. 34
18. 'There was a long queue': Robin Maugham *Somerset and All the Maughams* p. 121
    'The three older brothers': ibid. p. 123
19. 'My uncle always took dummy': *Of Human Bondage* 82
    'The walk through the darkness': ibid. p. 28
20. 'In winter it was as if': *Mrs Craddock* p. 273
21. 'the most delightful habit': *Of Human Bondage* p. 38
    'He did not know': ibid. p. 38
22. 'Tell him I stammer, Uncle': 'Looking Back' p. 11
23. 'I have never forgotten', 'He did not much like me', 'The Master was a Scot': 'Looking Back' p. 12
    'that engaging come-hitherness': *The Summing Up* p. 46
24. 'rose like the praise of men': *Of Human Bondage* p. 643

'because they amused him': ibid. p. 78

'that he seemed for a moment': ibid.

25. 'He was impatient and choleric': ibid. p. 68

'I adored him': *Cantuarian* December 1965

26. 'There was a wonderfully cobwebbed feeling': *The Vagrant Mood* (Mandarin 1998) p. 192

'an odd feeling in his heart': *Of Human Bondage* p. 74

27. 'In fact, I did not like either': *Cakes and Ale* p. 64

'accepted the conventions': ibid. p. 87

'We thought London people vulgar': ibid. p. 36

'He prayed with all the power': *Of Human Bondage* p. 57

28. 'someone I went to bed with': Alan Searle interview with Robert Calder 16.3.77 Jenman

'since our mother died': Robin Maugham *Conversations with Willie* p. 56

'I chose the name Ashenden': WSM to Mollie Ashenden 9.2.54 KSC

29. 'I made up my mind': 'Looking Back' p. 13

'I knew exactly what to do': ibid.

'In a flash there appeared': *Of Human Bondage* p. 99

# CHAPTER 2: AT ST THOMAS'S HOSPITAL

31. 'He did not much like me': *The Summing Up* p. 58

32. 'The whole horrible structure': *Of Human Bondage* p. 131

34. 'honestly mistook his sensuality': ibid. p. 135

35. 'the delights of those easy': *The Summing Up* p. 187

36. 'There emerged the vague rumour': *Of Human Bondage* p. 84

'If you don't get up at once': *Cakes and Ale* p. 109

37. 'in such a way as to': *Of Human Bondage* p. 182

39. 'I complained of the abnormality': *The Summing Up* p. 67

'I tried to persuade myself': Robin Maugham *Escape from the Shadows* p. 232

'The friendship of animal attraction': *A Writer's Notebook* p. 10

'I do not remember': ibid. p. 11

40. 'I entered little into the life': *The Summing Up* p. 60

'I was writing': WSM to the *Academy* 13.9.1897 Princeton

'[James] was greeted with such an outburst': *The Vagrant Mood* p. 163

41. 'Why, this is fine!': T. F. G. Jones *The Various Lives of Wentworth Huyshe* (Campden & District Historical and Archaeological Society 1998) p. 53

'I can never forget': WSM to Wentworth Huyshe 30.8.1897 HRHRC

43. 'did not want large airy rooms': *Of Human Bondage* p. 647

'treated like a crowned head': WSM to Norman Horne 19.3.37 Lilly

'I was bitterly disappointed': *Purely for My Pleasure* p. 6

'I lived laborious days': *The Painted Veil* p. viii

'I admired everything Ruskin told me': *The Summing Up* p. 96

44. 'such was my innocence': *The Painted Veil* p. viii

'They could write and draw and compose': *The Summing Up* p. 72

'That was strong meat': *Purely for My Pleasure* p. 6

46. 'The waiting for work': Viscount Maugham *At the End of the Day* p. 59
'The other day I went into the theatre': *A Writer's Notebook* p. 31
'the most enchanting spot': *The Summing Up* p. 96

47. 'I thought it all grand': ibid.

48. 'Its reputation as a decomposer': Compton Mackenzie *Extraordinary Women* (Secker 1929) p. 25

49. 'dear companion of my lonely youth': Frederick T. Bason *A Bibliography of the Writings of William Somerset Maugham* (Unicorn Press 1931) p. 9
'Few realised the exhaustion': *The Vagrant Mood* p. 192

50. 'There was a part': *The Narrow Corner* p. 40
'Really, the things that go on': *An Ideal Husband* Act II sc. ii

51. 'Oh, I should hate to be old': *A Writer's Notebook* p. 16
'Gentlemen, woman is an animal': ibid. p. 13
'up stinking alleys': *Liza of Lambeth* p. vi

52. 'There is some ability in this': Edward Garnett 20.7.1896 Berg

53. 'I had at that time': *Liza of Lambeth* p. vii

54. 'I described without addition': *The Summing Up* p. 161
'the first of the realistic descriptions': WSM to Paul Dottin 14.9.26 HRHRC
'I caught the colloquial note': *The Summing Up* p. 109
'It wasn't 'is fault': *Liza of Lambeth* p. 99

55. 'They sat there for a long while': ibid. p. 70
'This is the story': Raymond Toole Stott *A Bibliography of the Works of W. Somerset Maugham* p. 17
'A very clever realistic study': Anthony Curtis and John Whitehead (eds) *W. Somerset Maugham: the Critical Heritage* p. 22
'Unwin is indeed a most troublesome person': Charles Scribner 14.6.1897 Princeton

56. 'The whole book reeks of the pot-house': *Daily Mail* 7.9.1897
'Readers who prefer': *Athenaeum* 11.9.1897
'great and well-deserved success': *St Thomas's Hospital Gazette* June 1898
'I've just finished reading Liza': 20.7.1897 Frederick R. Karl and Laurence Davies (eds) *The Collected Letters of Joseph Conrad* vol. I 1861–1897 (Cambridge University Press 1983) p. 361

57. 'Mr Arthur Morrison may afford': *Academy* 11.9.1897
'I have not yet had': WSM to the *Academy* 13.9.1897 Princeton
'a most unpleasant book': private collection

58. 'He had no feeling for the old man': *Of Human Bondage* p. 626
'I think I learned pretty well': WSM to Barbara Kurz April 1961 HGARC
'I am sorry I abandoned': *The Merry-Go-Round* (Penguin 1976) p. 126
'I told him that I was throwing': *Liza of Lambeth* p. viii
'I was no longer interested': *The Summing Up* p. 161

## CHAPTER 3: A WRITER BY INSTINCT

60. 'Life was before him': *Of Human Bondage* p. 671
61. 'I came to it after weary years': *The Land of the Blessed Virgin* p. 51
62. 'have no openness as have the French': ibid. p. 148
    'In Spain the blood of youth is very hot': ibid. p. 48
    'How old are you?': *Don Fernando* p. 53
63. 'But when I write of Spanish women': *The Land of the Blessed Virgin* p. 84
    'a young thing with green eyes': *The Summing Up* p. 98
    'life was too pleasant': ibid.
    'Your successful man of letters': George Gissing *New Grub Street* (Oxford World's Classics 1998) p. 38
64. '[Unwin] did me thoroughly in the eye': WSM to J. B. Pinker 22.9.09 HRHRC
    'Seduced by this bad advice': *The Summing Up* p. 163
65. 'So far as we can see': Edward Garnett readers' reports Berg
    '[Mr Maugham] has written a good novel': *Spectator* 6.8.1898
    'A writing-desk littered with papers': *A Man of Honour* p. 1
66. 'loved the smell of smoke': *The Merry-Go-Round* p. 164
    'He was very good-looking': *Looking Back* p. 25
    'I had a natural lucidity': *The Summing Up* p. 22
    'Of course I was disappointed': WSM to Maurice Colles 28.2.1899 Lilly
67. 'It is true that "Stephen Carey"': WSM to Maurice Colles 10.11.1898 Berg
    'are all a little flat': Edward Garnett readers' reports Berg
    'Daisy as Dick Whittington': *Orientations* p. 252
68. 'Daisy walked down the High Street': ibid. p. 276
    'at the time was not very familiar': *Liza of Lambeth* p. xvi
69. 'an average book, fairly readable': *London Bookman* July 1899
    'The best writing we have yet seen': *Athenaeum* 17.6.1899
    'Mr Maugham begins to be interesting': *Academy* 1.7.1899
    'the dark brown eyes': Louis Marlow *Seven Friends* (Richards Press 1953) p. 144
    'The world is an entirely different place': *A Writer's Notebook* p. 221
    'I saw no reason to subordinate': *The Summing Up* p. 88
    'almost continuously in love': WSM to Kate Bruce 3.4.29 Berg
    'He is a fearfully emotional man': Barbara Belford *Violet: The Story of the Irrepressible Violet Hunt* (Simon & Schuster 1990) p. 116
70. 'a little strong' WSM to Maurice Colles 10.11.1898 Berg
    'too indecent for publication': *Colles v. Maugham* in the High Court of Justice, King's Bench Division 1908 HRHRC
    'finally I have erased': WSM to Maurice Colles 31.7.1899 Berg
    'I should have lost a subject': *The Summing Up* p. 187
    'as merely an insignificant curiosity': speech to Library of Congress 1950
71. 'Young writers were not introduced': Osbert Sitwell *Noble Essences or Courteous Revelations* (Macmillan 1950) p. 38

'the most interesting and consistently amusing': *The Summing Up* p. 4
'I never ceased to be fascinated': *The Moon and Sixpence* p. 10

72. 'a curious little home life': Nancy Mitford *The Water Beetle* (Hamish Hamilton 1962) p. 41
'He was not what people call': *The Vagrant Mood* p. 28
'I do not think he was': ibid. p. 26
'innately and intensely frivolous': WSM to Dean 10.2.50 Maryland

73. 'God is a gentleman': Cecil Roberts *The Pleasant Years 1947–1972* (Hodder & Stoughton 1974) p. 129
'an intolerably tedious' *The Vagrant Mood* p. 4
'I prefer to call the conveyance': ibid. p.39

74. 'the conventional rules were swept away': Lady St Helier *Memories of Fifty Years* (Edward Arnold 1909) p. 187
'Do you like cigars?': *The Vagrant Mood* p. 38

75. 'Often it turned out': Raymond Mortimer interview with Robert Calder 2.11.72 Jenman
'You were different': 'Looking Back' p. 27
'the first rent': *A Choice of Kipling's Prose* p. xx

76. 'the recollection of Mary came back': *The Hero* p. 305
'To James . . . that physical repulsion': ibid. p. 340
'The touch of her fingers': ibid. p. 40
'is ugly and beastly': ibid. p. 208
'an honest piece of work': *Liza of Lambeth* p. xvii
'an oak tree, just bursting into leaf': *The Hero* p. 333
'The western clouds of the sunset': *A Writer's Notebook* p. 34

78. 'Bertha looked at him': ibid p. 257

79. 'Women are like chickens': ibid. p. 88
'It puzzled him sometimes': ibid. p. 45
'My recollection lingers with most pleasure': *Books & Bookmen* May 1922
'[Gerald] was certainly not at all shy': *Mrs Craddock* p. 224

80. '[If] you are afraid': *Bookman* December 1902
'a substantial success': *Liza of Lambeth* p. xviii

## CHAPTER 4: LE CHAT BLANC

81. 'it seemed less difficult': *The Summing Up* p. 109

82. 'The shriek of execration': Michael Meyer *Ibsen* (Penguin 1985) p. 686

83. 'You don't know what it is': *A Man of Honour* p. 154
'brimming over with other people's ideas': *The Summing Up* p. 112
'very vain & full of self-conceit': WSM to Maurice Colles 7.11.03 Beinecke

84. 'Went to the first night': Kate Bruce unpublished ms private collection
'I'm glad my little brother': Robin Maugham *Somerset and All the Maughams* p. 164
'a long Scandinavian night' *Athenaeum* 28.2.03
'Not for a long time': *Sunday Special* 1.3.03

'is admirably conceived and written': *Saturday Review* 28.2.03

'I was not satisfied': *The Summing Up* p. 111

85. 'Now that the author': *Illustrated London News* 27.2.04

'There is no reason to suppose': *Saturday Review* 5.3.04

'I can see now the shy young author': Raymond Mander and Joe Mitchenson *Theatrical Companion to Maugham* p. 20

'Harry told me that my plays': Robin Maugham *Conversations with Willie* p. 56

'He needed a lot of understanding': Robin Maugham *Somerset and All the Maughams* p. 163

'Very much homosexual': Rebecca West interview with Robert Calder 14.9.76 Jenman

86. 'I'm sure it wasn't only failure': Robin Maugham *Somerset and All the Maughams* p. 165

'pale and grave': unpublished ms private collection

'violently pessimistic': *The Summing Up* p. 27

87. 'must at some time have been ill-treated': unpublished ms private collection

'both wept easily at plays': unpublished ms private collection

'Times are very hard': WSM to Wentworth Huyshe n.d. HRHRC

88. 'If you hear of anyone': WSM to Maurice Colles n.d. HGARC

'I was anxious to see you': WSM to Maurice Colles 19.7.02 Lilly

'Behold three short stories': WSM to Maurice Colles 3.7.04 Berg

'an honourable condition': *The Magician* p. vi

'The whole thing was, of course': Laurence Housman *The Unexpected Years* (Cape 1937) p. 202

89. 'I rather like her': James T. Boulton and Linden Vasey (eds) *The Letters of D. H. Lawrence* vol. V (Cambridge University Press 1989) p. 98

'My "affair" is over': WSM to Violet Hunt n.d. Berg

'I am wishing I need never write': WSM to Violet Hunt n.d. Berg

90. 'I think you have done it': WSM to Violet Hunt n.d. Cornell

'chiefly, I think, because it was called': WSM to Edward Marsh 1.4.43 Berg

'between the aestheticism of her early youth': *The Moon and Sixpence* p. 13

91. '[Reggie] told her little scabrous stories': *The Merry-Go-Round* p. 40

'careless into what abyss': ibid. p. 100

'I wrote with affectation': *Liza of Lambeth* p. xix

'I was simply dying for a fag': *The Merry-Go-Round* p. 284

'a certain primness of manner': ibid. p. 10

92. 'If she had been beautiful': Leon Edel *Henry James* (Collins 1987) p. 226

'a queer lot': preface by WSM to Doris Arthur Jones *What a Life!* (Jarrolds 1932)

'didn't quite come off': WSM to David Cecil September 1957 Jenman

'[at least] I am not a porter': Max Beerbohm *Around Theatres* (Hart-Davis 1953) p. 4

93. 'you, my boy, are not one': *Saturday Review* 4.4.08

'He little knew': *Plays* vol. I p. vii

'a strong man, of no very easy temper': *The Merry-Go-Round* p. 35

'Most of what one writes': WSM to Violet Hunt n.d. Cornell

'because I was at the time': *The Summing Up* p. 164

94. 'quite the most dazzling figure': Douglas Goldring *Odd Man Out* (Chapman & Hall 1935) p. 54

'a nice fellow': Keble College, Oxford

'I was constantly failing': Harry Philips to Joseph Dobrinsky 16.9.66 Texas A&M

'We took a great liking to each other': ibid.

'I cannot help thinking': WSM to Gerald Kelly n.d. HGARC

95. 'She had a certain hold over him': *The Merry-Go-Round* p. 171

'Money was like a sixth sense': *The Summing Up* p. 112

'I see that you have charged me': WSM to Maurice Colles 28.8.04 Lilly

'I should like you to observe': ibid. 12.2.04

'[Mr Maugham] has his pen well under control': *Times Literary Supplement* 26.5.05

'I wrote with jealousy gnawing': *Liza of Lambeth* p. xiii

96. 'It was all very nice': *The Magician* p. vi

'When I am with my brother': WSM to Violet Hunt n.d. Berg

97. 'his whole face was just one colour': *Sunday Times* 24.1.54

'Both of us obstinately refused': ibid.

'to my shame': *The Magician* p. vii

'My dear Gerald, I am very sorry': WSM to Gerald Kelly 26.7.05 HGARC

98. 'Willie was a duck': *The Times* 18.3.69

'who has the ingenious idea': WSM to Gerald Kelly n.d. HGARC

'I cannot say that I was his secretary': Harry Philips to Joseph Dobrinsky 16.9.66 Texas A&M

'He was exceedingly kind': ibid.

99. '[Willie's] interest in paintings was immense': ibid. 14.11.66

'Maugham adored a laugh': ibid. 16.9.66

100. 'I began this letter three days ago': WSM to Gerald Kelly 25.4.05 HGARC

'I suspect he was a tragic figure': Clive Bell *Old Friends* (Chatto & Windus 1956) p. 164

'but unfortunately he took an immediate dislike': 'Looking Back' p. 28

'coldly and bitingly virulent': *The Vagrant Mood* p. 183

101. 'After a moment's hesitation': 'Looking Back' p. 28

'a bed bug, on which a sensitive man': Aleister Crowley *The Spirit of Solitude: An Autohagiography* vol. II (Mandrake Press 1929) p. 243

'I took an immediate dislike to him': *The Magician* p. viii

102. 'like a managing clerk': *The Vagrant Mood* p. 183

'Willie – with his impeccable French accent': *Sunday Times* 24.1.54

'I am dreadfully afraid': WSM to Arthur St John Adcock 14.5.08 Lilly

'[Maugham] has a very calm almost lethargic demeanour': Flower (ed.) *The Journals of Arnold Bennett* vol. I *1896–1910* p. 208

'I didn't very much like him': *The Vagrant Mood* p. 186

103. 'I've told her about you': ibid.

'a very lovable man': ibid. p. 183

'I never saw Maugham moved': Belford *Violet* p. 116

'I was somewhat ashamed': Harry Philips to Joseph Dobrinsky 16.9.66 Texas A&M

'I miss you sadly': WSM to Gerald Kelly 15.4.05 HGARC

104. 'You are a downy old bird': *Loaves and Fishes* p. 38

105. 'I think I have got you a new client': Arnold Bennett to J. B. Pinker 11.6.05 HRHRC

106. 'I think we must agree to differ': WSM to Maurice Colles 29.7.05 Beinecke

'because they have no one': WSM to J. B. Pinker 12.11.05 HRHRC

107. 'We have been here nearly a week': WSM to Gerald Kelly n.d. HGARC

'In the process of making a complete failure': E. F. Benson *Final Edition* (Longmans Green 1940) p. 106

108. 'I'm sure a lot of people will think': WSM to Gerald Kelly 19.9.05 HGARC

'It was there I decided': Harry Philips to Joseph Dobrinsky 16.9.66 Texas A&M

109. 'one places all one's love': *A Writer's Notebook* p. 42

'By the time I received the money': *The Summing Up* p. 164

'Has the *Lady's Realm*': WSM to J. B. Pinker 3.7.06 HRHRC

110. 'irked my conscience': *Liza of Lambeth* p. xii

'Have no fear; I will come back': *The Explorer* p. 204

'I *do not like* it': WSM to Violet Hunt 10.4.07 Berg

'The people were too heroic': WSM to Gerald Kelly 25.3.07 HGARC

111. '[and] Maugham told me afterwards': George C. Tyler *Whatever Goes Up* (Bobbs-Merrill 1934) p. 208

'feeling pretty melancholy': ibid. p. 209

'I began to think': *Plays* vol. I p. viii

112. 'Your letter filled me with exultation': WSM to Golding Bright 16.9.07 HRHRC

'I went to Cook's': *Plays* vol. I p. ix

113. '[I was] very short of money': Toole Stott *A Bibliography of the Works of W. Somerset Maugham* p. 274

# CHAPTER 5: ENGLAND'S DRAMATIST

114. 'The years between the beginning': James Agate *A Short View of the English Stage 1900–1926* (Herbert Jenkins 1926) p. 68

'I reflected upon the qualities': *Plays* vol. I p. vii

115. '[Lady Frederick] wears a kimono': ibid. p. 67

'Now for the delicate soft bloom': ibid. p. 73

'D'you suppose I don't know': ibid. p. 89

116. 'I surmised you were in some trouble': *The Merry-Go-Round* p. 234

'Exhilarating entertainment': *The Times* 28.10.07

'a delicious evening': *Academy* 2.11.07

'as an accomplished dramatist': Beverley Nichols *Twenty-Five* (Penguin 1935) p. 233

'it is not a moment at which I commonly feel': WSM to Kelly n.d. HGARC

'You succeeded in making Paradine': WSM to Charles Lowne 28.10.07 Lilly

117. 'I happened to look up': *The Summing Up* p. 115

118. 'inconceivably silly': WSM to Kelly 26.1.08 HGARC
    '*The Waltz Dream* & my dealings': ibid. 20.2.08
    'not much of a success': ibid. 8.3.08
    'My success was spectacular': *The Summing Up* p. 115
    'I was much photographed': ibid. p. 116
    '[and] I thoroughly enjoyed myself': 'Looking Back' p. 36
    'Great ladies cultivate those': *Plays* vol. III p. viii

119. 'Who is Edgar Wallace?': *The Vagrant Mood* p. 197
    'When the ladies retired': *Cakes and Ale* p. 3
    'One has to go back': *Sunday Times* 3.5.08
    'the hero of the year': *Saturday Review* 20.6.08

120. 'light as a feather': *Sunday Times* 29.3.08
    'suddenly became much sought after' Harry Philips to Joseph Dobrinsky
    16.9.66 Texas A&M

121. 'the most finished comedian of his generation': W. Somerset Maugham (ed.)
    *The Truth at Last from Charles Hawtrey* (Thornton Butterworth 1924) p. 5
    'I tried to get a small part': WSM to Gerald Kelly 20.2.08 HGARC
    'she had the most beautiful smile': 'Looking Back' p. 30

122. 'He had acquired calmness of demeanour': *Of Human Bondage* p. 293
    'I have often acted a passion': *The Summing Up* p. 77

123. 'a woman of whom I had been extremely fond': Graham Young 'Somerset
    Maugham' *Daily Mail* 27.1.53
    'came of common family': Derek Hudson *For Love of Painting: The Life of Sir
    Gerald Kelly KCVO, PRA* (Peter Davies 1975) p. 51
    'had a very happy love affair': Gerald Kelly to Richard Cordell 20.8.59 Lilly
    'the most perfectly realized woman': Gerald Kelly to WSM n.d. HGARC

124. 'I opened the door': *Cakes and Ale* p. 139

125. 'desperately in love': Hudson *For Love of Painting* p. 51
    'She posed beautifully': Gerald Kelly interview with Robert Calder 4.2.70 Jenman
    'When I went to the first rehearsal': 'First Rehearsal' ms 1935 Lilly

126. 'To lose one leg': *Plays* vol. I p. 172
    'Noticed in myself': Flower (ed.) *The Journals of Arnold Bennett* vol. I *1896–1910*
    p. 287
    'D'you know him at all?': *The Summing Up* p. 117
    'I regularly wrote one act': WSM to Joseph Dobrinsky 1.8.57 Texas A&M

127. 'I hated poverty': *A Writer's Notebook* p. 73
    'the great, the insinuating': Louis Marlow *Two Made Their Bed* (Gollancz 1929)
    p. 9
    'Sometimes after an evening with Willie': *Books & Bookmen* May 1980
    'See him standing in the centre': *Saturday Review* 20.6.08
    'Somerset M., a dramatic genius': 3.5.07 ms journal Cornell

128. 'Practically nothing remains': WSM to Maurice Colles 29.11.07 Jenman
    'I have always thought that publishers': *Liza of Lambeth* p. xii
    'I, as you know, make a point': WSM to Gerald Kelly 25.3.07 HGARC
    'I wanted to consult you': WSM to J. B. Pinker 5.10.06 HRHRC

129. 'had a palpitating horror': *Liza of Lambeth* p. xix
'Margaret . . . horribly repelled': *The Magician* p. 118

130. 'I hear that Maugham has crucified us': Jonathan Benington *Roderic O'Conor* (Irish Academic Press 1992) p. 95
'an appreciation of my genius': John Symonds *The King of the Shadow Realm: Aleister Crowley, His Life and Magic* (Duckworth 1989) p. 129
'Maugham had taken': Crowley *The Spirit of Solitude* vol. II p. 129
'the many things in the East': *The Magician* p. 35

131. 'I daresay you are quite right': WSM to Violet Hunt 31.12.06 Berg
'with the title SON OF A BITCH': WSM to Gerald Kelly n.d. HGARC
'a real thrill of horror': *Spectator* 12.12.08
'First and last things': Stanley Weintraub *Reggie: A Portrait of Reginald Turner* (George Braziller, NY 1965) p. 163
'I am amorous of thy body': *The Magician* p. 98
'It is not for anyone to censure': speech to the Royal General Theatrical Fund 26.5.1892 Berg

132. 'You are a perfect dear': Jonathan Fryer *Robbie Ross: Oscar Wilde's True Love* (Constable 2000) p. 200
'the most amusing man': *The Vagrant Mood* p. 173
'I didn't want to hurt his feelings': WSM to David Cecil n.d. Jenman
'Ah, it's my second editions': Harry Philips to Joseph Dobrinsky 16.9.66 Texas A&M

133. 'I really think Reg': David Cecil *Max* (Constable 1964) p. 109
'I remember that the room': WSM to David Cecil n.d. Jenman
'I received the impression': *The Vagrant Mood* p. 174
'I'm sure there are various old women': Max Beerbohm to WSM 5.2.28 HGARC
'Max, Reggie Turner, George Street': WSM to David Cecil n.d. Jenman

134. 'Her conversation was artificial': Sitwell *Noble Essences* p. 130
'*Write a light comedy at once*': Julie Speedie *Wonderful Sphinx: The Biography of Ada Leverson* (Virago 1993) p. 166
'My dear Sphynx, It is too kind': WSM to Ada Leverson 2.7.09 Beinecke
'a great honour': ibid. 23.4.08

135. '[Maugham's] visits were looked forward to': Violet Wyndham *The Sphinx and Her Circle: A Biographical Sketch of Ada Leverson 1862–1933* (Deutsch 1963) p. 77
'I wish you would ask me': WSM to Ada Leverson n.d. Beinecke
'"something nice" . . . because the author': Wyndham *The Sphinx and Her Circle* p. 167
'My dear Sphinx, I am very sorry': ibid.

136. 'by the young woman': WSM to Joseph Dobrinsky 1.8.57 Texas A&M
'was like a force of nature': introduction to Isaac F. Marcosson and Daniel Frohman *Charles Frohman: Manager and Man* (John Lane, The Bodley Head 1916)
'[Charles Frohman] is the most wildly romantic': *The Times* 10.5.09

137. 'I want to tell you how glad I am': WSM to Charles Frohman 28.1.09 HRHRC
'I should much like to know': WSM to Golding Bright 20.9.08 HRHRC
'relieved and pleased to hear': ibid. 12.11.08

138. 'It astonished me a little': Irene Vanbrugh *To Tell My Story* (Hutchinson 1948)
p. 78
'the hurried lunch at a restaurant': *The Summing Up* p. 101
'I tried to go to my own first nights': ibid. p. 105
'I read that I had neither decorum': *Plays* vol. II p. vi
'I venture to suggest': WSM to 25.12.11 private collection

139. 'I was always nervous with Maugham': Vanbrugh *To Tell My Story* p. 79
'The brave has not yet won the fair': WSM to Gerald Kelly 3.3.08 HGARC
'she was not a particularly good actress': *Looking Back* p. 48
'the stoic and impeccable maid': *Sunday Times* 10.1.09
'I think it wants a good long stay': WSM to Gerald Kelly 8.3.08 HGARC

140. 'I implore you to take advantage': ibid. 25.3.07
'I look upon Orpen': ibid. n.d.
'All my friends had been to bed with her': 'Looking Back' p. 49
'the only man she ever really loved': Hudson *For Love of Painting* p. 51
'There was no one I liked better': 'Looking Back' p. 49

141. 'One has to be very strong': *A Man of Honour* p. 156

142. 'What has stayed clear in my memory': Marlow *Seven Friends* p. 144
'pale, dark, and rather handsome young man': Ada Leverson *The Limit* (Grant
Richards 1911) p. 51
'He behaved like anybody else': ibid.

143. 'Knowing that Miss Luscombe': ibid. p. 181
'who is coarse and common': ibid. p. 219

144. 'I was very fond of him': interview with Sir Julian Hall Victoria & Albert
Museum
'Lovely day. Golf afternoon': private collection

145. 'I am neither so happy': WSM to Gerald Kelly n.d. HGARC
'Really it is with the greatest difficulty': ibid. 23.4.09
'the fantastic conventions and prejudices': Gerald Kelly to Reginald Pound
26.1.53 Berg
'To me England has been a country': *The Summing Up* p. 95
'An amiable person has offered': WSM to Gerald Kelly 25.3.07 HGARC
'I met an Egyptian pasha': ibid. 9.9.07

146. 'a living link with Oscar': Louis Marlow to Llewellyn Powys 8.3.39 private
collection
'Ah, yes, yes, I know': Marlow *Seven Friends* p. 143
'I think the difficulty of play-writing': *Plays* vol. II p. vii
'If light comedy is the only form': *Saturday Review* 9.1.09
'for the wide divergency of tastes': *Nation* 16.1.09

147. 'They were just cynical enough': Desmond MacCarthy *William Somerset
Maugham: The English Maupassant* (Heinemann 1934) p. 4
'The critics accused me': *The Summing Up* p. 116
'The intelligentsia, of which': ibid.
'I am tired & bored': WSM to Golding Bright 20.10.09 HRHRC
'You've got through the world': *The Tenth Man* p. 197

148. 'It went very flat': WSM to Ada Leverson 27.2.10 Beinecke

'worked his puppets too long': *Saturday* Review 22.10.10
'were neither frankly realistic': *The Summing Up* p. 118
'I was happy, I was prosperous': *Of Human Bondage* p. 2
'one of London's wittiest bachelors': Elsa Maxwell *The Celebrity Circus*
(W. H. Allen 1964) p. 20
'If she was not at home': *Listener* 28.1.54

149. '[He] had started to dress himself': Roberts *The Pleasant Years* p. 135
'You will not know 6 Chesterfield Street': WSM to Charles Frohman n.d.
HRHRC
'with the reserve and detachment': MacCarthy *William Somerset Maugham:
The English Maupassant* p. 4
'still talked as though': *The Summing Up* p. 2

150. 'My dear Mrs Allhusen': WSM to Dorothy Allhusen n.d. Beinecke
'Thank you so much': ibid. n.d. Garrick
'I want to make a compact with you': 'Looking Back' p. 36
'My dear Sphynx, Pray thank your friend': WSM to Ada Leverson 21.2.10
Beinecke

151. 'during the dreary time of public mourning': WSM to Violet Hunt n.d. Berg
'is one of the greatest successes': WSM to J. B. Pinker 12.2.09 HRHRC
'I am sailing by the Caronia': WSM to Charles Frohman 9.10.10 HRHRC
'like Christopher Columbus': WSM to Golding Bright 16.10.09 HRHRC

# CHAPTER 6: SYRIE

152. 'I am booked up for luncheon': WSM to M. L. Fleming 3.11.10 Jenman
153. 'host of social entertainments': *New York Times* 5.11.14
'with his swallowtails': Billie Burke *With a Feather on My Nose* (Peter Davies
1950) p. 91
'We were not members': ibid.
'I note that you have found me': WSM to M. L. Fleming 29.9.12 Jenman
154. 'The great novelists, even in seclusion': *The Vagrant Mood* p. 168
155. 'I protested that I was perfectly capable': ibid. p. 166
'There was a striking family likeness': Robin Maugham *Somerset and All the
Maughams* p. 42
156. 'Barrie thinks it far & away': WSM to Gerald Kelly n.d. HGARC
'The public goes & laughs': ibid.
'People are shocked': WSM to Dorothy Allhusen n.d. Beinecke
'I think it possible': WSM to Gerald Kelly n.d. HGARC
'which will bring me in anything': ibid.
157. 'Howard has been very kind': ibid.
'one of the best things you have done': ibid.
'I have never been so comfortable': ibid.
'a gay discreet bandbox of a house': Hugh Walpole 'William Somerset
Maugham' *Vanity Fair* 1920
'This morning I walked': WSM to Gerald Kelly n.d. HGARC

158. 'with pictures of Bangkok': *Of Human Bondage* p. 537
     'I have half a mind to join you': WSM to Gerald Kelly n.d. HGARC
     'After submitting myself for some years': *Of Human Bondage* p. 2
     'I had all that stuff choking me': WSM to Joseph C. Smythe n.d. Jenman
     'Now that I am well on with it': WSM to Gerald Kelly n.d. HGARC

159. 'I brought my book away with me': WSM to Dorothy Allhusen n.d. Beinecke
     'to clear my brain & rest': WSM to Gerald Kelly n.d. HGARC
     'The book is not ready': WSM to William Heinemann 9.7.12 Random House
     'I am working hard': WSM to Gerald Kelly n.d. HGARC
     'a disastrous failure': ibid.

161. 'His insignificance was turned to power': *Of Human Bondage* p. 603
     'not all the incidents are related': *The Summing Up* p. 188

162. 'She was tall and thin': *Of Human Bondage* p. 306
     'it was absurd to care': ibid. p. 309
     '[Philip] was sick with anguish': ibid. p. 427
     'He never even kissed her now': ibid. p. 549

163. 'Though he had always been poor': ibid. p. 564
     'He turned away and walked slowly': ibid. p. 625
     'He lost his head': ibid. p. 685
     'it was no self-sacrifice': ibid. p. 699

164. 'I sought freedom': *The Summing Up* p. 190
     'I can't tell you how pleased': WSM to Gilbert Clark n.d. Jenman
     'Willie used my stuff': Gilbert Clark May 1914 Jenman

165. 'undoubtedly an episode in our friendship': Harry Philips to Joseph Dobrinsky
     16.9.66 Texas A&M
     'You wait, my boy': WSM to Gerald Kelly 19.9.05 HGARC
     'he exercised peculiar skill': *Of Human Bondage* p. 259

166. 'I am aware that in the past': WSM to William Heinemann 6.8.14
     Random House
     'I am sorry to have been so fussy': ibid.
     'Were I given freedom of choice': George H. Doran *Chronicles of Barabbas
     1884–1934* (Harcourt, Brace 1935) p. 148

167. 'It is on the grand scale': *New Statesman* 25.9.15
     'Here is a novel': *New Republic* 25.12.15
     'two of the most notable, satisfying contacts': Doran *Chronicles of Barabbas* p. 148

168. 'partly on account of the weather': Marcosson and Frohman *Charles Frohman*
     p. 407
     'I want a new play from you': ibid. p. 270
     'I well remembered the shock': *Plays* vol. II p. xiii
     'a good deal of discomfort': WSM to Gerald Kelly 1.1.6.13 HGARC
     'that curious and intense life': *Plays* vol. II p. xiii
     'My God, what a life they lead': WSM to Mabel Beardsley 29.12.12
     Jenman

169. 'I give her board and lodging': *Plays* vol. II p. 247
     'You're nothing but an ignorant woman': ibid. p. 284
     'For God's sake take it': ibid. p. 298

170. 'the audience of course knew nothing': WSM to Gerald Kelly 3.12.13 HGARC

'the leading part loses': ibid.

'In scene after scene': ibid.

'was a beautifully written but dreary': Burke *With a Feather on My Nose* p. 98

'gives an altogether incorrect': *Edmonton Journal* 4.4.14

'No Canadian man would dream': *Daily Bulletin* (Edmonton) 10.4.14

171. 'The Pygmalion of Mr Maugham': *English Review* May 1914

'If I meant to marry': *The Summing Up* p. 190

'Do you really think': WSM to Alfred Sutro n.d. private collection

172. 'I've come to ask you': 'Looking Back' p. 48

173. 'My schemes for going round the world': WSM to Gerald Kelly 3.12.13 HGARC

'I guessed at once': 'Looking Back' p. 48

'I knew how careless she was': ibid.

'a much better husband': ibid.

174. 'It happened that I had nothing': ibid. p. 56

'I wish we didn't have to go': ibid.

175. 'She hoped I would come': ibid. p. 57

'After that I saw Syrie': ibid. p. 58

179. 'is furnished in a pleasantly fantastic manner': *Plays* vol. III p. 123

180. 'a courtesan just past her prime': Glenway Wescott interview with Ted Morgan, Jenman

'the most charming man in London': ibid.

181. 'It was all very delightful': 'Looking Back' p. 61

'Uncle Willie brought Mrs Welcome': Kate Bruce unpublished ms private collection

'locked horns in an endurance contest': Maxwell *The Celebrity Circus* p. 20

182. 'I didn't want to tell you': 'Looking Back' p. 61

'I have got a great deal to tell you': WSM to Gerald Kelly 4.5.14 HGARC

183. 'still madly devoted': WSM to M. L. Fleming n.d. Jenman

'they had tastes in common': Faith Compton Mackenzie *Always Afternoon* (Collins 1943) p. 90

184. 'The bundle of papers that arrived': Faith Compton Mackenzie *As Much as I Dare* (Collins 1938) p. 269

'treated poor Brooks very badly': Compton Mackenzie to Grenville Cook 1.5.66 Lilly

'He had fine perceptions': Benson *Final Edition* p. 243

'I don't know what I shall do': Compton Mackenzie *My Life and Times: Octave Four 1907–1915* (Chatto & Windus 1965) p. 233

185. 'To me the very shape of England': *A Writer's Notebook* p. 128

186. 'She made me feel a brute': 'Looking Back' p. 64

'There are no candles': WSM to Gerald Kelly n.d. HGARC

187. 'There seemed not to be more than two doctors': *A Writer's Notebook* p. 75

'Conversation mingled with groans': ibid. p. 78

'Mais non, mon vieux': 'Looking Back' p. 63

'I saw a battle between aeroplanes': WSM to Alfred Sutro n.d. private collection
'I was lucky enough': WSM to William Heinemann 27.12.14 Random House

188.  'I had done no work of this kind': *A Writer's Notebook* p. 76
'I was a trifle vexed': *The Summing Up* p. 78
'The war had a most important influence': MacCarthy *William Somerset Maugham: The English Maupassant* p. 14

189.  'We are either rushed off our legs': WSM to M. L. Fleming n.d. Jenman
'It makes sightseeing a matter': WSM to Gerald Kelly n.d. HGARC
'The work was hard and tedious': *A Writer's Notebook* p. 82

190.  'When I remarked on it': MacCarthy *William Somerset Maugham: The English Maupassant* p. 5
'She took no notice': 'Looking Back' p. 64

# CHAPTER 7: CODE NAME 'SOMERVILLE'

191.  'I'm sorry, but is there anything': Robin Maugham *Conversations with Willie* p. 18
'From you or from life?': ibid. p. 20

192.  'a habit of walking across': *Of Human Bondage* p. 18
'charmed the birds from the trees': Arthur Marshall interview with Robert Calder, Jenman
'charming, full of kindness': Hugh Walpole ms diary HRHRC
'jolly and delightful': *Listener* 7.2.74
'perennially young': Harold Acton *Memoirs of an Aesthete* (Methuen 1948) p. 188
'very masculine ... with a hard tarty face': Peter Quennell interview with Robert Calder, Jenman

193.  'He had an air of dissipation': *Up at the Villa* p. 17
'a rosy roly-poly': Sara Haxton to Louise Sharon 19.3.96 Bancroft

194.  'I am leading the dullest': ibid. 1.1.01
'without anyone knowing anything': 'Looking Back' p. 64

195.  'It is bitterly cold here': WSM to William Heinemann 10.2.15 Random House
'If only I am able to write': WSM to Gerald Kelly 1.2.15 HGARC
'Did I tell you that my banker': WSM to William Heinemann 7.3.15 Random House
'She took it as the most natural thing': 'Looking Back' p. 68

196.  'She cried bitterly': ibid.
'I am very glad to know': WSM to Al Hayman 10.6.15 Fales

197.  'a dazzling icy glitter': Mander and Mitchenson *Theatrical Companion to Maugham* p. 8
'An excoriating ... and exceedingly interesting': *New York Times* 13.3.17
'no playwright since Vanbrugh': Louis Kronenberger *The Thread of Laughter: Chapters on English Stage Comedy from Jonson to Maugham* (Knopf 1952) p. 291
'remarkable ... [and] mercilessly amusing': *New Statesman* 6.10.23
'one of the most brilliant plays': Agate *A Short View of the English Stage* p. 107
'Owing to various rumours': Mander and Mitchenson *Theatrical Companion to Maugham* p. 122

198. 'She was very amusing': 'Looking Back' p. 65
'I wish you wouldn't call me girlie': *Plays* vol. III p. 63
'a handsome youth of twenty-five': ibid. p. 20
'I wish you wouldn't constantly ask me': ibid. p. 63

199. '[Mr Maugham] and Mrs Wellcome': Wellcome Library collection
'I was at a loose end': 'Looking Back' p. 69

200. 'You'd be a fool to marry her': ibid. p. 74

201. 'If we were married': Robin Maugham *Conversations with Willie* p. 35
'Tu n'as pas encore perdu': Georges de Porto-Riche *Amoureuse: Théâtre d'amour*
vol. III (Albin Michel 1928) p. 87
'It positively made my blood run cold': WSM to Gerald Kelly 12.11.15 HGARC

202. 'I am thankful it is over': ibid. 26.2.16
'You will be doubtless seeing her': ibid. 28.2.16
'The whole matter has been a great distress': WSM to F. H. Maugham 12.3.16
HRHRC
'high comedy at its very best': Vanbrugh *To Tell My Story* p. 112

203. 'light as a feather': *Sunday Times* 13.2.16
'the quintessence of natural gaiety': *Daily Mail* 8.2.16
'Well, ma'am, my belief': *Plays* vol. III p. 158
'Don't you know how you feel': ibid. p. 188
'one of the best performances': ibid. p. v
'I have never had such an enormous success': WSM to F. H. Maugham 12.3.16
HRHRC

204. 'If you do well': *Ashenden* p. 4

205. 'He had charming manners': ibid. p. 30
'I know nothing so tedious as coding': ibid. p. 215
'[The code] was in two parts': ibid. p. 105

206. 'as orderly and monotonous': ibid. p. 109
'Geneva, the centre of all rumours': WSM to Gerald Kelly 12.11.15 HGARC
'it was absurd to think': *Ashenden* p. 108

207. 'had been doing us down': Christopher Andrew *Secret Service: The Making of the
British Intelligence Community* (Heinemann 1985) p. 152
'[Ashenden] gave him his orders': *Ashenden* p. 19

208. 'no more than a tiny rivet': ibid. p. 7
'hours of infinite drudgery': Edward Knoblock *Round the Room* (Chapman &
Hall 1939) p. 208
'[Wallinger's] Swiss show so far': Michael Occleshaw *Armour Against Fate: British
Military Intelligence in the First World War* (Columbus 1989) p. 225

209. 'I wanted to recover my peace of mind': *The Summing Up* p. 192
'I was willing to marry Syrie': 'Looking Back' p. 75
'There is a great deal of sympathy': WSM to Gerald Kelly 15.10.16 HGARC

210. 'for beauty and romance': *The Summing Up* p. 193
'I was convinced that by going to Tahiti': 'Looking Back' p. 76

211. 'On a journey by sea': ibid. p. 90
'not a tramp, not a sailing vessel': *A Writer's Notebook* p. 90
'it is an empty desert': *The Trembling of a Leaf* p. 14

212. 'a more devoted, generous': WSM to Klaus Jonas 29.8.56 HRHRC
'She had a cabin two removed': Wilmon Menard *After Dark* December 1975
'hot lallapalooza from Honolulu': Menard *The Two Worlds of Somerset Maugham* p. 307

214. 'rather handsome travelling companion': ibid. p. 316
'I entered a new world': *The Summing Up* p. 193
'I rarely went to my ship's cabin': Menard *After Dark* December 1975

215. 'from a hint or an incident': *The Summing Up* p. 195
'the writer cannot afford to wait': WSM to Michael Watkins 4.7.54 private collection
'dressed in a sleeveless singlet': *A Writer's Notebook* p. 94
'His face was red and blotchy': *The Trembling of a Leaf* p. 122
'The first time you saw him': ibid. p. 128

216. 'What is your name?': ibid. p. 144
'[Mrs W.] spoke of the depravity': *A Writer's Notebook* p. 94
'to have Sadie [Thompson]': Menard *The Two Worlds of Somerset Maugham* p. 108

217. ''I want her to accept': *The Trembling of a Leaf* p. 294
'[Sadie] gathered herself together': ibid. p. 301
'After supper we went on deck': *A Writer's Notebook* p. 96

218. 'a flat-nosed, smiling dark native': ibid. p. 117
'"How much will it cost?" I asked': ibid. p. 118

219. 'the first completely beautiful': Glenway Wescott interview with Robert Calder, Jenman
'Maugham adored Haxton': George Rylands to Robert Calder, Jenman
'he was noisy and boastful': *Up at the Villa* p. 28
'But for him I should never have got': 'Looking Back' p. 90

220. 'a sheer masterpiece of sardonic horror': *Saturday Review* 5.11.21
'One of the evil limitations': James Michener to Klaus Jonas 13.2.5 HRHRC

221. 'There is no object more deserving of pity': *The Moon and Sixpence* p. 160
'I felt that I had been put': 'Looking Back' p. 97
'who first sentenced the drunk': *Saturday Review* 14.10.61

223. 'I do not know whether it is intended': WSM to William Wiseman 7.7.17 Jenman

224. 'It was tantalizing': WSM to Gerald Kelly 25.9.17 HGARC

225. 'Mr Somerset Maugham is in Russia': Wiseman mss File 90-42, E. M. House Collection, Yale University Library
'In his cold and uninteresting way': *Ashenden* p. 220
'I realized that I could not count': 'Looking Back' p. 80

226. 'looked very unhealthy': *A Writer's Notebook* p. 165
'in the middle of his speech': Louise Bryant *Six Red Months in Russia* (Heinemann 1918) p. 117
'as he faced now one': *Daily News* 27.9.17
'I've never seen a man': Glenway Wescott interview with Robert Calder, Jenman
'With Sasha acting as hostess': 'Looking Back' p. 82

227. 'I am receiving interesting cables': Calder *W. Somerset Maugham and the Quest for Freedom* p. 282

228. 'The endless talk when action was needed': *The Summing Up* p. 197
229. 'In the birch trees rooks were cawing': *A Writer's Notebook* p. 154
'I am longing for news': WSM to Edward Knoblock 1.10.17 Berg
230. 'we in the Hotel Europa': Emanuel Victor Voska *Spy and Counterspy* (Doubleday, Doran 1940) p. 232
'I know that you have friends': WSM to Edward Knoblock 1.10.17 Berg
'You won't reveal you had lunch': www.ochcom.org
'It organised a certain amount': *The Autobiography of Arthur Ransome* (Cape 1976) p. 190
231. 'Delightful lunch with Willie Maugham': Hugh Walpole ms diary HRHRC
'I am very sensual': ibid.
'He watched Russia as we would watch': Walpole 'William Somerset Maugham' *Vanity Fair* 1920
'the secret agent of reactionary imperialism': Rhodri Jeffreys-Jones *American Espionage: From Secret Service to CIA* (Collier Macmillan 1977) p. 96
232. 'I must make the Russian soldiers understand': WSM to Wiseman 18.11.17 Wiseman mss Yale University Library
233. 'I can't do that': 'Looking Back' p. 85
'I fear this [is] of only historical interest': Private Secretary Archives 1917–24 Balfour, PRO FO 800/205
'I failed lamentably': *The Summing Up* p. 196
'[I thought] that it was only sensible': 'Looking Back' p. 86

## CHAPTER 8: BEHIND THE PAINTED VEIL

235. 'I delighted in the privacy': *The Summing Up* p. 197
236. 'There is something that would appeal': WSM to Edward Knoblock 24.2.18 Berg
'The post is always the great thrill': WSM to Alfred Sutro n.d. private collection
'Meant to be nothing': WSM to Paul Dottin n.d. HRHRC
'a play so negligible': *New Statesman* 6.10.23
237. 'a very truthful account': WSM to Paul Dottin n.d. HRHRC
'[Willie's] mysterious bosses': A. S. Frere to Ted Morgan 11.3.78 Jenman
'He was not happy unless he was settled': *Ashenden* p. 67
'He was travelling with a brand-new passport': ibid. p. 171
238. '[Giulia] staggered. She put her hand': ibid. p. 143
'with a politeness to which no exception': ibid. p. 215
239. 'Mr Harrington was a bore': ibid. p. 283
'When Ashenden himself was reading': ibid. p. 279
'He was so well-meaning': ibid. p. 283
'A half-hour later I heard firing': Voska *Spy and Counterspy* p. 232
'He lay on his face': *Ashenden* p. 325
240. 'often spoke about': Kenneth Clark to Robert Calder 29.12.81 Jenman
'It was true that he was an important person': *Ashenden* p. 52
'They desired the end': ibid. p. 263

241. 'The modern spy story began': *New York Times Book Review* 13.9.81
     'The Ashenden stories were certainly': Ted Morgan *Maugham* p. 313
     '*Ashenden* is unique': Raymond Chandler to WSM 13.1.50 HRHRC
242. 'a specimen of Somerset Maugham': *New York Times* 15.4.28
     'We find they are nothing': *Vogue* (London) 20.7.28
     'a strange outcome for a series': WSM to Desmond MacCarthy n.d. Lilly
243. 'What will happen in the future': WSM to M. L. Fleming n.d. Jenman
244. 'He and Maude spent a long time': Robert Hichens *Yesterday* (Cassell 1947)
     p. 254
     'I should have thought': Hugh Walpole ms diary HRHRC
     'Has it occurred to you': *The Moon and Sixpence* p. 40
245. 'You don't want me to talk': ibid. p. 145
     'They must be very pleasant': ibid. p. 212
     'I am always sure': *Sunday Times* 24.1.54
246. 'one of those unlucky persons': *The Moon and Sixpence* p. 83
     'hackneyed and vulgar beyond belief': ibid. p. 66
     'an agitated guinea-pig': ibid. p. 90
     'had the true instinct': ibid. p. 213
     'We must be shown something': *Athenaeum* 9.5.19
247. 'I am making my plans': WSM to Gerald Kelly 14.10.18 HGARC
     'He wasn't nasty about it': *Listener* 7.2.74
     'in which all the characters': *Plays* vol. V p. vi
     'a triumphantly tactful evening': *The Times* 28.3.19
248. 'gave dinner parties to end all': Glenway Wescott interview with Ted Morgan,
     Jenman
     'I had naturally bad taste': Kate Bruce unpublished ms private collection
249. 'Syrie simply didn't understand': Robin Maugham *Conversations with Willie* p. 33
     'You have driven me to talk to you': 'Looking Back' p. 100
250. 'I didn't have a voice in it': *Listener* 7.2.74
     'I think that if Syrie hadn't fallen in love': Glenway Wescott interview with Ted
     Morgan, Jenman
     'I was forty-three when we married': 'Looking Back' p. 100
252. '[Willie] looks ill and bored': Hugh Walpole ms diary HRHRC
     'I flatter myself': *Plays* vol. III p. 231
     'I confess that sometimes': ibid. p. 288
253. 'The difference between men and women': ibid. p. 235
     'style, wit, elegance': *The Times* 1.9.19
     'succeeded in turning herself': Sheridan Morley *Gladys Cooper* (Heinemann
     1979) p. 79
     'more or less unconsciously': ibid.
254. 'gives you everything': WSM to Robin Maugham 10.6.37 HRHRC
     'You have thrust your hideous inventions': *On a Chinese Screen* p. 95
255. 'At its foot were a number': ibid. p. 106
256. 'an experience that really enriches': WSM to Robin Maugham 10.6.37 HRHRC
     'one of the pleasantest places': WSM to David Horner 15.6.35 HRHRC
     'very nasty smells': *On a Chinese Screen* p. 88

'I have got a good deal of material': WSM to Golding Bright 12.1.20 HRHRC

257. 'p. 124 I am inclined to criticize': WSM to H. I. Harding 7.10.21 private collection

'A fascinating volume': *New York Times* 4.2.23

'His descriptions are not so much natural': *Saturday Review* 13.1.23

'the only novel I have written': *The Painted Veil* p. ix

258. 'As far as I can make out': ibid. p. 67

259. 'Am I the father?': ibid. p. 137

'fierce, oddly hysterical too': ibid. p. 25

'One may doubt whether': *Times Literary Supplement* 14.5.25

260. 'He was self-conscious': *The Painted Veil* p. 26

'Convivial amusement has always': *The Summing Up* p. 76

'willing to chatter all day long': *The Painted Veil* p. 26

'There's hardly anyone here': ibid. p. 8

261. 'In married life there are times': WSM to M. L. Fleming 3.1.20 Jenman

'I seem to live in an atmosphere': 'Looking Back' p. 96

262. 'You are very pleasant to travel with': ibid. p. 95

'were always particularly kind': *The Times* 1.8.55

'Syrie had a very heartless side': Glenway Wescott interview with Ted Morgan, Jenman

'it was easy to be fascinated': Richard B. Fisher *Syrie Maugham* p. 47

263. 'Her hospitality did not spring': Michael Burn *Childhood at Oriol* (Turtle Point Press 2005) p. 242

'a little dull and lacking in drama': *The Times* 10.8.20

'The third act does not come off': WSM to Gerald Kelly n.d. HGARC

'I was a little frightened of him': Liza Maugham in conversation with Pat Wallace, Frere Family Archive

264. 'I think he must have had a picture': ibid.

'He never stammered': ibid.

265. 'If you come near me': ibid.

'There are only two courses': 'Looking Back' p. 95

# CHAPTER 9: 'A WORLD OF VERANDA AND PRAHU'

266. 'In all production': WSM to Edward Knoblock 1.2.25 Berg

'A play is very like a suit': WSM to Paul Dottin n.d. HRHRC

'the drama is in a state of unrest': WSM to Edward Knoblock 1.2.25 Berg

'I cannot *imagine* that anything is likely': WSM to Fred Bason 28.9.23 Lilly

267. 'Words fail to describe': Kevin Brownlow *The Parade's Gone By* (Secker & Warburg 1968) p. 277

'the obscene Cecil': WSM to Edward Knoblock 17.8.21 Berg

'I look back on my connection': ibid.

'I am sure it is not difficult': WSM to Barbara Back 7.11.37 HRHRC

'The technique of writing': *North American Review* May 1921

268. 'I was shoved roughly': Menard *After Dark* December 1975

269. 'Say, this is the real life': *A Writer's Notebook* p. 177

270. 'more bother than you can imagine': WSM to Bert Alanson 17.5.25 Stanford
'If all else perish, there will remain': *Sunday Times* 19.12.65

271. 'He tells us – and it had not been said before': *100 Key Books of the Modern Movement* chosen by Cyril Connolly (Alison & Busby 1986) p. 73
'Most English households of the day': Arthur Grimble *Pattern of Islands* (John Murray 1969) p. 1
'A sahib has got to act': George Orwell *Collected Essays* (Secker & Warburg 1961) p. 19

272. 'a combination of awe, envy': *A Writer's Notebook* p. 213

273. 'Most people living in out-of-the-way places': *The Casuarina Tree* p. 130

274. 'they were more lonely': *First Person Singular* p. 10
'They are bored with themselves': *A Writer's Notebook* p. 188

275. 'was like a very big doll's house': *Ah King* p. 176
'[Izzart] wondered whether': *The Casuarina Tree* p. 216

276. 'to get a boy was easier': Ronald Hyam *Britain's Imperial Century 1815–1914* (Batsford 1976) p. 137
'brides coming out from England': John G. Butcher *The British in Malaya 1880–1941* (Oxford University Press 1979) p. 203
'The blinds on the verandah': *The Casuarina Tree* p. 165

277. 'I think of those thin black arms': ibid. p. 195
'It was the elder of his two sons': ibid. p. 201
'had real trouble on their hands': Menard *The Two Worlds of Somerset Maugham* p. 36
'The chief disadvantage for ladies': Captain R. L. German MCS *Handbook to British Malaya 1926* (Malay States Information Agency 1926) p. 46

279. 'Crosbie grew very red': *The Casuarina Tree* p. 293
'was clearly marked by a trail': Victor Purcell *The Memoirs of a Malayan Official* (Cassell 1965) p. 271
'It is interesting to try': *Straits Budget* 7.6.38

280. 'are all ghastly betrayals': Edwin Tribble (ed.) *A Chime of Words: The Letters of Logan Pearsall Smith* (Ticknor & Fields 1984) p. 86
'I tried to make use of them': Menard *The Two Worlds of Somerset Maugham* p. 31
'I made acquaintance with them': *The Summing Up* p. 200
'[when] sitting over a siphon': *The Gentleman in the Parlour* p. 32

281. 'I'm sorry, I'm sorry': Menard *The Two Worlds of Somerset Maugham* p. 35
'Do write to me': WSM to Edward Knoblock 17.8.21 Berg

282. 'a bit dreary': *Ah King* p. 185

283. 'I thought the best thing': *A Writer's Notebook* p. 184

284. 'a necessity, and if I am deprived': *The Summing Up* p. 88
'I have the greatest admiration for Racine': *Ah King* p. 165
'have the opportunity of living': WSM to Thring 10.2.22 HGARC

285. 'It seemed strange to me': *Vogue* (New York) 1.9.53
'I am dreadfully put out': WSM to M. L. Fleming 10.10.21 Jenman

286. 'You are a wonderful friend': WSM to Bert Alanson 26.2.21 Stanford
     'You were as ever wonderfully good': ibid 9.2.49
     'One delicious situation follows another': *Life* 29.9.21
     'the best English comedy': *Theater Magazine* November 1921
     'one of the very few creditable high comedies': Louis Kronenberger *The Thread of Laughter* (Knopf 1952) p. 294
     'this brilliant playwright': James Agate *A Short View of the English Stage* (Herbert Jenkins 1926) p. 86
287. 'One sacrifices one's life': *Plays* vol. IV p. 78
     'You can't expect a man': ibid. p. 57
     'gift [that] sprang from a clear-sighted': *New Statesman* 6.10.23
     '*The Circle* is one of the best plays': ibid. 19.3.21
288. 'each separate tale is begun': *Saturday Review* 5.11.21
     'My short stories have been a very great success': WSM to Bert Alanson 28.1.22 Stanford
     'one of the most agreeable persons': WSM to Edward Knoblock 16.10.24 Berg
289. 'in their ill-fitting, ready-made': *A Writer's Notebook* p. 171
     'Maugham seems to fancy me': Sinclair Lewis to Grace Lewis 3.2.22 HRHRC
     'restless, clownish, and intense': C. R. W. Nevinson *Paint and Prejudice* (Methuen 1937) pp. 179–80
290. 'I think you have done a very clever thing': WSM to Gerald Kelly 5.5.20 HGARC
     'Willie Maugham came to tea': Hugh Walpole ms diary HRHRC
291. 'My dear Marsh, Thank you very much *indeed*': WSM to Edward Marsh 5.7.19 Berg
292. 'With the strength of a typhoon': Cecil Beaton *The Glass of Fashion* (Weidenfeld & Nicolson 1954) p. 204
     'She has exquisite taste': *A Writer's Notebook* p. 174
293. 'I have a notion that children': *The Gentleman in the Parlour* p. 35
294. 'my constant companion': WSM to Reginald Turner 31.12.21 Craig V. Showalter Collection
     'You cannot think how impatient': WSM to Bert Alanson 25.7.22 Stanford
295. 'Another piece of work like this': *Spectator* 9.9.22
     'We have got quite an arsenal': WSM to Bert Alanson 25.10.22 Stanford
     'cherishing and fortifying': George Orwell *Burmese Days* (Penguin 1989) p. 69
297. 'I trusted that after he left': *The Gentleman in the Parlour* p. 93
     'A great deal of course was exquisitely boring': ibid. p. 62
298. 'Neither wet sheets nor ice packs': ibid. p. 127
299. 'I am often tired of myself': ibid. p. 9
     'I guess Egbert would like': ibid. p. 144
300. 'Never was Mr Maugham more readable': *New York Herald Tribune* 20.4.30
     'was a most amusing companion': *Cosmopolitans* p. 124
     'He was fearless': 'Looking Back' p. 148
     '[Gerald] who set the pace': Beverley Nichols *A Case of Human Bondage* p. 146
     'Will you invest $5,000': WSM to Bert Alanson 25.5.23 Stanford

## CHAPTER 10: SEPARATION

302. 'Middle age has its compensations': *Vanity Fair* December 1923
'It is simply magnif': *Arnold Bennett's Letters to His Nephew* (Heinemann 1936)
p. 141

303. 'so roomy and spacious': WSM to Bert Alanson 6.10.23 Stanford
'For your own sake as well': WSM to Edward Knoblock 21.1.23 Berg

304. 'You must expect to pay something': WSM to M. L. Fleming n.d. Jenman
'charming but *very* naughty': Norman Douglas quoted in Robin Maugham
unpublished diaries Beinecke
'He was a naughty boy': Nichols *A Case of Human Bondage* p. 147
'was probably the only person': Rebecca West to Beverley Nichols 4.5.66
Delaware
'the handsome young man': Nichols *A Case of Human Bondage* p. 144

305. 'ambiguous telephone calls': Evelyn Waugh *Vile Bodies* (Penguin 1938) p. 110
'Willie's sex life was not necessarily': Glenway Wescott interview with Ted
Morgan, Jenman
'Gerald Haxton was wonderful': George Cukor unpublished interview with
Jesse Hill Ford, Margaret Herrick Library
'I personally had much affection': WSM to Bert Alanson 27.8.23 Stanford

306. 'a very substantial, comfortable sum' ibid. 25.10.23
'It was quite an experience': ibid. 6.10.23

307. 'Take your freedom': *The Gentleman in the Parlour* p. 137
'I cannot tell you how much': WSM to Bert Alanson 14.1.24 Stanford
'I steered clear of Haxton': Basil Dean *Seven Ages: An Autobiography 1888–1927*
(Hutchinson 1970) p. 233

308. 'a perfectly amazing letter': Bruce Kellner (ed.) *The Letters of Carl Van Vechten*
(Yale University Press 1987) p. 72
'I must confess that I am disappointed': WSM to Edward Knoblock 16.10.24
Berg
'I feel that two such literary Englishmen': D. H. Lawrence to WSM 24.10.24
Jenman

309. 'no loss: a bit sour': 29.10.24 James T. Boulton and Lindeth Vasey (eds) *Letters of
D. H. Lawrence* vol. V (Cambridge University Press 1989) p. 158
'He answered crossly': Frieda Lawrence *Not I, But the Wind* (Heinemann 1935)
p. 139
'It would be hard to find': *Vogue* (London) 20.7.28
'a sick man of abnormal irritability': *W. Somerset Maugham's Introduction to
Modern English and American Literature* (New Home Library 1943)
'just like Atlantic City': WSM to Edward Knoblock 1.2.25 Berg

310. 'We are drawing near to the end': ibid.

311. 'I am not so anxious': WSM to Charles Towne 23.11.24 Beinecke
'He just sent it out like a parcel': ibid. 25.9.25
'It never occurred to them': *The Painted Veil* p. 13

312. 'is to eat cold mutton': Kate Bruce unpublished ms private collection

'My father was fifty years old': Robin Maugham *Somerset and All the Maughams* p. 172

314. 'Needless to say I could not work': WSM to Golding Bright 18.3.25 HRHRC
'I do not of course know': WSM to Edward Knoblock n.d. Berg
'Don't expect us to be two roses': Boulton and Vasey (eds) *Letters of D. H. Lawrence* vol. V p. 445

315. 'she did desperately mind': Liza Maugham in conversation with Pat Wallace, Frere Family Archive
'sweating at every pore': *The Constant Wife, Plays* vol. IV p. 146
'Resistance only exasperated her': *Ah King* p. 323
'I realized that what she was chiefly': Gerald McKnight *The Scandal of Syrie Maugham* p. 122

316. 'was incapable of realising': Frank Swinnerton to Robert Calder 28.9.76 Jenman
'Did you have a nice day': Liza Maugham in conversation with Pat Wallace, Frere Family Archive
'I had a great feeling': ibid.

317. 'S-S-Syrie d-d-didn't really imp-p-prove matters': Rebecca West to Beverley Nichols 4.5.66 Delaware
'Willie took this without protest': ibid.
'writing like a chambermaid': A. S. Frere interview with Ted Morgan, Jenman
'She had a miniature, rather touching dignity': Burn *Childhood at Oriol* p. 177

318. 'I think I should warn you': Nichols *A Case of Human Bondage* p. 82
'[Syrie] for a time': Cathleen Nesbitt *A Little Love and Good Company* (Faber 1975) p. 142
'Some of Syrie's activities': 'Looking Back' p. 92

320. 'We called him Mr Know-All': *Cosmopolitans* p. 74

321. 'is really a very charming little place': WSM to Bert Alanson 17.5.25 Stanford

322. 'He caught my eye and shouted': Nichols *A Case of Human Bondage* p. 27

323. 'I went over to Le Touquet': WSM to Edward Knoblock n.d. Berg
'I am so thrilled at getting off': WSM to John Ellingham Brooks 3.10.25 HRHRC
'Mr Somerset Maugham and his secretary': *Malay Mail* 15.2.26
'He could cook, he could valet': *Ah King* p. 2

324. 'It was very agreeable': *The Summing Up* p. 214
'I seemed to develop the sensitiveness': ibid. p. 200

325. 'I felt that all the depictions': WSM to Klaus Jonas 3.7.51 HRHRC
'The width of observation': *Listener* 23.12.65
'Maugham achieves an unspoken ferocity': Connolly *100 Key Books* p. 73

326. 'I don't think there's much about niggers': *The Casuarina Tree* p. 120

327. 'Ginger Ted would rape her': *Ah King* p. 135

328. 'The journey on a French boat': WSM to Bert Alanson 15.3.27 Stanford

329. 'I cannot but think': WSM to Edward Knoblock n.d. Berg
'I have made a very agreeable arrangement': WSM to Bert Alanson 20.5.26 Stanford

330. 'I will not conceal from you': WSM to Charles Towne 2.7.26 NYPL
    'You seem now to have bound me': ibid. 24.4.26 Beinecke
    'I am sure you will make an excellent editor': ibid. 2.7.26 NYPL
331. 'Twenty minutes before starting': WSM to Bert Alanson n.d. Stanford


# CHAPTER 11: THE VILLA MAURESQUE

332. 'I have at last found a place': WSM to Gerald Kelly n.d. HGARC
333. 'I hadn't reckoned on the temptation': *Strictly Personal* p. 3
    'The great luxury on the Riviera': ibid. et seq.
    'The swimming pool is a great success': WSM to Bert Alanson 1.8.27 Stanford
334. 'Miss Cooper's acting . . . was superb': *Sunday Times* 12.2.27
    'I place Somerset Maugham': Gladys Cooper *Gladys Cooper* (Hutchinson 1931)
    p. 245
    'The majority of authors': ibid.
335. '[We] have to content ourselves': Barry Day (ed.) *The Letters of Nöel Coward*
    (Methuen 2007) p. 227
    'Maugham lacked genuine enthusiasm': Dean *Seven Ages* p. 177
336. 'I'm tired of being': *Plays* vol. IV p. 157
    'Are you as great a fool': ibid. p. 180
    'What is a wife': ibid. p. 160
    'You were the mother': ibid. p. 179
    'Refuse to speak to him': ibid. p. 146
337. 'I suffered agonies': WSM to George Cukor n.d. Margaret Herrick Library
    'vain as a peacock': WSM to John W. Rumsey 21.11.24 Beinecke
    'Quite early in rehearsals': Dean *Seven Ages* p. 304
    'Maugham and his wife': ibid.
338. 'Mr Maugham was out of form': *Saturday Review* 16.4.27
    'nice enough but it had the disadvantage': 'Looking Back' p. 108
    'Crowds and crowds at the party': *Arnold Bennett's Letters to His Nephew* p. 188
    'spent three whole nights': unpublished ms copyright the Literary Estate of the
    late Sir Cecil Beaton
339. 'My mother had a very bad': Liza Maugham in conversation with Pat Wallace,
    Frere Family Archive
    'I always hated Gerald Haxton': ibid.
    'I was hysterical': ibid.
    '[Willie] watches Gerald losing thousands': Ruth Gordon *My Side* (Harper &
    Row 1976) p. 371
340. 'We lunched tête à tête': 'Looking Back' p. 108
    'Your mother dragged me through the mud': Liza Maugham in conversation
    with Pat Wallace, Frere Family Archive
    'Everything is absolutely finished': WSM to Barbara Back 16.5.29 HRHRC
341. 'I made a mistake': 'Looking Back' p. 110
    'She made my life utter hell': Robin Maugham unpublished diaries Beinecke

'abandoned liar': WSM to Barbara Back 22.4.29 HRHRC

'tart who ruined my life': Robin Maugham unpublished diaries Beinecke

'[opening] her mouth as wide': WSM to Kate Bruce 16.1.31 Berg

'I have learned from the papers': WSM to Barbara Back 16.5.29 HRHRC

'very unimportant detail': WSM to Richard Cordell 29.6.36 Lilly

'For those who seek a moral': Harold Acton *Washington Post* 2.3.80

342.  'He wrote it at my request': Nichols *A Case of Human Bondage* p. 102

'help one up one's little ladder': ibid. p. 70

'With drink Beverley's tongue': unpublished ms copyright the Literary Estate of the late Sir Cecil Beaton

'I have been very fortunate': Godfrey Winn *The Infirm Glory* (Michael Joseph 1967) p. 92

343.  'that Willie had fallen for him': Pat Cavendish O'Neill *A Lion in the Bedroom* (Jonathan Ball 2004) p. 295

'an attractive young person': *Strictly Personal* p. 94

'it was sentimental slush': ibid. p. 96

'[If] you were laughing': ibid. p. 100

'Don't be a fool': Anton Dolin *Last Words* (Century 1985) p. 74

'a delicious creature': Robert Phelps (ed.) *Continual Lessons: The Journals of Glenway Wescott 1937–1955* (Farrar Straus & Giroux 1990) p. 91

344.  'jugged. You don't know the kind of life': Hugh Walpole to Virginia Woolf in Nigel Nicolson (ed.) *Letters of Virginia Woolf* vol. IV (Hogarth Press 1978) p. 250

'a modified version of rough trade': Glenway Wescott interview with Ted Morgan, Jenman

'He was wonderful': Raymond Mortimer interview with Robert Calder, Jenman

'my starry eyed little friend': Guy Little to Alan Searle 16.1.34 HGARC

345.  'but if you'll have dinner with me': Alan Searle interview with Robert Calder, Jenman

'the less Syrie knows': ibid.

346.  'Perhaps we should all look': *Plays* vol. V p. 298

347.  'Stage dialogue has been simplified': ibid. p. x

'another of Mr Maugham's': *New York Times* 20.11.28

'I know that I am for it': WSM to Alfred Sutro n.d. private collection

'Isn't it grand that *The Sacred Flame*': WSM to Kate Bruce 3.4.29 Berg

'our business went up': *Gladys Cooper* p. 270

348.  'For some reason (chiefly I suppose': WSM to Bert Alanson 15.9.28 Stanford

350.  'I was prepared to spend': *Strictly Personal* p. 3

'the raffinement de luxe': Terence de Vere White (ed.) *A Leaf from the Yellow Book: The Correspondence of George Egerton* (Richards Press 1958)

'a haven of comfort': Ann Fleming *Spectator* 17.5.80

'The arms would drop back again': Roderick Cameron *The Golden Riviera* (Weidenfeld & Nicolson 1975) p. 42

351.  'I am silent with pleasure': Hugh and Mirabel Cecil *Clever Hearts* (Gollancz 1990) p. 294

352. 'He had about him': Nichols *A Case of Human Bondage* p. 19
    'Haxton was a most amiable creature': George Cukor unpublished interview
    with Jesse Hill Ford, Margaret Herrick Library
    'very jolly and delightful': Raymond Mortimer interview with Robert Calder,
    Jenman
    'charmed the birds': *Listener* 7.2.74
    'It was Gerald Haxton': Robin Maugham *Escape from the Shadows* p. 96
353. 'Fundamentally Maugham was a formal man': Cameron *The Golden Riviera*
    p. 45
    'I have never been able to persuade': *The Summing Up* p. 229
    '[and] word followed word': 'Looking Back' p. 5
    '[As Darwin] never worked': article by Kenneth Allsop *Daily Express* n.d.
354. 'I have always had more stories': *The Summing Up* p. 80
    'Then I go over very carefully': WSM to Paul Hackbest 15.11.30 Lilly
    'the most enthralling of human activities': *The Summing Up* p. 222
    'the useful little imp': *Plays* vol. V p. viii
355. 'I am no longer interested': WSM to Klaus Jonas 14.5.56 HRHRC
    'anything you do': Glenway Wescott *Images of Truth* (Hamish Hamilton 1963) p. 85
    'who had lingered in my mind': WSM to Paul Dottin 1.1.31 HRHRC
    'I swear I never thought': *Daily Telegraph* 29.9.30
356. 'Oh, I don't know': Garson Kanin *Remembering Mr Maugham* p. 101
    'by the time I have finished': WSM to Joseph Dobrinsky 16.2.61 Texas A&M
    'I am just finishing a novel': WSM to Gerald Kelly 30.5.29 HGARC
357. 'I have noticed that when someone asks': *Cakes and Ale* p. 7
358. '[Her] manner with Mrs Driffield': ibid. p. 128
    'She told me the hardest job': ibid. p. 178
359. 'I had long had in mind': ibid. p. 1
    'the yellow hair of a girl': *The Gentleman in the Parlour* p. 46
    'who neither read the books': *Cakes and Ale* p. 41
360. 'was very amiable to the authors': ibid. p. 154
    'I'm going to take a bus': ibid. p. 160
    'in which he showed quite definitely': ibid. p. 123
    'viceroy of the literary world': Peter Daubeny *My World of Theatre* (Cape 1971)
    p. 34
361. 'he was mean as cat's meat': Thomas Brady 'The Eighty Years of Mr Maugham'
    *New York Times Magazine* 24.1.54
    'I knew Hugh Walpole': John St John *William Heinemann: A Century of
    Publishing 1890–1990* (Heinemann 1990) p. 358
    '[I had] a considerable affection': *Cakes and Ale* p. 8
    'I'll tell you the sort of book': ibid. p. 98
362. '[Alroy Kear's] views on marriage': ibid. p. 18
    'one of the most memorable': Anthony West *New Yorker* 23.8.52
363. 'Read on with increasing horror': Hugh Walpole unpublished diaries HRHRC
    'I can't see any resemblance': A. S. Frere interview with Ted Morgan, Jenman
    'contains a most envenomed portrait': Michael Holroyd *Lytton Strachey* vol. II
    (Heinemann 1968) p. 680

'your laudable fiendishness': E. M. Forster to WSM 24.11.30 HGARC

'I hear poor Hugh': Jessica Brett Young *Francis Brett Young* (Heinemann 1962) p. 172

'the red-hot poker': Tribble (ed.) *A Chime of Words* p. 86

'thoroughly just, accurate': Brett Young *Francis Brett Young* p. 172

'cried aloud to be caricatured': Beverley Nichols *All I Could Never Be* (Cape 1949) p. 232

'I can see why Maugham': Henry Hardy (ed.) *Flourishing: Letters 1928–1946* (Chatto & Windus 2004) p. 193

'No English writer': *New York Times* 12.10.30

'supreme adroitness and ease': *Graphic* 15.10.30

364. 'a model of construction': MacCarthy *William Somerset Maugham: The English Maupassant* p. 9

'perfect novel': Gore Vidal *United States* (Deutsch 1993) p. 250

'superb . . . [as well as] a textbook': *Listener* 23.12.65

'[Driffield] gave you the impression': *Cakes and Ale* p. 89

'I am really very unlucky': WSM to Hugh Walpole n.d. HRHRC

365. 'piteous, writhing & wincing': Anne Olivier Bell (ed.) *The Diary of Virginia Woolf* vol. III (Hogarth Press 1980) p. 328

366. '[After *Cakes and Ale*] Maugham's reputation': Frank Swinnerton *Figures in the Foreground* (Hutchinson 1963) p. 35

## CHAPTER 12: MASTER HACKY

367. 'As what I have was invested': WSM to Messmore Kendall 13.1.29 HRHRC

'He was warm, affectionate': A. S. Frere to Anthony Curtis 31.12.73 private collection

368. 'had an inestimable gift': A. S. Frere interview with Ted Morgan, Jenman

'Willie to me is the most interesting': Nelson Doubleday to Eleanor Palffy 29.6.44 Princeton

369. 'last of the great': Cyril Connolly *Enemies of Promise* (Penguin 1961) p. 93

'He has a sense': MacCarthy *William Somerset Maugham: The English Maupassant* p. 8

'I can tell you nothing': David Garnett to Ted Morgan 25.1.78 Jenman

'I know just where I stand': Dean *Seven Friends* p. 160

370. 'If you have a snap-shot': WSM to Fred Bason 25.12.30 Lilly

'We Cockneys try to repay': attached to WSM to Fred Bason 28.9.34 Lilly

'No, I do not think': ibid. 13.11.31

371. 'This was my *Glorious* chance': Fred Bason to Grenville Cook n.d. Lilly

'You know quite well': WSM to Fred Bason 25.10.35 Lilly

'you are at perfect liberty': ibid. 11.5.26

'the toil and struggle': *Plays* vol. VI p. viii

'I haven't the desire': ibid.

372. 'you cannot have that intimate': ibid.

'Fashions change in the theatre': Winn *The Infirm Glory* p. 249

'led by the brisk but determined': *A Traveller in Romance* p. 27

'a picture of a gentleman': reproduced in Cole Lesley, Graham Payn and Sheridan Morley *Noël Coward and His Friends* (Weidenfeld & Nicolson 1979) p. 209

'red-eyed and miserable': Jack Hawkins *Anything for a Quiet Life* (Hamish Hamilton 1973) p. 43

373. 'businesslike, quiet, coolly cynical': *Cakes and Ale* p. 31

'to see the brilliant castigator': Louise Morgan *Writers at Work* (Chatto & Windus 1931) p. 58

'I dote really on the smell': WSM to David Horner 19.8.37 HRHRC

'the most entertaining game': *The Traveller's Library* p. 1

'I've lost hundreds': Maxwell *The Celebrity Circus* p. 19

374. 'The student of human nature': *The Traveller's Library* p. 1

'I do not flatter myself': WSM to Pfeiffer 26.9.31 HRHRC

375. 'Qu'importe sa vie': Sibyl Colefax Collection Bodleian

'light as thistledown': Cecil Roberts *Sunshine and Shadow 1930–1946* (Hodder & Stoughton 1972) p. 328

'she was like a little parrot': Jerry Rosco *Glenway Wescott Personally* (University of Wisconsin Press 2002) p. 97

'it was impossible to be bored': Acton *Memoirs of an Aesthete* p. 213

'were delivered with the artistry': Cecil Beaton *The Restless Years: Diaries 1955–63* (Weidenfeld & Nicolson 1976) p. 13

'The talk goes rocketing round': Basil Bartlett unpublished diaries private collection

'I have to keep my youth': Brian Masters *Great Hostesses* (Constable 1982) p. 137

376. 'I remember being terribly hurt': Liza Maugham in conversation with Pat Wallace, Frere Family Archive

'It was the most terrible shock': ibid.

377. 'There was a trace of subservience': Robert Rhodes James (ed.) *Chips: The Diaries of Sir Henry Channon* (Weidenfeld & Nicolson 1967) p. 32

'A strange little gathering': E. Phillips Oppenheim *The Pool of Memory* (Hodder & Stoughton 1941) p. 85

'J'ai un secrétaire': Horace de Carbuccia *Adieu à mon ami anglais* (Editions de France) p. 5

378. 'He was a gangster': *Strictly Personal* p. 29

'The people he puts before you': *The Vagrant Mood* p. 178

'My dear William . . . During a time': Odette Keun *I Discover the English* (John Lane The Bodley Head 1934)

379. 'It is not true': Odette Keun to WSM 4.1.34 HGARC

'For Barbara, because she never calls': *The Narrow Corner* Sotheby's catalogue of the sale of the Villa Mauresque 20.11.67

380. 'Your letters are a boon': WSM to Barbara Back n.d. HRHRC

'She is the least self-centred writer': WSM to Kate Bruce n.d. Berg

'I think they all': WSM to Barbara Back n.d. HRHRC

'Oh, Mr Maugham': S. N. Behrman *Tribulations and Laughter* (Hamish Hamilton 1972) p. 302

381. 'Willie had told him': Alec Waugh interview with Ted Morgan, Jenman
'Somerset Maugham may have misunderstood': *Rylands* introduction by Victor Rothschild (Stourton Press 1988)
'his taste appeared to me faultless': *The Summing Up* p. 21
'Lunch would have been going': Arthur Marshall *Life's Rich Pageant* (Hamish Hamilton 1984) p. 88

382. 'marvellously entertaining': Arthur Marshall *New Statesman* 25.2.77
'he loved to make one laugh': Anthony Curtis *The Pattern of Maugham* p. 15
'it would be idle to deny': Rebecca West *Nash's Magazine* October 1935
'It is exasperating': Harriet Cohen *A Bundle of Time* (Faber 1969) p. 180
'Willie hated to be touched': Glenway Wescott interview with Ted Morgan, Jenman
'carping at everyone': Rosco *Glenway Wescott Personally* p. 45

383. 'naturally happy temper': Day (ed.) *The Letters of Noël Coward* p. 229
'debonair and dashing': Alec Waugh *My Brother Evelyn and Other Profiles* (Cassell 1967) p. 280
'I lead a peculiarly quiet life': WSM to Gerald Kelly 14.12.33 HGARC
'no mincer of words': Acton *Memoirs of an Aesthete* p. 188
'He was a delightful creature': Jane Kelly *Listener* 7.2.74
'The mental domination': Beverley Nichols Foyle's Luncheon speech 1966
'No matter how badly': Arthur Marshall interview with Robert Calder, Jenman

384. '[Maugham] venait généralement': Carbuccia *Adieu à mon ami anglais* p. 8
'And did you masturbate?' Arthur Marshall interview with Robert Calder, Jenman
'What a place that is': Herman to Alan Searle n.d. HGARC

385. 'just this side': Kenneth McCormick interview with Ted Morgan, Jenman
'I'm p-p-perfectly aware': Robin Maugham *Conversations with Willie* p. 50
'Thank you again for your kindness': Gerald Haxton to Bert Alanson 6.8.28 Stanford
'He was a bad, bad, loud drunk': Jerry Zipkin interview with Ted Morgan, Jenman
'*Why* do you have to drink': Robin Maugham *Conversations with Willie* p. 52

386. 'You do not know what it is like': Winn *The Infirm Glory* p. 280

387. 'Gerald couldn't help resenting': Robin Maugham *Conversations with Willie* p. 20
'Gerald now likes the bottle': Arthur Marshall interview with Robert Calder, Jenman
'I could not bear the thought': *A Writer's Notebook* p. 217

388. 'I don't know about you': Robin Maugham *Escape from the Shadows* p. 84
'[Gerald] is getting more peaceful': WSM to Barbara Back 22.12.30 HRHRC
'It is really very pleasant': ibid. 21.4.32
'Wretched creature, Why don't you write': WSM to Alan Searle n.d. HGARC
'I am so very glad': ibid.

389. 'makes his relations with H[axton]': Paul Levy (ed.) *The Letters of Lytton Strachey* (Viking 2005) p. 639
'You know what I want': WSM to Alan Searle 2.4.34 HGARC
'The artist should never allow': WSM to Tammy Ryan 26.10.46 private collection

'I have never seen you': WSM to Gladys Cooper 23.9.31 Jenman

390. 'One morning when he had been': *First Person Singular* p. 140

391. 'I think some of them are very nice': ibid. p. 212
'After all, I am an Oriental': ibid. p. 193
'Though he spoke facetiously': ibid. p. 204

392. 'It was a large, square building': *The Narrow Corner* p. 111
'Mainsail and foresail were hoisted': ibid. p. 34

393. 'She was just aching for it': ibid. p.162
'I wanted him simply frightfully': ibid. p. 202
'Maugham's one and only': Gore Vidal *Sexually Speaking* (Cleis 1999) p. 174
'Oh God. If I'd known': *The Narrow Corner* p. 166
'Erik was worth ten of her': ibid. p. 198
'He was a slim, comely youth': ibid. p. 28
'Under his bushy grey eyebrows': ibid. p. 7
'He was an agreeable companion': ibid. p. 15
'This matter, which I supposed': *Plays* vol. VI p. v

394. 'I live on the Continent': *Daily Express* 3.11.32
'She wants a man': *Plays* vol. VI p. 126
'The day's long past': ibid. p. 127

395. 'We were the dupes': ibid. p. 164
'I was stirred to indignation': *Daily Express* 17.11.32
'the work of a man': *Sunday Times* 6.11.32
'My dear Lulu, Somerset Maugham's': 17.11.32 Louis Wilkinson to Llewellyn Powys private collection
'My dear Louis, *For Services Rendered*': 23.4.33 Llewellyn Powys to Louis Wilkinson private collection

396. 'You are Bessie Legros': *Plays* vol. VI. p. 293

397. 'To tell you the truth': ibid. p. 300
'a perfectly straightforward': WSM to Raymond Mortimer n.d. Princeton
'so as to make it more palatable': WSM to Joseph Dobrinsky 1.8.57 Texas A&M
'It seemed to be conceived': John Gielgud *Early Stages* (Macmillan 1939) p. 220
'I was very nervous': ibid.

398. 'Shakespeare will out': *Sunday Times* 17.9.33
'I almost bowed in acknowledgement': Noël Coward to WSM n.d. HGARC
'[It] was the last play': WSM to Joseph Dobrinsky 1.8.57 Texas A&M
'I cannot tell you': Day (ed.) *The Letters of Noël Coward* p. 227
'With all its glamour': Kanin *Remembering Mr Maugham* p. 45
'I can never get over': WSM to Alan Searle 8.4.44 HGARC
'I want to write novels & stories': WSM to Bert Alanson 21.1.33 Stanford

## CHAPTER 13: THE TELLER OF TALES

400. 'seven hundred colleges in America': WSM to Alan Searle n.d. HGARC
401. 'Beloved by unliterary, unofficial': Wescott *Images of Truth* p. 65

'the mahatma of middlebrow culture': Robert Mazzocco *New York Review of Books* 23.11.78

'Mr Maugham's short stories': *Spectator* 29.9.33

'His extraordinary knowledge': *New Statesman* 25.8.34

'Maughamesque short story': Charles Drazin (ed.) *The Journals: John Fowles* vol. 1 *1949–1965* (Knopf 2003) p. 165

'His plots are cool and deadly': Frank MacShane *The Life of Raymond Chandler* (Cape 1976) p. 75

'the transforming passion': V. S. Pritchett *New Statesman* 8.10.49

'I have never pretended': *Selected Prefaces and Introductions* p. 69

'I find it often': *A Writer's Notebook* p. 219

402. 'She is not mondaine': Rebecca West to WSM n.d. HGARC

'sunny place for shady people': *Strictly Personal* p. 156

'He had a certain dreadful circle': George Rylands interview with Robert Calder, Jenman

'He was too much impressed': *Sunday Times* 19.12.65

403. 'It was a representative Riviera party': *Collected Short Stories* vol. I p. 265

'It was their fat that had brought them': ibid. p. 227

'the long-limbed English': ibid. p. 229

'an enclosure covered with glass': ibid. p. 231

404. 'In front of Beatrice': ibid. p. 239

'The cure at Bad Gastein': WSM to Sibyl Colefax 28.8.34 Bodleian

405. 'We went to a lovely performance': WSM to Alan Searle n.d. HGARC

'[and] expects to make': WSM to Alan Searle 29.7.34 HGARC

'easily the nicest character': Robin Maugham unpublished diaries Lilly

406. 'Judge and Author Bereaved': *Daily Telegraph* 27.7.35

'Charley's death was expected': WSM to Gerald Kelly 4.8.36 HGARC

'"kinky clients" . . . [and] the only time': Honor Earl unpublished ms private collection

'alone with my parents': Robin Maugham *The Search for Nirvana* p. 41

'a well-dressed attractive man': Robin Maugham *Escape from the Shadows* p. 26

407. 'I'm not saying I think there was incest': Glenway Wescott interview with Ted Morgan, Jenman

'This is only to say': WSM to Robin Maugham 5.6.34 HRHRC

'We met him the first night': Robin Maugham *Escape from the Shadows* p. 84

408. 'I learned many things in Vienna': ibid. pp. 86 et seq.

'I had a lovely party': Liza Maugham in conversation with Pat Wallace, Frere Family Archive

'She was wrapped up in cotton-wool': McKnight *The Scandal of Syrie Maugham* p. 137

'almost mechanical correctness': *Daily Telegraph* 22.4.36

409. 'What do you think': WSM to Barbara Back 28.3.34 HRHRC

'gay, fantastic & amusing': ibid.

'odious charmer': Alan Pryce-Jones *The Bonus of Laughter* (Hamish Hamilton 1987) p. 226

410. 'a distinctive trait of the homosexual': *Don Fernando* p. 141

'St John of the Cross': *New Statesman* 29.6.35
'This is Mr Maugham's best book': *Spectator* 21.6.35
'kind, very considerate': WSM to Barbara Back n.d. HRHRC
'I have been playing golf today': WSM to Alan Searle 11.2.35 HGARC
'The fleet is in': ibid. 18.7.35

411. 'Things are going very badly': WSM to Alan Searle n.d. HGARC
'The doctor tells me': ibid.
'fantastic contracts': WSM to Alan Searle 18.11.35 HGARC

412. 'small, neat, impeccably dressed': Leon Edel *Saturday Review* 15.3.80
'Maugham was leaning forward talking': Alec Waugh *The Best Wine Last*
(W. H. Allen) p. 216
'Gerald has been behaving': WSM to Alan Searle 24.11.35 HGARC
'The place is picturesque enough': WSM to Alan Searle 16.12.35 HGARC

413. 'The West Indies are disappointing': WSM to Juliet Duff 23.2.36 HGARC

414. '& gave me a couple of murderers': ibid.
'The guillotine is in a small room': *A Writer's Notebook* p. 232
'of all the men I questioned': WSM to Juliet Duff 23.2.36 HGARC
'I got one very good story': WSM to Alan Searle 6.2.36 HGARC
'I have been thinking much of you': ibid. n.d.
'My happiness would be complete': ibid. 22.12.35

415. 'I can quite see that the prospect': ibid.

416. 'grim and cold . . . I had goose-flesh': 'Episode' *Collected Short Stories* vol. IV
p. 136
'Of course what I should like': WSM to Alan Searle 24.11.35 HGARC
'but felt it only right to remind her': 'Looking Back' p. 114
'She was very frank': *Horizon* January 1959
'J'ai dû être remplacée': Flora Groult *Marie Laurencin* (Mercure de France 1987)
p. 233

417. 'I found myself positively in danger': Ted Berkman *The Lady and the Law*
(Little, Brown 1976) p. 215

418. 'Mr Maugham anatomises emotion': *New Statesman* 27.3.37

419. 'with his puckish humour': *A Writer's Notebook* p. 319
'very serious rumours': Nigel Nicolson (ed.) *Harold Nicolson: Diaries and Letters
1930–1939* (Collins 1966) p. 276
'I am a writer': WSM to Juliet Duff 10.12.36 HGARC

420. 'I'm afraid I am not a very good partner': Robert Boothby *Boothby: Recollections
of a Rebel* (Hutchinson 1978) p. 195
'I think she had a very difficult role': WSM to Charles Towne 18.3.37 NYPL
'I am leaving Cannes tomorrow': Wallis Simpson to WSM 7.3.37 HGARC
'What many people did not understand': Winn *The Infirm Glory* p. 337
'Gerald is in bed': WSM to Alan Searle 24.12.36 HGARC
'[Alan] is being very sweet': WSM to David Horner 15.1.37 HRHRC
'Searle was more pussy-cat': Daniel Farson *Never a Normal Man* (HarperCollins
1996) p. 77
'So far as I am concerned': WSM to Barbara Back 24.3.37 HRHRC

421. 'is a ghastly mess': WSM to Robin Maugham 9.2.35 HRHRC

422. 'It is very wonderful': WSM to Bert Alanson 15.3.38 Stanford
'There is no reason why your father': WSM to Robin Maugham 6.5.38 Lilly
423. 'Well-dressed, attractive and slim': Robin Maugham *The Search for Nirvana* p. 52
'I am tired & want a change': WSM to Charles Towne 27.10.37 NYPL
424. 'Yesterday Anthony Blunt & a friend': WSM to Alan Searle n.d. HGARC
426. 'an injured and defensive heart': V. S. Pritchett *Christian Science Monitor* 23.3.38
'I think you must know grammar': WSM to Edward Marsh 27.1.37 Berg
'p. 28 Has "massivity" any advantage': Christopher Hassall *Edward Marsh* (Longmans 1959) p. 692
'I like to think they may have adorned': WSM to Edward Marsh 8.10.38 Berg
427. 'Never have I read an autobiography': G. B. Stern *And Did He Stop to Speak to You?* (Henry Regnery 1958) p. 164
'that both the main interest': *Criterion* XVII 1938
'been to pretty well every': WSM to Alan Searle n.d. HGARC
428. 'so far as stories were concerned': WSM to Karl Pfeiffer 26.2.38 HRHRC
'[I] only regret that the shadow': WSM to E. M. Forster 24.2.38 King's College, Cambridge
429. 'I can understand that when people say': *A Writer's Notebook* p. 261
430. 'and when I told her that I had spent': *The Memoirs of the Aga Khan* (Cassell 1954) foreword p. ix
'I was enthralled to meet him': M. M. Kaye *Enchanted Evening* (Penguin 1999) p. 227
431. 'As for getting any insight': WSM to Karl Pfeiffer 26.2.38 HRHRC
'I remained in that state for so long': *A Writer's Notebook* p. 252
432. 'Bhagavan [the Maharshi] and Somerset Maugham sat': www.beezone.com/Ramana/somerset_maugham.html
'We have been much disturbed': WSM to Alan Searle 15.3.38 HGARC
'while Gerald painted the town red': Harold Acton *More Memoirs of an Aesthete* (Methuen 1970) p. 335
433. 'It really is the perfect holiday': Nicolson (ed.) *Harold Nicolson: Diaries and Letters 1930–1939* p. 351
434. 'I do not think there is any danger': WSM to Bert Alanson 13.5.38 Stanford
'I have not waited until I received': WSM to Herman Ould 26.6.38 HRHRC
'That young man holds the future': Nigel Nicolson (ed.) *The Diary of Virginia Woolf* vol. V (Hogarth Press 1984) p. 185
'like a dead man': Anne Olivier Bell (ed.) *The Diary of Virginia Woolf* vol. V (Hogarth Press 1984) p. 185
435. 'Well, we've escaped war': WSM to Bert Alanson 23.10.38 Stanford

## CHAPTER 14: AN EXERCISE IN PROPAGANDA

436. 'I think it an abuse': *Selected Prefaces* p. 10
437. 'had a fearful reality': *Christmas Holiday* p. 250
438. 'maladroitly handled': *London Mercury* March 1939
'the completely normal Charley': *Boston Evening Transcript* 21.10.39

'For pure technical felicity': *Spectator* 17.2.39

'I am now advised': David O. Selznick to Daniel T. O'Shea 24.3.39 HRHRC

'Here in Italy everyone seems convinced': WSM to Bert Alanson 12.6.39 Stanford

439.  'there was a feeling of gentle excitement': *Strictly Personal* p. 26

440.  'I am hoping . . . [to] get some sort of work': WSM to Desmond MacCarthy
5.9.39 Lilly

'I much fear that I shall be left': WSM to Robin Maugham 7.10.39 HRHRC

'Willie and I are . . . feeling very aged': Gerald Haxton to Robin Maugham
28.9.39 HRHRC

'This raised my spirits': *Strictly Personal* p. 60

441.  'private reports': ibid. p. 136

'What difference will it make': 'The English Family' unpublished typescript
Jenman

'Méfiez-vous de cet Anglais': Carbuccia *Adieu à mon ami anglais* p. 40

'I was entertained by generals': 'Looking Back' p. 146

442.  'The officer in command told me': *Strictly Personal* p. 88

'I was determined to write': ibid. p. 108

'The impression I received': ibid. p. 80

'I cannot attempt to describe': *France at War* p. 41

443.  'There are plenty of empty houses': ibid. p. 29

'These wretched people': *Strictly Personal* p. 105

'pleasantly democratic . . . Orders are given': *France at War* p. 65

'I had not been able to help': *Strictly Personal* p. 115

444.  'arrived in London': ibid. p. 124

'I am glad that your father': WSM to Kate Bruce 30.9.39 Berg

445.  'It means that the second Viscount': WSM to Bert Alanson 4.4.39 Stanford

'Robin dear, I am settling $25000': WSM to Robin Maugham 20.11.39 Berg

'I am very glad': WSM to Robin Maugham 11.2.39 HRHRC

'I am told on all sides': WSM to Robin Maugham 20.11.39 Berg

'It was very quiet on the Riviera': *Strictly Personal* p. 137

'Everyone is bored': WSM to Ellen Doubleday n.d. Princeton

446.  'It never struck any of us': *Strictly Personal* p. 152

447.  'Don't struggle . . . Open your mouth': ibid. p. 162

448.  'Many broke down then': ibid. p. 171

449.  'Willie got home! . . .' Kate Bruce unpublished ms private collection

'Would it be possible for me to visit': WSM to Alan Searle n.d. HGARC

'In Alan Searle it seemeth me': unpublished HGARC

450.  '[There is] practically no night-life': *Daily Express* 1.10.40

'Willie! Thank God you're safe': Liza Maugham in conversation with Pat
Wallace, Frere Family Archive

451.  'But it didn't work': ibid.

'After my three weeks': *Strictly Personal* p. 239

'Willie Maugham was palpably bored': Kenneth Young (ed.) *The Diaries of Sir
Robert Bruce Lockhart* vol. II *1939–1965* (Macmillan 1980) p. 79

'[I] shouted at her to take cover': Michael Swan *Ilex and Olive* (Home & Van
Thal 1949) p. 75

452. 'You know we've had some air raid warnings': WSM to Alan Searle n.d.
HGARC
'W. Somerset Maugham is in this country': *New York Times Book Review*
24.11.40

453. 'Just as the best novel': Edward Weeks *Writers and Friends* (Little, Brown 1981)
'When, in this war': *New York Times* 24.10.40

454. 'the crisis was destroying': *Strictly Personal* p. 261
'On his arrival Maugham was given': Robert Calder *Beware the British Serpent*
p. 121
'looking old, tired and shrivelled': *The Vagrant Mood* p. 181
'she managed to create': WSM to David Horner 11.10.44 HRHRC
'though frequently complimenting me': Phelps (ed.) *Continual Lessons* p. 97

455. 'I said that for my part': ibid. p. 91
'I had the feeling': Liza Maugham in conversation with Pat Wallace, Frere
Family Archive
'I can't bear this': Glenway Wescott interview with Ted Morgan, Jenman

456. 'a large ginger moustache': Farson *Never a Normal Man* p. 41
'If by any chance we are beaten': 'The English Family' unpublished typescript
Jenman

457. 'in his hardest, narrowest voice': Glenway Wescott interview with Ted Morgan,
Jenman
'The vast majority are ready': WSM to F. H. Maugham 14.1.41 private
collection
'Naturally we should keep confidential': David O. Selznick to Daniel T. O'Shea
14.3.41 HRHRC

458. 'So far I have only been allowed': WSM to Alan Searle 1.4.41 HGARC
'poor & poorly acted': ibid. 15.4.41
'fictional drivel': *Nation* 3.5.41
'worst novel': *New Republic* 19.5.41
'talking in his sleep': *Newsweek* 7.4.41
'an unscrupulous scamp': *Up at the Villa* p. 105
'He had immense vitality': ibid. p. 28
'Why didn't you leave him? . . .' ibid. p. 29

459. 'the most tedious job': WSM to Robin Maugham 4.6.42 HRHRC
'It is two miles from the sea': WSM to Ellen Doubleday 3.6.41 Princeton
'Of course it wasn't true': Liza Maugham in conversation with Pat Wallace,
Frere Family Archive

460. 'J'étais dans une grande soirée': Gerald Haxton to Louis Legrand 24.2.41 Stanford
'fast-disappearing career': *Film Weekly* 29.3.35
'I see something of the stars': WSM to Kate Bruce 27.6.41 Berg
'one little ray of sunshine': WSM to Osbert Sitwell 9.10.41 HRHRC

461. 'I went to my last the other day': WSM to G. B. Stern 20.7.41 HRHRC
'I meet few people who interest me': WSM to Karl Pfeiffer 20.7.41 HRHRC
'You mean about Mickey Rooney?': Karl G. Pfeiffer *W. Somerset Maugham:
A Candid Portrait* p. 69
'Which one is he supposed to be now?' Wilmon Menard 'Maugham in

Hollywood' *American Film* April 1979

'demure in black silk': *A Traveller in Romance* p. 96

'I was so pleased to see Willie': Katherine Bucknell (ed.) *Christopher Isherwood Diaries* vol. I: *1939–1960* (Methuen 1996) p. 142

'an old Gladstone bag': Brian Finney *Isherwood* (Faber 1979) p. 180

'that delightful, strange man': Swan *Ilex and Olive* p. 70

462. '[climbing] all over him': Bucknell (ed.) *Christopher Isherwood Diaries* vol. I p. 142

'I am afraid this is no more': WSM to Alan Searle 25.7.41 HGARC

'I have read scripts and reviewed': David O. Selznick collection 25.4.41 HRHRC

463. 'I loathe the people': WSM to Kate Bruce 27.6.41 Berg

'I know very well': WSM to Edward Marsh 1.3.43 Berg

'Writing, writing, writing': WSM to Alan Searle 24.10.41 HGARC

'the result so far': ibid. 13.11.41

'Now that America is in the war': WSM to Glenway Wescott 12.12.41 Maryland

464. 'The countryside [is] wild, lonely': WSM to Karl Pfeiffer 28.1.42 HRHRC

'[They] have captured my sympathy': WSM to Robin Maugham 4.6.42 HRHRC

465. 'quite nice, a little shy': WSM to Barbara Back 8.7.33 HRHRC

'Ellen ran the worst household in America': Jerry Zipkin interview with Ted Morgan, Jenman

'I have grand gallops': WSM to Alan Searle 16.4.42 HGARC

466. 'It's no good your telling me': WSM to Edward Marsh 1.3.43 Berg

'Of course I should miss him': WSM to Alan Searle 10.5.42 HGARC

'I know that people used to come': Glenway Wescott interview with Ted Morgan, Jenman

467. 'three long, long, long weeks': John Keats *You Might as Well Live* (Simon & Schuster 1970) p. 237

'Thank you very much for the recipe': WSM to Eleanor Roosevelt 1.3.45 Library of Congress

'What a distinguished profile': ibid. n.d.

468. 'too hot to do anything': WSM to Alan Searle 26.6.42 HGARC

'The hall was packed': WSM to Barbara Back 6.2.44 HRHRC

'Our stock is falling lower': WSM to Alan Searle 30.6.42 HGARC

'[Willie] does not mind so much': Phelps (ed.) *Continual Lessons* p. 90

469. '& next day when he was being taken': WSM to Alan Searle 22.7.42 HGARC

'The book has been a great pleasure': WSM to Karl Pfeiffer 12.5.43 HRHRC

471. 'I dare say I shall go to Paris': *The Razor's Edge* p. 143

'I had written nothing more': ibid. p. 340

472. 'calls more countesses': *Our Betters* p. 15

'[Willie] was fascinated by him': A. S. Frere to Anthony Curtis 31.12.73 private collection

473. 'By meditation on the formless one': *The Razor's Edge* p. 284

'Larry sat with his arm stretched out': ibid. p. 202

'sheer delight': *New Statesman* 26.8.44
'I will not pretend': WSM to Edward Marsh 1.6.44 Berg
474. 'It has given me a lot of satisfaction': WSM to Diana Marr-Johnson 18.10.44 private collection
'Gerald is working very hard': WSM to Robin Maugham 6.10.43 HRHRC
'[He] is delighted really': WSM to Alan Searle 23.11.43 HGARC
'[and] it is a wonderful relief': WSM to Karl Pfeiffer 24.11.43 HRHRC
475. 'who will give me, I think': ibid. 12.1.44
'I worked as usual in the morning': *A Writer's Notebook* p. 319
'I was disappointed, but not distressed': WSM to Edward Marsh 1.6.44 Berg
'I have been in great trouble': WSM to Barbara Back 9.7.44 HRHRC
476. 'Though I have long known': WSM to Ellen Doubleday n.d. Princeton
477. 'to breathe a little better': WSM to Barbara Back 9.7.44 HRHRC
'coughing & spitting convalescents': WSM to Ellen Doubleday 16.7.44 Princeton
'I think going to see him twice a day': WSM to Barbara Back 9.7.44 HRHRC
'I am afraid he is growing weaker': WSM to Edward Knoblock 2.10.44 Berg
'I have to face the prospect': WSM to Diana Marr-Johnson 18.10.44 private collection
478. 'There is a slight hope': WSM to Alan Searle 3.11.44 HGARC
'Gerald's death has been a bitter blow': WSM to George Cukor 18.11.44 Margaret Herrick Library
'Please don't write & sympathize': WSM to Charles Towne 28.11.44 NYPL
'the tempestuous grief': WSM to Alan Searle 20.12.44 HGARC
'I don't want to see you!': Roberts *Sunshine and Shadow, 1930–1946* p. 376
'He had his habitual composed': Behrman *Tribulations and Laughter* p. 288
479. 'I suppose I shall give it a trial': WSM to David Horner 11.10.44 HRHRC


CHAPTER 15: THE BRONZINO BOY

480. 'For thirty years he has been': Day (ed.) *The Letters of Noël Coward* p. 229
'Tout me le rappelle': WSM to Louis Legrand 15.5.45 Jenman
'The best years of my life': WSM to Robin Maugham 26.6.44 HRHRC
481. 'I found Willie overwhelmed': Robin Maugham *Escape from the Shadows* p. 140
482. 'It has happened to me from time to time': *New Yorker* 8.6.46
'He has always disliked me': WSM to Ellen Doubleday 9.8.46 Princeton
'Everyone here is of course': WSM to Alan Searle 9.5.45 HGARC
483. '[Willie] was very, very kind to me': George Cukor interview with Jesse Hill Ford, Margaret Herrick Library
'I'd never bought a picture': *Purely for My Pleasure* p. 17
484. 'in grateful acknowledgement': *Traveller in Romance* p. 132
'You would be doing me a great favour': WSM to the Earl of Halifax 6.7.45 Margaret Herrick Library
'I know that at one time': PRO FO 371/44582, Donnelly minute 14.9.45 quoted in Calder *Beware the British Serpent* p. 132

'Alan arrived, very heavy': Glenway Wescott interview with Ted Morgan, Jenman

485. '[Alan] is a great comfort to me': WSM to Bert Alanson 22.1.46 Stanford
'it recalled a pain': *Traveller in Romance* p. 132
'for the kindness and the generosity': ibid.
'I am very grateful to you': WSM to Ellen Doubleday 9.8.46 Princeton

486. 'My old servants are back': WSM to Tammy Ryan 13.8.46 private collection

487. 'Voila votre Colonel d'Amerique': n.d. Stanford
'[I lived] in Maugham's Paris apartment': David Posner to Ted Morgan 28.3.77
Jenman
'gigantic Jewish poet': Glenway Wescott interview with Ted Morgan, Jenman
'I was starry-eyed': David Posner to Ted Morgan 22.2.77 Jenman

488. 'Willie just cut his head off': Glenway Wescott interview with Ted Morgan,
Jenman
'People are strangely apathetic': WSM to Nelson Doubleday 20.10.46 Princeton
'I hope I shall like her next husband': WSM to Bert Alanson 10.4.47 Stanford
'said mother, aged 67': WSM to Nelson Doubleday 12.9.46 Princeton
'even richer than Shaw . . .!' *Daily Herald* 5.10.50

489. 'In the last week I have had': WSM to Ann Fleming n.d. private collection
'Millionaires & such like': WSM to Sibyl Colefax 15.12.44 Bodleian
'Does Mr Maugham realize': *Daily Telegraph* 17.4.47

490. 'overcome [by] the indifference': Raymond Mander and Joe Mitchenson
*The Artist and the Theatre* (Heinemann 1955)
'I wish I could enlist your help': WSM to J. B. Priestley 12.1.48 HRHRC

491. 'I think you have been harsher': WSM to Edward Marsh 9.2.48 Berg

492. 'I cannot tell you what a relief': WSM to Glenway Wescott and Monroe
Wheeler 22.8.48 Maryland
'rice, oil, bacon, sausages': WSM to Tammy Ryan 13.8.46 private collection
'very much pleased': WSM to Ellen Doubleday 26.1.47 Princeton

493. 'as right as rain for William': Phelps (ed.) *Continual Lessons* p. 162
'[the perfect] nanny': Morgan *Maugham* p. 494
'I loved him with all my heart': unpublished ms Margaret Herrick Library
'I am, I think, very happy': Alan Searle to Ellen Doubleday 27.12.46 Princeton

494. 'I'm so glad you're here': Morgan *Maugham* p. 565
'The family were all fond': Nicolas Paravicini to author private collection
'Liza and the children are here': Alan Searle to Bert Alanson 21.8.47 Stanford
'He is a pompous donkey': WSM to Ellen Doubleday 11.9.53 Princeton
'which adds greatly to the gaiety': WSM to Nelson Doubleday 19.8.48
Princeton

495. 'Ostensibly, he is cutting down': Ellen Doubleday to WSM 15.12.47 Princeton
'Nelson has created a vast empire': WSM to Douglas M. Black 15.9.46 Jenman
'I am not so foolish': WSM to Ellen Doubleday 14.1.49 Princeton

496. 'It's good enough': Julian Maclaren-Ross *Collected Memoirs* (Black Spring Press
2004) p. 247

497. '[The Queen] was very nicely dressed': WSM to Bert Alanson 23.7.54 Stanford
'But don't you see': George Rylands interview with Robert Calder, Jenman
'I am the greatest living writer': F. J. Shirley *Cantuarian* December 1965

'You will remember how astonished': WSM to Antony Darnborough n.d. Jenman

498. 'soulful damsels': WSM to Diana Marr-Johnson n.d. private collection
'People I haven't seen': Robin Maugham unpublished diaries Beinecke
'I am not a monkey in the zoo': WSM to Kate Bruce n.d. Berg

499. 'When he emerges [from the pool]': Kanin *Remembering Mr Maugham* p. 27
'Willie arrived punctually at eight': Young (ed.) *The Diaries of Sir Robert Bruce Lockhart* vol. II p. 684
'the whole air of hanky-panky': Patrick McGrady *The Youth Doctors* (Arthur Barker 1968) p. 97

500. 'I feel strange': Kanin *Remembering Mr Maugham* p. 139
'We had Willie Maugham and his catamite': Artemis Cooper (ed.) *Mr Wu and Mrs Stitch: The Letters of Evelyn Waugh and Diana Cooper* (Hodder & Stoughton 1991) p. 261

501. 'as though they were gauleiters': *The Vagrant Mood* p. 179
'One could never be quite certain': Liza Maugham in conversation with Pat Wallace, Frere Family Archive
'He imposed a regime': Peter Quennell *The Wanton Chase* (Collins 1980) p. 162
'That's what you'll be doing': Peter Daubeny *My World of Theatre* (Cape 1971) p. 98

502. 'all I had done': *Sunday Times* 3.4.66
'we were enjoying a nightcap': *Paris Review* no. 165 p. 205
'his face is the wickedest tangle': Charlotte Mosley (ed.) *In Tearing Haste: Letters between Deborah Devonshire and Patrick Leigh Fermor* (John Murray 2008) p. 20

503. 'It goes with a swing': WSM to Ian Fleming n.d. Lilly
'No. [It's] not that I didn't mean': ibid.
'Do you remember Paris': WSM to Gerald Kelly 8.12.48 HGARC
'I had wanted the Queen': Gerald Kelly to Bert Alanson 3.3.53 Stanford

504. 'Your father bore with grim disapproval': WSM to Robin Maugham 3.2.50 HRHRC
'You may well be right': Robin Maugham *Somerset and All the Maughams* p. 189
'only two hearts': Gerard Noel *Ena: Spain's English Queen* (Constable 1984) p. 282

505. 'Frank says, "Hiya, baby!"': Kanin *Remembering Mr Maugham* p. 191
'Far too many people': Graham Payne and Sheridan Morley (eds) *The Noël Coward Diaries* (Papermac 1982) p. 382

506. 'M. Cocteau talks for the benefit': James Lord *Some Remarkable Men* (Farrar Straus & Giroux 1996) p. 127
'It has always been an ambition': WSM to Bert Alanson 30.4.49 Stanford
'He liked a picture': Acton *Memoirs of an Aesthete* p. 189
'I do not think Utrillo': *Life* 1.12.41

507. 'It was the picture': *Purely for My Pleasure* p. 24
'a fantastic absence of feeling': Nicky Mariano (ed.) *Sunset and Twilight: From the Diaries of Bernard Berenson* (Hamish Hamilton 1964) p. 439
'was remarkably perceptive': Kenneth Clark *The Other Half* (John Murray 1977) p. 116

508. 'The first time I saw it': *Daily Express* 16.11.51 quoted in Roger Berthoud *Graham Sutherland* (Faber 1982) p. 141
'carried caricature as far': Edmund Wilson *The Fifties* (Farrar, Straus & Giroux 1986) p. 204
509. 'Although I wouldn't like Graham to know': WSM to Kenneth Clark 16.4.51 Wake Forest

## CHAPTER 16: BETRAYAL

510. 'On the continent of Europe': *A Writer's Notebook* p. 318
'not a great fan': William Plomer to Jocelyn Brooke 14.5.53 Jenman
'don't think I'm at all': Angus Wilson to Jocelyn Brooke 5.5.53 Jenman
'May I be excused?': William Sansom to Jocelyn Brooke 5.5.53 Jenman
'[cannot] because of the novel': Elizabeth Bowen to Jocelyn Brooke 24.3.53 Jenman
'truly and deeply sorry': Noël Coward to Jocelyn Brooke 16.6.53 Jenman
'[I] shall produce 2000 words': Raymond Mortimer to Jocelyn Brooke 27.4.53 Jenman
511. 'those thousands of readers': *Author* 25.1.54 Lilly
'Anybody else would have sat down': St John Ervine to Richard Church 19.2.54 HRHRC
512. 'he will tell you everything': *New Yorker* 29.10.49
'I really cannot stand': WSM to Richard Cordell 23.1.39 Lilly
'he tears everything': Phelps (ed.) *Continual Lessons* p. 166
513. 'I had held on to those letters': Jerry Zipkin interview with Ted Morgan, Jenman
'Your kids of Paravicini': Louis Legrand to Liza Maugham 15.4.64 private collection
514. 'I must tell you that this has come': Robin Maugham to Alan Searle 28.12.62 HGARC
'I've had an offer from the American': Robin Maugham to WSM 14.2.62 HGARC
515. 'I promise you here and now': ibid. 20.2.62
'[Mr Maugham's] celebrity in Europe': Alan Searle to Bert Alanson 29.1.53 Stanford
516. 'smiling . . . heavily perfumed': Georges Rosanoff *Racontez Docteur* (Guy le Prat 1977) p. 13
'[Alan] was not in himself': Phelps (ed.) *Continual Lessons* p. 162
'a namby-pamby': Jerry Zipkin interview with Ted Morgan, Jenman
'muddle-headed . . . [and] not very bright': Douglas Cooper to Robert Calder 10.9.78 Jenman
'I think you are a darling': Alan Searle to Jane Clark 17.4.52 Wake Forest
'[you are] such a darling': Alan Searle to Jerry Zipkin 10.3.59 HGARC
'I have few friends': ibid. 15.11.50
'he enjoyed the complaining': Jerry Zipkin interview with Ted Morgan, Jenman

517.  'Thank you for all those wonderful picture books': Alan Searle to Jerry Zipkin
      28.12.54 HGARC
      'Oooh, you should have seen': Camilla Chandon de Briailles unpublished
      private collection
      '[Mr Maugham] was generous to me': unpublished ms George Cukor
      Collection Margaret Herrick Library
      'Alan Searle was a knight': Liza Maugham in conversation with Pat Wallace,
      Frere Family Collection
      '[who] said in his entire life': Glenway Wescott interview with Ted Morgan,
      Jenman

518.  'Mr M.'s popularity in Japan': Alan Searle to Klaus Jonas 25.11.59 HRHRC
      'He still felt he had something': Jeffrey Meyers *Somerset Maugham: A Life* p. 317

519.  'He's a white man': James Lees-Milne *Diaries, 1942–1954* ed. Michael Bloch
      (John Murray 2006) p. 435
      'I have been reading Kipling': WSM to G. B. Stern 6.2.51 HRHRC
      'is our greatest story writer': *A Choice of Kipling's Prose* p. xxviii
      'The fact is that, like drinking': WSM to Bert Alanson 5.9.54 Stanford
      '[My] fertile invention': WSM to Klaus Jonas 14.5.56 HRHRC
      'Writing with me': *Daily Express* 20.1.58

520.  'the last one "The Delicate Nature"': WSM to H. E. Bates 22.9.53 private
      collection
      'I have good servants': WSM to Kate Bruce 18.1.51 Berg
      'It would be hypocrisy': WSM to Barbara Back 10.8.55 HRHRC
      'Tra la la, no more alimony': Robin Maugham *Somerset and All the Maughams*
      p. 20

521.  'I am like a passenger': *A Writer's Notebook* p. 333
      'an iguana sunning itself': Calder *Willie: The Life of W. Somerset Maugham* p. 43
      'with his pale deeply furrowed face': Frances Partridge *Everything to Lose:
      Diaries 1945–1960* (Little, Brown 1985) p. 131
      'reminded of the lizards': Harold Nicolson to Robin Maugham 17.12.58 Lilly
      '[Willie] was shapely but tiny': Glenway Wescott interview with Ted Morgan,
      Jenman
      'a seedy relic of the Edwardian era': WSM to Douglas M. Black 30.1.57
      Jenman
      'Things I could do with pleasure': WSM to Gerald Kelly 2.7.59 HGARC
      'a poor old celluloid doll': *Beaton in the Sixties: The Cecil Beaton Diaries as He
      Wrote Them 1965–1969* introduction by Hugo Vickers (Weidenfeld & Nicolson
      2003) p. 17
      'If you think I'm g-g-g-ga-ga': Behrman *Tribulations and Laughter* p. 308

522.  'Robin's handicap has always been': WSM to Kate Bruce 2.2.57 Berg
      '[Robin] is as frivolous': WSM to Bert Alanson 28.7.55 Stanford
      'It has been my ill-fortune': *A Choice of Kipling's Prose* p. xxii

524.  'Alan is not nearly as simple': James J. Berg and Chris Freeman (eds)
      *The Isherwood Century* (University of Wisconsin Press 2000)
      'Parents subjected me': unpublished ms George Cukor Collection Margaret
      Herrick Library

'I'm always thinking about the future': Alan Searle to Bert Alanson 12.1.50 Stanford

'What will become of me': Alan Searle interview with Robert Calder, Jenman

525. 'I want you to know': Liza Maugham in conversation with Pat Wallace, Frere Family Collection

526. 'It will also be very nice for you' ibid.

'Dearest Daddy, You really are making me': ibid.

527. 'As far as he's concerned': ibid.

'Alan must have had a hand in it': ibid.

'his vile so-called daughter': Alan Searle to Jonas 17.4.63 HRHRC

528. 'a scavenger . . . a bitch': Alan Searle to Jerry Zipkin 21.8.63 HGARC

'Alan incites Willie against Liza': Mark Amory (ed.) *The Letters of Ann Fleming* (Collins Harvill 1985) p. 184

'There is something in her': Diana Marr-Johnson to Alan Searle 12.4.62 HGARC

'I only hope that he': Alan Searle to Robin Maugham 1.6.62 HGARC

529. 'dire et declarer nul': private collection

'I am peace-loving': Alan Searle to Sam Behrman 26.7.63 Jenman

'He is devoured by retrospective hate': Payne and Morley (eds) *The Noël Coward Diaries* p. 508

530. 'I am thrilled': Alan Searle to Lord Beaverbrook 11.11.61 Parliamentary Archives BBK/C/293

'a very imperfect and tormented creature': 'Looking Back' p. 144

531. 'Everyone is fully aware': anonymous 14.11.62 HGARC

'Entirely contemptible': Payne and Morley (eds) *The Noël Coward Diaries* p. 511

'shabby, sordid, embarrassing': Kanin *Remembering Mr Maugham* p. 68

'the ancient Maugham mined': Vidal *United States* p. 237

'I believe neither in the existence': 'Looking Back' p. 128

532. 'The maps are out': Alan Searle to Jane Clark 11.2.55 Wake Forest

'Never again will I stir': Alan Searle interview with Ted Morgan, Jenman

'Rarely sensible, and in acute misery': Alan Searle to Jerry Zipkin 21.8.63 HGARC

'Poor, poor Willie': Alan Searle to Robin Maugham 1.12.63 HGARC

'even today the pain': *Sunday Express* 26.1.64

'I have been shut up': Alan Searle to Robin Maugham 5.4.65 HGARC

'He lives in some terrifying world': Alan Searle to Jerry Zipkin 5.4.65 HGARC

533. 'I have a good many': Alan Searle to Glenway Wescott 2.7.65 Maryland

'like a malignant crab': Robin Maugham unpublished diaries Lilly

'black double-breasted quilted smoking jacket': Robin Maugham unpublished diaries Lilly

'Willie is now completely': Alan Searle to Ellen Doubleday 27.11.65 Princeton

534. 'It wasn't sexual': Mary Dawson interview with author 18.5.06

536. 'The first little splutter of interest': WSM to Karl Pfeiffer 1.5.46 HRHRC

'the most enthralling': *The Summing Up* p. 222

'can tell his secret': *Mrs Craddock* p. 221

# Select Bibliography

## EDITIONS OF THE WORKS OF SOMERSET MAUGHAM REFERRED TO IN THE TEXT

*Liza of Lambeth* (1897; Vintage 2000)
*The Making of a Saint* (1898; Farrar, Straus & Giroux 1966)
*Orientations* (Fisher Unwin 1899)
*The Hero* (Hutchinson 1901)
*Mrs Craddock* (1902; Vintage 2000)
*A Man of Honour* (Dramatic Publishing Company 1903)
*The Merry-Go-Round* (1904; Vintage 2000)
*The Land of the Blessed Virgin* (1905; Knopf 1920)
*The Bishop's Apron* (Chapman & Hall 1906)
*The Explorer* (1907; Heinemann 1922)
*The Magician* (1908; Vintage 2000)
*The Tenth Man* (Heinemann 1913)
*Landed Gentry* (*Grace*) (Heinemann 1913)
*Of Human Bondage* (1915; Vintage 2000)
*The Moon and Sixpence* (1919; Vintage 1999)
*The Trembling of a Leaf* (Heinemann 1921)
*On a Chinese Screen* (1922; Vintage 2000)
*Loaves and Fishes* (Heinemann 1924)
*The Painted Veil* (1925; Vintage 2001)
*The Casuarina Tree* (1926; Oxford University Press 1985)
*The Letter* (Heinemann 1927)
*Ashenden* (1928; Vintage 2000)
*The Gentleman in the Parlour* (1930; Vintage 2001)
*Cakes and Ale* (1930; Vintage 2000)
*First Person Singular* (Heinemann 1931)
*The Narrow Corner* (1932; Vintage 2001)
*Ah King* (1933; Oxford University Press 1986)
*Don Fernando* (1935; Vintage 2000)
*Cosmopolitans* (Doubleday, Doran 1936)
*Theatre* (1937; Vintage 2000)
*The Summing Up* (1938; Vintage 2001)
*Christmas Holiday* (1939; Vintage 2001)
*France at War* (Heinemann 1940)
*Books and You* (Doubleday, Doran 1940)

*The Mixture as Before*  (Heinemann 1940)
*Up at the Villa*  (1941; Vintage 2000)
*Strictly Personal*  (Doubleday, Doran 1941)
*The Hour Before the Dawn*  (Doubleday, Doran 1942)
*The Razor's Edge*  (1944; Vintage 2000)
*Then and Now*  (1946; Vintage 2001)
*Creatures of Circumstance*  (Heinemann 1947)
*Catalina*  (1948; Vintage 2001)
*Great Novelists and Their Novels*  (John C. Winston 1948)
*A Writer's Notebook*  (1949; Vintage 2001)
*The Writer's Point of View*  (Cambridge University Press for the National Book
    League 1951)
*The Vagrant Mood*  (1952; Vintage 2001)
*Points of View*  (1958; Vintage 2001)
*Purely for My Pleasure*  (Heinemann 1962)


*Collected Short Stories*  vol. I (Vintage 2000)
*Collected Short Stories*  vol. II (Vintage 2002)
*Collected Short Stories*  vol. III (Vintage 2002)
*Collected Short Stories*  vol. IV (Vintage 2002)


*The Plays of Somerset Maugham* (Heinemann 1931–4)
Vol. I: *Lady Frederick, Mrs Dot, Jack Straw*
Vol. II: *Penelope, Smith, The Land of Promise*
Vol. III: *Our Betters, The Unattainable (Caroline), Home and Beauty*
Vol. IV: *The Circle, The Constant Wife, The Bread-Winner*
Vol. V: *Caesar's Wife, East of Suez, The Sacred Flame*
Vol. VI: *The Unknown, For Services Rendered, Sheppey*


*The Traveller's Library*, compiled and with notes by W. Somerset Maugham
    (Doubleday, Doran 1937)
*Tellers of Tales*, selected and with an introduction by W. Somerset Maugham
    (Doubleday, Doran 1939)
*W. Somerset Maugham's Introduction to Modern English and American Literature* (New
    Home Library 1943)
*A Choice of Kipling's Prose*, selected and with an introductory essay by W. Somerset
    Maugham (Macmillan 1952)


*Selected Prefaces and Introductions of W. Somerset Maugham* (Heinemann 1963)
*Seventeen Lost Stories by W. Somerset Maugham* compiled by Craig V. Showalter
    (Doubleday, Doran 1969)
*A Traveller in Romance: Uncollected Writings 1901–1964: W. Somerset Maugham* ed.
    John Whitehead (Anthony Blond 1984)

# WORKS ABOUT SOMERSET MAUGHAM

Richard Aldington *W. Somerset Maugham: An Appreciation* (Doubleday, Doran 1939)

Frederick T. Bason *A Bibliography of the Writings of William Somerset Maugham* (Unicorn Press 1931)

L. Brander *Somerset Maugham: A Guide* (Barnes & Noble 1963)

John Brophy *Somerset Maugham* (Longmans 1952)

Ivor Brown *W. Somerset Maugham* (International Profiles 1970)

Robert Lorin Calder *W. Somerset Maugham and the Quest for Freedom* (Heinemann 1972)

Robert Calder *Willie: The Life of W. Somerset Maugham* (Heinemann 1989)

Robert Calder *Beware the British Serpent: The Role of Writers in British Propaganda in the United States 1939–1945* (McGill-Queen's University Press 2004)

Bryan Connon *Somerset Maugham and the Maugham Dynasty* (Sinclair-Stevenson 1997)

Richard Cordell *Somerset Maugham: A Biographical and Critical Study* (Heinemann 1961)

Anthony Curtis *The Pattern of Maugham* (Quality Book Club 1974)

Anthony Curtis *Somerset Maugham* (Weidenfeld & Nicolson 1987)

Anthony Curtis and John Whitehead (eds) *W. Somerset Maugham: The Critical Heritage* (Routledge & Kegan Paul 1987)

Paul Dottin *Somerset Maugham et ses romans* (Perrin 1926)

Paul Dottin *Le Théâtre de Somerset Maugham* (Perrin 1937)

Richard B. Fisher *Syrie Maugham* (Duckworth 1978)

Klaus W. Jonas *The Gentleman from Cap Ferrat* (New Haven, Connecticut Centre for Maugham Studies 1956)

Klaus W. Jonas *The World of Somerset Maugham* (Greenwood Press 1959)

Klaus W. Jonas (ed.) *The Maugham Enigma* (Peter Owen 1954)

Garson Kanin *Remembering Mr Maugham* (Hamish Hamilton 1966)

Desmond MacCarthy *William Somerset Maugham: The English Maupassant* (Heinemann, 1934)

Gerald McKnight *The Scandal of Syrie Maugham* (W. H. Allen 1980)

Raymond Mander and Joe Mitchenson *Theatrical Companion to Maugham* (Rockliff 1955)

The Rt Hon. Viscount Maugham *At the End of the Day* (Heinemann 1954)

Robin Maugham *Somerset and All the Maughams* (Heinemann 1966)

Robin Maugham *Escape from the Shadows* (Hodder & Stoughton 1972)

Robin Maugham *The Search for Nirvana* (W. H. Allen 1975)

Robin Maugham *Conversations with Willie* (W. H. Allen 1978)

Wilmon Menard *The Two Worlds of Somerset Maugham* (Sherbourne Press 1965)

Jeffrey Meyers *Somerset Maugham: A Life* (Knopf 2004)

Ted Morgan *Maugham* (Simon & Schuster 1980)

Beverley Nichols *A Case of Human Bondage* (Secker & Warburg 1966)

Karl G. Pfeiffer *W. Somerset Maugham: A Candid Portrait* (Norton 1959)

Frederic Raphael *Somerset Maugham and His World* (Thames & Hudson 1976)

Charles Sanders *W. Somerset Maugham: An Annotated Bibliography of Writings about Him* (Northern Illinois University Press 1970)

Raymond Toole Stott *A Bibliography of the Works of W. Somerset Maugham* (University of Alberta Press 1973)

# Illustration Credits

# Index

Works by Somerset Maugham (WSM) appear directly under title;
works by others under author's name